From Hiroshima
to Glasnost

From Hiroshima to Glasnost

AT THE CENTRE OF DECISION

A MEMOIR

Paul H. Nitze

WITH ANN M. SMITH AND STEVEN L. REARDEN

WEIDENFELD AND NICOLSON
LONDON

First published in Great Britain in 1990 by
George Weidenfeld and Nicolson Limited
91 Clapham High Street London SW4 7TA

ISBN 0 297 81053 7

Printed in Great Britain by
REDWOOD BURN LIMITED
Trowbridge, Wiltshire

To Phyllis

Contents

Introduction

Those who know me moderately well will say that I am an assertive, hard-nosed pragmatist. I guess that judgment comes from the fact that I have a firm belief that the world can turn out to be better than it otherwise would be depending upon what individuals, particularly those who have luck on their side, do about it. What is more, I believe Americans, to quite a disproportionate degree, have luck on their side.

It is my view that belief is the underlying and basic element of policy and action. First one must sort out matters of belief: who one is, in what relationship to whom, and what general direction in the realm of values is up and what direction is down. Then clear and rigorous logic, based upon a cold and unemotional assessment of the objective evidence concerning the relevant facts, and a careful analysis of the probable outcomes and probable material and moral costs of alternative courses of action, can help to get one from where one is to where one wants, and should want, to be.

How have I come to that view? From my grandfather, my parents, and my sister I absorbed a deep interest in ideas. Early in life, as a witness to the limitless tragedy of World War I, I felt grow in me a determination to act, to work with others to influence the course of history and not supinely to accept what, in the absence of will and action, might be the world's fate.

I came to Washington in the summer of 1940 with Jim Forrestal. I have been here, with short exceptions, ever since. For almost five decades I have played some role in the affairs of state, working with others to bend what otherwise might have been called the "inevitable trends of history." Some of the outcomes were wholly satisfactory, some marginally successful, and some were failures—but, on the whole, they were better, I think, than would otherwise have come about.

On balance, we were fortunate in the opportunities for significant action the fortune of history opened up for us. It cannot be the good fortune of all mankind to live in Athens under the leadership of a Pericles, in Florence under the Medici, in the United States under a Washington or a Lincoln. Nor is it the usual fate of mankind to live under a Cleon, a Nero, a Stalin or a Hitler and thus have an unambiguous case for withdrawal from government or opposition to it. The usual case is a mixed one in which the task of the man of general wisdom and with a taste for politics is to manage, to deal with, to nudge the existing situation toward the best that is within the realm of the politically possible, to find such scope as he can for his courage, his fortitude, and his willingness to view facts with an open mind. When given half a chance, the combination of courage and an open mind can do wonders.

I believe that a certain pride is justified in what we were able to accomplish, given those opportunities, and also the very real difficulties we faced. A war was won. Europe and the Far East, shattered by that war, were largely restored. The spread of totalitarianism was checked. A third world war has been avoided. But dangers for the future remain.

The problems and opportunities facing the present and coming generations are no less, perhaps greater, than those we faced. I hope that some of our experiences may provide insights useful to them. In any case I am grateful to have had the good luck to participate in the history of a fateful era.

And now, from the beginning: My paternal grandfather came to this country from Germany on a "grand tour" shortly after the American Civil War. He decided to stay, settled in Baltimore, and became the managing partner of Robert Garrett & Sons, bankers for the Baltimore and Ohio Railroad. My father was born and raised in Baltimore and received his undergraduate degree at the age of eighteen from Johns Hopkins University. He received his doctorate in philology at twenty-three.

He then lectured at Columbia University until he won an appointment at Amherst College in Massachusetts and in 1905 became head of the Department of French Literature. There I was born five years after my sister, Libby, on a cold winter morning in January 1907, the only son of the oldest surviving son, of the oldest surviving son, et cetera, for six generations. I have in my possession the dark and scowling portraits to prove it.

When I was two we moved to the University of Chicago where my father joined a particularly distinguished faculty under the inspiring leadership of its first president, William Rainey Harper. My father remained there as head of the Department of Romance Languages and Literature for over thirty years—an eminent scholar and enduring fixture at the university. My early years there among scholars who were at the forefront of their fields, as well as among the gangs that terrorized the South Side of Chicago, were—in addition to being diverse—happy, challenging, and satisfying.

The university was an enclave in a part of the city best described in James Farrell's novel *Studs Lonigan*. When the wind was from the west it brought the stench of the stockyards; from the east it brought the soot and cinders from the steel mills of Gary and south Chicago. We lived on Fifty-sixth Street. On Fifty-fifth, just one block away, lived and operated some of South Side Chicago's toughest gangs. My mother insisted on dressing me in a Buster Brown outfit, complete with flowing tie. In this attire, I walked the gauntlet to and from school every day.

I soon received my first lesson in power politics. The gang on the block bounded by Fifty-fifth Street, Woodlawn and Kimbark avenues, would waylay and soundly beat me up every day on my way home from school. For protection, I joined the Scotti brothers' gang on the neighboring block run by the sons of an Italian family. The eldest brother was a charismatic leader, a blue-eyed, blond Italian, full of courage and paternal kindness to his gang. He inspired great loyalty in me; I did whatever he asked, without concern for the fine distinction between legal and illegal activities.

Of course, a good part of this admiration came from intense gratitude, for from the moment I joined his gang, they defended me. Thereafter I was able to live in relative peace in that part of Chicago's jungle.

From the time I was seven I was treated as a full member of the family council and was expected to share the responsibilities that go with it. There were times, however, when I would have welcomed firmer direction and guidance. Nevertheless, I believe it was useful to have been given individual responsibility at an early age.

By far the greatest influence in my life was my mother. At times the intensity of her love was overwhelming. She was small with immense vitality, warmth, wit, and energy. She shocked the Chicago community because she smoked and spoke her mind at a time when the duties of a professor's wife consisted of pouring tea and making polite conversation. She had many liberal and outrageous friends; among others, Sally Rand, Isadora Duncan, and Clarence Darrow (for whom she mortgaged our house in order to provide bail for a left-wing agitator he was defending). Her taste in the arts was more eclectic than most Americans at the time. She admired the music of Richard Strauss, the works of Franz Kafka, the

Impressionist painters—Cézanne, Gauguin—and the German Postim-
pressionists. Her zest for life soon made her a favorite, not only at the
university, but also on the more fashionable North Side of Chicago.

We spent six months in Europe every other year; my father was able
to combine two of his annual three months' vacations for research and
to meet with his European colleagues. Some of my earliest recollections
are of Europe. The one that made the most lasting impression was our
visit to Austria in 1914. I was then seven. We—my mother, my father, my
sister, and I—were mountain climbing in the southern Tyrol, a part of
Austria which is now part of Italy. We stopped at a peasant's cottage just
below timberline, where my sister and I were each given a glass of warm
and frothy milk straight from the cow by the mistress of the cottage. We
continued our climb along the mountain trail to the top. We stopped to
say good-bye to the peasant woman as we wound our way down the
mountain and found her in tears. Her husband had been ordered to
report for mobilization in the Austrian army. A few weeks earlier, on
June 28, the Archduke Francis Ferdinand had been assassinated at
Sarajevo.

The Austrians and the Serbians appeared to be on the verge of war and
there was imminent danger that Russia would intervene. The situation
seemed ominous in Austria and my father bundled us all on a train to
Munich, where he thought we would be safer. We arrived the following
morning after a night of excitement and intrigue, mostly invented by
Libby, who had a high sense of drama. At Munich, however, the drama
was starkly real. A terrorist bomb had exploded in the train station and
the scene was one of destruction and chaos. There we learned that overnight Germany had ordered mobilization and declared war on Russia.
World War I had begun!

We watched from the third-floor windows of our *pension* as German
soldiers marched down the principal boulevard in Munich on their way
to the front. Flowers were stuck jauntily in the barrels of their guns and
the people lined the streets to cheer them on with roars of patriotic
enthusiasm. While we were still in Munich, England declared war on
Germany. Because we spoke English, we were harassed wherever we
went. My father had us wear small American flags on our clothes—which
helped, but not much.

In August, during the Battle of Tannenberg, we stayed with some of
my mother's relatives in Frankfurt. Their eldest son kept a map of the
progress of the battle on the Eastern Front and the developments that led
to the encirclement of the Russian forces at Tannenberg. Within a year
he had been killed fighting on that front.

My father was trying frantically to book passage for us back to the United States. This proved to be difficult since he was far from alone in his single-minded pursuit. He finally got us on a small Dutch steamer, the *Nordam,* in September. It brought us safely home as the Battle of the Marne raged on the Western Front.

From my recollection of both wars, I would say that the emotional dedication of the people on both sides in the First World War was far greater than it was in World War II. Even though more lives were lost in the Second World War, the impact of the First on the structure of civilization, the disillusionment and brutalization of man and his humanity, were such that the civilized world was never again the same.

Five years later, in 1919, I was in the sixth grade at the University Elementary School in Chicago. Our current events class called for us to role-play individuals who were involved in important current issues. Our subject, one day, was the final sessions of the Paris Peace Conference. I played the role of Walther Rathenau, the German foreign minister, who had made an impassioned plea for his country based upon the inconsistency of the peace terms with President Woodrow Wilson's Fourteen Points.[1] I shared his view that the peace treaty lacked justice, consistency, and proper purpose.

My father's academic colleagues discussed the terms of the Treaty of Versailles at length that summer, and none of them, as far as I could tell, believed in its wisdom. They were, in my estimation, as distinguished a group of scholars as had ever been brought together, but it was evident that they were powerless to influence events.

It was then, at the age of twelve, that I decided when I grew up I wanted to be in a position where I could participate in world events and be close to the levers of influence. Distinguished scholarship did not appear to offer that opportunity.

I attended the university elementary school and high school, both affiliated with the university's Department of Education, which I completed at the age of fifteen. My father—perhaps owing to his own experiences—decided I was too young for college, so I was packed off for two years at

---

[1]President Wilson, in an address to Congress in January 1918, outlined a far-reaching program to govern the peace terms with Germany and the postwar world. The German request for a peace based on Wilson's Fourteen Points in November 1918 had been granted by the Allies, but these terms receded into the background as conflicts of views and interest materialized during the Paris Peace Conference.

Hotchkiss, a preparatory school in Connecticut whose graduates, for the most part, go on to Yale.

My two years at Hotchkiss were full of camaraderie, athletics, girls, and studies—and pretty much in that order. I enjoyed mathematics and considered the possibility of becoming a physicist. Latin, I discovered with the beauty of Virgil, was not the subject that I had found so tedious at U High in Chicago. I was developing my own taste in literature and Hotchkiss' approach to the subject left me less than enthralled. This approach, I had heard, would be carried on at Yale.

So I selected Harvard rather than Yale, to the surprise of my father and the dismay of my brother-in-law, Walter Paepcke, who wanted me to follow in his footsteps. After I expressed some interest in Harvard, he invited me to the annual Yale Club dinner in Chicago but I was not particularly impressed by the Elis. The Princeton Club guest was the wittiest of the speakers, but a man from the Harvard Club, in my view, made the best speech. Partially as a result, I found myself at Harvard in the fall of 1924. Had I attended a Harvard alumni dinner in those days of Prohibition and excessive drinking, I probably would have ended up at Yale.

At Harvard, I became so involved in the friends I made through my participation in football and rowing on the crew that increasingly I slighted my studies. By my senior year I had come to regret my cavalier attitude toward academic requirements. Not only did I have to take five courses rather than four in that year, but I could not afford to do less than well in any of them and qualify for honors. I did well in the economics courses I took and received summa cum laude on my senior thesis. I missed graduating magna cum laude by a small margin.

I had worked excessively hard that year, however, and came down with a serious bout of hepatitis in the spring. The medical field then knew little about the disease and failed to warn me to avoid alcohol until I was completely recovered. After turning in my senior thesis and completing final exams, I joined some friends in celebration.

After we toasted the end of our college years and vowed eternal friendship, Freddy Winthrop, in a conversation with Morton Eustis, boasted of the seaworthiness of a canoe he had just bought. Morton bet him two hundred dollars that he couldn't paddle the canoe from the Ipswich River north of Boston to the Yacht Club landing in New York. I joined Freddy in accepting the challenge.

The next morning at dawn we climbed into the canoe with two cans of baked beans and a pocket knife. Eight cold and windy days later, after two close encounters with death, we arrived at New York, flushed with the excitement of having beaten the odds and having survived a dangerous adventure. We gladly paid the hundred dollars to ship the canoe back to Boston.

The next weekend we celebrated our victory at North Easton in Massachusetts, where the large and interesting Ames family all had houses. We put on a track meet and I entered the sixty-yard dash. For me, the meet ended at thirty yards, where I collapsed and was carried off to the hospital with a serious recurrence of hepatitis. My doctor didn't believe I would make it. It was six months before I fully recovered.

The study of economics revived my interest in finding a path to understanding and influencing the real world, which I saw as something quite different from the world of either academia or social relationships. Economics bore on the world of business and international trade, but only abstractly. Its analyses were logical but depended on carefully defined sets of assumptions which were not self-evident and only partially valid. In certain contexts those assumptions differed from common sense and personal experience. In particular, value judgments could not be derived from economics. Economics depended on assumed and vastly oversimplified value judgments.

In sociology I hoped to find the discipline that would relate practical life to basic values. I supplemented my studies in economics with a course in sociology, a field to which I would return almost ten years later in search of answers to questions that had emerged over the decade. In this search for understanding, I found help at Harvard, but not enough. The same was true of my years on Wall Street, but the two experiences managed to complement each other and helped me in the decade of the fifties to explore those questions in greater depth with some notion of the direction in which to look for answers.

After graduation in 1928 and a decision to go into the world of business rather than graduate school, I served a stint in the cost-accounting office of a boxboard mill of the Container Corporation of America in Philadelphia and then Bridgeport, Connecticut. As instructive as that was, I soon thought I had learned all that I wanted to learn about accounting. It was time to move on.

I struck a bargain with William T. Bacon, a friend of my father's and senior partner of the brokerage firm of Bacon, Whipple and Company in Chicago. He agreed to pay my transportation to Germany in return for a report on whether German securities might be a better investment than American securities at their current excessively high prices. If the report proved to be of value, the firm would make an additional payment for my time and other expenses.

The next eight months found me in Europe, armed with letters of introduction from several bankers, professors, and others, including one from Clarence Dillon, head of Dillon, Read and Company, investment bankers in New York City.

I met with Mr. Dillon prior to my departure. He was, I sensed, a man of extraordinary intelligence. He invited me to lunch in his private dining room on the fortieth floor of the Equitable Building on Nassau Street. We were interrupted by one of the firm's partners, a younger man named Forrestal. In a letter I wrote at the time, I described my impression of James Forrestal at that first meeting: "It was an extraordinary experience. I left feeling small and ineffectual. Forrestal impressed me as being very keen and forceful. A much finer specimen than anything I have seen for a long time."

After seven months in Paris, Berlin, and other parts of Europe, and shortly before my return to the United States, I made my first visit to the Soviet Union. The year was 1929 and the visit was not on my itinerary. I ran into Freddy Winthrop in Berlin while I had a little time on my hands, and we decided to do some hiking around Lake Inari in northern Finland. The lake was almost two hundred miles north of the Arctic Circle. Except for a few settlements of Laplanders on the shore of the lake, the entire area was uninhabited.

The sun circled overhead twenty-four hours a day at that time of year, but the sky was overcast, and a fine rain penetrated our clothing. We headed north toward the little Finnish town of Petsamo (now Soviet and renamed Pechenga) on the Barents Sea. There were no trails, and after three days of walking in the rain we were lost. Unknowingly, we had crossed the border into the Soviet Union and might still be there, buried in a Soviet prison, if we had not run into a Good Samaritan, a Russian fishing on a desolate lake. He told us we were in the Soviet Union and had better get out fast. He showed us a trail that would lead us back to Finland and told us that if he were we, he would run. And run we did until we had recrossed the border! We came out near the beautiful village of Boris Gleb with white houses in a birch forest and a handsome church with onion-domed spires astride a huge river, the Pasvik, which flows into the Arctic. After resting up in Boris Gleb, we then walked to Kirkenes in Norway. There we caught a ship around the North Cape.

Returning to Chicago in September, I stopped in New York to see Mr. Dillon to thank him for the letters of introduction. He asked to see my report. While the logic of the report was simple, I don't believe anyone else had laid it out for him in quite the same way. '

The essential facts, as I saw them, were that the German economy could not withstand much strain and the political structure of Germany was even weaker. In order to meet the reparation payments demanded of them, the Germans had resorted to enormous short-term loans, increasingly from American banks. If there were to be a recession in the world economy, particularly in the United States, the banks would not renew their loans. The German government would have to impose a repressive deflationary economic policy on its economic scene in order to compensate for the withdrawal of capital from the country. The political structure was not strong enough to tolerate that kind of economic depression. This being the case, my conclusion was that anyone contemplating investing money in Germany ought to have his head examined.

Clarence Dillon took an interest in me and invited me to spend the weekend at Dunwalke, his estate in New Jersey. On the drive out in his Rolls-Royce, I asked him whether he thought we were headed for a recession. "No," he said, "it will be the end of an era."

He went on to explain that throughout history, societies have been dominated by one element of society or another—by priests, by royalty, by the military, by politicians from either the common folk or from the aristocracy, and from time to time by wealthy financiers. This last element had found its way to the top of the hierarchy for a while in ancient Greece, in Rome in the days of Lucullus, in the city-states of Italy during the days of the Medici, for a while in France, and then in Austria. In the United States the New York banking community had wielded more influence than politicians in Washington since the Civil War. History, he said, has shown us that periods dominated by men of finance have been of relatively short duration.

No, he said solemnly, we will not have a recession; we will have a depression, which will be far more serious than anyone now thinks possible. After which, he predicted, Wall Street will no longer control the levers of power and influence; it will be reduced to a secondary element in our society.

That is why, he continued, he was disbanding the company's entire national distribution network and would retain only a core of people in the New York office. He said he had given notice to some four thousand well-trained, good, able people employed by Dillon, Read and Company around the country. At the moment the market was achieving daily new highs and all those people could get jobs tomorrow. If he were to delay another month, he doubted they would be able to do so.

I was sobered by his words, but I found it difficult to believe that we were heading into disaster in those heady days before the market crash. His predictions, however, turned out to be correct.

I returned to Chicago and delivered my report to Mr. Bacon, who did not appear to be particularly interested. I was offered some stock the firm was selling at the firm's cost rather than the market price—and a job. I declined the former—since I had little money—and accepted the latter. I had only been there a few days when I received a telegram from Mr. Dillon asking me to come to work for him. I jumped at the chance, and on the first of the month, just before Black Tuesday, in October 1929, I became number fifty-one on the roster of employees at Dillon, Read and Company. I was very likely the last man hired on Wall Street for many years thereafter.

Fortune was good to me in spite of the Depression that darkened the world economy. I worked with some of the most distinguished men on Wall Street and rubbed shoulders with some of its biggest crooks. It was a useful education to be exposed as a young man to the barons and wizards of high finance. The experience left me with little awe of the great and perhaps with excessive confidence in my own abilities and judgment.

The theories of John Maynard Keynes came as no surprise to me and my contemporaries when his book *The General Theory of Employment, Interest and Money* was published in 1936. Keynesian economics may have been a revelation for the academic world, but among the young men of Wall Street, his theories were a confirmation of what we had learned through daily practical experiences. It was evident to us that the Depression had been caused by a competitive and self-exacerbating search for financial liquidity. It could be reversed with the help of massive deficit spending by the government, but only after the Depression had been carried to an obvious extreme as it had in 1932.

I expressed this theory at a dinner party in 1932 with almost disastrous results. Just recently I had met Phyllis Pratt, with whom I was immediately smitten, for she was lovely, gay, and blessed with a sunny smile that would light the darkest corners. In due course, I was taken home to be inspected by her family and to meet her somewhat formidable mother,

Congresswoman Ruth Pratt, from the Blue Stocking district of New York City. It was an elegant dinner party; another guest was Sir Montaqu Norman, a distinguished British gentleman and governor of the Bank of England. In response to a question from Mrs. Pratt, he said that the Great Depression was the result of universal overproduction. I was not over twenty-five years old, but that did not stop me from voicing my disagreement.

"Overproduction is not the problem," I said. "The world needs much more than is being produced. The problem is lack of ability to pay because of a worldwide competitive search for economic security through excessive banking liquidity."

There was a moment of silence as my impertinence hung in the air at the dinner table, but Sir Montaqu was interested in the subject. Our debate dominated the rest of that evening's discussion.

Somewhat later, Phyllis told me that after the guests had left, her mother asked her whether she might be serious about this brash young man. When Phyllis confessed that she might be, her mother said she was going upstairs—she felt she was going to be ill. But Mrs. Pratt thought her children could do no wrong and quickly accepted me into the family. Over time we developed a lasting affection for each other.

Phyllis and I were married in December 1932, a union that lasted for over fifty-four years. Two of our children, Heidi and Peter, were born a few years later. Our other two children, Bill and Nina, made their appearance during the forties after we had moved to Washington. Phyllis attempted over the years to soften the edges of her sometimes abrasive husband, without, I fear, a great deal of success.

Before my marriage to Phyllis, I shared an apartment on East Eighty-second Street with a series of roommates, including, in 1932, Sidney Shepard Spivak, a man of exceptional talent and wit, who always had a scheme of some kind under way. Spiv, as we fondly called him, was an ardent supporter of Franklin Delano Roosevelt.

I also supported Roosevelt. I had come to the conclusion that Herbert Hoover and his economic advisers lacked understanding of the way the domestic economy—and its relation with the international economy—worked. That failure had led to an unwise expansion of credit in 1927, to the stock market crash in 1929, and to a contraction in government expenditures and in bank credit in 1930, which converted the Wall Street crash into the worldwide Depression of 1931 and 1932. I saw no hope for getting these policies reversed other than through a change of administration. Despite Roosevelt's talk about balancing the budget and trying to protect the United States from the worldwide Depression through increased trade barriers, I thought he would be more susceptible to new ideas and to reversing himself than would the Republicans.

During the presidential campaign, I became engaged in conversation with a gentleman who sat down next to me on the Lexington Avenue subway. I was so interested in what he was saying that I invited him to dinner the following evening in the apartment I shared with Spiv.

William Bullitt had been a member of our delegation to the Paris Peace Conference in 1919. He told us a fascinating tale about a clandestine visit to Moscow in 1919, where he had gone at the request of President Wilson to investigate the stability of the Bolshevik government. He had come back with a plan approved by Lenin that he hoped would improve relations between the two countries. President Wilson had ignored Bullitt's recommendation that he adopt the plan and Bill resigned from the delegation with some bitterness.

He came back to the United States after spending some time in France and moved on to other things. His continuing interest, however, in improving our relationship with the Soviet Union was apparent. The three of us—Bill, Spiv, and I—became friends and we continued to dine together from time to time.

Through Spivak, Bill became involved in Roosevelt's campaign and was able to persuade the presidential candidate that upon his inauguration, the United States government should recognize the Soviet Union and that he, FDR, should appoint Bullitt the first United States ambassador to the Bolshevik government in Moscow.

In 1935 Lady Luck truly smiled on me. At the invitation of a friend I joined with some twenty others to build a laboratory here in the United States for two French scientists who had developed a new vitamin-mineral product. In return they gave us the exclusive rights to market their products in the United States.

Visynerall, which is what we called the initial product, was a smashing success. Later the laboratory developed a number of other excellent pharmaceuticals, including a pill for certain types of diabetes. Fifteen years later we sold out to Revlon for a large amount of its stock. Thereafter I was financially independent.

In the spring of 1937, Phyllis and I took our first extended vacation since our honeymoon. We motored around Europe in a Model A Ford, much of the time in Germany. We saw ominous signs in villages proclaiming JEWS ARE NOT WELCOME HERE! We heard Hitler rant and rave at enormous crowds in Munich and in Rothenburg with evident effect. What concerned me most was passing a group of youths of sixteen or so—members of Hitler's Jugendkorps—on a road in Bavaria. They were healthy and handsome, but hard, with a look of arrogance and disdain that sent a shiver of apprehension down my spine.

I thought back to World War I and the armistice, to Versailles, to Keynes' *Economic Consequences of the Peace,* and to my own experiences in Germany during the inflation of 1922 and again in 1929 and 1930. Danger was in the air, danger that a chain of events could lead to spreading totalitarianism and to war. The question was, what could one do, what could I do, to mitigate that danger?

When we returned to New York, Phyllis and I went salmon fishing on an isolated river in the central forest of New Brunswick. I read again a book I had first started in 1931: Oswald Spengler's *The Decline of the West.* At that time my reaction was that it had all the faults of the German temperament; it was brilliant, full of profound feeling and thought, but dogmatic, rough, tactless. Along the peaceful banks of the Upsalquitch River, I pondered the flaws in its logic. How could the tendencies toward cultural decay, socialistic Caesarism and war, which he saw as being irreversible, be countered and reversed? I knew of no one who had a lucid and persuasive opinion on those issues.

I resigned from Dillon, Read and Company, moved my family to Boston, and matriculated as a graduate student at Harvard in the field of sociology, with philosophy and constitutional and international law as supplementary fields. It was a memorable year. I learned much about sociology, something about philosophy, and a little about law, but I received almost no answers about Spengler, the trends of the future, and what could be done to affect those trends. At the end of the year we returned to New York, the questions more clearly formed in my mind, but still without answers.

I found investment banking and working out reorganizations and mergers involving multimillion-dollar deals exhilarating. I found it difficult to keep from getting involved in what appeared to be interesting opportunities. In 1938 I formed Paul H. Nitze and Company, which consisted of me, one associate, and a secretary for the two of us.

Operating my own company was exciting and challenging and eminently successful. But even with the help of law firms, engineering firms, accountants, and banking firms, it still involved working under enormous strain. I developed a streptococcus infection in 1939 that stubbornly persisted. In those days there was no penicillin to combat this bacterium.

After I recovered, I decided that running my own business was just too strenuous and obviously detrimental to my health. Jim Forrestal was then president of Dillon, Read and Company, although Clarence Dillon still retained control. I told Jim that I would like to return to Dillon, Read, that I preferred the peace and quiet of the double bed to the hurly-burly of the chaise lounge. Little did I know that in less than a year I would return to the hurly-burly of the chaise lounge, this time in the city of Washington.

PART I

I

War and the Heritage of War

When Adolf Hitler's German armies invaded Poland on September 1, 1939, I was visiting my parents at their ranch, the Constant Spring Ranch, high in the Rocky Mountains of Colorado. The six-hundred-acre ranch covered the lower side of a mountain called the Twin Sisters and the bottomland along the stream that flowed between the Twin Sisters and Longs Peak, the highest mountain in the Continental Divide range. The Twin Sisters is a long, dark, forested mountain with twin humps that dominate much of the skyline when one looks west from the plains of northeastern Colorado. The stream had become a series of beaver dams and ponds backed up behind them. The main income of the ranch came from the annual trapping of beavers by the U.S. Department of the Interior for translocation on the headwaters of the Mississippi and Missouri rivers. My parents' house was on the slope of the Twin Sisters looking directly across the valley at the perpendicular face of Longs Peak where it drops into Chasm Lake at its base. My sister and I had spent our summers in those mountains and knew every foot of terrain west to Grand Lake and north to the Wyoming border.

My father made it a practice each summer to invite one of his graduate students from the University of Chicago to spend the summer at the ranch, helping with some of the chores, but largely to absorb wisdom. That year the student was Claude Bakewell from a distinguished St. Louis family. His field was philology, but later he became a Jesuit priest.

Upon hearing the news of Hitler's invasion, I decided to return immediately to New York. Claude volunteered to drive me into town to catch the next plane east. The crisis had been building for some time, but it is not possible fully to anticipate the actuality of such an event. During the drive we became involved in a conversation about purpose. The momentous news of the war and the lonely drive on a starry night in the mountains made us wonder about the imponderable. Was there a purpose to life, was there a purpose to the universe? If so, was it possible for a

3

human mind to have some approximate understanding of that purpose? Was it possible to formulate a statement of purpose which was more satisfactory than other statements? We finally turned that around to an examination of whether one could formulate a statement of purpose of the universe which was less satisfactory than some other statement. If it was thus possible to formulate a hierarchical ladder from bad to worse, should it not be equally possible to formulate a hierarchical ladder from better to still better? If it were possible for the human mind to do this, then it should be possible to have some dim and approximate but still not wholly worthless intimation of what not only the world, but the whole universe surrounding us, was about, with its immense diversity, energy, and drive. It was with these ponderous thoughts swirling in my mind that I entered the years of World War II.

By the time I arrived back at my desk at Dillon, Read and Company, in New York, the United States had declared its neutrality, a decision in which I concurred. Being of German-American ancestry, I had been deeply committed to U.S. neutrality at the outset of World War I. But when the United States entered that war, I did what I could to help us win it. I was too young for the Army, so I looked for something else to do. To my surprise I found I was able to sell a large number of Liberty Bonds to people in our community. I believed in Wilson's Fourteen Points and was deeply shocked when they were abandoned at the Versailles Peace Conference. I believed firmly in John Maynard Keynes' thesis in his book *The Economic Consequences of the Peace* that the Versailles treaty was punitive and destined to sow the seeds of future conflict. In the early years of Hitler's rise, I was ambivalent about the impressive economic revival which had occurred in Germany, contrasted with the obvious dangers to be anticipated by his extremist methods. I was equally concerned with the dangers which might ensue from Joseph Stalin's ideas and methods in the Soviet Union. It seemed to me that the United States should keep out of that contest. This caused me to sympathize with the America Firsters in the United States. The Munich debacle, followed shortly by the German invasion of Czechoslovakia, persuaded me that the major danger was from Hitler. But in 1939 I still believed that neutrality was the proper course for the United States.

Many of my friends felt otherwise. Billy Fisk, who had been my assistant at Dillon, Read, and who four or five years earlier had discovered the beauties of Aspen, Colorado, and had persuaded me to join him in its development as a skiing area, flew off to England to join the Royal Air Force. He was the last fighter pilot to die in the Battle of Britain the next year. My college friend Morton Eustis drove a truck for the Friends

Service Corps and was killed during the German invasion of France. Stewart Alsop, another Harvard friend, joined the British army and survived the entire war.

On the morning of April 9, 1940, German troops crossed the Danish border and launched the lightning assault that in a matter of weeks crushed the resistance of the Low Countries, drove what remained of Britain's expeditionary army off the continent of Europe, and forced the surrender of France. France and Poland were gone, Stalin was Hitler's ally, and the British army was severely crippled. Thoroughly shaken by those developments, I did not see how Hitler could be defeated.

While brooding over these ominous developments, I walked into the office of my boss, Clarence Dillon, and asked him what hope he saw for the future. He said, "Paul, you are overly discouraged. The situation is extremely serious but not hopeless. Let us analyze it together. In this war, modern technology, as exemplified in the tank and the airplane, is of enormous importance. In the long run, Detroit can outproduce the Ruhr. The question then is one of time. Can England hold out long enough for Detroit's superior production capability to be transformed into effective military power? Today, England's principal defensive asset is the English Channel. As long as the French fleet does not fall into German hands, the British fleet should be able to so dominate the Channel that the Germans cannot invade." He went on to say that he had just placed a transatlantic call to his friend of many years Lord Beaverbrook, the publisher of the London *Daily Express* and a close associate of British Prime Minister Winston Churchill, to urge that the French fleet be sunk before the Germans could get their hands on it. The call came through while I was in the room. I stepped out. Not many days later the British did, in fact, sink the bulk of the French fleet at Mers el-Kébir, Algeria.

The startling success of the German Blitzkrieg caused a dramatic and profound change in the mood, if not the policies, of the United States. Technically, we remained neutral and were obliged by the Neutrality Acts passed in the 1930s to isolate ourselves from any direct involvement in the fighting. But the realities of the situation were such that our action policy deviated more and more widely from our declared policy. The more Germany conquered, the more endangered became our own security.

During the spring of 1940, President Roosevelt became persuaded by events that the time had come for the United States to prepare for possible involvement in the war. The extent to which he could act was limited, not only by legislation but by opposition in the Congress and in the country at large. Not all of the America Firsters, of whom I was one, had become persuaded of the necessity or desirability of American involvement. In addition, Roosevelt had thoroughly alienated the American business community. His basic political strategy throughout the 1930s had been to paint American business—and particularly Wall Street—as malefactors of great wealth and to depict himself as the defender of the common man. After the fall of France, he came to the realization that it was no longer useful to describe American businessmen as the hostile "they" opposed to the "we" of the bulk of American people led by the Democratic party under his guidance. What was now needed was to unify the country, to pull it together into a common "we." The threat— the menacing "they"—had become Hitler and his Nazi adherents. The time had come to rebuild links between Washington and American business, beginning with Wall Street.

During the 1930s, Dillon, Read and Company was one of the most profitable firms on Wall Street, but it was small in terms of personnel. There were approximately fifty of us, including clerks and stenographers; the partners, or officers, of the firm numbered about fifteen. Clarence Dillon, who controlled the firm, had turned over much of the day-to-day responsibility to the other partners, particularly to James V. Forrestal who was designated president. I was one of several vice presidents.

One day in June 1940 Jim called me into his office and said he wanted my advice. Paul Shields, a Wall Street broker, a Democrat, and a friend of President Franklin Delano Roosevelt's, had just left him with an intriguing proposal. Only recently Congress had authorized the President to appoint six special administrative assistants—the "silent six" as they were later known. Paul had said that Roosevelt had decided to rebuild his relations with the business community to face the difficult times that lay ahead. He wanted someone from Wall Street, preferably a Democrat, to come down to Washington and be one of these six. Paul had suggested Jim's name, and the President in turn had authorized Paul to find out whether Jim would accept.

Jim was obviously uneasy about taking the job. His entire life had been wrapped up in business and he had had no experience in government or politics. He was not at all sure that he could be effective or useful in Washington; he asked me what I thought he should do. I replied by asking him what would happen if he took the job and it did not work out satisfactorily. "Under those circumstances," he replied, "I guess I would return to Dillon, Read." I said I thought that he himself had answered his own question. "If you go and it turns up heads, you win," I said. "If it turns up tails, you lose very little. And if you don't go, will you ever regret having possibly missed the opportunity of working in a framework of wider scope?" He said he would.

Forrestal went down to Washington almost immediately. I found myself a few weeks later in Louisiana working out some financing for the United Gas Company (now Pennzoil). One evening when I returned to my hotel in Shreveport, I found waiting for me a telegram which read: "Be in Washington Monday morning. Forrestal." The order seemed clear enough, as far as it went, but it hardly explained much. The next day I found Jim's office in the old State-War-Navy Building, now the Old Executive Office Building, next to the White House. The only staff the law authorized him to have was one secretary. He told me that he wanted me to occupy a desk in his office, live at the house he had just rented in Washington, and help him as best I could. The government could not pay me, so I was to remain on the payroll of Dillon, Read. In this wholly illegal fashion my career in Washington began.

Latin American Problems

In the summer of 1940 the State-War-Navy Building was the hub of the executive branch. That single building, with its high ceilings, slatted doors, and a fireplace in each office, housed the entire State Department as well as the President's executive staff. Among those who were now taking up residence here and elsewhere in Washington were a substantial number of people who previously had been persona non grata in FDR's administration. I am speaking, of course, of people who had been, like myself, part of the business and financial community. They included many registered Republicans. Although I had initially been a registered Democrat, I had switched parties in 1937 as a result of my belief that Roosevelt's attempt to pack the Supreme Court was contrary to the spirit of the Constitution.

For living accommodations, I accepted Jim's offer to stay with him at the house he had rented on Woodland Drive. Among those who would come to dinner, the most frequent guests were Arthur Krock, who ran the Washington bureau of *The New York Times*, and Thomas G. Corcoran and Benjamin V. Cohen, who were both members of FDR's White House "inner circle." Krock fancied himself a Washington kingmaker. He was smart, cynical, knowledgeable about the ways of the town, and in those days the most powerful and influential member of the Washington press corps. His knowledge of the personalities in the administration and Congress was unparalleled. For the two of us who were fresh to Washington, his experienced advice was invaluable. Tommy Corcoran and Ben Cohen were the principal authors of FDR's New Deal, its programs and its legislation. Tommy was ebullient, effervescent, full of optimism that the New Deal—based on spend and spend, elect and elect, tax and tax—was the answer to every prayer and could go on indefinitely. Ben, I felt, took a more enlightened and responsible view. Between them they had done much to make FDR's domestic program work, in the sense of rescuing the country from the worst of the Great Depression.

One of the first specific tasks assigned to Forrestal by FDR concerned South America and the Caribbean. No one was quite certain where Hitler would make his next move after the fall of France. One possibility was that German divisions might go through Spain and continue down the African coast perhaps as far as Dakar, thus assuring control of the western approaches to the Mediterranean and cutting off Britain from the Suez Canal. A German presence at the point of Africa closest to South America, coupled with German and Italian subversion in South America, could present a threat to the southern half of the Western Hemisphere. A number of actions was indicated. One of these was to assure air control over the Caribbean, both for strategic reasons and as a counter to German submarines in the Gulf of Mexico. Forrestal and I worked out a secret arrangement with Juan Trippe and Henry Friendly, who were president and general counsel, respectively, of Pan American World Airways, under which Pan Am urgently constructed six airfields in the Caribbean which could, if necessary, be converted to military use.

The more difficult problem that Jim and I encountered was to put together a way of coordinating U.S. cultural and commercial policy toward Latin America. Despite the "Good Neighbor" initiative taken in the 1930s, our relations with the peoples and governments of Latin America were far from close. The threat of "Yankee imperialism" continued to dominate their attitude toward the United States. Moreover, because of cultural and business ties, many Latin Americans felt bound to Europe and tended to identify themselves with the Axis, as the Rome-Berlin alliance was called. During the 1920s and 1930s there had been a sharp increase in immigration from Germany and Italy; many of those immigrants had set up companies that, in some instances, dominated the local economies. With much of Europe now under German occupation, the export markets on which a number of Latin American states had depended were effectively under the control of Berlin. The threat seemed all too real: If Germany could succeed in subverting the Latin American republics through economic, psychological, and other pressures, the United States might find itself standing virtually alone without friends or allies on its southern flank.

No one agency in the government was clearly in charge of addressing the problem. To complicate matters, there were three competing points of view in the government. Henry Wallace, then secretary of agriculture, urged support of the radical Left in Latin America in order to be in the forefront of what he saw as the wave of the future. Secretary of the Treasury Henry Morgenthau, Jr., sought to make Europe our primary focus and wanted us into the war as quickly as possible in order to destroy Hitler and punish Germany for having persecuted the Jews. Secretary of State Cordell Hull was fixed on the idea that wars were the result of trade barriers and that a mutually beneficial system of multilateral trade would remove the seeds of future conflicts. Faced with this conflicting and competing advice, Roosevelt had recently brought Harry Hopkins into the White House to help sort out matters of strategy. But Hopkins was ill and had neither the time nor the energy to devote to our difficulties in Latin America. At the President's request, Forrestal agreed to do what he could to straighten out the situation.

As Forrestal and I began to dig into the matter, we found the State Department under Cordell Hull almost totally lacking an organization for strategic policy-making. Most of the people in the State Department at that time had been brought up in the school of diplomacy that emphasized reporting; few were oriented toward the formulation and execution of strategic policy per se. We concluded that the State Department was inadequately staffed and not intellectually equipped to deal with the radically new situation brought about by the war.

The solution Jim and I decided upon was to create an Office for Coordination of Commercial and Cultural Relations Between the American Republics, later renamed more simply, the Office of the Coordinator of Inter-American Affairs. What we had in mind was a separate agency, directly responsible to the President rather than to any cabinet head, that could devote full-time effort to strengthening hemispheric commercial and cultural relations. Jim approved a draft of the office's charter that I had prepared with the assistance of Jim Rowe, another of the White House silent six.

I urged that we place the matter before the President without delay, but Forrestal resisted, demonstrating that in the short time he had been in Washington he had learned more about how one can be effective in government than had I. He said, "Paul, what you propose isn't the way to do it. You have to assure political backing for what you want done. If I were to put this forward with no further preparation, top people would be against it. But if I let them talk this thing out, they'll finally come to the conclusion that this is the only practical solution."

I was annoyed with Jim for what I thought was unnecessary delay, but his instincts proved to be right. Cordell Hull and many in the State Department were skeptical of the idea of a coordinator's office; they saw it, quite justifiably, as circumventing their authority. Had Jim made a direct appeal to the President, Hull would have tried to block the idea and probably would have been successful. Eventually, Hull decided it was necessary and approved it in essentially the same form as we had originally conceived it.

The most serious difficulty we encountered in setting up the Coordinator's Office was finding a director who was acceptable to FDR. The person Forrestal and I wanted for the job was William L. "Will" Clayton of Houston, Texas, an exceptionally talented businessman whose company, Anderson, Clayton and Company, had been doing business for years in Latin America. Others on our list of possible candidates included Ferdinand Eberstadt, Nelson Rockefeller, and John Hay "Jock" Whitney, who were also able and knowledgeable with respect to the subject.

Forrestal took our list to the White House to discuss it with the President. I wasn't present at the meeting, but I recall the story as Jim related it to me upon his return. At the mention of Clayton's name for the post, FDR drew back and proclaimed him to be unacceptable because of Will's past associations with anti–New Deal business groups and because it was rumored that Will had contributed $25,000 to Wendell Willkie's 1940 presidential campaign. He also turned down Eberstadt, feeling that Ferd, though brilliant, had too prickly a personality and was too controversial. But he found Nelson Rockefeller acceptable; he had received a campaign contribution of $25,000 from Nelson.

Forrestal told me that he had urged the President to reconsider his decision. If, however, he was determined to appoint Nelson, he ought to appoint Will Clayton as his deputy. He had told the President that although Will had the greater competence, he was not someone to stand on prestige and position. He would, Forrestal thought, be prepared to accept the position of deputy. He could then give his wisdom and expertise to the organization and Nelson could give it the imagination, drive, and public support it needed. Forrestal said that at this point Mr. Roosevelt smiled and said, "Well, I guess Will will be all right for the deputy job because Mrs. Clayton contributed ten thousand dollars to my campaign."

Nelson Rockefeller came down from New York and over dinner one evening at the "F" Street Club, Jim and I urged him to accept the top job. He accepted, and on August 16, 1940, Mr. Roosevelt issued an executive order establishing the coordinator's office. Will Clayton accepted the post of deputy and the task of getting the Office of Coordinator of Inter-American Affairs under way appeared to have been completed.

Marshall and Selective Service

My work in Washington with Forrestal ended abruptly in August 1940, when President Roosevelt nominated him to the newly created post of under secretary of the navy. The news, when it came over the radio, was a total surprise, not only to me but to Forrestal. A week earlier Secretary of the Navy Frank Knox had invited Jim to go out on the Potomac on the Navy's yacht, the *Sequoia*. They had had dinner and had talked about world politics and sundry matters, but there had been no suggestion that he was being considered for the deputy's position. The President made the announcement without talking to Jim in advance.

When Forrestal's appointment took effect, I returned to New York to resume my association with Dillon, Read. It turned out to be a brief stay. Not long after I had returned to New York, I received a telephone call from William Draper, a former Dillon, Read partner who had long served in the Army Reserve and was now on active duty in Washington with the rank of colonel. Congress was then debating the desirability of a selective service act and Bill was part of an Army team assigned to getting the legislation designed, enacted, and implemented. He asked whether I would come down to Washington and lend a hand.

The term "systems analyst" did not then exist, but that was what he wanted me to be. Back in Washington I found myself joining a group that had already set up shop at Fort McNair to work out a draft of the proposed legislation and the particulars of the selection and deferment process under what was to become the Selective Service Act of 1940. In addition to Bill Draper and myself, our group included Major Lewis Hershey, and four or five junior officers. The chief of staff of the Army, General George C. Marshall, took a special interest in what we were doing. It was through Marshall that I received an exceptional and vivid introduction into the principles and practical processes of effective democratic government.

My recollections of Marshall are of a man totally committed to doing what was right, politically acceptable, and effective under the American democratic system. Though destined to become one of the truly great leaders of his day, Marshall was then barely known outside the Army. His reputation was that of a coolly efficient staff officer who was almost totally devoid of emotions. I came to know him in a different light. To General Marshall, American history lived, the Constitution was a vital and most precious document, and the American people were a group whose proper interests and concerns were to be given priority over all lesser considerations. He not only spoke eloquently on the practical consequences of these ideas, he lived them, radiated them, and infused them into those who worked with him.

Those of us who had spent our lives on Wall Street had been mainly concerned with solving problems; we rarely found it necessary to give much thought to how our actions might impinge on the democratic system. Marshall educated us. We were now working in a totally new environment, one in which problem solving had to take into account more than the mere mechanical results. Draft selections and deferments were a case in point. It was obvious that if the United States became involved in the war, it would need a vast number of men in uniform. Marshall's point was that men should be selected or granted deferments on the fairest and most equitable basis possible, for if they weren't, there could be a serious public backlash against the administration, a loss of confidence in the government, and a crippling of the war effort.

I was profoundly impressed by Marshall's attitude. Matters of fundamental principle were involved. We had to be able not only to decide but also to explain to the satisfaction of the country why certain occupations were placed in a deferred status and why others were not; how regional equity was being maintained despite the fact that certain cities, such as Detroit with its many highly trained workers, would have a high number of deferments. (I should add that for reasons I can ascribe only to the vagaries of fate, my draft number never came up and I was never inducted into the armed forces, even though I was eligible to be selected throughout the war. Despite jobs that would have entitled me to an exemption, I had decided at the outset of the war not to ask for one if or when I was called up.) The system had to be workable, but it also had to be fair and democratic in order to enjoy popular support.

On September 16 President Roosevelt signed into law the Selective Service Act of 1940, which had passed Congress by one vote. We were ready to implement it promptly. Millions of Americans were drafted under it. There were inevitably a number of errors in that implementation, but I am unaware of any serious criticism during World War II of the theory underlying the structure of the act.

Latin America—Again

In the summer of 1941 I once again changed jobs, this time becoming the assistant for financial matters to Nelson Rockefeller in the Office of the Coordinator of Inter-American Affairs. Will Clayton had already been lured away by Jesse Jones to the Reconstruction Finance Corporation, but in the meantime Nelson had managed to recruit a varied and interesting staff. Two with whom I worked closely were Anna Rosenberg, who later became assistant secretary of defense, and Carl Spaeth, a classmate of Nelson's at Dartmouth, a Rhodes scholar, and later dean of the Stanford Law School. Carl and I quickly became close friends.

The Rockefellers, the Spaeths, the Nitzes, and from time to time Enrique de Lozada, a Bolivian diplomat, lived together that summer in Nelson's house at 2500 Foxhall Road. My friendship with Nelson dated back to our days together in New York in the 1930s, when I had been with Dillon, Read, and he had been director of Rockefeller Center. Nelson was energetic, had an engaging manner, and invariably put vitality into an organization. But he had an enormous ego that needed to be stroked constantly; he demanded total loyalty from everyone on his staff.

One of Nelson's close friends was the new vice president, Henry Wallace, who would visit the Foxhall Road house frequently to join in the general camaraderie, play tennis, or practice with his boomerang, which he enjoyed throwing and did with remarkable skill. Everything went along reasonably well until FDR signed an executive order creating the Economic Defense Board and placed it under Henry Wallace's direction.

The board's charter gave it worldwide coordinating authority over economic activities—an authority that impinged directly on Nelson's in Latin America. The question at issue was how to resolve the conflict of jurisdiction. At first, it seemed that Henry and Nelson would arrive at a settlement on their own. They were good friends and appeared to agree on policy, but as they talked over the details, irreconcilable differences emerged.

As the disputes dragged on, those of us at the working levels of Nelson's organization and of the Economic Defense Board grew increasingly concerned. It appeared more and more probable that we would be brought into the war any day, and that we just did not have the time for extended haggling. In an attempt to settle the dispute, Carl Spaeth and I met with Henry Wallace's deputy, Milo Perkins. We three agreed that economic policy toward Latin America should be decided by Nelson and Henry jointly, but that implementation of that policy should be left to Carl Spaeth and me. We thought this arrangement might work, but in practice Henry and Nelson remained at loggerheads. Since time was slipping and we were getting no guidance, Carl and I decided we had to act on our own best judgment. When Nelson found out what we were doing, he was outraged. He took particular exception to Carl's involvement and accused him of personal disloyalty. The upshot was that Carl got fired and went over to the State Department, while I was transferred to Henry Wallace's organization to be in charge of coordinating Latin American economic matters. In the reshuffle, Nelson's office lost effective control of economic matters and wound up becoming little more than a coordinating staff for cultural affairs.

Much of this took place while I was away. In November 1941 I became part of a joint State-Treasury-Coordinator fact-finding mission to our embassies in South America. The head of the team was Christian M. Ravndal, a career Foreign Service officer, whose father had also served in the State Department. James Mann represented the Treasury, and I represented the coordinator's office. I had previously tended to accept the stereotype of the Foreign Service officer as being cautious, discreet, slow moving, and pantywaisted. Chris was nothing of the sort; on the contrary, he was both an effective diplomat and a dynamo of energy, wit, and decisiveness.

Our investigation confirmed our suspicions that the urgency felt in Washington was not shared in the field and that the organization of our embassies was then weak in all areas other than diplomatic representation and reporting. Walter Donnelly, the economic counselor in Rio de Janeiro, Brazil, for example, was an outstandingly able man, but his staff consisted of a single clerk who had been recruited in Rio some twenty years earlier. Later, after the United States became involved in the war, the U.S. mission in Brazil amounted to some one thousand people, many of them engaged in the development and procurement of strategic materials essential to the war effort.

When we arrived in Montevideo, Uruguay, the ambassador invited us to have dinner with the principal members of his staff. After the dessert course, the ambassador asked Chris to brief the group on our mission.

Chris began his remarks in eminently diplomatic style, from time to time referring to his host as "Mr. Ambassador." He described in detail the instructions he had received from Sumner Welles, the under secretary of state. But his final remarks were directly to the point. The United States, in collaboration with William Stephenson, who headed British intelligence, had developed a list of people in Latin America who were actively sympathetic to Germany and Italy. This was called the "Proclaimed List." By executive order of the President, all American citizens were forbidden to do business with those on the list. Ravndal pointed out that in Uruguay, the American ambassador had not implemented the President's instructions and that some of the people on the list were the ambassador's personal friends and acquaintances. When Chris got to this portion of his remarks, he said that Sumner Welles' final instructions to him concerning Uruguay had been to "goose" the ambassador. By morning the ambassador had acted.

It was during this trip, while on a stopover in Asunción, Paraguay, checking into our hotel, that I heard the news of the Japanese attack on Pearl Harbor on December 7, 1941. That an attack by the Japanese had taken place did not surprise me; relations between the United States and Japan had been steadily deteriorating for some time. When Roosevelt imposed an embargo on the export of critical materials to Japan, I had begun to fear the worst. As the embargo became tighter, the Japanese had grown more desperate, feeling that their just place in the world was at stake. The question in my mind was where and when they would make their move. The answer came with dramatic suddenness at Pearl Harbor. We hurriedly completed our mission in Bolivia, Chile, Peru, Ecuador, and Colombia and returned to Washington. What we found was a city radically changed in mood from when we had left.

Economic Mobilization for the War

Shortly after the Japanese attack on Pearl Harbor, the Economic Defense Board became the Board of Economic Warfare (BEW). At first the change of title appeared inconsequential since it carried with it no new powers or duties. But within a few months, as the nation moved into high gear for the war, the BEW began to acquire additional responsibilities. Hitherto, the board's primary function had been to control exports. On April 13, 1942, President Roosevelt issued another executive order that expanded the board's activities into the control of imports as well. More importantly, the board also acquired the power to determine the policies, plans, and procedures of all federal departments and agencies with respect to the procurement and stimulation of production of imports essential to the war effort. It was a broad mandate and it naturally touched off a great deal of resentment among competing agencies, especially the State Department and the Reconstruction Finance Corporation (RFC).

My own duties at this time underwent a similar change. From dealing with purely Latin American affairs I was transferred to a new job with responsibility for policy affecting the worldwide procurement of metals and minerals. The actual procurement was originally done by the Reconstruction Finance Corporation and its subsidiaries—the Metals Reserve Company, the Rubber Reserve Company, and the U.S. Commercial Company. What we in the BEW did was to issue directives to those operating subsidiaries of the RFC stating what contracts should be negotiated and executed. This procurement was not only for the United States; we were doing it for the British and our other allies as well. The Combined Raw Materials Board decided the international allocation of the materials acquired and the War Production Board decided the domestic allocation.

After the war I found that all of the belligerents had faced similar problems of mobilization. There were differences, of course, but there were also many striking similarities, a fact which became evident when I interrogated Albert Speer, Germany's minister of war production, at the end of the war. All of the major powers had been deficient to one degree or another in some essential raw materials and had had to find ways of coping with chronic shortages. One way, prior to the war, was by stockpiling. All countries stockpiled, though in Germany and Japan it was done on a much more intensive basis. In Japan the critical items were iron and oil because Japan had practically no natural reserves of either. Much of Japan's steel was smelted from scrap iron purchased before the war from the United States. Germany faced a similar problem, but dealt with it in a somewhat different fashion. Although Germany did have some iron ore reserves, it was not high-grade ore, so Germany imported most of its high-grade ore from Sweden. It had guaranteed access to that by its successful attack on Norway. Fortunately, the United States had a great abundance of natural resources, but we too faced shortages of such things as copper, lead, zinc, tin, rubber, quartz crystals, and mica, to name only a few, much or all of which had to be imported from abroad.

When war broke out a primary goal was a vast acceleration of the production of armaments. The immediate problem was to allocate the more critical materials in such a way as to optimize and maximize production. Not surprisingly, since almost everything was in short supply at the outset, there was considerable competition over who would get what. The approach taken in the United States and in most other countries was to articulate the scheme of control around the one critical war material which cut across the entire range of war production. In our case it was steel. If the Army decided it needed so many tanks, someone would have to estimate the steel requirements for those tanks and settle on the priority they should have in the allocation of steel. There were other subordinate requirements as well, which usually fell in line behind the principal allocation, though special shortages continually plagued the system. Overseas procurement, which was my responsibility, constituted an essential part of dealing with these shortages.

In general, I found my boss, Vice President Henry Wallace, to be an intelligent and serious man, not the bumbling "good heart" as he was so often portrayed in the press. Born and raised in Iowa, he felt a special kinship to the American farmer. Both his grandfather and father were prominent farm journalists, and his father had also served in the 1920s as secretary of agriculture in the Harding and Coolidge administrations.

Among Henry's early accomplishments were the invention of new statistical methods for more accurately measuring farm output and the development of a new high-yield strain of hybrid corn that helped contribute to the enormous increase in farm production in World War I. After the war, however, overseas demand for American farm products declined and there was a sharp drop in agriculture prices, resulting in a depression across the farm belt. Henry blamed the Republicans and in 1928 he jumped parties and supported Alfred E. Smith, a Democrat, for president. Four years later he joined the Roosevelt administration as secretary of agriculture and in 1940 he was FDR's running mate.

Henry Wallace was a man dominated by a vision of an increasingly egalitarian future. He and his deputy, Milo Perkins, saw the future of American interests abroad in terms of supporting left-wing movements. Not surprisingly, the BEW became a haven for leftists—Marxists, radical nonconformists in the Populist tradition, and a number of avowed (and some unavowed) Communists. Wallace himself had visions beyond the war and hoped to see a postwar revitalization of the underdeveloped world through unleashing the mass of the population from what he viewed to be the oppression of their masters, in some cases European colonialism. I fully supported his basic goal, but his methods and insistence on unreasoning support of the Left caused me numerous problems. One of his policies, for example, was that our contracts for the purchase of raw materials should include a "labor clause" committing each foreign producer to engage in fair labor practices such as we had in the United States. It may have seemed reasonable from Henry Wallace's standpoint, but in countries like Chile and Bolivia, it was viewed as unwarranted U.S. intervention in their domestic affairs and aroused bitter resentment.

Matters came up daily that required me to deal with a wide range of people, problems, and ideas. A particularly serious problem arose shortly after the Battle of Kasserine Pass in North Africa, where General Erwin Rommel's Afrika Korps inflicted a humiliating defeat on our forces. After-battle assessments indicated that a major factor in the defeat was the ability of Rommel's people to listen in on the radio communications between our tanks and their battalion commanders. The reason for this was that we had only one or two frequencies for communication with our tanks, this owing to the few oscillator plates in our radio sets. Rommel's tanks, on the other hand, had more sophisticated radios with many more possible frequencies, which they changed regularly to prevent our side from listening in. As a result of these findings, the army revised its requirements for the number of frequencies in our radio sets, increasing the need for quartz oscillator plates by some tenfold. Quartz crystals only occur in a geological formation called a "pegmatite deposit," and those occur only in certain parts of the world, Brazil and India being virtually the only sources.

It was necessary, therefore, that we find a way greatly to increase the production of quartz crystals. I went down to Brazil with a team of about forty geologists and mining engineers to seek out new sources of supply and to arrange for the delivery of mining equipment to bring new mines into operation as quickly as possible. We roamed through the state of Minas Gerais on horseback for weeks trying to locate additional pegmatite deposits. We found some, but the prospects of a large and immediate increase in production were not encouraging.

Upon returning to Washington, I discovered that the problem had already been solved, not through the discovery of any new sources of supply but by an advance in technology. Previously, only three companies—Western Electric, General Electric, and Westinghouse—had been in the business of producing oscillator plates. All used essentially the same process, which involved testing the crystals for malformations before grinding or "lapping" them to the desired thickness. Many crystals failed the test and the entire crystal was then discarded. But then a small company in Chicago, the Delta Machine Company, asked permission to take the rejected crystals, cut them into plates, lap them, and then test them. Most of them worked! Unexpectedly the lapping process straightened out malformations in the crystalline structure. Within a brief time, instead of a shortage of oscillator plates, we actually had a surplus.

Similar solutions were often found for other problems. Items that were scarce at the beginning of the war were often available in overabundance by the end, sometimes by finding new technologies or substitutes, but more often than not simply through hard work. Take the example of aluminum. At the outset of the war Isador Lubin, a White House economist, suggested to FDR that he announce a production target of a hundred thousand airplanes a year. Most people, including me, thought this a fantastic and unattainable goal. The amount of aluminum needed to produce a hundred thousand planes is immense. It required that we develop Alcoa's and Reynolds' metals facilities in British Guiana (now Guyana) and Dutch Guiana (now Suriname) and encourage Aluminium Ltd.—now ALCAN—greatly to expand its production in Canada. The effort was considerable, but it paid off in the end; we succeeded in meeting the production target.

One of the more bizarre episodes in which I found myself involved occurred early in 1943 around the time of the Casablanca Conference between Roosevelt and Churchill. One day a request appeared on my desk for the procurement of large amounts of green tea. I had no idea at the time what this was all about and only later learned that it was part of the "Darlan deal" that brought the French in North Africa over to our side. As part of the deal, to placate the Arab sheiks in the area, the United States agreed to supply them with green tea, considered a delicacy by the sheiks.

The only place in the world where green tea could be procured was China. Much of the tea-producing region of China had already fallen to the Japanese, so procurement in large amounts usually involved smuggling through enemy lines. After difficult negotiations, I finally arranged with the Washington representatives of the Chinese National Resources Board to acquire the amounts of tea we needed. The next problem was to get it out of China, no mean feat at the time since our principal means of access to China was through the air over the "Hump"—the mountain chain dividing India from China.

I went over to the State Department and located the officer working on Chinese affairs to enlist his help. His name was Alger Hiss. I had seen Hiss before at meetings, but this was my first face-to-face encounter with him in negotiations. I had difficulty persuading him to support the allocation of space for my tea on the return flights from Chungking to India.

With some people you quickly sense that they are frank and open and have nothing to hide. Alger was not that way; I had the feeling that he was holding something back. I couldn't quite figure out what it was, but it made me feel uneasy.

It turned out that Alger was a good friend of Laurence Duggan's, who lived around the corner from our house in Washington on Woodley Road. During the war years gasoline was rationed, so we organized a car pool that included Larry and another neighbor, John Dickey, who later became president of Dartmouth College. Then it became convenient to add a fourth member and Larry suggested Alger Hiss. So for a while Alger and I were in the same car pool. After the war, when the House Un-American Activities Committee became active, it subpoenaed Larry Duggan to testify on alleged Communist activities. To the horror and amazement of his friends and acquaintances, Larry, rather than submit to questioning, committed suicide.

Shortly after Duggan's suicide the loyalty investigation of Alger Hiss by a Senate subcommittee headed by Richard Nixon began. The day the hearings opened, Charles E. "Chip" Bohlen and I were having lunch together at the Metropolitan Club, which in those days had a ticker tape that spewed forth the day's news as it came across from the wire services. Before going upstairs for lunch, Chip and I stopped to check the tape and saw a summary of Alger's testimony relating to the 1945 Yalta Conference between Roosevelt, Churchill, and Stalin. Chip said, "What Hiss said about Yalta isn't the way it happened. I know. I was Roosevelt's interpreter. I don't know why Hiss is doing so, but he is lying." That revived my initial skepticism about Alger Hiss. From then on I doubted the truthfulness of his testimony.

Not all the problems I encountered were overseas. Some were here in Washington and involved bitter interagency jealousy and rivalry. As time went by, it became evident that the activities of the BEW were generally resented by the State Department. In fact, Wallace was in a continual battle with Cordell Hull, the secretary of state, whom he considered to be far too conservative. One day some miners were killed during the course of a strike at the Catavi tin mines in Bolivia. Wallace denounced to the press Cordell Hull and the State Department's policy toward Bolivia and insinuated that the department was responsible for what he referred to as the "Catavi Massacre." President Roosevelt was forced to intervene in this internal row; he decided to send a three-member team to investigate the affair. The chairman of the group was a judge named McGruder. Mr. Hull was to nominate the second member, and Henry Wallace was to pick the third. Wallace nominated me, as I had been actively concerned with the Bolivian situation, particularly the procurement of tin, of which we were then in very short supply.

Henry called me into his office to give me guidance before I was to leave Washington and to fill me in on the current U.S. ambassador to Bolivia, Pierre de Lagarde Boal, a career diplomat who had been born in France but raised in the United States. He told me that when World War I broke out, Boal had rushed to Europe to join the French cavalry and later became one of the first members of the Lafayette Escadrille. Twice wounded, he had won both the Legion of Honor and the Croix de Guerre. He was a man of complete integrity, courage, and judgment. There was no doubt in Henry's mind that Boal had acted with all propriety in the Catavi incident, but that was not the point. Henry was certain that after the war the wave of the future would be to the left. It was important that the United States establish itself during the war as being in the forefront of that wave of the future. He indicated that his own hopes of being able to make an adequate contribution to history required him to lead in this movement. The substance of the message was that I was to find Boal guilty of disregarding the miners' rights regardless of the facts, and that this was justified by what Henry personally conceived to be the proper objective of U.S. policy. I told Henry that he must nominate someone else; I could not carry out his guidance.

As time went on Wallace found himself involved in a bitter quarrel with Jesse Jones, head of the Reconstruction Finance Corporation, that eventually brought down the BEW. The quarrel stemmed largely from the fact that the BEW was directly dependent on the RFC for the financing of its operations abroad. We relied on the RFC and its subsidiaries to provide the necessary loans and credits for our foreign purchases. Wallace and Jones had never been friends; in fact, they had long been political rivals. So it was not surprising that the cooperation we received was less than enthusiastic. Transactions that should have taken a day or two to complete took weeks or even months. Wallace grew frustrated, then irritated, and finally in the spring of 1943 he tried to secure the transfer of the U.S. Commercial Company, the RFC subsidiary, to the BEW so that we could do our own financing. Jones never came out directly against the transfer, but it was clear that he was much opposed.

As the quarrel between Wallace and Jones surfaced in the newspapers, President Roosevelt became concerned and directed James F. Byrnes, his newly appointed "czar" for wartime economic matters, to settle the matter as quickly and expeditiously as possible. Wallace and Jones were too personally involved to come to any reasonable settlement. In mid-July 1943, after Byrnes had held several fruitless talks with Wallace and Jones, the President announced the abolition of the BEW and the consolidation of its functions, along with those of the U.S. Commercial Company, in a new organization known as the Office of Economic Warfare under Leo T. Crowley. For Wallace, personally, it was a stunning setback that hurt him deeply.

Leo Crowley and the FEA

The Office of Economic Warfare, or OEW, turned out to be an interim agency, the first step toward the complete consolidation of governmental economic activities abroad into a single organization. In September 1943 the OEW was superseded by the Foreign Economic Administration, or FEA, which acquired all the responsibilities of the old Board of Economic Warfare and its subsidiary corporations, the Office of Lend-Lease Administration, and several agencies previously attached to the State Department, including the Office of Foreign Relief and Rehabilitation and the Office of Foreign Economic Coordination.

The head of this new organization, Leo T. Crowley, was a stalwart in the Wisconsin Democratic party. I found Crowley a thoroughly incompetent and corrupt individual. He used politics and his political connections to further the personal ambitions of his former business associates. Though he styled himself a midwestern Populist, I doubt whether he ever really had any firm political convictions like Henry Wallace, who truly was a midwestern Populist. The small bank Crowley had presided over, like many other banking institutions in the Depression, had failed. It was later disclosed that he had avoided personal bankruptcy only by obtaining a loan with wholly improper strings attached from a New York financier.

In 1944 President Roosevelt named Will Clayton, who was then deputy director of the RFC, to supervise the disposal of surplus property at home and abroad. Will delegated responsibility for the disposal of surplus property overseas to Leo Crowley, who in turn directed me, in addition to my procurement duties, to prepare plans and recommendations on how surplus property abroad should be dealt with. To avoid red tape, I consulted directly with General Lucius Clay, who was then Jimmy Byrnes' deputy in the Office of War Mobilization and Reconversion.

After examining the problem, I came to the conclusion that there was no point in trying to sell surplus property abroad at the end of hostilities because few, if any, of the countries involved would have the necessary foreign exchange. The principal problem we were likely to encounter with many countries after the war was one of finding enough assistance for them to assure their recovery; it should not be one of exacting payment for property that was inconvenient for us to return to the United States. For some time I had been interested in the question of the postwar strategic position of the United States and the steps we should take in case the coalition against Hitler fell apart after Germany's defeat. It seemed to me that the security of the United States would be greatly enhanced if we had control of a series of island bases around the perimeter of the Eurasian landmass.

Having these thoughts in mind, I talked to General Clay and suggested to him that we work out an arrangement with our Allies. We would turn over to them the surplus military equipment and other surplus U.S. property located abroad at the end of the war in return for long-term leases on those island base facilities which would contribute to our mutual long-term security. It was Clay's view that at the peace conference which would follow the conclusion of the war we would be in a position to ask for and get whatever was necessary for our long-term security; accordingly, he saw no need for action prior to a peace conference. I had the highest respect for Clay's abilities, but in this instance I felt he was being exceedingly shortsighted and overly optimistic. Indeed, the postwar peace conference he envisioned has yet to take place.

I proceeded, even though I had no formal designation of authority, to assemble the necessary staff to deal in detail with the surplus property tasks Crowley had assigned to me. I "borrowed" about forty or fifty people from other parts of the agency, but I could not go to the Bureau of the Budget or Congress for permanent positions and funds to keep the operation alive without Crowley's authorization. So I appealed to Crowley and asked him to sign a directive I had had the legal staff prepare. Crowley refused to sign it. "Paul," he told me, "you know what I'd really like is Will Clayton's job as director of surplus property disposal; if I sign this and you fellows do a good job of handling it, the credit will all go to Will Clayton, because he's in charge of the overall enterprise. If this thing lays an egg, the responsibility for that will rest with Will Clayton, which will improve my chances of getting his job."

I said, "I understand you clearly, Mr. Crowley, but under those circumstances I can't do my job. I resign." Crowley was dumbfounded for a moment and refused to believe me. Finally he replied. "I don't want you to resign, Paul," he said. "I'm just telling you what I want you to do." When I insisted that I *had* resigned and that it was all over, Crowley became threatening. He said, "You know, I'm an important figure in the

Democratic party and I will guarantee you that if you do this you will never again get a job in a Democratic administration." Crowley's threat notwithstanding, I stuck to my guns; having handed in my written resignation, I took a taxi to the Pentagon, and within two hours signed on to a job with the U.S. Strategic Bombing Survey.

2

The U.S. Strategic Bombing Survey

In the fall of 1944, after four years in Washington working mostly on economic problems connected with the war, I was given a new assignment—that of assisting Franklin D'Olier in organizing and conducting the U.S. Strategic Bombing Survey (USSBS), initially as one of the survey's directors and, later, as its vice chairman. One evening, shortly before my resignation from the FEA, Phyllis and I had dinner with Colonel Guido R. Perera and his wife, Faith, both of whom we had known for years. Guido asked whether I might be interested in becoming involved in a new project he was helping to organize—a study of the effects of strategic bombing on Germany. I gave it little thought until my confrontation a few days later with Leo Crowley, after which I had grabbed the taxi to the Pentagon to see D'Olier and his deputy, Henry Alexander. After about half an hour of discussion, D'Olier asked whether I would serve as one of the directors of USSBS. I accepted on the spot.

D'Olier was a distinguished elderly man, who had been a colonel in World War I and had served as an aide to General John J. Pershing. He had been the first head of the American Legion. For many years he had been president of the Prudential Life Insurance Company. Alexander was a highly competent lawyer, who had left the Davis, Polk law firm to become a partner in J. P. Morgan and Company. D'Olier had been asked to be chairman and Henry Alexander vice chairman of the USSBS (which we pronounced "uzz-buzz").

George Ball, another FEA refugee and, later, one of the directors of USSBS, was also present at the interview. D'Olier wanted the appointment to go through promptly and asked Ball how it could best be expedited, since the appointment of USSBS directors required presidential approval. George, noting that Colonel D'Olier had an appointment with President Roosevelt the next day, suggested that D'Olier take the matter up with the President at that time. To expedite things George reached into his briefcase and drew out a sheet of White House stationery which he seemed to have handy for just such emergencies. He put the sheet in the typewriter and proceeded to type out the appropriate language. FDR signed it the next day. Thus, within twenty-four hours of having been told by Leo Crowley that I would never again get a job in a Democratic administration, I had been appointed to a new post in the Roosevelt administration.

The Task Begins

When I joined the bombing survey, it was still little more than an organization on paper. But because of Guido Perera's advance preparations, we were able to assemble our study teams fairly quickly. The survey was almost wholly a civilian operation from start to finish, with necessary staff and logistical support provided by the Army Air Forces. The major requirement in selecting the directors of the project was that they know nothing whatsoever about strategic bombing in order to assure that they would approach the problem with an objective attitude. In addition to Henry Alexander and me, J. Fred Searls, deputy director in Jimmy Byrnes' Office of War Mobilization and formerly the president of New-mont Mining, was brought in to be in charge of studying ordnance and vehicle production; Harry L. Bowman of the Drexel Institute of Technology headed the physical damage division; and Rensis Likert, a specialist in opinion sampling from the Agriculture Department, was put in charge of studying the effect of strategic bombing on enemy morale. Later, as we felt the need for someone to assess the overall economic impact of strategic bombing, John Kenneth Galbraith, then on the staff of *Fortune* magazine, joined our organization. My particular assignment at the outset was to evaluate the effects of the air campaign on the German ball-bearing and machine-tool industries.

On November 4, 1944, having completed our preliminary briefings in Washington, a group of ten of us, led by D'Olier, boarded a plane for England to begin accumulating data for our study. After a few days in England, D'Olier, Henry Alexander, and I flew to Paris to talk directly with General Carl "Tooey" Spaatz, who commanded the U.S. Strategic Air Forces in Europe.

General Spaatz had recently established a forward headquarters next to General Dwight D. Eisenhower's just outside Paris. D'Olier and Alexander were billeted at Spaatz's headquarters while I shared a room with a Colonel Peters, who was organizing an administrative support staff for USSBS adjacent to General Eisenhower's headquarters. Peters had developed a close friendship with a young woman named Kay Summersby, an attractive British girl who was one of Ike's chauffeurs. When she was not driving for Ike, she served as my chauffeur. For three or four days Peters, Kay Summersby, and I went everywhere together. Later, rumors began to circulate that General Eisenhower had fallen in love with her and was persuaded by General Marshall not to divorce Mamie so that he could marry Kay. I had thought she was Peters' girl.

In our meeting with General Eisenhower I was astonished by the shallowness of his strategic judgment; I was, however, favorably impressed by his effectiveness in handling administrative matters. One of the questions we needed to settle was whether the survey should rely on General Eisenhower's forces for its logistical support or whether it should organize its own logistics with its own jeeps, living quarters, and communications. Ike advised us to organize our own; if we relied on his subordinate commanders to take care of us we would find ourselves in continual argument and delay. He was quite right. But on matters having to do with strategy of the air war and the targets to be attacked, his judgment seemed naive. For example, he advocated that inasmuch as food was a fundamental requirement for the German people, strategic bombing should concentrate on burning down barns on German farms. There were literally hundreds of thousands of barns in Germany and they could be rebuilt in days.

Upon my return to England, one of my first concerns was to find a competent analyst to assist me in evaluating the effectiveness of the Army Air Forces' massive and repeated attacks against the German ball-bearing industry. My criteria for an assistant were straightforward: He had to have, first, a Ph.D. degree, as evidence of his research ability, and second, a close knowledge of Germany, including the language, in order to work, after the conclusion of hostilities, with Germans to produce and evaluate data. He need have no specialized experience since the field was virgin territory; no one had researched a similar problem before. The Army obligingly made a check of available personnel and eventually came up with twenty-five names, including one man who prior to the war had been Vincent Astor's butler!

The most promising candidate on the list was an Army sergeant named Philip J. Farley, who was to go on to have a distinguished career after the war in government, serving as deputy director of the Arms

Control and Disarmament Agency in the early 1970s while I was a member of the U.S. SALT delegation. When I first met Farley in World War II, he was a clerk at one of the American air bases in East Anglia. I interviewed Sergeant Farley and told him that I was looking for a man to work primarily on assessing the impact of strategic bombing on the German ball-bearing industry, one of the AAF's top priority targets. Farley expressed interest in the job and I decided to give him a trial period of a week to see if he would work out. It became clear in just that short time that he was not only able, but could absorb information faster than any of the rest of us.

It was during this period that I came to know General Orvil A. Anderson, one of the most colorful and interesting figures in the AAF. His reputation was that of a man with great confidence in his own judgment and little respect for authority. But he had an extremely keen mind and provided a wealth of information, having been part of the original group that after Pearl Harbor had worked out the details of the air offensive against Germany. Like many others in the AAF, Anderson saw strategic air power as the key to victory.

Anderson explained to us that the year before, in 1943, he had been involved in planning and executing the heavy raids against the Schweinfurt ball-bearing factories. By and large those raids, from the standpoint of U.S. planes and airmen, had been a disaster. In one raid in October 1943, the AAF had sent over 291 planes. Twenty percent had been shot down and of those that returned, over eighty percent had suffered some degree of damage. Each crew member had to fly thirty missions before he could be rotated back to the United States. With the average loss rate being nine percent per mission, the chances of surviving thirty missions were pretty slim. It turned out that if the crew survived its first mission, the chances of surviving the second and third and so forth steadily increased. The best crews, as they gained experience, did in fact survive thirty missions, even though the odds were against it. But with loss rates as high as they were, there was a serious problem in keeping up morale.

Anderson knew that continuing loss rates such as these would be intolerable. The problem stemmed mostly from the effective defense mounted by the German Luftwaffe's fighter aircraft, which our AAF had hoped it could destroy through attrition, that is, it could down more enemy planes in the course of bombing German targets than the Germans could replace. As our early experience showed, things were working out the other way around, with our losses well in excess of theirs. In keeping with his reputation for impatience with incompetence—no matter where it lay—and contrary to the directive then in existence, Anderson ordered his bombers to draw out the German fighters, and then instructed his bomber commanders, when threatened with attack, to return to base or scatter. The fighters could then concentrate on attacking the Luftwaffe, unhampered by having to defend the bombers. In a matter of weeks, the air war had turned in our favor and our planes could carry out their strategic bombing missions almost at will. The results of Anderson's unauthorized decision were an undisputed success.

In order that we might become more familiar with the problems of strategic bombing, Anderson suggested that I spend some time at a divisional base where actual operations were planned and executed. The base chosen was that of the Fortieth Combat Wing at Bury St. Edmunds, commanded by Colonel Frederick Castle. The AAF was generally composed of relatively young men; Fred was somewhat older than most. He had been in the Army Air Corps as a young man, but had left the service to join the Sperry Gyroscope Company, where he rose to become a vice president. When he reentered the service after the outbreak of the war in Europe, he was given the rank of colonel rather than what he should have been—a general officer—had he served without a break.

Rarely have I been so impressed by any single individual as I was by the capacity and courage of this man. I lived with Fred Castle in the same shack for about a week, watched everything he did, and listened closely to what he said. Despite the pressures of his responsibilities he seemed to enjoy educating me on all the manifold problems of his command and also speculating on those of the postwar world, and how the United States might best go about dealing with them.

His command included three airfields and about forty thousand men. It was a round-the-clock operation, seven days a week. Orders would come in from High Wycombe, the headquarters of the Eighth Air Force, around six o'clock each evening designating the next day's targets. Then Castle's division would work out its operational plan specifying who would do what. The planning was usually finished by midnight and Castle would then sleep for perhaps three hours. Before dawn he would get up to supervise final preparations and watch the planes take off. Once a week he would pilot the lead aircraft himself because he felt he could command his unit more effectively if he knew exactly what his men were experiencing. It was on one of these missions, two months after I left, that his plane was shot down and he lost his life.

First Forays into Germany

By the end of 1944 the strategic bombing survey was largely in place and ready to commence its substantive work. We had a basic organization, part of it headquartered in Washington, part of it in London in offices adjacent to the American embassy in Grosvenor Square. We also had a fairly sizable and growing staff of some eight hundred military officers and enlisted men and another three hundred civilian analysts. We also had gathered a considerable amount of information—targeting directives, intelligence studies, routine flying reports, and other data. What we did not have was the one thing essential to the success of our project: access to Germany—the only place where we could obtain the detailed factual information necessary to draw relevant conclusions and to demonstrate their validity to skeptics.

One of the reasons the survey was authorized when it was—in September 1944—was the expectation of many, from President Roosevelt on down, that the war in Europe would be over before the end of the year. The success of the D-day invasion, followed by the breakout from the Normandy beaches and the swift march across France, had given rise to wide expectation of an early victory. At one point it appeared that a single, well-directed thrust into Germany could swiftly end the war. Unfortunately, the failure of the Arnhem operation—a daring but unsuccessful raid in force aimed at securing an Allied bridgehead on the Rhine—had dispelled most of the optimism. In December, just as I was returning from a brief visit to the United States, the Germans launched a massive counterattack. As the Battle of the Bulge raged, hopes diminished even further for an early end to the war.

Consequently, it was not until the spring of 1945, after the Allies resumed their offensive, that our field teams got their first glimpse inside Germany. We quickly discovered that any delay in arriving at a target site we wanted to investigate could jeopardize our finding the information we needed. Ground combat, looting, and a host of other factors could change local conditions to such an extent that it might prove impossible to obtain accurate information on the effects of strategic bombing. So it was imperative that our field teams be on the front lines as quickly as possible following in the wake or even sometimes in advance of the attacking armies. The danger to our personnel, especially to the "spearhead" teams we sent out to secure an area for later study, was considerable.

One such incident involved the disappearance of a field team near Leipzig (one of the few forays into territory designated for Soviet occupation that the survey was able to make) just before V-E Day. When I heard the news of the team's disappearance, I immediately set off on a personal investigation. Not until after the surrender, when I located one of the survivors in a hospital, did I fully learn what had happened. They had run into a German roadblock and enemy soldiers had fired on them. Two of our men had been killed and the other two had been wounded, one rather seriously. The two survivors were captured by the Germans. The head of the team, a machine tool company executive from Ohio, was less seriously wounded. After an hour or so, a German colonel appeared and asked him if he would accompany him to see his commanding general. The general, it turned out, thought his position was hopeless and offered to surrender what remained of his corps. Our executive from Ohio said he would be delighted to accept the general's offer, but in order to make it official he would have to get back to the front lines of the Allied forces, whereupon the general had him escorted safely back to the lines and our team leader returned with the accepted surrender in his pocket!

The Interrogation of Albert Speer

As the war in Europe drew to a close, the survey shifted the focus of its operations to the continent and moved its central field headquarters after V-E Day to Frankfurt, which we knew by its code name, "Dustbin." The Germany I returned to on V-E Day was a study in sharp contrasts. The big cities were almost totally in ruins, but the countryside was virtually untouched. In spite of having seen Germany at all seasons of the year, I cannot recall that country being any more beautiful than in that spring of 1945. Not only southern Germany, but the country north to Frankfurt, all of Thuringia, and even Schleswig-Holstein were indescribably lovely. To my surprise, the people appeared friendly and looked healthy, reasonably well fed, and certainly better dressed and neater than the people in England. The most serious threat to the economy was the extensive damage suffered by the transportation system. The outward appearance of the population notwithstanding, I had no doubt that the German people were in for difficult times. However, I judged that the situation was not hopeless.

As our field teams moved into Germany they spread far and wide in search of information. From the voluminous data we finally accumulated, the survey was able to demonstrate that not one end item of German war production had been delayed a single day by virtue of the attacks on the ball-bearing industry. The buildings of the ball-bearing plants had been blown into rubble, not once, but time after time. The screw machines, lathes, and grinding machines that actually made the ball bearings were of heavy construction and could be dug out of the rubble, put back in working order, and reerected at some other location. While the cost to the Germans to restore ball-bearing production was high, involving the dispersal of factories and even the building of underground plants, they were able to offset the damage within the time they had to repair their losses. This appeared to answer one of the questions we had hoped to answer—whether concentrated attack on one small but essential component of industry would seriously check a country's war production machine. The evidence indicated that if the time and effort necessary to repair and/or relocate plants by dispersal or by building underground could be fitted into the time available, then the air attacks would not accomplish their purpose.

Most of the time our field teams were able to locate the information we were seeking. But sometimes our efforts resulted in bitter disappointment, as in the case of tracking down the official records of Hitler's minister of armaments and the mastermind behind Germany's war production effort—Albert Speer. Our intelligence indicated that the Germans had evacuated Speer's files to a secret hiding place in the Harz Mountains. We checked out the report, but before our team arrived on the scene, the Germans destroyed the records. What our team found instead, however, was something no less intriguing—an underground tunnel complex, built in the 1930s, that housed the main production and assembly facilities of the V-1 and V-2 rockets that had terrorized London during the war. The main complex totaled thirty-five miles of three interconnecting caves, with twenty-eight additional caves for storage.

The most important catch was Albert Speer himself. We heard reports that Speer had escaped Berlin just before Soviet troops entered the city. But it was not until May 10, 1945, that Lieutenant Wolfgang G. Sklarz and Sergeant Harold Fassburg, members of our G-2 Interrogation Section, stumbled across Speer in Flensburg on the North German coast. At the time of the discovery of Speer's whereabouts, I was in London. The next morning I hastily organized my materials and flew to Germany to participate in Speer's interrogation.

We found Speer living in Schloss Glucksburg, the castle of the dukes of Holstein, near Flensburg. At the time the area in and around Flensburg was under the control of a "rump" German government headed by

Admiral Karl Doenitz; it was the only part of Germany that the Allies had not yet occupied, so in a sense we were moving in hostile territory. Speer had no objection to being interviewed. On the contrary, he valued the attention we paid him. Most importantly he knew he was a candidate for war criminal prosecution and hoped against hope that if he cooperated, his chances of acquittal would be improved. Our interrogations stretched over some ten days. We would arrive in the afternoon at about two and talk until six or seven in the evening. His own secretary did much of the note-taking and translating.

As the interrogation progressed, it became obvious that Speer was enormously proud of what he had been able to accomplish in increasing Germany's war production, particularly during the final six months, when the damage caused by our bombing had become irreparable. Now that Germany was defeated, he saw it in the best interests of the German people to have the war against Japan brought to a swift conclusion. He spoke freely of his experiences, and told us where to find those of his papers, including his personal reports to Hitler, that had escaped destruction.

After nine days of interviews, word arrived that the Doenitz government was about to be arrested, including Speer. We decided therefore to conduct one final, exhaustive interrogation to extract as much information as possible, not only on the German war effort but on Speer's views of the underlying reasons for Germany's collapse. For five hours Speer recounted in detail his experiences and feelings. In the final analysis Speer attributed Germany's defeat to the softness, stupidity, and incompetence of the group around Hitler, particularly Goering, Bormann, Himmler, Sauckel, and certain Gauleiters, the regional Nazi party leaders. For Hitler he expressed his personal admiration. During the period of spreading defeat he described Hitler's progressive separation from reality. Even in the Third Reich's final days, when Speer refused Hitler's direct order to pursue a scorched earth policy in the face of the advancing American, British, and Russian armies, Hitler had not turned on him as he had on some of the others. Speer came from a prominent, well-educated family, a fact that he felt set him apart from Hitler's other lieutenants. Being mostly from working-class backgrounds with little education, they fully exploited their newly found power and position and acquired insatiable tastes for luxuries and creature comforts. It was, in Speer's view, literally a regime of wine, women, and song. Toward the end Goering and a number of others turned to drugs or alcohol to numb the reality of impending doom. Hitler did not interfere for two reasons—he was disposed to let his subordinates conduct their private lives in whatever manner they chose, while they themselves cooperated with one another in concealing their excesses from him.

The manner in which Germany's leaders conducted themselves, Speer believed, had a direct bearing on the war effort. The determination of this group to protect its standard of living led it to reject sacrifices necessary to win the war. Unlike Britain and the United States, Germany suffered no critical defeat early in the war—no Dunkirk or Pearl Harbor—to focus attention on the problem or galvanize the country into action. As a result, Germany allowed its enemies to capture the initiative. By the time German war production reached its peak in 1944 and full mobilization was declared, the tide of battle had turned so decisively that the cause had already been lost.

During the course of Speer's justification of his position, one of our group, Captain Burton H. Klein, became so angry he could no longer restrain himself from intervening. He asked how Speer could have worked with Hitler's gang and let himself be associated with the inhumanities and the stupidities of which they were so guilty. Speer replied that it was difficult for anyone who had not had a similar experience to put himself in his place. He had been torn by loyalty to his country and its government, on the one hand, and yet caught in a political climate in which survival and power could only be achieved by working alongside of, and competing with, people of whom he deeply disapproved.

Lessons Applied

Although the interrogation of Speer told us much that we needed to know, we had yet to interview Speer's chief statistician, Rolf Wagenfuehr. I was in Frankfurt when news reached me that Wagenfuehr had been located in Soviet-occupied East Berlin. The survey had a DC-3 assigned to it, so transportation was assured.

There was very little left of the Berlin I remembered from the 1920s and 1930s. Whole districts that I had known as thriving commercial and residential areas, with open-air cafés, lush gardens, and elegant apartment buildings, were now piles of rubble. What the American and British air forces had not destroyed had been finished off by the Red Army. We found Wagenfuehr living in one of the few habitable buildings in the eastern sector of the city. Wagenfuehr had already decided to cast his lot with the Russians and there seemed no way we could persuade him to come over to the West. So one evening several members of the survey's staff slipped into his house, kidnapped him, in effect, and flew him out to Bad Nauheim for interrogation. Not until after he had given us all the information he could, did we allow him to return to Berlin.

While in Berlin, I received a garbled telephone message saying I was to be at the Frankfurt airport at dawn the following morning. I drove all night in a jeep we had flown into Berlin. When I got to Frankfurt a plane was standing by to take me to Prestwick, Scotland. George Ball, General Orvil A. Anderson, and Colonel John D. Ames were waiting to fly on with me to Washington. Our plane departed immediately that same day, June 7, and two days later we began a round of meetings with the members of the Joint Target Group of the Joint Chiefs of Staff. We had been summoned back by none other than the commanding general of the Army Air Forces, General Henry H. "Hap" Arnold, in preparation for stepped-up air attacks against Japan. General Arnold wanted to be sure that, in designing a new air campaign against Japan, he made full use of what USSBS had learned in its study of the strategic bombing campaign against Germany.

At the time of our return to Washington, our findings were still incomplete, but we had accumulated sufficient information to draw tentative conclusions. Looking over the interrogations with Speer and other evidence, I felt that strategic bombing was likely to cause the greatest disruptions if it concentrated on basic industries and services, such as oil and chemicals, steel, power, and transportation. Unlike the ball-bearing and airframe plants, these basic industries, once severely damaged, could not be quickly restored to full production nor could stocks be readily replaced. Speer had spoken to us at length of this situation and the measures he had introduced to keep his basic industries in operation. So strongly had he feared attacks on them that in many instances he had resisted the construction of underground plants for finished products, arguing that if the Allies were denied these targets, they would go after basic industries, which by their nature could not be successfully concealed. In other words, he had used finished product plants as diversionary targets to lure Allied bombers away from attacking more vital industries.

The most significant finding, I thought, concerned the effects of strategic bombing on the oil refining and chemical plants and on the German transportation system. These in the end were the most decisive blows that the air campaign inflicted on the German economy. The destruction of the oil refining and chemical plants denied the Germans all but a trickle of gasoline and, as a by-product, denied them the ingredients for the manufacture of explosives. The attacks on the transportation system had left the production of factories stranded on loading platforms, disrupted vital coal shipments, and finally brought the German war economy to a standstill.

It soon became clear in our meetings with the Joint Target Group that their projections for air operations against Japan differed widely from our conclusions in Germany. Our group assigned to me the job of writing out an alternate strategy for the air attack on Japan.

I spent the Fourth of July with my family that year at our country place on Long Island. Phyllis had insisted that I leave Washington to celebrate the Fourth and I agreed, but I brought paper and pencil with me to continue my work on the alternate strategy. A picnic had been planned on Jones Beach with children and friends. Most of the time, however, I was busily writing away on yellow foolscap. Occasionally, however, I would go for a swim or build sand castles with the children. I would give the yellow sheets to Phyllis to hold for me and she would stuff them in her beach bag. On our way home we stopped at a drugstore in Glen Cove for ice-cream sodas for the children. When we arrived home and I asked Phyllis for the yellow sheets, she opened her bag and they were nowhere to be found. "Good God!" I cried in dismay, and dashed for the door. We retraced our steps, ending up at the drugstore, and there at the foot of the chair pedestal was a little heap of yellow paper which depicted in detail the alternate strategy for the air attack on Japan.

The plan I devised was essentially this: Japan was already isolated from the standpoint of ocean shipping. The only remaining means of transportation were the rail network and intercoastal shipping, though our submarines and mines were rapidly eliminating the latter as well. A concentrated air attack on the essential lines of transportation, including railroads and (through the use of the earliest accurately targetable glide bombs, then emerging from development) the Kammon tunnels which connected Honshu with Kyushu, would isolate the Japanese home islands from one another and fragment the enemy's base of operations. I believed that interdiction of the lines of transportation would be sufficiently effective so that additional bombing of urban industrial areas would not be necessary. My plan of air attack on Japan was approved but not my estimate of when it would cause Japan's capitulation.

While I was working on the new plan of air attack, Fred Searls came to see me to get my views on a new project he had recently undertaken for his former boss Jimmy Byrnes, who had just been sworn in as Truman's secretary of state. Fred said that leading members of the scientific community thought they could win the war through the building of a fantastic and still highly secret new weapon—the atomic bomb. He told me that he had examined the work of something called the "Manhattan Project" (the code name for the organization that was building the bomb) and was skeptical whether it would succeed. We concluded that even without the atomic bomb, Japan was likely to surrender in a matter of months. My own view was that Japan would capitulate by November 1945. However, the Joint Chiefs saw matters differently. The upshot was that they unanimously recommended that plans go forward for an early invasion of the Japanese home islands. President Harry S. Truman, who had succeeded FDR on the latter's death that April, was then left with the choice of using the atomic bomb against Hiroshima and Nagasaki, or of authorizing the attack against Kyushu and the Tokyo plain. He opted for the atomic bomb and in so doing opened a new chapter in the history of modern warfare.

Reassignment to Japan

Toward the end of the summer, I returned to Washington, where an advance group of the survey had set up headquarters and was beginning to write the final report on how and to what extent the strategic air campaign had contributed to Germany's defeat. By then the war in the Pacific was also over and President Truman had decided that the effectiveness of the air war against Japan should be the survey's next subject of inquiry. In addition, there were four other questions he said he wanted us to address: (1) the reasons for Japan's attack on Pearl Harbor, (2) how Japan arrived at its decision to surrender, (3) the effects of the atomic weapons dropped on Hiroshima and Nagasaki, and (4) our recommendations, based on the survey's findings in these other matters, for the postwar reorganization of the U.S. armed forces and the role that should be accorded air power.

It turned out that most of the civilians who had worked on the European phase of the survey did not want to continue with it in Japan. D'Olier was uninterested in remaining as chairman and it was with some difficulty that General Arnold persuaded him to stay on, at least in name. Henry Alexander, the survey's vice chairman, wanted to go back to J. P. Morgan and Company, and George Ball wanted to resume his law practice. Ken Galbraith, who had been in overall charge of the economics division in Europe, volunteered to come over to Japan in a temporary capacity for a month or so, but not longer. Rensis Likert, head of the morale division, also dropped out, but he provided us with a first-class replacement in a sociologist named Burton R. Fisher. Of those of us who had been in Europe together, I was one of the few who chose to stay with the survey and see it through to the finish.

I remember flying into Japan in early September over Tokyo Bay on a beautiful pale blue day—light clouds, Fujiyama on the left, and directly ahead of us, a small island rising out of the harbor mist supporting a very Japanese-looking pine tree. I quickly came to the conclusion that from the air, at least, Japan was the most beautiful country I had ever seen. Then we got down on the ground and could see just how devastating the war had been for Japan. Whole cities had been burned to the ground by the air raids, and since Japan had very few good roads to begin with, the war's disruptions had brought transportation almost to a halt. The people, especially the peasant class, appeared graceful and hardworking, but they were confused and totally demoralized. My own feelings were likewise confused. I thought Japan was a marvelous country populated by the most hateful people on earth. Like other Americans at that time, I could not forgive the Japanese for Pearl Harbor.

After landing I went directly to report to General Douglas MacArthur, the Allied supreme commander, who proceeded to give me a four-hour lecture on air power and its role in the Pacific theater. I found that there were points on which he and I were in disagreement, so I asked whether another interpretation might not be possible. MacArthur was a little annoyed at having his presentation interrupted, but he listened as politely as he could. Finally, he said, "I have a bit of advice. I don't want to see you again and I hope you so conduct yourself that you don't have to see me again. But if you feel yourself getting into trouble, then I want you to come and see me before you *really* get into trouble."

And I said, "All right, fine. I understand and I'll go about my business."

Much to my astonishment, I received word two days later that MacArthur wanted to see me again. I wondered what I might have done or what had happened to change the general's mind. This time the meeting lasted six hours, during which he again went into detail on the role of air power, incorporating virtually all the points that I had raised at our previous meeting. I was delighted that I might have influenced his thinking and felt that we had become friends. Indeed, we had. I became part of "the group," which made the rest of my stay in Japan much more enjoyable.

I became a frequent dinner guest at his house and came to enjoy greatly the company and hospitality that he and Mrs. MacArthur provided.

The general was a truly intriguing and complex man, one of the more fascinating personalities I have known. My regard for him as a military commander and for his accomplishments during the war was high. Very few others in either the Army or the Navy possessed his sense of strategy and tactics or his capacity for leadership. But he was also vain, suspicious, and contemptuous of higher civilian authority.

About a month after our first meeting, MacArthur called me into his office and asked me if I would be interested in becoming his new principal economic adviser. I told him that I would have to think it over and returned to my office, where I mentioned MacArthur's proposal to Major General William F. Marquat. Marquat had been MacArthur's principal artillery officer during the war, so he knew MacArthur's way of thinking and his approach to problems from his own experience.

He said, "If I were you, I would tell General MacArthur you will do it but only on certain conditions. One is that you would like to report directly to his chief of staff, not through the usual chain of command. If you have to report through channels, your life will be so complicated that you can't get anything done."

I said, "Yes, but I also doubt that one man can do this job by himself. I believe I should insist that I be allowed to go back to Washington and recruit four or five people to help me. Another point is, I don't think it's possible to run the Japanese economy except in coordination with general U.S. economic policy toward the Far East. Therefore, I ought to have someone back in Washington who is backstopping the operation so that it can be properly coordinated with U.S. economic policy elsewhere."

Marquat said, "Yes, I think that makes sense."

A short while later I went back to MacArthur and told him that I was prepared to accept the job, but only on the conditions that Marquat and I had discussed. MacArthur blew up. He said, "I have absolutely no use for the people in Washington, including the President. Nobody in my command is going to have any relationships with anybody in Washington. And what's more, I don't think you need additional people. You can use other people in my command but you're not going to go back and recruit other people that I don't know. I will not accept your conditions."

I said, "Well, General, I don't think one man can make a success of dealing with the Japanese economy unless he has somebody's help in the United States and support for the things that are needed here."

MacArthur said, "Don't worry about that. U.S. industry will bring sufficient pressure on President Truman so that he'll have to do the things that are right."

When I insisted that I was serious about the conditions I had suggested, MacArthur brought our conversation to an abrupt end. "All right," he said, "I understand." And that was that. The job was no longer mine to be had, and the whole matter was closed as though it had never even happened. MacArthur was like that. If you stood up to him and refused to kowtow, he usually respected you for it, but he was also very careful to protect himself. In this case, I doubt that our relationship was affected one way or another. He later appointed General Marquat to the job. Marquat had no prior experience for the job, but he wound up doing it more successfully than I had thought possible.

Mission Accomplished

The survey worked to complete its mission quickly. Our main headquarters were in the Dai Iichi building in Tokyo. Some of us stayed in the Imperial Hotel, while others who were not on field assignments lived aboard the USS *Ancon*, a freighter converted to a command ship known as "the admirals' go-cart" because it was often used to carry high-ranking officers and officials. I set December 1, 1945, as the terminal date for the field investigation and told my staff that if they would work twelve hours a day, six or seven days a week, we just might make it home for Christmas.

Of the problems President Truman had asked us to examine, I was especially intrigued by the question of why the Japanese had attacked Pearl Harbor. It seemed to me that the key person to interrogate on this subject was Prince Fumimaro Konoye, who had been replaced as prime minister by General Hideki Tojo shortly before the Pearl Harbor attack. By and large, the interrogation was a disappointment. Konoye, while cooperative, offered almost no information of importance. A few days later, however, his secretary appeared at my office in the Dai Iichi building and asked to see me. He said that Prince Konoye had the feeling that he had "not done well" in his interrogation. In further answer to the questions I had raised, Konoye, through his secretary, now presented me with his personal diary, a narration of events leading up to Japan's decision to go to war. Shortly thereafter, in December 1945, Konoye committed suicide.

In addition to Konoye's "memoir," the survey also obtained the records of the *zaibatzu*, Japan's largest industrial firms which played—and still play—a leading role in Japanese politics. It took some time to sort out the facts, mainly because of a group of economists sent to assist us by the Federal Trade Commission. While these FTC representatives may not have been Communists, they clearly shared a Marxist interpretation of economics and history which skewed their judgment. Shortly after their arrival, they produced a report, based on theory rather than research, that Japan had been prodded into the war by the intrigues of the seven leading *zaibatzu* families, who saw the war as a means of gaining control of natural resources and foreign markets.

A cursory glance at the FTC report led me immediately to question its conclusions, since it was totally contrary to the evidence we had accumulated through our interrogations of Konoye and others. I asked Ken Galbraith, who had come for a limited visit, to look into the report and find out whether there was any foundation to its claims. Ken came back in a week or ten days and presented me with strong evidence to the contrary. He had found a German intelligence officer in a prison camp in Japan who had served in the German embassy during the war and who had kept copies of the cables he had sent to Joachim von Ribbentrop, the German foreign minister, prior to Pearl Harbor. Over and over in these messages the German officer had bemoaned the fact that the *zaibatzu* were reluctant to see Japan enter the war and had fought tooth and nail against it. This evidence confirmed that the answer to the President's question was, in fact, the reverse of the draft report by the Federal Trade Commission people.

In addition to Konoye, I also interviewed Marquis Koichi Kido, head of the Imperial Household and one of the leaders of the peace faction that had ousted Tojo in 1944. My interrogation of Kido lasted several hours, but like the interview with Konoye, it seemed to go nowhere. I remember asking, "When did it first occur to you, Marquis Kido, that Japan had lost the war?" All I got in response was unintelligible mishmash. After this went on for a while, my interpreter, a young Navy officer who had been given a crash course in Japanese at the University of Michigan, turned to me and said, "Mr. Nitze, you know if you ask the question in that way, you'll never get an answer."

I said, "In that case, how should the question be asked? You understand what I want to know. How would you ask the question?"

He replied, "I would phrase the question by asking, 'Marquis Kido, when did it first occur to you that the Will of Heaven demanded that the emperor review his policy and perhaps seek a different course?' "

"All right," I said, "ask the question your way and see what happens."

The result was that Marquis Kido then gave me, in the most precise and accurate detail, exactly what I wanted. He said, "This first occurred to me after the Battle of Saipan." Then he went on to describe at length his negotiations with the emperor's advisers, the difficulties that had arisen, the negotiations with the Russians, and so forth. It all boiled down to asking the question in a way that was not offensive or humiliating by Japanese standards of proper behavior.

As part of its investigation in Japan, the survey also conducted a careful study of the effects of the atomic bombs dropped on Hiroshima and Nagasaki. At that time newspapers in the United States were filled with speculation, some of it proclaiming the atomic bomb to be of limitless power—the ultimate weapon. The survey's task was to measure as precisely as possible the exact effects of the two bombs—in other words, to put calipers on the problem so that people back home would have a factual frame of reference within which to draw conclusions about the bomb's true capabilities as well as its limitations.

When I arrived at Nagasaki, the visual evidence alone demonstrated the immense power of the weapon. About a mile and a quarter from ground zero (the point directly below where the bomb exploded in the air), there were some houses with tiled roofs. Although the houses were still standing, their tiled roofs were deformed with bubbles that had boiled up from the intense heat radiated by the explosion. Some distance away were several gas tanks which a steel structure had partially screened from the heat and radiation accompanying the explosion. Where the gas tanks had been shielded from the heat, they retained their original color, but where they had been exposed, the paint on them was burned.

Much of the evidence we accumulated came from interviews with survivors, who told of some striking anomalies. For instance, in Nagasaki, the railroads were back in operation forty-eight hours after the attack. Most of the rolling stock in the city had been destroyed, but the tracks suffered relatively minor damage. In Hiroshima, we learned that a train had been going through the city when the bomb went off. People sitting next to open windows suffered few cuts or other injuries from broken glass, but because they were directly exposed to radiation, many of them fell ill and later died. On the other hand, people sitting next to the closed windows, even though many were cut by flying glass, generally survived because the windows shielded them from the radiation. We also found that even in the immediate blast area, people who had taken to simple air raid tunnels emerged unscathed, indicating that the bomb's effects were largely confined, like most conventional weapons, to aboveground targets. But in Nagasaki the air raid warning sounded nearly ten minutes after the bombing when only four hundred people were in tunnel shelters.

As a wartime precaution the Japanese had partially evacuated Hiroshima and Nagasaki before the attacks took place. Nonetheless, casualty figures were high—70,000 to 80,000 killed in Hiroshima (about a quarter of whom were conscripted Korean laborers) and another 35,000 to 40,000 killed at Nagasaki. Yet these were not the most devastating air attacks that Japan had suffered. In one firebomb raid against Tokyo in March 1945 the AAF inflicted casualties of 83,600 killed and destroyed nearly 16 square miles of the city. The significance of the atomic bomb was that it compressed the explosive power of many conventional bombs into one and thus enormously enhanced the effectiveness of a single bomber. With each plane carrying ten tons of high explosives and incendiaries, the attacking force required to equal the effects of a single atomic weapon would have been 210 B-29s at Hiroshima and 120 B-29s at Nagasaki.

These findings influenced my perception of how the postwar military establishment should be organized. In considering the postwar structure of our defense establishment, as Mr. Truman had requested, I thought that we had to take into account the possibility that our enemies would have weapons as powerful and as destructive as our own. I became convinced therefore that any postwar reorganization of the armed forces should include provision for, first, a vigorous research and development program, to assure the optimum exploitation of science and technology for national defense; second, a vastly improved system of intelligence gathering and analysis to avoid a repetition of the Pearl Harbor disaster; and lastly, closer coordination of the armed forces under an integrated department of defense oriented toward weapons systems based upon modern technology. Under it there would be three services, each with precisely defined missions.

We recommended that one of the services, the Department of the Navy, have the mission of achieving and then exploiting, as directed, control of the surfaces of the sea, the waters below, and the air above; it would be authorized to use whatever weapons systems and basing arrangements were best suited to carrying out that task. The second, the Department of the Army, would have the mission of achieving control of land masses as directed; it would be authorized whatever weapons systems were best suited to carrying out its task, including close air support forces. The third would be the Department of Strategic Forces. It would have two tasks. One would be deep strategic attack against an enemy's heartland and the defense of our heartland against such an attack by an enemy. The second task would be to achieve general control of the air through the progressive destruction of enemy air forces. It would be authorized control over all strategic forces, including submarines with long-range missiles should these eventually be developed.

The postwar debate over service unification, and the escalating quarrel between a Air Force and the Navy over aviation and its uses, made roles and missions a problem of central importance. The Air Force wished to maintain full command and control over all land-based air and wanted no responsibility for strategic defense. The Navy, on the other hand, did not wish to be excluded from the strategic nuclear mission. The Army did not wish to take responsibility for close air support. I considered these to be narrow-minded, parochial objections. Shortly after returning to Washington, I strongly advocated my ideas to Jim Forrestal, as well as to Major General Alfred M. Gruenther, Admiral Forrest Sherman, and General Lauris Norstad, who were then working on legislation to unify the armed services. They all agreed that my proposals were basically sound from a military standpoint, but they doubted whether they were politically workable. The objections within the services were simply too deep-seated.

The services finally met together at Key West, Florida, in 1948 and worked out their own compromise as to their respective roles and missions, or rather which weapons systems each service should be authorized to acquire. But despite the Key West agreement, bickering among the services continued and is still much in evidence today. I believe that the approach taken to solving the roles-and-missions problem has been a serious detriment to the development of a sound U.S. military organizational structure. Had the problem been addressed properly and objectively at the beginning, I am confident that the military establishment in the United States would be in far sounder shape today than it is.

As the principal author of the survey's final report on the Pacific War, I avoided any implication that either land-based or sea-based air had "won" the war. Both, I felt, had been vital at different stages of the war. In the beginning, carriers served an essential function by establishing control of the seas, allowing U.S. forces to "leapfrog" across the Pacific to bring land-based bombers within range of the Japanese home islands. From that point on, with her fleet crippled and with her air forces reduced to kamikaze (suicide) missions, Japan's defeat became inevitable. Our Air Force flew practically unopposed, leveling Japan's cities and factories. Even without the attacks on Hiroshima and Nagasaki, it seemed highly unlikely, given what we found to have been the mood of the Japanese government, that a U.S. invasion of the islands would have been necessary.

In January 1946, after the *Ancon* returned to the United States, the strategic bombing survey was largely disbanded. Only a handful of us stayed on to write the final *Summary Report on the Pacific War*, which was released to the public that July, together with a large number of supporting studies, the most important being those on the effects of atomic weapons and on Japan's struggle to end the war. With the project now effectively finished, the USSBS came to an end, having performed, to my mind, a difficult and demanding task with energy, objectivity, and dispatch.

3

The Marshall Plan

With the publication of the final summary report on the Pacific War in the summer of 1946, my mission with the bombing survey came to an end. What had begun in 1940 as a seemingly temporary assignment to help Jim Forrestal had stretched out to six years of continuous government service. I then tentatively agreed to return to New York to be the original managing partner of J. H. Whitney and Company, the venture capital company Jock Whitney was organizing. But Phyllis and my children wanted to stay in Washington. Also, my basic thinking and interests, as a result of my various wartime experiences, had changed. When I received an offer from Will Clayton to join the State Department as deputy director of the Office of International Trade Policy, I therefore accepted and canceled my plans to join Jock Whitney.

New Job—New Problems

The State Department in those days still had its main offices in the old State-War-Navy Building next to the White House. Although the War and Navy departments were now housed elsewhere, office space remained at a premium. To ease the strain, the department had taken over from the Army a building which it called "New State," at Twenty-first Street and Virginia Avenue in what was then a seedy part of town known as "Foggy Bottom." However, most of us in the economic or "E" section of the State Department continued to use the old building. I had the good fortune of inheriting Will Clayton's office overlooking the White House and its gardens. It had high ceilings and a magnificent fireplace. When later I joined the rest of the staff at New State, I acquired an office which, while almost devoid of character, had a novel feature (for that time) called "air-conditioning" that was supposed to, and generally did, make life more bearable during Washington's hot, muggy summers.

Early in my new job a Swedish delegation came to Washington to negotiate a revision of the 1935 U.S.–Swedish reciprocal trade agreement. The head of the delegation was a very able economist named Dag Hammarskjöld, who later became secretary-general of the United Nations. Like many other countries after the war, Sweden had overextended itself and was running a chronic balance of payments deficit. The Swedes decided that the way to relieve the strain was to put discriminatory tariffs on their imports from the United States. At the outset of our discussions, Hammarskjöld produced a large number of graphs showing the most important indices having to do with the Swedish economy and its internal and international financial situation. After studying Hammarskjöld's figures, I became persuaded that Sweden was indeed in need of significant relief. So, notwithstanding the department's policy of promoting free trade, I proposed changes in our reciprocal trade agreement permitting sharp but temporary Swedish restrictions on imports from the United States. Hammarskjöld thought I had gone too far and insisted that Sweden could get along with less.

"According to your own data," I told him, "it looks to me as though your country needs the full amount of help I have suggested."

He said, "No, we don't need that much. We can do it with less."

I said, "If you won't accept it, I can't force it down your throat."

We thereupon drafted an exchange of aide-mémoire temporarily modifying the treaty to reflect the terms that Dag thought adequate. In less than two months, it turned out that Hammarskjöld had underestimated Sweden's requirements and wanted to reopen negotiations. I agreed. Out of this second round of talks emerged another agreement, tailored closely to what I had originally proposed.

No sooner had the negotiations with the Swedes concluded than a similar problem arose with Canada, which also wanted relief from a serious balance of payments deficit. I wondered what country would be next to apply for relief. On the basis of statistical data I pried out of the Treasury Department, I found the sum and substance of the problem to be this: The United States was currently running a balance of payments surplus of over five billion dollars annually, meaning that the rest of the world, overall, was running a five-billion-dollar deficit. Thus the United States was eating up the rest of the world's foreign exchange reserves. One by one, like Sweden and Canada, these countries would become unable to service their debts and sooner or later they would run into serious difficulties. Unless something were done to reduce the U.S. trade surplus and ease the situation, the coming months would doubtless witness a worldwide chain of financial crises, resulting in spreading financial and political chaos.

Early in 1947, after studying the Treasury's figures, I drafted a memorandum and forwarded it to Will Clayton, who was now under secretary of state for economic affairs. What I had in mind was a worldwide effort totaling twenty to twenty-five billion dollars stretched over a four- to five-year period. My suggestion was not unique, since others in Washington had by this time drawn similar conclusions. Jim Forrestal, for example, was urging something along the same lines and later George Kennan, one of the department's leading Soviet experts, came up with a plan for economic assistance to Europe only. Their plans were more political than economic and they fastened their attention on the spread of Communist and Soviet influence in Europe. At that time there was a consensus in Washington that the Soviet threat came primarily from political intrigues and subversion. A major opportunity for such tactics to succeed would spring from spreading economic disarray in Western Europe. If that were not forestalled, there was a serious possibility that local Communist or radical parties in Italy, Germany, and France and eventually England would achieve takeovers of power. I did not at that time see much of a threat of military action by the USSR against Western Europe. I thought that that threat would not arise until after the completion of the three five-year plans that Stalin announced immediately after the war. My worry was with the general worldwide economic situation, including Europe but not Europe alone. I thought our efforts should be global in scope.

Will had yet to be persuaded that the situation was as serious as I considered it to be. Nonetheless I was confident in my assessment. The world economy, as I saw it from Washington, was steadily worsening, especially in Europe. Some of the coldest weather of the century had struck Europe that winter with devastating effect. For lack of adequate transportation to move coal, fuel supplies had run short in many places; and without power, industrial activity had slackened to about three-quarters of its prewar production level. Since the prewar figures we used for comparison were for a period of economic depression, the current situation had all the makings of a looming catastrophe.

The political implications of this situation were all too apparent—strikes that further crippled the economies of France, Italy, and other countries; a rising tide of social discontent, aggravated by Communist agitation; and the steady weakening of governments friendly to the

United States. In Greece there was the additional problem of an escalating guerrilla war against the Athens government by Communists who were receiving guidance from Moscow and aid and support through Albania, Yugoslavia, and Bulgaria. At the same time Turkey was under heavy Soviet pressure, but of a different sort. Using a combination of threats and propaganda, Moscow demanded concessions that, if made, would soon have reduced Turkey to the status of another Soviet satellite.

Since the end of the war Greece and Turkey had both relied on Britain for political support and military and economic aid to keep themselves going. In February 1947 the British advised us that because of their own economic problems, they could no longer sustain this assistance. A turning point had been reached—a decision had to be made whether to let the Communists have Greece and possibly Turkey as well, or whether the United States should undertake a major initiative.

The key figure in the decision was Dean Acheson, then under secretary of state for political affairs. Heretofore Dean had been one of the most able and persuasive supporters of the maintenance into the peace of the East–West wartime alliance. He had been a major figure in the creation of the Bretton Woods agreements of 1944 leading to establishment of the World Bank and the International Monetary Fund. He had actively contributed to the creation of the United Nations. And he had been closely involved in the interim economic assistance programs to Britain and other European countries. He believed we should work for Soviet cooperation on the major issues, rely on the UN to deal with the intermediate issues, and expect the usual British diplomatic skill and acumen to handle the day-to-day tactical problems of world politics. The experiences of 1946 and the beginning of 1947 caused him to change his point of view. Moscow's intent to achieve control over all of Central and Southern Europe was all too obvious, the UN had proven to be next to useless for settling such disputes, and the weakness of the United Kingdom was now a matter of record.

A contributing factor in Dean's change of view was the Russian refusal to consider modifying the Supreme Allied Agreement with respect to Japan. In that agreement the Allies had agreed to fix very low "levels of industry" to keep Japan from having the economic strength to rearm. For instance, one provision was that Japan should not be permitted more than three million tons of steel production per annum, and that all Japanese steel mill capacity in excess of that figure was to be dismantled and the machinery turned over as reparations, primarily to the USSR and to some degree to China. Here we were, carrying the occupation burden amounting to hundreds of millions of dollars a year, with no hope of getting Japan economically back on her feet or of reducing those occupation costs unless there were a higher level of industry in Japan, which could not be done without increasing steel production. The Soviet Union's refusal to agree to a change in the level of production, thus forcing us unilaterally to breach the level-of-industry agreement, was another reason that caused Dean to reassess the situation. When Acheson finally switched sides, he took enough of informed Washington opinion with him to move the majority view from a policy of inaction to a policy of action.

It did not take much imagination to see what had to be done in Greece and Turkey. Acheson and Loy Henderson, who was then director of the Office of Near Eastern and African Affairs, headed up a group to do the staff work; they asked me to handle the details on the economic side. Following a hasty round of deliberations, Mr. Truman went before Congress on March 12, 1947, to proclaim his determination "to support free peoples who are resisting attempted subjugation by armed minorities or by outside pressures." To support this purpose he asked Congress to appropriate four hundred million dollars in economic and military aid. Thus were born the Truman Doctrine and the Greek-Turkish aid program. To many Americans it may have sounded as if the United States were embarking on a world crusade. But actually the Truman Doctrine was used only to support aid to Greece and Turkey; it was not called upon to justify intervening against the threat of Communist or Soviet expansion elsewhere. But it set in motion a series of events that were to shape American foreign policy for the next generation.

A significant by-product of the Truman Doctrine was the attention it drew to the deteriorating situation in Europe. About a month after the President's speech, General George Marshall, by then secretary of state, named George Kennan to set up a small group of analysts, organized as the Policy Planning Staff, and asked them as their first task to develop recommendations for a larger, more inclusive program addressed to the problems in Europe. Kennan had little knowledge of, or experience in, economic matters and asked me to serve as his deputy. I agreed, but before I could go to work he had to clear my transfer with Dean Acheson. Dean had known me for years, but resented my activities during the war, which he thought (to some extent correctly) had undercut State Department policy control over wartime economic matters. He said, "George, you don't want Nitze. He's not a long-range thinker, he's a Wall Street operator." The upshot was that I stayed where I was in the Office of International Trade Policy and George picked another deputy. However, it turned out that my duties over the next two years brought George and me into regular and frequent contact. So it happened that George would often "borrow" my services when the need arose.

Acheson soon resigned to resume his law practice. His successor was Robert Lovett, whom I had known from my days on Wall Street. His father had been chairman of the board of the Union Pacific Railroad. Bob was one of the leading partners of Brown Brothers, a New York merchant banking firm. He was widely admired for his wit and negotiating skill. During World War II he had been assistant secretary of war for air and had had great success in leading our air buildup. As Marshall's deputy in the State Department, he concentrated his efforts on relations with Congress and on dealing with the European ambassadors in Washington. He was wise, skillful, and knowledgeable in his dealings with them. I considered his abilities to be more in the direction of tactical skill than profound analysis. But I thought him to be one of the great men of that age. I still have his picture hanging on my office wall.

George and the group he assembled ultimately produced a series of reports that outlined in general terms the steps that needed to be taken. One paper dealt specifically with the problem of the recovery of Europe from the political and economic chaos which had resulted from the war. It differed from my earlier paper in concentrating only on Europe. It took the position that the economic problems of the rest of the world would sort themselves out if Europe were to recover economically. Despite my preference for a more global approach, the important thing was to get an offset to our persistent balance of payments surpluses into the stream of international payments as swiftly as possible. For this purpose it could well be argued that Europe was indeed the most crucial area.

In addition to working on these reports, George contributed a most remarkable essay that he published anonymously that summer in *Foreign Affairs* under the title "The Sources of Soviet Conduct." It was this article that provided the overall rationale for the policy that would guide U.S. foreign policy for the next generation. Here he introduced the concept of containing Soviet and Communist expansionism, but he was vague on what might be required to achieve successful containment. Walter Lippmann, the veteran journalist, and a number of others saw this flaw and immediately pounced on it. Even so, I found George's underlying argument persuasive—that "a long-term, patient but firm and vigilant containment of Russian expansive tendencies" would eventually produce fundamental changes in the Soviet system, making it less menacing toward the West. However, George did not venture to predict when we might expect these changes to occur. I concurred with George's assessment of the situation. Since then, I have noted many changes in method, approach, and personalities in the Soviet system, particularly after Mikhail S. Gorbachev became general secretary. But it has taken much longer than I had once hoped to anticipate significant change in the underlying doctrine animating that system.

In dealing with the more immediate problem of Europe's growing instability, I thought that we should attack it at its source and restore confidence where it was needed most—in the economic sector. Twice before in my memory we had sat back and let events take their course— first, in the 1920s, when we had let the German reparations question get out of hand, and again in the 1930s, during the Great Depression, when we had retreated into political and economic isolation. In both instances the most disastrous consequences had ensued. We could not afford again to be blind to the probable consequences of American inaction.

The concerns that many of us had addressed in private finally received a chance for public expression when in April 1947 Dean Acheson canvassed the department for suggestions on a speech he had been asked to give early the following month before the Delta Council in Cleveland, Mississippi. Dean deputized his speechwriter, Joseph Jones, to prepare a draft; Joe asked me to help him. That speech, as I remember it, was the department's first public attempt to focus attention on the deteriorating conditions in Europe. It was a good speech, well received by its immediate audience, but it drew little national interest.

Equally important, as it affected the department's readiness to deal with the problem, was the change in Will Clayton's thinking. Will had gone to Geneva that April for a further round of talks on the General Agreement on Tariffs and Trade (GATT); during a subsequent trip to France, Germany, and the Low Countries, he finally became persuaded that the gravity of the problem demanded immediate corrective action. Neither my memo nor those produced by George Kennan and the Policy Planning Staff could convey the sense of impending crisis as effectively as actually seeing what was happening.

While Will was in Europe, Congress had taken up consideration of a bill to impose a sharp tariff increase on wool imports into the United States, an action that threatened to scuttle the GATT negotiations in Geneva. Will returned to town on May 19, 1947, and immediately assembled a group of us from his office for lunch at the Metropolitan Club to discuss not only the wool tariff bill but also the general situation in Europe. Will was genuinely alarmed that Europe was on the brink of disaster. The thing that had made perhaps the strongest impression on him was the unwillingness of the European farmers to sell their produce to the cities, because the cities had nothing to sell in return. While the farmers were hoarding food in the country, people in the cities were starving. Something had to be done to break the impasse, to get industry and agriculture moving again, and to restore a sense of confidence in the economic and political system.

After lunch, Will returned to the office and finished dictating a memo for Secretary Marshall that he had started writing on the plane. His concern was as much for the welfare of our own country as for the future stability and health of Europe, though for all practical purposes the two were inseparable. "The facts are well known," he argued. Only with a quick and substantial infusion of U.S. aid, founded on "a strong spiritual appeal to the American people to sacrifice a little of themselves," did Will feel that disaster could be averted.

From this point on, events moved rapidly, culminating on June 5, 1947, with Secretary Marshall's proposal in his Harvard commencement speech offering American aid to those European countries willing to coordinate their efforts for economic recovery. The key contributor to drafting the speech was Charles "Chip" Bohlen, who wrote the first and most of the second draft of Marshall's speech. As he related in his memoirs, Chip relied primarily on three sources—the Policy Planning Staff study that Kennan and his colleagues had prepared pursuant to Secretary Marshall's request; Clayton's memorandum to the secretary, from which Chip garnered many key phrases; and "a general idea of what was in Marshall's mind." Although Marshall subsequently made several changes in some of the wording, the essence of the speech came from Chip's pen. It was his idea that our initiative should not be directed against any one country. Rather, it should be open to all the countries of Europe—East and West alike—and it should aim at eliminating basic problems—hunger, poverty, and disease. All these ideas were Chip's. That the Soviets and their East European satellites later denounced our offer as "American imperialism" and decided not to participate revealed the essential difference between their objectives and ours. Our goal was to revive Europe economically and spiritually and make it thrive again; theirs was to perpetuate squalor and chaos in the hope that eventually all Europe would fall to Communist control. Had they chosen to cooperate, I believe we might have avoided much of the bitterness that followed. But the essential point is that the United States was finally committed to a definite, constructive course of action. Had we delayed any longer it appeared wholly probable that a succession of Communist takeovers would have swept the Continent.

Developing a Program

Reactions to the secretary's offer of assistance caught us off guard. We had anticipated a favorable response, especially from abroad, but the press coverage that the secretary's speech received was modest. However, Acheson had alerted Ernest Bevin, the British foreign secretary, beforehand; it was Bevin's enthusiastic response that caught the press's attention. Suddenly, the State Department was deluged with requests for the details of what we intended to do, a rather embarrassing situation since, in fact, nothing had yet been done in the way of detailed planning. The Marshall "plan" was nothing more than the concept outlined in the speech at that point. No one knew what it would cost (though we had some rough ideas and knew it would be expensive) or what would be needed to implement it and how.

The first step, as in any major undertaking, was to assemble an organization capable of converting the concept into a working plan. Some preliminary work had already been done by Colonel George A. "Abe" Lincoln, the Army member of an ad hoc committee that was part of an advisory body known as the State-War-Navy Coordinating Committee. During the war, Abe had served on General Marshall's staff in the Operations and Plans Division of the War Department, where he had demonstrated a remarkable ability to bring together talented officers. One of his protégés was Dean Rusk, who eventually went on to be secretary of state in the Kennedy administration; another was a young colonel named Charles "Tic" Bonesteel, whom the Army had detailed to the State Department after the war. Tic became overall coordinator for European recovery and I was named head of a group in charge of compiling data for estimating Europe's needs.

The team I assembled consisted initially of the same people who had assisted me on the negotiations with the Swedes and Canadians, including Robert Tufts, William T. Phillips, and William H. Bray, Jr. As the work became more complex, requiring specialized talent that my part of the State Department could not provide, I began recruiting people on "loan" from other departments and agencies.

One of the first problems to be overcome was a dearth of reliable statistical data on conditions in Europe. We knew the situation was serious, but we needed more facts before we could plan in detail to assure that U.S. assistance would have the maximum effect. So we put together a questionnaire and asked the European participants to fill it out. Very few of the European countries could quickly come up with this kind of information. The British kept fairly accurate and useful records; the French, on the other hand, were almost totally devoid of records that could help us. They assigned the job of filling out the questionnaire to one of their foreign service officers who later confessed to me that none of his figures had any basis in hard data. Rather, he had concocted out of his head what appeared to him to be reasonable estimates. As it turned out, his estimates were as accurate as any other country's "data."

Our policy toward European recovery was that the Europeans should themselves take the lead in assessing their needs and in setting objectives. Accordingly, they assembled in Paris a working group known as the Committee of European Economic Cooperation (CEEC), chaired by Sir Oliver Shewell Franks of Great Britain. The CEEC was supposed to be a totally European organization, independent of the United States. But it seemed clear—on both sides of the Atlantic—that there ought to be some degree of coordination lest the CEEC come up with recommendations that were out of line with what was reasonable and feasible for us in Washington. So in August 1947 I flew to Paris and arranged to stay at the same hotel where Franks and other members of the CEEC were staying.

Most of my meetings—all entirely unofficial and technically off the record—were with Franks and his deputy, Denny Maris, at breakfast or lunch. One of the issues we discussed was whether, and if so to what extent, the European countries could achieve closer coordination of trade, banking, and other aspects of their economies. Franks finally became persuaded to recommend to his government that as part of the recovery effort, they swing to the side of an integrated European customs union. He returned to London over the weekend to see the foreign secretary, Ernest Bevin. Bevin took the matter up with the cabinet and the idea was rejected. I concluded that the time had not yet come to press the issue of true European integration.

A little later the German question caused me to take another trip to Paris. It had been decided that the U.S. ambassadors to the CEEC countries, together with Robert D. Murphy, the political adviser to the American military governor of occupied Germany, should meet in Paris under the chairmanship of Jefferson Caffery, our ambassador to France, to discuss whether we should make Marshall Plan aid available to Germany.

When it came around to Bob Murphy to express his opinion, he said something along the following lines: "Today there is no possibility of a political problem arising in Germany. The average daily ration provides 950 calories, sometimes even less, which is close to starvation. When people are starving they think only of food, not of politics. They don't have much energy and we control the food. If you want to keep Germany politically docile, continue our present policy. The question is whether the American people will long stick to a policy of keeping them close to starvation." We all agreed that that was highly unlikely. Bob then went on to say: "In that event, you must not only make Marshall Plan aid available to Germany, but should think about restoring Germany to a position of full membership in the community of nations. Once you feed them adequately, they will be interested in politics, and you can't afford to go only halfway." His remarks carried the day and it was agreed that Germany should be included.

Having decided to include Germany in the Marshall Plan, we had then to prepare the German economy for full integration into the rest of Western Europe, starting with such basic steps as currency reform. By late 1947 the harsher and more punitive aspects of our occupation policy in Germany (i.e., those features associated with the Morgenthau Plan to "pastoralize" Germany) had given way to more enlightened treatment aimed at encouraging the German people to make a better life for themselves and concurrently to reduce the economic drain on us. However, it seemed to me that these measures were only the beginning of what had to be done. In particular, we had to give up the idea—at least for the time being—of trying to reunite Germany under one central authority and make it clear to the Soviets, who occupied the eastern half of Germany, that we would rather see the emergence of separate eastern and western German states than continue the charade of so-called four-power control.

As a necessary part of getting the German economy going again, currency reform seemed to me long overdue. In planning the postwar occupation of Germany, the War and Treasury departments had arranged to print a special scrip that was supposed to be used alongside the German Reichsmark only by occupation authorities on a limited basis to pay troops, purchase supplies, and so forth. However, Harry Dexter White, who worked for Henry Morgenthau in the Treasury, gave the Soviets copies of our printing plates. A few years after the war the House Un-American Activities Committee conducted an investigation. The committee suspected White and members of his staff of having pro-Communist leanings and of having intentionally compromised our policy in Germany. There was no doubt that White had made the decision to turn the plates over to the Soviets. The avowed purpose was to permit them to print the currency they needed in their portion of Germany. This turned out to be an enormous amount. Inflation, which had been rampant in Germany toward the end of the war, grew even worse from

V-E Day on. When asked by the committee about this and other decisions he had made, Harry Dexter White repeatedly took the Fifth Amendment to avoid answering. It was never proven that he was a member of the Communist party. It was my view that he was such a dominating and objectionable character that the Communist party would have had doubts about admitting him to membership. But he certainly worked closely with the Communists.

In an effort to restore fiscal stability, the U.S. military governor, General Lucius Clay, and Under Secretary of War William H. Draper, Jr., persuaded Joseph M. Dodge, a prominent Detroit banker, to come over to Germany and head a commission looking into a comprehensive reorganization of Germany's currency and finances. The commission's report, completed in May 1946, urged a number of far-reaching reforms, including the prompt introduction of a new currency called the Deutsche Mark at an exchange rate with the old currency of one to ten. A copy of the report crossed my desk shortly after I joined the State Department later that summer. I urged implementing its recommendations as soon as possible, but because of opposition from the French and the Soviets, nothing happened for nearly two years.

By early 1948 it was increasingly clear that currency reform involving the whole of Germany would probably never take place because of continuing Soviet resistance. Clay and Murphy therefore proposed that as an interim measure they be allowed to go ahead with currency reform in the bizonal area under U.S. and British occupation. Inclusion of the French and Soviet zones could be arranged later, should it become possible. I concurred with their recommendation, but General Marshall and Ernie Bevin counseled patience; they wanted to make a final attempt in the Allied Control Council to win Soviet acceptance of the new currency. If that failed, then Clay could proceed with the introduction of the new currency on a bizonal basis.

As it happened, the Soviets walked out of the Control Council on March 20, 1948, even before the currency question could be brought up again for discussion. Around this same time Clay and Murphy returned to Washington and contracted with the U.S. Treasury to print literally tons of new money (readily distinguishable from the old currency), which was then flown secretly into Germany. The date chosen for the currency changeover was June 1, but at the last minute the French decided to participate in the conversion as well, so the date had to be pushed back. Finally, on June 20, 1948, the conversion took effect, leaving the Berlin occupation marks printed by the Soviets and not properly submitted for conversion not convertible into U.S. dollars. In retaliation the

Soviets blockaded Berlin, thus precipitating one of the most serious crises of the postwar period.

Though European recovery matters claimed much of my time, U.S. economic policy toward Japan was also in my sphere of responsibility. Unlike Germany, however, Japan was not subject to four-power control; rather, it was subject to a different regime springing from the agreement that had set up the wartime Supreme Allied Command in the Pacific. William Walton Butterworth, Jr., who ran Far Eastern affairs in the State Department, and I agreed that the situation was intolerable. We were paying for the full support of Japan and were restrained from letting Japan get back on its feet economically. We recommended to Acheson, then under secretary of state, that we unilaterally lift the level of industry constraints. He agreed. The Soviets, as I thought they would, protested immediately, but dropped the matter after a few days. I think they were surprised that it had taken us so long to come to our senses.

Thereafter I recommended to General Draper that Joe Dodge be sent to Tokyo to help straighten out Japanese finances, which were even more confused than those in Germany. The economic stabilization measures that Dodge recommended early in 1949 and that MacArthur proceeded to impose were exceedingly severe—the Japanese were already experiencing a very low standard of living and were being told that they would have to do even more belt tightening. It was a difficult sacrifice, but together, lifting the level of industry constraints and stabilizing the yen made possible Japan's great economic miracle.

Washington Agent
for the Marshall Plan

The measure of the Marshall Plan's effectiveness was, of course, its ability to stimulate economic recovery. After my return to Washington from the CEEC meetings in the summer of 1947, we stepped up the pace of our preparations and began analyzing the available data in closer detail. Our investigation confirmed that the balance of payments aspect of the problem was crucial, but it was by no means our sole concern. Had it been, we could have simplified matters merely by giving the Europeans cash grants to pay off their debts. Though grant aid was involved to a considerable extent, it was not intended to be the focal point of the program. Rather, the program was meant to be one of cooperative economic self-help and reconstruction. The goods and services to be supplied would generate proceeds in the currency of the country to which they were supplied. Those local currencies, which we called "counterpart funds," should be put to constructive use; they should be recycled back into the local economies to stimulate further reconstruction.

To expedite the processing of data, I persuaded the Army to let us use its computers. These were rather primitive devices by today's standards, but their use greatly speeded up the many laborious calculations that developing the program's requirements involved. This was one of the first instances, insofar as I know, of a program of this kind being developed with the assistance of a computer. Our first "run" demonstrated a major error in our planning assumptions. In the first year of the program we estimated the requirement for U.S. Marshall Plan funds to be five billion dollars, but in the second year the computer showed it going up to eight billion dollars, and then showed it jumping in succeeding years. It was evident that we had put excessive weight on the demand side of the equation. We had assumed that the prime objective was the most rapid European recovery that could be achieved; the principal limiting factor we had initially entered into the program was the available supply of raw materials, including food, and oil from abroad. As availability of such supplies increased year by year, so did European capacity usefully to absorb financial assistance.

Most of us who worked on the problem at this, the "technical" level, had focused on its economic side—how to revive production, restore trade, strengthen financial markets, control inflation, and so forth. Secretary Marshall had a different perspective that reflected his experience in the 1920s and 1930s, when the mood in the United States had been strongly isolationist. "You know," he told me, "the country at some time is going to return to that kind of isolationist mood, and it is essential that these programs that you are now working on be self-liquidating. It's all right at this time to request appropriations from Congress of the size you think necessary, but they must be decreasing, and they must work themselves down and eventually out, because the country won't stand for this over a long period of time."

He was, of course, right. An open-ended program with increasing costs would doubtless have been attacked as ineffective and as a "give-away" that could have triggered the kind of reaction that Marshall feared. So we redesigned our program to reflect a declining availability of aid, starting in the first year with five billion dollars, then four billion, then three billion, and so forth until aid ceased entirely after the fifth year. As it turned out, the Marshall Plan lasted only four years.

During this phase of the work I had a horrid shock. I had borrowed from the Treasury Department a man named Harold Glasser to help with balance of payment projections. Harold was a brilliant economist and did a first-rate job. One afternoon he came into my office and told me he was resigning. "Good Lord, Harold," I said, "you can't resign; you're running all the work on balance of payments and you're doing a superb job. It's one of the most important parts of the whole thing."

Harold said, "No, I must resign. I have no choice. It has to do with my relations with Harry Dexter White and the Treasury during the war. I can't tell you what it's about, but I just have to resign." And so he did.

Shortly thereafter, as I've mentioned, Harry Dexter White appeared before the House Un-American Activities Committee to answer charges that he was a Communist. I then learned why Harold Glasser had resigned. He and a number of others who had been on White's staff during the war were also under investigation. The committee's hearings were inconclusive, but Harold took the Fifth Amendment so many times that he totally compromised his credibility.

After recovering from this disruption, we next undertook to obtain congressional authorization and funding—not made any easier by President Truman's growing difficulties with the Republican-controlled Eightieth Congress. We knew we would have a fight on our hands with some of the die-hard isolationists and would have to have our facts straight to demonstrate that we knew what we wanted to do and that the program would actually do it. So my staff and I began assembling what we called the "brown books," which laid out in detail for each country the financial situation and evolving balance of trade and payments, the needs of each recipient country, and the type and level of aid we proposed the United States offer. We then developed a legislative program that Mr. Truman submitted to Congress on December 19, 1947. To reach this point we had worked practically around the clock. Spending Saturdays and Sundays at the office became routine.

Sometime after we began our planning work, I was handed the job of explaining the program to the press. I remember John Scali, then an Associated Press correspondent, asking me what I estimated the program would cost in the initial year. I answered $5 billion. When all the dust settled, Congress appropriated $5.025 billion for that year.

In the meantime a series of outside committees had been established to provide wider participation in the development of the program. The most important of these groups was the committee headed by W. Averell Harriman, the U.S. ambassador to Moscow in World War II and an influential figure in the Democratic party. Harriman's deputy was my close friend the economist Richard M. Bissell. They arrived at their findings independently, but their estimates and recommendations were almost exactly the same as those our group developed in the executive branch. Another group, headed by Secretary of the Interior Julius Krug, looked into the availability of raw materials to support the program. Acheson, who had recently returned to private life, organized yet a third committee to foster public support for the plan. In addition, the Brookings Institution was commissioned by the Senate Foreign Relations Committee to report on the optimum way in which the U.S. government should organize and administer the program. In short, support for the program was broadly based; all involved worked hard to make it a success.

A Christmas skiing vacation to Canada with Phyllis and the children helped relax me and got me in shape for the next round—the congressional hearings, which opened on January 7, 1948, before the Senate Foreign Relations Committee. Lewis Douglas, our ambassador to the Court of St. James's, had been brought back to Washington to coordinate the testimony. My job was to serve as his backup in case he needed help in explaining the details of our proposals, which turned out to be quite often. On occasion, Douglas could be brilliant, but under intense congressional pressure he tended to crack. I learned then and there that one needed nerves of iron to go through a long and important congressional hearing. At one of the sessions Will Clayton joined us and it was like a breath of cool clear air.

The Senate Foreign Relations Committee hearings proved fairly routine. I can recall no major congressional problems until it came time for hearings before the House Foreign Affairs Committee, where Ernest Gross, legal adviser to the State Department, and I presented much of the department's testimony. At that time the Foreign Affairs Committee had only two staff assistants—Charles Burton Marshall, soon to become one of my closest friends and colleagues, and William Yandell Elliott, a professor of government and former tutor of mine at Harvard, known to many of us as "Wild Bill." Being short of staff, the chairman of the committee asked Ernie and me to act in a dual role, not only as witnesses for the State Department, but as staff assistants to the committee. It was a highly unusual arrangement but we agreed.

The House hearings dragged on and on. Finally, we received word on a Thursday that the Rules Committee had scheduled debate before the full House on an authorization bill the following week and that the Foreign Affairs Committee had to have its report in the hands of each congressman by 9 A.M. Monday. The job of drafting the report fell upon the staff, such as it was, consisting of Burt Marshall, Ernie Gross, Wild Bill Elliott, and myself.

Late that Thursday afternoon we assembled in Burt's office. Though the committee had received a great deal of testimony and technical information, the data had yet to be sifted and put together in a draft report. Fortunately, somewhat earlier, acting on a suggestion by the committee chairman, Burt had prepared a short paper which provided us with a conceptual framework. However, by morning we were still far from finished. The committee reassembled but quickly became bogged down debating details, paragraph by paragraph. By Friday evening, tired from lack of sleep and somewhat exasperated, we were back in Burt's office, no further along than we had been that morning.

It was at this point that Burt decided to take charge. He went to his stationery cabinet, pulled out a pair of scissors and a ream of typing paper, laid the blank pages on the floor, and began taping them together into a single sheet at least twenty feet long. I asked him what he was doing.

"It's an old technique," he said, "called 'cut-and-paste.' I learned it as a journalist in El Paso, and it is the same technique I used to write my Ph.D. thesis at Harvard. I will take this raw material we have, dictate my analysis of it to my secretary, and she will type it on that long sheet of paper. Meanwhile, you fellows will be reviewing what I've dictated. Then, when we have a change or correction to make, we can just cut a piece out, type the insert, and paste it all together again. It's the only way I can think of to get the report done in the time remaining."

So that was how we wrote the report. Burt dictated and his secretary typed, while the rest of us offered whatever comments we had to make. At one point Bill Elliott tried to usurp command of the operation and Burt threatened him with a chair! Wild Bill beat a hasty retreat and was quiet as a mouse from then on. We worked through the night, tired though we were, and the next morning had our copy retyped and submitted it to the committee. No doubt the Rules Committee never thought it could be done.

While Congress debated what it should authorize, a group of five or six of us from various agencies across Washington began meeting for lunch, at my instigation, at the Metropolitan Club every Friday to discuss the actual running of the program. The group included Dick Bissell from the Harriman committee, Thomas C. Blaisdell, Jr., from the Commerce Department, William McChesney Martin, Jr., from the Treasury, and several others. We worked from no preset agenda and never signed any papers at these meetings. They served merely as a means of informal exchange, but in the process became the essential basis for effective inter-departmental coordination.

The plan of organization that was eventually adopted placed adminis-tration of the program outside the State Department under a special administrator for economic cooperation. To fill this post, Bob Lovett, Acheson's successor as under secretary of state, suggested the name of Paul Hoffman, president of the Studebaker-Packard Corporation, who was in Tokyo at the time advising General MacArthur on the Japanese reparations problem. We sent him a telegram offering him the job and he returned to Washington to talk about it. I met him at the airport and brought him back to our house, where Phyllis and I wined and dined him that evening. After much persuasive effort on our part, he accepted the job. Will Clayton recommended that Hoffman hire me as his deputy, but he refused. Instead, he hired Dick Bissell, who, I hasten to add, did a first-rate job.

Deliberations Culminate in Congress

On April 3, 1948, legislation authorizing the Marshall Plan finally cleared Congress and went to Mr. Truman's desk for his signature. The next step was to secure appropriations. Once again I found myself spending most of my time testifying at committee hearings on Capitol Hill.

The first round of hearings took place before "Honest" John Taber's House Appropriations Committee. After opening remarks by Bob Lovett and Paul Hoffman, I was left to justify the appropriation request in detail. I arrived armed with the various "brown books" which we had prepared earlier and which we had already turned over to the committee to study. Taber had other ideas.

"We're not going to use your brown books," he told me privately on the eve of the hearings. "I don't believe in balance of payments justifica-tions, and these brown books of yours are geared entirely around balance of payments problems. I want to start with the countries in alphabetical order. That means we'll start with Austria. We'll take the list of things that you've proposed be delivered to Austria in alphabetical order. You, Mr. Nitze, will justify why each one of these items is necessary, in the amount you propose, to the economic recovery of that country."

So the next day we started with Austria and moved haltingly down the list of proposed aid items. When we reached the letter *p*, we came to an item of twenty-five thousand tons of pulses, a type of bean. Taber's nose began to quiver as he asked me why it was necessary to go to the expense of shipping pulses to Austria instead of growing them there. I replied that that proposal came from the Department of Agriculture and that their experts could explain it better than I could. I said it was my understanding that Austria had never produced the full amount of food necessary for its population and had always had to import food.

"I know," Taber replied, "but pulses are things you can raise pretty readily and easily on a small acreage. Do you have anyone who knows about that? Pulses are the easiest things to raise from every standpoint; it takes very little acreage, and there is not any reason in the world why they should not raise their pulses themselves. I do not know whether any of you knows anything about agriculture or not, but it seems to me that somebody should look into this thing who knows about such things."

By now it was obvious that Taber was trying to stall action on the appropriations request. He wanted to make it appear that our program was poorly thought out and that I, in particular, as the State Department's principal spokesman, had not the faintest idea of how to handle the taxpayers' money. It was an effective tactic and he was in a commanding position to make it succeed.

After the pulses, we moved on to a discussion of a proposal to ship 120 tractors to Austria. Taber wanted to know why these were needed.

"I am more familiar with the European situation as a whole than I am as to Austria with respect to tractors . . . ," I told him, but before I could finish my sentence, he cut me off.

"I do not care about going into Europe as a whole," he declared. "I think we have to go into each country on this tractor business and if we can, get information on it."

So we continued to talk about Austria's need for tractors, but still Taber was not satisfied. "It was understood," he said, "that we were to proceed and develop the needs of these countries. We are not getting the information. If we do not get it, there is no use of our wasting our time here. We ought to have somebody here who knows the answers."

My reply was that he could indeed have his answers if he would allow me to bring in my expert witnesses, as I thought had been agreed.

"No," he said, "the statement I made last night is that I wanted to develop the needs of each country first before we went into the question of our capacity to supply; because I do not want to ask an organization what we are able to supply until I know what the need is. I cannot pass on that question until I know what the need is. And I do not see how we can do it in any orderly way unless we get that information first."

At this point, Taber got up and went into an office adjoining the hearing room to use the phone. Nothing happened for half an hour. Then Taber reappeared and startled everyone with a complete about-face. "Mr. Nitze," he said, "you can call your experts. We'll adjourn the hearing now, and you have them here tomorrow morning."

It was not until I talked with Bob Lovett back at the State Department that I learned what had happened. "John Taber called me," Bob explained, "and described the full horror of your presentation, particularly your inability to justify the need for pulses, the fact that you'd never grown them, and that you had not been to Austria to learn whether they could grow there." Bob said he had listened to Taber until he had completed his full catalog of horrors. Then Lovett said to Taber: "You know, I could ask you a question that you couldn't answer. For example, 'How many rivets are there in a B-29 wing?'" To this Taber replied, "You would know that better than I because you were assistant secretary of war for air in World War Two." "Well," Bob said, "that's just the point. Some people are more knowledgeable about certain matters than other people. So why don't you let Nitze have his experts there to answer these technical questions?" But before Taber could answer, Bob asked him another question: "If it takes eight yards of pink crepe paper to go around an elephant's leg, how long does it take to kill a fly with a flyswatter?" Taber said, "That's a nonsensical question." Bob told him, "Of course! Now why don't you stop asking Nitze nonsensical questions?" And Taber agreed.

That exchange between Taber and Lovett over the phone saved the Marshall Plan. Bob Lovett understood Taber's mentality. They had worked together many times before and over the course of their dealings Bob had learned how to handle him, how to present a problem to get around Taber's prejudices. A conservative with isolationist leanings, Taber was deeply skeptical of the Marshall Plan; his line of questioning was designed to find any legitimate excuse to block action on the program. He knew that if and when the bill cleared his committee, he would be the one who would have to lead the floor fight in the House for its passage. If he finally decided to support the bill, he wanted to be able to demonstrate to his colleagues that having taken the bill apart piece by piece, he knew it thoroughly; he wanted to anticipate and be able to answer any criticism. Though I came to understand Taber's position and what he was trying to do, I found his methods tedious and time consuming. I had lost fifteen pounds by the time those hearings ended some forty sessions later!

After the appropriations bill cleared the House, we moved to the next phase of the ritual—hearings before the Senate Appropriations Committee. Several days before the hearings were about to begin, Secretary Marshall called Chip Bohlen and me into his office; he told us that the committee wanted him to testify at its opening session. He proposed that Chip and I write a statement for him to make. Chip would write the first part, dealing with the political considerations, and I would do the second part on the economics of the program. We stayed up much of the night, prepared our two drafts, and married them into a finished statement the following morning before going to see General Marshall.

After reading our paper, Marshall leaned back and thought for a moment. Then he said, "You know, I don't think I'll use this statement of yours." Chip and I were both shocked! We had worked hard, felt we had our facts straight, and couldn't imagine what we'd done wrong.

General Marshall immediately recognized our disappointment and sought to reassure us. "It isn't that I disapprove of what you've written," he said. "The problem is a different one. This committee doesn't really want to know about the European Recovery Program; they want to know whether *I* know anything about it. If I go up there and deliver a prepared statement, they will know that it was prepared by my staff in the State Department and not by me. It won't help our cause a bit. I didn't ask to appear before this committee; they've asked me to appear and they've set the hearing for eleven A.M. As it happens, one of my fellow officers from the Army, a general, has died today and his funeral is at ten A.M. on Monday. I will go to the funeral, and I will be late appearing at the Senate Appropriations Committee hearing. Everybody will expect me to have a prepared statement. I will have no prepared statement. I will say that I have come at their request and that I'm ready to answer any questions they may have. In the meantime, over the weekend, I will have studied this paper that you two have drafted for me. No matter what the questions are, there will be some way I can use all that information in my replies to the questions that the Senate asks me. The information in your document will be in my answers."

Marshall's approach worked like a charm. The committee was completely won over by the way he handled himself and the appropriations bill sailed through the Senate without a problem. Like Lovett, Marshall knew the people with whom he was dealing and how to gain their cooperation. This is a most useful art if one wants to get things done in Washington. I can think of no one who surpassed Lovett and Marshall for their wit and tact in this regard. Dean Acheson, who succeeded Marshall as secretary of state, was a more intelligent and brilliant man, but often he could not resist humiliating people whose support he could have used.

Point Four

The Marshall Plan, without question, turned out to be one of the most successful and positive contributions in the history of American foreign policy. In a somewhat different category I place the Point Four program, which, though similar in some ways to the Marshall Plan, lacked its sense of purpose and high degree of commitment.

The occasion for announcement of Point Four is still vivid in my mind. It happened on January 20, 1949—that cold, blustery winter day when Mr. Truman was again sworn in as President, following his stunning and unexpected victory the previous November over his Republican challenger, Thomas E. Dewey. Like many Americans, I had expected Mr. Truman to lose, but I was tempted into betting on his winning when an associate of mine in the State Department, Samuel Hays, offered me odds of fifty to one. Hays was a specialist in public opinion polls and was convinced that the margins in favor of Dewey shown by the polls were so large as to make a Dewey victory a certainty. "Anyone who would bet on Mr. Truman," he told me one day, "even at odds of fifty to one, would be crazy. Making a bet like that would be like taking candy from a baby." I asked, "Do you really mean that?" And he replied, without hesitation, "Certainly." So he accepted my two-dollar bet. It was an easy hundred dollars.

In his inaugural speech Mr. Truman listed four foreign policy objectives that he hoped to pursue over the duration of his presidency. Last on the list, an item quickly dubbed "Point Four" by the press, was the proposal of "a bold new program for making the benefits of our scientific advances and industrial progress available for the improvement and growth of underdeveloped areas."

I had met a few months earlier with "Abe" Lincoln, who told me that he thought our entire approach to economic assistance, as exemplified by the Marshall Plan, was much too Europe-oriented. I knew Colonel Lincoln to be an intelligent and able man. The more I mulled over his criticism, the more I became convinced that he was partly right. By and large, our Asian policy since the end of the war had concentrated on two problems—China, into which we had pumped billions of dollars in economic and military aid to virtually no avail; and Japan, which we still occupied and were now trying to reconstruct into a peace-loving country, with a democratic economic and political system. We were also involved in Korea, but we thought of it as a less important country that attracted attention largely because its economic problems seemed so intractable. The rest of Asia, except for the Philippines, stretching from the Persian Gulf to the Pacific, was generally unfamiliar territory that festered with problems—anticolonialism, social unrest, overcrowded populations, and economies that despite their resources and potential wealth remained underdeveloped.

I did not believe that anything like the Marshall Plan, which depended on strong local multinational initiative, integration, and cooperation, would be feasible or appropriate in dealing with the problems of Asia and other underdeveloped countries in that area. It occurred to me that during World War II there had been experiments in Latin America with something called the *servicio* program, sponsored by the Institute for Inter-American Affairs. The Americans who participated in the *servicio* program were technical advisers, paid jointly by the United States and the host country, to work on problems such as public health, sanitation, and agriculture. I thought that something along similar lines should be authorized to assist our work in Asia, so I consulted with the Bureau of the Budget, which reported my idea to Clark Clifford, special counsel to the President, at the White House and his assistant, George Elsey.

All this occurred around the end of 1948 when Clifford and his staff were preparing the President's inaugural address, which was supposed to set the administration's agenda for the next four years. Using the *servicio* program as their point of reference, they expanded on it, dressed it up so to speak, as a major new initiative to help less fortunate countries and sent it back to the State Department for comment. Bob Lovett referred it to Chip Bohlen and me. I thought that the proposed program should be dropped from the President's address, not because I felt it was an inherently bad idea, but because the executive branch had not yet had time to think through and flesh out the details of a program of the indicated magnitude. Chip agreed with me, and Bob Lovett signed a memorandum to the President endorsing our position. But Clark Clifford thought that the speech needed a humanitarian initiative and overruled us; the proposal thus went into the President's speech.

When Point Four eventually got started, the results were initially disappointing. Though a number of projects were launched, the program's accomplishments were minimal, even by the standards of its most ardent proponents. A basic problem was the absence of a clear-cut definition of the program's aims. It was run by the Technical Cooperation Administration, an agency which prided itself on its independence from foreign policy guidance. It was soon dominated by people who were interested in technology for the sake of technology, with no consideration for our foreign policy aims. The basic idea did, however, eventually produce some notable results, including contributions to the "green revolution," which has at least temporarily relieved the world food problem to the current distress of American agriculture.

4

The Berlin Blockade,
the Palais Rose Conference,
and Jim Forrestal's Suicide

The continuing impasse over Germany and the ongoing Soviet blockade of Berlin were the focal issues during most of the first half of 1949. Since the Soviets had imposed their blockade the previous June, tensions in Europe and the United States had risen and fallen with a certain regularity. The success of the Allied airlift in bringing millions of tons of food, fuel, and other essentials into Berlin had effectively thwarted a Soviet takeover of the city, but it had not eliminated the possibility that some incident might trigger an armed confrontation that could lead to a third world war. Throughout the crisis, all hoped for the best and steeled themselves for the worst.

By 1949 our aims in Germany had changed significantly from what they had been at the close of World War II. We were still committed to denazification and demilitarization. But the less enlightened and punitive features of our policy—the harsh and sometimes brutal practices associated with the Morgenthau Plan of reducing Germany to an agrarian existence—had long since given way to more constructive endeavors in the western two-thirds of Germany under U.S., British, and French occupation. In the eastern zone, where the Soviets were in control, the creation of a one-party state politically and economically subservient to Moscow was well along.

Given the course of events since the war, German reunification did not appear to be a practicable short-term objective. The Russians had no intention of withdrawing from their zone on any acceptable terms. Nonetheless, reunification remained our declared policy and a long-term objective deeply held by the German people. It was vigorously and repeatedly supported in policy statements by the West. Many doubted that security for Europe could be achieved until German reunification had been accomplished. Even those who feared the strength of a reunited Germany saw no prospect of its being accomplished and therefore saw no danger in supporting it as an objective.

The Palais Rose Conference

The first serious consideration of German reunification, as a program rather than merely as an objective, followed the lifting of the Berlin blockade in May 1949. As a condition for lifting the blockade, the Russians had insisted, and the United States had agreed, that there be a meeting of the Council of Foreign Ministers in Paris to discuss "matters arising out of the situation in Berlin and matters affecting Germany as a whole," including Austria.

At the time the meeting was agreed upon, I was deputy assistant secretary of state for economic affairs, which placed me in a key position because of the issues involved. The Berlin blockade had arisen in the first place from a dispute over what currency was to be used in Berlin. I was assigned to work with George Kennan, director of the Policy Planning Staff, to develop a plan for U.S. proposals at the upcoming meeting. Initially, George concentrated on the political aspects of the plan, while I concentrated on the economic aspects. But as time passed, the line demarcating our areas of work became blurred. I thus found myself deeply involved with George in the political plan as well.

George and I were uncertain as to what it was the Russians wanted to accomplish at the meeting or what they would propose. One possibility was that they might consider, or possibly propose, the withdrawal of all foreign forces from Germany, to be followed by reunification. We developed two alternative proposals for consideration by the Western delegation. One was called "Plan A," which contemplated the phased withdrawal of foreign forces from Germany (except for an American access port at Bremen), reunification under free elections, and limitations on German rearmament under four-power control. "Plan B" contemplated no commitment to withdraw military forces from Germany. It endeavored to go as far as might be practicable within that limitation toward German reunification; it included limitation of unilateral controls by the individual occupying powers in their respective zones, and four-power control operating by majority vote on other issues, except for certain basic limitations on German rearmament which could be changed only by unanimous agreement among the occupying powers.

Dean Acheson, who had succeeded General Marshall as secretary of state in January 1949, finally decided to base the Western negotiating position on Plan B rather than Plan A. This was done because most believed the Russians would not in fact agree to any plan requiring the withdrawal of their forces from the Eastern zone. Still, Acheson was determined to explore every option. He therefore asked Chip Bohlen informally to sound out the Soviets on whether they would entertain a proposal similar to Plan A. On the first day of the conference Chip had lunch with General V. I. Chuikov, the Soviet high commissioner for the Eastern zone. Eventually, Chuikov turned the conversation to the subject of a general withdrawal of forces.

"The Germans hate us," Chuikov volunteered. "It is necessary that we maintain our forces in Germany." Even after four years of occupation and day and night indoctrination, the Russians still did not trust the East Germans and looked on them as a potential enemy—a wolf dressed now in Marxist-Leninist sheep's clothing. In any case, Chuikov's remarks put an end to any further discussion of Plan A.

Immediately preceding the actual opening of the Palais Rose Conference we held a briefing for our delegation on what we should expect the Soviet position to be and what we should hope to accomplish. Chip handled the political matters and I spoke on the economic angles. In keeping with the spirit of bipartisanship that infused our foreign policy at that time, the delegation included John Foster Dulles, the Republican party's leading foreign policy spokesman.

I had known Foster Dulles before from several dealings with him on Wall Street and from these I had formed a negative opinion of his character. This was our first encounter in the realm of international politics. A time had been set aside for questions after Chip and I finished our briefing. Foster was the only one who spoke. I do not remember his exact words, but they unambiguously suggested that our whole negotiating position was excessively tough, that we were ignoring legitimate Soviet interests, and that he, Foster, wanted the record to show his protest. Acheson raised no objection. Thus, the conference commenced, with Foster recorded as being basically opposed to our position.

During the Western consultations preceding the opening session, Ernie Bevin, the British foreign secretary, had made it evident that he hoped to establish a role for himself as arbiter between Andrei Vishinsky, the Soviet foreign minister, and Secretary of State Acheson.

At the first substantive exchange, Acheson spoke first, then Robert Schuman, the French foreign minister, then Vishinsky, and finally Bevin. Vishinsky took such an extreme, assertive, and nasty position that Bevin found it impossible to find middle ground; he began to side with Acheson. In a later round the question arose as to whether we should let the city authorities in Berlin run the city as best they could unless the occupying powers were unanimous in overruling them. At one point,

Acheson asked Vishinsky whether the USSR really meant to insist on the right to veto even the appointment of a janitor in the Berlin National Art Museum. Vishinsky replied, "Of course! They might appoint some dreadful person such as Mayor Reuter [the honored mayor of Berlin] to be janitor. We couldn't permit that." From then on Bevin was the most convinced and eloquent spokesman on the Western side.

It quickly became obvious that on the two major issues—an overall settlement for Germany and the unification of Berlin—there was no possibility of reaching an agreement with the Soviets. After a few days, the light dawned on Foster and he came to Acheson to request that his dissent over our position be expunged from the record. Acheson agreed to do so. Later, after the conference, I read an article in *The New York Times*, written by my next-door neighbor James "Scotty" Reston, which credited Foster with putting backbone into our negotiating stand. I asked Scotty where he had got such nonsense. "Where else?" he replied. "I got it from Foster Dulles, off the record, of course, just after he returned from Europe and held a private press briefing up in New York."

Despite the inability of the conference to settle the major questions, we did not give up entirely. The problem was to find out whether any lesser agreements in the direction of a modus vivendi in Germany and Berlin or an agreement on an Austrian peace treaty were possible.

In collaboration with the French and British delegations, we developed two package proposals, one relating to a modus vivendi in Germany, the other to Austria. We wanted to improve our access facilities to Berlin and we welcomed an increase in trade between the eastern and western areas of Germany, provided it was balanced as to composition and value. We also welcomed ad hoc meetings of the Berlin commandants provided there was no agreement which would give the USSR a veto; and we had been persuaded by our people in Germany, who had checked the problem with the State Department's German economic desk, that we had more to gain than lose by direct negotiations between the West Germans and the East Germans, provided all negotiations were ad referendum to the occupying powers. We thought there was some possibility that if we could get trade going again between East and West Germany and develop ad hoc procedures for resolving minor problems, we would slow down the freezing of the division of Germany and improve the long-run chances for the reunification of the country on terms satisfactory to the West.

The Austrian treaty question was complicated owing to the fact that there were Yugoslav claims to be settled and assets in Austria formerly owned by the Germans and now owned by the Russians. Our Austrian proposal suggested that Austria pay $150 million in marks for the Russian-held German assets, other than certain oil and shipping properties, which the USSR would retain. The Russians, in turn, would waive the Yugoslav claims and a group of deputies would meet to resolve eight other relatively minor disagreed points no later than September 1.

Unfortunately, the Soviet delegation could not make such decisions on its own. Almost everything had to be referred to Moscow for approval. So, on June 12, when we presented our proposals to Vishinsky, he advised us that he would need two days to obtain instructions.

On June 14, Vishinsky said he had received his instructions, which were generally favorable. Only our proposal that the Soviets share control of the Autobahn to Berlin received a categorical rejection. Vishinsky said his government did not believe the situation justified a "Danzig corridor" through East Germany, a reference to the thin strip of land separating East Prussia from the rest of Germany before World War II, giving Poland access to the Baltic Sea through the port of Danzig, now called Gdansk. He had some amended wording of the other points we had raised, and this necessitated considerable detailed negotiations over the next few days.

As usually happens at conferences like these, the foreign ministers turned these problems over to their "technical advisers." My Soviet counterpart at these technical-level discussions was the Soviet deputy minister of finance, P. Malietin. The most important measure Malietin and I worked out was the clearing arrangement to facilitate increased trade between the Eastern and Western zones of Germany. It still exists today.

I remember at one point in our conversation asking him whether he was a trained economist. "Of course not," he replied. "Economists in my country have nothing to do with finance. They devote their entire careers to the esoteric study of how best to predict the timing of the collapse of capitalism. They are useless on any practical matter."

On another occasion, the question of inflation came up. I asked Malietin how the Soviet Union went about controlling inflation. "Certainly, we have the problem of inflation," he said. "As a matter of fact, I am the one who is in charge of controlling the problem. We have everyone's bank account on computers. This enables us to follow all the ins and outs of what happens with respect to the flow of money and payments in the USSR. It became evident in 1948 that we had too much money chasing too few goods. To solve the problem, I worked out a program under which we one day announced that all ruble currency and all deposits in the banks were declared worthless, except bank deposits beyond a thousand rubles or so up to one hundred thousand rubles were convertible into new bank deposits at a ratio of one hundred to one. Lesser amounts of currency or bank deposits could be exchanged for new rubles at lesser ratios. We put through this currency reform and, suddenly, we had no more inflation."

Malietin was a shrewd and intelligent negotiator. Gradually, piece by piece, we worked out an agreement and sent it up to the foreign ministers for final approval. On the basic settlement relating to Austria we had proposed, Vishinsky said he was authorized to agree. But as the discussion progressed, it became evident that there was not a full meeting of minds. Schuman and Vishinsky got into a considerable debate as to whether the formerly German-owned assets to be transferred to Austria for $150 million in marks were to be free of all other claims, and whether payments with regard to them could be taken out of Austria without regard to the Austrian government's foreign exchange controls. Vishinsky said some of these facilities had been improved since 1945 and these improvements might involve additional claims.

Two days later Vishinsky received instructions permitting him to negotiate an agreement on this point, but new difficulties arose with respect to the freedom of the USSR to transfer payments due them in connection with these properties. Vishinsky wanted language that would have assured his country the right to transfer profits or other income either in kind or in freely convertible currency. We were willing to agree that the USSR could transfer profits in kind or in the currency in which the profits arose, but objected to language that might put on the Austrian government a foreign exchange burden of undisclosed magnitude. We also could not understand the meaning of "other income" and Vishinsky could give no satisfactory explanation.

On the Sunday before the final session there was a long discussion of the export-of-profits paragraph in the Austrian paper. It seemed that everyone was in agreement as to the substance of the matter. The only remaining difficulty was one of wording. Vishinsky still insisted that payments for such property be in freely convertible currency. We and the British remained opposed. As a compromise, Secretary Acheson suggested a sentence which ended with the words "subject to clarification by the Deputies with respect to the export of freely convertible currency and the definition of 'other income.'" Vishinsky said he would have to get instructions from Moscow before accepting this sentence. Acheson pointed out that the final session had been agreed for Monday. Vishinsky said that if he did not receive his instructions by then, we should eliminate the entire paragraph from the conference communiqué and refer the whole matter to the deputies for further discussion.

Later that evening, Chip Bohlen, Llewellyn "Tommy" Thompson, and I met with members of the Soviet delegation to draft the conference communiqué. The Soviet representative at this meeting was Georgiy N. Zarubin, Vishinsky's deputy for Austrian matters. Everything moved along without difficulty until we came to paragraph *g,* which dealt with the transfer of currency free of Austrian foreign exchange controls. Zarubin said he doubted whether he would receive instructions from Moscow in time and proposed, therefore, as Vishinsky had indicated earlier, that the paragraph be stricken from the communiqué. The rest of us were stunned that the Soviets would really agree to this procedure, since without paragraph g the Austrian government could exercise full control over the rate of exchange at which the Soviet receipts would be converted; this would give us more than Acheson's compromise language would have done. I asked Zarubin whether he was sure that this was what he wanted to do. He said, "Yes. I have talked to Mr. Vishinsky about it and that is what he wants to do."

So paragraph *g* was dropped. The next afternoon, after a brief plenary session, the communiqué was issued without any reference to the terms of conversion of Soviet receipts free of Austrian currency regulations. We all drank champagne, toasted the success of our endeavors, and made ready to go home.

Several hours later I was in my room at the Crillon Hotel, finishing my packing to go home, when the phone rang. Chip Bohlen was on the other end. "Paul," he said, "you can't go. All hell has broken loose. French intelligence has been listening in on the telephone circuits between Paris and Moscow and they picked up a telephone conversation between Vishinsky and his deputy in Moscow, Andrei Gromyko. You won't believe what was said!"

The sum and substance, as Chip reported it, were that Moscow was furious with Vishinsky. In the West, Vishinsky had a reputation as a tough operator, a reputation he had acquired in the 1930s as the chief prosecutor at the highly publicized purge trials of Stalin's rivals. We now saw Vishinsky for what he really was—just another of Stalin's lackeys. Gromyko, although technically Vishinsky's subordinate, called him all manner of foul names and told him that he had been tricked by the Americans into giving up Soviet claims against Austria. When Gromyko learned that the communiqué had gone out, he was horrified and told Vishinsky: "You get hold of Acheson, Bevin, and Schuman and you reconvene the conference right now—*or else!*"

Within minutes after his talk with Gromyko, Vishinsky was on the phone to Acheson. He demanded that the conference be reopened. Acheson balked. "We can't reconvene the conference," he said, "because all the documents have been signed. The communiqué has gone out and the conference is over." Vishinsky was adamant. "I insist," he said, "that the conference be reconvened and that it be done tonight, at the Quai d'Orsay [the French Foreign Ministry] at eight o'clock."

Acheson refused to reconvene the conference, but did agree to a special meeting at the Quai d'Orsay that evening. He and others from the Western delegations arrived just ahead of the Russians. I remember standing near the entrance, watching Vishinsky and his translator, Pavlov, enter the building. Never have I seen two more destroyed-looking individuals. They looked pea-green, as though the end of the world were near. And for Vishinsky that may well have been the case. Not long after he returned to Moscow, Stalin fired him. His career was finished and he was seldom heard from again.

At the Monday night special meeting after the communiqué had already been issued, Vishinsky said he must have paragraph *g* reinserted, reading as follows: "That Austria shall not put any obstacles in the way of the export of profits or other income (i.e., rents) in the form of production or any freely convertible currency received." Mr. Bevin still did not feel that the definition of "other income" was sufficiently precise and Secretary Acheson suggested the additional words, "subject to clarification by the Deputies." Vishinsky said that his government wanted agreement on this point prior to the time the deputies met. Acheson said the problem was too complicated to be firmly agreed that night, but if the USSR wanted it agreed prior to the deputies' meeting, there was no reason why this could not be done through normal diplomatic channels. Vishinsky agreed and the meeting broke up with everyone under the impression that subject to further clarification of this one sentence, through a procedure that had been agreed upon, the Austrian matter had been successfully concluded. Of course we were all mistaken. The Austrian treaty negotiations dragged on for five more years and did not culminate in a settlement until 1955.

Forrestal's Death

During the Palais Rose Conference word reached me of Jim Forrestal's death. Either he accidentally fell or intentionally jumped from the top floor of the Bethesda Naval Hospital, where he was being treated for acute depression. I was deeply saddened, for Jim had been my partner and mentor for many years. Throughout his life Jim had viewed everything he did as a challenge. Dillon, Read had been a challenge and he had risen to the top. The Navy had been a challenge, and he had reshaped it to help win a war. Then, after Congress passed the National Security Act that unified the armed services in 1947, he became secretary of defense, the greatest challenge of his career. He thought he could do whatever he set out to do. He had a host of friends and associates who had generally helped him once he had had a chance to explain what he was trying to do and why. The straw that broke him to the point of suicide was that he finally found that he could not persuade Mr. Truman of his point of view and that some whom he had considered to be his friends were working against him. It became more than he could bear.

After Jim became under secretary of the navy in 1940, we saw each other less frequently than before, though we remained close personal friends. By the time World War II ended, it seemed to me that Jim was under growing personal pressures that were detracting from his objectivity. I recall one instance, in February 1946, just after Stalin had announced three five-year plans devoted to building up the Soviet military establishment so that it could "deal with any eventuality." From the context it was clear that "any eventuality" meant a war with the United States. That speech, I concluded, could be interpreted as a delayed declaration of war against us. I went over to see Forrestal about it; he fully concurred in my opinion. But he said he could not find anyone else in Washington who felt the same way. Jim was deeply worried and asked me to talk to Dean Acheson, who was then under secretary of state and whom Jim considered to be a seminal source of weakness in the government. I went to see Dean, as Jim had asked, and found him wholly unsympathetic to my reading of Stalin's speech. He said, "Paul, you see hobgoblins under the bed. They aren't there. Forget it!"

My conversation with Acheson drew Jim's closest attention. "Paul," he told me, "I believe the evidence is conclusive that there are Communists in the State Department. They are having a very damaging effect on our national policy." He refused to tell me where he got his information, but I suspected that it must have come from the Office of Naval Intelligence. Jim was persuaded that the State Department harbored Communists working for the Soviet Union and, further, that Dean and others in the department were making a serious mistake by underestimating their influence.

One of Jim's problems was that he sometimes lacked a light touch. A few months later, when we were rushing to complete the USSBS report on the Pacific war, I had stayed at the office late one evening discussing with Paul Baran, a brilliant Moscow-born economist, what the Communists might be up to. It was a Thursday night, nothing special scheduled on my calendar, so I asked him to come home and join me and Phyllis and the children for supper. Paul and I arrived at home and all of us assembled in the kitchen, it being the cook's night off. In the middle of preparing dinner we heard the doorbell ring. There on the front steps stood Jim Forrestal, dressed in black tie, accompanied by Lady Cochran, the beautiful wife of the British naval attaché, in elegant evening wear. They had arrived for dinner but they were a day early! Phyllis started scurrying around to see how she could deal with the situation. Then Paul Baran intervened. Announcing that he was an able chef, he took over in the kitchen and prepared a sumptuous second meal, much more elaborate than the simple one we had started, with many of the same ingredients Phyllis had planned for Friday's party. The bridge table was erected in the library and four of us sat down to dine. Jim seemed to be embarrassed by the mix-up, but I considered it an entertaining mistake and hoped Jim would look upon the occasion with the same amusement that I did. Jim did not relax, however, until Paul Baran had emerged from the kitchen and after Ken Galbraith and George Ball had dropped in to gossip. Only then did he become engrossed in the conversation. A little after midnight, Forrestal and Lady Cochran drove off into the night, taking Paul Baran, still deep in serious conversation, with them. It was an odd combination. I understand that Paul subsequently resumed his association with the Left.

It later became obvious to me that Jim was in bad shape psychologically. During the debate over the unification of the armed services, Jim was the leading spokesman for the Navy, which opposed unification. Then, after the 1947 National Security Act cleared Congress, President Truman named him secretary of defense, a job that thrust him into the middle of the fierce postwar feuds between the Air Force and the Navy. I had had a taste of their bickering during my work with the bombing survey, so I knew firsthand the problems Jim would face. Forrestal, trying as best he could to mediate their disputes, became the target of attack from both sides. The stress and strain on his mental stamina were enormous. Just before the new law took effect, Lieutenant General Lauris Norstad, then deputy chief of staff for operations of the Army Air Forces, came to me to inquire—all very unofficially and off the record—whether

I would be interested in serving as first secretary of the air force when the National Security Act separated the AAF from the Army. It was an appealing offer and I indicated that I would be willing to accept if the job were offered. But when Norstad told the White House that I was a registered Republican, I was dropped from consideration. The job went instead to Stuart Symington, who had previously been assistant secretary of war for air.

Symington had been one of Forrestal's close friends for years. Back in the 1930s, Stuart had been president of a corporation that made stainless steel, the Rustless Iron and Steel Company of Baltimore. It practically went bankrupt and finally was sold to the American Rolling Mills Company. After losing his job, Stuart turned to Jim, who helped arrange his selection to run the Emerson Electric Manufacturing Company in St. Louis. Stuart did this with great success. Then, during the war, Stuart came to Washington and succumbed to a serious case of "Potomac fever."

As secretary of the air force, Symington was technically Forrestal's subordinate, but Stuart thought he had better political instincts and understood better what Mr. Truman wanted. Stuart was an able salesman and he did all he could to "sell" the Air Force to the public as the nation's first line of defense. Jim favored "balanced" forces—an army, a navy, and an air force with integrated capabilities to project our military power wherever it might be needed, on land, on sea, or in the air. As far as Stuart was concerned, the Army and the Navy were largely superfluous. The Air Force, he insisted, could do it all. (Later, in 1960, when he was seeking the Democratic nomination to be president, Stuart was the strongest voice in support of there being a missile gap and for unification of the armed services under Air Force dominance.) Why Jim tolerated Stuart's open criticism of his policies—why he did not fire him as many urged him to do on numerous occasions—is a question I could never answer.

The limits of their friendship became fully apparent during the weeks before and immediately after the 1948 election. Jim, believing that the secretary of defense, like the secretary of state, should be above politics, declined to campaign for Mr. Truman. Stuart, on the other hand, became actively involved in the election and struck up a friendship with Louis Johnson, chief fund-raiser for the Democratic party. It was widely rumored that Truman had promised Johnson that he could have any job in Washington he wanted for his efforts, and Johnson picked the Defense Department. Stuart sensed the direction the winds were blowing and promptly shifted his loyalty from Forrestal to Johnson. Stuart became one of those whispering that Forrestal had betrayed Truman during the campaign. Others, including Arthur Krock, a classmate of Jim's at Princeton and then head of *The New York Times* Washington bureau, joined the movement to force Jim out. In the end, the defection of his friends, added to his other problems, left him a deeply troubled, demoralized, and broken man.

5

The H-Bomb Decision and NSC 68

From all outward appearances it was a routine patrol off the coast of Alaska by an Air Force WB-29 weather reconnaissance plane. Such flights were almost daily occurrences, though for this plane the mission was part of what was then a closely guarded secret. It was not in fact a typical weather plane, but a unit of the Air Force's Long Range Detection System that had been established less than a year earlier to monitor the Soviet Union's atomic energy program. Equipped with sensitive instruments using specially treated filter paper to pick up any radioactive dust that might be in the air, these planes would loiter for hours at high altitudes off the Soviet coast, downwind from where U.S. intelligence analysts suspected the Soviets' test range for atomic devices was located. The results of the flight this day—September 3, 1949—showed an abnormally high count of radioactive particles. Upon closer inspection, they confirmed what we had feared would eventually happen—that sometime the previous week the Soviets had detonated a nuclear device. With this one event, the threat posed by the Soviet Union acquired a new, more ominous and dangerous dimension.

At the time I learned about the Soviet detonation, I was just settling into a new job as deputy director of the State Department's Policy Planning Staff, or S/P as it was identified on the department's organization charts. ("S" stood for "Secretary," indicating that it was part of the secretary of state's immediate office, and "P" stood for "Policy.") As I mentioned earlier, it was created in 1947 at the direction of George Marshall as a planning and advisory body to the secretary of state. S/P had no operating responsibilities; its task was to study longer-range problems and recommend solutions which, if approved by the secretary, would then guide the department's operating divisions. In practice, of course, things were rarely this simple. But it did mean that there was a group in addition to the secretary and the under secretary that was not specialized either in a particular area, such as Europe, Asia, or the Middle East, or in a particular function like economics, and that could worry about troublesome problems that cut across the board and appeared likely to have long-range significance. In collaboration with the Joint Staff and the Joint Strategic Survey Committee in the Pentagon, S/P became a significant part of the President's politico-military advisory support mechanism.

To my mind, the success and effectiveness of this system in the late 1940s and early 1950s when I was part of it were the result of President Truman's unwavering confidence in his senior advisers, especially Secretaries Marshall and Acheson. As I look back on it, the relationship between Truman and Acheson was probably the best between a president and his secretary of state in this century. They knew each other's thoughts and, more importantly, they had the deepest respect for each other. Mr. Truman realized that he needed someone with Dean's foreign policy experience and analytical mind, while Acheson realized that he needed Mr. Truman's down-to-earth commonsense qualities. Mr. Truman never tried to hide anything from Mr. Acheson and he, in turn, never tried to hide anything from the President. They worked together as a team.

Mr. Truman was a man of strong opinions and convictions; one of the hallmarks of his presidency was that he never shirked decisions and rarely second-guessed those that he made. Had he confronted the Cuban missile crisis, I have no doubt that he would have taken a course similar to that chosen by John F. Kennedy, but with a great deal less agonizing. I remember one episode around 1952 when we were involved in a reassessment of our policy toward Spain. The Joint Chiefs deemed Spain a highly desirable location for important air and naval bases, and we on the Policy Planning Staff had accordingly initiated a review of our policy aimed at normalizing relations with Spain. At the time, Spain was under a fascist dictator, General Francisco Franco, who had leaned toward the Axis in World War II. Having completed the necessary analytical work and having secured all the necessary concurrences short of the President's, we placed our proposals before the NSC for Mr. Truman's consideration. I accompanied Acheson to the meeting. Mr. Truman came in, took a look around the room, and said, matter-of-factly, that he had a brief announcement. "I am not going to approve this proposed change of policy," he said. "Mr. Franco was an associate of Mr. Hitler and Mr. Mussolini in the last war, and I do not approve of people who once kept company with those men." And with that, he declared the meeting adjourned and left the room. Later, he changed his mind and the process of normalization began, but he gave in only with the greatest reluctance.

I confess that my initial impression of Mr. Truman, formed during World War II, was less than favorable. My first contacts with him were while I was in charge of overseas procurement for the Board of Economic Warfare. At the time, he was chairman of a Senate committee investigating fraud, waste, and abuse in the war effort. The committee's general counsel was a man named McGhee (no relation to George McGhee, later the State Department's Middle East expert), who sometimes showed up in my office to relay complaints from Mr. Truman about my procurement activities. Mr. Truman felt that we should buy as much as possible from domestic suppliers to help the people and economy in this country. This was not always possible, since the quality of some imported materials, like mica, for example, was often so far superior to what we could buy here in the United States that the domestic product was worthless. Mr. Truman's attempts to intervene in this fashion seemed to me grossly improper. When he became President I had visions of the country being turned over to political cronies of his like McGhee.

My wife Phyllis caused me to change my mind about Mr. Truman. When I came home from Europe in 1945 I found her convinced that the Trumans—Mrs. Truman, in particular—were wonderful people of great integrity. Through her wartime volunteer work she had met Mrs. Truman and had formed a favorable opinion of her and of her husband. My respect for Phyllis's invariably sound and perceptive judgment of others told me that I must have underestimated Mr. Truman; she was, of course, right. Mr. Truman had the utmost respect for the office of the presidency, and while he did keep a few cronies like General Harry Vaughan around for company, his respect for the office of the presidency kept him from letting them meddle in decisions he considered to be presidential.

After his meetings with the President, Acheson would come back and brief his immediate staff on what had transpired. Dean was easy to work for because he kept his immediate associates fully informed and up-to-date. I could go over to the Pentagon and talk to the Joint Chiefs, for example, knowing that what I said correctly reflected not only the secretary's views but those of the President. So, even though I was a senior civil servant, not a presidential appointee, I was able to speak with authority and helped take some of the burden from Acheson's shoulders.

Acheson was an exceptional individual, a commanding presence wherever he went, distinguished in appearance, well dressed and witty, and entertaining in speech. Among his greatest joys were the long walks he regularly took with his close friend Justice Felix Frankfurter; they would discuss everything from the major events of the day to the latest Washington gossip. Their common interest was, of course, the law, which Dean saw as bringing out into the open and reflecting the true values and central issues of American life. In contrast to General Marshall, his predecessor as secretary of state, a man of impeccable character, who represented the best that middle-class America can offer, Dean Acheson had the grace and bearing of an aristocrat. Both were great men, though vastly different in style, but both worked well with Mr. Truman and with each other.

How S/P Operated

Under George Kennan, the Policy Planning Staff acquired a reputation as an organization of "deep thinkers." A specialist on the Soviet Union, George normally handled Soviet affairs himself. He was fluent in Russian, knew the literature of the country, and was deeply steeped in its culture and history. No one in the department, except Chip Bohlen, could rival his knowledge and experience in dealing with the Soviets. As an aide to Ambassador William C. Bullitt in the 1930s and, later, during World War II as chargé d'affaires of our Moscow embassy, George had acquired an intimate familiarity with the Soviet Union that justifiably accorded him a leading role in developing this aspect of our foreign policy. His celebrated "X" article, published in *Foreign Affairs* in 1947, identified him as one of the principal architects of the policy to contain Soviet expansionism.

While I worked for him, George ran the Policy Planning Staff as a highly personalized operation. He was frank in what he said to us and he was keenly interested in the ideas we had to contribute, but after the discussion had reached the point where he felt he had gotten from us everything we had to offer him, he would go off with his secretary, Dorothy Heisman, to a little office he kept in the Library of Congress. There, undisturbed by anyone, he would draft and come back with a superbly written report.

With justified pride in the excellence of his prose, George was reluctant to alter any of the reports that he personally had written. Having taken the pain and effort to tap others for ideas, to do additional research if need be, and to do the final writing, he looked upon each report he prepared as etched in steel. Then he would hand it over to the secretary of state, who could either agree or disagree with George's analysis and recommendations.

Soon after I came on board as deputy director in the summer of 1949, George made clear that he would like to step down. He was convinced that his usefulness as policy director was near an end and that he should leave the Foreign Service to do research and to write. But George did not adjust easily to being separated from the mainstream of foreign policy. One day in the summer of 1950, shortly after he had taken up residence at the Institute for Advanced Studies at Princeton, he came back down to Washington and had lunch with Acheson and me. After Dean and I had discussed some of the issues we were then working on, George said, "When I left the department, it never occurred to me that you two would make foreign policy without having first consulted me."

When I succeeded Kennan as director of policy planning on January 1, 1950, I adopted a different approach. During the war years, while I was handling the procurement of strategic commodities abroad, I had learned that it was often necessary to delegate responsibility to others, even though I often believed that the results could have been better had I done the work myself. Most of the time, of course, I was wrong; the procurement business during the war was so vast and complex that it was simply beyond the capabilities of any one person to manage all of it. After joining the State Department I found that the same was true of foreign policy.

During my tenure as director of S/P, most of the papers we turned out were a joint product of a number of us on the staff. I would ask one member to write the first draft, someone else to write a second, and so on until we had something that covered the complex aspects of the problem and seemed clear and to the point. In the last analysis I would take responsibility for deciding the staff's position and for the wording of the final report, even if a majority, or all, of the other members were against me. But that rarely occurred.

Fortunately, I had Dean Acheson's trust and support. His philosophy was that policy percolates up from the bottom as much as it filters down from the top. What he wanted was the most objective advice we could provide, unadulterated by considerations of congressional or public opinion or domestic policy. He once told me: "These factors must at some point be taken into account, but that's my job and Mr. Truman's, not yours. I don't want it being done twice." He was highly skeptical of a theoretical approach to problems. He encouraged his advisers, particularly those of us on the Policy Planning Staff, to come up with our own ideas and to fight for them vigorously. He was sharp enough in cutting us back down to size when we came up with what he considered to be stupidities. But when he made a decision either for or against our ideas he did it in the presence of those involved and gave us a clear understanding of why he had decided the matter in the way he had.

The H-Bomb Decision

Soon after I joined the Policy Planning Staff, two problems came to the forefront. One, of course, was the discovery of the Soviet detonation of an atomic device; the other was the approaching consolidation of Communist rule on the Chinese mainland. Though neither event was a total surprise, the fact that they had occurred almost simultaneously suggested that we were on the verge of a fundamental change in the balance of power. The question was: How should we react to these developments?

George had been studying these two problems for some time. As to China, it was his view that we could do nothing useful to influence the situation there; it would be best if we did nothing, at least for the time being. On the atomic question, he believed that the time had come to put a halt to reliance on nuclear arms and to reopen negotiations with the Soviets on international control of atomic energy. It was his judgment that nuclear weapons were likely to be more damaging than helpful to the support of our foreign policy. He concluded it was dangerous to have them around, and that we should get rid of them at the earliest opportunity. It was a cogent and appealing argument, but it seemed to me one-sided and less than realistic. It struck Dean Acheson, who had earlier done much of the work leading to the Baruch Plan for an acceptable system of international control of atomic energy, much the same way. So the question remained: What should we do?

A crucial aspect of the problem was whether to move forward with the development and testing of a thermonuclear weapon, or H-bomb, or to continue to hold our scientists under wraps. Our military believed that something had to be done to preserve our margin of nuclear superiority over the Soviets, the only area other than naval capabilities where our armed forces enjoyed an effective edge over theirs. Not surprisingly, George weighed into the debate strongly on the side of those who opposed developing the H-bomb. But his arguments had little impact on Dean Acheson's thinking. My own view was that we should have as much information as possible before recommending a course of action to the President.

Atomic energy information (or "restricted data," as it is known officially) was in those days a matter of the utmost secrecy and was not available to anyone outside the Atomic Energy Commission (AEC) except for a handful of people. So sensitive was this information that Mr. Truman refused to keep any of it in his White House safe! I first learned of the possibility of an H-bomb from Robert LeBaron, who was then serving as atomic energy adviser to Secretary of Defense Louis Johnson. In view of my ignorance of the matter, LeBaron arranged a briefing for me by a group he called the "Atomic Colonels"—three colonels who were working for the Joint Chiefs on atomic energy matters. The idea was to build a weapon based on the fusion process, rather than the fission process used in the Hiroshima and Nagasaki bombs. A fusion weapon might attain as much as a thousandfold increase in the yield or power of the explosion of what was possible with a fission weapon. Although theoretical studies done in the 1930s had shown such a bomb to be possible, not much had been done in the United States since then to carry the work forward because of doubts among many scientists that a fusion device was feasible or desirable.

These estimates by the Atomic Colonels were not readily confirmed from my conversations with members of the scientific community. The State Department's chief consultant on atomic energy matters was J. Robert Oppenheimer, who was also chairman of the AEC's General Advisory Committee, composed of the country's leading nuclear physicists. "Oppie," known as the "father" of the A-bomb for his brilliant work on the Manhattan Project in World War II, was considered to be the leading expert on atomic energy. He opposed further research and development aimed at testing a fusion reaction. He told me he did not think such a reaction could be brought about. If it could be brought about, he did not believe it could be harnessed to produce a usable weapon; the equipment required would be so massive and heavy that it could not be fitted into an airplane. Furthermore, the amounts of nuclear material required to produce a single fusion weapon would be so great that it would be more effective to make a number of fission weapons out of that material than to make a single fusion weapon. His final argument was that Soviet scientists lagged behind ours because of excessive secrecy; their scientists were not allowed to publish—therefore scientific knowledge was excessively compartmentalized in the Soviet Union. Even if a fusion weapon was theoretically feasible, the Soviets would be able to develop it only if we had earlier demonstrated that feasibility; in other words, it would be a mistake for us to demonstrate the feasibility of such a weapon even if it were possible. All in all, he concluded, the world would be much better off if no one had such weapons.

After my talk with Oppie, LeBaron suggested that I meet with Edward Teller, who was one of the few scientists at Los Alamos conducting feasibility studies on the H-bomb. The next day Teller arrived at my office to give me a two-hour briefing on his work. Teller had a clear and powerful mind and could make his ideas understandable even to one who was not a professional physicist. He went to the blackboard and showed me two different approaches to solving the problem. He was uncertain whether either of them would succeed but he was confident that something along the lines of one or the other would. The essence of his bomb design was to contain a configuration of deuterium, lithium deuteride, and tritium in a confined space and subject them to the extreme heat and enormous radiation pressure from a fission reaction for the necessary part of a millionth of a second to cause the isotopes of hydrogen to fuse themselves into helium atoms, thus releasing unheard-of amounts of energy. I became persuaded that what he had outlined might well be done. But I continued to be troubled by Oppie's last argument that if we restrained ourselves from demonstrating feasibility the Soviets would be unable to succeed on their own.

LeBaron was anxious that I should side with him in supporting the development of the H-bomb. So he asked me to talk with Ernest O. Lawrence, director of the University of California's Radiation Laboratory in Berkeley. Lawrence flew to Washington for the appointment. He strongly supported Teller and questioned Oppie's argument about the effect of secrecy and nonpublication of experimental results on Russia's ability to solve scientific problems. He said the Soviet nuclear weapons program was no more and no less secret than the one in the United States. In both countries work on nuclear weapons matters was highly classified and scientists working on these matters were seldom, if ever, allowed to publish their findings. Most of the real advances that occurred here, Lawrence added, were made by physicists under the age of thirty. What motivated them was their sense of pushing forward the frontiers of knowledge and the prestige resulting from the appreciation of their work by their peers. This was enough to stimulate creative work in the United States and it was probably the same in the Soviet Union. The freedom to publish meant little in these circumstances. He saw no reason why the Russians could not progress as rapidly as we.

To settle the question of whether to build the H-bomb, Mr. Truman on November 19, 1949, appointed a Special Committee of the National

Security Council, composed of the secretaries of state and defense and the AEC chairman, David Lilienthal. They, in turn, appointed a working group of deputies to develop specific recommendations. LeBaron, as Louis Johnson's chief adviser on atomic energy, represented the Defense Department; Henry D. Smyth and Gordon Dean, both members of the AEC, represented the commission whenever Lilienthal was absent; and R. Gordon Arneson, the secretary of state's atomic energy adviser, and I were delegated by Acheson to represent the State Department.

For the next few weeks we thrashed over the issues in an effort to come up with an agreed course of action. The views of the AEC representatives differed so radically from those representing the Pentagon that an agreed position was impossible. LeBaron favored a crash program to build the bomb, while Lilienthal opposed development altogether. That left the State Department with the swing vote. I tried to look at the problem as objectively as I could. I agreed with the judgment of Oppie and others who opposed trying to build the "super" bomb that the world's future prospects would be better if it proved beyond the power of technology to build such a weapon. But I also suspected that Oppenheimer was not being totally straightforward with me on other arguments—that he was letting his political views cloud his scientific judgment.

In the last analysis, it came down to this: If, as Teller believed, such a weapon were technically feasible, and if, as Lawrence suggested, the Soviets possessed capacity similar to ours, then our operating assumption had to be that the Russians were already working on an H-bomb. That they might eventually succeed in developing one could not, therefore, be ruled out. The crucial question was how disadvantageous would such a development be if we had decided not to proceed? My estimate of the situation was that we could not afford to run that risk. After weighing all the factors, I concluded that we had to see whether the bomb was in fact feasible, not necessarily on a crash basis as LeBaron wanted, but through a deliberate effort.

Lilienthal was hard to persuade. His resistance rested on moral grounds as much as anything. Having been charged with the awesome responsibility of overseeing the nation's atomic energy program, he did not think that a decision of this magnitude should go forward without a clear understanding of its possible effects on our foreign policy. I agreed, but I thought that the decision to begin the research should not be postponed. I therefore drafted a paper incorporating his views and merging them with my own. It recommended:

1. That the President authorize the A.E.C. to proceed with an accelerated program to test the possibility of a thermonuclear reaction;

2. That no decision be made at this time as to whether weapons employing such reaction will actually be built beyond the number required for a test of feasibility;

3. That the N.S.C. reexamine our aims and objectives in the light of the USSR's probable fission bomb capability and its possible thermonuclear capability;

4. That, pending such a review, no public discussion of these issues on the part of those having access to classified materials in this field be authorized.

Acheson accepted my suggestions, but as might have been expected he had trouble persuading Secretary of Defense Johnson. Though Johnson fully endorsed working on the H-bomb, he objected to the idea that it be developed in conjunction with a review of our basic national security policy, probably because he knew that such a review would undermine his credibility by exposing critical deficiencies in our military posture. But if he wanted Acheson's backing for the H-bomb, his only choice was to acquiesce in the policy review. It was the necessary price.

The H-bomb internal debate closed undramatically, with a brief meeting between the President and the Special Committee on January 31, 1950. Afterward, Acheson told me what had happened. At his urging, Lilienthal had led off with a short recapitulation of arguments against the H-bomb, including his own moral qualms. But it quickly became apparent that Truman had already made up his mind. "Can the Russians do it?" he had asked. Assured by the committee that they did indeed possess the necessary capabilities, he had cut short further discussion and signed off on the committee's recommendations and a press release announcing his decision. The meeting had lasted less than ten minutes.

Much has been written in retrospect as to whether Truman made the right decision. I think he did, chiefly because he had no way of knowing what the Soviets might do. In fact, what many of us suspected at the time was true—it did not take a demonstration by the United States to convince the Soviets that the H-bomb might be feasible. What we did not know was that Stalin actually had given the go-ahead for the Soviet H-bomb around November 1, 1949—a full three months before Mr. Truman made his decision. What the Soviets wound up producing, though, appears to have been significantly different from what we initially produced.

The first test of a fusion device by the United States took place in November 1952 and yielded an explosion of over 10 megatons, but this device was far too large to be a deliverable weapon. In fact, it weighed some ten tons and took up an area the size of a small house. The Soviets tested their first thermonuclear device in the summer of 1953. But it had a yield of less than three hundred kilotons, leading some scientists to suspect that it may have been a "boosted" device—a fission bomb with tritium and other elements added to produce a larger than normal explosion. The Soviets tested a true fusion weapon, with a yield of over a megaton, in 1955. Thus, they succeeded in turning out usable thermonuclear weapons much earlier than we did. The Soviets were fully committed to developing an H-bomb before Mr. Truman made the decision that we should do the same. There can now be little doubt that had Mr. Truman not acted when he did, the Soviets would have achieved unchallengeable nuclear superiority by the late 1950s.

Some years later, while I was involved in the SALT II negotiations, I learned from my Soviet counterpart, Aleksandr N. Shchukin, a physicist who had worked with Andrei Sakharov on the Soviet H-bomb, the pressure under which they had achieved their breakthrough. One day during the negotiations the U.S. delegation invited the Russian delegation to join us for a boat trip on Lake Geneva. The trip lasted several hours. It was a glorious, clear sunny day, so Shchukin and I went to the top deck for a leisurely conversation. "You know, Mr. Nitze," he said, "I have never knowingly lied to you, but I did once tell you an untruth. It concerns what I said about the heart attack I had in the 1950s. I said that it happened after returning from a forty-kilometer cross-country skiing trek from my dacha outside Moscow. That was not correct. It really happened while I was working with Sakharov on the H-bomb project. The project was being supervised for Stalin by Lavrenty Beria, the head of the Soviet secret police [now the KGB]. Beria drove us without mercy, day and night, the most demanding taskmaster one could imagine. The strain was intense, with Beria hurling a continuous series of threats at us as to what would happen if we didn't produce faster. Then one day we received word that Beria had been killed. A great burden had been suddenly lifted; my relief was so great that it was then that I had my heart attack!"

The Origins of NSC 68

While the AEC began serious work on building an H-bomb, a State-Defense group was formed to examine the national security implications of the President's decision. The group had no chairman. Secretary Acheson and Secretary Johnson had joint responsibility. On the State Department side, since the study involved matters of long-range policy, the Policy Planning Staff was responsible for the staff work.

Dealing with the Defense Department in those days was tricky. Johnson had promised Mr. Truman that he would hold the military budget to thirteen billion dollars, a figure that was becoming more unrealistic with each passing day. He believed the State Department was conspiring with the armed services to make it impossible for him to carry out his promise. So he issued an order that all contacts between the military and the State Department had to go through his immediate office. It was, of course, an unworkable and impractical arrangement; it posed significant difficulties in carrying out the President's study directive.

One of Johnson's principal aides was a retired Army officer, Major General James H. Burns, whom Johnson had called back into service as his deputy for politico-military affairs. As such, Burns was the Pentagon point of contact with the State Department. Burns was a wholly decent man, interested in cooperating as best he could; but his health was not the best and he usually worked only half a day. We needed a full-time contact and we also wanted direct access to the Joint Chiefs of Staff. Johnson, after some delay, reluctantly approved the appointment by the Joint Chiefs of a representative to work directly with the Policy Planning Staff. They chose Major General Truman "Ted" Landon, who was then the Air Force member of the Joint Strategic Survey Committee. I found him to be a wise, straightforward, and competent collaborator.

We worked intensely from mid-February 1950 until early April, when we submitted our final report (NSC 68) to the National Security Council for the President's consideration. It was my view that the investigation should take a broad perspective and examine both where we stood and where we should wish to be in the future in terms of a broad conception of our national security.

One of our first concerns was the security of Europe, where our North Atlantic Treaty Organization (NATO) allies were in serious need of reassurance that the balance of power was not tipping in favor of the Soviet Union. Now that the Soviets had acquired an atomic capability,

Acheson and I concurred that NATO could not for the indefinite future rely primarily on the threat of nuclear retaliation to deter or, if necessary, to stop a Soviet invasion. We had to strengthen our position with other means and this meant a buildup of conventional forces. Since the European economy could not yet sustain such a buildup, some share of the money and resources would have to come from the United States.

The writing of NSC 68 fell almost entirely to the Policy Planning Staff. John Paton Davies authored some of the more telling phrases. One of his contributions was the phrase "to frustrate the Kremlin's design." Foster Dulles later borrowed that phrase and inserted it into the 1952 Republican platform. Bob Tufts, who had worked with me since the Hammarskjöld negotiations back in 1946, made major contributions, as did Robert Hooker, who helped write those portions having to do with the ideological struggle between East and West. Practically everyone on the staff participated in one way or another to make it a joint effort from start to finish.

The Defense Department members of the policy review committee did not initially accept our assessment of the situation. Louis Johnson had so drummed into their heads the need for holding the military budget to thirteen billion dollars that they found it hard even to contemplate a proposal that might result in a military budget increased by more than five billion dollars per year. Initially, they wanted a few more air groups, a couple of additional divisions, and a few more ships, but that was about all. It was not until we had had a week or two of discussion that General Landon accepted the idea that we were engaged not in a mere horse-trading budget exercise, but in a fundamental reassessment of the requirements of our national security policy, as the President had directed. From that point on, things progressed smoothly as we wrote our report with growing consensus on what the thrust of it should be.

After becoming director of the Policy Planning Staff, I joined Secretary Acheson every morning in his small staff meeting room or dropped by his office, which was adjacent to mine, to check with him on important developments. Thus, Acheson stayed current on what the group was doing. Johnson, on the other hand, had sought to divorce himself from the entire affair and, except for an occasional memo from General Burns, he knew virtually nothing of our deliberations. Believing that Johnson must be fully informed about the progress on a report for which he was to share responsibility with Acheson, I arranged with General Burns for a briefing for Johnson and Acheson to be held on March 22 in the Policy Planning Staff's conference room.

The State Department group assembled around three in the afternoon, but with no sign of Louis Johnson. Johnson and General Omar N. Bradley, the chairman of the Joint Chiefs, accompanied by their aides, arrived about fifteen minutes later. Johnson entered the room in a towering rage and announced that he had no intention even of sitting down. He said the entire effort was a conspiracy by me and General Landon to subvert his attempts to hold down the military budget. All of us were astonished and practically dumbfounded. Finally, Acheson spoke. He told Johnson, "You and I are supposed to deliver this report and these are the people we've appointed to do the staff work for us. I can't understand why you won't let yourself be briefed on what they've done. After all, the report is going to be yours and mine, not theirs. We're the ones who are going to have to sign this document."

Johnson refused to listen. "No," he replied, "I won't have anything to do with this conspiracy." And with that, he ordered Bradley and the others to follow him and stalked out of the room. General Burns—visibly distraught—stayed behind. I thought he was going to burst into tears. He said, "I've done everything I could do about this. I've kept my secretary advised. He agreed to this meeting and now he humiliates me this way. I'm going to have to resign."

I did all I could to reassure Burns. I said, "For God's sake, don't resign. You're the essential link between the two departments. You've got to stay; otherwise this report will never be finished." So Burns agreed not to resign and we proceeded with completion of the study.

When the final report was circulated near the end of March, Johnson was out of town attending a meeting of the NATO defense ministers at The Hague. Everyone else, including Acheson, the three secretaries of the military services, and each of the Joint Chiefs, promptly endorsed the report. When Johnson returned he greeted what amounted to a fait accompli. He could have lodged a dissenting opinion, but he would have looked foolish doing so given the endorsements the report had already received. Johnson may have suffered from numerous defects of character, but he knew when he was beaten; in this instance he tried to make the best of the situation by adding his approval of the report and by recommending that Mr. Truman accept it.

The report itself, some sixty pages long, addressed what I have considered throughout my career to be the fundamental question of national security: How do we get from where we are to where we want to be without being struck by disaster along the way? NSC 68 began by defining the basic U.S. purpose, quoting from the Preamble of the Constitution, and then discussed the nature of the Soviet threat. Here we drew a clear distinction between the aims of the United States, which were to protect and preserve the institutions of a free society, and those of the Soviet Union, which centered on preserving the Soviet Communist party and its base, the USSR, but also on extending the Kremlin's domination outward as far as practicable. What we found most disturbing was not that the Soviet Union would espouse such objectives, but that it had developed a political, economic, and military structure designed specifically for their eventual realization. It followed that if the United States were to deal effectively with this threat, it had no choice other than to take the lead in initiating "a substantial and rapid building-up of strength in the free world . . . to support a firm policy intended to check and roll back the Kremlin's drive for world domination."

Truman was properly cautious about the budgetary implications of NSC 68. He reserved final judgment on those issues until the agencies and departments had submitted their implementing requests and his budget advisers had had a chance to go over them in close detail. My personal estimate was that the buildup recommended in the report would probably require annual appropriations of around forty billion dollars for the next four to five years. But the report itself contained no money figures. I told Secretary Acheson what I personally estimated the program might cost and he advised against any mention of specific sums. "Paul," he said, "don't put any such figure into this report. It is right for you to estimate it and to tell me about it, and I will tell Mr. Truman, but the decision on the amount of money to be requested of the Congress should not be made until it has been costed out in detail. One first ought to decide whether this is the kind of policy one wants to follow. The extent to which one actually implements it with appropriations is a separate question which involves the domestic economy and other considerations. So don't get into that hassle at this stage."

Following Acheson's advice, our final report contained only a general reference to costs, though we made no attempt to disguise our belief that the recommended program would require expenditures well in excess of the current thirteen-billion-dollar ceiling. One question was whether the economy could afford it. I discussed this matter with Leon Keyserling, the acting chairman of the President's Council of Economic Advisers. He and I agreed that a forty-million-dollar defense budget could be sustained, provided the administration took the necessary concomitant steps in taxation and control of scarce materials. Keyserling wanted to spend the money elsewhere than on defense, but he saw no serious problem as far as the general capacity of the economy was concerned. My own preference was to raise taxes rather than to resort to deficit spending, but raising taxes was a politically unpopular course and one that the Bureau of the Budget later resisted. During the Korean War, I recommended, for example, a steep excise tax on automobiles, rising sharply with horsepower in excess of a hundred; the idea was to cut down on civilian consumption of steel, rubber, and petroleum products while also raising substantial revenue. My suggestion was laughed at. Predictably, the economy had to suffer the adverse effects of heavy government borrowing to offset annual deficits during the Korean War. The seeds of our persistent inflation since then were sown at that time.

The often expressed contention that NSC 68 urged a buildup of our forces because we anticipated a war with the Soviet Union sometime in 1954 is incorrect; it is a misreading of the paper. In the light of the intelligence reports we had at the time, we judged that, if in the meantime we were to undertake no measures to offset the projectable increases in Soviet capabilities, 1954 would be the year of "maximum" danger—the point at which the Soviets would have atomic weapons and delivery aircraft in sufficient number to threaten extensive (even unacceptable) damage to the United States. But we did not believe that the Soviets operated from any kind of master plan that automatically decreed that they would launch an attack on such and such a date at such and such a time, like the schedule Hitler had adopted for the conquest of Europe in World War II. Soviet doctrine is, in fact, exceedingly flexible. It assumes that capitalism will eventually fail and that Communism will prevail, but it makes no attempt to predict when this will come about.

Equally erroneous is the contention that NSC 68 recommended a sharp departure in U.S. policy. On the contrary, the report concluded by calling for the reaffirmation of what was already approved policy in NSC 20/4, a general policy paper covering our relations with the Soviet Union. That report, masterminded by George Kennan in 1948, had described the serious nature of the Soviet threat and had gone on to recommend "timely and adequate preparation" to combat internal and external Soviet moves that might jeopardize our security. The major change recommended in NSC 68 was a stepped-up level of effort to counter recent developments, with emphasis on strengthening our military capabilities in the face of significantly increased Soviet capabilities. Heretofore our foreign policy had stressed economic assistance, as under the Marshall Plan, and collective security through the North Atlantic Treaty, backed by a very modest program of military aid to our allies. These measures, while obviously important, did not appear to me to be sufficient. I did not think that under the proposed buildup, the United States and its allies could or should attempt to match the Soviets soldier for soldier or tank for tank, nor did I consider a policy of rearmament as necessarily implying the futility of negotiations or the imminent possibility of a shooting war. Rather, I viewed the recommended policy as the logical response to an evident danger that was not likely soon to go away and that could only grow worse the longer it was ignored.

In the final drafting of NSC 68, Chip Bohlen and I had a serious discussion about the language of the report dealing with the purpose of the Soviet Communist party leadership. Chip insisted that I had gotten Soviet priorities wrong. He insisted that they were most interested in maintaining their power base within the Soviet Union, that their second priority was maintaining control over their satellites, and that their ambitions for further expansion afield were only a third priority. I changed the language in the relevant paragraph of NSC 68 to conform more closely to Chip's judgment as to Soviet priorities. Later, however, Chip continued to complain about NSC 68 and this paragraph in particular. He claimed that NSC 68 gave too much emphasis to Soviet ambitions for expansion. I could never get clear from him how he wanted the language further amended. This disagreement came to the attention of Secretary Acheson. He decided to call us both in and arbitrate our dispute. Acheson listened to us argue for an hour or so and came to the conclusion that he could not understand how Bohlen wished the language changed. So the language stood as we in the NSC study group had drafted it. Even so, Chip continued to believe that we had put too strong a case for Soviet expansionism.

NSC 68 was the first of what later became a series of basic national security policy papers produced each year through the Truman and Eisenhower administrations. At the time it was completed and handed to Mr. Truman, I was by no means certain that its recommendations would be accepted and acted upon. (In fact, Mr. Truman did not officially approve the conclusions of NSC 68 until September 1950, though they were operative policy well before then.) However, I felt reasonably sure that events would bear out the accuracy of the report's analysis. I was not alone in this belief.

Not long after NSC 68 was finished, I was paid a visit by a friend of mine from my Wall Street days, Alexander Sachs. Born in Czarist Russia, he had emigrated to the United States and had worked his way up to become the senior economist with Lehman Brothers in New York. Sachs had many friends in the scientific community, including Albert Einstein, Enrico Fermi, Leo Szilard, Edward Teller, and others who were involved in nuclear physics. In 1939, fearing that Nazi Germany might be developing an atomic bomb, they had prevailed upon Sachs to take a letter written by Einstein to FDR, expressing their concern and urging that the

United States launch its own program to explore the feasibility of this new type of weapon. It was thus that the Manhattan Project came about.

When Sachs arrived at my office that day in 1950, it was with a similar sense of urgency. He brought with him three papers. The first was an analysis of Soviet doctrine concerning the correlation of forces; the second argued that the Soviets would view their successful atomic test and events in China as a favorable change in the correlation of forces; and the third analyzed where and when they might try to exploit this changed situation. Sachs thought that Moscow was naturally cautious and would try to minimize risks by acting through a satellite. He predicted a North Korean attack upon South Korea sometime late in the summer of 1950. It seemed to me a logical analysis and one that deserved closer study.

Our ambassador to South Korea at that time was John Joseph Muccio, who happened to be in Washington shortly after Sachs visited my office. I had lunch with him and asked him what he thought of Sachs' analysis. Muccio thought such an attack was quite possible and mentioned numerous instances of armed clashes along the 38th parallel, the dividing line between North and South Korea. The reason he was in town, he said, was to persuade the military assistance people in the Pentagon to give South Korea an additional ten million dollars for fighter aircraft, ammunition, and fast patrol boats to catch North Korean infiltrators. However, since 1947, the Joint Chiefs had maintained that the United States had no strategic interests in Korea and that therefore it should limit its obligations and commitments there. One result was that military assistance policy for South Korea specifically prohibited any action that might result in the creation of a South Korean "air force" or a South Korean "navy." It appeared highly unlikely that Muccio would get what he was asking for. I agreed to support his requests, but I knew that until NSC 68 was approved and implemented, we would continue to address our problems in piecemeal fashion. Muccio and I did succeed in getting approval for the fast patrol boats needed to reduce clandestine infiltration into South Korea from the north, but that was the limit of what was then possible.

I next heard from John Foster Dulles, who arrived at my office one day armed with a memorandum he had written, addressed to me and Dean Rusk, who was then serving as assistant secretary for Far Eastern affairs. Foster had recently been named a consultant to the department for the purpose of negotiating a Japanese peace treaty and was about to leave for Tokyo for talks with General MacArthur. Before leaving, he wanted to register his disagreement with comments Secretary Acheson had made in January before the National Press Club. In that speech, Dean had referred to our "defense perimeter" in the Pacific in terms that excluded Korea and Taiwan. Dean was reiterating the strategic advice of the Joint Chiefs. General MacArthur had made similar remarks almost a year earlier, quoted in *The New York Times* on March 2, 1949. Although Dean was later accused of having "invited" a North Korean attack, I could see no basis for such an accusation, especially in view of Dean's added comment that we would honor our commitments no matter on which side of the defensive perimeter a violation might occur.

Foster's memorandum demonstrated that he was not half as much worried about Korea as he was about what might happen to Chiang Kai-shek and the Nationalists who had swarmed to Taiwan after the Communist victory on the mainland. The thrust of his memorandum was that if we were to let Taiwan fall to a Chinese Communist invasion force, it would set a bad example, weaken our prestige and influence among our friends and allies in the Far East, and invite further Communist aggression.

I pointed out to Foster that the secretary had said nothing to indicate a withdrawal of our support from either Korea or Taiwan, and that he had phrased his remarks to accord with the military advice of the Joint Chiefs. Foster still took issue. "You've been asking whether Formosa is necessary to us militarily," he said. "Suppose you ask the Chiefs what their attitude would be if the President were to decide that from the political standpoint, it was important to defend Korea. Then, would it be militarily feasible and prudent to do so?" I agreed that that was a different formulation of the problem and said I would consult the Chiefs. But even after I had reformulated the question in the way Foster had suggested and discussed it at length with the Joint Strategic Survey Committee, the response from the Chiefs came back that, without additional forces or a reduction of obligations elsewhere, we should make no commitment to defend either Korea or Taiwan.

Even this did not satisfy Foster. Just prior to the invasion he went to Korea, where he toured the front lines along the 38th parallel and delivered an address to the South Korean parliament. Reaffirming our concern for the South Koreans' fate, he pledged unspecified American support under the UN Charter in case of trouble, though he really had no authority from Washington to make such a statement. Still, his was a fairly accurate depiction of our position, one we would feel called upon to uphold sooner than any of us, including Foster, expected.

6

War in Korea

Like the Japanese attack on Pearl Harbor, the North Korean invasion of South Korea occurred on a Sunday—June 25, 1950. It took the United States by surprise. Despite Sachs' predictions and Muccio's warnings, our intelligence emanating from General MacArthur's headquarters in Tokyo hinted at nothing to provoke undue worry or alarm over an impending invasion. I suspected—and had so warned repeatedly during the preparation of NSC 68—that the Soviets might be planning some kind of action, but where it would take place was difficult to foresee. Yugoslavia or Berlin were likely targets and Southeast Asia seemed a possibility also. Korea, although obviously a potential trouble spot, had not provoked the same degree of concern.

Because I was not in Washington when news of the invasion broke, I have no firsthand recollections of how Washington reacted to the initial shock of the invasion. This being the beginning of the vacation season, many of the senior officials were out of town. Mr. Truman was at his home in Independence, Missouri. Dean Acheson had gone to his country house, Harewood Farm, in Maryland. I also had taken some days off to join my family and a friend, Fred Eaton, for salmon fishing on the Upsalquitch River in a remote region of New Brunswick. Thinking that I had left the cares of the world behind in Washington, my most immediate concern was what fly, put down at what spot, would tempt the wily salmon.

Our main camp was fifteen miles from the nearest road; to get there we were pulled up the river by a barge pulled by horses. We were totally out of touch with civilization, except for a portable radio that one of our guides carried. One evening, after Fred and I had had our supper and were sitting by an open fire at a remote pool upriver from the main camp, one of our guides came to us and said, "There's a report that the North Koreans have just attacked South Korea." At dawn the next morning we broke camp, got into our canoes, and raced down the river to where I had left my car. I drove at breakneck speed to the nearest town with an airport, and flew immediately to Washington.

During the flight to Washington, my mind raced back over the years and events that had led up to the current crisis. As alarming as the invasion was, it seemed to me the inevitable consequence of a policy that from the beginning had been grossly shortsighted. Our involvement in Korea dated from 1945, when, as a matter of military expediency, the United States and the Soviet Union divided Korea—then a Japanese colony—at the 38th parallel into two zones of occupation. The intention, as stated in the 1943 Cairo declaration, was that Korea should "in due course" become a free and independent country under a single government. While the Soviets disarmed Japanese soldiers north of the line, American troops disarmed those south of it. It was never envisioned by us that the 38th parallel should become a fixed or permanent boundary, but rather that it should serve as a temporary line of demarcation, separating the two occupation forces, until the Japanese were gone and elections could be held to reunify the country.

The turning point occurred in 1947, by which time negotiations to reunify Korea had reached a total impasse. Two choices, neither of them satisfactory, presented themselves. We could either accept the situation as it stood, withdraw our forces, and let the South Koreans fend for themselves, or we could ensure a perpetuation of the stalemate but with small hope of achieving a settlement. The first course seemed to me foolhardy since I seriously questioned both whether South Korea could, without U.S. assistance, defend itself against North Korea, which was receiving extensive Soviet help, and whether the South Korean economy could sustain itself. The south had most of the population and agriculture, but it lacked an industrial base and access to natural resources, nearly all of which were in the Communist-controlled north. In retrospect, my assessment of South Korea's economic potential was grossly pessimistic. The "economic miracle" that years later swept South Korea then seemed to me well beyond that country's possibilities.

In 1947 the Joint Chiefs of Staff urged a policy of withdrawal from Korea. At the time, General Eisenhower was Army chief of staff in Washington. Eager to withdraw his forces, which then numbered some forty-five thousand troops, Eisenhower persuaded the other members of the JCS to endorse a memorandum to the National Security Council recommending that our troops mount out at the earliest practicable opportunity. He used the argument that Korea was of no strategic importance to the United States in a war with the USSR and that therefore an early withdrawal would not harm our strategic position. Opinion in the

State Department, from Secretary Marshall on down, questioned the advisability of the Chiefs' recommendation. Most of us suspected—and our intelligence analysts concurred—that an American withdrawal would be followed in time by a Communist attempt to achieve control of the south through subversion or direct aggression. But under continuing pressure from the Army, President Truman finally acquiesced to Eisenhower's demand. In July 1949, the last U.S. combat troops departed, leaving behind a five-hundred-man military advisory group to help train and equip the South Korean armed forces.

By 1949, when the removal of our troops from Korea took place, Eisenhower had left the military and was working in New York as president of Columbia University, with one eye on eventually moving to the White House. Eisenhower said a number of things which I found difficult to forgive, even in a military man turned politician, during his 1952 campaign for the presidency. Forgetting or ignoring that the withdrawal of our forces had been done on his recommendation, he blamed the Truman administration for having made a tragic political blunder that, in effect, had invited the North Korean attack. Such duplicity and double talk by Eisenhower, coupled with his subsequent refusal to stand up for General Marshall against the pernicious and unfounded accusations of Senator Joseph McCarthy, led me to doubt his judgment or honesty or both. I switched my voter registration from Republican to Democratic in 1952, just before the election.

I arrived in Washington two days after the invasion had begun in June 1950. The UN had already passed a resolution condemning the attack and President Truman had ordered General MacArthur to provide air and sea support to the South Koreans. These decisions having been made, it was only a matter of a day or so before the President would have to decide whether to intervene with ground troops as well. Given the limited ground forces we had in the area and the possibility of emergencies elsewhere, a strong argument could have been made that it would have been imprudent to commit them on the Korean peninsula. The realities of the situation, reinforced by Mr. Truman's determination not to allow aggression to go unpunished, argued against such prudence. Further delay would have produced a total disaster in Korea. The South Koreans were taking a terrible beating and their resistance had all but collapsed as they retreated in the direction of the Han River and eventually to Pusan.

On June 30, 1950, Mr. Truman accepted the necessity of sending American ground troops to Korea to block the invasion. This decision led next to consideration of the command structure these forces should be under.

We wanted the world to realize that the North Korean attack was an act of aggression being met by international resistance, so we made certain that all actions we took had the sanction of the United Nations. Thus we accepted—and sought to establish in everyone's mind—the principle that ultimate responsibility for the retaliation being directed by General MacArthur rested with the UN.

To underscore this point, the British offered to sponsor a resolution in the Security Council reaffirming that the UN was in charge and requesting the United States to designate a commander of the forces fighting under the UN flag. Burt Marshall, who had joined the Policy Planning Staff just a few weeks earlier, took one look at this resolution and promptly showed up in my office urging that it be withdrawn or rewritten. Burt did not know MacArthur personally, as I did, but he was familiar with the general's reputation for independence amounting to insubordination and suspected that it would be a mistake for MacArthur to receive his appointment through the UN. It made no sense, Burt argued, to grant a commander like MacArthur the authority to act for the UN and still expect him to abide by the orders he might receive from the President.

I took Burt's objections up with the head of State's office of UN affairs, John D. Hickerson, who was coordinating the effort to secure passage of the resolution. Jack agreed that there was ample room under the resolution for MacArthur to make mischief. But he pointed out that the language of the resolution had already been agreed upon in the Security Council. Any attempt on our part to change the wording at this point would raise awkward questions which we could not fully or candidly answer. The implication would be that we did not trust our own military. I reported all this to Secretary Acheson. He, too, concurred that there was potential for conflict inherent in the UN resolution, but he nevertheless decided that the political realities justified the risk. Thus on July 7 the Security Council adopted the resolution as presented.

A question that was on everyone's mind, especially Mr. Truman's, was what to expect next from the Soviet Union. Was Korea an isolated instance of local aggression or was it part of a general Soviet-directed offensive? The Policy Planning Staff was assigned the task of preparing a report on that subject to the NSC. Nothing in the evidence I saw contradicted my belief—shared by others, I should emphasize, from the President on down—that the Soviets were behind the assault. But as we dug for more information to clarify what they were up to, we came away virtually empty-handed. The best our intelligence community could provide was an estimate saying that while the Soviets were likely to attack anywhere at any moment, such attacks might not necessarily take place. No doubt Mr. Truman found this assessment as unenlightening as we did in the Policy Planning Staff.

At the risk of oversimplifying a complex series of events, let me say that the Korean War fell into four phases. The distinction was not always clear at the time and often problems overlapped one another. But in trying to recall the course of the war and my involvement in it, it helps to work from a few benchmarks.

The first phase lasted from the outbreak of fighting in late June 1950 until MacArthur's landing of UN troops at Inchon on September 15, 1950. Throughout this period American and South Korean forces were constantly on the defensive, pinned down to an area shrinking to the outskirts of Pusan on the southern tip of the peninsula. In Washington there was intense criticism of Mr. Truman's leadership by the Republican minority in Congress. Our intelligence, however, showed that the Communists had overextended their supply lines. By August I knew that MacArthur was planning a counteroffensive. Though not privy to the details, I suspected that it would be some form of landing along the Korean coast and then a thrust inland to exploit the North Koreans' vulnerability.

A related development was Mr. Truman's decision in early September to replace Louis Johnson as secretary of defense with General Marshall. I had heard rumors for some time that Mr. Truman was dissatisfied with Louis Johnson's performance, so I was not surprised when he was finally fired. The news reached me while Dean and I were in New York conferring with the British and French on the German rearmament question. These were difficult negotiations, as the French were reluctant to see Germany rearmed. During a private meeting of the U.S. delegation, a call came in for Acheson from Averell Harriman in Washington. I knew at once from the expression on Dean's face that he had heard good news. "Johnson has just been fired," he announced. "Bring out the champagne." And with that we adjourned to the next room to the sound of popping corks!

Johnson's departure, followed shortly by MacArthur's brilliantly successful Inchon invasion, supported by U.S. and British naval units, ushered in phase two of the war. After Inchon, it became apparent that MacArthur had scored a stunning military victory by trapping the North Korean army between his own forces and those of General Walton Walker, who had launched a simultaneous counteroffensive in the south. Also by this time, British and Australian ground units were beginning to reach Korea in substantial numbers, giving MacArthur's command a growing edge over the enemy. In a matter of days North Korea's army collapsed and ceased to offer any significant organized resistance.

By this time, also, Mr. Truman had become persuaded that the conclusions and recommendations in NSC 68 were in essence correct and that they should be fully acted upon without further delay. On September 30, 1950, he approved an implementing directive. Broadly speaking, we had three objectives. We aimed, first of all, to bolster our conventional capabilities not only to deal effectively with the emergency in Korea, but also to be in a better position to respond should similar emergencies arise elsewhere. Second, we wanted to strengthen our strategic nuclear forces to present a more credible deterrent of aggression against our truly vital interests. And finally, we wanted to assist our allies, especially in Europe, to improve their deterrent military posture.

Meanwhile, the elimination of the North Korean army had raised a question that we in Washington had debated off and on since summer: What should be our policy once the North Korean aggression had been stopped and our forces had regained the ground lost south of the 38th parallel? Should we cross that line and attempt to reunify Korea, an objective we had long espoused? Or should we halt at the 38th parallel, reestablish and strengthen the regime in the south, and let matters in the north sort themselves out on their own?

Prior to Inchon, I judged it impossible to reach definite conclusions on these difficult questions. I therefore recommended to Acheson, who agreed entirely, that we should postpone a decision pending the results of our planned counterattack. The NSC worked up a paper to this effect and in early September, Mr. Truman added his concurrence.

After the stunning success of Inchon, the debate in Washington resumed. The Joint Chiefs, supported by General Marshall, who was now secretary of defense, thought that MacArthur should be given leeway to use his forces as he saw best. They supported a flexible policy that did not automatically preclude crossing the 38th parallel. Dean Rusk and his deputy, John Allison, among others in the State Department, concurred with this view. Among the military in this country, it was accepted as a time-honored principle that the commander in the field, being closer to the immediate situation and being responsible for the safety of his forces, be allowed the final word in deciding how to deploy and use them. The assumption is that he should not operate under constraints—that is, orders from far away—that might deny him the flexibility of being able to exploit opportunities as they arise in the immediate situation. It is a philosophy that has been part of American military doctrine since Grant's day, and in most instances it has worked well. But in this case, with my personal knowledge of MacArthur's contempt for Washington and Truman in particular, it was my view that he should be given unambiguous direction on the central issues of U.S. policy.

In the Policy Planning Staff we tried to assess the situation in terms of its long-range implications. Those who argued in favor of crossing the 38th parallel had a strong case on their side. A reunified Korea was a logical and desirable objective. To stop at the 38th parallel would have been tantamount to a restoration of the status quo ante. The North Korean regime would be left in place and the Soviets would no doubt help it to rearm. The threat from the north would be revived, obliging the United States, in all probability, to keep sizable forces in the south indefinitely.

This line of reasoning, though appealing in its superficial aspects, had one principal flaw—it failed to take into account the possibility that China, the Soviet Union, or both might intervene if our forces moved too close to their borders. It seemed to me that rather than risk widening the war, which might well result from crossing the 38th parallel, we should consolidate what we had gained by the Inchon victory and seek peace terms that would guarantee the security of the South Korean regime. If this could be done, we would avoid the necessity of having to keep troops in Korea after the peace. The plan I had in mind would result in effective demilitarization of the north. We would agree to liberal peace terms as far as the continued existence of the regime in the north was concerned, but in return insist upon no expansion in the number or capacity of airfields and no increase in the size of their military forces from its then greatly depleted strength.

With these ideas in mind I set about reducing them to paper in a form that Secretary Acheson could present to Mr. Truman. Events soon effectively scuttled my efforts. On September 29, 1950, General Marshall sent MacArthur a secret cable assuring him, "We want you to feel unhampered tactically and strategically to proceed north of the 38th Parallel." I knew a message of some kind had been sent, but I had no information that MacArthur had been told he was free to go above the 38th parallel in pursuit of the enemy. I assumed instead that an effort had been made to get Washington thinking to MacArthur without specifically directing him what to do.

The next day, September 30, the Joint Chiefs, with Mr. Truman's approval, issued new instructions designed to curb any impulse MacArthur might have had to conduct unlimited operations. "Your military objective," the directive read, "is the destruction of the North Korean Armed Forces." But in doing so, MacArthur was enjoined from going near either the Soviet or Manchurian borders; and he was further advised to adopt a defensive posture at the first sign of Soviet or Chinese intervention. To my mind, the intent of these orders should have been clear. Although MacArthur could go above the 38th parallel to clean up pockets of resistance, he was not authorized to engage in large operations that might provoke the Chinese or Soviets and thus jeopardize chances for an early negotiated settlement of the conflict. But MacArthur, as I had suspected he would, interpreted this order differently.

Then, a week later on October 7, the UN adopted a loosely worded resolution calling for reconciliation between the warring parties and the holding of elections under UN auspices to establish a new Korean government representing all factions. MacArthur seized upon this resolution as a UN call for North Korea to surrender. The mistake of having earlier given him his command through the UN now became apparent. Since technically his authority derived from the UN he felt at liberty to disregard the caveats contained in his September 30 directive from the President and the Joint Chiefs. On October 9, insisting that his mission was "to enforce the decrees of the United Nations," he broadcast a demand for unconditional surrender of the North Koreans and threatened full-scale invasion of the north if they did not comply. Efforts to negotiate a settlement, based on the terms under study in the Policy Planning Staff, were now hopelessly compromised.

At the Wake Island meeting later in October, MacArthur assured Mr. Truman that the chances of Soviet or Chinese intervention were remote. Philip C. Jessup, then ambassador-at-large, had brought along his secretary, and it was she who served as note-taker at these meetings. When Mr. Truman returned to Washington, she filled us in on the details of the conversations. I had seen reports—most of them emanating from our embassy in New Delhi—that the Chinese were threatening intervention if UN forces crossed the 38th parallel. The source of most of these reports was India's ambassador to Peking, K. M. Pannikar, who had a reputation of being pro-Chinese and pro-Communist. Because of the source of these reports, I did not take them at face value, but neither did I reject the possibility that they might prove to have substance.

In the meantime, MacArthur marched his troops north in two widely separated columns in a manner inviting a counterattack. He promised his men that they would be home with their families for Christmas. Advance units reached the Yalu River, the border between Korea and Manchuria, on November 22. A few days later came a massive Chinese counterattack by substantial forces that had infiltrated to positions between and behind our lines. Our units fell into headlong retreat back down the peninsula with heavy casualties. MacArthur publicly blamed everyone but himself for the disaster. His comments in the press accused unnamed politicians in Washington of having tied his hands.

A further problem concerned the scale and scope of our rearmament efforts. The initial program, which Mr. Truman had approved in late September 1950, aimed at extending the buildup through June 30, 1954. But in November 1950, Chinese intervention in Korea induced a reassessment of that timetable. The inescapable conclusion was that we had underestimated Soviet and Chinese intentions, that the dangers were even more grave than we had originally feared, that the risk of a larger conflict could not be ignored, and that we should accelerate the pace of our preparations. Mr. Truman agreed and late in 1950 he ordered, on the advice of the NSC, that the buildup he had approved earlier be completed by June 30, 1952—two years prior to the date initially envisioned.

Despite "revisionist" historians who have since asserted that the Truman administration overreacted, there was no doubt in my mind at the time that the danger of the war's spreading was serious and that the situation called for more vigorous measures than we had theretofore contemplated. I did not, however, share the view of the "doom-and-gloom" prophets—Stuart Symington chief among them—that we should prepare ourselves for a full-scale preemptive nuclear attack on the Soviet Union. I did not believe the Soviets wished to provoke a nuclear war, and therefore would not intervene in Korea unless our actions posed a direct threat to their Far Eastern provinces.

China's intervention ushered in the third and, to my mind, the most difficult and dangerous period of the war. Eventually, the U.S. retreat halted and a battle line stabilized back around the 38th parallel. It was the view of those who seemed to me to have the best judgment of what was then going on in Korea that our troops simply got tired of running, turned around, and said in effect: "No more retreat!" MacArthur's command had little to do with stemming the Chinese advance. Our troops just dug in and fought. It was now the Chinese who were overextended and, as a result, they took tremendous casualties.

MacArthur had either grossly misjudged the enemy's reaction to his move north, or he had misjudged Mr. Truman's willingness to expand the war by initiating the use of nuclear weapons. Meanwhile, I learned, from intercepts of cable traffic coming across my desk, that MacArthur's real aim was to expand the war into China, overthrow Mao Tse-tung, and restore Chiang Kai-shek to power. It was clear that MacArthur was headed in a most dangerous direction. I concluded that as difficult and unpopular as it might be to do so, the President sooner or later would have to replace him. The longer he stayed in command, the more I despaired that we would find a sensible course of action.

Part of the problem was that MacArthur had not been briefed on the extremely limited size of our nuclear weapons stockpile, which was then largely under the custody of the Atomic Energy Commission. I had gone over the matter with General Herbert B. Loper, who was responsible for monitoring the stockpile for the military, to determine exactly what was available. Loper and I agreed that the stockpile was not large enough to mount an effective attack against China and still have sufficient weapons to deal with the Soviets if they, too, decided to intervene.

At about this same time I went in to see Acheson. I said I had a recommendation to make. He should propose to Mr. Truman that he relieve General Harry Vaughan, the President's immediate commanding officer in World War I, who was now improperly exploiting his White House connections, and William O'Dwyer, our ambassador to Mexico and another crony with a doubtful reputation.

To this Dean replied: "Paul, if I go over and see Mr. Truman and suggest what you propose, he'll just throw me out of his office."

And I said, "I don't doubt that's what he'll do. But do you disagree with my analysis? Do you disagree that Mr. Truman will eventually have to relieve General MacArthur?"

Acheson said, "No, I don't disagree with that."

I said, "Do you agree that this will then become a most serious political problem?"

He said, "No, I don't disagree."

"Do you agree that Mr. Truman would be in a better position to meet the criticism he's bound to encounter if he first put his own house in order?"

"Yes," Dean said, "he would be."

And finally, I said, "Then aren't you duty-bound to recommend to the President what you believe to be the wise course, even if you doubt it is a recommendation he is likely to accept?"

"Damn you!" he exclaimed, and threw up his hands.

So Dean did as I had suggested. He went over to Blair House, where Mr. Truman was living while the White House was being remodeled, and advised him that Harry Vaughan and William O'Dwyer should be relieved of their official duties. And just as Dean had predicted, he was thrown out.

MacArthur's repeated public outbursts finally became so reprehensible that on April 10, 1951, Mr. Truman fired him. The day before, I accompanied Acheson to a meeting at the White House where Mr. Truman made the decision. General Bradley, the chairman of the Joint Chiefs, was also at the meeting. He suggested that representatives of the State and Defense departments together draft an order relieving MacArthur. The dubious honor fell to me and to Colonel Chester V. Clifton, who was General Bradley's aide at the time.

The plan was to have Secretary of the Army Frank Pace, who happened to be in the Far East at the time, personally deliver the order we had drafted to MacArthur at his headquarters in Tokyo. But before the necessary cables could be sent, rumor spread that a "leak" had occurred and that the *Chicago Tribune* was going to publish the story. Around the White House there was genuine concern that MacArthur might upstage the President and resign his command rather than be relieved. A press conference was hastily arranged and at one in the morning on April 11, Mr. Truman announced what he had done. The news reached MacArthur in Tokyo via the wire services. Though reports I later read said he accepted the President's decision without the slightest protest, I am sure he must have been deeply hurt. But my regard for him as an individual whom I knew and respected did not erase the fact that his behavior had been disloyal and had thus been a discredit to his profession and could very well have ended up threatening the security of the country he claimed he was duty-bound to serve.

Opening an Avenue of Negotiations

Around the same time as MacArthur's dismissal, in the spring of 1951, it appeared to us on the Policy Planning Staff that the time might be ripe to resume the search to negotiate an end to the war. Relations between Peking and Moscow appeared no longer to be necessarily as monolithic as previously. The Chinese had suffered immense losses as a result of their intervention and appeared to be militarily stalemated. The Soviets appeared to be holding back from giving them full support. All this pointed to the possibility of a developing rift in the Communist camp that we might exploit to bring the war to a satisfactory conclusion.

After the rapid advance of UN forces through Pyongyang and beyond, a team including Richard M. Scammon from the Policy Planning Staff went to North Korea to search for documents dealing with the planning that had gone into the surprise attack and the background of subsequent significant decisions. The documents they obtained thoroughly supported what had theretofore been mere speculation that the Soviets had been deeply involved in the plan from the beginning. The North Korean division that had spearheaded the attack had been trained in the USSR. Their air force equipment was entirely Soviet built. Many of the planes in the North Korean air force were being flown by Soviet pilots. On all strategically important points, Kim Il-sung, the North Korean leader, had turned to Moscow for guidance.

At one point, the Policy Planning Staff prepared a paper we called "Removing the Fig Leaf from the Hard Core of Soviet Responsibility." It dealt in detail with the evidence which linked the Soviet Union to the attack against South Korea. We scrapped the paper because we were unprepared to advocate doing anything significant to punish the Soviets for their actions; we had too much on our hands as it was.

A major barrier to opening talks was the lack of any means of communication with the Chinese. Historically, it has usually been the policy of the United States to grant diplomatic recognition to whatever government is actually governing a country. But in the case of mainland China this had proved impossible, owing chiefly to the continuing strong support that Chiang Kai-shek enjoyed from his friends and supporters in the United States, including many right-wing Republicans in Congress. But even if we had had diplomatic relations, the situation might still have been the same. The British had recognized the Peking regime in 1950, but had gained nothing from it. In fact, their ambassador was kept in a position of virtual house arrest.

So we had to find other avenues. A college professor on the West Coast put us in touch with a Chinese scholar studying in the United States who claimed to know how we might make contact with Peking. At Acheson's suggestion, Burt Marshall flew out to Hong Kong to explore further this possibility. Using some additional contacts recommended by the CIA, Burt succeeded in establishing indirect communications with Chou En-lai, the Chinese Communist foreign minister. The Chinese at first appeared willing to talk, but for reasons we were never able to ascertain, they suddenly broke off contact, leaving Burt no choice but to return home. However, Burt did not return empty-handed. He brought with him many keen observations and insights which he subsequently reduced to memoranda and circulated throughout the department. It turned out to be some of the most reliable and accurate political intelligence available, a great help later during the negotiations.

In May 1951, I received a telephone call from New York from Andrew Corry, one of the junior men on our delegation to the UN in New York. He described to me a talk he had had with Semen K. Tsarapkin, one of the Soviet disarmament specialists who was then serving as deputy to

Jacob A. Malik, the head of the Soviet UN delegation. Tsarapkin had spent thirty minutes denouncing the United States and all its works but said some words at the end which could only be interpreted as indicating a Soviet interest in an armistice in Korea, if the United States shared such an interest, and would make the first move.

I told Corry to fly down to Washington immediately to give us all the details. I talked to Burt Marshall and Acheson about it. We decided that we should follow up this lead but that we should take care that it not appear to be an American initiative. Accordingly, we got in touch with George Kennan, now no longer in government, who agreed to act as a go-between. He knew Malik well and arranged a meeting with him at Malik's summer house on Long Island. If the Tsarapkin move was serious, something might come of such a meeting. If it was not, the U.S. government would in no way appear a supplicant for an armistice and thus damage its bargaining position.

When he saw Malik, Kennan said that he personally was interested in possible Soviet views as to an armistice. Malik's response was predictably noncommittal, but he said he would refer the matter to Moscow for consideration. I took this response to be a positive sign and decided to initiate staff work on the intricate policy and tactical problems involved in negotiating an armistice. Admiral Forrest Sherman was at that time the chief of naval operations. I had come to know him well during the writing of the Pacific report of the U.S. Strategic Bombing Survey. It was to him that the Joint Chiefs of Staff turned to supervise their work on the issues involved in a possible armistice. After some discussion we both agreed that General Matthew Ridgway, MacArthur's successor as UN commander in Korea, and Admiral C. Turner Joy, the commander of U.S. naval forces in the area, needed to be consulted; the only question was when.

One weekend early in June the telephone rang while Phyllis and I were out at our farm in southern Maryland. On the other end of the line was Sherman, who said he was flying out to Tokyo and Korea in his personal plane early the next morning. He wondered if I would be free to accompany him. I protested that I had no money, no clothes other than my farm clothes, no passport, no travel orders, and no permission from the secretary to undertake such a trip. Sherman said, "Why don't you go ahead and check with Acheson? You won't need anything else."

I then called Acheson to clear matters with him. "What's the problem?" he said. "Go ahead and go!"

The next day Forrest Sherman and I boarded a plane headed for the Orient, the first time I had been back there since the days of the Strategic

Bombing Survey. Along the way we stopped in the Aleutians at Attu, refueled at Shemya, and from there flew to Tokyo, where we spent several days conferring with General Ridgway and his staff. Then we went to Korea for a firsthand look at the front lines. Traveling by helicopter, we flew over an area known as the "Punch Bowl" near the 38th parallel where fighting at that time was especially intense. On several occasions we came dangerously close to being shot out of the air. After observing the action around the Punch Bowl we boarded the battleship *New Jersey* and sailed up the coast to Wonsan harbor, where our fleet was heavily engaged with North Korean shore artillery. We were lobbing shells at them and they were lobbing shots right back at us. Captain Arleigh Burke, who was then commanding a task force giving naval gun support to the eastern edge of the battlefront, came aboard the *New Jersey* to brief us.

While Admiral Sherman and I were discussing with General Ridgway and members of his staff possible negotiating positions, word arrived that Malik, on June 23, 1951, had made a speech on a UN–sponsored radio program confirming the Soviet Union's interest in seeing an armistice negotiated as early as possible. Overnight, our deliberations in Tokyo took on a new and more serious sense of urgency.

The first problem was how to organize the talks. Since we had no diplomatic relations with China the only solution was to conduct the talks through military channels. It had been agreed in Washington that the negotiations would be handled through the Joint Chiefs rather than through the State Department. As their principal agent, the JCS nominated Admiral Sherman. He in consultation with Ridgway had decided that actual negotiations would be under Admiral Joy, who in turn chose Arleigh Burke as his principal assistant.

The second question was where the talks should be held. Originally the site agreed upon was Kaesong, which was close to the front lines. But this turned out to be too near to the actual fighting, and in October 1951 the talks moved to Panmunjom.

A few days after Malik's radio talk, Admiral Sherman received a message directing him to return immediately to Washington. It had been decided that I, however, should stay in Tokyo to work with Admiral Joy on the development of our negotiating position.

The main issues could readily be foreseen. One was the location of the armistice line: Should it be at the 38th parallel, the existing forward edge of the battlefront, or should it be somewhere else? From our standpoint the best solution would be a line from Wonsan harbor to an indentation in the western coastline of Korea just north of Seoul. This would have been the shortest and most defensible line for both sides.

The second point was the return of all UN prisoners of war or, at least, a guarantee of their freedom to choose to return.

The third point was more difficult: Should we agree forceably to return all North Korean prisoners to North Korea as guaranteed by the Geneva Convention (to which we were not a signatory) or should we merely give them the right to choose whether they wished to return or to stay in South Korea?

These issues had not been fully resolved on the U.S. side when Admiral Joy and Captain Burke went off to initiate the negotiations at Kaesong. Then a few days after Admiral Joy left for Kaesong, I received a telegram from Acheson directing me to return to Washington by the earliest means, which I did.

With the beginning of negotiations in 1951, the fighting in Korea gradually subsided into a war of attrition. Many pitched battles remained to be fought and just before the armistice was signed in 1953, the Chinese, in an effort to improve their negotiating position, launched a major offensive that took a heavy toll on both sides. But compared with the first year of the war, the second two showed a marked drop in casualties. The Chinese dug in and our troops dug in, forming opposing lines running the width of the peninsula at approximately the same place where the conflict had begun—the 38th parallel. An agreement ending the war might have been signed then and there, in 1951, had it not been for one issue—the prisoners of war.

It was clear from the beginning of negotiations that the prerequisite to any agreement was the return of our prisoners from camps in the north. The question at issue was what to do with the more than a hundred thousand North Korean and Chinese POWs, many of whom resisted repatriation. The Geneva Convention allowed no exceptions on returning prisoners of war, but the United States had never officially joined the convention and in this instance I seriously questioned the justice of its provisions. Chip Bohlen had been deeply troubled by a similar problem that had arisen in Europe after World War II, when thousands of Russian POWs in German prison camps had asked not to be sent back to the Soviet Union. Our policy at that time had been to repatriate them regardless of their personal preferences, with the result that many were shot by the Soviets or sent to "reeducation camps" in the gulag. I came to the conclusion—and Acheson fully supported me—that we should not be party to a repetition of such horrors in Korea.

The Pentagon, citing the Geneva Convention, came to a different conclusion. Its attitude was to get the war over with as quickly as possible and expedite the return of American servicemen being held by the Chinese and North Koreans. Our military were therefore prepared to concede on the POW issue and send every one of the North Koreans and Chinese home, including those who did not want to go. I remember early in 1952 a series of meetings at which Acheson, Chip Bohlen, and I argued this out with Bob Lovett, William C. Foster, the deputy secretary of defense, and the Joint Chiefs. We became hopelessly deadlocked. Finally, Acheson said, "Well, the only way to resolve this question is to take it up with the President." And, he added, "I feel confident that Mr. Truman will back up the viewpoint I am taking." And so he did. Once again, Dean's instincts and reading of the President's mind proved correct.

Much to his regret, Mr. Truman was unable to secure an armistice before he left the presidency. As a result, negotiations carried over into the Eisenhower administration, which took office in January 1953. The bottleneck in the talks was still the POW question. One day, as if out of the blue, Syngman Rhee, the South Korean president, announced that the North Korean POWs his government was holding were free to go. He simply opened the gates of the POW camps and let everyone out. Although there were angry reactions from the Eisenhower administration in Washington, Rhee's unilateral action proved to be the first step toward breaking the POW impasse; shortly thereafter the armistice was signed, thus ending a war which could well have been avoided.

7

Building "Situations
of Strength"

No war is an isolated event; wars have broader ramifications. In the case of Korea the side effects in some respects dwarfed events on the battlefield. Militarily and psychologically, the United States was unprepared for the conflict when it erupted. This became evident during the early days of the war in the summer of 1950, when our forces suffered a succession of setbacks and defeats. The success of the Inchon invasion retrieved some of our lost domestic support and restored some of our lost prestige abroad. However, it temporarily blinded many to the limits of our available military power. The reality did not sink in completely until the Chinese intervened. After that, it seemed obvious to me and others, including Dean Acheson and Mr. Truman, that we could no longer delay; we had little real choice but to step up the pace of building what Acheson called "situations of strength."

Avoiding a "Pax Americana"

Indicative of the seriousness and immensity of the problem we faced was the question of what the United States ought to aim to achieve should a direct confrontation with the Soviet Union prove unavoidable. The question first arose in August 1950 in a request for guidance from the Joint Chiefs, who were then worried that the conflict in Korea might escalate into a full-scale global war with the USSR. The NSC passed the task on to the Policy Planning Staff. My immediate response to the Chiefs' request was conditioned by my experience in World War II and by my reading of the histories of other conflicts. Neither provided me with much confidence that specific war aims could be defined in advance, adhered to during a war, and ultimately realized. In World War I, for example, German and Allied war aims became increasingly demanding as the war went on, with the result that they made a solution short of almost total devastation on both sides virtually impossible. In World War II, FDR abandoned trying to frame Allied war aims in advance and went to the other extreme of substituting "unconditional surrender" as our sole objective. This gave our enemies no incentive whatsoever to negotiate their capitulation. It was true, of course, that in dealing with Italy and Japan the Allies repudiated their own stated policy and made concessions. Hitler, however, at great cost in lives to Germany and to our side, took us at our word and held out until the bitter end, convinced that he had no other choice. What we had had was a policy that was sometimes "unconditional," sometimes not.

Given the historical record on such matters, I was not confident that we should or could undertake a project as ambitious as the Chiefs' request appeared to be—that is, to delineate war aims for a hypothetical conflict. But after Philip Jessup, the department's troubleshooter in matters like these, sounded the Chiefs out further and determined that their request was serious, I agreed that we should give it a try.

With the war going on in Korea and the difficulties of trying to implement NSC 68, the war-aims paper (now dubbed NSC 79) did not rate top priority. When he had time, Burt Marshall worked on it, but after several drafts, which developed important ideas but which he considered unsatisfactory, Burt concluded that the project was impossible. He came to me asking to be relieved of it. "Trying to decide war aims," he said, "is like asking: 'When you play bridge next week, what should you lead?' " I did not press him to continue.

After Burt Marshall opted out of the project, I gave his draft to Bob Tufts and John Paton Davies to see what they could do. Like Burt, they found the problem perplexing, though they also came up with some useful ideas. The next person to work on it was Louis Halle, who spent several months on the task; he later told me that he found it the most interesting paper he had ever worked on. Just before leaving town for a conference in London, I sent a copy of Lou's draft to Dean Acheson for his advice and comments. A few days later Acheson left to see Schuman in Paris on his way to London.

Fifteen minutes before he was to leave for Paris, Acheson called Lou into his office to talk to him about his draft of the NSC 79 report. Lou told me later that Acheson had obviously read the paper with care, since he asked questions about specific paragraphs on specific pages. Lou said that Acheson was enthusiastic about the paper, but told him: "It's too bad it can't be published; it is the only paper that I have ever seen which might make an impact on the world as great as Keynes' *Economic Consequences of the Peace."*

The first portion of the paper had survived from Burt Marshall's draft. It dealt with our military aims during such a war, stressing the importance of radically reducing the Soviet Union's nuclear capability while minimizing losses to ourselves and our allies, the object being to shift the balance of remaining military power in our favor as a basis for negotiation of a settlement, not the capture of territory per se.

Recently, Lou told me that what he remembers best about the paper was the portion that dealt with what our policy toward Russia should be: It recommended that we take the position that our quarrel was with the Communist leadership, not with the Russian people, and that it was not our aim to dismantle the Soviet Union, even though it would be necessary to restore full independence to the Baltic States and the Soviet satellites behind the Iron Curtain.

My recollection, refreshed by the recent rediscovery of a copy of Lou's paper that had somehow found its way into my secretary of the navy files, is of the portion to which I had given much attention. This concerned the broad policy question of how best to deal not only with the Soviet Union, but with the world as a whole, assuming an American victory over the Soviet Union. That section of the paper first analyzed three alternative courses of action—the establishment of a Pax Americana, a world government, or an international balance of power system—and rejected all three.

Pax Americana would be contrary to the American ethos, and it would invite enmity and opposition to us on the part of other peoples and nations. Moreover, it was beyond the capacity and will of the United States to enforce. World government would not work either—either it would be a cover under which we wielded the reins of power on basic decisions, in which event it would be seen as a disguised Pax Americana, or else it would be run by others, in which event it was likely that the rest of the world would gang up on the United States. Balance of power as a policy also had risks and shortcomings, particularly the likelihood that most of the stronger states would be aligned against us after a victory over the Soviet Union had made us by far the strongest single power in the world. They would wish to maximize the prospects of increased power and freedom of action for themselves by joining with others to diminish ours.

The recommendation of the paper was that we adopt a policy embodying an element of each of the three alternatives. In a peace treaty with the Soviet Union we should insist on the total elimination of Soviet nuclear weapons and facilities to produce them. We should urge (indeed, insist) that all nations join us in turning over their nuclear weapons and production facilities to a UN agency which would operate under an international mandate and international control, but over which the United States would have effective veto power. Under this basic security umbrella we should strive for reduction of conventional armaments, adherence to the basic provisions of the UN Charter, the maintenance of worldwide liberal trade and monetary policies, and opportunities for economic development. In order to keep this system going we should address ourselves with subtlety and care to forming ever-varying dominant coalitions of partners to support a working system of order more useful to the rest of the world in general, and to us, than could be envisioned under any alternative formula.

When I got back from England I discussed Lou Halle's draft with Phil Jessup and George Perkins, assistant secretary of state for European affairs. They understood the paper and were in basic agreement with it, but Acheson concluded that the paper was too "hot" for general distribution; he thought that its subject matter, the analysis, and the recommendations would be misunderstood if they somehow leaked. He therefore ordered that all copies but one be destroyed and that that one be kept in my personal safe.

While the project did not result in a published paper, it was a most useful and thought-provoking exercise, for it clarified certain basic realities underlying world politics and brought into sharper focus the basic problems the United States faced as a superpower. Soviet spokesmen would argue that their view of a world in which they would be the strongest power in a Communized world is quite different. However, now that Communist ideology has lost much of its persuasive power, their objective of a Pax Sovieta must present them with similar difficulties.

NATO and the German Question

In addition to exposing our own military weaknesses, the Korean War made it abundantly clear that something should be done to help our European allies strengthen their military capabilities. Though the progress made under the Marshall Plan had been considerable, Europe's economy was still in a fragile condition and therefore limited in its ability to support increased defense burdens. Much of the cost was therefore likely to fall on us and add substantially to the cost of the fledgling military assistance program that we had initiated in 1949. But if financial problems had been the only obstacle, they might have been cleared away relatively promptly. As it happened, the dominant and most troublesome problems were political and would take years to work out. Some of these problems are still with us today.

The immediate issue had two parts. First, what was the United States prepared to do? And second, what would our European allies be prepared to do? Under the collective security provisions of the North Atlantic Treaty signed in April 1949, our obligations to one another were to treat an attack in the treaty area upon one member as an attack upon all. It followed that if the alliance were to carry out its mission, it would need the military capabilities to do so. But despite its outward appearance, NATO had not been conceived as a military organization; rather, it was at the start a political concept, the main objective of which was to restore and preserve members' confidence through assurance that we would all face a threatening USSR together. As such, by the summer of 1950, NATO, from a military standpoint, was still a paper alliance, with no command structure, no troops, and no immediate plans for acquiring any.

Under the 1949 Mutual Defense Assistance Act, NATO agreement upon an "integrated" defense of the North Atlantic area had to be achieved before Congress would allow any significant amounts of military aid to be made available. To meet this condition, NATO adopted a broad strategic concept, which in turn became the basis for a Medium Term Defense Plan, containing the first estimate of the land, sea, and air forces that the alliance would need in order to acquire a reasonable ability to defend its territory against a Soviet attack. The most striking feature of the plan was the immensity of what would be required to do so— almost 100 ready and reserve divisions, approximately 8,000 aircraft, and more than 2,800 ships of varying types. It was a tall order—taller than the Europeans themselves could fill, even with our help, without seriously interfering with their economic recovery.

Lurking in the background was another, more sensitive issue—the question of whether, and if so, to what extent, West Germany should be included in NATO's plans. On a purely objective level, the arguments strongly favored some level of German participation, not only to take advantage of West Germany's large manpower and industrial potential, but also to offset recent Soviet actions, which had resulted in the creation of a militarized East German "police force." Without a West German contribution, it was difficult to imagine that NATO would ever be in a position to mount a viable defense. However, in the months and weeks preceding the outbreak of the Korean War, political emotions held sway, especially among our European allies, who still vividly remembered the blows they had received from the German war machine in World War II. Despite suggestions from our Joint Chiefs that German rearmament would vastly improve NATO's posture, Acheson at that time still adhered to a policy of continuing to enforce German demilitarization. "There is no discussion of doing anything else," he said. "That is our policy and we have not raised it or revalued it."

Apart from important policy considerations, there were personal reasons why I was reluctant to raise the German rearmament question, since in the past I had been publicly accused of being pro-German. In 1948 a group calling itself the Society for the Prevention of World War III published an issue of its journal devoted entirely to allegations of my pro-German sympathies. Included was the accusation that I could have been involved in the sinking of the French luxury ocean liner *Normandie* at her dock in New York harbor during World War II. The implication of the piece was that I was secretly a German agent who wanted to see Germany remilitarized to dominate Europe. I was infuriated by these accusations and immediately consulted with Edward Burling, founder of the firm of Covington & Burling, for advice as to how I should proceed to sue for libel. He and his partners advised against it, saying that the law of libel as it affects a public figure was such that I would be wasting my time and money.

I was dissatisfied with this advice and hired George Ball, who had left the government to run the Washington office of a leading New York law firm, to prepare two briefs for me. One was to cover everything that would be needed to prove that the allegations were false and malicious, and the other to cover the law of libel. The second brief fully confirmed Covington & Burling's advice. George took the first brief, showed it to the owner and publisher of the magazine, a man named Isidore Lipschutz. George told him that we were prepared to go to trial, but if he agreed never again to mention my name in his publication, he would urge me to drop the proceedings. Lipschutz agreed and I was not bothered again.

After the North Korean attack, attitudes on both sides of the Atlantic began to change. For Acheson, the question was no longer whether but how Germany should be brought into the general defense plan for Europe, at the earliest opportunity, and in the least disruptive manner. Realizing now that the fate of Europe might hang in the balance, many

Europeans reluctantly agreed. Indeed, it would have been ridiculous for the other European nations to make substantial, additional military efforts and cut back on civilian production and consumption, while Germany was permitted to manufacture and consume on a "peacetime" basis. Nevertheless, it remained politically impossible to rearm German manpower or convert German industry to military production as long as the European peoples saw in such action the risk of a resurgence of German militarism. A truly common effort appeared the only practicable solution.

On July 31, 1950, Acheson and Truman discussed the problem at some length. They felt that to create a German military system, complete with a revived general staff and Ruhr munitions industry, would weaken rather than strengthen Europe's position and result ultimately in a repetition of past errors. In reviewing other options, they agreed that the preferable solution would be the creation of a European or NATO army, complete with an integrated command and supply system, which would have the additional advantage of drawing Germany even closer into the politico-economic integration of Western Europe.

Meanwhile, on August 9, Charles Spofford, our representative on the NATO Council of Deputies, returned to Washington to report that without a substantial increase in American ground forces in Europe, our allies were unlikely to undertake the added sacrifices of stepping up their own rearmament. Concluding that the time for decisions had come, Acheson in mid-August asked the Defense Department for its views on a multifaceted proposal to strengthen our forces in Europe and to make them part of a European Defense Force with a unified command and integrated staff. Part of the idea, of course, was the eventual inclusion of German forces, though in putting the proposal before our allies, as he planned to do at the next meeting of the North Atlantic Council, scheduled for mid-September, Acheson saw no immediate need to raise this controversial and potentially divisive issue. Acheson believed that it would follow logically, once the European Defense Force was a fait accompli, that German participation was not only necessary but desirable as well.

Despite Acheson's request for a prompt response, the Defense Department—still under Louis Johnson's control at this time—chose to procrastinate. Our proposals, we were told, were under study and a response would be forthcoming in due course. In an effort to expedite matters, Acheson authorized me to conduct a discreet exploration of the problem directly with Defense Department representatives. I spent the next several weeks at the Pentagon, accompanied by Henry Byroade of our German affairs bureau and Assistant Secretary of State for European Affairs

George Perkins. Our counterparts were Rear Admiral Thomas Hinckley Robbins, Jr., who represented the Joint Chiefs of Staff, and Colonel Royden E. Beebe, who was General Burns' deputy in charge of NATO affairs in the Office of the Secretary of Defense. We kept no minutes of our discussions and circulated no papers, except our final recommendations to our superiors. Because of European sensitivities, we took every possible precaution to avoid leaks.

My recollection of these meetings is that we were in general agreement as to the overall policy, but divided over how it should be implemented. Robbins made it clear that the Joint Chiefs were adamantly opposed to half measures. If there were to be a program to reinforce deterrence in Europe through the buildup and closer coordination of allied capabilities, the Chiefs insisted that all the necessary components be agreed to as a package deal. Those components included West German participation, the stationing of substantial U.S. forces in Europe, sufficient military contributions by the other NATO countries, and agreement that there be unified command of all these forces in wartime. If all of these conditions were met they would recommend that General Eisenhower be asked to serve as the initial NATO supreme commander. However, they emphasized that their support was contingent on the entire package being approved. My rejoinder was that this approach would entail numerous hazards; should one part or another fail of adoption, the entire package could come undone. But it seemed that my warnings fell on deaf ears. It was not long before we were deadlocked.

On August 26, Mr. Truman summoned his senior advisers to the White House, chiefly to deal with the growing problem of General MacArthur, but also to explore how we might achieve a breakthrough in our talks at the Pentagon. To spur matters along, Mr. Truman issued a letter, listing a number of specific questions he wanted answered, and set a deadline of September 1 (later extended to September 5), for the secretaries of state and defense to make up their minds.

Though the President's letter helped somewhat to accelerate our discussions, progress was still painfully slow. What finally emerged was a policy, approved by Mr. Truman on September 8, that in effect made liberal concessions to the Defense Department point of view. Not only did it endorse a unified command, increased American forces, and a rearmed Germany, but more importantly it placed all of these measures together on a single agenda for NATO's consideration. When the time came for our delegation to go up to New York for the conference, we were accompanied by the JCS representative, Admiral Robbins, whose main apparent job was to make sure that we adhered faithfully to this policy. We promptly nicknamed him "One Package Robbins."

One of the more touchy aspects of the problem was how to broach our policy to our allies, especially the British and French, who customarily met with Mr. Acheson for private talks prior to the convening of these conferences. Though Mr. Truman had released a public statement indicating our readiness (subject to congressional approval) to increase the strength of U.S. forces in Europe, he had glossed over the question of German rearmament. A list of "tentative" conclusions, forwarded to the British and French embassies on September 2, was little more enlightening. In fact, the first real inkling that our allies received of our position came from the newspapers while Bevin was still at sea and just before Schuman boarded his flight to New York. At a meeting with members of the press on Saturday, September 9, the U.S. high commissioner to Germany, John J. McCloy, who was also a member of our delegation, made what he thought were off-the-record remarks to the effect that Germany could conceivably contribute ten divisions to NATO's defense. The *Washington Post* correspondent, Ferdinand Kuhn, decided that McCloy's comments were too hot to suppress; the next morning his paper featured an article containing an exceedingly accurate summary of our policy.

Preliminary meetings between the Big Three foreign ministers— Acheson, Bevin, and Schuman—began on September 12 at the Waldorf-Astoria Hotel in New York. One of the first items of business was how we would pool our resources to achieve an equitable distribution of NATO's economic burdens, an issue that had been tossed back and forth ever since the appearance of the Medium Term Defense Plan. At issue was how costs should be computed and the extent to which American economic and military assistance should bridge the gap between NATO's requirements and our allies' ability to contribute.

At one of our regular departmental staff meetings a few days before the conference began, Acheson had explained how he intended to handle this problem. "When it comes up, as surely it will," he said, looking at me, "I will nominate you, Paul, to head a committee to find a solution." Knowing just how complex and controversial were the issues involved, I was less than thrilled with this dubious honor. I also knew that I would be hard pressed to get out of it. On the first day of the conference, Bevin and Schuman approved Acheson's suggestion and designated Oliver Franks and Hervé Alphand as their respective representatives on the committee. As the basis for our discussions, I produced a list of suggestions that were promptly dubbed the "Nitze paper." But despite a wide-ranging examination, the result was inconclusive. It was decided to pass the issue on to a more permanent group of which Averell Harriman was the original chairman. They were called the "Wisemen" and the study they undertook was called by some the "Burden-Sharing Exercise," by others the "Nitze Exercise." It went on for some years. I later met a number of British and French diplomats who said they had wasted what should have been their most productive years on it and put the blame on me.

The more immediate question that preoccupied everyone's thinking was what to do about Germany. Amid a tense atmosphere, Schuman let it be known not only that he opposed the single package we were offering, but that he would resist it to the end. France had suffered dearly at Germany's hands in the last war, and it was too soon, in his opinion, to contemplate reviving that awful nemesis. As an alternative, he suggested a formula almost identical to what Acheson had wanted to do from the start. Not until NATO had been strengthened and its forces integrated, Schuman maintained, was there any reason why the question of German participation should be addressed. Later in the talks, as if to underscore his country's sensitivity on this point, he was joined by France's defense minister, Jules Moch, whose son had been tortured and executed by the Nazis in World War II. For Moch, the rearmament of Germany was not merely an unwise policy, it was a horror beyond his imagination.

Bevin, as I had suspected, proved more flexible. After cabling London for instructions from the Cabinet, he emerged with a counterproposal that fell somewhere on middle ground. While admitting that his own military advisers concurred with ours that a rearmed Germany was crucial to NATO's defensibility, he agreed with Schuman that the time for such a decision was no more ripe in Britain than in France. Why not start on a smaller scale, he suggested, beginning with the arming of a West German gendarmerie to counter the similar force being organized in the East? From this modest beginning more might come. I remember him telling Acheson, "You've got the right idea, me lad, but you're goin' about it the hard way."

When the full North Atlantic Council assembled on September 15, the outlook on the German question was far from encouraging, though on practically everything else there proved to be unanimity growing out of a common recognition that the emergency in Korea necessitated closer cooperation than ever before. In its communiqué issued at the end of the conference, the council announced its agreement that "at the earliest date" steps would be taken to create "an integrated force under centralized command," complete with a supreme commander supported by an international staff. But as for the other major issue on the agenda, the document hedged, saying only that the question of how best to elicit a contribution from Germany to Europe's defense should be the subject of further study.

These results showed cause for hope as well as disappointment. That NATO needed strengthening, all agreed, thereby establishing a consensus for future progress. The question was how to proceed, and on this score it was obvious that the ticklish question of Germany would continue to be a hindrance. A period of stocktaking was in order, not only for ourselves but for our allies as well.

Our decision was to change tactics, not policy. Having tried and failed with the single-package approach, Acheson was no longer under obligation to the Pentagon, nor was the Defense Department, for its part, inclined to insist on what was clearly impossible. In fact, shortly after the conference adjourned, General Marshall, who had replaced Louis Johnson by this time, asked the Joint Chiefs to review their position on an integrated NATO defense force. Though the inclusion of German troops, he said, would come about eventually, it was not to be regarded as a prior condition but rather as a subject for further international negotiation.

Another favorable sign was a change of attitude on the part of the French, though as we probed their position, it became apparent that the concessions they were offering were exceedingly limited. The apparent breakthrough—actually a rejoinder to our earlier proposal of an integrated NATO army—came in October, when the French Assembly, by an overwhelming vote, endorsed the so-called Pleven Plan, put forth by French Premier René Pleven, calling for the creation of a European defense force, complete with a single defense minister, a common budget, and a European assembly. Though provision was also made in the plan for the inclusion of German units at the battalion level, there were so many strings attached that it would have been many years, if ever, before a German contribution became a reality. Acheson was understandably annoyed; he dismissed the plan as a subterfuge to keep Germany permanently disarmed. Not surprisingly, leaders in West Germany evinced similar irritation and resented the implication in the plan that their country should be permanently relegated to second-class status.

Still, it seemed to me that by offering the Pleven Plan, the French were conceding that it was beyond their power and capacity to block German rearmament indefinitely. I was not surprised therefore that when the NATO Council met again in December in Brussels, the French dropped their opposition to a German contribution in exchange for a tacit understanding from us and the British that we would join with them in exploring the creation of a European defense community—what became the ill-fated EDC concept. Acheson had little enthusiasm for the idea or confidence that it would work, but he found it preferable to further delay on the appointment of a supreme commander and the creation of an integrated NATO army. But in achieving our larger objective of securing a German contribution to Europe's defense, we had barely begun. Months and even years would pass before German troops appeared in any significant numbers.

Debate over the Middle East Command

Even though the strength being created under NATO may have been inadequate as against the requirements, strength was being built nonetheless. A considerable deterrent to Soviet aggression in that theater was gradually emerging. In the Far East, our intervention in Korea had brought at least a temporary check to the progress of Communist aggression in that area. Ways to meet the requirements for increasing Japanese strength, improving the capabilities on Formosa, and of stabilizing the situation in Southeast Asia could be roughly foreseen. In the Middle East, however, the general picture was one of continuing weakness—so much so that it offered an open invitation for the Soviets to shift pressure to that area if they were blocked elsewhere.

Traditionally, the defense of the Middle East had been a British responsibility. But by the early 1950s the capabilities available to the British had become wholly inadequate to defend the Middle East against a Soviet attack. At the same time, Britain was under mounting pressure from the Egyptian government to relinquish control of the Suez Canal and from the Iranian government to grant it a fuller share of proceeds from Iranian oil sales.

The British in May 1951 came forward with a proposal to establish an allied Middle East Command (MECO) under a British officer acting as Supreme Allied Commander, Middle East (SACME). It was intended to be entirely a planning organization.

Shortly after the British broached their Middle East Command proposal, I met with Rear Admiral Arthur C. Davis, director of the Joint Staff, at the Pentagon to discuss with him the status of Middle East planning. Davis explained that the Middle East had long been considered a British responsibility. Accordingly, the JCS had not prepared military plans for that region.

It so happened that at the very time I was discussing these matters with Davis, representatives of the British chiefs of staff were just down the hall conducting a briefing on their plan. Davis and I joined them. Rather than attempt a general defense of the region, coordinated with the forces of other countries, like Syria and Iraq, British plans called for an orderly withdrawal to their Suez bastions, leaving the rest of the Middle East to be overrun. I came away from this briefing convinced that the time was not ripe for creation of a Middle East Planning Command. A plan for the British to withdraw on threat of attack would be politically disastrous. Shortly thereafter, the British proposal for MECO died.

In July 1952 a group of disgruntled Egyptian army officers toppled King Farouk's government and sent him into exile. The nominal leader of the coup was a general named Mohammed Naguib, but the real power behind the scenes was a young, ambitious colonel—Gamal Abdel Nasser. The new regime was even more anti-British than its predecessor.

Iran, the Shah, and Mossadegh

Toward the end of my tenure as director of policy planning, I became involved in another aspect of our Middle East policy, this time concerning a dispute between Iran and Britain over the latter's oil concession. By 1951, when the matter came to my attention officially, negotiations between Iran and the Anglo-Iranian Oil Company (AIOC), which was half owned by the British government, had become bogged down in details over a new supplemental revenue-sharing agreement. The most important points concerned Iran's twenty percent share of the company, increased royalties, and increased Iranization of the company. The Iranians were fully aware of the greater royalties enjoyed by other producing countries in the Gulf and in the Western Hemisphere, and originally demanded an agreement modeled on Venezuela's fifty-fifty profit-sharing plan. At the time Iran was getting twenty-two-cents-a-barrel profit; Britain offered to increase Iran's royalties to thirty-three cents, which was the same as Saudi Arabia was receiving, but still significantly less than the eighty cents a barrel that Venezuela received. If Iran accepted the supplemental agreement, her receipts would go from thirteen million pounds sterling per year to twenty-two million pounds.

Despite personal misgivings, the young shah of Iran had signed the supplemental oil agreement and had presented it in June 1950 to the Iranian Majlis (parliament), where it was rejected after a highly emotional debate. The leader of the opposition to the agreement was a charismatic politician named Mohammad Mossadegh, who was also head of a special oil negotiating commission appointed by the Majlis. Mossadegh and his followers on the commission now declared the supplemental agreement null and void and broke off further talks with the British. The Communist-dominated Tudeh party was again becoming active and the National Front, a radical body whose support Mossadegh openly courted, was reported to be urging nationalization of the oil fields.

To head off a confrontation George McGhee, the State Department's leading expert at the time on Middle East politics and oil, flew to London to try to persuade the British to make concessions; they refused. Then, late in 1950 Aramco, the American consortium in Saudi Arabia, announced a new contract with the Saudis giving them royalties equivalent to a fifty-fifty split of gross profits. This encouraged the Iranians to expect similar concessions from the British and to hold out for a better deal. In late February 1951 came hints that the British would offer Iran a fifty-fifty split modeled on Aramco's arrangement with Saudi Arabia. But on March 7, before an agreement could be concluded, Iranian Prime Minister Ali Razmara was assassinated by a religious zealot. Overnight, the country was thrown into turmoil.

Out of the confusion following Razmara's murder, Mossadegh and his extremist followers emerged triumphant. The Majlis promptly passed a law nationalizing the oil fields and all AIOC property,[1] including the huge Abadan refinery, then and still the world's largest facility of its kind. To the Iranians, the Abadan oil refinery was as clear a mark of colonial status as the British bases in Suez were to the Egyptians. To be his new prime minister, the shah reluctantly appointed Mossadegh, who served notice on the British that there was nothing left to negotiate. (I later learned that Mossadegh had canceled the negotiations partly out of personal pique. Neville Gass, who as vice president of AIOC had been in charge of the British side of the talks, had at one point apparently made an offhand remark that he and his company were not in the "carpet buying business." Mossadegh, an aristocrat, took this as a personal insult.)

In October 1951, Mossadegh came to New York to argue Iran's case

---

[1]Or so it seemed at the time. Later, in private conversations with George McGhee, Mossadegh insisted that the Abadan refinery had not been nationalized. The account is in George McGhee, *Envoy to the Middle World* (New York: Harper and Row, 1983), 395–96.

before the UN General Assembly. While there, he had a number of informal talks with George McGhee and Colonel Vernon Walters, then an Army interpreter and later U.S. ambassador to the UN. Acheson asked me to look into the matter to see if I could provide some fresh ideas that might lead to a breakthrough at these discussions. Although I made no claim to being an expert on the Middle East, I was familiar with the area and with the oil business from my days with Dillon, Read and Company, when I had helped negotiate a number of oil deals. I was not sure what I could contribute, but I agreed to do what I could.

My first meeting with Mossadegh occurred on October 17 while he was still in New York staying at the Ritz Towers Apartments. From this and subsequent conversations we were to have, I formed some definite and lasting impressions of Mossadegh—many of them sharply at odds with the public's perception of him and how he came across in the news media. From what I had heard and read about Mossadegh, I expected to meet a weeping lunatic. He turned out to be nothing of the kind. On the contrary, I found him to be a totally rational and sane individual, in control of himself at all times, leading me to conclude that his reputation as a "weeping madman" was nothing more than the result of the acts he put on to get the attention of the press and to appeal to his followers back home.

His background further belied his reputation. He had been trained as a lawyer at universities both in Germany and in France. As a result, he spoke excellent French and German. Although he practiced the politics of a populist, he came from an old landowning aristocratic family. He was much interested in improvements to the unique irrigation system in Iran. He had become the leader of the Nationalist Front of which the Moscow-oriented Tudeh party was a member. As far as I could tell, he himself was neither a Marxist nor a Communist. He dismissed the ruling Pahlavi family as nothing more than a pack of usurpers, and spoke disparagingly of the shah's father, who had been a sergeant in a cossack regiment before he seized power. No one knew how old Mossadegh was, though it was generally believed that he was in his late seventies or early eighties. He was canny, witty, and hard to pin down, a shrewd and tricky politician, but in my view, far preferable to the shah and his regime.

Pleading a need for medical attention, Mossadegh came down to Washington and was admitted to Walter Reed Army Hospital for treatment. George McGhee and I met him at Union Station and escorted him to the hospital, where our talks resumed. Later, when the doctors could not diagnose what was ailing him, Mossadegh moved into a suite of rooms at the Hotel Shoreham. Often when we met, he greeted us dressed in what appeared to be pajamas and sitting in bed. George and I agreed that George was to be cast as the great and good friend of Iran and I as the villain. My job was to insist upon those things not attractive to Mossadegh, but which were unavoidably necessary to make the deal work, while George was to dwell on the wonderful benefits that would come Iran's way if Mossadegh would agree to a framework for negotiations acceptable to the British.

To prepare for our talks with Mossadegh, I found myself doing more homework than I had done in years on such matters as oil cost-price comparisons, freight rates, currency conversion rates, marketing patterns, and so forth. Mossadegh was also well informed as to the intricacies of the oil business, and being a tough negotiator, he did not give in easily. His distrust of the British and his hatred of the AIOC blinded him to the realities of the situation. Not only did he insist on prices that were well above those on the world exchange, thereby making Iran's oil almost impossible to market, but also he heaped insult on injury by categorically refusing to allow British technicians, who had been thrown out when Iran nationalized the Abadan refinery, back into Iran. Moreover, he appeared to be under such heavy political pressures back home that it was nearly impossible for him to make the necessary concessions that would have led to an equitable settlement. Had he done so, no doubt he would have risked alienating one group or another on whose support he depended. Hence, his strategy was to temporize in the belief that the longer he held out, the more frightened we would become of a Communist takeover and the more likely it would be that we would put pressure on the British to come forth with most of the concessions.

At one point, to break the routine, George invited Mossadegh to spend a day at his farm in Middleburg in the heart of Virginia's lush hunt country. Mossadegh, who took an avid interest in farming, readily accepted the invitation. During the drive out to Middleburg, Mossadegh and I became involved in a conversation about Iran's politics and its forthcoming elections. It quickly became apparent that Mossadegh was not the populist that he appeared to be, but rather that he was very much an old-fashioned elitist. He thought that previous elections in Iran had been truly representative only in Teheran, the outlying districts being effectively controlled by the AIOC through the landlords. Mossadegh said that one of his goals as prime minister was to "reform" the system by allowing only the literate to vote. I asked him how this was supposed to result in a more representative government. He answered that such a system would free the healthy nationalist mass from Communist influence, on the one hand, and the AIOC, on the other. He described Iranian politics as being divided into three parts—the Anglophiles on the right, the members of the Tudeh on the left, and the nationalist center, which would remain anti-Communist so long as it perceived the government to be protecting its interests.

Part of Mossadegh's strategy was to drive a wedge between the United States and Britain by showing how selfish and self-centered the British had been and how their actions were the cause of all of Iran's problems. On one occasion he even ventured to predict that the United States might have to intervene with troops to restore order, just as it had had to intervene to save Korea. He then suggested that to avoid such consequences, the United States should come in and help Iran run its oil business. This, of course, was the last thing we wanted to do, for it would have looked to the British that we were trying to steal their concession and were not negotiating in good faith for an equitable deal. I told Mossadegh flatly that we had no interest in his oil other than seeing the refinery restored to production, supply resumed to Iran's former customers, and Iran proceed with its economic development.

Though our talks with Mossadegh offered few signs of encouragement, Acheson was determined to break the impasse and get negotiations started again, preferably by coaxing the British into a new initiative. In November he raised the matter at a meeting in Paris of the NATO foreign ministers, including the new British foreign secretary, Anthony Eden. Eden was quite willing to resume negotiations with Mossadegh, but he was no more eager to go against the AIOC management than his predecessor had been. Like Mossadegh, Eden believed that time was on his side. He thought that eventually the Iranians would make sweeping concessions or that Mossadegh would be overthrown, with results in either case favorable to Britain's interests. Acheson and I did not share Eden's optimism. Should the situation continue to deteriorate, we saw the possibility of the army collapsing, assassinations, and rapid movement toward the Tudeh party.

By this time, Acheson was thoroughly fed up with the stubbornness he had encountered on both sides. He was not inclined to press the matter further until he saw evidence of serious interest in a settlement. This left matters dangling. Meanwhile, it was my view, developed as the result of a fact-finding trip to London in February 1952, that we should work out a new and more practical initiative. Since it was evident that Mossadegh would not agree to restore the AIOC as the prime concessionaire, the only other practical solution seemed to me to be an international consortium made up of American and European firms. I began holding preliminary discussions with oil company representatives that spring, worked out most of the details over the summer, and by the fall of 1952 had a finished proposal ready for Mr. Truman's desk.

Before permitting me to broach my plan, Acheson wanted to be sure that we would be on solid legal ground and not run into trouble because of a pending antitrust suit against several of the country's major oil companies. On October 8, 1952, we outlined what we had in mind to Secretary of Defense Robert Lovett, the chairman of the Joint Chiefs, General Omar Bradley, Treasury Secretary John W. Snyder, Attorney General James P. McGranery, and Leonard Emmerglick of the Justice Department's antitrust division. During the meeting Lovett and Bradley both emphasized the strategic importance of the Middle East; why it was crucial that Iran not go Communist; and why this was likely in the event that no solution was found for Iran's problems. I remember Bradley saying at one point that the United States had spent billions of dollars on defense and was now proposing to throw it all "out the window" because of antitrust laws that threatened to block creation of the consortium. McGranery hesitated to offer a firm opinion, but Emmerglick raised so many objections that it became impossible for the meeting to reach a consensus on what to recommend to the President. Emmerglick was a dedicated trustbuster; he was determined to press the Justice Department's pending suit against the majors, no matter what the consequences might be for foreign policy or national security. Our plan, he argued, would undermine that lawsuit and be in direct violation of the Sherman Antitrust Act. Turning to General Bradley, he expressed shock and amazement that the Joint Chiefs did not agree and proceeded to argue that illegal collaboration between the oil companies over the years had held down production and increased prices enormously. This, Emmerglick contended, was of far greater military significance than anything Bradley had yet mentioned. And so it went. By the time the meeting finally broke up, Bradley was nearly purple with rage.

Fortunately, Mr. Truman was on our side and decided that the State Department should hold further exploratory talks with the major oil companies to determine whether they would be interested in joining the proposed consortium. Largely because of my long experience in dealing with the oil industry, Acheson designated me to represent the department in these discussions. I talked with officials from Standard Oil of California, Standard of New Jersey, Texaco, Socony Vacuum (now Mobil), Gulf, and a number of the independents. The person most interested and sympathetic among the majors was B. Brewster Jennings, the chairman of Socony Vacuum. Standard of New Jersey was reluctant, as were Texaco and Standard of California. Since there was a glut of petroleum on the world market at the time, none of these companies needed Iran's oil; to market it each would have to curtail purchases or production elsewhere. But if a strong enough case could be made that a joint effort was politically necessary and if legal protection from antitrust actions could be guaranteed, then it appeared to me that the majors would cooperate. Eventually, we did work out an arrangement, satisfactory to the American oil companies, AIOC, Royal Dutch Shell, and the Justice Department. Each of the majors agreed to offtake and market a share of Iran's production while an additional share was to be divided among a number of the interested independents.

Though the signs from London seemed favorable to our plan, those from Teheran were not. As the price for his cooperation, Mossadegh wanted a U.S. loan, which had been a matter of off-and-on discussions for several years. He now said his country would accept nothing less than fifty million dollars. At the time we had no aid program under which such a loan could be made, so I called Henry "Joe" Fowler, who was then head of the Defense Production Administration, to see if he could arrange something. After studying the problem for about a week, Joe assured me that the money could be found through his agency. Loy Henderson, our ambassador in Teheran, kept Mossadegh informed of what we were attempting to work out. I flew to London in October and again in December with Fred Eaton and Walter J. Levy, a leading oil consultant, to enlist British backing for our plan. We talked to the relevant people in the Foreign Office, the Ministry of Fuel and Power, and the Treasury, all of whom expressed support for the new approach we proposed to take. As a result, by the end of 1952, it appeared that a solution was at last in sight. Early in January 1953, Mossadegh gave his final approval and we thought everything was settled. A few days later, however, Mossadegh changed his mind, probably in the mistaken belief that he could cut a better deal with the incoming Eisenhower administration.

When Foster Dulles became secretary of state, I strongly urged him to continue the negotiations from where they had left off, to demonstrate to Mossadegh that he could do no better than our agreed arrangement. However, Foster refused to authorize Henderson and me to reopen the negotiations. I soon realized that Foster thought we had been too tough on Mossadegh, and that we had been dealing with the Middle East from the wrong end. He believed that Egypt rather than Iran was the key to that part of the world, and that Nasser should be made the wheelhorse of our Middle East policy.

Financially, Iran became more of a shambles. As the economy deteriorated, so too did the political situation, producing what Foster, at one of his press conferences, publicly termed "growing activities" on the part of the Tudeh party and "great concern" on the part of the U.S. government. It did not surprise me that Foster turned with the help of his brother, Allen, director of Central Intelligence, to more direct methods of solving the Mossadegh problem.

The usual explanation for Mossadegh's fall from power is that the CIA intervened in August 1953 to bring down his regime through a military coup. I have no reason to doubt that this was basically the case, but I was told a more precise version of events by Kennett Love, who was a *New York Times* Middle East correspondent at the time. His normal base of operation was Cairo, but for two months he had been in Teheran as things finally came to a boil. There had been fighting between pro- and anti-shah forces for some days and it appeared that Mossadegh's supporters had gained the upper hand. Love was covering the fighting near Mossadegh's house, where mobs paid by the CIA were trying to break in despite the fire of three tanks protecting it. Kennett was very nearly killed by .50-caliber machine-gun fire. He got away to a radio station controlled by anti-Mossadegh forces. This was the only one from which he could report to the outside world what was going on, since all the others had been shut down by Mossadegh.

The battalion commander, whose forces controlled the radio station, had thought the fighting was going badly for his side. He was planning to withdraw his forces from the city, following the example of General Fazollah Zahedi, head of the anti-Mossadegh forces, who had already fled the city. On hearing Kennett's description of the fighting in front of Mossadegh's house, he changed his plan and took his six tanks there. They overwhelmed the three tanks defending the house and it was Mossadegh who then had to flee. Zahedi and later the shah returned to Teheran. The CIA-sponsored coup had succeeded, but it was a very near thing. The irony of what happened is that Kennett personally was on Mossadegh's side and thoroughly disapproved of the management of AIOC, Zahedi, and the shah.

With Mossadegh removed from power, the day-to-day problems concerning Iran took on a quite different aspect, and tended now to reflect the idiosyncrasies of the shah, rather than those of Mossadegh. At the same time, though, the underlying strategic and political problems were essentially unchanged. The Iranian people remained difficult to govern, given to fanaticism and xenophobia, and as fiery as ever. The economic problems continued and were exacerbated by the shah's ambition to become the dominant military power in the Persian Gulf. The Soviet interest had not diminished.

In late 1953, Herbert Hoover, Jr., took over the position of deputy secretary of state from Walter Bedell Smith, who had fallen victim to cancer. To Hoover fell the task of working out an oil settlement among Iran, the British, and the international oil community. There was little difference between the deal he finally succeeded in working out in 1954 and the deal we had almost succeeded in negotiating in January 1953. The eventual economic consequences were beyond anything any of us had seriously contemplated at the time. When George McGhee and I were negotiating with Mossadegh, the question was whether we could persuade someone to commit to marketing 32 million barrels of oil a year at a price of around $1.10 per barrel. By 1974 Iran was producing 6 million barrels per day and receiving $60 billion a year for it, a two thousandfold increase!

The magnitude of the resulting upward revolution in Iranian living standards dissolved whatever remained of the glue of the customs and traditions that had held Iranian society together for a thousand difficult years. The Shiite Muslims under Ayatollah Khomeini were the one group that had maintained its cohesion and therefore had little difficulty taking over from the generally corrupt and weak elements supporting the shah.

Mossadegh had tried to ride the tiger in the Iranian search for a way into the modern world. Perhaps Iran was destined all along to fall victim to a radical and destructive cultural revolution, but I don't regret having made the effort to help it avoid that fate.

PART II

8

The Eisenhower Succession

In the spring of 1952 the nation stood at the threshold of another presidential campaign. After serving in a Democratic administration for over a decade, I still considered myself a Republican. Robert Taft, a conservative senator from Ohio, was the leading candidate for the Republican nomination. General Eisenhower had not yet announced his candidacy, but the date was fast approaching. I was in a personal quandary.

Having been an active participant in the development of our foreign policy over the last few years, I was not about to support Taft, who had done everything he could to thwart our policies in the Congress. On the other hand, I was uncertain what kind of president Eisenhower would make. I was inclined to believe, however, that General Eisenhower had a better chance than Taft to pull the country together, to give it a renewed sense of unity and integrity, and thereby the fortitude to meet what I considered to be the real dangers ahead.

The Chicago convention in July brought about a rethinking of my position. The foreign policy plank put forward by the Republican Platform Committee, and drafted by John Foster Dulles (I was told—perhaps incorrectly—with the advice of McGeorge Bundy, who was then on the Harvard faculty), promised to be an effective vote-getter, but I considered it to be bad policy. It contained a vicious indictment of most of the policies followed by the Truman administration since the end of World War II. With the rapier thrusts of a prosecuting attorney, it leveled one false charge after another against the preceding administration, including wholly unjustified charges of widespread corruption, incompetence, and disloyalty by top officials.

General Eisenhower enthusiastically reiterated the charges in his campaign, although he must have been well aware that on the important decisions in which he had participated, the charges were false. In disgust, just before the election, I changed my political affiliation back to the Democratic party.

I was even more profoundly disturbed when I learned that fall that General Eisenhower, in a meeting at Morningside Heights in New York City with Senator Taft, had promised not only "to cut the fat out of the defense budget," but specifically to cut five billion dollars in actual outlays in 1954. (That translates to more than thirty billion in 1988 dollars.)

A large amount of that so-called fat was cut from the procurement program for the B-52 strategic bomber, developed in the Truman administration to replace the B-36. President Eisenhower authorized procurement of the bomber in October 1953, two months after the Soviet Union unexpectedly exploded its first thermonuclear weapon. Unfortunately, not only was the rate of deployment set at an insufficient level, but in keeping with his "new look" defense policy, massive cuts were made in our general purpose forces. It was not until the 1956 presidential campaign, under strong domestic pressure, that Eisenhower reluctantly agreed to increase the production rate of the B-52 bombers. In the meantime, the administration stressed the procurement of strategic and tactical nuclear weapons as a cheaper alternative to conventional forces.

I strongly doubted that the policy was wise merely because it appeared neat, bold, and decisive, and that wise courses appeared difficult, expensive, and complex. I was convinced that our problems were going to become more difficult in the future than they had been in the past and that we needed a policy designed to meet the foreseeable tasks.

Immediately after the inauguration ceremony Foster Dulles, the new secretary of state, called me into his office. He began by saying that he had no quarrel with Acheson's policies (a surprising statement, but one I had no reason to doubt), but he thought Acheson had mishandled the Congress. No administration had gotten as much constructive foreign policy through the Congress as had the Truman administration, but Dulles thought he could do better. The new administration, he said, had come into office with a mandate for what he called a radically different foreign policy. Since I was known as one of Acheson's principal lieutenants, he thought it unwise to keep me as head of the Policy Planning Staff.

He told me that he thought the work of the Policy Planning Staff was of the utmost importance, but since it dealt principally with national security issues rather than diplomatic affairs, he thought its work should be placed directly under the control of the National Security Council. He hoped to devote ninety-five percent of his own time to those issues, leaving to his deputy, Bedell Smith, the responsibility for running the State Department and the conduct of foreign affairs. He said he didn't know many people at the working level in the field of foreign policy or national security; he therefore wanted me to stay on until Bedell or I could find a suitable replacement. Eventually Robert Bowie, who had worked with John McCloy in Germany, agreed to take on the job.

In the meantime—within a month after Eisenhower's inauguration, in fact—I became deeply concerned by what was happening to our foreign policy. On the one hand, the new administration was making bold gestures which substantially increased our commitments and the risk of confrontation. On the other hand, one by one, the tools we needed to carry out our commitments were being systematically dulled.

After the death of Josef Stalin on March 5, there was a scramble to determine how we should react to the crisis in the Kremlin. There was no dearth of suggestions from all spheres of American society—from the crackpots to the captains of industry. One major industrialist, Charles "Electric Charlie"[1] Wilson, president of General Electric, wrote the President a dramatic proposal. He urged Eisenhower to offer the Kremlin "a plan for peace," which he left, of course, unspecified. Eisenhower, Charlie Wilson contended, would be able to convince the Soviet people of his sincere desire for peace. He assured the President that that would advance the cause of peace and mean more to the people of the world "than any event since the Prince of Peace came two thousand years ago."[2]

In a conversation in mid-March with Emmet John Hughes, his principal speechwriter, the President said he thought it would be asinine to indict the Soviet regime once again. Instead, Emmet reported him saying, what do *we* have to offer the world to improve the chances for peace? Peace, he said, can bring us schools, hospitals, food for the hungry, a better world, instead of armaments for war. An arms race, he said, can lead us at worst to nuclear war, at best to robbing the peoples of the world of the fruits of their labor.

The specifics and not just generalities were what we needed. The President's proposals were to be unveiled on April 16 before the American Society of Newspaper Editors. We had a month to translate a general approach into a speech.

C. D. Jackson, White House special assistant and formerly associated with *Time-Life* publications, Emmet Hughes, Chip Bohlen, and I were selected to provide the means by which this metamorphosis was to take place. C.D. came to the drafting table unconvinced that the Soviets would

---

[1]To distinguish him from "Engine Charlie" Wilson, the former head of General Motors, and at that time Eisenhower's secretary of defense.

[2]As quoted by Emmet John Hughes, *The Ordeal of Power: A Political Memoir of the Eisenhower Years* (New York: Atheneum, 1963), 101.

be willing to give up their global ambitions by "genial, bourgeois talk about schools and hospitals for the ignorant and sick."[3] He was the first to try his hand at drafting the speech and from there the number of drafts multiplied, with each of us contributing uncounted revisions. I ended up working on the final drafts in close consultation with Emmet. We carefully filtered out any remarks that would obscure the main thrust of the speech, such as provocative references to the "liberation" of Eastern Europe or the "unleashing" of Chiang Kai-shek.

Foster Dulles was hostile to the effort, although his opposition was somewhat muted in the face of the President's enthusiasm. He was not inhibited from voicing his opinions to Emmet and me, however. Foster did not want to compromise the support we were giving to Chiang Kai-shek on the island of Formosa, or end the Korean War without obtaining radical concessions from the Chinese Communists. When the Communists appeared to be pressing their own peace initiatives, with Chou En-lai offering a Korean prisoner-exchange and Premier Georgii M. Malenkov agreeing to support Dag Hammarskjöld's nomination as secretary-general of the United Nations, Foster believed that the "peace offensive," as he called it, was due to the external pressures we and the West were bringing to bear on Moscow. The United States, he said, should see to it that those pressures were maintained, and if possible increased. By responding with a peace initiative of our own, he argued, we would be falling in with the Soviet scheme of things.

He left Washington about a week before the speech was to be given for a short vacation at his home on Duck Island in Lake Ontario. Before he left, however, he urged us to include in the speech a statement that the United States would be willing to sign an armistice agreement ending the Korean War *only* if the Chinese Communists would agree to keep their hands off Southeast Asia. Emmet and I ignored Foster's advice. The President brought the subject up in a meeting we had with him a few days before the speech was to be delivered.

I arrived slightly early at the White House Sunday morning for the eleven o'clock meeting and was directed to the President's quarters on the second floor. Opening a door at the end of the hall, I walked into a room to find the President changing his clothes after officiating at a ceremony at the Pan American Union. I caught him standing in nothing but his undershorts. His wife Mamie, who was sitting in a chair near the window, grinned, but the President flushed with annoyance. You're in the

[3]Ibid., 107.

wrong room, he said; go to my study at the end of the hall. Thus ended my only claim to intimacy with Dwight Eisenhower.

I retreated in haste and made my way down the hall, where I was joined shortly by Emmet, Bedell Smith, the President's brother Milton, and the President.

The President asked me about the specific objections Foster had to the speech. I told him that Foster objected to our proposal for an armistice in Korea without requiring a commitment from Communist China that it would forgo its ambitions in Southeast Asia.

If we insist on that, I said, there will be no armistice. The Chinese will never agree to that precondition. And, I warned, if the Korean War continues, you will have to reverse your commitment to Senator Taft to cut five billion dollars a year from the defense budget.

The President looked around the table. The others agreed with me. Okay, the President said, let's get to work, and we turned our attention to the text.

Foster was furious when he returned to Washington to find that the President had rejected his advice. It didn't help my relationship with Foster either.

The President delivered his speech, "The Chance for Peace," under great difficulty. The night before he had suffered his first attack of the ileitis that required—several years later—a serious operation. He described the attack in his memoirs as "one of the most miserable periods, physically, of my life."[4] The world, however, was unaware of his distress and welcomed his offer of peace.

Press reaction was immediate. *The New York Times* said that the speech was magnificent and deeply moving. Even *Pravda* and *Izvestia* printed the text of the speech in full. The talk in capitals and pressrooms around the world revolved around the President's speech and a bright, new hope for the future.

While the world waited expectantly for the promise to be translated into deed, the President's cabinet met the next day to discuss the difficulties of dealing with the tariff problem in Congress, the 1954 elections, and the plight of the post office, among other things unrelated to the President's new foreign policy initiative. The President did not attend the meeting; he had retired to Augusta, Georgia, after the speech to recuperate from his painful illness.

[4]Dwight D. Eisenhower, *Mandate for Change, 1953–1956* (Garden City, N.Y.: Doubleday, 1963), 147.

Emmet lamented the fact that the "peace initiative" was not being vigorously pursued by the Eisenhower administration. It did not bring about an understanding with the Communists on Germany and Berlin, but I believe the speech opened the way to the Korean armistice three months later and the conclusion of the Austrian peace treaty in 1955.

Shortly after the President's speech in April, Foster Dulles decided to take into his own hands the question of what to do with me. He suggested to Henry A. "Hank" Byroade, then assistant secretary for Middle Eastern affairs, that he become the new director of the Policy Planning Staff and that I take over Hank's job.

Neither Hank nor I was enthusiastic about the trade; Hank, because he preferred action to policy and planning, and I, because of the potential criticism that would ensue because of my German heritage. To be suspected of an anti-Jewish bias, no matter how unjustified, would be a handicap not only to performing my job, but to our foreign policy initiatives in that region as well. When Hank and I explained our objections to Foster, he agreed with us.

A week or so later I was approached by Eisenhower's new secretary of defense, Charles E. Wilson, whom I had never met. After an exchange of pleasantries, he told me that Foster Dulles had highly recommended me for the job of assistant secretary of defense for international security affairs. Frank Nash, then the incumbent, was seriously ill and planned to retire. Wilson asked if I would come to the Pentagon as Frank's deputy and be prepared to assume his position when it became available.

"But you know nothing about me," I said in surprise.

"I have investigated your record thoroughly," he said, "and with Foster's recommendation, I want you on my team."

It turned out he wanted me on his team within the week, but I told him that after my hard stint as director of policy planning, it was essential that I take a vacation before assuming a new post. I told him that I could report on June 15. He agreed.

In the meantime there were sounds of discontent emanating from Capitol Hill. Chip Bohlen's nomination as our ambassador to Moscow had not been well received and the confirmation proceedings were stormy. He had been branded as "worse than a security risk" for his role at Yalta, and the McCarthy contingent was out for his blood. Chip was the President's personal selection and he insisted that Chip's nomination be pushed through the Senate against all opposition. Everyone ended up slightly bloody and bowed from that confrontation. While Chip finally was confirmed, the White House agreed with the Senate leadership that there would be no more Bohlen cases.

The first hint that more trouble was brewing appeared in an article in the *Washington Times-Herald* two days before I reported to the Pentagon. "Paul H. Nitze, 46 and wealthy, one of the principal shapers of the European recovery plan, is the latest Truman-Acheson lieutenant contemplated for retention in a powerful position under the Eisenhower administration." The right-wing newspaper, recognized as being a voice for McCarthy, warned that I was a product of Wall Street and was partly responsible "for pouring billions into Europe. Enormous profits were reaped by Wall Street from this program," the article stated.

While I seethed at this slander, I reported to my new post in the Pentagon, fresh from my month's holiday and ready to go. I was told that the papers concerning my appointment had been lost in the White House, but that I should start to work anyway.

The morale in the office was at low ebb with poor Frank away much of the time, but it sprang to life when given some energy from the top. The able civil servants and military officers assigned to the office were ready to turn cartwheels for anyone who knew the business and who was willing to take responsibility.

Within a week or so, as I was settling in with my new duties, Frank and I met with the secretary of defense to brief him on several issues that were to be discussed at a meeting of the National Security Council that morning.

Charlie Wilson brushed aside our briefing papers and turned to me: "Paul," he said, "I'm having trouble over you because of your past associations."

I reminded him that he had been fully aware of my work for Dean Acheson and the Policy Planning Staff. He said something to the effect that perhaps the importance of my work in the State Department was exaggerated by some, but there were those who said that I was the principal architect of much of Acheson's foreign policy, not merely an implementer of that policy.

I told him that as a senior civil servant in the State Department and as director of the Policy Planning Staff I made many recommendations to the secretary of state, as had Frank Nash to the secretary of defense. I was proud of the role I had played during those years. Frank agreed.

Wilson, somewhat embarrassed, explained that influential Republican senators were opposed to my appointment and that this might affect the passage of legislation important to the Defense Department. In addition, he said, if the White House sent my name to the Senate for confirmation, it would violate the agreement the President had made with the Republican leadership that there would be no more Bohlen cases.

"Very well, Mr. Secretary," I said, "I didn't ask for this job. You will have my resignation on your desk Monday morning."

I went back to my office and started writing my letter to Wilson asking that I be relieved from my agreement to accept an appointment in the Defense Department. I decided to check with Foster to be sure he agreed with the statement in my letter that I had not requested the appointment and that it had been arranged between him and Charlie Wilson. To my surprise, Foster not only agreed, but helped me hone the letter into a more forceful, precise statement.

Over the weekend the word spread about this business and many of my friends who were holdovers from the last administration were trying to make up their minds whether they should resign in a mass protest. On Wednesday, Joseph and Stewart Alsop wrote a column in which they indicated that Senator Robert A. Taft, the Republican majority leader, was responsible for stonewalling my appointment. Senator Taft denied that he had been consulted about me at all or that he even knew me. I was convinced that he was telling the truth. The press had a field day trying to solve the mystery as to who did blackball me if it wasn't Taft.

As far as I could piece it together, McCarthy and his stooges stirred the thing up in the first place by getting the *Times-Herald* to publish the article accusing me of masterminding the Marshall Plan to make profits for Wall Street. Major General Wilton B. Persons, the President's liaison man with Congress, became worried, so he sat on my papers.

General Persons and the vice president, Richard Nixon, decided to talk with the Republican leadership about the matter. In the absence of Senator Taft, who was ill, they saw Senator William F. Knowland of California. Knowland told Nixon and Persons that the party couldn't stand another Bohlen case and the story got back that the Republican leadership on the Hill was against me.

So ended my official government service for the duration of the Eisenhower administration.

I would be remiss if I did not record in this memoir the more immediate and personal impact of the McCarthy era on the nation and on the State Department in particular. McCarthy raged from the floor of the Senate, while innuendo and secret lists abounded. President Eisenhower and John Foster Dulles turned their backs on the turmoil and disruption within the State Department.

I had thought that a Republican administration would blunt the attacks from the Republican side of the Congress, but the appointment of Scott McLeod as the State Department's new chief security officer soon dashed those hopes. McLeod was a former FBI agent and aide to Senator Styles Bridges, a staunch supporter of Senator McCarthy in his attacks on the State Department. I soon realized our troubles were just beginning.

Among those who were struck down and banished from the halls of government was a close personal friend and colleague, John Paton Davies. John had served with me on the Policy Planning Staff; I had been deeply impressed by his wisdom and foresight. His gentle manner and lively intelligence and his lovely wife, Patricia, gained them both a warm spot in our hearts. Phyllis and I spent many happy hours in their company.

John had been born in China of missionary parents and served there with the Foreign Service before and during World War II before moving to our embassy in Moscow in January 1945. In my estimation he had the best understanding of China, and the strategic relationship among China, Japan, the USSR, and the United States, of anyone in our government.

John made the mistake of being prematurely correct by twenty years. Near the end of the war, he recommended that we try realistically to develop the pro-American and nationalistic tendencies of Mao's group at Yenan, the Communist refuge during World War II, contrary to the popular wisdom of the day. He believed that the Soviet Union's policy had been long dominated by a desire to keep China, as well as Japan, alienated from the United States, and that it was important that we keep China, the sleeping giant, and the Soviet Union from joining forces.

It was with helpless despair that John's friends watched as one security investigation after another—nine in all—undermined his position as a loyal and valuable public servant. After nine security investigations had cleared him of all charges, John Foster Dulles, under pressure from Senator McCarthy, dismissed him in November 1954 on grounds that he lacked "judgment, discretion and reliability."

I had left government service by then, but during that fateful period, Pat and John were staying with Phyllis and me at our house on Woodley Road. The morning after John's dismissal, our breakfast was interrupted by a telephone call for John from Foster Dulles. For the final touch of irony to this tragic situation, Dulles told John that he imagined John would be looking for a job and offered to furnish him a *character* reference. When it came to carrying out his offer, however, Foster backed away on the advice of Arthur Dean, his successor as senior partner of the law firm, Sullivan and Cromwell. Arthur reminded him that his purported grounds for dismissing John were incompatible with a character reference, and that he would be subject to criticism.

John's friends had hoped that it might be possible to clear his name with the change of administrations in 1961. On the eve of President John F. Kennedy's inauguration, I wrote John in Peru, where he was then living with his family:

> I have told Dean Rusk that I think one of the important things the new administration should get at is straightening out the record of your case. You know how the wheels of bureaucracy grind. Maybe nothing will come of it, but I sincerely hope so.

Unfortunately I was right; the wheels ground very slowly indeed. It was not until 1968 that John's name was cleared.

John's case was only one of a large number of Foreign Service officers whose lives and careers were unjustly damaged by Joe McCarthy's charges. Most of them we eventually straightened out, but it was a deeply disturbing period.

I saw enough of McCarthy during this period to form an opinion of the man. He was crude, brutal, and ugly in his behavior toward others. When I first met him, he seemed to me to be a left-wing radical because of his opposition to the steps we were taking to assist NATO Europe assure its security. It was only later that he positioned himself on the far right. He, Roy Cohn, and David Schine found that publicity was to be had from exploiting trumped-up rumors that people in the State Department were Communist agents. I developed a deep loathing for all three men.

9

The Loyal Opposition

My concern that the Eisenhower administration would be unable to come up with a sound defense policy increased when Dulles addressed the members of the Council on Foreign Relations in New York on January 12, 1954. Reviewing the accomplishments of the new administration's first year, he said:

> . . . the President and his advisers, as represented by the National Security Council, had to take some basic policy decisions. This has been done. The basic decision was to depend primarily upon a great capacity to retaliate, instantly, by means and at places of our choosing.

I was seated at a table with Frederick Eaton and Douglas Dillon at the dinner given by the council when Foster Dulles announced this doctrine of massive retaliation. We looked at each other in amazement as his words sank in.

As a partisan defense of the Eisenhower administration in the most important segment of the executive branch's responsibility, national security, the speech showed the qualities that had built Foster Dulles's reputation as an outstanding advocate of what he conceived to be his client's point of view. It was, however, a blatant, and I thought extremely unwise, reversal of the policy behind which Dean Acheson and I—and many others—had so carefully labored to create a bipartisan consensus. The Republicans, having won the election, had lost interest in that policy and in continuing a bipartisan approach.

It would seem only prudent, I noted in a paper I wrote shortly afterward, that if we are speaking of a long-range policy—as Foster Dulles was—we should assume that, in any situation in which we may contemplate the use of nuclear weapons, nuclear weapons may well be used against us. Moreover, the probability of this happening would increase with each passing year. How, I asked, is the free world to decide the nature of its riposte to some distant act of aggression if the only sanction available is one that can be expected to result in the destruction of a major portion of its own factories and cities?

By 1955 it became clear that Foster's doctrine of massive retaliation was merely a declaratory policy, while our action policy was graduated deterrence. ("Graduated deterrence" can be defined as a policy of limiting wars—in weapons, targets, area, and time—to the minimum force necessary to deter and, if necessary, to repel aggression.)

In an article published in *Foreign Affairs* the following year, I argued for narrowing the gap between the two.[1] The difficulty with declaratory policy, I maintained, is that it tends to be ineffective in its political and psychological consequences if it deviates too far from action policy. To be clear as to the wisdom of a declaratory policy, one must be sure first that the action policy it suggests is one which is, and will continue to be, in conformity with our interests and with basic realities, and second that the political and psychological consequences of the declaration will be favorable.

(The dichotomy still exists; sometimes in the opposite direction. In the early years of the Reagan administration, the President made the statement that the Soviet Union had a margin of superiority in the strategic nuclear field. I believe few who knew the facts would have challenged the statement; what they did challenge was the wisdom of saying it. In other words, should one's declaratory policy—even with respect to a statement of fact—always reflect that fact, or should it sometimes be an unfactual statement calculated to support a mood of confidence? The debate continues.)

While Foster was "reshaping" American strategy, I retired to my farm in southern Maryland to lick my wounds after my resignation from government service in June 1953. The peace and quiet of the countryside on the Potomac River where it meanders down to join the Chesapeake Bay soon revived my sagging spirits and I became involved in raising tobacco, Hereford cattle, hogs, and children; not necessarily in that order.

As the summer progressed I became fit and tan as I involved myself in the operation of the farm. This included, incidentally, painting several large barns with the help of Emmet Hughes' wife, Eileen. Slowly my

[1]Paul H. Nitze, "Atoms, Strategy, and Policy," *Foreign Affairs* (January 1956).

focus shifted from concern over the latest policy decision of the Eisenhower administration to concern over the newborn calf in the barn.

The hot, summer days passed quickly and the bright colors of fall were upon us all too soon. I found that Phyllis, my sanguine spouse, had entered me in the annual horse race at the Charles County Fair. Although a reluctant participant, I surprised myself, my family, and my friends by winning by a length. I felt my spirits soar as the crowd in the stands roared their approval. I had never received recognition outside the halls of government—and I was proud of winning that race. Public acclaim can achieve marvels in restoring one's spirit.

I was ready when an opportunity came to return to Washington. Christian Herter, a close friend and member of Congress, left Washington in 1953 to become governor of the state of Massachusetts. (He would not return until 1957, when he accepted an invitation from President Eisenhower to become under secretary of state under Foster Dulles and then secretary of state in 1959 after Foster died of cancer.) For ten years Chris had served as president and I as treasurer of the Foreign Service Educational Foundation, a fund-raising and supervisory vehicle for the School of Advanced International Studies (SAIS) in Washington. I was invited to be his successor as president and I accepted with enthusiasm. So began a new career, with new challenges, and more importantly, the time to think and to analyze the lessons of the past decade.

Origins of SAIS

By the fall of 1953, my life was centered on the School of Advanced International Studies. The origins of the school went back to 1943, when Chris Herter and I shared a small house in Georgetown during the summer. He was then a congressman from a congressional district that included part of Boston. In those days, air-conditioning was almost unheard of in the homes and office buildings of the nation's capital. Our wives, who were cousins and close friends, and our children had deserted us for the cool breezes and swimming at Glen Cove, Long Island, rather than spend a hot, steamy summer in Washington. Chris and I therefore found ourselves each morning looking over our coffee cups at each other rather than our respective families.

As we discussed the problems our country would face in a postwar world, we saw the United States confronting unprecedented international problems, many already on the horizon: shifting centers of power, tensions about resources, changing cultural mores and traditional values, and the probable rise of the Soviet Union to world power with purposes antagonistic to our own. To Chris and me it seemed evident that the United States would have a growing role in the difficult, elusive search for a workable postwar order. To do so successfully, it was essential that our nation not recklessly dissipate knowledge so painfully acquired during four years of war.

Our discussions gave birth to the concept of an institution in Washington where the wisdom of the universities, business, and labor would merge with the knowledge and expertise of those currently engaged in government, foreign affairs, and international economic decisions. This wisdom and expertise could then be passed on to younger generations of Americans who, in turn, would be called upon to take on an increasing burden in the free world.

Together with other associates who shared these interests, we conducted a national educational survey to find out what programs were available for advanced students in international affairs. The only program at the graduate level was the Fletcher School of Law and Diplomacy at Tufts University. While other universities offered courses in political science or history, the field of contemporary international affairs was handled much like a high-school current events course, and was regarded as such by most scholars and students. Of course this situation has changed today, but in 1943 it was a relative wasteland.

Chris, with only minor help from me, managed to raise $165,000 toward a projected budget of $500,000 for the first five years of the school. With a $5,000 initial payment on the purchase of an old building on Florida Avenue—a former girls' school—the School of Advanced International Studies opened its doors with twenty-five students—twenty-two women and three men—in the fall of 1944. Halford Hoskins, the former dean of the Fletcher School, was its first director.

At the same time we applied for the privilege of granting the academic degrees of master of arts and doctor of philosophy from the District of Columbia. Our accreditation was received just one week before our first class graduated in 1945.

It was not until 1950 that SAIS—as the school is commonly known among its students and supporters—began its long and mutually beneficial affiliation with Johns Hopkins University.

Policy Planning in Exile

During the early postwar years, my support of SAIS had been in an advisory and financial capacity; but in the fall of 1953, after resigning from the government, I became intimately involved with its day-to-day operation in my new job as president of the Foreign Service Educational Foundation.

One of my first efforts was to establish a research center at the school. John H. Ferguson, Philip Watts, Robert Tufts, and Charles Burton Marshall, all of whom had been with me on the Policy Planning Staff, and Richard Bissell, who had worked with me on the Marshall Plan,[2] agreed to join me in this effort. The large foundations were unwilling to support this effort because of their concern that I wished to create a Policy Planning Staff in exile, manned by former members of the Truman-Acheson regime, and that doing so might tarnish their nonpartisan image and annoy the Eisenhower administration.

I remained unsuccessful until 1957, when the Rockefeller Foundation, under the direction of Dean Rusk, granted the school three hundred thousand dollars to establish the Washington Center of Foreign Policy Research.

Earlier I persuaded a friend, whose wife controlled a substantial private foundation, to support my projected research center, but when his wife saw our dilapidated building on Florida Avenue, she was horrified. She vetoed the project. This persuaded me that SAIS needed a new building.

Milton Eisenhower became president of Johns Hopkins University in 1956. I found Milton far more sympathetic to my approach to problems than was his brother. After Milton's appointment there followed a long period of collaboration between the two of us that lasted until his death.

Milton agreed that SAIS needed a new home. We worked out a plan to ask the leading foundations not for the two hundred thousand dollars I had found impossible to raise, but for close to five million for a much more elaborate program, which would include a new building.

With the help of Elmer Staats, who was then deputy director of the Bureau of the Budget and dealt with the disposal of surplus government property, I obtained a first-class building site for the school on Massachu-

[2]In February 1954, Richard Bissell joined the CIA and several months later became the director of the U-2 project that was then getting off the ground.

setts Avenue owned by the District of Columbia. An obscure statute permitted SAIS to acquire it for a tenth of its appraised value. With that start, Milton and I together raised the rest of the five million in a month or two, largely from the Ford, Rockefeller, and Carnegie foundations. The two hundred thousand for a research center had posed potential political difficulties for them; the five million did not.

After the research center was created, and the new building completed in 1963, SAIS came into its own as a focal point for intellectual work on the interface between theoretical analysis and the actual conduct of national security and foreign affairs.

The winter of 1954 blossomed into spring. I found I had the luxury of time to sit back and reflect on the issues that had been forced upon the world with the advent of the atomic weapon.

I began by sorting out my thoughts for my seminar at SAIS on the theory and practice of politics. This became an outline of a theory I hoped would be applicable to the entire spectrum of the political arena—domestic, international, business, as well as human relationships. I identified three fundamental elements on which I thought it helpful to focus, if one wished to understand the broad field of politics:

1. Structure (the shape and hierarchy of pertinent social relationships);
2. Purposes or value systems of the parts of that social scene; and
3. Situation (the objective situation in which the political contest takes place).

I sought to allow for a multiplicity of viewpoints ranging from that of a responsible member of a particular group at a particular time, say, the secretary of state today, or a less influential member of that group, or a member of an opposing group at another time, to one that approximates, as far as may be possible, that of a hypothetical observer from Mars studying the emergent characteristics of an interacting system of many cultures, races, states, classes over the full course of history. I suggested that a theory of politics should deal with both the realm of objective fact and the realm of purpose and value, as well as with the interrelations between these realms.

Obviously very few people go up and down these chains of thought before making up their minds how to act in any given instance. Instinct, tradition, education, leadership, and habit simplify the process in almost every specific case. But at certain points there is a moving edge of change in tradition, in education, or in leadership. Insofar as rational processes have a bearing on the course of developing change, it is at this moving edge that these considerations are pertinent.

I used this framework with my graduate students from 1954 until 1981. Together we put it under close scrutiny. With meticulous modification and clarification over time, this framework of theory became an invaluable tool in dealing with the complex problems I have confronted over the years.

My basic thoughts on this subject were elaborated in an article entitled "Necessary and Sufficient Elements of a General Theory of International Relations," published in a collection of works on related subjects in 1959.[3] I dealt with similar issues in a different context in "The Recovery of Ethics."[4] In it I focused the analysis on the most urgent ethical problem of the twentieth century—the role and use of nuclear weapons.

The origins of this small pamphlet go back to the day in 1958 when I addressed the board of trustees of The Church Peace Union, to which I recently had been elected. The union had been founded by Andrew Carnegie in 1914 with the mission to examine the relationship of ethics and foreign policy. William Loos, the executive director, asked me to expand my talk into an article for publication in their "Ethics and Foreign Policy" series of monographs. I agreed, and after much thought and many false starts, the article was published in 1960.

The question I asked myself as I began my task was, what kind of international order will prevail in the future? Will it be a world in which the ideas, principles, and political structures compatible with those we enjoy in the United States flourish while offering a place within that structure to Communist states? Or will it be an international structure designed by and compatible with the objectives of the Communist states while offering a possibility of coexistence to us and to other states similarly organized?

I could imagine a system compatible with our ideas under which the Soviet Union would have rights and responsibilities as great as those of any other single state. I also could imagine an international order basically designed by the Communists that would confer some degree of autonomy to the United States and other countries similarly situated. But the essence of the two systems would be quite different. I doubted the possibility of a truly halfway position.

[3]William T. R. Fox, ed., *Theoretical Aspects of International Relations* (South Bend, Ind.: University of Notre Dame, 1959), 1–14.
[4]Paul H. Nitze, "The Recovery of Ethics" (The Church Peace Union, 1960).

If there is little or no middle ground in the struggle for peace with justice, what resources of will and of national sacrifice are we entitled, or ethically called upon, to put into the effort to cause a system compatible with superior values to prevail? What risks are we entitled to take with the awful hazard of a nuclear war? What guidelines emerge from a comprehensive analysis of the full range of pertinent considerations?

The concept of an ethical framework that has objective validity, over and beyond the values of the individual or societal groups and to which man can aspire to have some degree of understanding, seemed to me to be necessary for there to be a well-founded sense of direction to a foreign policy.

Human will can be effective only at the margin of events. Freedom is not absolute either for individuals or for nations and much is determined by forces beyond their control, by events of the past, by accident, or by chance. At any given moment in time the margin of freedom left them may seem so small as to make it hardly worthwhile to exercise their will one way or the other. But the narrow margin of today becomes the foundation of the broader possibility for tomorrow. Over time the margin of freedom—the impact of will upon the possible—expands geometrically. The decision of today makes possible, or forecloses, ten decisions of tomorrow.

The accumulated wisdom and experience of the past do not always give unambiguous precedents for decisions and actions at the relevant margin of freedom of the present. A new integration of general purpose with the concrete possibilities of the present may then become necessary.

The most difficult issues of foreign policy and ethics arise when changes in degree, at some point, move so far as to become changes in kind, and dictate fundamental departures from past policy and direction.

There have been, from time to time, changes in the degree of destructiveness of weapons and of war. These changes, until recent decades, generally have been considered not to have invalidated the precepts of Western civilization and its antecedent cultures of the moral obligation to defend its freedoms, diversity, and cultural growth from tyranny, reaction, and cultural stagnation or death. But with the advent of the nuclear age, we are faced with a change in degree that threatens to become one of kind. The destructive nature of nuclear war dictates that we no longer regard war as merely the continuation of policy by other means.

The deterrence of nuclear war, until such time as technology provides a more reliable and stable method, must, for the United States, be based upon the capability to prevail if deterrence should fail. But this must be combined with an effort to join with other nations in the creation of a just international order. As I formulated these views, they appeared to be man's best hope simultaneously to preserve world civilization and Western culture and to decrease the likelihood of nuclear war.

While for the first time in years I was able to give sober reflection to these matters, my involvement with a number of technical committees advising the government acquainted me with the ideas and expertise of some of our most brilliant scientists, scholars, military and civilian officials. They helped pave the way for the evolution of my thinking on national security problems. This, in turn, bore upon my contribution to the conclusions reached in studies such as the Gaither Committee Report in 1957, the Fulbright Study of 1959, and the study prepared for presidential candidate John F. Kennedy in 1960 as a blueprint for national security.

I found that my earlier role in government and continuing access to information from friends still in policy positions gave me a broader view of the development of our national security policies than when I had had a responsible role within the State Department. I had a wider circle from which to draw information and exchange ideas both here and abroad; the Council on Foreign Relations and the Bilderberg Group,[4] to mention only two organizations outside of government, were forums for such exchanges.

Using SAIS as my base, I managed to keep abreast of academic affairs at the school, including my seminar on the theory and practice of politics, and a demanding schedule of speaking engagements, conferences, and government-sponsored studies. In addition I became involved in the Democratic party's presidential campaigns of 1956 and 1960.

In 1954, shortly after I left the government, I joined a group chaired by Thomas K. Finletter, a former secretary of the air force and later, in the Kennedy administration, our ambassador to NATO. The purpose of the group was to discuss and formulate progressive and innovative policy issues for the Democratic party in those lean years after the party's defeat at the polls in 1952, and prepare for the presidential campaign in 1956. The meetings were usually held in Tom Finletter's Man-

---

[4]The Bilderberg Conference was first convened in 1954 under the chairmanship of Prince Bernhard of the Netherlands to afford an opportunity for a free and frank exchange of views and to lay the foundations for improved understanding between Europeans and Americans on questions of common concern. The conference continues to serve its purpose in international affairs.

hattan apartment. The discussions were lively and useful, but my attendance was irregular.

The group was formed, in part, for the education of the candidate in things economic. Adlai Stevenson responded with interest but with little participation in the deliberations.

I was personally fond of Adlai, who had been a friend of mine and particularly of my sister's for many years. I spent long hours working on his behalf in the presidential race of 1956. Sometime after that defeat, Adlai asked George Ball and me to assist him as the representative of the President in preparations for an upcoming NATO summit meeting scheduled for December 1957. George and I both advised Adlai that the time was short to develop practical ideas for the NATO meeting. We also were concerned that Dulles's motives in asking for the participation of the defeated Democratic candidate were questionable. But Stevenson had just returned from a trip to Africa and was infused with the notion that NATO should change its spots and lead the industrial world in promoting the development of the Third World.

Foster Dulles had invited Adlai to participate in the preparations for the meeting in order, he said, to gain a measure of bipartisan support here in this country as well as among our NATO allies. In addition to George Ball and myself, Dean Rusk, Lloyd Garrison,[5] Tom Finletter, Charles Burton Marshall, and others, labored to educate Adlai on the delicate nature of the NATO meeting.

The problem for the United States was how to resolve with its NATO allies the disputes arising from the collective defense approach, how to reassure them of the reliability of the U.S. nuclear umbrella, and how to help them overcome their doubts about their own responsibilities to the Western alliance. We were unable to penetrate Adlai's preoccupation with the Third World and his insistence that we take this opportunity to reaffirm the "non-aggressive, peaceful purpose of NATO." We tried to impress upon him that the problem was not the peaceful purposes of NATO (which were understood even by the Soviets), but to maintain alliance coherence and a deterrent adequate for stability. Our efforts in that direction were to no avail. The entire episode proved to be an exercise in futility.

Adlai Stevenson was an attractive, somewhat tragic figure, with strongly held liberal views and an unparalleled facility with words. Un-

---

[5]Lloyd Garrison was an eminent lawyer active in labor relations and the American Civil Liberties Union for many years. He was a friend of long standing to Adlai Stevenson.

fortunately, he lacked the toughness to deal effectively with determined opponents—specifically with the Soviets.

After his defeat at the polls in 1956, Adlai was convinced that the Democratic Congress, led by Lyndon B. Johnson in the Senate and Sam Rayburn, the Speaker of the House, had failed to sharpen the issues and had gone out of its way to protect the Eisenhower administration from the consequences of its own folly. He believed that it was a mistake to allow the congressional wing of the party to be its only spokesman. He therefore urged the formation of a "shadow cabinet."

Thus was born the Advisory Council to the Democratic National Committee. In addition to Adlai, its membership boasted such names as Harry Truman, Eleanor Roosevelt, Averell Harriman, Senators Hubert Humphrey, Estes Kefauver, and John F. Kennedy.

Charles Tyroler II became the executive director of the council. He and his staff had offices in the LaSalle Building on Connecticut Avenue, which remained the home of the council—and of Charlie—for many years.

Again as executive director, Charlie assisted us in the founding of the Committee on the Present Danger in 1976 in the same suite of offices. In the years when I was the chairman of policy studies for the committee, I had the opportunity once again to sit at the large lozenge-shaped conference table, in my old chair with my name on the brass nameplate, in the austere surroundings of the room in which the Advisory Council once met.

A number of special committees were formed to assist the Democratic Advisory Council, one of which was the Advisory Committee on Foreign and Defense Policy. Dean Acheson was appointed chairman and I vice chairman.

After 1956, the Advisory Committee on Foreign and Defense Policy labored over the next four years to prepare position papers and statements. We issued a series of pamphlets under the auspices of the Advisory Council, culminating with the publication in 1959 of *The Military Forces We Need and How to Get Them*. This was a serious think piece on our defense posture and contained ideas that the Democratic party carried with it into the next decade.

10

Toward a Military Strategy

I received fresh insight into our chances for peace—as perceived by the West—in the summer of 1955. The occasion was a visit to Moscow with my family at the invitation of Chip and Avis Bohlen.

We arranged to meet Chip, who was then our ambassador to the Kremlin, in Berlin after the Geneva summit meeting in July of that year and to accompany him back to Moscow. The summit meeting had ended with the news media proclaiming a new era of détente (a word not yet entered into the lexicon of U.S.–Soviet relations), ushered in by "the spirit of Geneva."

As we drove from the Moscow airport past the University of Moscow with its modern, Stalinesque architecture and the homes of top members of the Politburo sprawled on the Sparrow Hills (now Lenin Hills) amidst lovely gardens and flowing fountains, our children were amazed by the opulence displayed in their first view of a Marxist society. After we crossed the Moscow River, however, the depressing reality of the city settled around us like a blanket of fog. Stretches of scarred earth greeted us where buildings had been stopped in midconstruction and abandoned years earlier. The scene became even more drab and somber as we drove into the center of the city, finally arriving at the small square in front of Spaso House, the residence of the American ambassador. A ruined church sagged at one end of the square and the pavement was in dire need of repair. Spaso House itself was a handsome, elegant mansion built by a wealthy nineteenth-century merchant.

We spent ten active and absorbing days in Moscow. The Bohlens were highly regarded by their Soviet hosts and members of the diplomatic corps and we were wined and dined at receptions and dinners. We were the first Americans to be taken through the Molotov truck plant. We went to the theater, the ballet, a burlesque show, and the circus. We visited the beautiful monastery at Zagorsk. We went to an agricultural fair, to GUM, the state store, to the market, and, of course, to the Kremlin. The Bohlens saw to it that we missed little that was of interest and available to foreigners in a xenophobic society.

Chip and Avis were an extraordinary couple. They were both attractive and wise in the ways of foreign policy and diplomacy and Khrushchev had a particular admiration for Avis. No American president could have asked for finer representation in a foreign capital.

Through Chip's influence with Vyacheslav Molotov, the Soviet foreign minister, I was invited to sit with Chip in a diplomatic box at a meeting of the Supreme Soviet when First Secretary Nikita Khrushchev and Premier Nikolai Bulganin gave their report on the Geneva summit meeting.

The experience was fascinating. There were some fifteen hundred members of the Supreme Soviet present representing the various regional and functional parts of the USSR. Our seats in the diplomatic box gave us a panoramic view of that sea of diverse ethnic dress, uniforms, and faces. I was puzzled when many in the audience nodded off while either Khrushchev or Bulganin—during their two- and three-hour speeches—dwelt on the "spirit of Geneva" and the new era of understanding between the Soviet Union and the United States. Yet there was wide acclaim whenever the speakers launched into an impassioned description of Western faults and shortcomings, the necessity for *mir*, and the actions the party proposed to take to achieve *mir*, the Russian word usually translated as "peace."

Chip explained that the primary meaning of the Russian word *mir* is "the world and those who live on it," and that concord among people and nations and the absence of war was only the secondary meaning. He went on to explain that, as the Soviets used the word, it meant a condition in the world in which socialism, the first stage of Communism, had triumphed worldwide, class tensions had been removed, and the conditions for true peace under the benevolent leadership and preeminence of the Soviet Communist party had come to pass.[1]

[1] In pre-October Revolution Russia there were two words spelled MИP and MIP in the Cyrillic alphabet, both pronounced in the same way. In 1918 the Russian alphabet was simplified; "I" was abolished and became "И." Thereafter there has been a single "MИP," transliterated as *mir* in our alphabet. Prior to 1918, MИP meant peace. MIP had two meanings: the universe or world and, its historical meaning, the village commune of elders which from time to time reallocated the cultivation of the village communal land among individual members of the village. (Isaiah Berlin in *Russian Thinkers* points out that for the pre-Marxist Russian revolutionaries and authors who created the foundations of the Russian populist, revolutionary, socialist movement in the 1840s, 1850s, and 1860s—such as Herzen, Belinsky,

The reaction of the members of the Supreme Soviet to Khrushchev's and Bulganin's remarks therefore indicated a lack of interest in the relaxation of tension exemplified by the "spirit of Geneva," but enthusiasm for the continuing struggle for *mir*.

This disparity with our perception of peace in a justly ordered world gave me new insight into the problem we faced with the Soviet Union. The disparity has surfaced repeatedly in our relationship over the decades since the Soviet Communist party took power. The Soviet phrase "peaceful coexistence" may sound like "live and let live" to non-Communist ears, but this is not the meaning that Khrushchev gave it in 1961 when he said:

> In conditions of peaceful coexistence favorable opportunities are provided for the development of the class struggle in the capitalist countries and the national-liberation movement of the peoples of the colonial and dependent countries. In their turn, the successes of the revolutionary class and national-liberation struggle promote peaceful coexistence.

During the Eisenhower years, a number of those in the national security business in government and a few of us outside government were giving intermittent but serious thought to questions of how most effectively to deter war, what forces in peacetime were required, and how large they should be. To arrive at even approximate answers, one had to judge how the Soviets might act in various tense peacetime crises, what factors would deter them from action, and what factors might induce them to go to war with us, despite the obvious risks involved. We also needed to judge how the United States might act and, in particular, what our strategy, tactics, and objectives might be in the event deterrence failed and we were to find ourselves at war with the Soviet Union. Finally, we needed to have a judgment on the dynamics of interaction between the United States and its allies and the Communist world in a serious crisis situation and in a situation in which deterrence had failed and war had actually come about.

We had all come to the conclusion that there was only one serious potential threat to the security of the United States. Many serious problems could be foreseen, but it did not seem possible that they could

---

Chernyshevsky, and Turgenev—"the village commune was the ideal embryo of those socialist groups on which the future society was to be based." Thus, *mir* (MVP) now has three meanings: the world, the commune, and peace.

threaten the security of the United States militarily unless they could lead to a conflict with the Soviet Union.

In those days, the U.S. nuclear deterrent forces consisted of intermediate-range bombers backed by a small number of heavy bombers capable of intercontinental range. But those heavy bombers counted on support from tanker aircraft which were also limited in number and concentrated on a few bases. This contributed to the growing vulnerability of our nuclear deterrent.

In the event of a crisis involving a serious possibility of war with the United States, how might the problem be seen from the Kremlin? Being careful planners, the Soviets undoubtedly would have carefully prepared war plans for a variety of contingencies. One could therefore theorize with some confidence that Soviet plans would include a disarming first strike against U.S. retaliatory capabilities. After absorbing a first strike, if we responded with the remains of the Strategic Air Command (SAC) by attacking Soviet base structure and nuclear attack facilities, the exchange ratios would go against us very quickly. In two, three, four, or at most five exchanges, the United States would be down to a woefully low level of capability while the Soviet Union could still be at a relatively high one. We could then be at their mercy. If we chose to attack their population, we would invite almost total annihilation in the United States.

Conversely, the United States could design a counterforce attack on the Soviet Union, provided we were prepared to make the first strike. This assumption in itself involved a large degree of political unreality. Initiating a first strike went against our culture and our self-image as a nation.

Given all these considerations, there were strong reasons, in developing war plans for the contingency of deterrence failing, to base them on the objective of effectively disarming the enemy rather than annihilating him. These considerations also indicated that our policy—in the event of general war—should be to avoid attacks on Soviet population centers. This, I thought, might well involve larger force requirements and perhaps a greater tolerance for the necessity of our striking the initial blow rather than adopting a policy of immediate retaliation against industrial and population centers.

In a situation in which two countries or blocs are more or less even in nuclear military capabilities, and those capabilities are vulnerable to destruction if struck before they are used, the value of an initial strike would be immense. This could result in serious instability in a crisis. The United States, for example, would look with grave suspicion on any action on the part of the Russians that would indicate they were preparing a first strike. This could well lead the United States to consider a preemptive strike. The Soviet Union, in an effort to keep one or two moves ahead of us, might well feel that it should strike even sooner than planned to head off our preemptive blow. I could foresee the possibility of a situation arising in which there would be such an interaction of fear that it would be almost impossible to conceive how statesmen could prevent the situation from degenerating into war.

Unless the United States managed to take action that avoided that situation, I could envision that the first phase of a war to disarm (or to annihilate, for that matter) might be of short duration, no more than four to seven days. In the second phase, the side that had been successful in the first phase and had the advantage could then move to consolidate its control of the land, the air, and the sea. In a third phase, the superiority of the side that had been successful in the first two phases should be such that it could force acceptance of its preferred peace terms.

The phases in this analysis are similar to a game of chess with an opening-game, a middle-game, and an end-game. The analogy fails, however, when one considers the opening move in a nuclear exchange relative to that of chess, because in a war arising out of a situation of crisis instability, it would make vastly more difference who moves first than who draws the white pieces in chess.

The Gaither Report

The Gaither Committee, as it became known with H. Rowan Gaither, Jr., in the chair, was an ad hoc committee of private citizens appointed by President Eisenhower to determine the requirement for and the feasibility of civil defense in the nuclear age.

As we studied the material supplied to us by top government officials, the CIA, and the military, we became convinced that the political leadership of the country had underestimated the gravity and extent of our strategic vulnerability. We were particularly concerned about the vulnerability to Soviet surprise attack of our strategic bomber force—then the heart of our deterrent. At Gaither's request, the charter of this survey was expanded to include this wider perspective.

Our early warning radar network could not assure sufficient warning time to our bombers to get them into the air before being destroyed on the ground. A program to train our bomber crews to take off quickly on warning was still an experimental concept. We calculated that ninety percent of our bomber force could be knocked out on the ground by a surprise Soviet bomber attack, let alone an attack by Soviet ICBMs.

Our U-2 flights, which began in mid-1956, brought back aerial photographs in the spring of 1957 of Soviet ICBM test sites at Kapustin Yar and Tyuratam, which prompted our intelligence people to judge that the Soviet Union had decided to emphasize strategic missiles rather than long-range bombers. In August the Soviets successfully flight-tested an intercontinental ballistic missile. By late 1957 our intelligence estimates predicted a Soviet production potential of one hundred ICBMs by 1960. We who were working on the Gaither Committee studies, however, were not informed of this new intelligence and updated estimate.

I was brought in as an adviser to the committee in the summer of 1957 and worked on several of the study efforts. Colonel George "Abe" Lincoln, my old friend and at that time a member of the faculty at West Point, and I assisted James Phinney Baxter in drafting the final report. Baxter was president of Williams College, an able historian, and a skillful writer, but Abe and I had been in the national security business for many years and had a more thorough knowledge and understanding of the substance of the study. Abe and I were mentioned as "project members" at the back of the report, which masked the fact that we shared importantly in shaping the substance of the final version. My affiliation with the Democratic party was not considered an asset by the incumbent administration.

The launching of Sputnik I by the Soviet Union in October 1957 was electrifying. Our space effort had been put on hold by an Air Force anxious to get on with the B-52 bomber program, which had been severely curtailed during the early years of the Eisenhower administration. As a result the Air Force had diverted funds from its program on satellite development into the B-52 program, which it felt was central to its mission. U.S. space technology was superior to that of the Soviet Union; the launching of Sputnik into space before our program was ready need not have happened.

The launching of Sputnik II came just five days before we presented our report to the President and the National Security Council on November 7. Sputnik II reinforced the major point in the report.

Our studies indicated that the major danger facing the nation was the vulnerability of our strategic forces. Our report emphasized that maintaining an effective second strike force should be our first priority. Deterrence, we warned, was not achieved by the force we had in being during peacetime, but by that portion of the force that was capable of surviving a Soviet first strike.

We urged that the United States improve its early warning network, train its SAC bomber crews so that that portion of bombers on alert could take off within the available warning time, accelerate our missile production program, and phase in hardened bases for our ICBMs as rapidly as possible. Because the members of the committee believed that a strategic nuclear balance would mean that local aggression would be the more likely form of warfare, the report recommended as a second priority that the United States train and equip adequate forces for conventional warfare.

Inherent budgetary limitations necessitated the assignment of priorities to our recommendations. The committee recommended a low-budget research program on the construction of civil defense shelters and other nonmilitary defense measures and assigned a still lower priority to the extensive and expensive passive defense, which had been the original focus of our work. In our analysis, the prior task was to assure deterrence and crisis stability.

President Eisenhower did not embrace the recommendations of our report. He was anxious to maintain his image as a man of peace and he was not about to approve a major expansion of our defense budget. Moreover, the Joint Chiefs of Staff assured him that our report contained no new proposals that were not already under consideration or in the process of implementation. John Foster Dulles was extremely hostile to our recommendations and surprised the members of the committee with his caustic remarks.

Dwight Eisenhower fell into that broad category of people who believed that nuclear war was "unthinkable," and therefore the effort to achieve a reliable deterrent capability was not urgent. He ended our meeting with him on November 7 with the comment that nuclear war was out of the question: "We don't have enough bulldozers to scrape the bodies off the streets."

While the Gaither Report recommendations had been made without dissent from the committee members, Jerome Wiesner, a brilliant scientist and frequent adviser to presidents, and others later said that the President's comment had marked a turning point away from their prior conviction that a technological solution could be found to the task of providing the West with a credible nuclear deterrent. Several members of the panel, who had great respect for General Eisenhower, adopted his apparent conclusion that defense against nuclear war was futile. They have since opposed most efforts on the part of the U.S. government to maintain and modernize its nuclear deterrent posture. A political solution, preferably in the form of arms control, or, failing that, what can only be described as a policy of preemptive surrender to a serious threat of nuclear war, became for them the only feasible course for the United States to follow.

Despite the President's unwillingness to approve the Gaither Committee recommendations, the high priority recommendations of the report were carried out. Sputnik, however, was the major incentive. In the course of the next few years we perfected our early warning capabilities and put a substantial part of our SAC bomber force on fifteen-minute-alert status, deployed our first Atlas ICBM squadron, successfully flight-tested the Titan ICBM, accelerated the Minuteman development program, and placed two Polaris submarines at sea. As a result, the relative strategic position of the United States vis-a-vis the Soviet Union rapidly became both more stable and more favorable to the United States.

The Fulbright Study

The Soviet ICBM test of August 1957 confirmed a drastic compression of the time required for the delivery of Soviet nuclear explosives at an intercontinental range, and a corresponding reduction in the warning time available to our deterrent forces. These effects, added to the fact that no active defense against an intercontinental ballistic missile in flight was then in sight, could gravely increase the temptation not only to the Soviets, but also to us, to initiate a nuclear strike in time of crisis before the other side did so. Our concern was heightened by indications that the Soviets planned to emphasize the deployment of ICBMs over long-range bombers.

In the SAIS study for the Fulbright Committee in 1959 on "Developments in Military Technology and Their Impact on U.S Strategy and Foreign Policy,"[2] we reported that an arms race was "likely to be of such scope and intensity as to provide each of the two great adversaries with repeated chances to seize an important lead in areas to which they assign

[2] The Fulbright Study was the result of a Senate resolution in 1958 authorizing the Committee on Foreign Relations to make a complete study of the factors that influenced United States foreign policy, its formulation and administration. The Washington Center of Foreign Policy Research at SAIS, instituted in 1957, was selected to conduct one of the basic research studies.

priority. . . . Range extensions will permit the global dispersions of ICBMs, but accuracy and warhead improvements will be of greater significance in their effect on the number of missiles required to destroy hardened military targets. The deterrent utility of fixed U.S. missile sites may be said to vary inversely with Soviet progress in these parameters."

The section of the report dealing with the concept of crisis stability and dynamic stability, in what I believe was the first in-depth study of the subject, was my principal contribution to the study. It held that in the strategic nuclear field a situation in which the nuclear forces of one side are vulnerable to destruction by an initial strike by some fraction of the nuclear forces of the other side is inherently unstable and therefore would lack "crisis stability."

The concept of "dynamic stability" evolves from the problem of relative changes in the strategic posture of nations. The fact that modern weapons systems take many years to develop and then to deploy in adequate number for strategic significance makes it difficult to avoid instabilities through prompt compensatory action. The periods of instability arising out of differences in time-phasing the development or deployment of weapons may therefore be quite extended and dangerous. Dynamic stability (as opposed to crisis stability) therefore may be defined as lack of need for significant change over time by either side.

My thoughts on national military strategy and stability continued to evolve over the decade of the fifties in tandem with the development of a theory of politics. I have found no reason to repudiate the basic thoughts in either. They have stood up well against much criticism to this day.

In Defense of the West

I made a stab at translating theory into proposed action in the spring of 1960. I was asked by E. Finley Carter, president of the Stanford Research Institute, to address the members of a national strategy seminar to be held at Asilomar on the Monterey Peninsula in California. He stressed that while the daytime presentations were to be serious exercises within the narrow boundaries of disciplined analysis, he wanted the two evening speakers—of whom I was one—to toss ideas to the audience from the "wild blue yonder" to stimulate new thought. The other evening speaker was Edward Teller.

Teller addressed the audience at Asilomar on Tuesday, April 26, while I followed on Thursday evening, the twenty-eighth. Ed told them that "openness" is the key to controlled disarmament. "If police methods and totalitarian methods disappear," he said, "then we shall have indeed made a positive step toward disarmament." But in dealing with the Soviet Union, he made clear that we had a totalitarian adversary that would not allow openness by any definition of the word. Thus he advocated "an eye for an eye, a tooth for a tooth"—no more, no less—in responding to Soviet aggression, together with passive defense and shelters for our civilian population. He found the concept of massive retaliation impractical because it was repugnant to the values of our society and the Soviet Union recognized that fact.

Teller, as usual, made good sense to me. I doubt, however, that he was in accord with my presentation two nights later.

The speech I made followed the precept that Carter had given me, which I thought was rigorous in its logic, but I was nevertheless dubious of its soundness. I warned my audience when I began my talk that evening that I had adopted one of the less widely accepted definitions of the economist; that is, "one who adroitly passes over the minor inconsistencies, the better to press on to the grand fallacy."

And press on I did, to the consternation of almost all of my listeners. I began by setting forth in precise terms eight judgments that would serve as assumptions governing the logic of the succeeding analysis. One of these assumptions was that a distinction could be drawn, on the one hand, between military preparations designed to put us and our allies (or the Soviets) in a position meaningfully to win a nuclear war were deterrence to fail, and, on the other hand, preparations designed merely to deny the other side such a capability. I called the first a Class A capability, the second a Class B capability. Another assumption was that the United States was not then doing, and was unlikely in the future to do, what was necessary to give itself a Class A capability.

I carefully set forth the strongest arguments I could find against my eight assumptions and found them less persuasive than the arguments in favor of them. I then drew the logical conclusion that we should try to get the maximum possible political benefits from open recognition of the fact that we were seeking a Class B, not a Class A, posture.

I then laid out a program consistent with that logic train. The actions I proposed were the following:

1. That the United States concentrate on building a variety of secure, purely retaliatory systems, preferably those exploiting mobility and concealment, and locatable away from population centers, in the air, under the sea, or in the deserts or tundra;

2. That, when we had such a mix of relatively secure systems, we scrap the fixed-based vulnerable systems that have their principal utility as components of a Class A capability;

3. That (in order to maximize the potential worldwide political gains from seeking only a Class B capability for the United States rather than a Class A) we multilateralize the command of our retaliatory systems by making SAC a NATO command; and

4. That we inform the United Nations that NATO will turn over ultimate power of decision on the use of these systems to the General Assembly of the United Nations subject to the following conditions—

> a. That we and our allies would assume continuing responsibility for manning, maintaining, and improving these systems;
> b. That UN inspectors would be invited to inspect and satisfy themselves that these are the only nuclear systems we are maintaining;
> c. That a UN order to use them would be honored only in the event some nation has initiated the use of nuclear weapons other than on or over its own territory in self-defense against military aggression.

In order to guard against the increased danger of local aggression, I proposed that we and our allies support a substantial increase in forces appropriate for limited war. A considerable stock of small tactical nuclear weapons might be maintained to be made available to any country subject to overt military aggression and desiring to use such weapons on and over its own territory in self-defense.

An intensified research and development program should be maintained to guard against the possibility that technological developments had, in fact, made a Class A nuclear capability possible. In other words, my sixth assumption (that neither side could achieve a true Class A capability against a determined effort by the other to deny it such a capability) might be wrong.

As part of the plan, the Soviet Union would be invited to take reciprocal action. In particular, it would be hoped that the USSR could give convincing demonstration that it too was prepared to restrict its preparation for the contingency of central war to a Class B capability.

It should be made clear that we and our NATO allies would reserve the unilateral right to modify or terminate the plan. New technological developments or evidence that the USSR was continuing to strive for a

Class A capability might well cause us to judge some new approach more conducive to the world's and our security.

Such, in outline, was the idea I offered for critical examination. I told my audience that they would probably be able to demonstrate it to be in fact the grand fallacy I had suggested in my introduction.

I concluded that the key to whether the suggestion I had put forward was worthy of further serious study, or should be quickly relegated to the scrap heap of other grand fallacies, depended upon whether the Soviet leaders showed themselves determined at all costs to strive for a predominant nuclear position, a true Class A capability, or whether they gave some indication that they perceived a common interest in a more stable nuclear relationship.

My audience of some five hundred military planners and strategists, government policymakers, and academics glared at me in stony silence. None of my friends in the Rand Corporation, an influential think tank in California, or the Air Force came to my support.

The bug in the speech, as I had suggested, was its assessment of what the Soviets would do. Would they opt for a Class B capability as we seemed to be doing? Or would they persist in striving for a Class A capability? Subsequently, in an article I published later that year in *Survival,* I endeavored to address these questions in some detail.[3] The more I thought about it, the more convinced I became that the Soviets would continue along their current course and continue to seek a Class A capability. Eventually, the threat posed by such a force could develop to the point where it would compel us to follow their lead and seek our own offsetting Class A capability. But by the time that point arrived, it might be too late for us to act in a way that would restore the strategic balance in our favor. I concluded, therefore, that despite the impression I may have left earlier with my Asilomar speech, a Class B posture—a posture from which one can retaliate but cannot hope to disarm the enemy—was, by itself, not a solid foundation for our political aims or our national security.

Nevertheless my foray into the "wild blue yonder" haunted me for a number of years thereafter. For more than a decade the Asilomar speech was used in an attempt to block my nomination or my confirmation for public office. In 1963, my confirmation hearings as secretary of the navy were dominated by grueling interrogations.

[3] "Political Aspects of a National Strategy," *Survival* 2 (November–December 1960): 219–26.

Stu Symington had advised me to emphasize the caveat I had used to introduce the speech and insist that the text was, in fact, a grand fallacy and not to be taken seriously. In spite of our differences over policy matters, I had great respect for Stu's sensitivity to the shifting moods of the Senate. I followed his advice.

The chairman of the Senate Armed Services Committee, Senator Richard Russell of Georgia, started the line of questions. I responded by attempting to set the speech in its proper context so that the committee would accept it as a creative and constructive intellectual exercise. "This speech," I said, "was meant to shock people into a realization of what the requirements of our security were, and what unpalatable alternatives we might have to face if we did not do things, many of which we subsequently have done, to improve our defense posture."

Unfortunately, while this appeared to satisfy the chairman, it did not appease Senators Strom Thurmond of South Carolina, Barry Goldwater of Arizona, or Harry Flood Byrd of Virginia, all of whom voted against my confirmation. Senator Robert Byrd of West Virginia, on the other hand, said he found it incredible that I could so carefully and logically present the considerations for and against a proposition I thought to be a grand fallacy. Nevertheless he applauded the frankness of my testimony, and voted for my confirmation along with most of the other members of the Senate.

PART III

II

The Kennedy Renewal

My first introduction to Senator John F. Kennedy was my appearance in 1959 before his Subcommittee on African Affairs after a fact-gathering trip to that continent for the Council on Foreign Relations. I was impressed by John Kennedy at that first meeting. He listened carefully, absorbing information and ideas for use when the occasion arose. He was young, intelligent, attractive, and energetic, all attributes I admired. Nineteen months later he became President of the United States.

Initially I had thrown my support behind Senator Hubert Humphrey for nomination as the Democratic candidate for the presidency in 1960. I contributed several thousand dollars to his campaign, specifically earmarked to pay the salary of Ernest Lefever, who had left SAIS to serve as foreign policy adviser to Hubert. I had been Ernie's adviser in his postdoctoral work at SAIS several years earlier, and I was aware that with a family to support he couldn't afford to leave his teaching post without some income.

Hubert's campaign was chronically short of funds, and I soon learned that Ernie was not receiving the pay he had been promised. The money I had contributed had been diverted to buy television time in the crucial West Virginia primary. Kennedy won that primary and Hubert withdrew. Hubert's presidential aspirations were put on ice for another eight years, and I—as did many of my Democratic colleagues—switched my support to John Kennedy. Ernie eventually received the money that was due him, thanks to my good friend W. John Kenney, who was Hubert's campaign treasurer.

Following Senator Kennedy's nomination as the Democratic party's candidate for the presidency, he appointed several task forces. He asked me to chair a four-member group to "consult . . . on national security problems with the ablest and most experienced authorities in the nation, without regard to party." The other three members were David K. Bruce, Roswell Gilpatric, and James Perkins.[1]

Senator Henry "Scoop" Jackson found a small room for us in his suite of offices in the Russell Senate Office Building. We talked with numerous people, on both sides of the political fence, including those within the Eisenhower administration who were prepared to share their views with us. We also talked with people in research institutions and think tanks, such as Rand, the Institute for Defense Analyses, MIT, and others, and we consulted with knowledgeable officials in Britain, France, Germany, and Canada.

We submitted our report to the president-elect on November 9, one day after he narrowly defeated Richard Nixon at the nation's polls. He directed that a copy of the report be furnished to each cabinet appointee involved in national security with the instruction that further analysis of the issues would begin from there.

In the report, we identified the principal national security issues the new administration was likely to encounter during its first months in office. The most urgent defense policy decision was whether we should attempt to achieve a politically meaningful "win" capability in general nuclear war, or settle for the more modest goal of being able to deny the Soviets such a capability through assuring ourselves secure retaliatory capability. From Kennedy's decision on that issue would flow the weapons systems and programs necessary to meet the chosen objective and the magnitude of the necessary supplements to the projected defense budget.

We urged him to make an early decision, bearing in mind that to have capabilities which would meet the more ambitious goal would be a tremendous undertaking, unlikely to be politically acceptable.

We strongly suggested that he make an early decision on where he wished to focus disarmament planning within his administration. The prevailing system, which gave both the Departments of State and Defense veto power but no positive authority, was unworkable. Our report recommended that the staff be placed under the direction of a top-level man reporting to the President through the secretary of state, thus presaging the creation of the Arms Control and Disarmament Agency (ACDA), mandated by the Congress in 1961.

Berlin remained in a state of permanent crisis, with the Soviet Union threatening to conclude a separate peace treaty with East Germany, thus

[1]David Bruce and Ros Gilpatric both served Kennedy during his administration, Bruce as our ambassador to Great Britain and Gilpatric as McNamara's deputy until 1963. James Perkins returned to his duties with the Carnegie Corporation and in 1963 became president of Cornell University.

terminating Soviet responsibilities to assure the West access to Berlin and leaving East Germany to be as arbitrary as it wished. Our report recommended that every effort be made to develop a common position on Berlin with the British, the French, and the West Germans, including a plan to cover the contingency of a renewal of a blockade.

Chancellor Konrad Adenauer of West Germany, we reported, appeared to have no idea what to do other than to remain intransigent in opposing any change in regard to Berlin. The British, it seemed, wished to work out an agreement with the Russians even if it was a bad agreement. The French, we believed, were prepared to stand reasonably firm.

Nevertheless, Charles de Gaulle was the most crucial problem facing us in our relations with our European allies. We predicted that it was unlikely that he could either be appeased or beaten down by frontal attack. The Suez crisis in 1956 had divided Britain and toppled its prime minister, Anthony Eden, but the crisis appeared to have united France. In Paris the United States was seen as having betrayed its allies. France had decided to act alone in protecting its interests in the future. Its nuclear program was spurred by this decision and added impetus was given to the formation of the Common Market.

Thereafter the only thing Charles de Gaulle—who had assumed the presidency of France in 1958—wanted from the United States was technological assistance in building his nuclear program. Here U.S. policy was often contradictory and somewhat arbitrary so that it stimulated not only divisiveness within the U.S. government, but contributed to the bitterness in Franco-American relations. De Gaulle, of course, wished nothing but an unconditional acceptance of his demands, which President Eisenhower had been unable to grant owing to the constrictions of the law and Washington politics.

By 1960 the explosive situation in Algeria had de Gaulle's full attention and he often seemed to favor a quarrel with Washington or London to gain support at home. Whether that was true or not, we didn't know, but it would not have been out of character for the determined French president. At the same time, de Gaulle nurtured an unfounded fear that the United States was waiting to move into the power vacuum in French-speaking Africa if France relinquished its claims there. John Kennedy's speech in 1957, while he was still a senator, in which he criticized the French for not granting independence to Algeria and the Eisenhower administration for supporting France, did not endear him to those in the Elysée Palace.

This then was the situation with de Gaulle in the fall of 1960. Our best strategy, we stated in our report to the president-elect, would be to rebuild our relations with the British, Italians, and others and bring the Germans around to cooperating with us rather than de Gaulle and thus restrict de Gaulle's freedom to disrupt the Western alliance. We recognized that our relations with France would be deeply affected by the position we took on Algeria. We were faced with a difficult dilemma since the Front de Liberation National (FLN) had turned to Moscow.

Other legacies that would require the urgent attention of the president-elect upon assuming office were Cuba, the Congo, Laos, and the "smoldering guerrilla war in South Vietnam." Because of limitations of time and space, our report made only brief stabs at sorting out the multitude of problems inherent in these global time bombs.

JFK and the Thirty-Second Decision

During the transition period, Clark Clifford asked me to recommend someone to be Kennedy's secretary of state. I suggested Dean Rusk. Clark said that Mr. Kennedy was not acquainted with Dean, and asked me to arrange a meeting as quickly as possible.

Dean was on vacation in the vast wilderness of the Olympic Mountains in Washington State, where he and his wife, Virginia, were on a camping expedition on horseback. I reached him—with great difficulty—through a forest ranger station; a puzzled Dean Rusk was brought to the telephone. He caught the next available plane to Washington to meet with the president-elect.

Mr. Kennedy was impressed by the soft-spoken, courtly president of the Rockefeller Foundation.[2] He recognized that Dean was a knowledgeable negotiator and a thoughtful and experienced planner and diplomat. Dean, however, had deep reservations; he told me that he would be unable to accept the cabinet post because he did not have the independent funds to support the job. I reluctantly told Clark Clifford that Dean was unavailable.

Later, Mr. Kennedy called Bob Lovett at the annual board meeting of the Rockefeller Foundation in Williamsburg, Virginia, and asked him to find out if Dean would accept the position. After Bob assured Dean that a generous termination allowance would be granted him as president of the foundation, Dean met with Mr. Kennedy and accepted the post.

That evening, Phyllis and I were having cocktails at our home in

[2]Dean once told me that he prided himself on looking like a bartender.

Washington when I received a telephone call from the president-elect. He said:

"Paul, I have a friend of yours sitting next to me and he has just agreed to become my secretary of state. He would like you to be his under secretary for economic affairs. Before you respond to this, however, you should know that I would like you to become either my national security adviser or deputy secretary of defense."

"How long do I have to make up my mind?" I stammered.

"Thirty seconds," he responded crisply.

My mind raced over the three possibilities. I quickly eliminated the job as under secretary of state for economic affairs; I had worked in economic affairs in State for many years and I was now interested in policy of a broader scope. As national security adviser, I would deal with broad policy but I could be stalemated by a Pentagon unsympathetic to the type of policy I thought was required. To bring it about, such a policy had to be supported by someone in a strong position in the Pentagon.

"I choose the post of deputy secretary of defense," I declared (within the allotted thirty seconds).

"Fine," he said, and hung up.

The rest is history, of course. Kennedy later asked Robert McNamara, then president of the Ford Motor Company, to be his secretary of defense, and McNamara would agree to accept the job only if given a free hand in the organization of the department and in the selection of his subordinates.

When Bob called me and asked if I would become assistant secretary of defense for international security affairs (ISA), I was—at first—much chagrined. I tried to reach John Kennedy in Palm Beach, Florida, at the private telephone number he had given me. I was told, "Mr. Kennedy doesn't wish to speak with you."

The message was clear. John Kennedy was embarrassed that he was unable to keep his commitment to me; his commitment to McNamara was of overriding importance.

While I was disappointed in the way that "thirty-second" decision turned out, it was the right decision considering the information I had at hand and the time available in which to make it. Many years earlier, Clarence Dillon had taught me to take all the time available to gather the facts and to analyze a situation thoroughly before making a decision. If, however, only a limited time is available, he told me to use it as best I could, but to *make* the decision. Never, he said, let a necessary decision pass you by regardless of the limited time you have in which to make it.

I had never met Bob McNamara, but he knew of me and my reputation for hard-nosed determination. He told Mr. Kennedy that he would prefer a deputy who would be his alter ego and carry out his programs without argument or confrontation. He felt that he would get along well with Ros Gilpatric, while he was concerned that our relationship—if I were to be his deputy—would be stormy. He was probably right; we disagreed on numerous issues over the ensuing years although our mutual respect and friendship continued to grow.

As it turned out, my job in ISA (known in Washington as the "little State Department") permitted me to do exactly what I had hoped to do. That was to assure the President and Dean Rusk Pentagon support for the type of policy they and I believed to be necessary.

Even during the transition period when I was as close an adviser to Kennedy as any other member of his team, I was not a member of the inner circle. After he took office there were times when he indicated he would have preferred a more direct personal relationship, but I strongly believed that I should not go over Bob McNamara's head to the President. That would have rendered me ineffective in my job in ISA.

The world had not stood still while the transition between Republican and Democratic administrations took place. Our relations with Cuba continued to deteriorate and Fidel Castro, the Marxist guerrilla who had overthrown Fulgencio Batista in 1959, remained a sharp thorn in our flank. Berlin was still the perennial problem, with Khrushchev continuing to threaten to sign a separate peace treaty with East Germany. The Congo was in an explosive situation and under the threat of direct Soviet intervention. Laos was a smoldering ember, waiting to burst into flames.

I was given a desk in John N. Irwin's office, my predecessor in the Pentagon, early in January—well before the inauguration—and immediately began dealing with some of these problems. I was asked to serve on two interdepartmental groups that were formed to deal with the more troubling and imminent crises then on the horizon—the Congo and Laos.

Shortly after I accepted the job as assistant secretary for ISA, Mr. Kennedy told me that he wanted my office to be the focal point in the administration for arms control. He asked for a thorough review of our policy before the nuclear test ban negotiations resumed on March 21. I became deeply involved in this review and preparations for the negotiations with the Soviet Union in Geneva. These matters, the Laotian and Congolese crises, and the budget review crowded my calendar. I turned over more and more of my other duties to my recently arrived deputy, William P. Bundy.

Bill Bundy came highly recommended by Dean Acheson. He was Dean's favorite son-in-law. I made Bill aware of all that was going on so that he could act in my place in the event of my absence, but we agreed that I would be primarily responsible for NSC-type policy issues and crisis management. Bill, we also agreed, would assume primary responsibility for the many complex problems in our military assistance program, which was a major part of the ISA operation.

The Bay of Pigs

Meanwhile the preparations for the Bay of Pigs operation gained momentum within the administration. The Cuban refugee force that had been trained and armed by the previous administration was eager to test its mettle, and the new administration was confronted with plans for an assault on Cuba, prepared under the direction of three holdovers from the past: Allen Dulles, director of Central Intelligence, Richard M. Bissell, CIA's deputy director for operations, and General Lyman L. Lemnitzer, chairman of the Joint Chiefs of Staff. All three were highly respected men in their field. I asked Bill to represent ISA in the planning, which was very closely held.

The days passed with my attention focused on other matters until I received a visit from General Edward Lansdale, an expert on counterinsurgency, whose assignment at that time called upon him to report to me. (Lansdale, incidentally, left ISA shortly thereafter. While reporting to me on his duties, he told me that he was working on a project, the nature of which he was not at liberty to tell me. I told him I could not accept that. If he could not confide in me the nature of the project, then I suggested he find another place to roost. He did. Ros Gilpatric took him under his wing.)

Ed was not directly involved in the planning for the Bay of Pigs, but he was uniquely qualified to judge the efficacy of the planning. While adviser to Ramón Magsaysay, later president of the Philippines, he had been instrumental in helping Magsaysay put down the Communist-led Hukbalahap (Huk) rebellion there. From 1954 to 1956 Lansdale was a political adviser in South Vietnam and helped establish the Ngo Dinh Diem regime. It was while serving there that he recommended the creation of a Vietnamese counterinsurgency force as opposed to a conventional force. He had been reassigned to the Pentagon in 1956 to help develop our Special Forces.

Ed took a very dim view of the planning for the Bay of Pigs operation. He told me that he was convinced that the project was badly organized, poorly prepared, and, on its current course, doomed to failure. Furthermore, he believed that the claim that the invaders would be supported by the Cuban people was poorly substantiated. Because of the experience his background gave him, I became uneasy and talked to Bill and to others who were involved in the planning. They all disagreed with Lansdale and I allowed my other concerns to crowd from my mind proper attention to this operation. That is, until I attended a meeting with the President in Dean Rusk's conference room on April 4.

The President had allowed the planning of the operation to continue since his inauguration, but he was far from convinced of its wisdom. He ordered that all preparation be such that the invasion could be halted up to twenty-four hours before its execution. He made it clear that plans were to be designed on the basis of no U.S. military participation.

My uneasiness about the operation stemmed from General Lansdale's uncertainty that it could be carried out successfully. In my mind, our moral right to try to stop the Communist menace from invading our hemisphere was not the issue. The Soviet Union had inserted itself in our backyard by stealth and deception in the form of the Castro regime in Cuba. Like a spreading cancer, it should, if possible, be excised from the Americas.

A few days before the meeting, the President had received a memorandum from Senator J. William Fulbright, who had become concerned about news reports of an impending invasion. The senator made an impassioned plea that the administration forgo its plans. He urged instead a policy of containment, with the recently inaugurated Alliance for Progress providing the necessary insulation from Castro for the rest of the hemisphere. "Remember always," Fulbright wrote, "the Castro regime is a thorn in the flesh; but it is not a dagger in the heart."

President Kennedy invited Senator Fulbright to join us at this critical meeting. Dean Rusk, I understand, had discussed his reservations about the operation earlier with the President. After the final plans were laid out by the CIA, the President started asking people around the table, in turn, what they thought: Should we or should we not go ahead with the operation? Fulbright was adamantly opposed and spoke eloquently on the immorality of the action.

As I have noted earlier, Ed Lansdale had caused me to doubt the practicality of our being able successfully to carry out the operation. But I had little doubt as to the morality of helping the Cuban people resist the consolidation of Castro's power through typical Communist methods, if the operation could be expected to succeed. Fulbright's presentation assumed the operation could succeed; his argument was that it would be wrong for us to try. When the President turned to me, I answered Fulbright's argument, saying that I favored getting rid of Castro if we could. But to my ultimate regret, I did not state my reservations as to the practicality of the invasion plan or Lansdale's doubts that it would stimulate an effective popular uprising.

The air strike, with obsolete, lumbering B-26s flown by the Cuban exile brigade before the invasion began, failed to destroy Castro's planes on the ground. Our cover story for this action was blown almost immediately and friends and foes alike condemned the strike as an unprovoked American attack on a tiny neighbor. At the last moment, the President called off the second air strike—planned to coincide with the invasion early Monday morning—on the advice of his secretary of state because of the international uproar caused by the first strike.

Richard Bissell and General Charles P. Cabell, deputy director of the CIA, protested to Dean Rusk when Mr. Kennedy called off the air strike, and Dean suggested that they present their arguments to the President. General Cabell said there was no point in pushing the matter further. The withdrawal of the air support, of course, doomed the operation even if all else had gone well.

The Meeting in Vienna

Shortly after the election, the Soviet premier informed our Moscow ambassador, Llewellyn E. Thompson, Jr., that he was interested in a meeting with the President. Mr. Kennedy wrote Khrushchev in February suggesting an early meeting. We assumed the whole idea would be postponed indefinitely after the Bay of Pigs debacle, but in May, Kennedy received an unexpected response from Khrushchev, who suggested a meeting in Vienna in June.

We arrived in Vienna on a gray, rainy Saturday morning and drove directly from the airport to the residence of the American ambassador. The talks with the Soviet premier were scheduled to begin shortly after noon. Khrushchev arrived at 12:45 and the two leaders retired to the music room, where the discussions began on a disastrous note.

The President allowed himself to be drawn into an ideological debate on Marxist-Communist theory and the role of historical inevitability. As Arthur Schlesinger (an aide to Kennedy) said, Khrushchev was a veteran dialectician and was operating on home turf from years as a Bolshevik agitator. While President Kennedy was impressed by the older man's vitality and debating skill, he was nonplussed by the harsh rhetoric and rigid dogma that were thrown up against his every appeal to reason.

Mr. Kennedy emphasized the danger of miscalculation in a world where one side or the other might tread on the national security interests of the other. Khrushchev bristled in response that social revolution needed no spokesman and that dams could not halt the flow of ideas. As the defender of wars of national liberation, the Soviet Union could not stand by while the United States intervened in the internal affairs of another country struggling against the yoke of feudalism and despotic leadership.

Kennedy somewhat lamely admitted that the United States was sometimes put in the position of defending dictators. We support free choice, independence, and change, he said, but we have difficulties with our allies and our actions are often dictated by strategic considerations. We are concerned by any shift in the balance of power.

If strategic considerations concern you, Khrushchev retorted, and you believe that Cuba represents a threat, how about Iran and Turkey for us, and Taiwan for the Chinese?

And so it went. The President's face was pale and strained when he and the Soviet premier emerged from the first meeting.

The minutes had stretched into hours for those of us who waited outside the music room while the discussions were going on. We were dismayed after the first session, although Llewellyn "Tommy" Thompson reminded us that such bellicosity was par for the course on the part of the Soviet premier.

Chip Bohlen and Tommy Thompson would huddle with the interpreters after the meetings, and the minutes would be dictated to a squad of secretaries. The typed transcript would not be available until ten or eleven o'clock at night—after the dinners and receptions provided by our Viennese hosts—at which time we would avidly read its contents.

Khrushchev had expected to find in Kennedy the pampered son of a rich man who would be no match for the burly, battle-scarred Communist who had gained his maturity in the mines of Stalino (now Donetsk). Khrushchev attempted to intimidate the young President and test him for possible reactions to future Soviet adventurisms. President Kennedy, after his initial wavering in the face of Khrushchev's brutal onslaught, began to hold his ground, particularly on the subject of Berlin.

There were only two days of meetings, involving five or six hours of discussion between the two leaders. The climate of the discussions did not improve as Khrushchev dealt one blow after another. The exception was Laos. The two men seemed to be in accord on the need to lower the heat of contention in the Laotian kingdom; Laos did not appear to be near the top of Khrushchev's concerns. The premier also assured President Kennedy that the Soviet Union would not resume nuclear testing unless the United States did so first. This, of course, was a cynical pledge inasmuch as the Soviet Union, without provocation, resumed its testing at the end of August for a two-month series of blasts, culminating with the most powerful explosion ever detonated. In fact, it was estimated by our scientists that the Soviets started specific preparations for their new test series in March about the time the first test ban conference got under way in the new administration.

Berlin was the most disappointing of the subjects broached by the two leaders. Khrushchev repeated his intention to sign a separate peace treaty with East Germany in December, thereby canceling all existing commitments, including occupation rights, administrative agreements, and rights of access. President Kennedy protested in vain and said, as the meetings came to a close, "Mr. Chairman, I see it's going to be a very cold winter."

The two leaders parted with cautious but mutual respect. Khrushchev in his memoirs expressed his admiration for John Kennedy's grasp of international issues in spite of their differences. He said that while President Eisenhower had been prompted on numerous occasions during their meetings in Geneva and Washington by first Dulles and then Herter, John Kennedy appeared to have complete command of the issues under discussion. "John Kennedy and I met man to man," he said, "as the two principal representatives of our countries."[3]

Nuclear Test Ban Negotiations

The principal snag in negotiating a test ban agreement since the negotiations began in 1958 had been verification. The United States had insisted on on-site inspection to verify unidentified seismic events and the Soviet Union had opposed the idea with equal vehemence.

Nevertheless, momentum toward agreement began in the early

[3]Nikita Khrushchev, *Khrushchev Remembers: The Last Testament,* trans. and ed. Strobe Talbott (Boston: Little, Brown, 1974), 497.

months of 1960 and increased hopes that a final agreement might be reached at the forthcoming summit meeting in Paris, scheduled to begin May 16.

On May 7, 1960, Premier Khrushchev announced that Francis Gary Powers and his high altitude U-2 reconnaissance plane had been shot down over Sverdlovsk on May 1. The summit was canceled.

After that it was all downhill for East-West relations. The delegations stayed at the table in Geneva doing little more than marking time until they adjourned on December 5.

Immediately after the inauguration, President Kennedy asked for postponement of the Geneva Test Ban Conference, scheduled to resume February 7, in order to review U.S. policy. The Soviets agreed and a new date of March 21 was set.

The review, in which I was heavily involved, began with a thorough examination of the transcripts of over 250 negotiating sessions in Geneva to determine the exact nature of Soviet complaints to our position. We were prepared to make the concessions necessary for an agreement, if by so doing there entailed no significant risk to our national security.

We met with the Soviets in Geneva off and on during the spring and summer of 1961 without resolving our differences. The pressure on the President to resume testing increased after the Vienna summit meeting. Arthur Dean, who led our negotiating team, was sent back to Geneva toward the end of August with instructions to make one more attempt to arrive at an agreement with the Soviets before the President made a decision about test resumption. Tsarapkin, the head of the Soviet delegation, showed no interest in our latest concession[4] and reiterated what had become the standard Soviet response at the negotiating table: A test ban could not be achieved except in the context of general and complete disarmament.

This exchange took place on August 28. On August 30, the Russian news agency, Tass, announced that the Soviet Union had decided to resume nuclear testing. Two days later the Soviets exploded in the atmosphere a 150-kiloton nuclear weapon.

The President was urged by many of his advisers to announce our intention to resume testing to demonstrate our resolution and to satisfy

[4]The Soviets were concerned that at the end of a proposed three-year moratorium on underground testing, we would be free to test below the 4.75 seismic magnitude threshold. Dean proposed that a panel of scientists convene six months before the end of the moratorium period to evaluate the degree to which the threshold could be lowered, or indeed if it could be eliminated completely.

domestic clamor. They were joined by some members of Congress as well as some in the scientific community. Moreover, a Gallup poll in July had shown a two-to-one margin of the American public favoring the resumption of testing. Nevertheless the President was reluctant to take that step.

Several days later, on September 3, the United States and Great Britain, the third member of our trilateral negotiations, released a joint proposal to the Soviet Union for an immediate atmospheric test ban which would involve no on-site inspection. Moscow's answer was a second test, followed by an immediate third.

The President announced our intention to resume testing on September 5. While he did not foreclose our option to test in the atmosphere, he said that he had ordered the resumption of nuclear testing in the laboratory and underground, thereby eliminating the danger of radiation fallout. The joint U.S.–British proposal, he said, would remain open until September 9.

It was on that date that Premier Khrushchev formally responded to the joint proposal. "Cessation of one kind of test only—in the atmosphere—" he said, "would be a disservice to the cause of peace." So, in the name of "peace" he rejected the proposal, which closely foreshadowed the Limited Test Ban Treaty signed by all three parties in 1963.

The tests continued. The Soviets completed a two-month series of atmospheric tests that culminated in the explosion of a fifty-eight-megaton bomb that our scientists told us would have had a yield of over a hundred megatons if the core of the weapon had been encased in uranium rather than lead. Hans Bethe, the Nobel Prize-winning physicist, said in a statement in September 1962 that "the kind of weapons the USSR tested showed that their laboratories had probably been working full speed during the whole moratorium on the assumption that the tests would at some time be resumed, and that it was likely that they started specific preparations in March 1961 when the Test Ban Conference reconvened in Geneva."[5]

The Joint Chiefs of Staff scoffed at the notion that nuclear testing constituted a health hazard. In a memorandum to the secretary of defense shortly after the inauguration, the Chiefs maintained that health hazards, if they existed at all, had assumed an importance far in excess of their significance in relation to the primary issue, the security of the United States. The Chiefs warned that the United States relied primarily on technological breakthroughs for its security and its ability to keep ahead

[5] Personal correspondence with Arthur Dean, April 25, 1979.

of the Soviet Union. Important developments, they said, could only be advanced through nuclear testing.

In my view, many of the concerns of the JCS were valid. While my earlier studies had confirmed the great hazards from prompt fallout from a multimegaton exchange of ground-burst weapons, the effects of high altitude tests in the atmosphere were quite different. The Soviets relied heavily on public fears of nuclear testing to maintain their superior knowledge of nuclear effects in the atmosphere. They fanned the flames of public opinion to pressure us into a one-sided test ban treaty. They had prepared for months for the resumption of their testing program in the fall of 1961, and every test, beginning with small explosions in the atmosphere to the final huge detonation, was carefully calculated to deliver the maximum amount of information, information that has eluded us to this day. Our knowledge of nuclear effects in the atmosphere is still mostly conjecture, while the Soviet Union has far more experimental information about such effects than we do. We have not been able to catch up with the knowledge gained by the Soviets during their atmospheric testing program from the fall of 1961 until July 1963, when they locked in their superiority with the Limited Test Ban Treaty.

It was not until April 25, 1962, that the United States began its first series of atmospheric tests subsequent to the voluntary moratorium on testing imposed by President Eisenhower in the fall of 1958. The series, designated Operation DOMINIC, included forty tests and did not exceed twenty megatons in total yield. On the other hand, the Soviet series the previous fall yielded almost ten times that amount.

The Soviet Union resumed its testing in the atmosphere in August. On August 27, the United States and Britain tabled two alternative draft treaties: one for a comprehensive test ban and the other for a limited test ban in the atmosphere, outer space, and underwater. We indicated our preference for the comprehensive treaty, which still required on-site inspections, although the number was left blank in the draft treaty text and subject to negotiation.

The Soviets promptly rejected both treaties and the conference recessed on September 7, not to resume until November 12. The Cuban missile crisis, to be discussed later, made it a fateful interlude.

Toward the end of April 1963, President Kennedy joined with Prime Minister Harold Macmillan in a letter to Premier Khrushchev offering to meet in private tripartite discussions to discuss the issues that remained to be settled in the negotiations, or, alternatively, "to send in due course very senior representatives who would be empowered to speak for us and talk in Moscow directly with you."

Khrushchev's response was full of recriminations, threats, and charges, yet he ended on a positive note: The USSR, he said, "would continue to seek agreement and would be prepared to receive your highly placed representatives." The Soviet premier continued publicly to testify to the duplicity and irascible nature of the Kennedy administration at every opportunity while signaling through private communications his willingness to reach agreement.

In June, the White House received a letter from Khrushchev agreeing to a meeting in Moscow and suggesting the date of July 15. The tone of the letter was hardly gracious, but another door had been opened in the negotiations.

The President named his favorite troubleshooter, Under Secretary of State Averell Harriman, to head the American mission to Moscow. Harriman was assisted by Carl Kaysen from the White House, Adrian Fisher from ACDA, John McNaughton from the Defense Department, and William Tyler from State. The British delegation was headed by Lord Hailsham (Quintin Hogg), minister of science.

Ten days of negotiations centered on a draft treaty similar to the one tabled by the West in August 1962 for a limited test ban covering all areas but underground and a short, less detailed draft treaty tabled by the Soviet Union.

All of this, of course, ignores the battles that raged within the executive branch leading up to our final position in Moscow, not to mention the harsh debates in Congress. The Joint Chiefs of Staff, when they realized that President Kennedy was indeed serious about concluding a test ban treaty with the Soviet Union, raised a storm of protest, as did the AEC laboratories.[6]

The principal objection raised by the Chiefs and scientists at Sandia and Livermore laboratories was the important gain the Soviets could make through clandestine testing under a comprehensive test ban, or even under a limited test ban.

General Maxwell Taylor warned that the Joint Chiefs might not be able to support a specific draft test ban treaty in hearings before the

[6]General Curtis LeMay, in testimony before the Senate Armed Services Committee on August 16, 1963, said that it wasn't until two days before Harriman left for Moscow that it dawned on him that we were really serious about trying to negotiate a treaty.

Senate Armed Services Committee scheduled for late June. He added that the Chiefs did not look forward to appearing before the Senate and revealing the disagreement within the executive office.

Secretary McNamara thought that a comprehensive test ban would freeze our current superiority over the Soviet Union. He also recognized that the Joint Chiefs did not agree with this conclusion and that it was important that we present a unified front to the Congress. He knew that the Chiefs relied on the AEC laboratories and the Air Force Technical Applications Center (AFTAC) for scientific data, and he believed that some issues had to be confronted and refuted on the record. Until this was done it would be difficult for the Chiefs to agree with his position.

I agreed with General Taylor's claim that the Soviets could conduct eighty percent of the testing they wanted to do without being detected. I believed, however, that while it was difficult to support a comprehensive test ban on national security grounds alone, it could be supported on foreign policy grounds.

Bob McNamara charged me with the responsibility for settling the dispute with the Joint Chiefs and the other agencies. There were some fifty technical issues that had to be resolved before we could face the Soviets and the Congress with a solid front.

Most of the issues involved our ability to detect clandestine testing by the Soviet Union, not only small detonations underground and in the atmosphere, but in such exotic places as the South Pacific just north of Antarctica, in outer space, and even behind the moon. There appeared to be endless speculation about where and under what circumstances it was possible to detect tests and where it was not.

I am not a scientist, and I did not see how I was going to bring about agreement among numerous bright and strong-minded scientific experts, each of whom was firmly convinced that he was right and others were wrong. Not only did the JCS have their scientific advisers but each of the agencies involved in the debate had its own.

Bob and I discussed the best way to bring about a consensus. We finally agreed on the following procedure:

1. That I identify each of the fifty principal issues on a 3 × 5 card.
2. That I take one card and one issue at a time, and call in all of the experts from all of the agencies on that particular set of issues, and let them all say what they had to say on that issue.
3. That at the end of each session I decide the probable truth on each issue as indicated by the balance of evidence presented, and so note it on the back of each card.

4. That after all of the issues had been discussed and I had made my decisions, I then circulate my tentative decisions on the fifty issues to all of the agencies involved. That I tell them that they had the right to réclama, but only if they had new evidence that had not been available at the original session. If they did, then they were entitled to another complete review of that issue.

After this review process had been completed, each agency was asked to develop its substantive position on the negotiations, subject to the condition that it not advance any argument of fact that did not correspond with the findings on those fifty cards.

To my delight, the procedure worked. There were only two or three issues on which there was serious disagreement with my judgment of what the probable facts were. I found that once there was general agreement on the facts, there was little difficulty in getting general agreement on the policy. Policy evolved ineluctably from the fifty decisions. Based on those decisions, a limited test ban could be adequately verified and made sense; a comprehensive one would not.

Some years later I checked on the current state of the art in this field and how it corresponded with the decisions I made in 1963. On some issues we were wide of the mark. By and large, we had been far more successful in our verification capabilities than had been originally anticipated. Our seismographs became far more sensitive than had been foreseen at that time. We were excessively conservative in the initial test ban treaty, but the decisions had to be made on the basis of the best information available at the time.

After this review the Joint Chiefs continued to voice their objections to a comprehensive test ban that would not be verifiable without on-site inspections. In addition, a private survey indicated that such a treaty would fail of ratification by ten votes in the Senate. The administration's position shifted to a limited test ban.

This shift was accelerated when Khrushchev, on July 2, in a speech in East Berlin indicated his willingness to consider a limited test ban agreement without mentioning the requirement for a moratorium on underground testing. At the same time, he proposed that the treaty be coupled with a nonaggression pact between NATO and the Warsaw Pact countries.

Averell Harriman was instructed to seek a test ban along the lines of the limited treaty tabled in August 1962. He was authorized to explore Soviet intentions concerning a nonaggression pact but not within the context of the test ban negotiations.

He was further instructed to inform the Kremlin that our primary interest was in concluding a verifiable comprehensive test ban agreement. This would entail, of course, on-site inspections, a condition the Soviets adamantly opposed. This subject was disposed of in the first day of meetings when Khrushchev left no doubt as to his negative position on the matter.

After ten days of negotiations, the Limited Test Ban Treaty, consistent with our review of the fifty factual issues, was concluded and initialed in Moscow on July 25, 1963.

12

The Little State Department

During the Eisenhower administration, as we have seen, United States nuclear strategy was dominated by the concept of massive retaliation to a Soviet attack here or abroad by attacking a combination of military, urban-industrial, and government control targets in one great spasm. This strategy was incorporated in NATO's strategic concept (MC 14/2, adopted by the North Atlantic Council in May 1957) which called for a massive nuclear response to any sustained Soviet attack, whether or not the Soviets used similar weapons.

General Lauris Norstad, supreme allied commander in Europe (SACEUR), introduced the idea of a "pause" before initiating a massive U.S. response to a Soviet attack. The "pause" concept was never fully defined, but the purpose was to recognize that failure of deterrence could be ambiguous, accidents do happen, and that we should have some alternative to an immediate and rapid escalation to general nuclear war.

When President Kennedy came into office in 1961 he had already made the decision that a stated policy of reliance upon the prompt use of nuclear weapons was not only dangerous but a liability to our foreign policy. He ordered a reappraisal of our defense requirements, including our strategic plans and the nuclear and nonnuclear capabilities of our forces.

I had long been an advocate of flexible military response and our task force report to the president-elect the previous November strongly supported this position. When Robert McNamara accepted the job of secretary of defense, he received a mandate from Mr. Kennedy to examine the broad spectrum of possible military responses to flare-ups around the globe.

Berlin Crisis, 1961

Events in Berlin came to a head even earlier than we had anticipated with the erection of the Berlin Wall in August 1961. Premier Khrushchev had demanded as early as 1958 that Allied occupation of Berlin end or he would sign a separate peace treaty with East Germany and turn over access control to the East German government. The West remained firm and the six-month deadline Khrushchev had imposed passed without event. In the fall of 1959, the Soviet premier softened his rhetoric somewhat at a meeting with President Eisenhower at the presidential retreat, Camp David, and agreed to a four-power summit meeting in May. A resolution on Berlin, of course, met the same fate as the test ban negotiations when Gary Powers was shot down over the Soviet Union in his U-2 aircraft nine days before the summit meeting was to begin.

The Western alliance was at odds. Chancellor Adenauer and President de Gaulle were not willing to negotiate anything that would alter the status quo,[1] while Macmillan and Eisenhower were prepared to negotiate with the Soviet Union over the status of Berlin. Without a unified position with our allies, hope for a negotiated settlement was futile.

Among our differences with the Soviet Union over this issue was the recognition of the East German state. A negotiated settlement on West Berlin, which would have guaranteed its freedom and the right of access, would have involved in one way or another the de facto recognition of the East German state. Bonn and Paris were not willing to pay that price.

I agreed with de Gaulle that we should stand firm on this issue and force Khrushchev to take the responsibility for his own actions rather than assent to his aggression through negotiations.

My position was that we should go to great lengths to avoid war, general or limited, over Berlin. But if we were to be routed out of a rightful position, we should not legitimize the act through a negotiated agreement. To come to terms on West Berlin under the circumstances would only mean concession and retreat as a result of an ultimatum, and that, in my dictionary, did not define a negotiation. If we had to accept defeat, we could at least avoid the casuist's error of calling the unavoida-

---

[1]The French president insisted that if we would just hold firm, the whole problem would go away. Chancellor Adenauer, on the other hand, was concerned that negotiations would lead to a permanent division of Germany.

ble ipso facto right. If we could not hold on in Berlin, we at least had to hold on to our sense of justice and honor.

By 1961 we were no closer to a resolution. In fact, as we learned at the Vienna summit, the problem was ripening into crisis proportions. The need for a capability to respond effectively to Soviet pressure with less than the full might of our nuclear arsenal was never more dramatically clear than during the Berlin crisis of 1961.

Our NATO contingency plans called for sending a small military force down the Autobahn to Berlin and, if resisted, moving to the nuclear response envisioned in MC 14/2.

As we were to learn again in the Cuban missile crisis, when you come face-to-face with the reality of a crisis situation, it takes on a different shade of meaning from when you are involved in contingency planning for a future possibility. The advantage of contingency planning, I believe, is that considerable time and effort go into establishing the parameters of thought and action. When the crisis occurs, minds are attuned to the possibilities for action; the precise action must still be decided. General Eisenhower once said, "Plans are worthless, but planning is everything," with his usual tendency toward oversimplification.

In March 1961, President Kennedy commissioned a study on Berlin from Dean Acheson. I worked with Dean on drafting the report. The final version was submitted to the President three weeks after Mr. Kennedy returned from Vienna.

Mr. Acheson advised the President that it was likely that the Kremlin would provoke a crisis on Berlin in 1961. He warned that a Communist takeover of the city in any form would profoundly reshape the alignment of power in Europe. Continental Europe, he said, would undoubtedly seek "adjustments." An American willingness to fight for Berlin, the former secretary of state said, was essential if the Soviet Union was not to dominate Europe and, by so doing, dominate Asia and Africa also.

Acheson recognized that we did not have the capability, against determined Soviet resistance, to open a ground corridor to Berlin or to maintain an airlift. We must convince the Russians, he said, that preventing the loss of Berlin was more important to the United States than gaining it by force was to the USSR, and that the United States should be prepared to run greater risks to achieve its purpose than the Soviets should be to attain theirs.

A battalion, he said, was too small to send up the Autobahn; an armored division, with another division in reserve, would present a formidable force and raise difficult questions for the other side. He recommended that preparations for a ground operation be lengthy, discernible, and ominous.

In line with this recommendation, he advised the President to publicly request from the Congress a large increase in the military budget, and that he do so as soon as the Soviet Union stepped up tensions on Berlin. He urged the President to declare a national emergency, which would allow him to mobilize the Reserves, extend terms of service, bring back dependents from Europe, and impress all concerned—particularly the Kremlin—with the gravity with which we regarded the situation.

While the President accepted many of the recommendations of Acheson's report, he chose to keep our military preparations to meet the crisis at a steady, low-key pace, with the exception of the public announcement of his July request for an additional 3.2 billion dollars from Congress for the military budget. He was advised by his Soviet experts that loud pronouncements at that stage of the game would compel the Soviets to respond with belligerent public statements and military measures of their own. He did not declare a national emergency, but he did request standby authority from Congress to call up the Reserves, and instigated other measures, including tripling draft calls.

At the same time, he decided to go forward with negotiations. The United States, he said, could not leave the initiative to the Kremlin. Moreover, his hope for a satisfactory diplomatic solution would fail if the Soviet Union presented a "peaceful" solution and we had none and refused to negotiate.

New ideas for our own solution were slow to come and the necessity of coordinating any new actions or diplomatic moves with our allies compounded the problem. As I mentioned earlier, while the British prime minister backed the President one hundred percent, Chancellor Adenauer and President de Gaulle staunchly opposed negotiations. At a NATO foreign ministers' meeting in Paris on August 4, which I attended with Dean Rusk, it became clear that our allies would back us in military action only in support of "vital Western interests" in Berlin. These were defined as the continued freedom and viability of West Berlin, free access to and from Berlin, and the continued presence of Allied forces in Berlin as a guarantee of those rights. Freedom of movement within the city was not included, nor was the meaning of "viability" made clear.

Access to West Berlin had been controlled by the Communists since 1951 and since then the number of crossing points had been progressively reduced. In July 1961, Walter Ulbricht, chairman of the East German Council of State, began to tighten severely the screws on the exodus. This heightened the anxiety among East Berliners, who feared the worst.

By the summer of 1961, 3.5 million East Germans and East Berliners had poured across the dividing line into West Berlin. This influx of refugees from the Communist sector was draining the lifeblood from the East German economy, still suffering from the devastation of World War II, in contrast to the booming prosperity of West Germany and West Berlin. The refugee camps in West Berlin were already packed and over-crowded when forty-seven thousand fled to West Berlin during the first twelve days of August, fearing the gates to the West would be closed permanently.

We had expected a confrontation over Berlin, but frankly we had not anticipated a serious move on the part of the Kremlin in August. Speculation had been that the crisis would gradually mount through late fall toward a possible blockage of our access to the city in early winter.

The President was in Hyannis Port on Cape Cod and I was in Maine vacationing with my family when on Sunday, August 13, I was torn from the cool breezes of Northeast Harbor and returned to the sultry heat of Washington. A wall of barbed wire and rubble had been thrown up overnight, dividing the city of Berlin, permanently separating, in many cases, parent from child, husband from wife, and friend from friend.

Upon my hurried return to Washington, I called together those on my staff in ISA and other officials in the Pentagon concerned with Berlin to discuss what now was to be done. Allied troops in Berlin had been put on alert but confined to barracks to prevent incidents. The wall, at this point, could easily be knocked down by a jeep or a truck, but it was not clear to anyone in the West whether the barrier was being constructed to keep the East Berliners in or to keep us out. Allied access to the divided city was our vital concern and on that score Mr. Khrushchev had assured us on several recent occasions that there would be no interference with allied traffic in and out of Berlin. Soviet Marshal Ivan Stepanovich Koniev had said much the same thing at a meeting of allied military commanders at Potsdam, in East Germany, on August 10, just two days before the barrier went up.

Washington had received no recommendation from our own people in Berlin or from the Federal Republic of Germany or from anyone else to knock down the barrier. I together with other Pentagon officials carefully considered whether we should recommend this action to the secretary of defense. Then, in the middle of our deliberations, we received intelligence information indicating that two East German divisions and elements of three Soviet divisions had been moved up surreptitiously to encircle Berlin. In our judgment, if the Soviets had been bluffing, they would have moved into position around Berlin openly in an effort to intimidate us. This covert deployment suggested they were planning a more serious trap, in which we would knock down the wall and they would respond by occupying all of Berlin. The situation could have escalated quickly into a general nuclear war for which neither we nor our allies were militarily or psychologically prepared. We decided against a recommendation to move against the wall.

It was not until Friday, six days after the wall went up during the predawn hours of the sleeping city, that President Kennedy reacted to the political problems caused by the crisis. As word reached Washington of the decline of morale in West Berlin, we became concerned that there would be a mass exodus from the city. West Berlin would be left an empty shell, no longer the bright beacon to those imprisoned behind the Iron Curtain. President Kennedy sent Vice President Lyndon Johnson to Berlin as his personal emissary, accompanied by retired General Lucius Clay, a hero to West Berliners since 1948, when he oversaw the airlift to the besieged city. Simultaneously, the President sent fifteen hundred American troops in armored trucks down the Autobahn through the East German checkpoints to Berlin. This small force certainly could not contain a Communist attack, but the President believed that West Berliners would benefit from this reminder of our commitment, and that the Soviet Union would understand that we intended to press our legal right of access to the stricken city.[2]

Throughout the remainder of the year, Washington continued to prepare for what appeared to be an inevitable confrontation with the Communists when and if Khrushchev actually signed a separate peace treaty with East Germany and access to the city of Berlin would be denied to allied powers.

I had expressed my concern to Bob McNamara as early as April regarding our military contingency plans in the event the Communists attempted to cut off our access to Berlin. He asked me to spearhead a review of those plans to assure that, if the contingency arose, the plans would provide for the use of substantial military force to reopen access to Berlin before resorting to nuclear weapons.

Toward the end of July, Bob McNamara and I flew to Europe to confer with General Lauris Norstad, who, at our request, had just set up a special Berlin planning unit known as "Live Oak" at SHAPE headquarters outside Paris. Norstad was from the old school of massive retaliation

---

[2]Eisenhower's comment when told about this the next day was that Khrushchev would merely chuckle over our small reinforcement of the Berlin garrison. Perhaps he did, but our troop convoy arrived in Berlin without Communist resistance.

and his preparations for the defense of NATO Europe, devised under the Eisenhower administration, strongly emphasized the early use of nuclear weapons in any major confrontation with the Soviets. This accorded with NATO strategic doctrine at the time, but was totally at odds with the flexible response approach that McNamara and I thought was preferable.

McNamara and I questioned General Norstad sharply about his plans to use nuclear weapons. In response he said he would not use them in the first instance. His preliminary plan was to open a salient as deep as it was wide at Magdeburg—a town on the Elbe River in East Germany about twenty-five miles from the dividing line between the zones—and hold that position as long as possible. He emphasized that he could not cross the Elbe no matter how many divisions he had. He saw no reason why our basic national security policy should be changed since we must, in the final analysis, rely on nuclear weapons. He pointed out that eighty-five percent of the targets threatening SACEUR were on that part of the SIOP[3] list scheduled for the recycle attack (the follow-on wave by bombers that had already executed one attack, returned to base, refueled, and were executing a second attack—hence, those targets would not be attacked for hours or even days after the initial assault). We must assure, he said, that those targets are taken out in time. Any change in NATO's strategic concept, he said, would send the wrong message to the Soviet Union and to our allies.

Our discussions on Berlin ended with Norstad finally agreeing with the general program developed thus far in Washington. He agreed, albeit reluctantly, that our military actions—a probe, for example—would have no credibility unless they were undertaken against a backdrop of increasing military strength.

McNamara and I toured our installations and corps headquarters along the central front and questioned the commanders about their nuclear targeting in support of NATO. Was there anything useful these theater nuclear weapons could do, we asked, independent of the SIOP? They were nonplussed by our question; it was obvious they had not considered that possibility. Our NATO allies thought only in terms of the psychology of deterrence, which posited that NATO would respond to a Soviet attack with the prompt, full use of our strategic arsenal. An initial nuclear exchange limited to targets in Europe was not what they had in mind. Our military in Europe shared this view. To my mind, this tension between our declaratory policy and the flexible response which

---

[3]Single Integrated Operational Plan, an integrated all-service plan for the use of all U.S. nuclear weapons.

McNamara and I thought should be our action policy posed a most serious problem.

In the meantime I had been asked to represent the Defense Department on an interdepartmental task force on Berlin, with Foy Kohler, assistant secretary for European affairs, representing State, and Major General David Gray representing the JCS. We met daily after the Berlin Wall went up and established a staff nucleus consisting of people from State, my office, and the JCS.

August ended with Khrushchev's announcement that he was resuming nuclear testing—another turn of the screw. By then I was hard at work with the Berlin task force and the military planning subcommittee of the Washington Ambassadorial Group.

The Washington Ambassadorial Group, made up of representatives from the United States, Great Britain, France, and, as of August 1961, West Germany, had been meeting off and on since 1958. In 1961 it was chaired by Foy Kohler. After the Berlin Wall was erected on August 13, I was asked to organize and chair a subgroup on military planning that would spell out what flexible military response might entail. These two groups, the quadripartite subgroup and the interdepartmental Berlin task force, were not in conflict, but represented different organizational facets of our approach to the same problem.

Our NATO allies had argued that the principal purpose—if not the only purpose—of military forces was deterrence, rather than their use, if deterrence failed, in the actual conduct of war. They claimed that since our deterrent in Europe was based on an expressed determination to meet any Soviet attack with nuclear weapons, a buildup of conventional forces would only weaken that deterrent by undermining its credibility. This argument was reinforced, of course, by the unspoken reluctance of European governments to incur the costs of a conventional military buildup (not to mention the opposition of their constituency), in spite of their mounting prosperity since the end of World War II.

In the Berlin task force, we soon discovered that our options were exceedingly few and not very attractive. There were advocates of another airlift, modeled on the one in 1948–49, in the event surface travel to Berlin became disrupted. But upon closer study, it became apparent that an airlift could be easily interdicted and therefore would not be reliable. Moreover, we believed it imperative to impress on the Soviets that we had a *right* to be in Berlin and that we would go to extreme lengths to protect our rights. It was essential that Khrushchev realized that maintaining our position in Berlin was more important to us than evicting us could possibly be to him.

The crisis atmosphere that had built steadily over the preceding months led to stepped-up planning both in Washington and at Norstad's headquarters in Paris. The outcome of our deliberations in the Berlin Task Force was the "Poodle Blanket" paper—which Mr. Kennedy approved on October 23, 1961.

The origins of the "Poodle Blanket" was the "Horse Blanket," an effort by my staff, notably Admiral John "Squidge" Lee, director of policy planning in ISA, and Lieutenant Colonel DeWitt Armstrong of his office. Under my direction, they made a list of all the actions the USSR might take against our access to Berlin; what actions the United States and the quadripartite powers (and, ultimately, NATO) might take; what response from the USSR might be stimulated by each Western action; and a general evaluation of the various courses of action.

The permutations expanded like possible successive moves in a game of chess and someone suggested that it would take a piece of paper the size of a horse blanket to write them all down. When it became clear that this effort was not only impossible but nonproductive—we reached a repetitive stage quite early—an abbreviated list of what we considered to be serious actions and reactions was dubbed the "Pony Blanket."

The Pony Blanket laid out the possibilities and the risks briefly and coherently, and later was used by me as chairman of the quadripartite military planning subgroup as my initial guidance. It helped the four governments to work toward a meeting of the minds on what we should do in a variety of contingencies. It went a long way toward persuading our NATO allies to accept the doctrine of flexible response that culminated belatedly in 1967 with the adoption of MC 14/3 as NATO's new strategic concept.[4]

In the Washington forum, the Pony Blanket became the subject of hot discussions. On October 10 it was the subject of a meeting at the White House, where minor adjustments were made in the order of operations. It was then approved by the President and issued as National Security Action Memorandum 109 and thereafter called the "Poodle Blanket."

The essence of NSAM 109 was its "preferred sequence," involving four phases of graduated response, ranging from diplomatic protest notes to all-out nuclear war. In case one response failed, we would go to the next and then the next, and so on. The first three phases involved pressure through diplomatic channels, economic embargoes, maritime harassment, and UN action, followed by or in combination with NATO

---

[4]My thanks to Squidge Lee for his excellent memory and for his willingness to share it with me. (Letter from Admiral John M. Lee, USN-ret., May 18, 1984.)

mobilization and then conventional military measures, such as sending armed convoy probes down the Autobahn, as we had discussed with Norstad. Phase four called for the escalating use of nuclear weapons.

At our meeting with the President, I suggested that since demonstrative or tactical use of nuclear weapons would greatly increase the temptation to the Soviets to initiate a strategic strike, it would be best for us, in moving toward the use of nuclear weapons, to consider most seriously the option of an initial strategic strike of our own. This, I believed, could assure us victory in at least a military sense in a series of nuclear exchanges, while we might well lose if we allowed the Soviets to strike first.

McNamara and I fully discussed the various possibilities of the fourth phase, but little was put on paper and his recollections of these discussions differ from mine. One of the alternatives we discussed was a worldwide maritime blockade of the Soviet Union. Subsequently, while secretary of the navy, I explored this option more fully through a rigorous assessment of our ability to conduct a war at sea without which it would be impossible to enforce a blockade.

As far as I know, phase four was never discussed in detail with anyone other than McNamara, General Curtis LeMay, who was by then chief of staff of the Air Force, and Major General Jerry Dentler Page, the SAC representative in the Pentagon. It is my recollection that McNamara and I discussed with General Page a possible plan for a strike against the three airfields on which Soviet heavy bombers were based and on their three forward staging bases in the Far North on the Arctic Ocean, where their surviving bombers would need to be refueled for an attack on the United States. We thought such an attack could be executed by two or three Polaris submarines, backed by a small number of heavy bombers. If successful it would eliminate a large percentage of Soviet forces capable of striking the United States. General LeMay thought we should strike with a much larger force. McNamara once told me that he had no recollection of this discussion.

All of the phases had serious problems, beginning with phase one. Certainly we didn't want to sacrifice large numbers of men by sending them down the Autobahn to certain defeat in a hopeless situation. This was why it was so important *at the outset* to relay to the Soviets our determination and will to maintain the freedom of West Berlin and our access to it.

In spite of our inferiority in military conventional forces in the European theater, we had, in my opinion, superior strategic capability behind us. Even though we very much wished to avoid a nuclear exchange, it was my opinion that the Soviet Union would wish to avoid one even more fervently. Even so, the risks were great and miscalculation on either side was our greatest potential enemy. To my mind, the Berlin crisis of 1961 was a time of greater danger of nuclear confrontation with the Soviet Union than the Cuban missile crisis of 1962.

Tensions eased somewhat in early November when Khrushchev announced he was postponing the December deadline for signing a treaty with East Germany, but harassment of Berliners and allied powers continued in the access corridors and confines of the city.

A little earlier I had asked Squidge Lee to prepare a "rationale" paper based on the Poodle Blanket paper (without spelling out the fourth phase). I wanted a definitive statement of U.S. strategy for the Berlin crisis—and recommended quadripartite and NATO strategy—that would encompass an evaluation of the situation, possible hostile actions, and appropriate Western response. With his customary efficiency, Squidge placed it on my desk within forty-eight hours. I took it in to McNamara, who thought it was a brilliant paper on strategy in the nuclear age, and within two hours it had received at least the preliminary approval of the President.

The rationale paper, of course, was extremely sensitive. In late November, McNamara and I presented the paper to the ministers of defense of West Germany and France, Franz Josef Strauss and Pierre Messmer, during their respective visits to Washington. We then flew to London in early December to present it to Harold Watkinson, the British minister of defense, during a visit at his home near Guildford. In each of these meetings, McNamara handed a copy of the document to the minister in absolute privacy, read it aloud, and then retrieved it. In other words, the minister would have the opportunity to consume the document through his ears and his eyes, but he was not permitted to retain a copy.

They all appeared to be impressed by the logic and clarity of the paper. They expressed concern, however, about the weakness of NATO's ground forces, particularly along the northern flank of the central front, and NATO's ability to hold the Soviets for a substantial period of time.

McNamara responded that the idea was to hold a Warsaw Bloc nonnuclear attack for a period sufficient to cause the Soviet Union to realize the gravity of the course upon which it had embarked and to call for negotiations. That was why, McNamara emphasized, the rationale paper visualized a NATO military buildup to a strength of thirty to forty divisions, plus additional aircraft and air defenses, in order to inflict greater conventional losses on the Warsaw Bloc than it could inflict on us.

Our British and German allies continued to insist that we must use tactical nuclear weapons at once, and the Russians must know we would use them. We can't fight a conventional war, they insisted, with any hope of success. McNamara agreed that was then true, but the objective of the NATO buildup was to change that situation.

Pierre Messmer, the French minister of defense, while supportive of the rationale strategy, obviously was under a different set of instructions. When he insisted, in a conversation with Dean Rusk during his visit to Washington, that we must accept the fact that France was already a nuclear power, Dean warned him that the USSR could incinerate France ten times over. Messmer conceded the point but said that de Gaulle reasoned that it mattered little if Russia could pulverize and irradiate France fifty times over, as long as France could return the compliment once.

These rash words were far from the real world. The French have never been in a position to do more than superficial nuclear damage to the Soviet Union as a whole.

Meanwhile, the search for a political solution continued. Before the opening of the disarmament conference in Geneva on March 14, 1962, Secretary Rusk and British Foreign Secretary Sir Alec Douglas-Home met with Soviet Foreign Minister Gromyko over the continuing problems surrounding allied access to Berlin. Rusk presented to Gromyko a new proposal, worked out by Henry Owen of the State Department's Policy Planning Staff and Martin Hillenbrand of the Berlin task force.

Rusk held out the prospect of an agreement that would prevent the spread of nuclear weapons, secure a nonaggression pact between NATO and the Warsaw Pact, establish several committees to be composed of equal numbers of East and West Germans to handle "technical" contacts between the two Germanys, establish an international access authority (with a seat for East Germany) to supervise travel between West Berlin and West Germany, and organize a permanent conference of deputies of the foreign ministers of the four powers (United States, Great Britain, France, and the USSR) to meet regularly on the Berlin situation. Gromyko appeared to be interested and the meetings continued over the next two months.

Word of this proposal leaked to the press in Bonn even before it was presented in detail to the Russians. Officials in Bonn denied that they were responsible for the leak, but it was clear that Chancellor Adenauer, who had been informed earlier of our intentions, was unhappy with our proposal. He believed that the proposal granted international recognition to East Germany by seating it next to West Germany on the international access authority and reinforced the division of Germany.

Washington held Bonn responsible for the leak to the press and an angry exchange took place through the press and diplomatic channels. It was in this atmosphere that I arrived in Hamburg on April 11, 1962, to address the Amerika-Gesellschaft and to give a talk in German at the University of Hamburg. The chairman of the Amerika-Gesellschaft was my old friend and skiing companion from the 1940s, Eric Warburg. Eric had returned to Hamburg after the war and had become a prominent banker.

Chancellor Adenauer saw a copy of my speech and invited me to visit him in Bonn after I left Hamburg. At our meeting, he was sympathetic to the content of my speech, which dealt with flexible response for NATO, but, as I remember it, he was displeased with some meeting Foy Kohler had had in Geneva with Gromyko. The chancellor threatened (and not for the first time) to "play the French card"[5] rather than continue to take a backseat in NATO.

Secretary Rusk continued his discussions with Gromyko but they arrived at an impasse over allied troops in West Berlin. Gromyko demanded that they be withdrawn, thus ending occupation and making Berlin a "free city." Rusk responded that the allied garrison was not negotiable. With neither side budging on the issue, the talks ended.

In truth, it was not until the finale of the Cuban missile crisis that the threat to West Berlin diminished. Until then, Khrushchev continued to test our will and determination through threats and harassment in every way he could without forcing a major response from us. I believe the placing of the missiles in Cuba was another step to test our will to resist intense Soviet pressure. I'm not sure we persuaded the Soviets of our seriousness even in that instance. Communist incursion in other areas—Southeast Asia, Africa, and now Central and Latin America—continued with little, if any, abatement.

As an epilogue to the events of the Berlin crisis, I might add that President Kennedy asked me, after the Cuban missile crisis, to think about a long-term solution to Berlin. He said that in Cuba we clearly had military conventional superiority, while the reverse was true in Berlin. He did not wish ever to have a crisis over Berlin similar to the Cuban missile crisis. What could we do, he asked me, to prevent this from happening?

[5]A reference to the French determination to look to its own defense, including an independent nuclear force, because the United States could not be relied upon to continue to carry the cost of European defense. Chancellor Adenauer had referred to this earlier in a meeting in November 1960 with Eisenhower's secretary of the treasury Robert B. Anderson over the balance of payments problem.

I realized this would call for radical steps. I recall that as I studied a map of East Germany, it occurred to me that we might try to make a trade with the Soviet Union. We would agree to recognize the independent state of East Germany if, in return, East Germany would release to West Germany an area along the access routes, plus a little extra, to make a triangle of land, the apex of which would go straight to Berlin. Western access to Berlin then would be secure and West Berlin would not be subject to the constant threat of blockade.

Tommy Thompson adamantly opposed this suggestion as nonnegotiable, as did the Bureau of European Affairs in the State Department. The President did not pursue the idea and no circumstances ever arose thereafter in which I thought such a proposal justified active pursuit.

A New Strategy for NATO

We began to seek allied acceptance of a new NATO strategy, based on the rationale paper, in January 1962, using the quadripartite Military Planning Subcommittee as the initial forum. Protracted discussions followed, sometimes interrupted for technical reasons. These talks covered the balance of forces and resulting restraints as well as the four-phase concept. An agreed quadripartite paper finally was submitted to the North Atlantic Council (NAC) in September. The paper, however, did not elaborate on what the fourth level of confrontation would entail.

Our allies favored a policy of controlled, limited use of nuclear weapons at an early stage. The U.S. position was that any use of nuclear weapons would introduce a new spectrum of violence that could readily lead to general nuclear war. I attempted on several occasions to impress on our allies the importance of a NATO conventional buildup. In Hamburg, for example, when I spoke before the Amerika-Gesellschaft in April, I told my audience that the objective would be to prevent the Soviets from isolating an area like Hamburg in a quick forward thrust with the troops they kept in East Germany. If the Soviets had to mobilize twenty divisions or more (and all that that would entail) in order to give them confidence that they could succeed in such a venture, they still would have been faced with a major fight and the clear danger that their aggression would bring on a nuclear response if they persisted. This being so, I reasoned, they would be less apt to initiate the action in the first place.

Deterrence, I repeated over and over to my audience, is a direct function of being ready and able to fight. Without an ability to meet a Soviet nonnuclear offensive along the central NATO front with a firmly held forward strategy, our only option for military action would be an immediate nuclear response. The difficulty was that it simply was not credible, particularly to the Soviets, that we or anyone else would respond to a given small step with the immediate use of nuclear weapons.

A representative of one of our allies, and a friend of many years, pointed out to me the distinction between accepting the merits of a military strategy and his country's capacity or willingness to meet the cost of carrying out that strategy. His candor was appreciated, and I believe he spoke for most of our NATO friends. Their arguments, however, usually rested on more dubious grounds; that is, the credibility of our nuclear deterrent would be diminished by the existence of large standing conventional forces.

We made every effort to assure our allies that in case of a massive conventional attack by the Soviet Union which would put any significant portion of NATO territory in danger of being overrun, the West would have to respond with all available means. This would include the use of nuclear weapons—a pledge that was meant then as it is today.

The unshakable conviction of our allies that the mere existence of nuclear weapons, regardless of what you could do with them in war, represented a shield against any and all Soviet aggression was incomprehensible to me and to McNamara. His concern was to ensure that the Soviets remained uncertain of military success if they attacked, and that we have alternatives to immediate nuclear confrontation. McNamara and I were in firm agreement on this score. At a NATO ministerial meeting in Athens in May 1962, he delivered an hour-long detailed exposition on American thought on major strategic problems. He told the assembled ministers that

> . . . if the deterrent should fail . . . despite our nuclear strength, all of us would suffer deeply in the event of major nuclear war.
>
> We accept our share of this responsibility within the Alliance. And we believe that the combination of our nuclear strength and a strategy of controlled response gives us some hope of minimizing damage in the event that we have to fulfill our pledge. But I must point out that we do not regard this as a desirable prospect, nor do we believe that the Alliance should depend solely on our nuclear power to deter actions not involving a massive commitment of . . . hostile force. Surely an Alliance with the wealth, talent, and

experience that we possess can find a better way than extreme reliance on nuclear weapons to meet our common threat.

His audience had listened in rapt attention during the course of his speech. It stirred a good deal of debate and resentment in Western capitals, but it did nothing to change the force structure in NATO. The defense budgets of most of our allies continued to decrease as percentages of gross national product as their prosperity increased.

Later that summer, a revaluation of Soviet conventional forces brought an additional reason to support a NATO conventional buildup. To our surprise our studies indicated that NATO and the Warsaw Pact had approximate equality in numbers of troops on the ground. In other words, Soviet forces appeared to represent a threat sufficiently modest to permit an extended conventional allied defense if NATO's deficiencies in weapons, modernization, and munitions were corrected.

Our NATO allies flatly expressed their concern that, in the event of a showdown, we would not risk the destruction of our homeland with a nuclear strike on the Soviet Union if called upon to do so. For this stated reason (but basically because of the added prestige of being nuclear powers), Britain and France were developing their own independent nuclear deterrent and the Federal Republic of Germany (FRG) was watching enviously from the sidelines. We were concerned, as were its European neighbors, that the FRG might decide to develop its own independent nuclear force, unless we made it clear that West Germany was regarded by other members of the alliance as a valued and indispensable member.

McNamara, in his Athens speech, tried to discourage our NATO allies from picking up the nuclear sword, telling them that their small nuclear deterrent offered no real threat to the Soviet Union, except to its cities, thereby inviting a preemptive strike on themselves in the event of a serious confrontation. Only a united nuclear force with coordinated targets represented a strong deterrent to hostile action initiated by the Soviet Union.

We had tried to lure Britain and France away with the idea of a multilateral nuclear force, or MLF, but France had shown no interest and only intermittent interest in a tripartite force composed of those countries already in possession of a nuclear capability (the United States, Britain, and France). Even then, de Gaulle had insisted that France would never allow foreigners to be in charge of weapons on its soil, which included, of course, the nuclear warheads to go with them. London was only lukewarm to the idea of MLF, while Bonn embraced the concept wholeheartedly with the thought that participation would give them equal status within the alliance and tie down the American nuclear commitment to NATO.

Washington was of two minds as to the value of a multilateral nuclear force, and President Kennedy was only lukewarm in his endorsement. He did not allow those in the State Department who were almost fanatical supporters of the concept to stand in the way of more practical objectives, such as enticing President de Gaulle into a strong French commitment to NATO.

In the spring of 1962, the President authorized me to explore with French General Gaston Lauvaud possible access to certain U.S. technologies for their nuclear program if we could arrive at an understanding in which the French would agree to certain commitments to NATO. It seemed to me that since the French were determined to have their own nuclear program, whether we helped them or not, it was time to give them assistance if, in return, they would commit themselves to NATO in a meaningful way.

General Lauvaud and I achieved an agreed minute, but it was rejected by President de Gaulle, perhaps because Mr. Kennedy, in an ill-timed press conference, mentioned that he thought it would be inimical to the interests of the allies for us to assist the French in developing an independent nuclear capability.

There were those in the State Department who opposed my negotiations with General Lauvaud because they suspected that France, after it had achieved a national nuclear capability with our help, would renege on its obligations to NATO. Moreover, they argued that this approach would undermine the prospects for the multilateral force and European unification. It was from these negotiations with General Lauvaud that a Greek chorus developed in support of the multilateral nuclear force.

The President was not opposed to the concept of a multilateral force, but he was always leery of any project that engendered fanaticism. He did not easily tolerate opposition to what he believed needed to be done, as in the case when he authorized my negotiations with General Lauvaud. As President, he was a firm believer in the lonely office he held, and that, for him, the final decision was his and his alone.

He agreed, however, to explore the feasibility of a multilateral nuclear force with our allies. In the summer of 1962, the Navy and my staff in ISA completed detailed studies for a multilateral force that called for the creation of twenty-five surface vessels armed with Polaris missiles with a range of 2,500 miles. The ships were to be manned with international crews, although the United States would maintain the right to veto a decision to launch an attack. The costs of $500–700 million a year over the next decade were to be shared by the participants.

McNamara and I opposed the concept of the MLF because of—among other considerations—the requirements for a unified strategic arsenal for a controlled and flexible counterforce strategy. We believed that when the Europeans fully considered the details of the plan and the costs involved, they would be adverse to the United States having a veto over the use of the force. I insisted that we keep our finger firmly on the safety catch. I thought it improvident for the United States to allow a lesser ally to get itself and us into a nuclear war. McNamara backed me in that view.

The issue was discussed in an NSC meeting in early 1963; the President decided it by straddling it. He gave Livingston Merchant, an experienced career diplomat, and Gerard C. Smith, then a consultant with the State Department, the task of examining with our NATO allies the practical and political feasibility of a multilateral nuclear force based on our Pentagon studies. He gave me the task of exploring an alternate approach that I had proposed, which was to bring our NATO allies more fully into our planning for the nuclear defense of NATO.

Gerard Smith and Livingston Merchant returned to Washington empty-handed; only Adenauer was still enthusiastic about the MLF and even he had reservations. President Kennedy still considered the MLF an exploratory plan to appease the clamor from our allies to share in our strategic nuclear planning. He was not yet ready to throw his weight behind the plan for several reasons, not the least of which was the ongoing test ban negotiations. The Soviet Union had complained that the multilateral force would violate the nonproliferation concerns that were an important element of the proposed treaty. Eventually President Johnson killed the whole concept of MLF in 1965.

While McNamara and I were convinced that MLF was not the answer, we wanted to lift the veil of secrecy from our strategic planning for our allies if only to give them some insight behind the new flexible and controlled counterforce doctrine. McNamara's Athens speech in May 1962 on the "no-cities" approach (referred to later) had been a first attempt to share our strategic planning with our NATO allies. Their hostile reaction to this plan, which appeared in part to stem from resentment over the fact that we had failed to consult with them over a fundamental change in our policy, came as a surprise to McNamara. We took every opportunity thereafter to speak with candor and openness to our allies.

Following President Kennedy's approval of my proposal for an alternate to MLF, I explored with our allies the formation of a high-level committee within NATO that would be an effective forum for political consultation on our nuclear planning. While I and others worked diligently with our counterparts in NATO to gain allied consensus, our efforts did not fully bear fruit until December 1966, when the Nuclear Planning Group (NPG) was formed. By that time I had been secretary of the navy for over three years and was out of the mainstream of nuclear planning. The NPG was composed of the defense ministers of Great Britain, West Germany, Italy, and the United States (France had withdrawn from NATO's military function by then) and three other representatives from the smaller NATO countries on a rotating basis.

Ever since April 1967, the NPG has met at the ministerial level twice a year on a wide range of subjects from ballistic missile defense in Europe to consultations on arms control. It has remained an effective forum for candid consultations with our allies and played a major role in convincing our NATO partners to accept the doctrine of flexible response.

13

The Cuban Missile Crisis

On October 11, 1962, McNamara and I attended the meeting held each Thursday with the Chiefs in the JCS Tank. As usual, the meeting began with an intelligence briefing. On that day a young Navy commander gave us information from various sources on Soviet shipping moving toward Cuba. He also informed us of detailed reports from the French, who still had an embassy in Havana, that they had seen trucks loaded with over-sized objects that looked like missiles covered with tarpaulins rolling through the streets of the city in the dead of night. I found his evidence persuasive not only that it was possible, but that it was probable, that Soviet offensive nuclear missiles were already in Cuba.

Over the weekend the Bohlens visited us at our farm in Maryland. I told Chip that I was convinced the Soviet missiles were in Cuba. He was dubious; almost everyone in the State Department and the CIA shared his view. They believed the Soviet leaders were too conservative to risk such a daring move. The notable exception was John McCone, head of the CIA, who was abroad, but continued to receive daily summaries of raw intelligence, including the information on which we had been briefed in the JCS Tank on Thursday. McCone had come to the same conclusion from that information as had I.

Since July our reconnaissance planes had reported an increase in shipping traffic from Soviet ports to Mariel in Cuba. What turned out to be a massive sealift immediately came under suspicion—in spite of efforts by Soviet Ambassador Anatoly Dobrynin and others from the Soviet embassy in Washington to assure government officials on several occasions that any weapons placed on Cuban soil would be defensive in nature. As late as October 18, Soviet Foreign Minister Andrei Gromyko personally assured President Kennedy, who managed to hide his outrage, that only defensive weapons were being furnished the Cubans.

Many Washington officials were lulled by Khrushchev's pledge after the Bay of Pigs that while the Soviet Union would resist any attack on

Cuba from the United States, he had no intention of establishing bases on the island. This was generally accepted here since the Soviet Union had not been known to place offensive nuclear missiles outside its national boundaries, even in Warsaw Pact countries. Not even the confirmation in late August that SAMs (surface-to-air missiles) had been emplaced in Cuba along with some twenty-two thousand Soviet personnel disturbed Washington's complacency.[1] It was assumed the SAMs were brought in to improve coastal and air defenses and the Russian personnel were technicians.

By late August the press had picked up the scent and members of Congress began to stir restlessly. Senator Kenneth B. Keating charged that the Soviet personnel were uniformed troops in spite of the fact that our intelligence indicated they were not uniformed and appeared to be technicians. On October 10 he maintained that it had been confirmed to him by "official sources" that bases for six intermediate-range ballistic missiles (IRBMs) were being constructed in Cuba. How Senator Keating could maintain that his information was verified by "official sources" remains a mystery to this day since no one in the intelligence community was able to verify the existence of the missile bases until October 14.

When Dean Rusk asked me to join him on the terrace outside the secretary's dining room on Monday evening, October 15, and told me that we now had incontrovertible evidence that offensive missiles did indeed exist on the island of Cuba, I was not surprised.

The occasion was a dinner for the German foreign minister, Gerhard Schroeder. I had become involved in a discussion with Hans-Albert Reinkemeyer about my concern that the Russians, frustrated in their threat to Berlin, might amplify it with a threat from Cuba. Reinkemeyer, a Soviet and Far Eastern expert nominally in the German Foreign Office but actually part of their intelligence service, argued that the danger was past; the Soviets no longer represented a threat to Berlin because they recognized that the risk of war was too great. My concern—which I mentioned to Reinkemeyer—was that the Soviets might be constructing the basis for a two-edged strategy. They might be currently lying low with respect to Berlin while they created a crisis in Cuba with the intent of trading one off against the other in some unforeseeable way. Rusk and Schroeder, who were sitting across the table from us, joined in the conversation.

---

[1]The large number of Soviet personnel was not known until the crisis was well under way. In August, the figure was thought to be 3,500. This figure, we now know, more closely approached 40,000 Soviet troops.

I noticed that Dean left the table, only to return in a few minutes—his bland face only slightly perturbed—and resume the conversation. Ten minutes later we arose from the table and Dean asked me to accompany him to the terrace outside the dining room. There, overlooking the glittering city and the dark calm of the Potomac, he told me that Roger Hilsman, director of the State Department's Bureau of Intelligence and Research, had told him that photographs taken by a recently authorized U-2 flight demonstrated beyond a doubt the presence of Soviet offensive missiles in Cuba.

We were both aware that the Pentagon had two contingency plans in the event that offensive missiles were placed on Cuba by the Soviet Union: one, an air strike on Cuba to eliminate the missiles, and two, an invasion preceded by an air strike. In addition a decision had been made earlier that month to alert Admiral Robert Lee Dennison, commander in chief of the Atlantic Fleet, to be prepared to implement a blockade of Cuba to prevent the missiles being replaced after they had been destroyed.

Now we were faced not with a contingency but with a reality. We knew that our allies, Britain in particular, did not share our view of the importance of Cuba and the political as well as military threat that Soviet missiles ninety miles off our shores represented to us. Dean and I agreed that we must move with deliberation and fully reconsider our contingency plans in the face of our confirmed suspicions.

McGeorge Bundy was immediately informed. He made the decision not to disturb the President's badly needed sleep and to wait until the following morning to break the news to the chief executive. Bundy also asked that no one change travel plans or cancel engagements that could alert anyone beyond a small circle of advisers of an impending crisis. It was important that our knowledge of the presence of the Soviet missiles be limited to as few people as possible until the President decided upon a specific course of action.

I had scheduled a trip to Knoxville the next day to address a meeting of the U.S. Civil Defense Council and I decided not to cancel that commitment. Therefore I was not present at the initial meetings with the President on October 16.

On the plane to Knoxville I jotted down some notes in an effort to clarify my mind on the central issues involved in the crisis that faced us. It seemed to me that one should start by trying to figure out how the Soviets would look at the situation. What were their objectives—not just what single objective did they have in mind, but the spectrum of objectives that might be behind their actions in Cuba? What might be their maximum objective, what might be their minimum objective, and what assets could they bring to bear to support their plan? Having sorted out what the Soviets might be up to, we could then better sort out what we should and could do about it, what our maximum and minimum objectives should be, and how we should relate means to those ends.

I decided that the Kremlin's preferred scenario was to see us put the blame for the missiles on the Cubans and for us to take action against Cuba, not the Soviet Union. The Soviet Union—in the eyes of the world—then would appear to be protecting an oppressed and threatened little country. The result could be that their support of Castro would not only succeed, but that the missiles would remain and they would have established a base for themselves in the Caribbean. This would balance in large part the disadvantages they felt themselves under because of the proximity of NATO forces—including U.S. forward-based forces—to their borders and our obvious strategic nuclear superiority at that time.

The corollary of this logic chain was that it would be a mistake to blame Castro for the presence of the missiles and to take action against Cuba. It would be far better to accuse Khrushchev and not allow him to assume the role of innocent friend and protector of the small and weak.

Max Taylor brought me up to date at a dinner party the evening I returned from Knoxville. He told me that the President had determined that the missiles must be removed from Cuban soil. The question, of course, was how?

In looking over the transcript recently of the two meetings on Tuesday the sixteenth (made available by the Kennedy Library in 1983), I was struck by the fact that military action was considered almost inevitable by almost all the participants, including the President and his brother. After an intelligence briefing, Dean Rusk had opened the meeting with a presentation of the options available to us. He had ended his presentation with the recommendation that we isolate Cuba by calling on the free world to halt all trade with that nation without, for the moment, invoking military action. But it wasn't until that evening, when McNamara laid out three possible courses of action, one of which was a declaration of open surveillance and immediate blockade against offensive weapons entering Cuba, that that alternative was proposed as our first response and not as the aftermath of military action involving an air strike, surgical or otherwise.

The President's advisers were highly concerned that, in response to any military action we might take, the Soviet Union would strike a retaliatory blow in any of a number of vulnerable areas important to us around the globe. Berlin was considered particularly vulnerable, as were the Jupiter missiles in Turkey—an early topic of discussion.

I joined the small group of the President's chosen advisers on this issue, the Executive Committee of the National Security Council, which became known as the "ExComm," Wednesday morning at the State Department. Among those who attended the meetings on a regular basis during those thirteen days were Robert McNamara, Roswell Gilpatric, and I from OSD, Maxwell Taylor, chairman of the Joint Chiefs of Staff, Dean Rusk, secretary of state, George Ball and U. Alexis Johnson, under secretary and deputy under secretary of state, respectively, Douglas Dillon, secretary of the treasury, John McCone, director of Central Intelligence, Robert Kennedy, the attorney general, McGeorge Bundy, national security adviser to the President, and Theodore Sorensen, presidential adviser. Dean Acheson was a frequent participant with General Marshall Carter, deputy director of Central Intelligence, and Sidney Graybeal of that agency briefing our group frequently with the latest intelligence from our reconnaissance flights over Cuba. Others joined us from time to time with many involved on the periphery, if not in our daily meetings. It was extraordinary that there was no leak.[2]

I was the only person authorized, or so I believed at the time, to keep notes on the meetings. The President recognized that the timeliness of military preparations was of the essence and that ISA was the natural focal point of liaison with the Joint Staff serving the Joint Chiefs of Staff. After each meeting I would debrief a small group in ISA consisting of Elmo "Bud" Zumwalt, Henry Rowen, John Vogt, and John McNaughton, who would then, in turn, work with members of the Joint Staff who would keep the services informed.

I adopted the practice of assigning different analytical tasks to each of these advisers. Frequently they had to respond within a few hours or less, timed to give me their written analyses to review, to revise, and to distribute and use at the next ExComm meeting. This practice frequently had the result that my views were the ones which the ExComm members used as the starting point for their discussions.

---

[2] *The New York Times* did get wind that a crisis was brewing with the Soviets over Cuba. They were tempted to publish the story, but James "Scotty" Reston, who was then my next-door neighbor, noticed that I had been leaving the house at dawn every morning for a week and rarely returned before midnight. He told the publisher that I was primarily involved with Europe and he thought the crisis was over Berlin. *The Times* decided not to publish the story. I learned of this only later, of course, when Scotty told me that he inadvertently had killed a scoop to his newspaper.

I was surprised to learn recently that the ExComm meetings were taped, although the transcripts, except for the first two meetings and the meetings on October 27, have not yet been released. I still have my notes on the meetings, but with each passing year they become more indecipherable. In a recent attempt to determine the participants of a conversation I found myself struggling to identify "A.J." After determining that the speaker was not Alexis Johnson, I realized that "A.J." was "Attorney General." Cryptic notes together with lousy spelling do not make an infallible record. Nevertheless, I have found my notes invaluable in putting together my recollections of the crisis.

On Wednesday the seventeenth the discussions continued with the added concern that we did not know what authority Soviet commanders in Cuba might have in the event of loss of communication with Moscow, or whether indeed there were nuclear warheads available for the missiles on the island. There was no evidence to indicate storage facilities for the warheads existed, although this in itself did not rule out the possibility.

We met in George Ball's conference room in the State Department and after a brief presentation by George, the discussion centered on why Khrushchev had decided on this dangerous course of action. Chip Bohlen, as reported in his memoirs, said it was arrogant, bellicose, daring, and dangerous (harebrained, the Soviet Central Committee said in dismissing Khrushchev in 1964). Bohlen said that Khrushchev believed that the threat would force the United States to agree to a settlement on Soviet terms of Berlin and the German question. He also believed that the Soviet premier calculated that this would answer the Chinese charge that he had abandoned the revolution. After the U.S. fiasco of the Bay of Pigs and his experience with Kennedy at Vienna, Khrushchev was confident that the American President could be bullied into accepting the missiles on our borders, where they would be a permanent basis for blackmail.

Khrushchev miscalculated. Whatever his failings may have been, John Kennedy did not lack courage in the face of imminent danger. Kennedy, of course, was supported at the time by the vastly superior U.S. conventional military capabilities around Cuba as well as by a superior strategic nuclear position. He also had an able group of men assisting him. But without that peculiar quality of courage that enabled him to call Khrushchev's bluff, subsequent history could have been quite different.

Tommy Thompson, for whom the President had the greatest respect, was the first to suggest that the Soviets might be trying to create a bargaining position to get our Jupiter missiles out of Turkey. This was a recurring theme throughout the long and difficult thirteen days. Most of us, myself included, believed that this was something to which we should not agree. Our NATO partners—Turkey, in particular—would be outraged at our weakness in the face of an immediate threat to our own security. How could they then count on our staunch support in the event of a threat to their security?

The Jupiter missiles were obsolete and vulnerable. Their only value lay in the fact that they presented the Russians with a targeting problem. In the event of serious danger of war, of course, these missiles could invite attack on their locations. But the Turkish government clung to them as a link coupling their security to U.S. nuclear forces and thus constituting a major deterrent against a Soviet attack on them. We had approached the Turks on several occasions in an effort to convince them that the missiles should not be deployed, but without success.[3] The President, as recently as late August 1962, had asked the Department of Defense to undertake a study on what action could be taken to get the Jupiter missiles out of Turkey.

The discussion then switched to our military alternatives, ranging from a single surgical strike at the Soviet missile sites in Cuba to an invasion of the island to thus rid ourselves of the Castro government once and for all. McNamara maintained that the missiles did not constitute a great enough military threat to justify military action to remove them. I argued that because of the military and political impact of the Soviet action on our posture a blockade plus surveillance was the minimum response we should consider.

The next morning—the eighteenth—the meetings continued at the White House with the President in attendance. With his powerful presence and dynamic energy, Robert McNamara tended to dominate any group in which he participated, and the ExComm was no exception. But in my view, in this instance, he put too much emphasis on the political considerations, which he understood less well than some of the others, and too little on the military issues. Or, to put it more succinctly, he put an excessively tactical slant on the military considerations without taking sufficiently into account the deep strategic considerations.

McNamara made the statement at that meeting on the eighteenth that the presence of the missiles did not change the strategic military balance. Our overwhelming nuclear superiority, he said, would deter the Soviet Union from actually using nuclear weapons. He had maintained from the beginning of the crisis that the military significance of the missiles was not unmanageable and could be offset without having to remove the

---

[3]The Italians, on the other hand, had told us earlier that they had no objection to the removal of the Jupiter missiles from their soil.

missiles. He agreed with the President, however, that the political consequences, both international and domestic, of allowing the missiles to
remain on Cuba dictated their removal. He did recognize the importance
of getting the missiles removed from Cuba before they became operational and before warheads were available, but I believe his concern was
due to fear of an irrational act by the Soviets, not a calculated move on
their part.

I disagreed with McNamara on his military analysis. I thought that
Soviet MR/IRBMs in Cuba could materially hasten the loss of our nuclear superiority, a loss we could ill afford because of our relative weakness in conventional capabilities in much of the world.

My disagreement with Bob McNamara over the military importance
of the Soviet missiles in Cuba deserves further explanation.

In the late fifties, we in the United States believed that the Soviets had
made the decision to deploy a large number of ICBMs and that we would
be unable to catch up with them for some time; hence the concern about
the so-called missile gap. Instead, the Soviets built over five hundred
medium- and intermediate-range ballistic missiles (MR/IRBMs), which
they deployed on their own territory.

My thesis was that behind this decision to deploy MR/IRBMs rather
than ICBMs (and I was aware they were having technical problems with
the design of their intercontinental ballistic missiles) was the desire of the
Kremlin to consolidate its holdings around the periphery of the Soviet
Union so that the Soviet Union could dominate the Eurasian landmass.
From there subsequent domination of Africa and Latin America through
client-states and direct coercion would be facilitated. As they worked
toward a more general nuclear superiority and access to the seas with
burgeoning naval forces, the oceans would fall under their control. The
free world would shrink slowly to within the boundaries of the United
States and we, in time, would be isolated. In a unipolar world, the United
States would be forced to yield to Soviet influence. This, I believed, was
the Kremlin's grand design to achieve—patiently, over as much time as
might be necessary—world domination without a nuclear shot being
fired.

To overcome U.S. strategic superiority in 1962—which threatened to
thwart their purposes—as quickly and as cheaply as possible, the Kremlin
made the decision to deploy MR/IRBMs on the island of Cuba, ninety
miles off our shores. We estimated that the Soviets planned an original
deployment of 40 launchers with 48 MRBMs (SS-4s with a range of 1,020
nautical miles), and 32 IRBMs (SS-5s with a range of 2,200 nautical miles).
This number of missiles would have provided one reload for each of the

40 launchers. As it turned out, the Soviets managed to ship only 42 MRBMs and no IRBMs before the shipments were terminated by our naval quarantine.

Had they completed their deployments both in Europe and in Cuba, the Soviet Union would have been able to target not only our European- and North African-based bombers, but most of our Strategic Air Command (SAC) bases here in the United States as well as many of our soft-based ICBMs under the penetration arc of their Cuba-based nuclear weapons. With the short flight-time of the Cuban missiles and the fact that we had no ballistic missile early warning system (BMEWS) or other early warning radar on our southern approaches, we would be in a difficult situation.

With the reliability and the accuracy of the Cuban missiles (1 to 1.5 n.m. CEP—considered good in 1962) and a warhead yield up to three megatons for MRBMs and up to five megatons for IRBMs, they represented a serious threat to our strategic deterrent capability.[4]

Raymond Garthoff, who was then with the State Department's Bureau of Political/Military Affairs, estimated in his report to the ExComm that, with the Cuban missiles, the number of surviving U.S. weapons after a Soviet surprise attack would be decreased by an additional thirty percent, and only fifteen percent of our preattack force would remain. He estimated that if unimpeded the Soviets could deploy in Cuba a force large enough to threaten the "entire strategic balance of power."[5]

McNamara, at that meeting on the eighteenth, recommended that we assume there were no nuclear warheads in Cuba at that time. Thinking aloud, he said that a limited air strike probably would be inconclusive and that the cost would not be worth the risk. A full invasion, he continued, should only be attempted if we were certain we were not operating against the threat of weapons armed with nuclear warheads. From those thoughts, he deduced that an intermediate level of attack would be a step beyond and more appropriate than a surgical strike on the missile sites. But he was concerned that we would not be able to stop there.

He recommended that we maintain our options by letting our first action be a naval blockade with the contraband list limiting only offensive

[4]Subsequent information indicated we had underestimated the ranges by ten to twenty percent and perhaps overestimated the yields by a larger amount. CEP (circular error probability) is the measure of the accuracy of ballistic missiles on point targets. It is the radius of a circle around the target within which half of attacking warheads can be expected to fall.

[5]See declassified memorandum, dated October 27, 1962, subject: The Military Significance of the Soviet Missile Bases in Cuba, in article by Raymond L. Garthoff, "The Meaning of the Missiles," *The Washington Quarterly* (Autumn 1982), 78–79.

weapons. This, he said, could be extended to petroleum products later and, if necessary, escalate to an air strike or even an invasion if the blockade failed. Nothing would be lost, he said, by starting at the bottom of the scale.

Maxwell Taylor urged that we move with speed and energy. The missiles could be operational at any time and the IL-28 bombers were still in their crates on the airfields. Now, he said, was the time to strike. The military, by and large, did not want to be responsible for accomplishing less than was expected of them and therefore wanted to err on the side of having more force available and authorized for use than might be needed.

The blockade offered at best an uncertain result: a slow, agonizing course of action during which time the missiles could become operational and we then would be under the Soviet gun.

Dean Acheson felt strongly that we should present Khrushchev with a fait accompli by removing the missiles and the IL-28 bombers in a surprise air attack "and then dealing with the consequences."[6] He held a dim view of the President's brother and scoffed at what he, Acheson, called Bobby's "ideological confusion."[7] This was in response to Bobby's allusion to a Pearl Harbor in reverse. Bobby Kennedy advised caution in our reaction to the Soviet provocation to the point of, what I considered, appeasement. He was often joined, not only by George Ball, Ros Gilpatric, and others, but at times by the President.

We were all aware of the dangers of a direct confrontation with the Soviet Union. If in the course of stopping a Soviet ship it became necessary to fire at it and perhaps sink it, the Soviet response could be to alert their submarines to sink our ship (an act that Khrushchev subsequently threatened in a meeting with American businessman William Knox the day the quarantine took effect). Or the Kremlin could respond by taking out the missiles in Turkey and Italy, our NATO allies. This would call for us to respond with a nuclear attack on the Soviet Union. An air attack on Cuba, on the other hand, while it probably would kill Soviet citizens, would not be an attack on a Warsaw Pact country and therefore would not require a response by the Soviet Union.

In spite of his opposition to a blockade, Dean Acheson lost patience with the quibbling over the legalities of a blockade. Such action, according to commonly accepted international law, can be declared only if there

[6]*Among Friends: Personal Letters of Dean Acheson*, ed. David S. McLelland and David C. Acheson (New York: Dodd, Mead, 1980), 245 (in an undated letter, ca. early spring 1963, to Patrick Devlin, justice of the British High Court, Queen's Bench Division).
[7]Ibid.

has been a prior declaration of war. To charges that if we acted otherwise we would be held accountable by friend and foe alike, he spoke out with characteristic impatience. Dean, who was considered one of this country's foremost experts in international law, explained to one and all that international law is merely a process based upon past precedent, that it continually evolves as new precedents are created. In this case we would be creating a new precedent. "If you object to the word 'blockade,' " he said, "why not use 'quarantine'?" Thus, the "quarantine" was born and the word "blockade" faded from the ExComm lexicon.

After meetings in the State Department that stretched throughout the afternoon and early evening, we met with the President in the White House late Thursday night. We all climbed into one or two government limousines for the ride in order to avoid attracting undue attention. We must have looked like the traditional twenty clowns in the circus climbing out of one small Volkswagen Beetle when we finally arrived at the Treasury Building next to the White House on Pennsylvania Avenue. To my surprise, since I was unaware it existed, we were led through an underground passage to the White House basement.

Mr. Kennedy listened to our differing recommendations, and then tentatively decided that in a televised speech he would reveal to the world the presence of the Soviet missiles in Cuba and our intention of implementing a naval quarantine.

On Friday morning we were back to square one. The Chiefs had asked the President to reconsider and order an air attack. Acheson, as I mentioned earlier, remained strongly opposed to the blockade. The President asked the ExComm to continue its discussions during his absence—he was leaving for a weekend of campaigning—to further weigh the pros and cons of quarantine versus military action.

Acheson left the group on Friday and retreated to his Maryland farm as the discussions centered on a naval quarantine. But he accepted the President's request that he leave for Paris immediately to confer with President de Gaulle, our most difficult ally, and Chancellor Adenauer in Bonn after the final decision was made late Saturday afternoon. "Of course I will do what the President asks," he responded when Dean Rusk called him that evening.

At the end of an afternoon meeting of intensive debate on Friday, Alexis Johnson and I retired to Alexis' office to try our hand at developing a time-phased scenario to cover the entire operation. We decided that the hour of the President's speech should be viewed as the focal point in time and that all of the necessary military and diplomatic moves should be allotted their appropriate time slots before and after "P" (for President's speech) hour.

Alexis and I agreed that he would prepare a time schedule covering diplomatic actions and I would prepare a time schedule covering the military actions. We scribbled these down on paper without the benefit of secretarial help. (We were still limiting the number in the small circle who were aware of the impending crisis to those with an absolute need to know.) Alexis dealt with the questions of how long before the speech the Soviets should be informed, when should the British, French, Germans, Canadians be informed, when should a meeting of the Organization of American States (OAS) be convened, when should the UN Security Council be brought in, when and how should ambassadors of other nations be briefed, and, most important, when should the congressional leadership be brought in.

For example, we agreed that the United Kingdom, as our closest ally, should be notified first; that de Gaulle's pride and our need for his support should make him second; Germany, Canada, Italy, and Turkey a close third; and other NATO allies and our Latin American friends, least likely to keep a secret, would be assembled an hour before the President's speech to be briefed and to listen to the speech.

This, incidentally, made Dean Acheson the irreplaceable man to see de Gaulle. He told me later that when he arrived in Paris with Sherman Kent, a senior CIA official, and the enlarged photographs of the missiles in Cuba, it was necessary to keep their visit a close secret to avoid letting the press know something was up. They stayed in an obscure hotel and were later led through a secret passage to the president's office in the Elysée Palace, with Sherman Kent laboring under the massive portfolios and cases of photographs. When Dean had briefed the general and then offered to show him the photographs as proof that the Soviet missiles did indeed exist on the island of Cuba, de Gaulle declined.

"That will not be necessary," he said, "your word is enough. Of course, you have my complete support," and cordially invited Dean to dine with him that evening.

Characteristically, the wily general once again confounded us. He had fought us on every issue for years and now, to Dean's surprise and relief, he gave his support freely when we needed it most.

I dealt with the questions of how long before or after the speech the naval quarantine forces should be in place, when and under what contingencies the fighter-bombers should be moved to Florida, what kinds of weapons they would need and when they could be made available, when the Marine divisions, their landing craft and protective naval forces could be ready, how and when civil defense headquarters should be alerted. We made an initial stab at dealing with all those questions as the evening lengthened toward midnight.

Since the presidential speech was the keystone of our plan, we asked Ted Sorensen to prepare a draft. He protested that the ExComm was still meeting and that no decision as to our course of action had been made. We finally convinced him to prepare a draft based on the President's tentative decision Thursday night for an initial naval quarantine, followed, if necessary, by an air strike and, if that didn't work, by an invasion. He went to work and produced a brilliant draft. Ted never ceased to amaze me with his capacity for producing apposite and dramatic prose.

Ted did the first draft of the speech Friday night, the nineteenth, finishing up about three Saturday morning. His draft was reviewed, amended, and generally approved Saturday morning at a nine o'clock meeting before the President returned to Washington.

At the next meeting with the President on Saturday afternoon—he had cut short his campaign trip—Ted's draft together with our scenario helped clear the many obstacles from the path leading toward a consensus on a final decision. The ideological debates that had tended to dominate and cloud the discussion were swept away by the scenario that focused on the naval quarantine as the initial action. It left open what additional military action might be required, and put into perspective the diplomatic moves and military preparations that would be required before the speech and those that could be deferred until after the speech. If the quarantine worked and the Soviets backed down, no further military action would be necessary. If the quarantine didn't work, the missile sites had to be taken out before they became operational. In order to do that, we had to take out their air defenses. If that didn't work, we had to be in a position to occupy the island through a military invasion.

It was no longer a question of either/or; it was a matter of being prepared to meet the possible contingencies—from a Soviet attack on the missiles in Turkey and Italy or a move on Berlin to a legal justification for the naval quarantine and properly preparing the diplomatic ground with the OAS and our NATO allies.

The central thoughts behind this, at least in my mind, were that (a) the missiles must be removed, (b) we should use the minimum military force necessary to accomplish this, being prepared for subsequent escalations if the initial response did not succeed, and (c) that we could take these steps with confidence that the situation would not get out of hand because of our unambiguous global nuclear superiority.

The logic underlying all this seemed to me to become clearer day by day during those crucial five days. The President had determined that the missiles must be removed. Normally the wisest course is to use the minimum forces necessary to accomplish one's objective. But we had no way of knowing what level of force would be adequate to assure removal of the missiles. McNamara had early argued that we would lose nothing by starting with the lowest level, a maritime blockade, while being prepared later for an air strike and then an invasion of the island. In this respect, he had my full accord.

The danger was that the Soviets might answer the initial action by an equal or greater response, including a nuclear response. As I've said, the crucial judgment was that they would not do so because at that time we had an unarguable position of global nuclear superiority. Certainly that was my judgment and I believe that of the majority of the members of the ExComm. I seriously disagree with McGeorge Bundy and a few other participants who now say that our nuclear superiority at the time had no bearing on their judgment. This is not to say that our nuclear superiority was the only factor bearing on the outcome. Our manifest conventional superiority in the area of Cuba also played a vital role.

An added complication appeared Saturday with the news that China had begun its attack on India over the Himalayas, which led some of us to wonder if Peking was moving in concert with Moscow on the other side of the globe. This was considered unlikely because Sino-Soviet relations were already suffering from a decided chill.

At that vital meeting Saturday afternoon, October 20, Adlai Stevenson, our UN ambassador, arrived from New York. He made a final plea that we not only utilize the United Nations and the OAS and pursue other diplomatic moves, but that we offer to withdraw from Guantánamo, our military base in Cuba since 1936, and to exchange our Jupiter missiles in Turkey for the missiles in Cuba before taking any provocative action, including the naval quarantine. Adlai maintained that we were unsympathetic to the viewpoint of the Russians, who were surrounded by their enemies and our nuclear weapons. I was outraged by his attempt at total appeasement. The President at first accepted and then courteously rejected Stevenson's last-minute appeal, although he recognized that the missiles in Turkey and Italy eventually would have to be removed.[8]

---

[8]Captain Zumwalt was sent later to the UN to deliver personally our final instructions to Ambassador Stevenson. He had difficulty in getting the ambassador to interrupt his work

Mr. Kennedy obviously was leaning toward a decision by the end of our meeting to impose a naval quarantine but it was not confirmed until Sunday morning when he spoke with General Walter C. Sweeney, Jr., commander in chief of the Tactical Air Command. General Sweeney told the President that even a major surprise air attack could not be certain of destroying all of the missile sites and nuclear weapons in Cuba.

Later that day, McNamara and I discussed in his office the directive to be issued to the Joint Chiefs and the Navy for the conduct of the quarantine. When we had worked it out in detail, I sent for Bud Zumwalt to write up the orders. The messenger caught up with Bud in the corridor near McNamara's office and he was brought in to receive his instructions. McNamara began to bark out orders to Bud in rapid sequence. Bud told me later that he memorized an acrostic so that he could re-create the instructions in their correct sequence since he was without pencil and paper. McNamara, noticing that Bud was not taking notes, picked up a pad and pencil and threw them at him. Furious, Bud continued to stand there, pad and pencil on the floor where they landed, until McNamara completed his instructions.

Bud thereupon dashed back to his office, where he dictated the instructions from memory to his secretary. He joined me in my office some twenty minutes later and I studied his directive. "Bud," I said, "I think you got it all. I want you to know that McNamara told me to fire you if you missed a single instruction."

McNamara approved the procedures and rules of the quarantine Sunday night. The proposed action was aimed solely at blocking further shipments of offensive weapons bound for Cuba and to do so with a minimum degree of force. Careful monitoring of every ship involved in the blockade force was essential, and insofar as possible, control of the situation at sea was to remain in the hands of fully responsible officials in Washington.

With the President's final decision for an initial naval quarantine, events were set into motion. Admiral Dennison on October 3 had taken the steps to prepare for the formation of a force adequate to enforce a blockade (or, as it turned out, a quarantine). Under cover of a large-scale amphibious assault exercise called "PHIBRIGLEX" 62 in the Caribbean, the Atlantic Fleet was moving toward a high state of readiness. Measures had been taken earlier to preposition bulk supplies (petroleum and ammunition) at Florida bases, reinforce our air defense capabilities in the

on his UN speech (to follow the President's announcement) long enough to receive the instructions.

southeastern United States, complete plans to reinforce Guantánamo, and prepare for the transfer of the Fifth Marine Expeditionary Brigade, with its associated amphibious shipping, from the West Coast to the Caribbean area. Two Army airborne divisions were brought to a high state of readiness and were prepared to move. SAC bombers and tankers were evacuated from Florida to make room for tactical fighter and defense forces. On October 23 the B-52 force was put on airborne alert, the B-47 fleet was dispersed to predetermined military bases and civil airports, and the entire SAC force was brought to an advanced combat readiness posture.

Subsequent to relocating the SAC bombers out of Florida, the Air Force tactical strike force was moved in, which represented at that time approximately one-third of the Air Force's worldwide tactical fighter resources. With the missile warning radars all oriented northward, several tracking stations throughout the Southeast were diverted to the job of watching Cuba. On October 22, Guantánamo was reinforced with over five thousand combat-ready marines and noncombatants were evacuated, just hours before the President's televised speech. As tensions heightened over the next week, an antisubmarine barrier was established southeast of Newfoundland and by October 30 over one hundred thousand U.S. troops were poised to invade Cuba, if that became necessary. By November 19 our military posture for operations against Cuba was at a peak and continued in that state until November 21, when the President officially lifted the quarantine. By the end of November our forces were rapidly returning to their pre-Cuban-crisis posture.

Our scenario went through many revisions up until the President delivered his speech on Monday evening, October 22, but it went like clockwork. An extract from the final version of the scenario appears in Alexis Johnson's memoirs.[9]

On national television the President revealed to the world the presence of Soviet offensive nuclear missiles on Cuba and our intention of implementing a naval quarantine of that island. The quarantine was put into effect at ten o'clock Wednesday morning, October 24.

We were braced for our first confrontation at sea, which we saw as the moment of significant danger. A few minutes after ten, two Soviet ships, the *Gagarin* and the *Komiles*, approached the quarantine line. We learned that a Soviet submarine was submerged between them. The President ordered the carrier *Essex* to move in for the interception with helicopters signaling the submarine by sonar to surface and identify itself. If it

[9] *The Right Hand of Power* (Englewood Cliffs, N.J.: Prentice-Hall, 1984), 384–86.

refused, the helicopters were to use small explosive depth charges until it surfaced.

As word came through that sixteen of the Soviet ships approaching the quarantine line had changed course or stopped dead in the water, we all breathed a little easier. The President ordered the *Essex* not to intervene, in order to give the *Gagarin* and the *Komiles* the opportunity to stop or turn around.

This, however, did not end the crisis. We were concerned that some of the deep-hulled ships that had changed course were on their way to rendezvous with other Soviet submarines, which would then attempt to escort them through the quarantine lines, thereby increasing the danger of confrontation. I argued that we should pursue one of the deep-hulled ships, board her, and establish to the world that the offensive nuclear missiles were aboard. Bob McNamara and others argued that we should avoid pushing the Soviets into a corner. We didn't know whether the warheads were already on the island, and while we thought the missiles were not yet operational, we couldn't be sure. The President accepted their argument.

In an effort to give Khrushchev time to think through his actions more carefully, Mr. Kennedy directed McNamara to make certain that Soviet ships approaching the quarantine line were followed and watched carefully but were not to be interdicted or boarded without fresh instructions from him.

The President believed that it was important to establish the principle of the quarantine without backing the Soviets into a corner. After a long discussion Thursday morning with the members of the ExComm, he decided that the first ship to be boarded should be from a Third World or Soviet-bloc country rather than from the Soviet Union itself.

Bud Zumwalt relayed this directive to the Navy. He appeared in the office of Admiral Ulysses S. Grant Sharp, who was then Op-6 (Plans, Policy, and Operations), with the new orders. Bud explained to the admiral that the President wished to give Khrushchev as much time as possible to think through his next move. It was very important that we take no precipitous action at that time. Admiral Sharp instructed Bud to go back to me and insist that the Navy be allowed to intercept a Soviet ship immediately to let them know we meant business. When Bud tried to protest, Admiral Sharp cut him off and told him to "follow orders."

When Bud came back and reported this conversation to me, I was outraged. I instructed Bud to return to Admiral Sharp and tell him that he was to carry out the instructions of civilian authority meticulously.

This, I am sure, did not sit well with either Admiral Sharp or his boss, Admiral George W. Anderson, the chief of naval operations.

Late that evening, I accompanied McNamara to the Navy Flag Plot, the command center for the quarantine operation. There Admiral Anderson dominated the small room and, as it turned out, jealously guarded his turf. In response to McNamara's sharp questions as to what exactly Anderson intended to do upon the interception of a deep-hulled Soviet-bloc ship at the quarantine line, Anderson replied there was nothing to discuss. The Navy, he said, had known all there was to know about managing a blockade since the days of John Paul Jones. McNamara responded that he didn't give a damn how John Paul Jones might have run a blockade; he wanted to know what he, the present-day chief of naval operations, Admiral George W. Anderson, intended to do upon intercepting a Soviet-bloc ship en route to Cuba.

The admiral, red-faced with rage, picked up a manual of naval regulations and waved it in the face of the secretary of defense and said, "It's all in here!" He then suggested that McNamara go back to his office and leave the running of the blockade to the Navy. McNamara directed that he be fully informed minute by minute during an interception so that he could consult with the President, and then the President and he would issue the Navy pertinent further instruction. He then turned on his heels and departed.

Admiral Anderson was not reappointed to his position when his term expired in June 1963. The President offered him the post of ambassador to Portugal, an appropriate kick upstairs.

Our first encounter with a Soviet ship was Thursday, October 25. The tanker *Bucharest* was allowed to pass through the quarantine line and proceed to Cuba after identifying herself and declaring that she carried nothing but petroleum.

But this was not before a low-flying surveillance plane the night before had dropped a flare near the tanker in order to get photographs. The flare made a loud explosive sound and the captain of the ship reacted by radioing Moscow that he had been attacked.

This incident, together with the accidental penetration of Soviet airspace by one of our U-2 planes several days later, I believe convinced the Soviets of the seriousness we attached to the presence of their missiles in our hemisphere. The Soviet's cautious behavior was in contrast to their belligerent remarks for public consumption.

Our sights were set on the Lebanese ship *Marcula* bound for Cuba under Soviet charter from the Baltic port of Riga, making it an ideal target for our purposes. Early Friday morning, the twenty-sixth, the *Marcula* was stopped without incident, boarded, inspected, and allowed to proceed, its cargo containing no contraband.

In the meantime, intelligence sources indicated that the missile sites were rapidly reaching a state of readiness and the IL-28 bombers were being uncrated. The Soviets were completing their work at a frantic pace, working day and night. We still had no evidence, however, that nuclear warheads were available.

In New York, UN Secretary-General U Thant desperately was trying to obtain a commitment from the Russians that there would be no further construction at the missile sites in Cuba, no further Soviet military shipments, and that the existing missiles would be defused in order that negotiations between the two superpowers could begin. He requested that we refrain from intercepting a Soviet ship while he performed this delicate task. We made every effort to comply with his request, but we dared not waver while the missile sites were being rushed into completion.

Getting the missiles dismantled and removed from this hemisphere was our immediate objective. If the Soviets refused U Thant's offer and the quarantine did not result in the removal of the missiles, what then?

That evening—the twenty-sixth—the State Department received the text of a letter to the President from Premier Khrushchev. In it he made a vague proposal that if the United States would agree to withdraw its quarantine and pledge not to invade Cuba, he would ship no more weapons to Cuba and he would dismantle or destroy those already there.

The next morning, Saturday, October 27, we met again with the President. Mr. Kennedy interrupted the discussion of Khrushchev's letter as he began to read the text of a public statement in the form of a *second* letter from the Soviet premier as it was received in the room. My worst fears were confirmed—the Soviets now demanded the removal of our Jupiter missiles in Turkey for their missiles in Cuba. The statement made no reference to the earlier letter from Premier Khrushchev. In fact, it was not clear that the new Soviet proposal did not include the denuclearization of all of NATO.

I urged the members of the ExComm to focus attention on this hemisphere. I reported that our ambassador to Turkey, Raymond Hare, had said it would be anathema to the Turks to pull our missiles out.[10] We

---

[10]William R. Tyler, assistant secretary of state for European affairs, and I had finally reached Ambassador Hare in Ankara by secure telephone after great difficulty the previous evening.

should inform Khrushchev, I said, that we were prepared to discuss only Cuba at that time. After Soviet offensive weapons had been removed from the island, I suggested, then we would be ready to discuss other issues.

The President gloomily said, "I don't think we can." He suggested that the only way we would get the missiles out of Cuba was by invading the island or trading our missiles in Turkey. We were in an insupportable position, he said, not to accept what would appear to others to be a rational, fair trade. He expressed dismay that we were now in a position of risking war in Cuba and in Berlin over obsolete missiles in Turkey.

Turkish Foreign Minister Selim Rauf Sarper had expressed outrage when Dean Rusk and I, under instructions from the President, had proposed to him in May 1961 that the Jupiters were already obsolete and should not be deployed in his country. We recommended to the President in June 1961 that in light of the Vienna talks and the vociferous objections of the Turks, it would not be advisable to cancel the deployment of the Jupiters in Turkey. Several attempts were made by other members of the administration over the next year and a half to approach the Turks on this delicate subject, but without success.

I suggested to the President that the Soviets might be trying a dual-track approach, one private, the other public. The public track was to confuse the public scene and bring additional pressure on us, while signaling privately that they were willing to make a deal limited to this hemisphere.

Our discussions carried through the day. General Taylor reported that the Chiefs recommended that we prepare for a major air attack on Cuba on Monday, followed by an invasion of the island.

Word arrived late that afternoon that one of our U-2 reconnaissance planes had been shot down over Cuba and the American pilot killed. This tragedy thickened the sense of impending danger.

Several attempts were made to draft a response to the second letter from Premier Khrushchev. There was disagreement as to whether we could ignore the new terms and little hope that the men in the Kremlin would now settle for Khrushchev's first proposal. Finally the President sent his brother and Ted Sorensen out of the room to draft an appropriate response. They came back in less than an hour with a letter that—after further discussion and refinement—was approved by the President and dispatched.

It responded to Khrushchev's first letter, accepting his proposal that in return for the immediate cessation of work on the missile sites and the dismantlement and removal of all offensive weapons under UN observation and supervision, we would pledge not to invade Cuba and we would lift the quarantine when the weapons had been removed. Our letter did not mention the central item in the second letter from Khrushchev— trading the missiles in Cuba for ours in Turkey. We were not hopeful that the Soviets would accept this response.

That evening the President approved McNamara's recommendation that we call up twenty-four air reserve squadrons in preparation for an invasion. He also authorized fighter escorts for our unarmed reconnaissance planes and directed that the fighters respond to any MiG attack.

Unknown to me—and a fact I did not discover until the publication of Robert Kennedy's memoir—Bobby Kennedy met with Soviet Ambassador Dobrynin earlier that evening.

He told the ambassador that the President had responded to Premier Khrushchev's first letter, accepting his proposal. When Dobrynin asked about the missiles in Turkey, Bobby informed him there would be no quid pro quo; that was a decision that would have to be approved by NATO. He went on to say, however, that the President had ordered their removal some time ago, and that he anticipated that within a short time the missiles would be removed from Turkish soil.

We all spent another uneasy night and convened Sunday morning at the White House. We were greeted by the full Tass text of Khrushchev's reply to the President, offering to withdraw Soviet offensive weapons from Cuba under UN supervision. We let out one collective sigh of relief.

Our attention then turned to the next step. At Dean Rusk's suggestion, we decided to pick up and accept the words Khrushchev had used to describe what it was he was prepared to remove from Cuba, that is, "offensive weapons."[11] The President suggested that we approach Khrushchev privately and ask that he withdraw the IL-28 bombers, which were capable of delivering nuclear weapons. He said he did not wish to get hung up on the IL-28 bombers, but we should make an effort to include them in the Soviet definition of "offensive weapons."

Our primary concern was that the Soviets stop construction at the missile sites immediately. Khrushchev had assured us that he had given orders for the Soviet missiles to be dismantled and removed from the island. The requirement for continued surveillance until the missiles were removed was imperative. The President suggested that we tell UN officials that they must carry out air reconnaissance or we would have to continue to do so.

---

[11] With my staff, I had already prepared a priority listing of the forces we would recommend the President press to have the Soviets remove. They were: (1) IRBMs, (2) MRBMs, (3) IL-28 bombers, (4) MiGs, (5) surface-to-air missiles (SAMs), and (6) Soviet troops.

UN officials were reluctant to start the surveillance flights immediately and, of course, the logistics involved made it impracticable to transfer the responsibility for this overnight. We were reluctant, on the other hand, to delay these overflights while Soviet missiles remained on the island. On Monday, the President authorized further reconnaissance missions, but agreed to suspend them Tuesday and Wednesday while the UN secretary-general was in Cuba to arrange inspection procedures for the UN observers. The President suggested that we leave ambiguous for the next twenty-four hours whether we would suspend the quarantine for those two days. U Thant had requested that we lift the quarantine, leaving our ships on station, since UN inspectors would be in all Cuban ports and would be able to report to us on all incoming and outgoing cargo.

The Soviets sent Deputy Foreign Minister Vasily Kuznetsov to New York to enter into negotiations with U Thant and our representatives, UN Ambassador Adlai Stevenson and veteran negotiator John McCloy, on procedures for the UN to carry out its mission of monitoring the removal of "offensive weapons" from Cuba. I sent Captain Elmo Zumwalt of my staff to work with them.

Kuznetzov reportedly said to McCloy when they met in New York that the Soviet Union would never again be placed in the humiliating position of retreat. Many here believe that the Soviet Union's scramble to achieve nuclear superiority dates from the Cuban missile crisis, when the Kremlin felt it had been at a strategic disadvantage.

However, Soviet budget expert William T. Lee—for whose work I have great admiration—tells me that nowhere can he find evidence that the Cuban missile crisis had a significant impact on the Soviet strategic nuclear buildup. He claims that most decisions on major weapons procurement through 1965 were made at the 22nd Party Congress in October 1961. "Given the lead-times involved," he stated in a 1979 article, "October 1961 is a much more plausible date than November 1962 for the decisions that resulted in the observed strategic missile deployments in 1966–1968."[12]

Monday evening we received word that the Soviet position, as stated by Kuznetsov, was that they would not permit on-site inspection of the missile sites until all the missiles had been removed. U Thant said that he was under the impression that this would take a week or two. At that time, UN inspection teams could go in to verify the removal of the

---

[12]William T. Lee, "Soviet Defense Expenditures in an Era of SALT," USSI Report 79-1, United States Strategic Institute, Washington, D.C., 1979.

missiles. The Soviets did agree to permit International Red Cross officials from neutral nations to inspect all cargoes at sea or at Cuban ports, if the Cubans had no objections. The Cubans, at this point, had refused to state their position until U Thant arrived in Havana on Tuesday.

And state their position they did. Fidel Castro was livid with Khrushchev for betraying his trust. Allowing the Soviets to place the missiles on Cuban soil had been risky for him, and now he felt that he had been a pawn for the Soviet premier in this power play. He refused to allow the UN team to implement its verification plans and even deployed the Cuban army around the missile base areas. "Whoever tries to inspect Cuba must come in battle array!" the bearded Cuban leader bellowed.

After Soviet Deputy Premier Anastas Mikoyan visited Castro on November 2, Castro withdrew his troops and allowed the removal of the missiles. Nevertheless, he still refused to accept the UN inspection team or to agree to the removal of the IL-28 bombers when this became an issue.

Which it very quickly did, because our continued air surveillance indicated the IL-28 aircraft were being rapidly assembled. Unlike the MRBMs in Cuba, which were to remain exclusively under Soviet control, the IL-28 aircraft were to be transferred to the Cuban government. In New York the Soviet negotiators argued that the bombers had been promised to the Cubans and could not be withdrawn without Cuban approval.

In Washington, the executive branch—as was its wont—was divided on what to do about the IL-28 bombers. The Joint Chiefs advocated removing the bombers by air attack. I and others recommended tightening the blockade by including petroleum products in order to force the Soviets and the Cubans to capitulate. Some in the State Department and Ambassador Stevenson argued that we should not press our luck now that we had achieved Soviet agreement to the withdrawal of the missiles, which had been our principal concern.

As tension mounted, we received word from the Soviets that they would permit close observation by our planes of their outbound missile-bearing ships. By Sunday, November 11, we had counted all forty-two missiles aboard Soviet ships making their way back to Soviet ports. But still on-site UN inspection teams could not verify the removal of all the missiles. In the meantime we had no choice but to continue surveillance flights over Cuba and to maintain the quarantine at sea to preclude reintroduction of the missiles.

As the problem of the removal of the IL-28 bombers remained unresolved, pressure mounted until it almost appeared that we would have a second crisis over the removal of the aircraft. The negotiations continued. We insisted that the bombers be removed prior to lifting our quarantine and that on-site inspection verify that no offensive weapons remained on the island. Not until these agreed measures had been completed would we give our assurances that we would not invade Cuba.

Finally, on November 19, under intensified Soviet pressure, Castro agreed to allow the withdrawal of the IL-28 bombers, which the Soviets promised to do within thirty days. The Cuban dictator, however, remained adamant concerning the prohibition of on-site inspection teams on Cuban soil.

The next day we agreed to lift the quarantine, and the last of the IL-28 aircraft departed Cuba on December 6 in open crates to facilitate our surveillance.

In a postmortem prepared in February 1963 by Walt W. Rostow's Policy Planning Staff in the State Department and some of my staff in ISA, we stressed the principal reasons for the successful conclusion of the Cuban missile crisis. First, we made it clear to ourselves and to the world that we considered the Soviet action a danger to our vital interests. Second, we began a broad front of political, economic, psychological, and noncombatant military moves against a background of massive military preparations. The Soviets could have had no doubt that we were prepared to take that next step toward combat operations.

The withdrawal of the missiles by Moscow, we noted in the document, did not come on the heels of the President's speech, in which he warned of full retaliation on the Soviet Union, nor did it come after the SAC alert that followed. It came only after noncombatant measures had been applied, and we had made it unmistakably clear that the United States was on the verge of destroying the missiles in Cuba or invading the island, or both, and was obviously capable of doing so.

I believed that we should have pushed our advantage with greater vigor. We had achieved our objective of getting offensive weapons removed from Cuba with a minimum amount of force. With the nuclear balance heavily in our favor, I believed we could have pushed the Kremlin in 1962 to give up its efforts to establish Soviet influence in this hemisphere. As it turned out, while the resolution of the crisis was seen as a triumph for the West, the Soviet Union achieved its goal of securing a guarantee from the United States to respect the territorial integrity of a socialist state in this hemisphere. Khrushchev said in his memoirs:

We forced . . . the US to demobilize and to recognize Cuba—not *de jure*, but *de facto*. Cuba still exists today as a result of the correct policy conducted by the Soviet Union when it rebuffed the United States. I'm proud of what we did. Looking back on the episode, I feel pride in my people, in the policies we conducted, and in the victories we won on the diplomatic front.[13]

Although the Soviets urged that we document our pledge not to invade Cuba, the matter was allowed to die on the vine in view of Castro's position on UN inspection teams. Then, in August 1970, the Soviets approached Henry Kissinger seeking assurances of American acceptance of the 1962 understanding. (This came just before the United States discovered that the Soviets were building a submarine base in Cuba.) Kissinger (who was then national security adviser to President Nixon) and the President agreed that this would be a good time to consummate the agreement. There followed an exchange of notes reaffirming the no-invasion pledge and the Soviet Union promised not to deploy offensive weapons in Cuba.

As my good friend Burt Marshall pointed out recently, understandings such as these—that is, an exchange of notes or other pledges between the President and other governments—are not the law of the land and therefore are not binding on successor presidents. He cited the 1817 Rush-Bagot Convention that demilitarized the Great Lakes and the U.S.–Canadian frontier. President James Monroe submitted the exchange of notes to a Senate vote, thereby making the Rush-Bagot agreement the law of the land when it was approved. This was not the case with the notes exchanged between the Soviet government and President Nixon in 1970.

---

[13] *Khrushchev Remembers: The Last Testament*, trans. and ed. Strobe Talbott (Boston: Little, Brown, 1974), 512.

14

McNamara's Pentagon

When the Cuban missile crisis was over, I was able to get home at a
reasonable hour for dinner for the first time in over a month. Phyllis and
I had cocktails while I regaled her with what I thought were entertaining
tales of what had gone on during the crisis. At that point, I was inter-
rupted by a telephone call from Bob McNamara, who said he was at the
White House discussing the Chinese invasion of India with the President.
They thought someone ought to go over there to deal with the situation.
There was a pause.

I said, "Yes?"

McNamara said they had decided I was the one who should go.

"When?" I asked.

He said, "There is no real urgency, you can wait until tomorrow."

Overnight I came to the conclusion that this was a foreign policy
matter and that someone from State, not Defense, should head the mission. In the morning I talked to McNamara, who agreed. We went to the
White House and talked to the President about it. He agreed and asked
Averell Harriman to head up a team that included General Paul DeWitt
Adams and me from the Department of Defense and Roger Hilsman
from State. General Adams was commander in chief of the Strike Command, a mobile force of corps strength to be called upon if U.S. ground
forces were needed in the defense of India or other nations in the Middle
East/Indian Ocean area. Carl Kaysen of the White House staff and other
staff experts completed the members of the mission that had been hurriedly put together in response to Jawaharlal Nehru's (the Indian prime
minister) appeal for help on November 19.

The Mission to India

When Nehru had made his appeal to Britain and the United States, his troops were in full retreat. The Chinese Communists surprised us all by declaring a unilateral cease-fire some twenty-four hours later. They said they would withdraw their forces, beginning in December, to positions some twelve miles behind their forward position of November 15, when they had started a major offensive, if the Indians would agree to a cease-fire and an armistice, and would not attempt to reestablish their posts in the Ladakh area of Kashmir.

This eighteen-thousand-foot desert plateau in the Himalayas that encompassed the bleak area of Aksai Chin lay in the path of the easiest and most direct route of the major road the Chinese were building to link Tibet with the province of Sinkiang. It was a difficult task for the Chinese, but necessary if they were to consolidate their hold on Tibet. According to Roger Hilsman, the value of the area to India was mainly symbolic to their national prestige and sentiment—part of the "sacred soil" of Kashmir.

We estimated that the Chinese intentions were limited, more political than military, but we couldn't be sure that their appetite for more territory would not be whetted by their successes.

The Kennedy administration viewed the Chinese cease-fire with caution and we were not at all sure the Indians should accept their conditions. To seek the answer to this and other questions, as well as to demonstrate to the Chinese our support for India, was our primary mission.

On November 21 we boarded the "McNamara Special," a KC-135 jet tanker, for our flight more than halfway around the world. It was unbelievably uncomfortable, with portable bunks and seats arranged in the windowless plane. There was no inner shell in the dimly lighted cabin area and the noise level prohibited normal conversation, much less the ability to discuss complex issues. The extremes of heat and cold added to our misery.

Eighteen hours after leaving Andrews Air Force Base in Washington, we landed in New Delhi on Thanksgiving Day. We emerged from the open hatch, blinking in the sunlight, like moles emerging from their dark underground tunnels on a sunny day. We were greeted by television cameras, the international news media, as well as our ambassador, John Kenneth Galbraith, his staff, and a crowd of Indians who hailed our arrival with warmth and enthusiasm. We were whisked to the prime minister's residence where we were welcomed by Nehru in a small, upstairs reception room. He was accompanied, to my great surprise, by my friend Barbara Ward, the well-known British economist and writer.

Barbara was lovely, dressed in white, as she appeared on the arm of Nehru, dapper and handsome in the traditional trousers and tunic of India and his personal trademark, a small rose in his buttonhole. She had been touring some of the Indian villages when the Chinese launched their attack and she was reporting to Nehru, an old friend, her impression of the reactions of the villagers.

Nehru was a charming, impressive man, who seemed somewhat out of touch with the practical realities and problems that faced his large, cumbersome, and fragmented nation. His daughter, Indira Gandhi, whom we met at the same time, impressed me as a competent, forceful, vigorous personality. There were rumors even then that she was being groomed as Nehru's successor.

After short discussions with Nehru and other officials, we were treated to a turkey dinner at the American embassy, and then immediately went to work. The next day the mission split into two groups. General Adams and I received military briefings and visited the two fronts. We could see from our plane the passes over which the Chinese forces had poured across the mountains. As far as we could tell, the Chinese would have had no difficulty in continuing their drive, but they had achieved their objective and withdrew unilaterally as they had pledged. This even though Nehru had rejected the terms of the cease-fire, in spite of Ken Galbraith's recommendation to Nehru that he accept the Chinese terms. He had said, however, that he would not upset the cease-fire as long as the Chinese continued it.

The long-term defense of India, in my mind, rested far more importantly on resolving the deep and sometimes bloody hostilities between India and Pakistan over the disputed territory in the Kashmir than on the military assistance we might agree to give them. A joint defense of the subcontinent was, I thought, essential to its success. The antagonisms between the two countries were driven by ancient religious differences and the bloody aftermath of partition after the British left India. Without a reconciliation, or at least an uneasy truce, I thought their survival as nations was in jeopardy. My thought was to extract a promise from Nehru to attempt a settlement with Pakistan in return for our military assistance. Ken was adamantly opposed to any U.S. efforts to bring about a settlement, believing that the subject was too sensitive to be broached to the Indians. I also had some difficulty in convincing Averell Harriman and Carl Kaysen of the wisdom of this approach. Duncan Sandys (Winston Churchill's son-in-law), who was in New Delhi on behalf of the British government, agreed with my suggested approach. This did nothing to help persuade Galbraith and Harriman.

At any rate, our efforts were futile. Although Nehru did agree to negotiate, he was unable to accept a compromise solution in the Kashmir due to the political temper of the times. The Pakistanis, whom we visited on our way home, recognized the practical requirement for a joint defense of the subcontinent, but they had little sympathy for India under attack by the Chinese. They were hopeful that enough military pressure from Communist China would induce Nehru to concede the disputed territory in the Kashmir to them.

On the other hand they voiced their concern about the military aid we were giving India and the fact that we could not guarantee that these arms would not eventually be used against them rather than Communist China.

We spent ten days in India and Pakistan conferring with officials, traveling to the front wherever it was necessary to see conditions first-hand, working and talking until the small hours of the night, with little opportunity for rest. After visiting Karachi and another eighteen-hour flight on that KC-135, we arrived back in Washington suffering from a good deal more than jet lag.

Back in Washington I turned over to Bill Bundy the task of working out the details of a military aid package to India. He headed that effort most ably but then he had to work out a comparable package of military aid to Pakistan. The entire operation seemed to me misguided. All that aid was used subsequently in fighting between India and Pakistan, not for the defense of the subcontinent against China or anyone else.

The Chinese had handled the situation with political sophistication and military skill. In 1959, after the Dalai Lama fled to India, they had destroyed the semiautonomy that Tibet had long enjoyed. The completion of the road after their successful foray over the Himalayas in 1962 allowed the Chinese to consolidate their hold and effectively suppress Tibet's ancient and honorable culture.

McNamara's Whiz Kids

Now let me go back to the beginning of McNamara's Pentagon administration and some of the organizational developments in the early days of his regime.

I did not meet Bob McNamara until the presidential transition period, when he asked me to become his assistant secretary for international security affairs. I was disappointed, of course, not to have received the post of deputy secretary, but I soon found McNamara to be a forceful leader with strong views on everything from civil rights, education, and fair housing to defense management. He had a single-minded, pragmatic approach to cost-effectiveness in the Defense Department and very little patience with the parochial tendencies of the military services. He was a liberal on domestic issues, although I believe, at the time, he was a registered Republican.

The term "whiz kids" was a label carried over from McNamara's own management group at Ford. The mantle rested easily on the shoulders of such self-confident young men as Alain C. Enthoven—thirty, brilliant, and intense. A Rand economist, Enthoven came to the Pentagon on the coattails of Charles J. Hitch, also from Rand, whom I had recommended to McNamara for the position of comptroller. Alain was soon ensconced over his own domain—the newly created office of systems analysis. His brilliance, unfortunately, was exceeded only by his arrogance, as he brought one general or admiral after another to the threshold of humiliation and quite often despair.

It's not surprising that the military top brass, with their decades of experience and accumulation of applied wisdom, were dismayed by an attempt to turn the Pentagon into a command post of theory and untried ideas. To come up with novel ideas is relatively easy; sometimes that is necessary and highly useful. What is difficult is first to achieve a solid basis for confidence that the ideas can be made to work, and, second, to make them actually work.

Bob McNamara was appalled at what he considered the extensive duplication of weaponry among the services and their research and development programs. In the first few weeks of the administration he asked the Joint Chiefs of Staff to come up with answers to some ninety-six questions in the Pentagon review of our defense needs. The Joint Chiefs simply did not have the machinery in place to generate adequate responses by the time McNamara expected them on his desk. Consequently Bob turned more and more to his handpicked civilian team in OSD for quick advice and action.

In May 1961, *Newsweek* magazine published an article by its Pentagon correspondent, Lloyd Norman, entitled "Top Brass vs. 'Whiz Kids' . . . The Crucial Conflict over Pentagon Policy."[1] I was depicted "as the

---

[1] *Newsweek*, May 29, 1961, 24–26.

leader of a cult of 'wooly headed' scientists, State Department idealists, and White House intellectuals . . . who, the military claim, want to disarm the U.S. of its massive nuclear power and stress limited war preparedness." Norman quoted one four-star general as saying: "This fellow Paul Nitze is one of our greatest headaches. He wants to throw the A-bombs out and fight with bayonets." After I became secretary of the navy, I was able to bring the military around (including Lloyd Norman, with whom I had been particularly angry).

Even before the inauguration, the president-elect had asked McNamara to look into the need for funds to supplement the Eisenhower defense budget for fiscal year 1961, and to recommend changes in the fiscal year 1962 defense budget request. Mr. Kennedy considered it essential that we get our recommendations for additions to or deletions from the Eisenhower budget to the Congress as quickly as possible in order to get the funds we needed to build greater flexibility into our defense capabilities.

McNamara undertook his job with the full energy and drive that are basic to his personality. He created four task groups. One, which he asked me to head, looked into our requirements for an adequate conventional military capability; another, headed by Charlie Hitch, examined our strategic nuclear force posture; the third delved into the field of research and development; and the fourth dealt with military installations.

The report prepared by my group was based on the posited need to deter a conventional attack upon our principal allies and to meet two limited war situations concurrently: one comparable to the Korean conflict and the other to a more limited engagement in Latin America or the Middle East. Our recommended figure amounted to the addition of three billion in 1961 dollars to the Eisenhower budget for conventional forces.

At the close of President Eisenhower's term of office, the United States had been relying almost entirely on nuclear forces for the defense of the West. When John Kennedy took office, some in the military, especially the Air Force, were reluctant to relinquish the simplistic security blanket of "massive retaliation." But the Army and the Navy worked closely with us in preparing our report to McNamara.

When McNamara reviewed the report of my task force, along with the reports from the other task groups, he slashed our recommendation to less than $1 billion. Together with this amount, he recommended that the President request an additional $1.8 billion for our strategic forces. This the President did in March. In July, however, with the Berlin situation heating up, President Kennedy went before Congress and requested an additional $3.2 billion for defense, nearly all of which was designated for conventional forces.

By August the full funds our task force had recommended and more were in hand. Kennedy had requested and received from an obliging Congress almost six billion dollars more in defense funds than Eisenhower had requested for fiscal year 1962. Over four billion of this amount was for conventional forces.

From the "No-Cities" Concept to Assured Destruction

The Joint Strategic Target Planning Staff (JSTPS) had been created by Secretary of Defense Thomas S. Gates in August 1960 to produce an integrated all-service plan for the use of all nuclear weapons possessed by U.S. military commands and for coordinating the plan with our allies.

From 1960 to 1974 the Single Integrated Operational Plan, or SIOP, designed by the JSTPS, gave the highest priority to urban-industrial targets, and second priority to nuclear threat and other military forces. Highest priority did not mean first in time or greater weight of effort; rather, it meant highest confidence in being able to destroy targets of overriding importance. Most time-urgent would be military targets, particularly nuclear threat forces. The option to withhold strikes against urban areas did exist and played an important role in the new SIOP of 1962, along with additional options and greater flexibility.[2]

Our ability to inflict major damage on Soviet cities had remained constant since the early years of the nuclear age. The Soviet Union's ability to damage American cities had, of course, increased significantly. The easier task for either side's offensive forces had been the destruction of the other side's urban structure. The more difficult task for each side was that of limiting damage to its own retaliatory forces, urban-industrial facilities, population, and similar assets of its allies. The more the Soviet Union increased its ability to inflict major damage on the United States

[2]The new SIOP announced by Secretary of Defense James R. Schlesinger in 1974 provided for less-than-massive options and emphasized lower collateral damage. For example, while war-related industrial facilities continued to be targeted, population centers were not. This pinpoint targeting capability was made possible by improved accuracy of our weapons delivery systems, thereby permitting the use of lower-yield weapons.

and its allies with its growing nuclear arsenal, the more important it became to limit damage to our side by destroying the other side's offensive capabilities.

The strategy of concentrating an attack on the military forces of the other side had been around since the Soviets first successfully tested a nuclear weapon in 1949. It was the basis for the estimate I had made in 1950 that we eventually might need ten thousand nuclear weapons. Rand analysts Herbert Goldhammer and Andrew Marshall concluded in 1959 that, from the point of view of damage limiting, the most effective strategy would be to target the other side's offensive nuclear forces, using high-yield weapons. They also proposed withholding a portion of SAC forces against selected targets in the event of a Soviet attack, with the threat that the remaining forces would strike Soviet cities unless the Kremlin agreed to terms acceptable to us.

It was not until Robert McNamara's presentation at the NATO ministerial meeting in Athens on May 5, 1962, and his commencement address at the University of Michigan at Ann Arbor the following month that the "no-cities" concept—or "controlled" counterforce strategy—was publicly articulated by a high government official. He said:

> The United States has come to the conclusion that to the extent feasible, basic military strategy in a possible general nuclear war should be approached in much the same way that more conventional military operations have been regarded in the past. That is to say, principal military objectives, in the event of a nuclear war stemming from a major attack on the Alliance, should be the destruction of the enemy's military forces, not of his civilian population.
>
> The very strength and nature of the Alliance forces make it possible for us to retain, even in the face of a massive surprise attack, sufficient reserve striking power to destroy an enemy society if driven to it. In other words, we are giving a possible opponent the strongest imaginable incentive to refrain from striking our own cities.

In our task force report to the president-elect on national security policy in the fall of 1960, we had urged him to make an early decision on whether to pursue a military "win" capability or a secure retaliatory capability. A military "win" capability was considered infeasible unless we had the ability to inflict a disarming "out of the blue" first strike on the military forces of the Soviet Union. We advised him, however, that a U.S. "win" capability probably was not feasible given Soviet capabilities and the political mood of the country.

When the President assumed office in January this question was addressed with mixed results. Bob McNamara and I were in accord on the need for a secure retaliatory capability. The feasibility of a damage-limiting capability was more doubtful. The question was, how much was enough to achieve what purpose?

Others were pushing for what was called "minimum deterrence." This school of thought maintained that numerical superiority or even equality was meaningless as a deterrent to strategic nuclear attack. Proponents of minimum deterrence believed a few invulnerable Polaris submarines with missiles aimed at Soviet cities would provide sufficient deterrent.

In contrast, General Thomas D. White, the Air Force chief of staff, advocated that we seriously strive for a first-strike capability effectively to disarm the Soviet Union. By then McNamara had come to the conclusion that it was not technologically feasible to disarm the Soviet Union by more than ninety percent. With the remaining ten percent the Soviets could cause nine to ten million casualties in the United States, a number he deemed unacceptable. I agreed that this was an unacceptable number—but with ninety percent of Soviet offensive forces destroyed, it would be an act of sheer desperation for them to pursue their attack. Furthermore, even if they did so, nine to ten million American casualties was better than the ninety to one hundred million casualties one could expect in the absence of a U.S. capability to deliver an effective counter-force strike.

The situation we should do our utmost to avoid—and this is as true today as it was then—is, as I have said earlier, one in which there would be comparable incentives on each side, in a crisis situation, to strike before the other did. In such a situation, to strike first would enable one to destroy a far greater proportion of the enemy's forces than one could destroy in a retaliatory attack. There *is* a difference between both losing ninety million people and losing the war and a situation in which you win a war and have nine to ten million casualties. You can't, however, say either is acceptable. What we must do is avoid being put into a position of inherent instability. It's worth an enormous amount of effort and cost to avoid it. One would wish it otherwise, but that's the way it is. Two plus two do equal four.

It was my view that the Russians in their own councils would consider a number of factors before they went down a course that they thought would lead to general nuclear war. One factor was the damage their civilian centers of population might suffer; another was their estimate of what might be the probable outcome of the initial phase of a nuclear exchange. If their generals told the high councils of the Kremlin that after successive phases of a nuclear war the United States would still have a residual capability considerably in excess of the remaining Soviet nuclear capability, and that the future of the world—insofar as it was controlled by military considerations—would then be dominated by those surviving U.S. forces, I believed this would be a stronger deterrent to Soviet leaders than the risk of losing large numbers of their population. They could do a number of things to protect their population by active and passive defense measures, including evacuation. And, of course, they had been brutal in World War II about accepting large numbers of casualties and still going on to win. Therefore, it seemed to me that the strongest deterrent to the Kremlin's initiating a nuclear strike was for them to see for themselves that our capabilities were such that the Soviet Union would come out second-best after the initial phases of a nuclear exchange, even if they struck first.

The President's first step was to strengthen our second-strike capability by accelerating our Minuteman and Polaris programs. This he did—at McNamara's recommendation—in his first request to Congress for supplemental funds to the Eisenhower defense budget for fiscal year 1961. The effect of this decision, along with others in the course of the next few years, was to reduce dependence for survival of our strategic force on early warning and quick response. While our B-52 bombers continued to rely on warning and alertness for their survival, our Minutemen in their hardened silos and Polaris missiles in submarines, at that time, did not.

The purpose of our retaliatory strike in a counterforce strategy would be to reduce the remaining Soviet nuclear capability after a first strike to a very small amount, not just in order to be able thereafter to dominate the nuclear equation, but also to limit damage to the United States from those remaining Soviet weapons. It was difficult to see in the early sixties how we could survive as a political entity after absorbing the enormous destruction of a Soviet strike from undamaged forces.

We began to explore the possibilities of a combination of active and passive defenses, including antimissile defense and weapons that would counter their submarines. We soon discovered that the requirements for damage limiting—in other words, the forces we needed in order to give us a shot at reducing the damage from an initial Soviet strike to manageable proportions—were greater than those we would need to assure the United States of a military win capability. In addition, it soon became evident that attempts to limit damage through active defenses at that time could be overcome by improvements in offensive forces, and at less cost. In other words, the cost of protecting populations versus the cost of destroying them was more by a factor of three, if we assumed the object of the attacker was to kill the opponent's population. The reverse was true of passive defenses, including civil defense.

McNamara was a firm believer that the United States could afford whatever was necessary for a strong defense. He also believed, equally firmly, that the Pentagon should request no more—and no less—than it needed from the Congress in defense appropriations. In other words, no margin in our requests to Congress was necessary.

The size of the budgetary requirements for a controlled and flexible nuclear strategic force oriented toward an effective counterforce capability soon cooled McNamara's ardor after the Cuban missile crisis of 1962. By then the danger of a nuclear confrontation with the Soviet Union appeared to have diminished and the costs of meeting it, if it were to come about, were thought to be far greater than he had originally assumed.

McNamara was unprepared, however, to drop his doctrine that the United States could afford whatever was necessary for defense and his assurance that he should and could with prospect of success ask the Congress for no more and no less than that. Therefore, because of the requirements of building up our conventional forces and his concern in 1963 that the country would not meet the cost of a ballooning defense budget, he changed his goals concerning our nuclear strategy and force structure. I objected strenuously to that way of justifying reduced military requirements. I thought it better to accept openly the practical necessity of living within the budget realities set by the Congress.

I argued that we should not shift our support for a counterforce, damage-limiting strategic doctrine even though we were not in a position at the time to obtain the required resources. I did not wish to go before Congress and defend a budget based on a revised strategy and force structure that did not reflect our true requirements. I realized, however, that we had to live within the budgetary limitations imposed upon us by the economic and political realities of the time. And that is the policy I followed when I became deputy secretary of defense in 1967. I instructed the services not to request more than eighty billion dollars (in 1968 dollars), which would give us a margin of five billion in the tug-of-war with the Congress. I knew that what we needed was more than we were going to get, and that what we were going to get was no more than about seventy-five billion. To let the military services ask for unattainable amounts would cause us to lose control over planning our program within a restrictive budget. But I did not change my view on what our strategic doctrine should be; that called for a counterforce, damage-limiting capability. To go after cities, if deterrence should fail, to my mind would be suicidal. It wasn't just a question of damage-limiting; I believed—and still do—that a counterforce doctrine and posture of sufficient scope would persuade the Soviet Union that it could not count on achieving a military victory in a nuclear exchange. This would assure effective deterrence.

McNamara, on the other hand, began to stress the doctrine of assured destruction as our central deterrent to a nuclear exchange; that is, having high confidence in our ability to inflict unacceptable damage on Soviet urban-industrial centers.[3] Thus, the marginal return from increasing our forces beyond one thousand Minuteman launchers, forty-one Polaris submarines, and some five hundred strategic bombers he did not consider worth the cost. This reasoning, of course, was instrumental in the decision to deploy penetration aids and MIRVs to overcome the Soviet ABM system, and short-range attack missiles (SRAMs) for our strategic bombers. Damage-limiting through refinement of our counterforce capability became a secondary objective. He now considered it essential to avoid any risk of a major confrontation with the Soviet Union. This seemed to me to be in conflict with a policy of maintaining a credible deterrent.

His interest in incorporating flexible options into the SIOP diminished. His Pentagon planners ceased their fevered activity in developing new options and, by default, our nuclear strategy, as reflected in the SIOP, became that of assured destruction, albeit with more control and flexibility and a growing list of targets.

By the end of 1963, as I prepared to move to the post of secretary of the navy, the debate was no longer focused on whether we should aim for a counterforce capability or an assured retaliatory capability but, rather, on the possibility of more subtle ways of dealing with a crisis. One that I wished to look into with care, as I mentioned earlier, was a naval blockade of the entire Soviet Union.

The Basic National Security Policy

Intermeshed with the struggle to achieve a capability for a flexible and controlled nuclear response and an effective deterrent to Soviet initiation of a nuclear strike, or an all-out conventional attack on our allies, was the

[3] The necessary damage criterion settled on by McNamara for this high confidence was the potential to destroy twenty to twenty-five percent of the Soviet population and fifty percent of its industrial capacity. This criterion then determined our strategic force requirements. He decided the forces already programmed met this criterion.

effort to revise the document known as the Basic National Security Policy, or BNSP.

The BNSP originated with NSC 68 in 1950. It continued to evolve throughout the Eisenhower administration as a broad outline of the aims of our national security strategy. The final debate on the language of the BNSP took place annually, usually in May. Budget guidelines were then issued and our military forces were structured to be compatible with budgetary limitations and the strategic concept set forth in the BNSP. The strategic concept remained fairly consistent throughout the tenure of the Eisenhower administration as it had in the Truman administration. In this way the President, through the National Security Council, which was responsible for supervising the preparation of the document, provided a measure of guidance to the Departments of State and Defense and the military services.

Problems arose when the BNSP would advocate a given strategic concept, and budgetary authorizations and appropriations failed to provide the means for its implementation. This too had been fairly consistent during the previous administration. For example, the BNSP would direct the Defense Department to rely on weapons to prevail in a nuclear war and also maintain flexible mobile forces for coping with smaller conflicts even though Congress had failed to provide the necessary funds for both.

In general, the document provided guidance so broad in nature that its practical applicability to concrete situations was limited. But it did lend general coherence to U.S. policy.

President Kennedy was advised by Richard Neustadt, who was then a professor of government at Columbia University, in a preinaugural memorandum, that a BNSP document would be used by the departments and agencies to further their pet programs and would reduce and hedge his freedom of action. I argued with McNamara that the Pentagon needed such a document. You couldn't achieve coherence, I said, among the six million people involved in our military forces and in their support elements without a comprehensive document giving a coherent explanation of our overall policy.

We in ISA, with the help of the State Department and the Joint Chiefs of Staff, attempted to coordinate a revised BNSP in the spring of 1961. But we soon ran into a series of disagreements with the Chiefs. While they acknowledged the merits of flexible military response, which we strongly advocated in our draft document, they argued that the paper was more appropriate for inclusion in a joint military planning document than as a statement of national security policy. A BNSP, they argued, should consist of a series of succinct policy statements which provide guidance as to objectives rather than attempt also to specify the means to be used to achieve those ends.

My staff, particularly Harry Rowen, worked doggedly on the revised BNSP with Walt Rostow in the State Department. General Andrew Goodpaster and I—he was then assistant to Maxwell Taylor, the chairman of the Joint Chiefs—reduced the areas of disagreement with the JCS to six. Andy and I sent a memorandum summarizing those issues to McNamara in the spring of 1963 and asked him to resolve them. He refused and sent it back with the comment that he didn't believe there was anything to be gained by the formulation of such a document. He suggested that a reading of the President's and his (McNamara's) public statements was sufficient to delineate our national security policy.

I persuaded William Kaufmann, then a professor at Massachusetts Institute of Technology, to spend some time with us in ISA and select the "right" portions of McNamara's speeches that would spell out our national security policy. The result was Kaufmann's book *The McNamara Strategy*,[4] but it provided no resolution of the six issues we had posed. I remember telling McNamara that I could find support for either side of those six issues in his speeches and those of the President's.

Neither the President nor McNamara wanted to be tied to decisions that might restrict his options in dealing with diverse contingencies that were appearing daily on the horizon. I understood the President's reluctance, but I believed more definitive guidance was necessary—if not essential—for both the State Department and the Defense Department. I also believed that some restraint on the President's options might not be a bad thing.

As it was, we tended to be in a perpetual state of reaction to one crisis after another rather than working toward long-term goals. Events, in other words, were shaping our policy, rather than we shaping events toward achieving a world environment in which those national purposes embodied in the Preamble to the Constitution could best be attained.

The evolution of policy during the Kennedy and Johnson administrations was ad hoc. We learned certain lessons from specific episodes, but these lessons were never amalgamated into a coherent policy structure. Events in Southeast Asia, for example, led us into a labyrinth from which it was difficult to recover.

[4] William W. Kaufmann, *The McNamara Strategy* (New York: Harper & Row, 1964).

Running the Navy

During the first four years of the Johnson administration, I served as secretary of the navy. By that time the service secretaries were excluded from participation in the mainstream of national security policy. Their tasks were to lead the effort to recruit, select, and train the personnel in their service; to develop, procure, and maintain the equipment their service needed; and to defend the interests of their service before the Congress and the public.

President Kennedy had an immediate need to nominate a successor to Fred Korth, the secretary he had had to relieve. He asked me to take the job. I had no desire to leave the mainstream of national security policy formulation. Kennedy assured me he would get me out of the Navy job and into the type of position I wanted in no more than six months. But within a month he had been assassinated. It was some four years later that President Johnson promoted me to succeed Cyrus Vance as deputy secretary of defense.

Once I became secretary of the navy I found myself wholly engrossed in the job. The top Navy senior officers were an exceptionally able group. After I had fired one admiral who persisted in refusing to follow my guidance, I found I had earned a certain respect. I recruited an outstanding group in the secretary's office to help provide civilian leadership. I was fortunate in the selection of the chief of naval operations, Admiral David L. McDonald, who served most of the four years with me. McDonald often differed with my judgment, but if, after he had had an opportunity to fully present his views, I remained unpersuaded, he would back me wholeheartedly. On many issues I came to consider his judgment superior to mine, particularly on the politics of the Washington bureaucratic scene.

Together we managed profound changes in the organization of the Navy, its personnel, its equipment, its strategy, and its morale. Much of the equipment the Navy now has—its nuclear carriers, its fighter-bombers, its submarines, its torpedoes, its radars and sonars, and its missiles—were developed, or the basic research for them done, during our time in office.

To administer and give direction to a large organization demand a quite different approach from the study, analysis, and bureaucratic infighting associated with national security policy formulation. There were more than 650,000 uniformed Navy personnel, more than 230,000 marines, and some million civilians supporting the Navy in one capacity or another working under my guidance.

I remember when a particularly unusual and unpleasant personnel problem arose, I complained to Bud Zumwalt, my principal naval aide, "Why does this have to happen to me?" His answer was, "If you have more than a million men working for you, every unpleasant problem that has one chance in a million of occurring will occur at least once."

Another essential of administering a large organization is to devote at least thirty percent of your time to management—not to what in a policy job I would call substance. The heart of the matter is the selection, assignment, compensation, and promotion (or selection-out) and supervision of key personnel. No single man can personally run a big organization with its array of diverse problems. He makes his contribution by welding together and perfecting the organization that actually does the work.

15

The Vietnam Imbroglio

On January 6, 1961, Nikita Khrushchev delivered the speech in which he vowed the support of the Soviet Union for "wars of national liberation." Hearing this on the eve of his inauguration, President-elect John F. Kennedy was sobered by the menace he heard in the words of his Soviet adversary. He asked his advisers to read the speech in its entirety to understand better the challenge facing us. We all recognized the challenge; how to deal with it practically and successfully in Southeast Asia eluded us.

President Kennedy faced a dilemma between his policy in Laos and his policy in Vietnam. The Eisenhower administration had chosen to back right-wing elements in Laos and by early 1961 the neutralists had joined the Communists in that country in their attack. President Kennedy made the decision to go for a political compromise and a military cease-fire in Laos rather than support the right-wing General Phoumi Nosavan, who had wrested control from the neutralist Prince Souvanna Phouma in December 1960.

Washington viewed the situation in Southeast Asia as an integral part of the global competition with Moscow. We considered it dangerous to give up ground too often. After our shift in Laos, the executive branch decided that if we then appeared to give up on Vietnam, the Kremlin was likely to doubt that we intended to stand firm anywhere.

In May, President Kennedy approved the objective stated in a task force report prepared by an interdepartmental group chaired by Ros Gilpatric. That objective was to prevent Communist domination of South Vietnam and to create in that country a viable and increasingly democratic society. So much for good intentions.

By September the Vietcong—North Vietnam's guerrilla arm in the South—had tripled the level of their attacks. The fall of a provincial capital only fifty-five miles from South Vietnam's capital at Saigon prompted President Ngo Dinh Diem to plead for a bilateral defense treaty with the United States (which he previously had spurned) and an accelerated American military buildup.

President Kennedy was bombarded with conflicting advice from Defense, State, and the CIA. The Joint Chiefs of Staff provided the estimate that 40,000 U.S. forces would be needed to clean up the Vietcong threat and that 128,000 additional troops could cope with intervention from North Vietnam or China.

In October the President turned to General Maxwell Taylor, who was then serving as his special military adviser, and asked him to go to Saigon with Walt Rostow to appraise the situation in South Vietnam and to advise him whether the United States should take a direct role with U.S. combat troops or continue training and support functions only.

General Taylor reported back to the President that he did not believe South Vietnam could be saved without the introduction of a U.S. military task force. He thought the introduction of U.S. combat forces was necessary to instill confidence throughout Southeast Asia.

The State Department was not at all happy with the report. Dean Rusk warned against troop commitment without reforms by Diem to broaden the base of his political support in South Vietnam. McNamara, on the other hand, along with Ros Gilpatric and the Joint Chiefs, gave the Taylor report an ambiguous endorsement. He cautioned, however, that General Taylor's military task force of six to eight thousand U.S. troops would represent only the first installment to a far larger and deeper commitment.

Several days later in a joint memorandum to the President with the secretary of state, McNamara somewhat revised his recommendation. While the two cabinet members agreed that the United States should commit itself to the clear objective of preventing the fall of South Vietnam to Communism, they recommended that U.S. combat forces be introduced *only if necessary* to achieve the objective.

This slight shift in McNamara's response followed a meeting in the State Department attended by—in addition to Bob McNamara and me—Dean Rusk, Walt Rostow, and Max Taylor at which the joint recommendation to the President was discussed at length. I argued strongly against the introduction of U.S. combat forces into the war in Vietnam. To commit any ground troops at all meant in the end to commit as many as might be required to ensure the security of those already committed. There was no such thing as being a little bit pregnant, and an open-ended commitment could well lead to an American involvement in another major ground war in Asia under unfavorable political and logistical circumstances.

At the price of some hard feelings, I won the day in that meeting. The President accepted the revised recommendations of McNamara and Rusk to introduce forces only if necessary, but my victory was short-lived. As the authors of the Pentagon study[1] of our involvement in Vietnam observed: "The dilemma of the U.S. involvement dating from the Kennedy era . . ." was how to achieve excessive ends while using excessively limited means. The best minds in Washington would be devoted to this problem for more than a decade.

Crossing the Threshold

By 1964, the first full year of the Johnson administration, I had assumed the office of secretary of the navy and as such was no longer involved in national policy planning or, for the most part, operational matters.[2] Therefore I was no longer a participant in the battle for the hearts and minds of the decision makers in Washington as to which road we should take in Southeast Asia.

When—after the introduction of two marine battalions in March— significant casualty reports began coming in on *my* marines in the spring of 1965, I decided, since the marines came under my jurisdiction, to go to South Vietnam to see the situation firsthand. After receiving a briefing in Honolulu from Admiral U. S. Grant Sharp, commander in chief of the Pacific, Admiral Roy Johnson, commander in chief of the Pacific Fleet, and General Victor H. Krulak, commanding general, Fleet Marine Force in the Pacific, I left for Southeast Asia in mid-June.

We landed on an aircraft carrier in the South China Sea and from there I flew by helicopter to Chu Lai, where the marines were trying to secure enough land to build an airfield and port facilities on the coast. Our troops were in a difficult position, surrounded by the Vietcong and fighting tenaciously to expand the small beachhead they had established between Route 1 and the sea. The Vietcong had control of Route 1 north of Chu Lai and the hills to the west of Da Nang, where, at night, our marines were surrounded by the enemy right up to the barbed wire

---

[1] In 1967, Robert McNamara commissioned a top-secret history of the American role in Indochina to be conducted within the Department of Defense. The narrators worked under my direction for the next year and a half. The result was forty-seven volumes that covered American involvement from World War II to May 1968. The completed history became known as the "Pentagon Papers" when it was purloined and parts of it published by *The New York Times* in 1971.

[2] I was sworn into that office on November 29, 1963.

around the periphery of the airfield. My helicopter pilot somehow managed to get us safely to Da Nang before we departed for Pleiku. Our outpost at Pleiku in the Central Highlands was isolated by fifty miles or more of jungle dominated by the Vietcong through which a solitary road led to the coast. The briefings I received in Saigon did nothing to ease my concern about our position in Vietnam, nor did General William C. Westmoreland, the American commander in Vietnam, or Ambassador Maxwell Taylor have any good news to offer.

General Westmoreland recently had submitted a requirement for 200,000 additional U.S. forces, a move that would increase American troops in Vietnam almost threefold. At a briefing at his headquarters in Saigon, I was disturbed to hear precise estimates of enemy forces based on what I considered to be inherently imprecise information. The subject of numbers had risen several days earlier at the meeting in Honolulu when General Krulak expressed his opinion that enemy force figures coming out of MACV (U.S. Military Assistance Command, Vietnam) were inflated. When I mentioned this to General Westmoreland, he took deep umbrage and said that I was accusing him of inflating enemy strength in order to justify lifting the ceiling on American forces in Vietnam.[3]

I returned to Washington pessimistic about our situation in Vietnam. In a conversation with Bob McNamara, I told him that I thought it would take many more than 200,000 men to accomplish our mission there, if we were able to do it at all. I doubted whether the effort to achieve our objective in South Vietnam, in the end, would be worth the cost to the United States in men and resources and in its strategic position in the world.

He looked at me with surprise and asked me whether I was recommending that we withdraw from Vietnam. I responded that I certainly

[3] In 1984 I testified on behalf of General Westmoreland in his libel suit against CBS. In the TV program "60 Minutes," CBS had implied (I believe with malice) that the general had led a conspiracy to deceive the President with underestimates of enemy strength during 1967, the year prior to the Tet offensive. The wide range of estimates of enemy strength in both 1965 and 1967 were indicative of the uncertainty of intelligence and of honest differences of opinions within the intelligence communities in Washington and Saigon. This was particularly true as to the categorization of the informally organized Vietcong villagers—consisting of women, children, and old men—who would harass and booby-trap when they could. Westy may not have been the greatest U.S. general, but he was the soul of honor. Furthermore, it would have been impossible for him to deceive official Washington, including the President, even if he had wished to do so. Estimates of enemy strength were inherently complex and uncertain, but we in Washington had all the basic information that Westy had.

didn't believe that we should send in 200,000 reinforcements, so I was indeed recommending that we withdraw.

He bore down on me with his piercing black eyes, and asked: "If we withdraw from Vietnam, do you believe the Communists will test us in another location?"

"Yes," I replied.

"Can you predict where?"

"No, I can't," I responded reluctantly.

"Well," he said, "under those circumstances, I take it you can't be at all certain that the difficulties of stopping them in the next area they may choose won't be greater than the difficulties of stopping them in South Vietnam."

"No, I can't," I said gloomily.

With that his eyes glazed over as he lost interest. "You offer no alternative," he said, and I could tell that as far as he was concerned the subject was closed.

I was privy only on rare occasions to McNamara's personal evaluation of the situation in Vietnam. This was due in part to my position as a service secretary, but even more, I believe, to President Johnson's and McNamara's obsession with secrecy and fear of leaks. Secondary and tertiary levels in State and Defense departments were shut off from the deliberations of the President and his top advisers. We found ourselves carrying out instructions without knowing how our roles fitted into the broader picture. When we were called upon to advise the secretary of defense, or, on rare occasions, the President, this compartmentalization tended to cloud our judgment.

By late June 1965, total U.S. ground forces in Vietnam stood at 75,000, and the administration was preparing to act on General Westmoreland's stated requirement for 200,000 additional troops. High-level meetings began in July. Robert McNamara prepared a report on his assessment of the situation and submitted it to the President at a meeting at the White House on July 21, a bare two days after his return from one of his frequent trips to Vietnam. This was one of those rare occasions when McNamara had made his evaluations available to me, although I did not attend this meeting with the President.

It was a gloomy assessment. In effect, it held that the tempo of the war was accelerating, the Central Highlands probably would fall in the monsoon season, six district capitals had already been lost and only one retaken, cities and towns were being isolated, and the economy was deteriorating. Terrorism was on the increase, the report continued, and the new government of President Nguyen Van Thieu and Premier Nguyen Cao Ky would not last out the year.

He recommended the deployment of an additional 100,000 combat troops by the first of October and preparations to deploy another 100,000 in 1966. He advised the President to ask Congress for authority to call up 235,000 Reserves, increase the regular armed forces by 375,000, and seek supplemental appropriations to pursue our objectives in Vietnam. He also recommended that we increase air sorties over North Vietnam from 2,500 to 4,000 a month while avoiding population and industrial targets.[4]

The next day, the President called in the Joint Chiefs of Staff and the service secretaries, as well as McNamara, Cyrus Vance, McGeorge Bundy, presidential assistant Jack Valenti, and Clark Clifford. President Johnson's military advisers supported McNamara's recommendations. When the President turned to me and asked for my views, I responded:

"In that area not occupied by U.S. forces, it is worse, as I observed on my recent trip out there. We have two alternatives, Mr. President. Support the Vietnamese throughout their country or stick to the secure positions we do have. We need to make it clear to the populace that we are on their side. Then gradually turn the tide of losses by aiding the ARVN [army of Vietnam] at certain points."

"What are our chances for success?" asked the President.

"If we want to turn the tide by introducing additional combat troops, I would estimate our chances of success to be about forty percent." I hastened to add we would need another 100,000 men in January in addition to the 100,000 we proposed to put in by October. He asked if we could do that. "Yes, sir," I replied.

The President appeared determined to dredge up every piece of information and listen to opinions from all sides before making his decision. Unfortunately the opinions he received were limited to those of his top advisers. He wanted answers, not opinions, from those in lower echelons. Ultimately, of course, the decision was his to make—it must have been a painful one. He approved McNamara's recommendation for an additional 200,000 troops and thereby crossed another threshold in Southeast Asia. The Americanization of the ground war in South Vietnam began.

Vietnam was as much a quagmire for Lyndon Johnson's personal ambitions as it was for the nation as a whole. His domestic programs were not a political gambit, but a strong conviction that grew out of his child-

---

[4]Operation Rolling Thunder, the sustained aerial bombing campaign of North Vietnam, had begun the previous February.

hood in his native Texas, where he had the opportunity to view firsthand the tragedy of hunger, illiteracy, and lack of opportunity. The war on poverty and the civil rights programs he pushed through Congress with threats, compromise, and the sheer force of his own will and personality were for him his legacy of hope and compassion for the American people. More than anything, he wanted to be loved by the American people and recognized by history as one of this country's greatest presidents. His failure to achieve either of these goals was his greatest personal tragedy.

I found President Johnson, in spite of his occasional lapses into coarse behavior, to be a man with drive, humanity, and depth of sensitivity, struggling with too large an ego and too little solid confidence. He felt a need wholly to dominate those around him, but those who could really be helpful to him would not let themselves be dominated. He thus came to rely on those not worthy of his own stature.

Shortly after Lyndon Johnson took office I was summoned to the Oval Office. The President had undertaken an economy drive and was looking in every direction to cut down the cost of running the federal government. Lights in government buildings, including the White House, were dimmed, and we found ourselves peering down darkened halls in the Pentagon. When I received word that the President wanted to see me the next morning, I assumed that he wanted to explore the possibility of getting rid of the *Sequoia* and the *Williamsburg*, the presidential yachts, which were maintained and administered by the Navy.

To be prepared, I asked my people to come up with every option they could think of to sell them, mothball them, sink them, or even maintain them and decree that they were primarily for the use of members of Congress. I was well prepared to discuss any possibility the President might have in mind. The President greeted me cordially, asked me to sit down in a chair next to his desk, and proceeded to go about the job of being President. He greeted visitors, chatted with staff, talked on the telephone, dictated to his secretary, and intermittently watched the three television sets he had arrayed in front of him in the Oval Office. From time to time he would look at me out of the corner of his eye to see whether I was duly impressed, and then would continue with his work. There was no mention of the presidential yachts or anything else that would have explained my presence at his desk. Finally, around one o'clock, I was permitted to leave.

Lyndon Johnson demanded absolute loyalty from his aides and it appeared that I was being tested for a position closer to him. But I was not impressed. I am sure he saw that I was not to be dominated or awed by his magisterial approach to the complex role of the presidency. There-after I continued to be treated with courtesy and respect by the President, but I was not to become one of his close advisers.

When Johnson made the decision in the summer of 1965 to American-ize the war in South Vietnam, opposition in this country to our in-volvement was just beginning to emerge. One of the focal elements of disenchantment became the youth of draft age. Many of those who had managed to avoid the draft by continuing their education had a hidden feeling of guilt. This caused some to demonstrate their readiness for action by attacking the administration. Many felt the draft system un-fairly favored college students as opposed to the less favored majority. I thought that there was considerable merit in their complaint. A differ-ent opposition group, which expanded its influence over the next few years, was a substantial segment of the press, particularly some of those reporting from Saigon. The cumulative effect of these two opposition groups was a Congress reluctant to support the executive branch in its requests for authorizations and appropriations needed to pursue its ef-forts in Vietnam.

I decided that a number of internal reforms were called for. I assem-bled a team from the Navy Bureau of Personnel to work out a reform of the draft procedures. They came up with a scheme in which all males, when they reached age eighteen, would be subject to selection by lot regardless of educational or occupational status. Everyone would there-fore have the same chance of being drafted. The principal problem was to work out a transition phase to deal with those already older than eighteen who had been granted temporary deferments. We proposed a five-year transition period during which time a significant number of those already deferred would be called.

While not perfect, this seemed to me to be as equitable a solution as was practically possible. This proposed reform was accepted with some amendments by the other services and then by McNamara. But President Johnson didn't like our scheme. He thought a greater percentage of young men from the East had obtained draft deferments on educational grounds than those from the Southwest. This inequality, he said, was not being wholly corrected under our proposal; therefore, it still favored what he called the "Eastern Establishment." Congress was not enthusias-tic either. This ended our effort to get the draft reform project autho-rized.

A second reform project concerned fiscal policy. McNamara and I both believed that to offset inflationary pressures, the increased defense costs brought about by our Vietnamese involvement should be offset by an increase in taxes. This would obviously be politically unattractive. McNamara tried the idea out on the Defense Industry Advisory Council, a twenty-seven-man group which included the chief executive officers of principal defense contractors. Charles B. "Tex" Thornton, who had had enormous success in creating Litton Industries, strongly opposed the idea. He thought a little inflation would be good for everyone. When a vote was taken, all of the members of the group but three sided with Tex. Those who backed our idea included only M. P. Ferguson, of Bendix Corporation, N. B. McLean of Edo Corporation, and Kermit Gordon, president of the Brookings Institution. With no backing from the defense industry and widespread opposition elsewhere, McNamara concluded the attempt would be politically hopeless and did not press it with the President.

A third project was to ask the Congress to give the President authority to call up Reserve units as he determined it to be necessary. The combat-ready army and marine units left in the United States were totally inadequate in number to meet a contingency requirement either in Vietnam or elsewhere. McNamara discussed this with the President, but Johnson correctly judged that such a request would trigger a full-scale debate on the Vietnamese war in Congress that could not be won in the prevailing negative political climate.

I thoroughly approved of McNamara's positive and enthusiastic approach to problem solving, but these experiences dampened any optimism about bringing the Vietnam War to a satisfactory conclusion in the face of such intractable domestic difficulties in getting sensible policy changes adopted and implemented. Although McNamara continued to keep his chin up, he too was similarly affected.

In July 1966 I again visited Vietnam and was impressed by the progress that our forces had made. We were well established at Pleiku, the airfield had been completed at Chu Lai, the airfield at Da Nang was secure, and we were engaged in clearing the Vietcong from the surrounding area. The marines had greatly increased the areas where they were able to provide the populace with an acceptable degree of security from the Vietcong. Their area of responsibility around Da Nang had expanded from about twenty square miles in 1965 to more than six hundred square miles in 1966. Expansion in other areas was equally impressive. The resurgence in civil activity in the form of small industry, schools, and road building indicated to me the confidence the populace had in the security provided. The morale of the American officers and men was high everywhere I went, including the ships and carriers of the Seventh Fleet, and all were operating at full capacity and efficiency.

One jarring note left an indelible impression on my memory—one I hope never to witness again. Our "harass and destroy" operations were carried out with the ARVN and consisted of the indiscriminate use of artillery in the countryside with Vietcong and villagers alike falling victim to the barrage.

During a visit to the Mekong Delta region, where the Vietcong were deeply entrenched, I saw our artillery bombard the countryside with lethal fire. Within the hour I visited a hospital and watched while a parade of dying and injured children were brought in for treatment, the innocent victims of our indiscriminate barrage.

This reflected the dark side of Lyndon Baines Johnson. General Krulak, a tough marine general who had fought at Guadalcanal and many other battles in World War II and killed many an enemy, came into my office one day after briefing the President. Krulak was visibly shaken. After being briefed on the difficulties the marines were encountering in locating and engaging the Vietcong, the President had risen from his chair, his face dark with anger, and with his fist pounding the desk for emphasis, exclaimed: "Kill the goddamn bastards, kill 'em, kill 'em, kill 'em!" The marine general said that obviously was a soldier's task, but the violence and brutality with which the President expressed this had shocked him.

When I returned to Washington after my second trip to Vietnam, I told General Goodpaster that I thought such tactics would win us more enemies than it would eliminate Vietcong. I suggested that our artillery cease their indiscriminate harass and destroy fire and be much more specific in their targeting. Andy agreed but he thought the military would resent it if the civilian side of the Department of Defense imposed such a limitation on military operations. He thought it better if the military commander were to appeal to the professional pride of the artillerymen to hit known targets with accuracy. Andy did this when he became deputy commander in South Vietnam under General Creighton Abrams in 1968. I believe he was largely successful.

Operation Rolling Thunder

Early in 1966 Bob McNamara had speculated that the number of enemy casualties exceeded our estimates of infiltration from the North and that attrition would soon turn the tide in our favor. I had doubts that a higher attrition rate alone was the answer. A concurrent objective was to halt the flow of troops and materials into South Vietnam, not merely to kill enemy soldiers.

I forwarded a study to McNamara on the effectiveness of the air strikes against North Vietnam prepared in the Office of the Chief of Naval Operations in October 1966, which recommended a halt in the air war until better intelligence on infiltration rates could be obtained. In my memorandum to McNamara I suggested that if the air strikes cut down on the number of troops and material flowing south, they were, perhaps, worth the effort. I noted, however, that there appeared to be a lack of hard data on which to make a decision one way or the other.

"It is significant," I wrote in the memorandum, "that (because of the inadequacy of available data) the analysts were unable to develop a logical case either for or against the current air campaign or higher or lower levels of air effort. This is not a criticism of the analytical effort, rather it is a reflection of the degree to which decisions in this area must be dependent on judgments in the absence of hard intelligence."

We had been unsuccessful, as far as we could tell, in raising the cost of the war to the North to an unacceptable level. When we launched our bombing campaign in early 1965, it was thought the destruction of Ho Chi Minh's hard-won industrial base, painfully constructed after World War II, would bring Hanoi to the negotiating table. As it turned out, the ability of the North Vietnamese to recuperate from their losses would have been amazing if this had not been clearly consistent with the conclusions of the U.S. Strategic Bombing Survey on the strategic bombing campaign in Germany in World War II.

Our efforts to destroy their oil storage depots through a major air offensive in the summer of 1966 had failed, as the North Vietnamese quickly dispersed their supplies in small drums throughout the countryside, which were then supplemented by continuing imports. This disappointing result, together with General Westmoreland's never-ending requests for more troops, began to dampen McNamara's confidence that we could achieve our objective within the politically practicable limits of time and resources.

By late 1966 and early 1967 the President and the secretary of defense were under increasing pressure from the JCS to intensify the bombing campaign in North Vietnam by striking at steel and power plants, locks, dams, and railways, and relaxing the restriction on targets near Hanoi and Haiphong. General Westmoreland asked for 200,000 more troops in March 1967, or a total U.S. force of 671,616. McNamara obviously was beginning to have second thoughts, not only about the bombing of North Vietnam, but about our commitment to the war in Vietnam.

At one of our regular Friday meetings in March, McNamara asked me how I thought we could settle the conflict. If, he said, we halt the air strikes and go to the negotiating table with the Communists, and despite a prior agreement, the North Vietnamese continue to filter south, the air war probably will resume and at a higher tempo. How do we break the cycle of events?

I suggested that we put less weight on negotiations and put ourselves and our allies in a position of strength that would permit some unilateral phasing down of U.S. forces. I recommended the creation of a high-level group to formulate overall plans for the war and to supervise their execution. I suggested Bill Bundy might head the group since he had the confidence of the President.

After giving the matter further thought, I suggested the following strategy and timetable:

September 1, 1967: Complete the destruction of power, steel, and cement plants in North Vietnam and mine inland waterways and coastal waters between the 17th and 20th parallels. Phase down air strikes in North Vietnam to RP I through IV.[5]

November 1, 1967: Complete the installation of strong points along the demilitarized zone (DMZ) to interdict infiltration.[6] Phase down air strikes to include only RP I and II.

January 1, 1968: Deploy regiment-size units to inflict high attrition on infiltrators as they enter South Vietnam. End air strikes in North Vietnam.

May 1, 1968: Complete large-scale search and destroy operations against North Vietnamese supply centers in South Vietnam.

At the same time, I recommended that we go ahead with our pacification program (an effort to give the South Vietnam population an increasing degree of security from the terrorizing tactics of the Vietcong guerrillas), taking into account the political situation in South Vietnam, and help the South Vietnamese exploit the military and pacification results so they could increase their authority and control. This would

---

[5]North Vietnam was divided into seven geographical regions, identified as Route Packages (RP). They were designed for the purpose of assigning responsibility for target development, collection of intelligence data, and target analysis. RP I through IV were in the southern section of North Vietnam.

[6]This is a reference to the electronic barrier concept at the DMZ that was under construction at that time. The DMZ was located at the 17th parallel, the demarcation between North and South Vietnam set by the 1954 Geneva accords. The 20th parallel was about seventy miles south of Hanoi.

have created a strong position without negotiations and would have enabled the United States to withdraw on a phased basis. Moreover, it would have allowed negotiations at any point with increasing U.S. bargaining power. These recommendations were not accepted.

In May the secretary asked the Joint Chiefs, the CIA, Harold Brown, as secretary of the air force, and me, as secretary of the navy, each to take an independent look at the effectiveness of the air campaign against North Vietnam and to examine our alternatives.

I put together a team in the Navy to explore the problem in depth, some of whom—including Rear Admiral Gene R. LaRocque[7]—were supporting the chief of naval operations in his capacity as a member of the Joint Chiefs. The major sources of equipment, ammunition, and essential supplies for the Vietcong and the North Vietnamese were the Soviet Union and Communist China, with large shipments arriving daily over the roads and railways crossing the Chinese border and through the port at Haiphong. Our analyses showed us that for every ton of material we destroyed along the transportation routes between Hanoi and the Chinese border and thence into South Vietnam, we used almost twenty tons of munitions. We further determined that even if we expanded that effort, we would not sufficiently lower the level of supplies reaching enemy forces in South Vietnam to interfere seriously with their ability to conduct the war. The CIA estimated that the daily import capacity into North Vietnam was 14,000 tons, although actually at that time it imported only 5,300 tons a day. Our optimum interdiction efforts could "at most" reduce the tonnage to 3,900, while the minimum requirement by the North Vietnamese—if it eliminated all but essential military and economic goods—was 3,000 tons a day. This volume could be handled comfortably by the Communists despite a major interdiction effort on the part of the allies.

We believed the mining of Haiphong harbor would represent an unacceptable risk with Soviet ships arriving daily with their war materials, and that it would just be a matter of time before another route could be found by the Communists to circumvent the harbor.

I recommended to McNamara once again that we concentrate our air strikes on the infiltration routes between the 17th and 20th parallels in North Vietnam, the narrow neck of the funnel flowing into South Viet-

[7]Admiral LaRocque has since become director of the Center for Defense Information, a group that later appeared to advocate minimum deterrence in the face of the rapidly expanding Soviet nuclear arsenal.

nam, to interdict the passage of troops and supplies south, rather than continue our effort to close the wide mouth of the funnel.

Harold Brown and his Air Force team came up with a similar analysis but different conclusions. They believed that pulling back the bombing to the 20th parallel would give the enemy a free ride. He therefore recommended air strikes on railroads on a harassing basis, cutting off Haiphong from the rest of the transportation system, and, in general, continuing the current effort.

The wild card was the supplies coming through the port of Sihanoukville (now Kompong Som) in Cambodia and then overland into South Vietnam. Proof of this route was not conclusive, however, and it was not until Richard Nixon succeeded Johnson as President that we received indisputable evidence of its crucial importance. Nixon secretly authorized expanding the air strikes into Cambodia in 1970, thereby creating an added furor of opposition on the American home front.

A major difference in the conduct of this war and World War II was that our war aims in World War II were to destroy the enemy and his war-making capabilities. In Vietnam the second part of that objective was not possible without broadening the conflict to include Communist China and the Soviet Union. That was something no one recommended.

Realistically, our efforts in Vietnam were doomed from the start if the American people, and therefore the Congress, would not back an all-out effort to drive the North Vietnamese out of the South and take our chances with intervention from the Communist world. Moreover, our efforts to meet the threat in Southeast Asia seriously impaired our readiness to deal with aggression in other areas of the world. Another confrontation in Cuba or Berlin or a major threat in the Middle East would have found us poorly prepared. Our military resources, particularly our strategic nuclear capabilities, were being stretched thin. But more importantly, by 1967 the American people had turned against what many saw as that "dirty, limited war in Vietnam."

In August the President made a new overture to Hanoi through Paris channels. It contained a significant change in U.S. terms for negotiation. Until then the United States had offered to end the bombing only if North Vietnam would stop its infiltration into the south. Hanoi, on the other hand, had demanded an unconditional end to the bombing before it would come to the negotiating table. In what became known as the "San Antonio formula," the President offered to stop all aerial and naval bombardment of North Vietnam if this would lead to prompt and productive discussions. The formula was left deliberately vague in order to elicit a response from Hanoi. By then I had been appointed deputy secretary of defense. I worked on the final drafts of the San Antonio formula with Nicholas Katzenbach, under secretary of state; Walt Rostow, the President's national security adviser; and Henry Kissinger, at that time a consultant to McNamara.

The President waited for a response to his initiative. When it arrived it was an emphatic rejection. Hanoi maintained that the overture was in the context of an ultimatum. After President Johnson repeated his offer publicly in an impassioned speech in San Antonio, Texas, on September 29, Hanoi rejected the offer once again as a "faked desire for peace" and "sheer deception." Our offer, however, remained open.

Under pressure from the Joint Chiefs of Staff and Senator John Stennis and his colleagues on the Senate Preparedness Subcommittee, President Johnson—in late October—lifted some of the bombing restrictions within the magic ten-mile circle around Hanoi and authorized an expanded air war against North Vietnam. Only the port of Haiphong retained its sanctuary.

On October 21, fifty thousand antiwar protesters marched on the Pentagon, where they confronted troops in battle gear (without, I might add, ammunition in their guns). Three of my four children were among the demonstrators—I suspect, more out of curiosity than for protest.

McNamara had given me the task of heading the preparations for defending the Pentagon. I worked closely with Warren Christopher, who was then deputy attorney general. We created a planning and operations center to be run by the Army. Decisions were made on how to organize the necessary troops and federal marshals. We decided not to furnish ammunition to our troops.

On the day of the march, McNamara took charge. He and I watched the marchers from his office window, then from a command post on the roof of the Pentagon, and finally from just behind the troops manning the line in front of the Mall entrance. In front of the troops was a thin line of federal marshals. The instigators of the march were using every device to provoke the troops to violence. The troops resisted every outrageous provocation. At one point, the marchers outflanked the line and some got into the building, but they were quickly ejected. By dawn the marchers had lost their energy and disbanded.

The student revolts of the sixties were a worldwide phenomenon comprising many subgroups with a wide range of asserted grievances. The actual causes are hard to decipher, even in retrospect. The words that excited many of the young of those days are now meaningless even to those who said them twenty years earlier. The vaguely Marxist authors whom they then considered inspirational, such as Dr. Herbert Marcuse and Noam Chomsky, are no longer read.[8]

Ten days after the march on the Pentagon, in a memorandum dated October 31, 1967, McNamara advised the President that an escalation of our role in Vietnam would produce continued but slow progress. But he questioned whether it would be possible in the current political climate to maintain our efforts for the time necessary to attain our objectives.

He recommended stabilizing our military operations in the South with a view to reducing American and Allied casualties and turning over more and more of the responsibility for conducting the war to the government of Vietnam. He also proposed halting all bombing in the North by the end of the year. This, he said, would either elicit a parallel reduction by North Vietnam or a move to negotiations, or both. In any event, a lack of response would demonstrate that it was Hanoi, not the United States, that was blocking a peaceful settlement.

The President showed McNamara's memorandum to several of his advisers, including Supreme Court Associate Justice Abe Fortas and Clark Clifford. They both repudiated McNamara's advice, Fortas on the basis that we must do what is right, not what the American people want, and Clifford on the grounds that it would be playing into the hands of Hanoi by demonstrating that we lacked the will to carry on the war. Their advice was couched in such terms as to be an indictment of the President's secretary of defense and sealed his imminent departure from the Pentagon. Their arguments carried the day with Lyndon Johnson. A meeting with his so-called wise men[9] in November confirmed him in this judgment.

Later that month McNamara decided his usefulness in the Johnson administration was over and accepted the President's offer to become president of the World Bank.

---

[8]Melvin J. Lasky, in the November 1988 issue of *Encounter*, in an article entitled "The Ideas of '68: A Retrospective on the 20th Anniversary Celebrations of 'the Student Revolt,' " deals with the phenomenon in his usual incisive and witty style.

[9]This advisory group was composed of former officials and advisers outside of government. They were Dean Acheson; George Ball, then in private law practice; retired General of the Army Omar Bradley; Ford Foundation President McGeorge Bundy; Arthur Dean, who had helped negotiate the Nuclear Test Ban Treaty during the Kennedy administration; former Treasury Secretary Douglas Dillon; former ambassador to Saigon Henry Cabot Lodge; retired diplomat Robert Murphy; General Matthew B. Ridgway, retired commander of UN troops in Korea; Maxwell Taylor; Abe Fortas; and Cyrus Vance, my predecessor as deputy secretary of defense.

The *Pueblo* Affair

Events appeared to be moving toward crises in other areas as well. In Korea serious incidents along the demilitarized zone were increasing— 566 in 1967 as opposed to 50 in 1966. On January 21, 1968, a commando force of North Korean raiders penetrated to within a mile of the presidential palace in Seoul and was repulsed after a bloody skirmish, leaving twenty-eight attackers dead and one wounded.

On January 23, 1968, the USS *Pueblo,* on an electronic intelligence mission off the North Korean coast, was seized in international waters and forced to proceed to the North Korean port of Wonsan with its eighty-three-man crew.

When I became deputy secretary of defense, I took over from Cy Vance the task of supervising the intelligence and communications activities of the department, including overhead reconnaissance (satellites and planes). The interdepartmental coordination of such operations took place through the 303 Committee,[10] which met every Thursday in the Situation Room at the White House. Reconnaissance aircraft flights were planned and carefully monitored by a small group attached to the Joint Staff—the Joint Reconnaissance Center. The Reconnaissance Center was directed then by an Air Force officer, Brigadier General Ralph D. Steakley, who was a true professional in the business and for whom I had a high regard.

The Navy had a number of ships that did similar intelligence work. They sailed wherever they could best intercept the electronic and radio traffic of the Soviet Union and its affiliates. Shortly after I became deputy secretary, a question arose as to whether their activities should also be planned and monitored by the Joint Reconnaissance Center. The Navy was bitterly opposed but I decided against the Navy.

The first issue to arise was a projected trip by the USS *Pueblo* in international waters along the coast of North Korea. General Steakley recommended a delay until he could carefully review all aspects of the mission. Since I had just ruled against the Navy by making the policy decision that Navy missions should be under the Joint Staff's control, I didn't want an Air Force officer immediately to hold up a Navy mission

[10]The 303 Committee was the interagency committee supervising covert intelligence activities. It was renamed the 40 Committee under President Richard M. Nixon.

on the mere suspicion that it had not been carefully planned. I denied his request. It was a serious error.

I remember being awakened in the middle of the night by General Steakley, who informed me that the *Pueblo* was being boarded by North Koreans. We immediately reached CINCPAC Fleet Headquarters at Pearl Harbor. It had no planes within range of the *Pueblo*. Our closest planes were on Okinawa, from where the Fifth Air Force dispatched aircraft more than two hours after we in Washington received the distress call from the *Pueblo*, an unaccountable delay. Flight time from Okinawa to the ship's last known location was an hour and twenty-three minutes, which caused our fighter planes to arrive more than three and a half hours after the request for help. This was too late.

General Steakley had been quite right. The mission had been sloppily planned on the overconfident assumption by CINCPAC Fleet that the North Koreans would not attack a U.S. Navy ship in international waters. CINCPAC hadn't bothered to alert the Air Force to have planes available to support the *Pueblo* if she were to run into trouble.

By eight o'clock the next morning, I was in a "crisis meeting," the first of several, in the White House Situation Room with McNamara, Walt Rostow, Bill Bundy, and General Earle Wheeler, chairman of the Joint Chiefs of Staff. The President joined us at ten.

Obviously our first objective was to get the crew back. A retaliatory attack, we judged, would be inconsistent with this objective. But could a nation such as ours afford to have a ship seized in international waters without retaliatory action? We examined every possible scheme but we were unable to come up with one that appeared to be to the net advantage of the United States. We took no retaliatory action.

Instead, we instigated negotiations to get the crew back. Our men went through unspeakable treatment for eleven months in their North Korean prison before we gained their release (with the exception of one who died) on December 23, 1968, by signing an apology and simultaneously repudiating it. Thus ended another tragic chapter in the American experience in Asia.

The Tet Offensive

On January 30, 1968, within hours after a thirty-six-hour truce had been called in honor of the Tet holidays and exactly one week after the *Pueblo* seizure, the Vietcong and the North Vietnamese launched an attack against virtually every major city and provincial capital, and most of the military installations in South Vietnam. In Saigon the insurgents penetrated the grounds of the American embassy and the presidential palace before they were repelled. There was intense fighting and the number of casualties, both civilian and military, mounted rapidly.

Allied forces fought well and drove back the enemy from Saigon, Da Nang, and elsewhere. The Communists suffered enormous casualties, with thirty to forty thousand killed or captured. Only in the provincial capital city of Hue did the fighting continue. There it lasted for nearly a month before the Communists were driven from their stronghold in the Imperial Citadel, the ancient walled section of the city.

Communist losses were largely Vietcong, who were committed to the offensive almost to a man. Thereafter they were never able to mount major military actions on their own. Reports indicated, however, that North Vietnam had committed only twenty to twenty-five percent of its forces. Politically the cost to us was high. The Tet offensive was a sobering experience for those of us in Washington as well as the American public, despite our net military victory.

By February we had slightly under 500,000 troops in Vietnam, with 525,000 authorized. The President sent General Wheeler to Saigon to confer with General Westmoreland on future force requirements. General Wheeler returned to Washington and submitted his report to the President on February 28, with a recommended course of action and a stated requirement for over 206,000 additional American troops by the end of 1968.

The President realized that if he met General Wheeler's request for 206,000 additional troops, it would mean a total American commitment to the war in Vietnam, huge additional expenditures, and an immediate call-up of the Reserves. He directed Clark Clifford, who was to be sworn in as secretary of defense on March 1, to conduct a thorough reassessment, from A to Z (at least that was my understanding of the President's directive), of U.S. strategy and commitment in Vietnam.

On February 28, Clifford convened the first meeting of what became known as the "Clifford Group." The principals were, in addition to Clark and myself, Bob McNamara; Dean Rusk; General Earle Wheeler; General Maxwell Taylor, then President Johnson's personal military adviser; Henry Fowler, secretary of the treasury; Nicholas Katzenbach; Walt Rostow, special assistant to the President; Richard Helms, director of Central Intelligence; Bill Bundy, assistant secretary of state for Far Eastern affairs; Paul Warnke, assistant secretary of defense for international security affairs; and Philip C. Habib, Bill Bundy's deputy. Neither Bob

McNamara, who then left the Pentagon, nor Dean Rusk attended after the first meeting.

Clifford told us at that first meeting that our task was to determine how and at what level we should meet General Wheeler's and General Westmoreland's request for additional troops. This task quickly evolved into a larger question, which Clifford put to us the next day. He told the assembled group that he believed the real problem was not whether we should authorize the 206,000 troops, but whether, if we continued to follow the present course, we could be successful with vastly more than the 206,000 requested. He asked us to examine our alternatives, the alternatives open to the enemy, the implications of the request—militarily, politically, and economically—and, in addition, negotiation alternatives.

Clark Clifford had a very different style of operation from Bob McNamara. Bob had arrived in the Pentagon and immediately jumped in with both feet. He wanted to have a better understanding and more detailed control over logistics, base structure, pay scales, and a thousand and one different things. He instituted the five-year force level and budget plan and numerous management tools which enabled him and his associates to see where the major issues were and to intervene with some degree of intelligence to bring about a more effective defense establishment. This required a tremendous amount of work, which resulted in his having a detailed and intimate knowledge of the complexities of the Department of Defense in a surprisingly short period of time.

Clark Clifford, on the other hand, had been an adviser to presidents for years, beginning with Harry Truman. Lyndon Johnson had consulted with him at least once a day and perhaps even more before Clark became secretary of defense. The President relied on this relationship and insisted that Clark remain his principal adviser as well as serve in his cabinet. This resulted in Clark spending much more time on the telephone with the President or over in the White House than did his predecessor. He was slow and deliberate as opposed to Bob McNamara's quick and decisive manner. Clark's decisions and recommendations were made only after lengthy deliberation and discussion. This left him precious little time to deal with the mass of detail that had to be addressed every day at the top level in the Defense Department. Clark left the running of the Pentagon, for the most part, to me as his deputy, while he concentrated on the White House, the war in Vietnam, the Congress, and the press.

Clark Clifford was a fire-breathing hawk when he arrived at the Pentagon to take over his duties as secretary of defense. He was a strong supporter of the President's policies in Vietnam and had opposed bombing halts throughout Operation Rolling Thunder.

He had been present at the preinaugural meeting between President-elect John Kennedy and outgoing President Dwight Eisenhower. Clark had been deeply impressed by President Eisenhower's prediction that if Laos fell, the rest of Southeast Asia would soon follow. John Kennedy, although he chose to follow a path different from that of his predecessor, was also convinced that we must hold on in Laos and South Vietnam or risk the collapse of the rest of the area.

Clark was a firm believer in the "domino theory" and when he arrived in the Pentagon, his opposition to a bombing halt remained intact. Even so, by his own admission, he was relatively naive about our involvement in Vietnam. Our daily staff meetings, as well as the meetings of the Clifford Group, were long, hard, exhausting expositions on the cruel, cold facts of American involvement and our frustrations in achieving our objectives.

Our morning staff meetings were dominated, although not exclusively, by Vietnam. We would begin at 8:30 and continue as long as it was necessary to clarify in Clark's mind the topics he wished to discuss in his daily meetings with the President and with the press. Since I was his deputy, it was usually up to me to argue with him until I was hoarse on what I considered to be the errors of his thinking on our course in Vietnam. There were times when I despaired of changing his mind.[11]

I urged the new secretary of defense not to take as absolute the objective of completely eliminating the subversion of South Vietnam by force. The means we were prepared to devote to that objective over time had not been defined at a national level, but it could not be an unlimited objective to be equated with the preservation of the United States. There were other foreign policy, defense, and possibly economic objectives which were more important to our survival than our objective in South Vietnam. Because the Vietnamese struggle had become the focal point of the more general conflict between East and West, it was no longer possible to view our objective there in isolation. There was a valid strategic principle, however, that cautioned against reinforcing weakness. The recurring issue in the history of our involvement in Vietnam had been that of reinforcing weakness or suffering from the humiliation of settling

[11]In addition to myself, George Elsey, Clark's civilian aide; Colonel Robert E. Pursley, his military assistant; Paul Warnke, assistant secretary of defense for international security affairs; and Phil G. Goulding, assistant secretary of defense for public affairs, were usually in attendance at the morning staff meetings.

for less than our original objective. The time had come, I suggested, for a review of our Vietnamese policy in the context of our global politico-military strategy.

These staff meetings paralleled the meetings of the Clifford Group with its objective of reappraising our policy in Vietnam from A to Z. I prepared two papers, one that encompassed the views I had tried to impress upon Clark Clifford, which I submitted to the Clifford Group, and the other a proposal for our immediate strategy in Vietnam. I had discussed the latter in detail with Bob McNamara before he left the Pentagon and later with Clark and subsequently submitted to the President.

For our immediate strategy, I urged a unilateral halt to the bombing and a call for negotiations somewhat like the San Antonio formula. "The essential point," I said, "in negotiating with the Communists is to give oneself plenty of trading room between one's original position and where one might end up, plenty of time and every opportunity to improve one's underlying strategic position while the time runs."

I suggested that protection of the population in South Vietnam, urban and rural, should have the highest priority. This meant, in my mind, a higher degree of integration of U.S. and Vietnamese armed forces, placing our priority on search and harass operations in the mountains rather than search and destroy, and greater effort to clear and hold in populated areas.

I wrote in my report: "The [government of Vietnam] structure and the [South Vietnam] people are the target of [North Vietnam] strategy and the key to the situation. If they fall apart there is little we can do militarily to save the situation. The most probable estimate is they will not fall apart, will not pull together as we desire and will continue to be the weak and perhaps the progressively weakening link in the situation."

What reinforcements we could get to Vietnam in the next 90 to 120 days were most important, I reported. It would be only a small percentage of the forces already there, but the additional forces in conjunction with other policy changes could, at the margin, make the crucial difference. We anticipated a second offensive by the Communists in May, and the outcome would be determined by which side was able to pick up the pieces first after the devastation of the Tet offensive. I suggested a deployment of 50,000 additional troops to give immediate advantage to allied forces. This, I pointed out, would deplete our active forces in the United States and would necessitate an immediate call-up of perhaps two divisions of Reserves and a call upon Congress for a budgetary supplement and a tax increase.

Domestically, I suggested, this would mitigate the opposition of the hawks, while the opposition of the doves would be somewhat mitigated by the cessation of bombing. A substantial call-up of the Reserves, not accompanied by a bombing halt, I predicted, would in all probability prompt the Soviets to increase their material and political assistance to North Vietnam. If we halted the bombing of North Vietnam, they would most likely put their most important effort into maneuvering the negotiations toward a termination satisfactory to themselves and the North Vietnamese.

The Clifford Group was split, with most civilian officials in the Pentagon, supported by Nicholas Katzenbach from State and excluding the new secretary of defense, advocating a change of policy. General Wheeler, General Taylor, Walt Rostow, and Henry Fowler came down on the side of more or less continuing our current course. Dean Rusk, I understand, believed military pressure was a necessary prelude to negotiation, but he did not support a troop increase.

My battles in the daily staff meetings, together with my supporters in the Clifford Group, were to no avail. The recommendation to the President from the task force made no effort to seize the opportunity to change directions. It urged an immediate deployment of 22,000 troops, holding in reserve the remaining troops requested by General Westmoreland contingent upon a week-by-week review of the situation. No bombing cutback was recommended, no peace-talk initiative, no A to Z reappraisal.

On March 12, in the New Hampshire Democratic primaries, Senator Eugene McCarthy, a strong opponent of our role in Southeast Asia, won over forty-two percent of the vote against Lyndon Johnson. Senator Robert Kennedy tossed his hat in the presidential ring on March 16, announcing his opposition to our policies in Vietnam.

The President was bombarded from within and without his administration to pursue a new course in the war, to halt the bombing, to withdraw, anything but continue to pursue his unpopular course. He was not without his supporters, however, who appeared to have his ear. He dug in his heels. At a meeting with his advisers on March 16 he said: "I am not going to stop the bombing. I have heard every argument on the subject, and I am not interested in further discussion. I have made up my mind. I'm not going to stop it."

On March 12, another incident occurred, which was destined to heighten my role in the President's final decision, announced to the world on March 31. The Senate Foreign Relations Committee began its annual hearings on the foreign aid bill (which included the military assistance program). A *New York Times* article had reported, for the first time, General Westmoreland's troop request and the deliberations of the Clifford Group. The Senate hearings were being televised and many of the senators on the committee decided this was an excellent opportunity to show their constituencies how much they shared popular opposition to our intervention in Vietnam.

Dean Rusk was the first to appear before Senator Fulbright's committee and the hearings quickly turned into a painful interrogation on Vietnam. Clark Clifford had been asked to appear after Dean, but the President suggested that he decline because of his inexperience in office.

At a meeting at the White House on Friday, the fifteenth, I was asked by the President to represent the Defense Department before the committee. I protested. I told him that I did not agree with the recommendations of the Clifford Group, which were to continue our current policy, and that I could not support that position before Congress. "Nonsense, Paul," he responded, "of course you can."

I spent a sleepless night, getting up in the early morning hours to scribble out a letter to the President. I explained why I could not testify on behalf of the administration, that I thought a thorough reappraisal was mandatory, enclosed a copy of my recommendations for an immediate strategy in Vietnam (as described earlier), told him I realized that he might well feel my usefulness was at an end, and offered my resignation.

I walked into Clark Clifford's office the next morning and placed the letter in front of him. He looked at me in astonishment. "Paul," he said, "I had no idea you felt so strongly about this." "Well, now you know," I replied. "I have been trying to tell you for the last twenty days and you haven't really listened."

"But you can't resign," he said. I admitted that I had no desire to do so. Clifford reluctantly agreed to convey my letter to the President but he insisted that I delete my offer of resignation. This I finally agreed to do.

Lyndon Johnson was not happy with what he regarded as my lack of support, and from that day I was no longer invited to attend the weekly Tuesday luncheons at the White House with the President and his closest advisers. Clark Clifford, on the other hand, was impressed by the strength of my conviction. He did not, however, wish to appear before the Fulbright Committee. Paul Warnke was recruited and he indicated his willingness to testify since the military assistance program came under his office, but Senator Fulbright refused to accept testimony from anyone but the secretary of defense or his deputy.

Faced with my refusal to appear on the Hill and the prospect of appearing before the bright lights of the television cameras to answer the hostile questions of the committee amid his own doubts, Clark Clifford reversed positions. Thereafter he led the opposition to our Vietnam policies and argued vehemently for disengagement as quickly as possible. I suddenly found myself in the position of counseling caution, building up our allies before withdrawing, rather than leaving them defenseless before the ferocious onslaught of Communist forces backed by the might of Communist China and the Soviet Union.

The President came under increasing attack from the Congress, members of his own administration, and the public at large. A poll indicated that forty-nine percent of the American people believed that we had been wrong to have become militarily engaged in Vietnam. The President "hunkered down," as he was prone to say, and called upon the support of the American people in speeches delivered in the Midwest before the National Alliance of Businessmen and the National Farmers Union.

The President was troubled, but gave no sign of his increasing doubts. He announced, however, on March 22 that he was calling General Westmoreland home to be Army chief of staff. Mr. Johnson replaced him several days later with Westmoreland's deputy in Vietnam, General Creighton Abrams.

He called in his group of "wise men" on March 25–26 and had them briefed extensively. The group that met over dinner with Clark Clifford included Dean Rusk, Averell Harriman, UN Ambassador Arthur J. Goldberg, Walt Rostow, Earle Wheeler, CIA Director Richard Helms, Nicholas Katzenbach, Bill Bundy, and myself. After dinner they received briefings by Bill Bundy on the prospects for negotiation, by Philip Habib on the political situation in Saigon, by Major General William E. dePuy, special assistant to the Joint Chiefs for counterinsurgency and special activities, on the military situation, and by George Carver of the CIA on the security situation.

The next day the "wise men" met with the President and gave him their verdict: Continued escalation of the conflict in Vietnam, intensified bombing of North Vietnam, and increased American troop deployments would not bring about a military solution. They recommended that the President seek a political solution at the negotiating table.

On March 31, President Johnson appeared before the nation on television. He renewed his offer of the previous August, based on the San Antonio formula, and asked that talks begin promptly. He informed the nation that he had ordered, that night, a cessation of bombing attacks "except in the area north of the demilitarized zone where the continuing enemy buildup directly threatens allied forward positions and where the

movements of their troops and supplies are clearly related to that threat."
A complete bombing halt, he said, would be determined by future
events.[12]

The President announced that he was sending 13,500 additional troops
to augment and support the 10,500 deployed in February to help meet the
Tet offensive. These were in addition to the 525,000 already authorized.
A portion of these men, he said, would be made available from our active
forces. The balance will come from Reserve units, which will be called
up for service. He called upon Congress to reduce the deficit by passing
the surtax which had been requested almost a year earlier.

And he ended his address with the bombshell: ". . . I do not believe
that I should devote an hour or a day of my time to any personal partisan
causes or to any duties other than the awesome duties of this office—the
Presidency of your country.

"Accordingly, I shall not seek, and I will not accept, the nomination
of my Party for another term as your President."

The narrator of the *Pentagon Papers* speculated that "the President's
decision to seek a new strategy and a new road to peace was based upon
two major considerations:

"(1) The convictions of his principal civilian advisers, particularly Secretary of Defense Clifford, that the troops requested by General Westmoreland would not make a military victory any more likely; and

"(2) A deeply-felt conviction of the need to restore unity to the American nation."

Four days later I issued a directive to the secretaries of the services and
the chairman of the Joint Chiefs of Staff placing a new ceiling of 549,500
on U.S. forces in South Vietnam.

The North Vietnamese responded tentatively to the President's call
for negotiations and, finally, in May, our delegation flew to Paris to meet
with them in what turned out to be unfruitful discussions.

I was convinced that we could achieve nothing in Paris that was not
won on the battlefield. The question was, in what area were we seeking
military success; against Ho Chi Minh or against the insurgency in the
South? In my mind, the answer was military success in the South. Fail-

---

[12]There was later some question on just how far north this allowed our bombers to go
as reports came in from Saigon that American military spokesmen interpreted this as
meaning we could bomb as far north as 200 to 250 miles north of the 17th parallel. Ambassador Averell Harriman urged the President to clarify this to avert the impression that he
had misled the American public and our allies. He recommended limiting the bombing to
south of Vinh, which was located about 150 miles north of the DMZ.

ure, however, marked the road at every turn in our futile efforts to gain for South Vietnam the right to determine its own destiny.

Thus ended my direct involvement in the Vietnam War. On January 20, 1969, David Packard took over my responsibilities as deputy secretary of defense, Henry Kissinger became head of the NSC staff, and Richard Nixon was inaugurated as President of the United States.

Shortly after Nixon took office, a group of former administration officials got together at the Rand Corporation offices in Washington to discuss—with the wisdom of hindsight—the lessons learned over the past eight years. We had agreed prior to our meetings that Vietnam would not be part of our discussions; otherwise we knew it would dominate the proceedings. It was impossible, of course, to ignore, since Vietnam had indeed dominated our waking hours for the greater part of the Kennedy-Johnson administrations. It reared its monstrous head continuously during our discussions at Rand, in spite of our best intentions.

We started with the premise that if we had known in 1965 that four years later we would be where we were in 1969, we would not have increased our involvement by making the fateful decision in July 1965 to commit an additional 200,000 U.S. forces to the war in Vietnam. During those four years we lost over 32,000 Americans in Vietnam and over 200,000 wounded, we lost 5,000 planes, we had a peacetime economy overburdened with enormous wartime expenditures, and we were no closer to our goals in Vietnam than we were in 1965. The damage to our position in the world and to our strategic nuclear capabilities in relation to the Soviet Union was incalculable. It was during this period that the Kremlin laid the foundation for passing us in the strategic nuclear field.

The speculation that followed this observation was: Where would we be in 1969 if we had not made the 1965 decision? South Vietnam certainly would have been lost to the Communists and we agreed that the "domino theory" was valid. Furthermore, the outcome of the attempted Communist coup in Indonesia in the fall of 1965 and the ensuing struggle over the next six months would not have ended as favorably as it did, from our point of view, if we had left a vacuum in Southeast Asia.

There was widespread support in this country up to 1965 for our efforts in Vietnam. The American public assumed (or was led to believe) that our investment would be limited, that we would achieve our goal in quick order and the boys would come home. Unfortunately, the decisions made in 1965 expressly and by design precluded public debate or even wide debate within the administration. When the Tet offensive showed that our goals, at least for some time, still would be beyond our reach, that we were apparently worse off than we had been three years earlier, and that more American boys would be killed in that distant land, America lost its stomach for the war and public support dwindled as it did with the Congress. Without this support, as George Marshall wisely stated many years earlier, a democratic nation such as ours will not provide the will and sacrifices necessary for military success.

PART IV

16

SALT I: Getting Started

As deputy secretary of defense from 1967 to 1969, I found myself devoting a growing part of my time and interest to arms control matters. Years earlier, even before Sputnik, I was among those who had become concerned about the stability of the nuclear relationship between the United States and the Soviet Union. Our strategic forces and those of the Soviet Union then consisted largely of heavy bombers, most of which were located on a small number of airfields. Because warning systems had substantial gaps between radars and could therefore be evaded, a well-executed surprise attack could destroy most of the strategic forces of the other side.

Sputnik, and the resulting prospect that the Soviets could field an ICBM threat to our bomber bases before we could do anything much about it, reinforced our worries. The result was an enormous U.S. R&D and deployment effort to avoid those risks. Total U.S. obligational authority for the direct costs of strategic programs during the six years from 1956 to 1962 averaged some forty-eight billion dollars a year, expressed in constant 1985 dollars. As a consequence of that effort, by 1962 the strategic relationship between the United States and the Soviet Union was reversed to our advantage. That favorable relationship continued on into the late 1970s.

In the mid-1960s, however, the United States decided to go down one line in its strategic program while the Soviet Union went down a quite different line. I was one of those who participated with Bob McNamara in the decisions of those years. Under a stable nuclear umbrella, what counted at the cutting edge of policy were, in addition to a strong political and economic posture, conventional forces adequate to deter other forms of pressure against our allies. Economic and budgetary considerations made it wise to cut the percentage of our GNP and defense budgets going into strategic forces. By and large, it is cheaper and in the short run more effective to make technological improvements than to increase the numbers of our forces. We decided to halt the Minuteman program at one thousand launchers, to halt the Polaris/Poseidon missile submarine program at forty-one boats, and to reduce substantially the size of our heavy bomber and air defense capabilities. Instead, emphasis was put on conventional forces and, as to strategic forces, on improved reliability, command and control, accuracy, and penetration capability, including penetration aids (i.e., balloons, dummy warheads, and thin strips of reflecting metal designed to confuse enemy detectors and tracking devices) and multiple independently targeted reentry vehicles (MIRVs). In 1967, as I shall relate in more detail, we decided to go forward with the Sentinel/Safeguard antiballistic missile technology, despite our doubts as to the cost-effectiveness of the system we then knew how to build. When these programs began to pay off, it became possible to reduce annual direct expenditures on strategic systems. By the mid-1970s they had been reduced by almost two-thirds.

The Soviets made a different set of choices. They decided, first of all, to equal and then to exceed us in the number of strategic missile launchers and greatly to exceed us in the average throw-weight of the missiles these launchers could carry. This left them with the option to improve the technical capabilities of this large-sized force. Not surprisingly, their expenditures on strategic systems greatly exceeded ours and continued to go up while ours were leveling off and going down.

Many people today emphasize the potentially destabilizing nature of technological progress. To me, the lesson of the last thirty years was quite different. Technology is inherently neutral; whether it is good or bad depends on the uses it is put to and whose ox is being gored. Without an enormous technological effort it would not have been possible for the United States to restore crisis stability by its efforts in the late fifties and early sixties. Whether we will need to make, and be able to make, a comparable effort in the future may ultimately be the most difficult problem we will face in fashioning forces and arms control agreements with which we can live.

Setting the Stage for Negotiations

The immediate issues that confronted those of us serving in the Johnson administration in the late 1960s were a continuing buildup of Soviet strategic offensive systems, both sea-based and land-based, with weapons that could directly threaten the retaliatory nuclear forces of the United

States; and growing evidence that the Soviets were on the verge of deploying a significantly expanded antiballistic missile (ABM) system. Neither development was wholly unexpected; taken together they indicated that the strategic balance was shifting in favor of the Soviet Union. At the same time as our offensive deployments were beginning to level off, those of the Soviet Union had accelerated to the unprecedented pace of 100 to 150 new ICBMs a year. At that rate the Soviets would have an ICBM force larger than ours by the early 1970s and thereafter would be in a position to achieve significant superiority in the absence of effective U.S. countermeasures.[1]

Also, there was the added danger of an intense competition in strategic defenses. By the mid-1960s it was evident that the Soviets were working on an ABM defense based on two types of systems. One type, Galosh, could be identified without question as an ABM system, and was being deployed around Moscow. The other type, Tallinn, was being deployed across the northwest approaches to Moscow and at a few other locations. It had rather confusing characteristics; it had the appearance of an air defense system with some ABM potential. We later learned that it had been designed to be capable of dealing both with the warheads launched by our submarine-based missiles, which reentered the atmosphere relatively slowly, and with our high-altitude bombers.

In January 1967, as evidence of his concern over Soviet increases in offensive and defense weapons, Mr. Johnson wrote Premier Aleksei N. Kosygin that he had instructed our ambassador to Moscow, Tommy Thompson, to be ready to participate in exploratory talks on measures to "curb the strategic arms race." The issue that was uppermost in his mind, the President said, was the apparent impending deployment of a Soviet ABM system and the resulting pressure this would create in the United States to deploy similar defensive systems, which were still in the research and development stage. Kosygin's reply in February was encouraging, but noncommittal. Later, the Soviets dropped hints that further discussion of the arms question would depend on the holding of a Kosygin-Johnson summit sometime in the not-too-distant future.

Determined not to lose the initiative, President Johnson continued to press the Soviets to set a date to start negotiations. A breakthrough of

[1]The following numbers give an idea of how the balance was shifting: In 1962, at the time of the Cuban missile crisis, the United States had 229 ICBM launchers and 144 SLBM launchers, compared with a Soviet force of approximately 50 ICBMs and 97 SLBMs. By 1970, the U.S. buildup had leveled off at 1,054 ICBM launchers and 656 SLBMs, while the Soviets were still adding to their forces, having by this time deployed 1,427 ICBM launchers and 289 SLBM launchers.

sorts finally came in early June 1967, when he and McNamara met with Kosygin in the small New Jersey college town of Glassboro. Both sides indicated a willingness to negotiate, but there was no consensus on what the talks should encompass. Johnson and McNamara stressed the need for controls on ABMs as well as other systems, while Kosygin talked mostly of the need for controls on offensive weapons. But he declined to commit himself to specific topics or to a time and place to begin negotiations.

Before I became deputy secretary of defense in June 1967, it had been agreed that the U.S. position to be put forward in the event of negotiations should be worked out through a Committee of Principals, chaired by Secretary of State Rusk. The committee's view was that initial exploratory talks, if agreed to by the Soviets, should look at the possibility of a freeze on strategic weapons as a first step toward halting the further buildup of arms. Included under the freeze should be ABMs and surface-to-air missiles (SAMs) that might be upgraded to have a significant ABM potential; fixed land-based strategic missiles; missile-launching submarines; and land-mobile ICBMs, and intermediate- and medium-range ballistic missiles (IRBMs, and MRBMs). Members of the group disagreed among themselves over the extent of the restrictions or reductions we should seek on top of a freeze, and the means by which compliance should be verified, whether by unilateral means or by on-site inspection.

The Joint Chiefs were understandably reluctant to rush into any agreement which would jeopardize what was then our superiority in strategic weapons, or which depended on unilateral means of verification. If, however, we did accept unilateral verification, the Chiefs wanted the agreement restricted to components that were fixed and verifiable as to character and number by satellite photography. This meant ABM interceptor launchers, ICBM silos, and similar components. The Chiefs also believed that as a precautionary measure we should not foreclose the option of an ABM system. They insisted that any agreement entered into by the United States should be in the form of a treaty, thus making it subject to approval by at least two-thirds of the Senate. Among its necessary clauses, the Chiefs believed that the treaty should include adequate provision for withdrawal if there were hostile acts of interference with our verification methods or evidence of deception or concealment by the Soviets.

My first and foremost concern was that an ABM agreement include a system of workable, yet effective, controls. I concluded that the basic controls should be on the phased-array radar systems that were essential to tracking incoming warheads. Much of what I learned about radars came from a physicist and engineer named Charles Lerch. Charlie had helped design and build the first large phased-array radar at Eglin Air Force Base in Florida. Most of the labor and expense connected with an ABM system is in its radars, not its interceptor missile launchers, which are relatively cheap and simple to produce. This argued against the Joint Chiefs' proposal.

In an effort to reconcile viewpoints, I suggested to McNamara that the committee appoint deputies to handle the detailed staff work that I thought would be necessary. Initially, McNamara resisted my suggestion. He believed strongly, as a matter of principle, that the most important staff work should be done at the top and not be assigned to subordinates. In the case of arms control, he felt he already understood the problem sufficiently and therefore saw no need for others to become involved. One of his worries was that if he turned the issue over to staff people, there would be leaks to the press, causing bad feelings all around and divisiveness within the government. I disagreed and urged him to reconsider. It seemed to me that arms control was such a complex problem that no one individual—even someone with Bob McNamara's amazing capacity—could master it effectively on his own. After going round and round over this for some time, Bob finally gave in and agreed to let a small group take a look at the various issues involved.

The result was the creation of a working-level group composed predominantly of State Department and ISA personnel who prepared a new set of proposals that were circulated to members of the Committee of Principals in September 1967. The paper assumed, first, that the Soviets would not agree to on-site inspection, and second, that the United States would proceed with the deployment of an ABM system. Accordingly, the paper proposed that the United States seek a freeze on the number of strategic offensive missile launchers currently in operation or under construction, limit anti-ICBM launchers to no more than a thousand, and accept the principle of unilateral verification.

Although I was optimistic that we might find limitations by which both sides would gain as a result of an arms control agreement, I knew that the reality of the situation was such that each side would more than likely try to achieve for itself gains relative to the other side. For example, the proposal to freeze land-based ICBMs was, in fact, a proposal to freeze the launch holes, or silos. The Soviets' missile silos were—and still are— larger than ours and could therefore accommodate larger missiles carrying a heavier and more powerful payload. A freeze would guarantee them this advantage indefinitely. Though I realized that assuring verification would be difficult, I thought that throw-weight, or the aggregate payload, on each missile was a more significant criterion of capability than the number of launchers and that we should seek to assure parity measured by that criterion.

General Wheeler, the JCS chairman, agreed with me. However, I found it hard to convince my other colleagues, who seemed to feel that American missiles would continue to be superior owing to their better accuracy. Most of them simply did not believe—or did not *want* to believe—that the Soviets could, in time, overcome our lead in the technology involved in accuracy; they could not foresee that at some point in the future the United States might be faced with an enemy whose missiles were not only larger than, and therefore capable of carrying more warheads, but also as accurate as our own.

Still, as long as the Soviets showed no apparent interest in negotiations, our efforts in Washington to devise proposals received low priority. Of more immediate importance to our strategic posture was President Johnson's decision, announced by McNamara in San Francisco in September 1967, that the United States would deploy a limited ABM defense, called Sentinel, chiefly to counter what then appeared to be an imminent threat from Chinese ICBMs, with the potential for expansion against Soviet missiles as well. The following January, in his annual budget message to Congress, President Johnson requested $1.2 billion to start production and deployment of this ABM system, along with additional funds for testing and possible deployment of MIRVs on our Poseidon and Minuteman missiles.

The extent to which these developments were responsible for shaking the Soviets out of their lethargy we do not know. What is clear is that by the late spring of 1968 there were finally signs of movement from the Kremlin, with Kosygin now suggesting an early exchange of views. We proposed that the subject matter of the negotiations be the limitation of strategic nuclear weapons and defenses against them. The Soviets wanted the subject matter of the negotiations to be "the limitation of strategic nuclear weapons and defenses against strategic nuclear missiles," thereby including heavy bombers capable of carrying nuclear weapons but excluding air defenses. Their formulation would limit an offensive system without simultaneously limiting the defenses against that offensive system, leaving the door open for the Soviet side to concentrate on their greatly superior air defenses.

Eventually, acting on advice from McNamara and Rusk, Johnson agreed to accept the Soviet formulation in order to get the talks under way before the end of his presidency. This decision caused us much difficulty in subsequent years. The upshot was a joint statement issued

in Washington and Moscow at the signing of the Nuclear Nonproliferation Treaty on July 1, 1968, announcing the intention of the United States
and the Soviet Union to enter into talks "in the nearest future" on the
limitation and reduction of "offensive strategic nuclear weapons delivery
systems as well as systems of defense against ballistic missiles."[2] The
expectation was that negotiations would begin around the middle of
October in Moscow in conjunction with a second summit meeting between Johnson and Kosygin.

Though the President's policy was clear, much still remained to be
done by the Committee of Principals to sort out the details of our negotiating position. Technically, my role in these deliberations was to back-
stop Clark Clifford, who by then had replaced McNamara as secretary of
defense. But since Clifford was unfamiliar with the intricate technical
issues involved, he tended to refer most such matters to me.

The basic problem was to find a negotiating position that would not
weaken our security, and yet at the same time would elicit a positive
response from the Soviets. In other words, we wanted the negotiations
to result in a non-zero-sum solution that did not wind up in an agreement
giving one side or the other a particular advantage. A few years earlier,
just before I left ISA toward the end of 1963, I initiated a paper that
endeavored to spell out in some detail the issues that would have to be
dealt with in such an agreement.

Some critics have since charged that the committee overlooked or
failed to consider perhaps the most important issue of all—MIRV. This
is not correct. Though MIRV was still in the experimental testing stage,
it had been under study since the early 1960s, its appeal being that it
provided a cost-effective means to increase one's offensive power. I, for
one, was much aware of the difficulties the MIRV question could pose for
arms control. I therefore suggested that in addition to our going-in proposals, we should develop a fallback position taking into account MIRV
in case the Soviets raised it. I thought that if at all possible, we should
try to obtain restraints on the MIRVing of fixed land-based ICBMs, but
that submarine-based systems should be exempted. My reasoning was
that fixed ICBMs were far more vulnerable than sea-based missiles and
therefore would be at far greater risk if the opposing side's ICBMs were
armed with MIRVs. However, the consensus among the other members
of the committee was that because of the verification difficulties, an agree-

---

[2]Quoted from Lyndon Baines Johnson, *The Vantage Point: Perspectives on the Presidency,
1963–1969* (New York: Holt, Rinehart and Winston, 1971), 485.

ment should not limit missile characteristics or qualitative improvements. Rather than attempt to force the issue, I agreed with my colleagues that we should await the results of further testing.

The outcome of our deliberations was not significantly different from the set of proposals that the committee had considered the previous year after the Glassboro summit. Our number one objective was still a freeze on fixed land-based ICBMs, IR/MRBMs, and submarine-launched missiles. We also hoped to negotiate a ban on land-mobile strategic systems, surface ballistic missile ships, and mobile ABMs; we were willing to accept deployment of at least one fixed, land-based ABM system, the number of launchers to be worked out in the negotiations. My greatest disappointment was that there was no provision for controls on throw-weight, though the option of negotiating such controls if the opportunity arose was not foreclosed.

As the committee neared completion of its task, the Soviet Union extended an invitation to President Johnson to visit Moscow around the middle of October. The White House arranged a news conference for August 21, 1968, to announce that the President had accepted the invitation. But the day before the scheduled meeting with the press, Soviet and Warsaw Pact forces invaded Czechoslovakia. Facing virtually no resistance, they swiftly brought down the Czech government headed by Alexander Dubcek, who had been moving in a direction too liberal for Moscow's liking. To protest the Soviet Union's outrageous behavior, Mr. Johnson canceled his trip to Moscow and reluctantly shelved plans to begin arms negotiations. I sensed that this postponement was another in what had become a long series of disappointments for him as he neared the end of his presidency. However, shortly after the election, I learned that he had approached Mr. Nixon with a plan to start the talks as soon as possible, before the new administration would take office. Not surprisingly, Mr. Nixon took a dim view of this idea (as did I) and it was promptly dropped. For the time being, at least until the incoming Nixon administration established itself, arms control was on hold.

Tenor of the New Administration

Hubert Humphrey's loss to Richard Nixon in the November 1968 election signaled the end of eight years of Democratic control of the White House and with it, my imminent departure once more from government service. That I would have a role in arms talks, should any materialize, seemed highly improbable. Though Nixon and I had known each other since the 1940s, our relationship had never been particularly close; therefore I could think of no personal reason why I might be asked to stay on in some capacity. Indeed, as a Democrat, who had once been a close adviser to President Kennedy, I could well imagine that Mr. Nixon would be glad to be rid of me at the earliest opportunity. It was something of a surprise, therefore, when in the summer of 1969 William Rogers, the new secretary of state, asked me if I would be interested in serving as ambassador to West Germany. After consulting with Mrs. N, I said I would. But owing to a misunderstanding by Bill Fulbright, that project misfired.[3] Bill Rogers then suggested that I be nominated as ambassador to Japan, but that did not materialize either. So I continued to make my office at SAIS and to involve myself in a host of other ventures.

At the outset of his presidency I doubted Mr. Nixon's interest in negotiating an arms control agreement with the USSR; other matters crowded his agenda. The major problems facing him were the country's growing disillusionment with its involvement in Vietnam, a general weakening of our relative strategic military posture and capabilities vis-à-vis the Soviet Union, a worsening of our economic position relative to Japan, South Korea, Taiwan, and the European Community, and a loosening of our ties to our allies and friends. Given these circumstances, he felt it advisable to seek a way out of the Vietnam quagmire, to normalize our relations with mainland China so as to lessen the impact of our possible withdrawal from Vietnam, and to work toward a policy of détente with the USSR, while trying to resist those at home and among our allies who wished to get away from confrontation so fast and with such little concern for the results as to turn control of the future over to our adversaries.

Initially, arms control took a backseat to other matters. However,

[3]The episode in question occurred in December 1967 while Fulbright was conducting hearings into the clash between U.S. and North Vietnamese naval forces in the Gulf of Tonkin in 1964. Fulbright had come to doubt whether the North Vietnamese attack had really taken place, and insisted that the Defense Department produce evidence. I was deputy secretary of defense at the time and agreed to brief the senator. The conclusive evidence, which I showed him, was intercepts of North Vietnamese radio traffic picked up by the National Security Agency. Fulbright, however, rejected this evidence because the North Vietnamese boasted in their messages that they had damaged one of our destroyers and had shot down one of our planes. This was, of course, incorrect, but Fulbright seized on it anyway. He thought I had produced these messages as part of a deliberate attempt to mislead the investigation. He held this against me when my name came up as possible ambassador to West Germany in 1969.

within a few months of taking office, Nixon found himself having to confront the problem head-on. The immediate issue was not arms control per se, but the status of our ABM program, which was coming up for an authorization vote in Congress. Opponents of ABM, concentrated mainly in the Senate, sought to kill the program. Whereas a few years earlier Congress had been a strong supporter of ABM, even voting unsolicited money for it, there was now a movement afoot to get rid of it. Nixon had said he needed Senate approval of the authorization bill because he wanted to enter into negotiations on limiting ABM defenses. He did not see how he could negotiate with any hope that the Soviets would make reasonable concessions if the Senate had turned down the program. Judging from my own experience with the Russians, I shared Mr. Nixon's concern and agreed that the United States would be in an exceedingly difficult position in the negotiations if the authorization bill failed to clear the Senate.

Those who opposed ABM, both in Congress and among the public, used a variety of arguments to try to show why an ABM defense was both unnecessary and infeasible. Some contended that we would be escalating the arms race, ignoring the fact that the Soviets had long had a vigorous ABM program under way, while others argued that we were wasting our time on a technology that, in their estimation, would never work. Such arguments ignored what was happening to our strategic posture and to our negotiating position. The more I looked into it the more I believed that the basis of the anti-ABM campaign was to be found in the country's disenchantment with the Vietnam War, in the widespread alienation from the government of former supporters of the nuclear defense program, and in the desire of many to wish away the problems of national security.

The most vocal and articulate opponents of ABM were the members of a lobbying group calling itself Citizens Concerned About the ABM, headed by Roswell Gilpatric and former UN Ambassador Arthur J. Goldberg. Another group, with the encouragement of Senator Edward Kennedy, produced a series of studies purporting to show that ABM would never work and that it was therefore a waste of time, energy, and good sense. The authors of these studies were by and large prominent members of the scientific-academic community who had become disgruntled with defense policy in general and Vietnam in particular. The behind-the-scenes organizer of this effort was a friend of mine, Cass Canfield, editor in chief of Harper and Row. Cass and his friends concentrated on putting pressure on undecided senators to vote against ABM.

To combat the anti-ABM campaign, I joined with Dean Acheson and Albert Wohlstetter, formerly the head of the mathematics division at Rand, in organizing the Committee to Maintain a Prudent Defense Policy. We sought no ties with either of the political parties and decided at the outset that we would not accept contributions from people in the defense business. We raised a total of fifteen thousand dollars, half of which I contributed myself. A sympathetic friend lent some vacant office space on Connecticut Avenue in Washington. Lacking funds to hire a full-time staff for research and writing, we recruited three young but exceptionally talented graduate students who agreed to work for expenses—Peter Wilson, Paul Wolfowitz, and Richard Perle. The papers they helped us produce ran rings around the misinformed and illogical papers produced by Cass's polemical and pompous scientists.

After a while, our committee attracted the attention of Kenneth Belieu, who had worked for me in the Navy and who was now a member of Nixon's White House staff handling congressional relations. Ken decided that our staff and budget were too small for us to have an adequate impact. He turned to William J. Casey, the President's longtime friend and later the director of Central Intelligence in the Reagan administration, to organize yet another lobbying group, the Citizens Committee for Peace and Security, which operated out of the Plaza Hotel in New York. Casey quickly raised a sizable sum of money, but he had no plan for its use. Ken told me of his problem; I suggested to Bill that he use his funds to gain publicity for the papers that we on the Committee to Maintain a Prudent Defense Policy were generating. This he agreed to do, with the result that our committee became the principal source of witnesses before the Senate Armed Services Committee on behalf of the authorization bill. The bill eventually cleared the Senate by one vote.

During the ABM debate, I received a phone call from Bill Rogers. This time he wanted to know whether I would be interested in serving as a member of the delegation that would be assigned the task of negotiating an arms control agreement with the Soviet Union. By now practically everyone was referring to these negotiations as the "strategic arms limitation talks," or, more simply, "SALT." The head of the SALT delegation was to be Gerard C. Smith, whom Nixon had picked as his director of the Arms Control and Disarmament Agency. My job on the delegation would be that of representing Secretary of Defense Melvin R. Laird, who had already agreed that I was a suitable candidate. I assured Rogers that I was indeed interested in the job.

Rogers then arranged that I meet with Mr. Nixon and his national security adviser, Henry A. Kissinger, at the White House. It had been some time since I had seen and talked with Nixon personally; I found him little changed. What continued to fascinate me about the man were the several opposing facets of his personality. To understand him, one had to appreciate the role that Eisenhower played in his life. To advance his career Nixon passed himself off as Eisenhower's protégé, though I seriously doubt that Ike ever thought of Nixon in those terms. What endeared Eisenhower to the American people was his apparent sincerity, which derived from his uncanny ability to be able to believe in two mutually contradictory and inconsistent propositions at the same time. As an example, while I was working on the Gaither Report in the 1950s, I recall attending a meeting with Eisenhower at which he flatly declared nuclear war utterly unthinkable. Then, in the next sentence he gave the Joint Chiefs detailed instructions on how they should prepare to go about fighting one! It was this "sincere" inconsistency that impressed Nixon with its effectiveness and, considering himself to be generally more intelligent than Mr. Eisenhower, he reasoned that if Ike could reconcile two mutually inconsistent propositions, he could do so with three or four or even more. As a result, Nixon wound up never being really sure of what he believed, though to many he came across as sincerely believing what he said. Even after the wide publicity given the evidence uncovered during Watergate, there were still many people who believed him when he said he had known nothing about it.

There were other interesting facets to his personality as well. Next to Eisenhower, the most influential people in his life were his parents. His mother was a Quaker and a frequent public speaker. While he never fully accepted Quaker teachings, he did learn much from his mother about how to deal with people by appealing to their sense of goodness and righteousness. Also, he had watched his father go bankrupt. The people he most admired and befriended were those who had followed the opposite course, who were self-made and had clawed their way up the ladder of economic success to achieve financial security and independence.

My personal recollections of Nixon date from the late 1940s, when he was a freshman congressman from California serving on the Herter Committee. At that time, my friend Philip Watts, who later became executive secretary of the Policy Planning Staff, was an adviser to the Herter Committee. This committee was instrumental in laying the groundwork for passage of the legislation that put the Marshall Plan into effect. At one point Phil and the committee visited Europe to get a firsthand view of the situation. When they returned, Phil told me that of all the members of the committee, the one who most impressed him was a congressman from California named Nixon. That was the first I had ever heard of him.

It was the Alger Hiss investigation that gave the American public its first close look at Nixon in action. That investigation also had a profound and lasting impact on him, as I found a few years later after he had been elected to the Senate. Nixon felt he needed to know more about foreign affairs and asked Phil Watts if he could recommend someone to brief him. Phil suggested that Nixon talk to me, so arrangements were made for the three of us to have a series of dinners together to discuss major topics of national security policy. At our first session, I started talking on the subject of NATO and was about twenty minutes into my exposition when Nixon suddenly interrupted and said: "Now that reminds me of an incident during the Hiss investigation. . . ." And away he went for the rest of the evening with a monologue on the Hiss trial. At our next dinner, the same thing happened. I was talking about the Middle East or some such problem area, when again Nixon interrupted and turned the rest of the evening's conversation to Hiss. Whether we ever got together for our third scheduled meeting, I cannot remember.

Henry Kissinger I had known almost as long as I had Nixon. My first introduction to Henry was in 1956. At that time the Council on Foreign Relations had asked me to join a study group it was sponsoring to look into the relationship between nuclear weapons and national security. Apparently, there was concern on the part of some that I might have too much influence on the group, so at the suggestion of Nelson Rockefeller, Henry Kissinger was brought in as the group's rapporteur, with the expectation that Henry—reputedly bright, aggressive, and resourceful— would counterbalance my influence.

The council's practice was to encourage the rapporteur to write up whatever findings the discussion produced or whatever new ideas might have occurred to him as a result of the discussion. This is how Henry came to write *Nuclear Weapons and Foreign Policy.* The study group itself I judged to be first-rate, producing many new insights based on what seemed to me to be sound analysis. Unfortunately, little of this found its way into Henry's book. I thought that Henry was wrong on some of the principal issues and on a number of important details. I rarely write book reviews, but when *The Reporter* magazine asked me to review Henry's book, I readily agreed.

After I had written the review I sent copies not only to the magazine but also to Henry. Several weeks went by and I heard nothing. Then one day while I was vacationing in Northeast Harbor, Maine, I got a call from

Philip Horton, the editor of *The Reporter*, wanting to know if I had my facts straight. I asked him what had caused him to ask such a question; he responded that *The Reporter* was being threatened with a libel suit by Henry Kissinger and the Council on Foreign Relations if it went ahead with publication of my review. After what I had just heard, I reread my review, made a slight change to soften what appeared to be a potentially offending sentence, but retained the essence of what I wanted to say. The review was published shortly thereafter.

A few months later I was at a meeting outside Rome of the Bildeberg group. Henry Kissinger was also there. As I was about to go up to my room, he called me aside into a small alcove and said: "Concerning that review you wrote of my book, I made a deal with *The Reporter* that they could go ahead and publish it but I would be entitled to publish a rebuttal of any length. For the last couple of months I have been working, off and on, on that rebuttal. And you know what? I got to page 147 of my rebuttal and decided that if the rebuttal took that many pages there must be something wrong!" We both had a good laugh and from that point on, for a time at least, were good friends.

One of my objections to Henry's book was his treatment of the potential of nuclear weapons. He had misunderstood the destructive power of the larger tactical ones and thought that each side could effectively use tactical weapons of up to 500 kilotons (KT) on a European battlefield without causing immense collateral damage. Henry had no realistic idea how destructive a 500 KT bomb would be and erroneously thought it would cause only somewhat more damage than a 10 KT weapon. At one point he said that the blast and heat effects of nuclear weapons increase only by the cube root of their stepped-up explosive power, and that the blast effect of the twenty-kiloton bomb exploded over Hiroshima was only ten times greater than a twenty-ton TNT blockbuster. The applicable rule of thumb is the square of the cube root, and therefore the ratio should be one hundred, not ten, to one. He also said that each German town of twenty thousand or more inhabitants would be an effective sanctuary for noncombatants. He did not realize that, because of the density of the population, there were few places in Germany where a 500 KT bomb could be detonated without collateral damage to some city of twenty thousand or more. In short, the book was disconnected from the elemental facts of geography and nuclear weapons. It was my sincere hope that Henry, as he made ready for SALT in his new position, was listening to advisers more knowledgeable than he.

The meeting that Rogers had arranged for me to have with Nixon and Kissinger proved especially memorable. Nixon began the conversation by expressing his reservations about both Bill Rogers and Gerry Smith. "Paul," he said, "I very much want you to take this job. I have no confidence in Rogers nor do I have complete confidence in Gerry Smith. I don't think they understand the arms control problem. So I want you to report anything you disapprove of directly to me." Then he described the back-channel JCS communications that I was to use. I told Mr. Nixon that I could not do what he was asking. As I recall it, I said, "Smith is head of the delegation and the delegation can only function effectively if there is teamwork and trust within it. If I am to be a member of the delegation, it will be as a member of Gerry Smith's team and not as someone reporting to someone else. And in any case, Smith reports to the secretary of state, who must have complete confidence in what Smith reports. That's the way it has to work!"

Nixon declined to see it my way. He renewed the same suggestion that I had just refused. Finally, he gave up, merely saying that I knew there was a channel of direct communication if ever I felt the need to use it. Thus ended the interview.

Preparing for Helsinki

Though I knew from the start that SALT might prove to be an unsuccessful endeavor, there was never any doubt in my mind as to the importance of the talks, both in terms of their potential impact on our security and as a political imperative. On occasions in the past, however, the Soviets had used similar forums largely for propaganda purposes. Care would have to be taken, therefore, to keep both aspects of the talks continually in mind.

Our delegation was an able and distinguished group, broadly representative of the various interests involved in the negotiations—political as well as military. Most of us had been involved in these matters before, which gave our delegation a solid foundation of experience and a strong sense of continuity. As I have already mentioned, the senior member and head of the delegation was Gerard Smith. His father, John Thomas Smith, was a well-known Irish-Catholic attorney, who had been part of the original group that had created General Motors. As a result, the family acquired considerable wealth while Tom came to preside over one of the most influential legal staffs in New York. Gerry, following in his father's footsteps, also became an attorney, but eventually found himself more interested in foreign affairs. After World War II, as our relations with the Soviet Union deteriorated, he set out to learn all he could about Russia, including the language, which he worked on for years. Choosing to specialize in nuclear matters, he joined the staff of the Atomic Energy Commission in 1950, and in 1954 moved to the State Department, serving first as special assistant for atomic energy matters and, later, toward the end of the Eisenhower administration, as director of policy planning, the same job I had once held.

My other colleagues were the State Department representative, Llewellyn Thompson, one of this country's leading experts on the Soviet Union; Royal B. Allison, a lieutenant general in the Air Force, who represented the Joint Chiefs of Staff; and Harold Brown, president of the California Institute of Technology and former director of Defense Research and Engineering (DDR&E) in the Pentagon, who served as a member-at-large, in effect representing the scientific community. At the outset of the talks, we were also joined by another old friend, Philip Farley, Gerry Smith's deputy at the Arms Control and Disarmament Agency (ACDA). The executive secretary of the delegation was a State Department official, Raymond Garthoff, who had long specialized in intelligence concerning Soviet affairs.

With one exception, the delegation remained intact throughout the negotiation of what became known as "SALT I." Tommy Thompson, because of ill health, was forced to leave the delegation in 1971; a year later he died. His successor, James Graham Parsons, known as "Jeff," was an experienced diplomat who readily admitted when he joined the delegation that he knew little about strategic matters. Fortunately, he was what one would call a quick study and proved of significant help in nailing down the language of the ABM treaty that, together with an interim freeze on offensive weapons, made up SALT I.

My two most immediate problems were to organize my own staff and to help work out our negotiating position. Out of the give-and-take between the senior members of the delegation, it became apparent that a consensus could not be found for any one view. We found ourselves often badly split both over the philosophy that should guide us and the goals we should strive to achieve, largely because we had no solid evidence on which to base a sound judgment as to Soviet attitudes and probable negotiating positions. The central point of uncertainty was whether the Soviet power structure would demand a counterforce, damage-limiting, war-winning capability to cover the contingency that deterrence failed, or whether they would place a higher priority on mutual deterrence and mitigation of strategic arms competition.

I recall that as we were preparing our negotiating position in 1969, an intelligence estimate approved by the Joint Chiefs came across my desk setting forth the judgment that once the Soviets attained parity they would cease the buildup of their forces, seeing no useful purpose in going further. I was curious what information they had to back this judgment. I telephoned Major General Daniel O. Graham, who was then head of the Defense Intelligence Agency, and asked him on what evidence this report was based. It turned out that they had no factual evidence whatever; the estimate merely reflected their own consensus based on guesswork and hope.

I concluded from this experience that in the absence of hard information to the contrary, the intelligence community was prone to assume that the Soviets would look at matters the way Americans would. I thought this unlikely. Accordingly, I persuaded ISA to put together a group of outside consultants—people not involved in SALT but well versed in Soviet affairs and arms control issues—to estimate what the Soviet objectives were likely to be once the talks began. The head of this "Red Team," as it came to be known, was my friend and former associate Charles Burton Marshall.

One of the reasons why I chose this approach was to avoid the "mirror-imaging" process that the intelligence community often applies in evaluating Soviet objectives and tactics. It had been my experience that the Soviets view their interests in a manner unique to themselves and that they tend to act accordingly. Burt Marshall and the members of his Red Team concluded that the Russians would look upon these negotiations as being merely one more arena in their ongoing confrontation with the United States. From this it followed that their principal objective would be to obtain the best results possible for the USSR and the worst results possible for the United States.

Many on our side hoped that the Russians would look at the talks as we did, from the standpoint of a non-zero-sum game in which both sides could profit from an agreement. It turned out, however, that Burt and his Red Team were correct in their assessment of Soviet aims and negotiating tactics. Throughout the talks, the head of the Soviet delegation, Vladimir Semenov, took the position that he was negotiating for the interests of his side alone and that it was up to the United States to protect its own interests. (We found that Semenov and most of his colleagues were totally unfamiliar with our "game theories" and initially had no comprehension of what was meant by a "non-zero-sum outcome"; the term was simply not part of their lexicon.) He found nothing at all embarrassing in taking preposterously one-sided positions and in making outrageous demands. The only thing that seemed to interest him and his superiors was that the

Soviet side aggressively pursue Soviet interests. My colleagues and I, for our part, were not prepared to accept this Soviet attitude as immutable. We hoped the Soviets would eventually come around and be more reasonable.

At the request of David Packard, who had succeeded me as deputy secretary of defense, I began developing detailed critiques of the various proposals up for consideration, with a view toward a synthesis of ideas that would ultimately prove generally acceptable to our side, including the Joint Chiefs. The overall strategy I found least appealing was that of trying to secure a "stop-where-we-are" agreement—in effect a freeze—not only because of verification difficulties (which were uppermost in the Chiefs' minds), but because it could allow the Soviets with their larger and more numerous weapons to gain a significant advantage sometime in the future. "I do not believe this is a sound approach," I told Packard. "The qualitative aspects which are not verifiable are exactly those which could make our forces vulnerable to a true first strike if we remain frozen where we are."

I recommended that we examine quite a different approach. To take account of known JCS views, it initially involved two phases, although I hoped it could eventually be simplified to become an agreed comprehensive plan. If that were to happen, it would call for each side to be limited to no more than 500 ICBM launchers, each capable of launching missiles with a volume of no more than 50 cubic meters. With their current technology, this would limit ICBM throw-weight to about a seventh of that then existing. Overall, the total number of SLBM, ICBM, and IRBM launchers would not be allowed to exceed 1,300. I believed that such limits on ballistic missiles, particularly on ICBM throw-weight, would make the resulting nuclear relationship much more stable than it otherwise was apt to (and has) become.

My colleagues thought we should go slowly on these matters and test the Soviets before making a decision. Though I reluctantly concurred, I worried that if we tried to negotiate on this basis, we could easily find ourselves making piecemeal concessions along the way, winding up with an agreement we might come to rue. In advising Secretary Packard of this possibility, I also expressed other concerns that I hoped he would pass along. "The President should be aware," I said, "that if the agreement expires under circumstances where continuation on the same terms would be disadvantageous to us, we may not then be able to negotiate an adequately improved agreement. Failure to negotiate a new agreement after expiration of the first could result in an arms race substantially more serious than the present one." Little was I aware exactly how prophetic these words would prove.

The Talks Begin

The first session of SALT began in Helsinki on November 17, 1969. The Finnish government spared no effort in making sure that both delegations were comfortable and attended to well. The choice of Helsinki as the initial negotiating site was at the insistence of the Soviets, who apparently wanted to be as close to home as possible. Thus while the American delegation arrived in Helsinki suffering the miseries and discomfort of jet lag from hours of being cooped up aboard a windowless Air Force transport, the Soviets arrived by train, refreshed and ready to do business that very day. For the second round, which commenced the following spring, the scene shifted to Vienna at our insistence. Thereafter, the talks rotated between these two cities until, finally, at the outset of SALT II the negotiations acquired a permanent home in Geneva.

Vladimir S. Semenov, the head of the delegation, was also a deputy minister of foreign affairs and, as such, outranked the chief of the U.S. delegation. His original number two was General Nikolai V. Ogarkov, deputy chief of staff, who outranked the senior military member of the U.S. delegation. The executive secretary of their delegation, Nikolai S. Kishilov, was a senior KGB officer who had some years earlier been thrown out of Finland when it was revealed that he and a woman posing as his wife were running two separate spy rings there. Another member of their delegation was Petr S. Pleshakov, who was minister of the radio industry that builds all the radars and electronic gear for the Soviet military. Academician Aleksandr N. Shchukin—my opposite number in the talks—was one of their most senior and respected scientists. At least a third of their staff had KGB experience. Many of their military advisers had affiliation with military intelligence.

Even at the outset of the talks, with much being made in the press of how important the negotiations were, I was deeply concerned that we were in for disappointment. For one thing, I knew that there was no consensus within the U.S. government on what our tactics should be. Early on in the negotiations the two delegations agreed that as one of the ground rules for the talks, there was to be no "linkage" of these negotiations to outside issues. In other words, we should not make trade-offs or bargains in arms control on the basis of agreements or accords reached on other problems, such as Vietnam, Berlin, or the Middle East, where U.S. and Soviet interests were in conflict. We now know from his memoirs that Mr. Nixon took an entirely different approach to the talks and that he viewed linkage between issues as a fundamental part of the negotiations even before they began.[4] I suspect that this was what was behind many of the concessions he made. I know he was desperate to do something about Vietnam, which was tearing the country apart, and may have felt he had a better chance of getting Soviet cooperation on Vietnam by making concessions on strategic weapons.

Nixon had such a passion for secrecy and such a lack of confidence in the reliability and judgment of what he considered to be the bureaucracy that not even Gerry Smith was kept precisely informed of what was happening at the presidential level. This went to such lengths that at discussions at the highest level, Nixon would rely on the Soviet interpreters rather than the more competent American interpreters, whose notes might be made available to others on the U.S. side. As a result, there were no precise U.S. records of what was said. Even the less precise memoranda of discussion, subsequently dictated by a member of Kissinger's staff, were not made available outside the White House. It was not even the practice to give a full oral briefing to those who had a need to know. Not only did this leave the members of the delegation in the dark much of the time, it also deprived the President and his immediate advisers of the available expertise to fine-comb the relevant detail. Such practices also resulted in unnecessary difficulties, some of significant consequence, in parrying Soviet strategy and negotiating tactics.

Another problem was that we entered the talks under strong domestic pressure to reach an agreement. In reality, there were two sets of negotiations going on. We were negotiating with the Soviets and, at the same time, we were negotiating among ourselves back in Washington, within the executive branch and between it and Congress, particularly the Senate Foreign Relations Committee. Influential members of the committee thought we were being too tough on the Russians and urged us to be more sympathetic and understanding of Soviet concerns. They considered it more important to cut a deal than to remain firm on significant points under negotiation. In short, there was general pressure on us to be flexible. As a result, we never did have a solid U.S. position to put forward, one that had the full support of Congress as well as of the administration.

[4]See Richard Nixon, *RN: The Memoirs of Richard Nixon* (New York: Grosset and Dunlap, 1978), 369–70.

The Soviets were fully aware of our difficulties and tailored their negotiating tactics accordingly. Indeed, they employed all manner of techniques to turn the talks to their advantage. At receptions they tried to ply us with liquor and food to get us to speak more freely and reveal more than we should. On one occasion during one of the Helsinki rounds, they went even a step further. Semenov invited the U.S. delegates for a weekend trip to Leningrad. After a tour of the city, including its magnificent art galleries, he took us to a dinner of caviar, sturgeon, and Persian dishes, served at the Semeramis, one of Leningrad's finest restaurants, reportedly managed by the KGB. Following the meal came musical entertainment, capped with a performance by a young diva of excellent voice and exceptional beauty. Semenov could see that she was a hit with his American guests. At this point he turned to me and, with a sly glint in his eye, inquired, "Would you like to have her?" I thought at first he was joking, but then I realized that he was serious. I politely declined his offer.

Such ploys were part of Soviet standard operating procedure. One of their favorites was a divide-and-conquer tactic of complimenting one member of our delegation while denigrating another, thereby hoping to sow dissension within our delegation. Semenov was a master at this. He used to tell me what a great person he thought I was and how marvelous Jim Forrestal had been. Obviously, he was well briefed and knew that Forrestal and I had been friends and business partners on Wall Street. He spoke at length about the various contributions I had made, all the while suggesting that the other members of the U.S. delegation were not very knowledgeable or professional. Then Semenov would go over to Gerard Smith and try flattery of him and criticism of me.

Equally irritating and disturbing was the way the Soviets were continuously trying to spy on us and listen in on our conversations. At the first round of talks in Helsinki, for example, the U.S. delegation had its offices in the American consulate, which was in the same compound as the American embassy. Across the street was an apartment building. We soon discovered that the Soviets had rented an apartment in the building facing the consulate and that they had installed eavesdropping equipment to listen to our conversations and high-powered cameras to photograph documents on people's desks. I rather doubt that these elaborate measures did the Soviets any good.

Usually, the opening round of a negotiation is largely exploratory; neither side wants to reveal its full hand, so there is a lot of picture taking and socializing, but not a great deal of substance. Those of us serving on the American SALT I delegation thought there was a chance to break that pattern, at least to the extent of making it clear to the Russians why we were there and what we hoped to achieve. We therefore set about preparing an opening statement that would be more than perfunctory. My recollection is that John P. Shaw, a Foreign Service officer specializing in Soviet affairs, and William Hyland of Henry Kissinger's staff prepared a first draft; I disliked it and wrote a different one. I sent mine around to the other members of the delegation for their suggestions and it became the basis for the statement we finally used.

The gist of the final paper used at the opening round in Helsinki was this: First, it was the intention of the United States—with or without an arms control agreement—to maintain a strategic posture fully adequate to deter anyone from attacking the United States or its allies. We assumed that it was the intention of the Soviet Union to maintain an analagous posture. Second, we deemed it possible to have an arms control agreement that would lead to a mutual improvement in the situation—neither side would gain an advantage at the expense of the other and both would benefit from an improved sense of security, that is, the non-zero-sum outcome. And finally, we thought that the greatest increase in security that both sides could hope to attain would be through a comprehensive agreement providing for deep cuts in strategic forces, though we recognized that this raised serious questions of verification. For our part, we favored a high degree of openness, allowing for the maximum possible capacity to verify any agreement. We hoped that the Soviet Union would reciprocate. If not, then any agreement would have to be narrowed to what could be effectively verified.

The Soviets, we found, were not as forthcoming. During this and subsequent sessions of SALT I (and for a long while during SALT II as well), I had the impression that the Russian delegation had not yet received any indication from higher authority—the Politburo—that a decision had been reached that they wanted an agreement. The Soviets spoke in terms of general principles and shied away (as did we, to a certain extent) from making concrete proposals. Their basic tactic was to wear us down until we would feel compelled to move toward their position. It was not until well into the second year of the talks that the Soviet side indicated that it had received word from the Politburo that it wanted an agreement.

Early on at Helsinki I came to the conclusion that if the talks were to succeed, we would have to establish different modes of communication between the two sides. In our official statements and informally we tried to impress upon the Soviets that whatever the outcome of the negotiations we intended to maintain a wholly adequate and reliable deterrent to defend the security of the United States and its allies. We assured them that we had no desire to weaken Soviet security either, and that we recognized their need for an equally effective deterrent to defend themselves. Within this framework, we pledged to work toward limiting nuclear weapons under agreements which would improve the security of both sides and make deterrence more solid, credible, and reliable. The Soviets thought about the problem of our relationship in an analagous but more directly confrontational way. What they consistently said, in effect, was that they regarded their security and that of their allies as inviolable and would not hesitate to destroy anyone who might endanger that security. The idea was much the same as what we were trying to put across, but the wording and sentiment behind it took on much more brutal overtones.

After the talks recessed just before Christmas, I returned to Washington, where work soon began on what positions to take at the next session, scheduled to begin around the middle of April 1970. Though I had not found the Soviets overly forthcoming at Helsinki, there appeared to be a strong underlying interest on their part in the ABM question. The problem was that their Galosh system and our Safeguard system were not oriented toward the same objectives. Theirs was being built around Moscow, presumably to protect what we referred to as their "National Command Authority (NCA)," while ours was being deployed primarily to protect our missile silos. I therefore suggested that we reexamine our ABM program, which was again under attack in Congress, and that we consider an offer either banning both sides' ABM altogether or limiting it to the protection of our NCA (i.e., Washington) and thus more symmetrical with theirs. I considered the protection of the President and of our central command authority to be of critical importance. Kissinger was lukewarm toward my suggestion; his concern was that it would only antagonize the anti-ABM clique in Congress. But Nixon thought the idea had merit and agreed that we should put it on the table at the next round of talks.

I also suggested that we lay before the Soviets a slightly revised version of my paper of the previous fall, calling for phased reductions in ICBMs and SLBMs until both sides reached a leveling-off point of a thousand launchers. Though I was by no means sure the Soviets would accept such an offer, I thought it should be made in any case in order to feel them out on the question of reductions. The major change from my original proposal was in the treatment of MIRVs, which I now recommended against trying to limit or ban. Two considerations predominated in my changed thinking: first, our greater reliance on MIRV technology; and second, my waning confidence that on-site inspection would solve the problem of monitoring a MIRV ban.

During the Helsinki round I had explored this latter issue informally with my Soviet opposite number, Academician Aleksandr Shchukin, who convinced me that even if his side were to agree to on-site inspection measures, means could be found to circumvent them. Shchukin was an extremely competent scientist and had closely studied this matter. The obvious way to determine whether a missile is MIRVed, he pointed out, was to take the front end apart with a screwdriver and look inside it. Even if both sides were to allow inspectors to take such action, Shchukin was still skeptical. "Suppose," he said, "you did have inspectors with screwdrivers or whatever else was necessary to verify that there were no MIRVs, and then along comes a crisis; we order your inspectors at our missile sites out of the area and you order our inspectors at your missile sites out of the area; how long do you think it would take to screw on a different front end, one with MIRVs?" I speculated somewhere around six hours. "Exactly," he said, "what you would have is at most six hours' notice; however, it is unlikely that inspectors would always be present at every missile, so you might not even have that much time." I found his argument persuasive.

From then on, I was skeptical whenever I heard mention of on-site inspection as an answer to all verification problems. I concluded that the effectiveness of on-site inspection depended on its purpose and the precise nature of the measures agreed upon. Moreover, we had a significant lead in MIRV technology, and MIRVing was necessary to assure that our SLBM warhead could penetrate Soviet defenses, especially if we failed to reach agreement to limit or to ban ABMs.

The upshot of our deliberations was a decision by the President that we would offer two proposals—one calling for the phased reductions I had advocated, the other a much more limited set of measures that would impose agreed ceilings on both sides' strategic forces at their current levels. Included in the latter was also a ban on MIRVs subject to on-site inspection for verification. Under both proposals, ABM would be banned or limited to the sides' national command authority, or NCA.

The Soviets, when talks resumed in Vienna, did not respond favorably to either of these proposals for limiting offensive arms, nor did they come forward with any constructive alternative suggestions. However, they did express interest in our NCA concept. Their main complaint was that neither of our offensive arms proposals took into account nuclear-capable forces such as land- and sea-based tactical aircraft that we had deployed in Europe, the Mediterranean, and elsewhere—what were referred to in SALT jargon as "forward-based systems," or FBS.

At the end of nearly a month of futile exchanges, the members of the American delegation got together to discuss amending our proposals to break the deadlock that had seized the talks. Since FBS appeared to be a major sticking point, the idea naturally suggested itself that we drop our insistence on including Soviet MR/IRBMs in exchange for Soviet agreement not to press for the inclusion of our FBS systems. With the FBS issue out of the way, we might then concentrate on an initial ABM agreement and on controls for the three central systems—ICBMs, SLBMs, and heavy bombers. Though inclusion of the last would mark a departure from any previous position we had taken, we felt it advisable if in exchange for reducing the number of our heavy bombers, we could get the Soviets to reduce the number of their ICBMs. We called this the "Vienna Option." Though I felt our tactic for presenting the proposal was improvident, as I shall explain below, I fully concurred with my fellow delegates that our two earlier proposals were not negotiable. On June 15, 1970, we advised Washington of our view and submitted our suggestions.

Shortly thereafter, we got our first taste of Henry Kissinger's back-channel diplomacy. As is now well known, Kissinger and Soviet Ambassador Anatoly Dobrynin were meeting regularly to discuss SALT and other aspects of U.S.–Soviet relations. At one of these meetings, held on April 9, Kissinger had effectively repudiated our initial Vienna proposals even before we offered them, telling Dobrynin that if the Soviet Union preferred something more limited, he would be happy to entertain it. Knowing in advance that the delegation's proposals were not backed at the top, the Soviets lost nothing by stalling. Weakness at lower levels is not that serious; those positions can be overruled. But weakness at the top leaves no recourse.

Then, in late June, Dobrynin came back to Kissinger with a Soviet proposal that the two delegations suspend efforts to reach an offensive-defensive treaty and concentrate only on an ABM agreement. Henry did not advise the full delegation of the new Soviet position. I later learned that he informed Gerry Smith in an eyes only cable on July 4. Smith immediately replied that in his view, what the Soviets were suggesting appeared too limited since it would deny us our strongest bargaining chip—ABM—and require nothing in exchange on offensive forces from the Soviets. Henry concurred and for the time being the matter was dropped, but it had indicated to the Soviet side that Nixon and Kissinger were weak in their position on demanding proper limitations on offensive systems. Some months later the Soviets returned with a virtually identical proposal.

Since only Gerry Smith was immediately privy to knowledge of the Soviet proposal, the rest of us on the delegation had to guess at what was happening behind the scenes. It appeared to me that the talks were drifting away from their original purpose; the only thing that interested the Soviets was to find ways of curbing our ABM program, without having to make serious concessions of their own on offensive arms. I concluded that the timing was not right for the initiative the delegation had recently proposed. Kissinger, however, thought otherwise, and on July 9 we received instructions, approved by Nixon, to proceed with an offer based on our Vienna Option. The specifics were these:

—ICBM and SLBM launchers and heavy bombers were to be limited to a total of 1,900 on each side.

—Under this ceiling there was to be a subceiling of 1,710 on missile launchers and a similar subceiling of 250 launchers on modern large (heavy) ballistic missiles, or MLBMs.

—ABM was to be banned or limited to the defense of one NCA on each side.

—Limitations on MIRVs and submarine-launched cruise missiles were to be left to future negotiations.

—Verification was to be by national technical (i.e., unilateral) means.

These proposals were discussed informally with members of the Soviet delegation, who indicated that they would probably be acceptable but that it was necessary that we *formally* present them. Otherwise, they said, it would be impossible for the Politburo to deal with so complicated a set of issues.

What bothered me was that our proposed initiative made a number of important concessions to the Soviets without concurrently assuring what we were to receive in return. Heretofore we had insisted on keeping bombers out of the negotiations; now we were including them. We had endorsed the idea of controlling MIRVs, including the use of on-site inspection; now we were giving up such controls and offering to accept unilateral verification. And we were conceding in toto on the MR/IRBM question, leaving the FBS issue still up in the air. I disagreed with Gerry Smith's contention that these were nonnegotiable positions to begin with. On the contrary, we had staked our negotiating position on them, and having done so, I felt we should not be making hasty concessions without being sure that we would obtain adequate compensation in return.

At bottom the question was one of tactics: Should we present these proposals as a single package, or should we try to negotiate each of them separately, demanding a quid pro quo for each as we went along? I believed we should start with offering to drop our demands for the inclusion of Soviet MR/IRBMs if they formally agreed to drop inclusion of our forward-based systems. I drafted a cable in Vienna setting forth my reasons, then flew to Washington. I did not want to carry a classified document with me on the plane, so I arranged for a member of my staff in Vienna to send the cable as though it were his own. When I saw Kissinger in Washington, he initially agreed with me, but Gerard Smith wanted our entire package put on the table at one time for the reason stated by the Soviet delegation. The current round of negotiations had been going on since April and it was apparent that everyone was tired, especially the Russians, who found the warm Viennese summer taxing on their health. After my last meeting with Kissinger, Gerry saw him again and persuaded him to reverse his previous decision. Gerry argued that we should move at once on the entire package so that the Soviets could go home and discuss it at length in the Politburo, then respond at the next round. On August 4 we complied with instructions to this effect.

Immediately following the plenary session at which we offered our proposals, I had a private chat with Shchukin. He seemed to cast doubt on the possibility that our initiative would be taken seriously. He said that, while he himself was optimistic about the talks, others were not, and that serious problems remained, particularly in Moscow and particularly with the military. He said that the senior military members of the delegation—Colonel General Nikolai Ogarkov and his deputy, Colonel General Nikolai Alekseyev—thoroughly understood the problems involved in the talks, but that others did not. Many back in Moscow, he explained, tended to take a scholastic view of East-West relations and drew a black-and-white distinction between "socialists" and "capitalists." They maintained that they had won World War II and, having done so, should not be constrained from carrying out whatever programs they deemed essential to Soviet national security. Overcoming this opposition, he implied, would be a formidable task.

Shchukin's remarks did nothing to alleviate my anxiety. As I suspected would happen, our gambit backfired. The Soviets pocketed each and every U.S. concession in our August 4 proposal and confirmed none of those expected of the Soviet side. When the talks resumed, the Soviets began the negotiations afresh, but on a more difficult basis from our standpoint; having already made substantial concessions, we had little left with which to bargain. It was a costly lesson—a mistake from which we were never able fully to recover.

Stalemate

In view of the important U.S. concessions that our August 4 proposal contained, we could prudently go no further and a stalemate could not be avoided. The Soviets, having won a great negotiating victory in Vienna at no cost to themselves, were now in a commanding position and could well afford to sit tight through the next session, which opened in Helsinki on November 2, 1970. This they proceeded to do with no embarrassment. They dismissed our August 4 proposal as "inadequate" and "one-sided," and insisted that the FBS issue was still very much alive.

The next round, held in Helsinki that winter, was in my opinion the nadir of SALT I, though not totally devoid of accomplishment. On lesser issues (almost invariably those where the Soviet position was indefensible) Soviet negotiators began to yield, perhaps in the belief that this would placate us and induce us to concede on issues of far greater importance. For example, they agreed that diesel-powered missile submarines should be counted as part of their strategic arsenal, not just nuclear-powered ones, as in their original position. They also agreed to bar special measures of concealment and interference in the collection of intelligence by national technical means. And they accepted an earlier U.S. proposal that a standing consultative commission be created to deal with possible ambiguities in any agreement that might be reached. But on the larger questions of limiting and controlling offensive and defensive systems, the Soviets remained as obdurate as ever.

Since the talks appeared to be going nowhere, the Soviets in December revived the idea they had floated without success the previous summer of negotiating a separate ABM treaty. They were not inclined to continue negotiating on controlling offensive systems, where they were rapidly adding to the number and power of their launchers. Over time the gap in the technical sophistication of their offensive weapons versus ours was bound to narrow; therefore they deemed it not in their interest to arrive at definitive long-term constraints on offensive systems at that time.

By the time the talks resumed in Vienna in March of 1971, a deal, nailing down our concessions to the Soviets, was already in the process of being worked out. For those of us serving on the delegation, a particularly galling point was the manner in which this came about through the "special channel" between Dobrynin and Kissinger. For all practical purposes, this meant that there had been two sets of parallel negotiations—those between the officially designated delegations, and those between Kissinger and Dobrynin. I suspected that that was happening, but like the rest of the members of the delegation, I was kept in the dark.

The "breakthrough," if one can call it that, came in an exchange of notes between Nixon and First Secretary Leonid I. Brezhnev on May 20, 1971. Instead of a single, comprehensive, long-term treaty covering both offensive and defensive systems, they agreed that there would be one treaty, the ABM treaty, and a temporary or "interim" agreement that would freeze offensive strategic missile systems roughly at the levels of those currently operational or under construction on each side, until permanent limitations could þe negotiated. The public announcement was delivered by Nixon himself to make it appear that he had personally intervened to "save" the talks.

Upon learning of this deal and the way it had been arrived at, Gerry Smith was so incensed that he talked of resigning in protest. I shared his hurt and anger, but I was more concerned about the potential substantive damage to our security than by hurt pride. There was now little choice but to carry on as best we could.

17

SALT I: Reaching
Agreement

Despite the May 20 accord, the stalemate continued, due partly to the ambiguous wording of the Nixon-Brezhnev statement. The Soviets chose to interpret it to mean that we were to concentrate on an ABM agreement before doing anything about offensive arms. Our interpretation was different. We interpreted the statement to mean that negotiations on offensive and defense weapons were to be conducted in parallel fashion. Accordingly, on July 27, 1971, we tabled drafts of both an interim freeze agreement on offensive weapons and an ABM agreement. Once again the Soviets balked, holding out until September before conceding that our interpretation was the correct one, by which time months had gone by with virtually no progress.

Since offensive weapons were to be subject to a freeze (the particulars yet to be agreed upon), it seemed to me that the most promising area for any initiative leading to real arms limitations was in the ABM field. Here we had at least some chance of getting something done, despite continuing opposition in Congress to our ABM program. The previous year the Senate Armed Services Committee had turned down an administration request to begin construction of an ABM complex around Washington, the reason being that providing protection for the capital would not look right to the voters back home who would have no similar protection. This meant that for all practical purposes the NCA concept was dead and that even though the Soviets had earlier seemed inclined to accept our NCA offer, we would have to develop alternative proposals. What we were left with as negotiating leverage were two partially completed ABM installations guarding Minuteman ICBM fields in the United States—one at Malmstrom Air Force Base in Montana, the other at Grand Forks, North Dakota. At this point the simplest course to follow would have been to press for a complete ban on ABMs, but this Nixon rejected on the grounds that a total ban would lessen our bargaining power when we later came to the negotiation of controls on offensive weapons, particularly the Soviet land-based ICBM force.

I concurred that the proposal of a complete ABM ban at this point would be ill-advised. For one thing, as the Soviets resisted controls on offensive missiles, some type of ABM defense would be necessary to mitigate the vulnerability of our Minuteman missiles. I thought that a Soviet strike against our Minuteman silos could best be countered by providing them with an ABM defense. I urged that we craft our ABM proposals accordingly.

It was during this period of the talks, from the summer of 1971 on, that I saw a great deal of my Soviet counterpart, Academician Aleksandr Shchukin. Though I have known a good many Russians over the years, Shchukin was one of the few with whom it was possible to develop more than a working relationship. Like myself, Shchukin was of the pre-World War I generation, though he was seven years my senior. Born in 1900 into a middle-class family with an academic background, he was raised in a household that placed a high premium on the arts and learning. In addition to his native Russian, he was fluent in French, which was the language he and I normally used in our conversations. We also shared a mutual love of music. As a young man, Shchukin had begun his formal education studying to become a music composer, but his training was later switched to that of a concert conductor. In 1917, upon reaching draft age, he was called up for duty in the czar's army. Later that year, when the October Revolution occurred, he faced the choice of siding with the White Russians or with the Reds. The Whites said they would continue the war against Germany, while Lenin and the Reds said they would seek an early armistice. Shchukin believed his country needed peace and opted for the Reds.

For the next few years, Shchukin served in the Red Army as a private and then as a radio operator at Tashkent in south-central Asia. When he resumed his studies at the end of the civil war, he decided to specialize in communications. He soon became one of the Soviet Union's leading authorities on the theory of the mechanics of radio, radar, and sonar waves while teaching at the Leningrad Electro-Technical Institute and the Leningrad Naval Academy. As a reward for his contributions he was elected to the Soviet Academy of Sciences in 1946; from then on he was pretty much free to pick and choose his own projects. One of these, as I have mentioned earlier, was the Soviet H-bomb, for which Shchukin designed much of the electronics.

Shchukin never said or did anything to raise any question about his loyalty to the Soviet Union, but neither, to my knowledge, did he ever intentionally lie or try to deceive me. He was a member in good standing of the Soviet Communist party and a recipient of the Order of Lenin. He was fully dedicated to strengthening and protecting the Soviet Union and the Communist party. But at the same time, owing perhaps to his background and training as a musician and as a scientist, Shchukin was more cosmopolitan and sophisticated than the other members of the delegation. What interested him were not merely the technical issues we were dealing with, but also their larger cultural and philosophic implications. Among Soviet negotiators, he was unique. Our conversations would often stray from the matter at hand to such subjects as the authorship of what we know as Shakespeare's plays or schools of thought on philosophy, physics, mathematics, and classical music.

The Walk on the Felsenweg

A potential breakthrough in negotiating the ABM treaty occurred shortly after we returned to the bargaining table in Vienna, in January 1972. One day Shchukin invited my wife, Phyllis, and me to join him and his wife for lunch in Baden, outside Vienna, where the Soviet delegation had its living quarters. The reason he gave was that he had brought back some new phonograph records from Moscow and wanted to share them with us. No one in the Soviet delegation had ever invited a member of the American delegation to a meal at its hotel in Baden, so there was surely more to it than listening to some records. I accepted immediately and then checked with Gerry Smith, who agreed with me that the Soviets appeared to be making some kind of overture and that I should pursue the matter without hesitation.

A few evenings later Gerry was at the opera, accompanied by the head of the Soviet delegation, Semenov. During a break in the performance Semenov turned to Smith and asked him if he had heard about the luncheon Shchukin and Nitze were scheduled to have. Smith replied that he had indeed heard of it and that it was his understanding that Shchukin had some records he wanted Nitze to hear. Semenov chuckled and said that that was his understanding, too. He added that as far as he was concerned, the meeting was to be totally off the record. Clearly, what the Soviets wanted was a private, substantive discussion.

The luncheon, which took place on January 19, began with a variety of hors d'oeuvres, followed by a soup course, lobster thermidor, roast lamb, and at least five different wines. I suspect that the elaborateness of the meal had something to do with the Russian sense of protocol. It reminded me of Chip Bohlen's descriptions of the sumptuous state dinners that Stalin had given for Roosevelt and Churchill at the 1945 Yalta Conference—the most lavish spreads imaginable even though the rest of Russia was practically starving. The irony of our luncheon with the Shchukins was that none of us touched more than a few bites.

After the meal, we adjourned to the Shchukins' bedroom, where they had their record player. Shchukin put on a record, but before it was half-finished he suggested we all go for a stroll up the Felsenweg, a path up a long rocky ridge. It was a pleasant day, warmer than most for that time of the year. The ladies soon dropped some thirty paces or so behind, giving Shchukin and me a chance to be by ourselves. Shchukin told me that he had chosen this rocky trail to give us a chance to talk where neither the KGB nor the CIA could possibly listen in.

Once we were up on the Felsenweg ridge, Shchukin wasted no time getting down to business. The purpose of our conversation, he said, was to explore whether a compromise might be feasible. Everything, he stressed, was to be off the record, just as Semenov had indicated. He said that his side, both in the delegation and in Moscow, had made a thorough analysis of our ABM proposals, including our most recent proposal to limit phased-array radar systems, in a permitted deployment area, to a specific number of Modern ABM Radar Complexes, or MARCs. These were to be circular areas of such small size that all radars, ABM missiles, and ABM launchers in them would be vulnerable to destruction by a single nuclear warhead. Shchukin said that his side was prepared to accept the MARC concept in principle, with a limit on their size to a radius of 150 kilometers, but that they were not yet prepared to discuss the specific number of MARCs or to agree to our proposed limitations on the power of the radars to be permitted within them.

Shchukin said that the Soviet acceptance of the MARC concept applied only to the defense of capitals. The rub was that we had said we did not want to defend Washington and were only interested in providing protection for our ICBM fields, while the Soviets were interested in providing protection for Moscow. To get around this problem, I suggested that instead of specifying the permitted purposes of the sites to be defended, we specify the types of components that would be allowed at these sites. Shchukin and I agreed that by combining limitations on the acceleration and range of interceptor missiles located outside an NCA and on the power aperture of the associated radars, such ABM systems would be capable only of the defense of silos and not cities.[1]

After my meeting with Shchukin, I briefed Gerry Smith and the rest of the delegation. Though all agreed that Shchukin and I had made progress, some, including Gerry, disapproved of the concept Shchukin and I had agreed to of permitting ABM systems of limited capability for the defense of missile silos only. The next day Semenov, Smith, Shchukin, and I met to figure out how much of the Felsenweg deal could be accepted by both delegations for referral to our respective governments. It turned out that Semenov also disapproved of the silo-only defense concept. At this point it was dropped from the negotiations and our side reverted to a proposal it had aired earlier, offering a choice between the defense of two ICBM sites or the defense of the national capital. The Soviets indicated that they would like to study the matter further, but as for the rest of the deal we had discussed, there seemed to be satisfaction all around.

The Final Round of Negotiations

Over the next several months, while we refined the ABM agreement that had emerged from my discussion with Shchukin into draft treaty language, our two delegations endeavored to sort out the details of an interim agreement freezing the level of offensive weapons. By now it was clear that we were working against a definite deadline and were expected to complete our task in time for signing ceremonies to take place at the upcoming Nixon-Brezhnev summit, scheduled for around the end of May 1972 in Moscow. But despite faster progress than we were normally used to, the Soviets were in no hurry and made no hasty concessions.

[1]The reasons for this have to do with the depth of the battle zone above the target. To defend a city, one must intercept the enemy's incoming warheads at a fairly high altitude, above 100,000 feet; otherwise, if the warhead goes deeper than that into the atmosphere and detonates, it will do considerable damage to the city. Also, the enemy can employ a number of penetration aids, such as decoys, which are difficult to distinguish from warheads until they reenter the atmosphere at an altitude of 300,000 to 250,000 feet. Consequently, the battle space for defense of a city is between 100,000 feet and 250,000 feet. Defending a silo, on the other hand, permits a much lower battle zone. Since the silo is protected with concrete and steel, it can normally withstand anything other than a substantial nuclear explosion within a few hundred feet. Hence, the defending system can select its targets at a later point, after the atmosphere has stripped away the light dummies and exposed the heavy warheads. The number of launchers required and the acceleration and range of the interceptor missile are accordingly lessened, as is the required capability of the defending radars.

Negotiating the Interim Agreement proved to be more complicated than had been anticipated. Was the freeze to apply only to systems that were operational or was it also to apply to systems that were under construction? It was eventually decided to include weapons in both categories. But then another question arose: What did the term "under construction" mean? The issue was especially critical with respect to missile submarines, because the Soviets used a different definition of "under construction" than our side used. They considered a submarine to be under construction when building of its reactor began, whereas we used the term to mean when the ship's keel was laid. Evidence of the latter could be obtained fairly easily from satellite photographs, but the same was not true for construction of a reactor, which occurred indoors and was therefore impossible to verify by national technical means.

The inclusion of missile submarines under the freeze was in fact a rather belated development. The question had first arisen back in 1971, when Kissinger and Dobrynin were working on what became the so-called historic breakthrough of May 20. Henry told me he had consulted with Nixon, who had said that he had no preference one way or the other on whether SLBMs should be included, and that he had informed Dobrynin of Nixon's ambivalence. He also told me—I now believe incorrectly—that I was the only member of the delegation who was privy to this information. Subsequently, the Joint Chiefs recorded themselves in favor of including SLBMs under the freeze. Henry now wanted the delegation to try to include SLBMs in the freeze, but it was difficult to bring the Soviets around because they knew Nixon was not interested and could probably be talked into concessions.

Consequently, as late as Saturday, May 20, 1972—the same day that Nixon took off from Washington for what the press was already calling his "historic meeting" with Brezhnev—there were still a number of important outstanding issues to be settled—two having to do with the ABM treaty, and two with the Interim Agreement. With respect to the treaty, there were still significant differences to be ironed out concerning phased-array radars. I had brought Charlie Lerch with me as a consultant on radar technology. He and Shchukin agreed on the basic formula by which one would compare the power of such radars. Its controlling elements were the area of the antennae measured in square meters times the power radiated through the antennae in watts (power aperture). We had suggested a cutoff between ABM-capable radars and those not so capable at 1×10^6 watt-meters squared. The Soviets insisted it be 1×10^{10}, the power aperture of their Dog House radar around Moscow, the largest and most powerful radar in the world, and ten thousand times what we were proposing. In effect, their proposal would make the limitation meaningless.

The other ABM issue concerned the location of ABM sites in the Soviet Union. By now we were agreed that each side would be permitted two ABM sites—one for the protection of an ICBM field, the other for protection of its national capital, though it was doubtful Congress would permit us to exercise our right to defend Washington. Our side insisted that the Soviet ICBM complex to be defended be east of the Urals. The Soviets earlier had indicated that they agreed with this in principle, but wished to formulate it as being outside the European portion of the USSR. However, the preceding week one member of the Soviet delegation had indicated that they now wanted to be free to place it without restriction.

The first of the two issues with respect to the interim agreement dealt with the definition of heavy ICBMs. We had, for over two years, proposed that this be defined as any missile larger in volume than seventy cubic meters, the volume of the largest of their nonheavy missiles, the SS-11. In the preceding week a Soviet negotiator had made it clear that his side did not wish to have heavy missiles defined at all. Their position was that they would agree not to convert their present light missiles, the SS-11, into missiles as large as the SS-9, but they would not agree that the follow-on to the SS-11 would not be substantially larger than the current missile.

The second issue with respect to the interim agreement concerned the status and number of submarines. The Soviets now indicated, first, that they were to have 62 modern submarines and we were to have no more than 41; and second, that they could build up to 950 SLBM missile launch tubes on those submarines, while we would be restricted on ours to 656. What submarines and missiles were to be included in these totals also remained to be agreed. At this point, the Soviet delegation had not received instructions from Moscow, so we in Helsinki were stymied in making progress on any of these outstanding issues.

Before the negotiations shifted from Helsinki to the summit meeting in Moscow, we received instructions from Washington that if it became necessary in order to reach agreement we were to drop our insistence on a definition of a cutoff between phased-array radars capable of performing ABM functions and those not so capable. After receiving those instructions, Gerard Smith and I discussed how we should implement them. I proposed that we wait until Thursday, May 25, before executing our instructions. I was hopeful that at the last moment the Soviet side would come in with a proposal that would move from their outrageous demand to a more reasonable one, closer to what we were proposing. After a preliminary reduction to 5×10^9, the Soviets finally came around on Wednesday afternoon with a compromise we could accept of 3×10^6.

Meanwhile, almost from the moment of their arrival in Moscow on Monday, May 22, the President and Kissinger found themselves deeply engrossed in negotiations with Brezhnev. On Tuesday night, we received a message from Henry that Brezhnev had been very forthcoming. He had asserted that the Soviet Union had no intention of increasing the volume of any of its missiles beyond their present size. Brezhnev proposed that both sides agree that there be no increase in the volume of replacement missiles over those currently deployed. We sent back a message to Kissinger pointing out that such an agreement would prevent the United States from continuing with its current program of substituting Minuteman IIIs for Minuteman Is, since the Minuteman III was some twenty-six percent greater in volume than the Minuteman I. During this period the Soviet delegation was receiving no new instructions from Moscow, nor, in fact, was it receiving any information on how the Brezhnev-Nixon talks were progressing. This made it impossible for us at Helsinki to help resolve the more important outstanding issues. When our delegations met on Wednesday, we got almost nowhere.

On Thursday evening, at approximately eleven o'clock, a message arrived from Kissinger telling us that the Soviet side had offered a text for the Protocol which would provide that the Soviet Union would limit itself to 950 SLBMs, but that they would begin to phase out SLBM missile launchers only when they had deployed 740 in modern submarines. We first sent back a message recommending against acceptance of this formula to represent the number of Soviet SLBM launch tubes then deployed or under construction. We later sent back a further message saying that we saw no way in which one could reconcile a 740 formula with (a) our intelligence estimates of their SLBMs currently deployed or under construction, (b) confidence in national technical means, and (c) the proposition that a replacement submarine met the definition "under construction" when the start of construction of the first additional SLBM launchers subsequent to the date of signing of the agreement began.

Shortly after midnight, May 26, the delegation returned to the Hotel Kalastajatorppa from a late-night session at the office. At four o'clock that morning my telephone rang and Ambassador Smith suggested that I join him and the others out in the corridor. A message had come in from Kissinger indicating the latest state of play in Moscow and asking for our comments. Gromyko had offered a compromise deal under which a further 28 existing Soviet SLBM launchers would be included under the 740 figure. Sometime after five we made up our minds and drafted a reply, suggesting that Henry postpone signing any agreement with such provisions.

Later that morning, at 9:30, we got another communication indicating that agreement had been reached in Moscow on the substance of the various remaining points and that we would receive full instructions shortly. After we had received those instructions we were to negotiate the necessary agreement language with the Soviet delegation, then fly to Moscow. The signing would take place that evening in Moscow at 7 P.M. their time, which was 6 P.M. Helsinki time.

We then waited for the promised instructions—normally communications from Moscow to us required about twenty minutes. An hour went by and we had not received the instructions. We telephoned Moscow on the open wire and were assured that the message had been sent. Howard Stoertz, one of our technical advisers, checked through his channels and could find no record that a message had been sent. An hour later, we were still waiting for the missing instructions. Half an hour after that we finally learned that Washington had a copy of the message and would relay it to us. At 12:30 P.M. the instructions finally came in.

We found it far from easy to translate what had been agreed in substance in Moscow into clear and consistent agreement language. It was not possible to meet the seven o'clock signing deadline. We recommended to Moscow that the signing be postponed until Sunday, when the President was to return from Kiev. We were told that this would be impossible, though the hour for signing could be delayed. We were now expected to arrive in Moscow in time for dinner at Spaso House at 8 P.M. The signing was to take place at 11 P.M. This implied wheels up from Helsinki at around four in the afternoon.

In an hour or two we had worked out language for Article III of the Interim Agreement and for the protocol that was to accompany it. Both seemed to us correctly to express our understanding of what had been agreed in substance in Moscow. The problem was to get the Soviet delegation to concur. They were evidently having problems similar to but perhaps greater than ours; they were not yet prepared even to meet. It was 3 P.M. before a meeting at our embassy between Garthoff and Kishilov could be arranged. It was decided that if the two executive secretaries could come to a tentative agreement on wording, the full delegations would meet immediately thereafter at the U.S. embassy. We then drove off to the U.S. embassy with Garthoff, who went into a separate room to negotiate directly with Kishilov. From time to time he came out to report the tentative agreements they had come to and the remaining differences. By 4 P.M. a text had been agreed and the Soviet delegation was requested to come to the embassy.

In the meantime, it had become evident that we had barely enough time to get the new text typed on treaty paper and get it to the airport in time to meet up with the two delegations, who would proceed directly from the American embassy to the airport when they had finished the final plenary meeting. Back at the U.S. SALT office were Jeannette Christian, Peggy Coyle, and Wanda Lewis, who were standing by to type the final text on treaty paper. As the language of Article III was read over the phone, they set to work. Wanda was given an electric typewriter with which she was unfamiliar. She ran into trouble with the initial pages and found that before she was through she had one sheet of treaty paper too few. Sid Graybeal, who was supervising the operation, made the decision that the last page of the fourth copy of the agreement package would be single-spaced rather than double-spaced, thereby saving a sheet.

The protocol to the interim agreement was the last issue to be resolved. It was too long and the language too tortuous to rely on telephone dictation, so Colonel Frank DeSimone brought it over in his car. In the meantime, the final plenary meeting of the two delegations was taking place. Originally, it had been planned that certain unilateral statements would be made by one delegation and replies made by the other side to perfect the record on the remaining outstanding issues and that, in addition, all the agreed interpretive statements would be read into the record and initialed by both sides. Ambassador Smith proposed that only the first task be carried out at the plenary and, since the second task presented no substantive problem, that it could be carried out on the plane when we became airborne. Semenov accepted Smith's offer. As a result, we were able to conclude the plenary by 4:30 P.M., and with a police escort we drove off to the airport.

Several days earlier, General Allison had arranged with the Air Force for a VIP configured C-118 to stand by in Helsinki ready to take us at a moment's notice to Moscow. Early on May 26, Ambassador Smith had invited Minister Semenov and a group of Soviets of his choice to ride with us in the U.S. aircraft to Moscow.

The U.S. delegation reached the airport in record time, the Soviet delegation arriving some ten minutes later. Finally, another five minutes later, Howie Stoertz drove up in a police car carrying with him the treaty text and an electric typewriter. We climbed aboard and flew off to Moscow.

On the plane the remaining actions with respect to the agreed interpretive statements were taken and the treaty text was checked. It was found to contain imperfections. In the U.S. text the "United States" was to precede the "USSR" wherever the two names appeared together, and in the Soviet text the "USSR" was to precede the "United States" in similar cases. This had not been consistently done. Furthermore, some of the copies read "President of the United States" instead of "President of the United States of America." It was therefore necessary to have some of the pages retyped upon our arrival in Moscow. It was arranged that Charles Bevans, the State Department treaty expert, and Curt Kamman of the U.S. embassy staff would meet Garthoff and Oleg Grinevsky of the Soviet Foreign Ministry and the electric typewriter in the VIP lounge in the airport immediately upon arrival. They would check the text and have the necessary corrections made. The rest of us were to proceed directly to Spaso House.

The Moscow Summit

We arrived at Moscow International Airport at 8:50 P.M. As Ambassador Smith went down the stairs to the tarmac, Secretary Brezhnev's aide came up to him in great agitation and said that he had instructions to take Ambassador Smith directly to the Kremlin. Ambassador Smith said that he had instructions from his authorities to go directly to Spaso House. Brezhnev's aide insisted that his instructions overrode those which Ambassador Smith had. Smith finally decided that the wiser course was to let himself be taken directly to the Kremlin. He then disappeared in a cloud of Soviet automobiles and police outriders driving at high speed out of the airport.

Car number 72 had been assigned to take me, General Allison, and Ray Garthoff to Spaso House. We stopped first at the VIP lounge so that Garthoff, Grinevsky, and the typewriter could meet up with Bevans and Kamman. We found the room empty. A Russian flight attendant appeared and told us that Bevans and Kamman had been there until a minute or two previously but had seen Ambassador Smith and a series of other cars leave at high speed. They had concluded that all of us had gone and had left in hot pursuit of the cavalcade.

Colonel Scott, the air attaché who had traveled to Helsinki to escort General Allison and the delegation to Moscow, told me that there was an American command center at the Rossiya Hotel. A telephone call put me through to a Mr. McGuire. I told him what had happened and asked him to find Bevans and Kamman. I told him that Garthoff, Grinevsky, and the typewriter were going off to MID, the Soviet Ministry of External Affairs, and that Bevans and Kamman should meet them there. McGuire said he would do his best. He in turn asked me whether we had an extra copy of the documents, as had been requested earlier, for the briefing of the press. I told him we had not had time to prepare an extra copy and that the press would have to wait until a copy could be made at the Ministry of External Affairs and gotten to them.

Garthoff, Grinevsky, and the typewriter then departed for MID. General Allison had been intercepted while getting off the aircraft and told that he was expected to be in uniform at the Spaso House dinner. He had been unable to find any place in the VIP lounge where he could change. Colonel Scott suggested the change be made in the Scott apartment in the U.S. embassy compound. With that, Allison departed with Colonel and Mrs. Scott for their residence to change into his uniform and agreed to meet me at Spaso House.

At this point, I was left alone with car number 72, a Russian driver who spoke no English, and Ambassador Smith's luggage, my luggage, and Ray Garthoff's luggage. We started off for Spaso House. By this time, it must have been 9:20 P.M. Everything went smoothly enough until we got to Tschaikovsky Boulevard, where one must turn left onto one of several side streets in order to reach Spaso House. At each one of the side streets there was a group of Soviet policemen whose task it was to maintain the security of Spaso House by letting no cars turn into the nearby side streets. After my driver had driven back and forth two or three times trying to find a way through the police cordon without success, I managed to get across to him by a series of gestures that he should try talking to the police and use my diplomatic passport as evidence that we should be let through. After two or three failures of this technique, he finally did find a group of policemen who let us turn left. We then found ourselves in the street which I recognized as being the one leading to Spaso House, but we were still more than a block away. It became evident that we could proceed no farther by car, the street being completely filled with police motorcycles waiting to lead the cavalcade of cars from Spaso House to the Kremlin for the signing ceremony. I got out of the car and managed to get through the motorcycle police force by waving my passport in their faces. I finally got to the front entrance of Spaso House and gave a sigh of relief as I saw American faces in the driveway.

I had walked about three paces into the driveway when I was seized from all sides and found myself in the clutches of the U.S. Secret Service. I protested that I was a member of the SALT delegation and was expected at the dinner. It was quite clear that they had never heard of SALT or of the delegation. I protested that they must let me speak to someone. They asked to whom I wished to speak. I suggested Secretary of State Rogers. By this time they were convinced I was either a nut or a member of the press corps. But they gave me one more chance and asked if there was someone else I wanted to see. I said, "Mr. Helmut Sonnenfeldt." They doubted whether that would be possible either. Secretary Rogers, Mr. Sonnenfeldt, and everyone else with the President's party were listening to a concert. They told me there was no one I could see and that I should go away. At this point, a Navy lieutenant commander with an aide's aiguillette came out of the door. I asked him whether he could help me, explaining that I was a former secretary of the navy. It appeared that I had merely succeeded in embarrassing him because he promptly disappeared without doing anything.

Then, a young man in a dark suit with a red button on his lapel appeared and asked me whether I was Mr. Nitze. I said I was indeed, and asked him who he was. He said he was associated with the Soviet Ministry of External Affairs, and he would like to be of help to me. He suggested that the wisest thing to do would be to go straight to the Kremlin and to give up trying to enter Spaso House. He said there was one difficulty, however; he did not have an automobile to get us there. I said that car number 72 had been assigned to me; I had left it a block and a half away. If he would find it we could use it. He went out and succeeded in finding car number 72 and in due course we started for the Kremlin.

As we approached the Kremlin there were police groups protecting the approaches just as there had been at Spaso House. It appeared that my Ministry of External Affairs friend did not have the necessary passes to get us through. Ahead of us he saw a car containing one of the deputy ministers. We slipped in directly behind him to get through the various barriers and arrived at the entrance to the Kremlin. At this point, the deputy minister emerged from his car and I emerged from mine; he proceeded into the Kremlin and I followed some ten paces behind. We went through corridor after corridor, all of which seemed to be totally empty. We finally entered a large room, Vladimir Hall, in which the signing was to take place. It was empty except for a small group in a far corner consisting of Semenov and two or three men unknown to me with whom he was deep in conversation. I walked up and greeted Semenov. It was clear that he wanted to continue his discussion with his associates. I went off and stood alone some distance away, waiting for something to happen. At this point, Semenov and his friends disappeared down a passageway at the rear of the room, leaving me all alone.

Some minutes later Secretary Rogers and First Deputy Foreign Minister Vasily V. Kuznetsov entered the room at the far side of the hall. Rogers greeted me with the greatest warmth and suggested that I join the two of them in the reception room behind the treaty signing room. Despite the fact that the last time I had seen anything of Kuznetsov was in connection with the Cuban missile crisis, we got along famously. Shortly thereafter, Marshal Andrei Grechko, the Soviet defense minister, entered the room, accompanied by the chief of staff of the Soviet General Staff, General Kulikov, and General Ogarkov. Kuznetsov introduced me to Marshal Grechko, who seemed to have a permanent grin. His comment was, "He is from that SALT delegation. The SALT group is the greatest bureaucracy ever invented." There was then much laughter on all sides.

At this point other Americans appeared, including U.S. ambassador to the Soviet Union Jacob Beam, Assistant Secretary of State for European Affairs Martin Hillenbrand, and Peter Flanigan, the President's assistant dealing with international economic affairs. From the other direction, Brezhnev, Soviet President Nikolai Podgorny, Kosygin, and the other members of the Politburo entered the room. Kuznetsov introduced me to them in turn. Brezhnev and Podgorny seemed to have the same kind of permanent grin that Marshal Grechko had. On the other hand, Kosygin and Gromyko never smiled at all. I had the impression that I was watching a group of actors pretending to be the Soviet Politburo. Then, Henry Kissinger, Ambassador Smith, General Allison, and others who had been at the press briefing entered the room. Kissinger seemed to be preoccupied and did not say hello and went off to a far corner deep in conversation with Bill Hyland, a member of his immediate staff.

At the same time Shchukin arrived with his friend Mstislav V. Keldysh, who was president of the Soviet Academy of Sciences. Keldysh said that Shchukin had often talked to him about me and I responded that Shchukin had often sung Keldysh's praises to me. Finally, President Nixon arrived. We were still in conversation when Brezhnev began to move toward the treaty signing room. The entire Soviet mass pushed, shoved, and jockeyed to ensure that each got exactly to his correct position. I found myself way at the end on the American side until Secretary Rogers pulled General Allison and me in to stand beside him and Ambassador Smith.

After the signing, Brezhnev, Kosygin and Podgorny began clinking glasses with those of us who were nearby and later Brezhnev went out of his way to walk across the bottom of the platform to clink his glass with Henry Kissinger. A very few minutes after the signing Brezhnev suddenly moved toward the door and the entire Soviet delegation pressed after him like a school of fish. President Nixon also made for the door and all in the President's party followed on after him. Within seconds there were only three people besides myself left in the room—Ambassador Smith, General Allison, and Herbert Klein, the delegation's press officer. Those of us on the SALT delegation had been told to stay to participate in a press briefing scheduled to follow the signing. We asked Herb Klein how to get there. Herb said that it was not at all clear that there would be a press briefing and that we should just relax; if we were needed someone would let us know.

Ambassador Smith said, "What do you mean, relax? I have no car, I have not had dinner, and no one has told me where I should go." Herb asked Ambassador Smith where he was staying. Ambassador Smith replied Spaso House. Finally, Herb offered to drive him to Spaso House.

With the departure of Ambassador Smith and Herb Klein, General Allison and I were the sole remnants. Before leaving, Herb had pointed out to us the tower of the Hotel Rossiya, which dominates the skyline, and suggested we might want to walk there. He told us that no one would bother us if we wandered around the Kremlin grounds nor would we have any trouble leaving. One only had difficulty getting into the Kremlin—not getting out. General Allison and I then wandered through the Kremlin grounds, which were illuminated and extremely beautiful that night. We finally walked out through Red Square and proceeded on to the Rossiya Hotel, where room service produced a small steak for me at 1:30 A.M. Around 2:00 A.M. I retired.

SALT Goes to Congress

From a public relations standpoint the Moscow summit was a great success. In the United States banner headlines hailed the agreements signed there as ushering in a new era in U.S.–Soviet relations, solidifying détente. However, it seemed to me that SALT I had produced mixed results. I thought that the ABM treaty, which I had had some hand in fashioning, was a definite step forward in arms control, a model perhaps for future agreements. It sailed through the Senate with little trouble. It was seen as putting a brake on what was potentially a wide-open competition in strategic defenses. Though it did not prohibit continuing research in this area, it set ground rules which, with one or two gaps and as long as it was adhered to, promised a more or less symmetrical pattern of development and deployment that would not allow one side or the other to achieve a threatening advantage.

The Interim Agreement covering offensive weapons, on the other hand, was flawed in that it did exactly the opposite—it tended to accentuate the asymmetries that already existed in favor of Soviet land-based missiles. It was, in other words, potentially destabilizing to the strategic environment unless we moved swiftly to replace it with a permanent agreement that would eliminate these dangerous features.

I will summarize briefly the specifics of the two accords. First, with respect to the antiballistic missile treaty, each side was permitted two limited ABM "deployment areas," one for protection of its capital, the other for protection of an ICBM launch site, each with one hundred interceptor missiles and one hundred launchers. To guard against the possibility of these two deployment areas becoming merged into a regional or nationwide ABM system, the treaty specified that the two sites to be defended had to be at least 1,300 kilometers apart. But as I have already mentioned, it was not probable that we on our part would deploy an ABM system around Washington, and as it turned out, the Soviets decided not to deploy a second ABM to protect one of their ICBM sites. The result in 1974 was the signing of a protocol amending the treaty to limit both sides to only one ABM deployment area with one hundred interceptors and launchers. In fact, the United States never did build up to the limits of the treaty. The Grand Forks site was the only one ever activated, and it was deactivated at the insistence of Congress in 1976. The Soviets, in contrast, continue to operate their system around Moscow to this very day.

The heart of the ABM treaty was its technical provisions, which though concise are complex. Shchukin once remarked to me that he thought it would take over a thousand pages to spell out all the technical parts due to their complexity. But we succeeded in reducing them to a few paragraphs, accompanied by a set of "agreed statements" for clarification purposes. In addition to the radar restraints I have already described, the treaty prohibited certain qualitative improvements in ABM technology, such as the development, testing, and deployment of ABM interceptor missiles with multiple independently guided warheads.

During the negotiations, President Nixon also instructed that we were to try to obtain prohibitions on ABM weapons based on technologies other than those used in then-existing ABM radars, interceptors, or launchers, such as lasers and particle beams. However, our instructions stated that we were not to press this issue if it appeared that by doing so we would hinder fulfillment of the deal worked out between Nixon and Brezhnev in their May 20 agreement. Though future technologies employing "other physical principles" were known to be under study in both countries and the subject of much discussion even in the open literature, their application still appeared remote. The Soviets tentatively agreed that it was desirable to have prohibitions on "future" systems, but when it came to the final writing of the treaty, their representatives on the drafting committee said they could not agree to the inclusion of any specific restraints on components of systems which no one then fully understood and therefore could not be defined. I discussed this matter on several occasions with Shchukin, who consistently took the view—as did other senior members of the Soviet delegation—that prohibitions on future systems, other than a blanket ban on their deployment, involved too many unknowns to be addressed effectively under the treaty. Consequently, we dealt with this problem not in the treaty itself but in an accompanying Agreed Statement D, which provided that if any ABM system or components capable of substituting for ABM radars, ABM interceptors or their launchers based on other physical principles were created in the future, they would be subject to future discussion and agreement. This implied that "creation," which was understood to include development and testing of such components, was not limited.

Some years later, when the Soviets tried to claim that our Strategic Defense Initiative (SDI) launched in 1983 violated the treaty, I went back over the negotiating record with the help of Judge Abraham D. Sofaer, then the State Department's legal adviser. This review refreshed my recollection that the Soviets did not agree in a manner they would consider binding on themselves that the restrictions under Article V of the treaty (on the development and testing of space-based ABM systems and components) were to apply to testing and development of devices based on physical principles other than the physical principles of then current ABM components.

The Interim Agreement on offensive weapons and the Protocol accompanying it took a wholly different approach to the problem of arms control. The purported aim was to freeze the offensive strategic arsenals on both sides at roughly equal levels, but the agreement covered only ICBM silos and SLBM launch tubes and embraced numbers that strongly favored the Soviet side since there were no constraints on finishing launchers that were under construction prior to July 1, 1972. This meant that while the U.S. arsenal was indeed effectively frozen because we had finished our construction program years earlier, the Soviet arsenal could continue to grow until construction was completed. At the time the agreement was signed, the United States had an operational force of 1,054 ICBM launchers, whereas the Soviets had an estimated 1,618 launchers either operational or under construction. The agreement specifically prohibited the replacement of light ICBMs with the heavy ICBMs like the much larger Soviet SS-9, but left replacement with missiles up to SS-9 size ambiguous. Modernization and replacement were not prohibited so long as the dimensions of silo launchers were not "significantly increased."[2] Not addressed by the agreement were such questions as MIRVed warheads, missile throw-weight capacity, and the status of mobile ICBM systems, though with respect to the last our side added a unilateral statement that we would consider deployment of such a system to be inconsistent with the objectives of the agreement.

The most questionable part of the freeze, in my view, was the limitation imposed on SLBM launchers and modern fleet ballistic missile submarines. These were treated both under Article III of the Interim Agreement and in the Protocol, which limited the United States to a maximum of 710 SLBM launchers and 44 modern ballistic missile submarines, 3 more than we actually had in service at the time. However, during the summit, Kissinger confidentially assured the Soviets that the United States would not build up to its allowed limit. Henry never told the delegation about this secret "unilateral assurance," nor did he mention it to Congress when he and Nixon returned to Washington with the signed agreement in hand.

Also, the Protocol more than offset this cushion by allowing the Soviets a ceiling of 950 launchers and 62 modern ballistic missile submarines, provided that any additional launchers above 740 were to be replacements for older ICBMs or SLBMs that had been retired. This represented an enormous numerical concession to the Soviets; we could have held out for a better deal had our side not been so eager for an agreement. Kissinger wanted to get the matter out of the way and proceeded to do so personally in Moscow during a negotiating session Wednesday night. His opposite number that evening was L. V. Smirnov, a deputy premier who headed the Communist party committee in charge of Soviet defense industries. Outside the Soviet Union, Smirnov was barely known and his sudden appearance across the bargaining table took Henry by surprise. The only reason I knew about him was that Shchukin had mentioned his

---

[2]After the summit an agreement was reached ad referendum in Helsinki on May 26, 1972, that further clarified this provision by limiting any increase in silo diameter to no more than fifteen percent. This may seem like a small amount, but increasing the diameter of a silo by fifteen percent allows for an increase in missile volume by over thirty percent and for much larger increases in throw-weight.

name during our discussion on the Felsenweg. Smirnov was shrewd and fully in command of his facts, while Henry knew little about the details of what the Soviets had under construction in their submarine program.

Subsequently, Henry and Dobrynin met privately in Washington on June 17, at which time they agreed to a "clarification" to the submarine deal Henry had negotiated in Moscow. Kissinger had found that the Soviets had interpreted the Protocol signed in May the way I had interpreted it at the time. Henry had had to negotiate a new agreement to make it conform to the incorrect description of it he had given in his May press conference.

Though I was critical of the SALT I Interim Agreement, I supported it when it went before the Congress for approval.[3] Both Gerry Smith and I came to the conclusion that, despite the agreement's defects, we should support it and urge Congress to do likewise so as to open the way to the subsequent negotiation of a more comprehensive, permanent accord. We also endorsed the so-called Safeguard program (not to be confused with the ABM system of the same name) proposed by the Joint Chiefs to protect against the possibility of failure subsequently to reach such an accord. This involved pressing ahead with the cruise missile program, a follow-on ballistic missile submarine (the Trident), the B-1 bomber, and an advanced technology ICBM (the MX). Many in Congress believed that SALT I had gone too far in making concessions. In adopting the joint resolution approving the Interim Agreement on September 30, 1972, Congress incorporated an amendment, sponsored by Senator Henry Jackson of Washington, which stipulated that in SALT II the goal should be a level of strategic forces not less than those of the Soviet Union.

[3]Though not a formal treaty like the ABM treaty, which required the advice and consent of the Senate, the SALT I Interim Agreement nonetheless needed congressional approval before it could take effect, as mandated by a provision in the 1961 Arms Control and Disarmament Act.

18

SALT II

Early in September 1972 Henry Kissinger paid a hastily arranged visit to Moscow to discuss, among other things, East-West trade, Vietnam, and security negotiations. Out of these talks came agreement that negotiations on arms control would resume in Geneva before the end of the year. The U.S. presidential election campaign was then just moving into full swing, and Nixon had little time to think seriously about what our opening negotiating position should be. As a result, we arrived in Geneva with barely any instructions. Nonetheless, both sides had consistently expressed an interest in a more complete agreement to replace the Interim Agreement; and it was Henry Kissinger's view (as well as mine) that we should do everything possible to preserve the momentum generated by SALT I.

At this stage in the negotiations, with SALT I just concluded and SALT II beginning, those of us involved in the arms negotiations continued to believe that a permanent agreement limiting offensive strategic nuclear arms would work to the benefit of both sides, especially now that there were comprehensive restraints on ABM systems. I was cautiously optimistic that the Soviets would see the situation in a similar light and draw the same conclusion. In approaching the upcoming SALT II negotiations, we based our expectations on two fundamental judgments: first, that constraints on ballistic missile defenses, particularly on large phased-array radars, which were deemed to be essential to ABM defense and which took many years to build, would prevent breakout or circumvention of the ABM treaty; and second, that with defensive systems thus limited, it would be possible in the next few years before the SALT I Interim Agreement expired, to negotiate equally comprehensive limitations on strategic offensive arms, thereby establishing a more stable deterrent balance at reduced levels on both sides.

Negotiations Resume

The atmosphere at the actual resumption of the negotiations in Geneva in November 1972 did not bode well. I began to wonder whether our earlier judgments were still sustainable. Since the U.S. delegation came virtually unprepared, except with general instructions to begin developing a work schedule for the talks, it was the Soviets who did most of the talking—a reversal of roles. As I expected, many old and familiar issues quickly resurfaced. Among other things, the Soviets indicated that they wanted the withdrawal of our forward-based systems, including all of our missile submarines based in Europe, and mutual "restraint" in the development of new strategic systems.

For many members of the American delegation and staff this was their last appearance at the SALT negotiating table. I was one of the few who carried over after the first session of SALT II. Gerry Smith had earlier indicated that he would like to step down, and it was clear that there would be other personnel changes as well. General Royal B. Allison, the JCS representative, had incurred the disapproval of Senator Henry Jackson by his refusal to acknowledge that U.S. Minuteman missiles might become vulnerable as Soviet ICBM accuracy improved. Jackson thought that the military should have a more forceful representative on the delegation. As one of the most influential members of the Senate Armed Services Committee, Jackson was not to be ignored. To replace Allison, the Chiefs, at Jackson's urging, picked Lieutenant General Edward Rowny, who was at the time serving as chairman of the NATO Military Committee in Brussels. In addition to Rowny, the other new faces were U. Alexis Johnson, an exceedingly able senior Foreign Service officer, who succeeded Gerry Smith as head of the delegation; Boris Klosson, the new State Department representative; and Ralph Earle II, who became ACDA's full-time representative on the delegation. Harold Brown agreed to stay on as the at-large delegate, but as president of the California Institute of Technology he was, as during SALT I, usually preoccupied with other matters.

What bothered me more than the shake-up in the delegation was the almost wholesale purge of personnel in the Pentagon following Nixon's reelection. When Melvin Laird indicated that he would not be staying on as secretary of defense in Nixon's second term, a number of his most competent assistants, including Johnny Foster, the director of defense research and engineering (DDR&E), and Gardiner L. Tucker, assistant secretary of defense for systems analysis, were fired by Nixon's White House aides. It was the loss of these people, more than any change that took place in the composition of the SALT delegation and its staff, that to my mind helped to cripple our negotiating capability.

Back in Washington that winter, we finally got around to sorting out what we hoped to accomplish in SALT II. In SALT I, neither side had obtained all that it wanted. Any negotiation to be at all successful and productive involves a process of mutual accommodation, which in turn involves concessions and compromises. The substantive question we faced going into SALT II appeared to be, then, whether and how, in view of the concessions and compromises made by our side in SALT I and those that would be necessary to make in SALT II, we could expect to achieve an agreement that would be in the interests of the United States. To start with, a consensus quickly developed that any replacement agreement should be based, as was the ABM Treaty, on the principles of equality in capabilities, increased stability in the nuclear relationship between the two sides, and a mutual desire to reduce the resources committed to strategic arms.

Our principal goal was to secure Soviet acceptance of the concept of "essential equivalence," as set forth in the Jackson amendment. This meant that both sides did not have to be exactly equal in each component of their nuclear capabilities but that overall the strategic nuclear capabilities of the two sides should be essentially equal to each other, preferably at levels lower than those programmed by the United States.

Because our MIRV program appeared to be significantly ahead of the Soviet Union's, the Joint Chiefs were understandably reluctant to make major concessions on this issue. They favored, at most, a freeze on the MIRVing of ICBMs which, if adopted, would have assured the United States a continuing lead in MIRV technology and in the number of targetable warheads. In return, they were prepared to accept continuation of the Soviet Union's forty percent advantage in the number of ICBM launchers. My reaction to this was one of considerable skepticism. I found it highly unlikely that the Soviets would ever agree to assure us a continuing lead in MIRV technology; on the contrary, it seemed to me only a matter of time before they initiated their own MIRV testing program. (In fact, they began such testing in the summer of 1973.) I continued to think that if we were ever to make progress in this area, controls on throw-weight should be one of our principal objectives. But when the throw-weight issue came up at an NSC meeting on March 8,

1973, just two days before negotiations were to recommence in Geneva, the discussion proved inconclusive. A thorough interagency review was ordered, but nothing of consequence came from this while I remained a member of the delegation.

When the talks resumed in Geneva on March 10, 1973, our negotiating position rested on obtaining Soviet acceptance of force levels consistent with establishing essential equivalence on all central strategic systems. As a first step, we proposed an equal aggregate on both sides of 2,350 strategic launchers. We had arrived at this figure by splitting the difference between our arsenal of roughly 2,200 launchers (including ICBMs, SLBMs, and heavy bombers), and the estimated 2,500 launchers that the Soviets had. We also indicated a willingness to discuss further restrictions such as separate ceilings on ICBMs and ICBM throw-weight, a MIRV freeze, a possible ban on intercontinental cruise missiles, and prohibitions of ballistic missiles aboard surface ships and air-to-surface strategic missiles. We did not propose, nor did we favor, any immediate or further restrictions on SLBMs, the least vulnerable element in either side's strategic nuclear arsenal and therefore the one that contributed most to what we called "crisis stability."

It quickly became apparent that the Soviets had a view different from ours as to what should be accomplished. Their negotiators held that in accepting the Interim Agreement we had conceded that the Soviet Union was entitled to an advantage for an indefinite time of some forty percent in the number of missile launchers and something better than double the average effective size, or throw-weight, of their missiles over ours. In working out a more complete and permanent agreement, all that was necessary, in their view, was to add strict and equal limits on bombers and other armaments, provide for the withdrawal of our nuclear forces capable of striking Soviet territory deployed in support of our allies, and halt our B-1 and Trident programs but not the "modernization" of their comparable systems. The one-sidedness of their position made it difficult for me to see how an agreement could ever be reached.

In October 1973 the Soviet delegation tabled a draft treaty which laid out their proposals. It confirmed what I had suspected for some time—that the Russians were intent on making permanent the temporary advantages in numbers and size of ICBMs and SLBMs specified in the Interim Agreement. In addition, they wanted us to remove our forward-based systems from Europe and to cease deploying nuclear-capable aircraft aboard our carriers. Were we to have agreed to their formula, the result in effect would have been to leave all of NATO Europe at the mercy of Soviet conventional forces, backed by unrestrained numbers of

Soviet medium-range, intermediate-range, and tactical nuclear weapons.

From this point on, the talks were effectively stalemated. Not only did Ambassador Johnson refuse to discuss the Soviet-proposed treaty text with them, but also, the gathering Watergate scandal tended increasingly to preempt attention in Washington. Then, on October 6, 1973, Egyptian and Syrian forces launched a coordinated attack against Israel, capturing Israeli positions on the eastern bank of the Suez Canal and on the Golan Heights, and bringing on two weeks of war that would change dramatically the military and political picture in the Middle East. The Soviets, who had advance knowledge of the attack, did not advise us. It was evident that their commitment to détente and to the various statements of principle we had negotiated with them was nil. That there would be repercussions in the arms control field I had no doubt.

The next month, as the negotiations in Geneva were about to recess, Alexis Johnson and I informally sounded out the head of the Soviet delegation, Vladimir Semenov, on how we should proceed when the talks resumed after the first of the year. I told Semenov candidly that so far as I could see, SALT II was going nowhere. The Soviet Union's proposals were so wholly one-sided that there was no way we could take them seriously or treat them as constituting the basis for an agreement. Were these, I asked him, serious proposals or was I misinterpreting the Soviet position? Semenov replied that while he would have chosen different words to describe the situation, my assessment was essentially correct. He added that, despite our protestations, he was confident that eventually we would come around to the Soviet Union's point of view and accept a treaty along the lines they had proposed.

I concluded from this conversation with Semenov that as long as the Watergate scandal dragged on, serious arms control negotiations were unlikely. Initially the Soviets had found it hard to imagine, at least from their perspective, that a president of Nixon's power and prestige could ever be in serious political trouble at home. But as time went on, they began to realize that Nixon was in a weakened position; they were fully prepared to exploit that weakness in the expectation that eventually he would make concessions to improve his image at home and salvage his presidency. He had given in on the SALT I Interim Agreement at a time when his political position was markedly stronger. Little wonder that the Soviets now expected him to do so again. As the Watergate scandal loomed ever larger, I concluded that it was destroying the prospects of a sensible and sane SALT II accord.

By this time, I began to wonder whether I was making an effective contribution by staying with the delegation. As a government official, I was constrained from speaking out on the issues; as a private citizen I would be under fewer constraints and could put my views before a wider audience in the hope of influencing the ultimate course of national policy. I had not yet decided to resign, but I began to look upon resignation as an option to be considered.

I returned to Washington and immediately set my mind to thinking how something worthwhile could yet be salvaged from the negotiations. The product was a paper in which I endeavored to lay out in some detail what I thought should be the hierarchy and interrelation of U.S. negotiating aims.

I distributed this paper on a limited basis to James Schlesinger, who had replaced Laird as secretary of defense, and to the members of the Joint Chiefs, among others, in the hope that it would eventually work its way over to the White House and Nixon's desk. The Chiefs reacted favorably, as did Schlesinger, but when I tried to clear my paper through Henry Kissinger's staff at the State Department, all I received were negative reactions. Not only were my recommendations somewhat at odds with the thinking in Henry's office, but also there was a general reluctance on the part of Henry and his staff to put competing proposals before Nixon for consideration. As they say in the journalism trade, Henry "spiked" my paper.

However, Fred Wikner, an official in the Defense Department, determined that it was essential that it reach Nixon. Wikner rented a cottage on Key Biscayne not far from Nixon's Florida White House and one day walked down the beach, persuaded the security guards to let him through, and actually talked either with Alexander Haig, the White House chief of staff, or perhaps Nixon himself. So the paper did get to the top, though with a different effect than he had hoped for. He was promptly fired.

In the wake of this episode, I became increasingly convinced that my talents and expertise could be put to better use elsewhere than on the delegation. I mentioned this to Jim Schlesinger, indicating that resignation was one option I was entertaining. Jim confided to me that he, too, wanted to resign and wash his hands of the entire mess, but he felt constrained from doing so because of his concern over what Nixon might do if impeachment proceedings went forward, as seemed increasingly likely with each new Watergate revelation. Jim said his particular concern was Haig, whom he regarded as unpredictable and fully capable of trying to organize a military coup d'état to keep Nixon in office.

Knowing that I was dissatisfied with the way things were going in Geneva, Schlesinger in late January approached me with an offer to step down from the delegation and move back into the Pentagon as assistant secretary of defense for international security affairs (ISA), the same job I had held in the Kennedy administration. Jim was afraid that Kissinger, who was known to be eager to work out a SALT II accord, might be tempted into improvident concessions; he thought that my presence in ISA would help to cool Henry's ardor and put a break on any hastily arranged or ill-advised initiative. Others, including Bud Zumwalt, who was then serving as chief of naval operations, urged me to accept Jim's offer. As Bud put it, "Paul, you know it's essential that somebody take over ISA and really run it, and that somebody is you."

I had held the ISA job before and was not attracted to doing it twice. But I knew from experience that ISA could help shape the content of national policy. And after the decimation of the Pentagon's upper staff echelons following Nixon's reelection, the Defense Department was desperately in need of rejuvenation. For these reasons, I was ready to help by doing whatever I could if Schlesinger requested it.

Again, I was subjected to the usual vetting before my nomination could go to the Congress. As part of the routine clearance process I was requested to supply answers to a series of questionnaires about my financial holdings, my political leanings (I was a registered Democrat), and sundry matters that might have a bearing on my "fitness" for confirmation. The final sentence in the most important of the questionnaires said that if there were anything else the White House should know about me before sending my name forward to the Senate, I should speak to J. Fred Buzhardt, the general counsel to the President.

One day in February I went over to the White House to see Buzhardt, who happened to be an old friend. Buzhardt asked me why I was there. I referred to the last sentence in the questionnaire. I said I thought the White House should know that I thought it probable that the President had committed impeachable offenses. Fred asked whether I had any proof. I said that I had none, but that I thought he and his superiors should know what I thought. Fred was relieved; he said that as long as I had no proof the nomination could go forward.

I returned to the negotiations in Geneva a few days later to await my confirmation. As it turned out, my nomination for the ISA job never went to the Senate owing to the strong opposition of Senator Barry Goldwater, who sat on the Senate Armed Services Committee. Eleven years earlier Goldwater had opposed my appointment as secretary of the navy. Later, Goldwater, a general in the Air Force Reserve, blamed me, as secretary of the navy, for having spoiled his chances for the presidency in 1964 by my counterattacks against his charges that the Democratic administration was weakening our defenses and favoring the Navy over the Air Force When the prospect arose that I might again be running ISA, the White House congressional liaison officer Tom C. Korologos grew worried that if my nomination went forward, Goldwater would vote against the President if he were ever impeached. I soon thereafter learned that the entire matter of my returning to ISA had been quietly dropped.

In retrospect it was probably best for me personally that my nomination and appointment to ISA failed to materialize. At the White House the deepening gloom of Watergate was taking a heavy toll both on Nixon himself and on the credibility of his administration. Many associated with it, including even those who had had nothing whatsoever to do with Watergate, found their reputations tarnished. I had known Nixon for a long time, so I was familiar with his behavior. I believed that in an effort to rescue his administration and to rally the public behind him before impeachment proceedings began, he would make imprudent concessions to the Soviet Union on arms control to strike a deal. I realized that if I resigned at this point, it would be seen merely as an act of protest. My resignation would have no immediate impact on the content of policy, nor would it prevent Nixon from taking some improvident step to save himself. But I could no longer function under the steadily darkening cloud of Watergate. I had to do something to escape the contamination that was enveloping the executive branch. Resignation seemed the only course to take.

On May 28, 1974, I wrote Secretary Schlesinger, expressing my thanks for his support and advising him of my decision to resign. "I believe," I told him, "that, if relieved of my present responsibilities, I can be freer to support the strong domestic, foreign and defense policies that present circumstances appear to me to require." The same day I notified President Nixon, asking him that my resignation take effect on May 31.

A week passed and I heard nothing from the White House. Then another week went by, and still nothing. One evening Phyllis and I were having dinner with Judge Gerhard Gesell and his wife. I described to him my problem. He recommended that I write the President another letter, but this time I should use the phrase "unilaterally terminate." I followed his advice and sent a second letter on June 14. It said simply: "My request of May 28th to resign not having been accepted, I now feel compelled unilaterally to terminate my appointment effective today." So that there would be no misunderstanding of the motives behind my action, I also issued a press release that voiced my deeply felt concern over the current situation and the debilitating effects it was producing. My statement read in part:

> Arms control is integral to the national security and foreign policy of this nation and they, in turn, are closely intertwined with domestic affairs. In my view, it would be illusory to attempt to ignore or wish away the depressing reality of the traumatic events now unfolding in our nation's capital and of the implications of those events in the international arena.

> Until the Office of the Presidency has been restored to its principal function of upholding the Constitution and taking care of the fair execution of the laws, and thus be able to function effectively at home and abroad, I see no real prospect for reversing certain unfortunate trends in the evolving situation. Time is now of the essence in establishing the preconditions for such a regeneration.

Shortly thereafter Nixon and Kissinger set off for their scheduled summit meeting with Brezhnev in Moscow, where arms control topped the agenda. Contrary to the impression conveyed by Kissinger in his memoirs, *Years of Upheaval,* it was never my intention to time my resignation to coincide with the summit and thereby undercut or embarrass him and his boss in those talks. I had tried to resign weeks earlier and Nixon had paid me no heed. Moreover, whatever damage may have been done to the U.S. negotiating position was done by Nixon himself, not by others. The erosion of Nixon's credibility and standing in the eyes of the American people was an accomplished fact. Nixon's presidency was already morally bankrupt and mortally wounded.

That the Soviets proved reluctant to discuss substantive matters with him in any serious way was hardly surprising. The sides were too far apart on controls of strategic offensive arms to be able to negotiate a permanent agreement paralleling the ABM treaty. As an alternative solution, Henry proposed—and the Soviets readily agreed—that the negotiations in Geneva should concentrate instead on a ten-year replacement agreement for the Interim Agreement, in effect postponing the issue until the mid-1980s. It was almost certain, given then-current trends, that by that time the Soviets would have a preponderance of strategic offensive nuclear power. This would leave Nixon's successors an almost hopeless task of negotiating an equal and stabilizing SALT III treaty.

The Vladivostok Accord

In the weeks and months following my resignation from the delegation, I was often asked whether I was optimistic or pessimistic about the prospects for a SALT II agreement. In reply I said there were really two questions to be considered. The first was: What are the prospects for a SALT II agreement? The second was: How useful an agreement could we expect if one proved possible?

As to the first question, I said that I could see some grounds for optimism. For one thing, I expected the Soviet leaders to be more anxious to make progress and to be more flexible in their approach than they had been in the last two years, and, in particular, more so than during the Nixon-Brezhnev summit in the summer of 1974. The situation had changed after Nixon's resignation on August 9, 1974. Gerald Ford, his successor, could be expected to remain in office at least until January 20, 1977. The Interim Agreement was scheduled to expire later that same year. As I analyzed it, the Soviets would try to secure some kind of agreement to replace or extend the Interim Agreement before the election of 1976. Secondly, I thought that as Soviet leaders looked at what was happening to the economic and political foundations of Western Europe, Japan, the non-Organization of Petroleum Exporting Countries (OPEC) of the Third World—and even in the United States—they would probably judge that new opportunities were opening up for them. Furthermore, I believed that they saw their relative military position improving as they deployed their new family of weapons, especially a new series of ICBMs and a new intermediate-range missile, the SS-20, all of which they had been developing and testing over recent years. In these circumstances, I did not expect the Soviets to rock the boat too much. I thought they would try to maintain détente and their special relationship with the United States and, at the same time, press ahead with negotiation of an arms control deal, though not in a way reflecting much eagerness for one.

On the second question—how useful an agreement would be if one were possible—I said I believed the answer would have to be much less hopeful. The Soviets in the past had taken an extremely one-sided position with multiple built-in possible fallbacks. Even if they were to show new flexibility, I doubted they could justify to themselves giving up the superior position they saw within their grasp. With our three-hundred-billion-dollar budget ceiling, our chronic balance of payments problems, and the approaching onset of double-digit inflation adding further to our economic woes, they had to see some prospect of our not adding to our strategic programs sufficient additional real resources to change the relative trends. I therefore said I did not see how, under current conditions, we could expect to achieve an agreement which would significantly alleviate our growing defense problems arising from a potential shift from parity to Soviet superiority and from assured to significantly less than assured crisis stability.

It was against this background of concerns that I viewed and assessed the results of the meeting between President Ford and General Secretary Brezhnev at the Siberian port city of Vladivostok in November 1974. The agreement reached there provided for equal ceilings of 2,400 on the number of ICBMs, SLBMs, and heavy bombers that each side could have over the next ten years; it also provided for equal ceilings of 1,320 on the number of MIRVed missile launchers. The accord carried over from the Interim Agreement a restriction on building fixed ICBM launchers at new locations and limited the modern large ballistic missile (MLBM) launchers to those operational or under construction in May 1972—308 to 320 on the Soviet side and none on the U.S. side. It provided for freedom to mix between various systems under these limitations. Airborne ballistic missiles with a range of more than six hundred kilometers were to be counted. At first, in explaining the deal he had helped work out, Kissinger indicated that limits, if any, on cruise missiles, whether air, land, or submarine launched, remained to be settled and would be taken up at Geneva. Later, he modified his position, saying that this was not entirely clear from the negotiating record. Our forward-based systems deployed on carriers, in Europe or in the Far East, were not to be counted, nor were the British and French systems, though the Soviets reserved the right to raise these issues later. Still to be negotiated were the verification procedures to be used. There was also no agreed definition of what a heavy bomber might be, although Kissinger indicated that the negotiating record precluded inclusion of the new Soviet Backfire bomber.

Thus the Soviet side did make some concessions from their previous extreme positions. The accord gave an appearance of equality. It did not, however, deal with the crucial question of throw-weight—the most useful verifiable measure of relative missile capability, either MIRVed or unMIRVed; nor did it deal definitively with the nagging question of forward-based systems. It was difficult to see how the accord reduced, in a meaningful way, the U.S. strategic defense problem posed by the new panoply of Soviet missiles and bombers which were completing test and evaluation and whose large-scale deployment was then beginning. If we did not add new strategic programs to those already programmed, the United States was likely to end up the ten-year program with a half to a third of the Soviet MIRVed throw-weight. The Soviet side would thus have more or larger reentry vehicles. The United States would also end up with a half to a third of the Soviet unMIRVed missile throw-weight. The bomber forces of the two sides, in view of our lighter air defense, would have approximately equal capability.

Much to Henry Kissinger's regret, he was never able to translate the Vladivostok Accord into a SALT II treaty. One of the problems he encountered was a rather abrupt change of attitude on the part of the Soviets and a toughening of their stand on certain issues. Over lunch one day in January 1975, Henry recounted to me the troubles he was having and cited a recent conversation he had had with Soviet Ambassador Dobrynin, shortly before Dobrynin returned to Moscow for routine consultations. According to Henry, Dobrynin had expressed grave reservations about the investigations then being launched in Congress by the Church and Pike committees of alleged misdeeds by the FBI and the CIA. Dobrynin had said that he would have to report to his superiors that the U.S. executive branch was without authority and that there was no point in dealing with it. Kissinger of course had strongly disagreed. He insisted that the administration was now far sounder and more secure than when Nixon was in office. But Dobrynin was unconvinced and had told Henry: "Any government that can't protect its intelligence and security agencies is not to be taken seriously."

Although Henry and I often disagreed, we respected each other's opinions and decided that it would be helpful to both of us to stay in touch and exchange ideas. At Henry's suggestion, arrangements were made whereby I would receive regular briefings on the status of the arms negotiations and other national security matters in which I might be interested. This was intended to give me a continuing source of generally authoritative and reliable information. He agreed that, as an exception to the usual State Department regulation, I was not to be inhibited from speaking out on the issues, the reason I had decided to leave government in the first place. However, the arrangement Henry had proposed was never implemented by the State Department.

Private Citizen—Public Concerns: The 1976 Election

My departure from government in 1974 did not mean my departure from public life, though it did give me the welcome opportunity to devote more attention to some long-neglected business matters, to resume teaching my international relations seminar at SAIS, and to spend more time with my family. For a base of operations, I accepted the invitation of Ronald Easley, who had been head of the OSD SALT Support Group, to become a resident consultant to his research firm called System Planning Corporation, which had its offices in the Washington suburb of Rosslyn, Virginia.

My intention to write and speak out on issues of national concern, especially those affecting the national security, led over the next several years to a series of articles in *Foreign Affairs* and other journals setting forth my views on the current strategic balance and its implications, both foreign and domestic. It seemed to me evident that the Soviets were making rapid and significant progress in their strategic force program and that the net consequence, from the Soviet perspective, was a shift in the correlation of forces in their favor. Neither SALT I nor the projected SALT II agreement that appeared to be taking shape had yet had—or promised to have—any discernible effect in arresting the trend toward an increasingly large margin of Soviet offensive strategic superiority.

My computations indicated that we should be able to counter these trends only if we adhered closely to a long-term program of strategic modernization, no aspect of which should be in conflict with arms control measures I thought we should be seeking. This meant deployment of 550 MX missiles in a multiple-aim-point mode, deployment of the Trident II missile in an appropriate number of Trident submarines and improvement of their accuracy and reliability to the levels which seemed technologically feasible, and production in planned numbers of the B-1 bomber augmented with strategic cruise missiles. Such developments and deployments would, however, cost money and take time. During the interim, in order to retain sufficient deterrent capabilities during the time required to restore a stable strategic balance, urgent attention should be given to providing the quick and possibly temporary fixes necessary to meet the problems likely to emerge in the late 1970s and early 1980s. Among the "quick fixes" I favored were the rapid development and deployment of a movable ICBM transporter-erector-launcher and a hardened capsule for our Minuteman IIIs, a variety of simplified point defenses, provision for a potential rapid increase in bomber and SLBM alert rates, and testing of reliable and appropriate methods to launch Minuteman from under verified large-scale attack against our silos.

There was a further problem in that the Soviet Union had in recent years been paying increasing attention to projectile power, including air mobility, longer-range tactical air capabilities, intermediate-range missiles, and projectile sea power. To counter such threats in the absence of confidence in the adequacy of our nuclear deterrent could be difficult and imprudent. Not to be able to counter them could leave us with wholly inadequate tools of policy.

Around the same time that I stepped down from the delegation, I received a phone call from Averell Harriman, who had recently been authorized by the Democratic Advisory Council to organize two task forces—one on domestic issues, the other on foreign policy. The task forces were to be convened promptly to commence the preparation of position papers for submission to the council as suggestions or statements of party policy to help guide candidates in the 1974 and 1976 elections. At Averell's request, I agreed to serve as a member of the foreign policy task force's defense and arms control study group.

As is often the case in situations like these, there was a wide diversity of viewpoints. My view was that the study group should strive for a middle position that would pull the party together. During the late 1940s and early 1950s, it had been a Democratic administration that had led the way toward the economic and political recovery of those great areas of the Eurasian landmass which had either been devastated by World War II or had to face the difficult transition from colonialism to independence. In support of this policy, the Democratic party had consistently endorsed a strong defense posture and the development of an alliance structure consistent with the principles of the United Nations Charter to enhance individual and collective security against aggression. But by the mid-1970s, this consensus had largely broken down under the divisive effects of Vietnam and the unsettling political atmosphere generated by the Watergate affair.

The culmination of the study group's work was a report entitled "Priorities for Defense 1977–1981," issued in April 1976. All of us who had participated in the study group concurred that there was an urgent need for new directions in our foreign and defense policy, that we should continue to strive for arms control and better relations with the USSR, and that we should make a thorough and realistic reassessment of our obligations abroad and the threats we faced. But while I believed that the foreign policy called for in the report was, in general, sound, I thought that the military forces estimated to be necessary to back it up would prove inadequate in view of growing Soviet power. In the sphere of strategic nuclear deterrence, I believed that my colleagues (with the exception of Henry Rowen, who also voiced dissent) underestimated what was required. I did not think we should delay production of the B-1 bomber and I did not find it advisable to halt production of the Trident missile submarine until a cheaper follow-on SLBM had been designed and readied for production. Further, I favored proceeding with urgency in developing an alternative basing mode for our fixed ICBM force.

I also took exception to the report's recommendations with respect to general purpose forces. I believed that the requirements for a usable counterintervention force were large and that its costs could not be met from judicious savings in our current general purpose forces. In fact, I believed that the U.S. defense budget would have to go up to support the foreign policy outlined in the report—not down, as the report implied.

Nuclear proliferation was another important problem, but again I disagreed with my colleagues, who seemed to feel that nuclear proliferation was a greater danger than the growing imbalance and instability in the nuclear and conventional balance between the United States and its allies and the USSR. In my opinion, it was that growing imbalance which made the possession of nuclear weapons appear necessary to third countries. And finally, I believed that it was essential for the United States to keep its foreign policy aims and the political and material means necessary to support those aims in prudent balance, in particular because of negative developments in the international situation. Where we had gone wrong in the past was where we had permitted such a disjunction to arise.

The debates within the study group were reenacted again and again over the course of the summer and on into the fall campaign. In the meantime, I turned my attention to the primaries and the upcoming convention that would produce the Democratic party's nominee for president. As usual, there had initially been a large field of candidates. My preference at the outset of the campaign, early in 1976, was Scoop Jackson, who, to me, had a keener appreciation of national security problems than anyone else seeking the nomination. When Jackson's candidacy faltered, I began looking at others in the race. My children thought I should give consideration to a newcomer who had been the governor of Georgia, Jimmy Carter. They thought he was a fresh face with worthwhile new ideas, a younger man who, like Jack Kennedy a decade and a half earlier, seemed to radiate hope and optimism.

Although I supported Carter for president in 1976, I did so without a great deal of enthusiasm. I found his attitude toward politics grounded in a hortatory Wilsonian approach, which had been impractical even in Wilson's day, and which seemed even more out of tune with the realities of the 1970s. I further questioned whether his frequent mea culpas about the United States as a nation were helpful. We had not, as a nation, ignored Latin America or the Third World or engaged in military adventurism, as he often implied; nor, though we may have acted imprudently in involving ourselves in Vietnam, did we do so from evil motives.

I realized, of course, that no matter who the candidate might be, he would find himself under pressure to hold down defense expenditures. It was my belief that certain savings in defense through improved manning and better overall direction and management could be achieved. I estimated them at around five percent of the current rate of defense expenditures. On the other hand, the trends in U.S. capabilities in comparison with those of our potential opponents had been for some time adverse and needed correcting. I pointed out in my dissent from a Carter study group report that this would require additional outlays. We needed to improve our conventional capabilities, which had deteriorated sharply since Vietnam, and, most important of all, we needed to strengthen our strategic posture.

Shortly after he received the Democratic party's nomination for the presidency, Carter held a strategy session with his principal advisers on defense and foreign policy at his home in Plains, Georgia. I was among those he asked to attend. At the time I was involved in some other matters for System Planning and was about to embark on a CIA project which would lead later in the year to the celebrated "Team B" study. But I had the distinct impression from our earlier conversations that Carter was favorably disposed toward what I had to say and wanted my advice. Having been involved only in state politics, he was naturally more comfortable and familiar with domestic matters than with foreign and defense affairs, despite his training at Annapolis and experience in the Navy. If I could make a constructive contribution, I was anxious to help.

Early on the morning of July 26, 1976, I flew down to Atlanta for the meeting, returning to Washington that evening. Upon arrival at Hartsfield Airport I was greeted by Stuart Eizenstat and Jack Watson, two of Carter's political advisers, who were helping him organize his campaign. They had chartered a bus to drive us to Plains. To give us something to do during the drive, they distributed some reading material, including a paper on defense policy and arms control originally written by Harold

Brown and recently revised by Wolfgang Panofsky, the Stanford physicist, and Paul Doty, director of Harvard's Program on Science and International Affairs.

The position taken in their paper I found to be even more inclined to reducing our defense effort than that in the study group report. I turned to Harold Brown, who was sitting next to me on the bus, and asked, "Harold, wherever did the ideas in this paper of yours come from? Surely, this isn't representative of your thinking, is it?" He concurred that these really were not his views and insisted that he had had no part in writing that portion of the paper. "But your name is on it as one of the authors," I said. "How can you feel comfortable being associated with ideas like these?" To this he offered no reply.

Later that day we gathered for our meeting at the Pond House on Carter's estate, a kind of gazebo overlooking a small lake. Among those attending the meeting, besides Carter, were his wife, Rosalynn, Cy Vance, Paul Warnke, Harold Brown, James Woolsey, Barry Blechman, Lynn Davis, and I. Vance led off the discussion with a generally glowing picture of our strategic position and applause for Carter's recent announcement that he would cut the defense budget by seven billion dollars if elected president. Harold Brown then spoke up, essentially repeating those points made in the paper I had read on the bus, followed by Warnke, Blechman, and Davis, who made similar remarks. Finally, I was asked to speak. I had brought along some charts and tables showing my projections of our deteriorating position vis-à-vis the Soviets in the coming years and what we should be doing to repair the situation. Only Jim Woolsey supported me. My remarks were unpersuasive to Carter. Given the tone of the other presentations and the rosy picture they painted, I was not surprised. Later, toward the end of his presidency, Carter did in fact ask for substantial increases in the defense budget, but his inclination at the time of the Pond House meeting was wholly in the opposite direction.

I was somewhat surprised when, after the meeting, Carter asked me to prepare a report on what I thought we should do in the area of arms control. The view contained in my report when I presented it in September was that we should concentrate, in the first instance, on obtaining a SALT II agreement which, like the ABM treaty, would be of unlimited duration, would accord the right to roughly equal capabilities to both sides, and would do this in a manner which would promote strategic/crisis stability. This would mean not only the deferral, probably until SALT III, of efforts aimed at a lowered ceiling on U.S. and Soviet strategic delivery vehicles; it would also require some modernization of U.S. offensive forces along the lines I had suggested at our Pond House meeting and in a then-recent *Foreign Affairs* article entitled "Assuring Strategic Stability in an Era of Détente."

Carter did not wish me to deliver my report to him personally; he wanted me to give it to one of his aides, Anthony Lake, who lived in Washington. One evening I drove over to Lake's house. He greeted me at the door dressed in an apron and surrounded by a tribe of unruly children, from which I gathered that his wife was out for the evening and that he had been left at home in charge. Since Carter never acknowledged my paper, I assumed at the time that it never reached him and that it had got lost somewhere between Lake's front door and his dinner table. However, I was mistaken. Some years later, after Carter left the presidency, I was told by Ambassador Jaakko Iloniemi of Finland that Carter had told him on a trip to Plains that he regretted not having heeded the advice in a paper on arms control written by Paul Nitze early on in the presidential campaign. I doubt whether Carter was aware at the time of the election that arms control was destined to become one of the two issues (the other was the economy) that would prove the undoing of his presidency.

Team B and Creation of the CPD

Despite my earlier involvement, I did not play a part in Jimmy Carter's 1976 campaign, which culminated in his election that November to the presidency. I had done what I felt I could to influence his thinking, but my ideas had not been well received. There being no opportunity to be an active participant in formulating government policy, I devoted my time and energy to special projects.

That fall I took part in the Team B study. Following a recommendation by the President's Foreign Intelligence Advisory Board, a number of outside experts were chosen to conduct an analysis parallel to that being done inside the intelligence community, of Soviet strategic defenses, missile accuracies, and strategic objectives. Under the rules laid down earlier that summer, both groups were to use the same data and come to their conclusions independently of one another. Our group— called "Team B" to distinguish it from the in-house group, or Team

A—was headed by Richard Pipes, a professor of Russian history at Harvard.[1]

What sparked the Team B inquiry was a growing body of evidence that the intelligence community's National Intelligence Estimates, or NIEs as they are called, had for some years persistently miscalculated progress in Soviet strategic capabilities. In 1974, Albert Wohlstetter, a close friend and one of the leading experts on strategic matters, published a series of articles in *Foreign Policy* magazine demonstrating that since the "missile gap" episode of the early 1960s, our intelligence analyses had been in error by increasing margins year by year; having earlier overestimated Soviet strategic offensive capabilities, they had gone to the opposite extreme in recent years of underestimating them. Members of the President's Foreign Intelligence Advisory Board, the oversight body for the intelligence community, had expressed concerns similar to Wohlstetter's. As a result, there was considerable pressure on the CIA to bring in an outside group to double-check the agency's findings and analytical methods.

The theory of the NIEs is that they look outward, do not concern themselves with U.S. capabilities, and therefore should not attempt to make either current or forward net assessments. However, theory and reality, in the case of the NIEs, seldom correspond. In fact, the most important part of any NIE is that dealing with forward projections. The interaction between what we perceive the Soviet side to be doing and what we actually decide to do, and vice versa, is often overemphasized, but nevertheless it is a very real and tangible component of such decisions. Our decision in the late 1960s to MIRV our ICBM and SLBM forces was, in part, a result of an NIE projection that the Soviets in the foreseeable future would build a large number of exo- and endoatmospheric ABM intercepters. That the Soviets did not do so was in large measure due to the fact that we decided on an elaborate MIRV and pen-aid program which the Russians correctly judged their then-current technology could not counter.

As I began the Team B investigation, I had gained the impression that

[1]Besides Pipes and myself, the other members of Team B included General Daniel O. Graham, the former director of the Defense Intelligence Agency; Professor William Van Cleave, a specialist in strategic matters at the University of Southern California; Paul Wolfowitz of the Arms Control and Disarmament Agency; Thomas Wolfe, a retired Air Force officer and an expert on the Soviet military establishment who was then working at Rand; Seymour Weiss, former director of the State Department's Bureau of Politico-Military Affairs; and General John W. Vogt, Jr., recently retired as commander of U.S. Air Forces in Europe.

some in the CIA had reacted to this episode with a sense of guilt. Their estimates, which appeared to have caused the United States to open the destabilizing MIRV competition, turned out to be wrong. Therefore, the NIEs should not forecast future Soviet arms developments or deployments to which the United States could be expected to react, unless there was positive and unambiguous evidence of those developments and deployments. In case of doubt, reassuring rather than worrying statements were in order. Reinforcing this, I discovered, was a tendency to imagine that Soviet decision makers act or react in given circumstances in a manner analogous to the way in which U.S. decision makers might react in similar circumstances. The result had been a fairly consistent record since that time of understating future threatening developments.

As the Team B study progressed, we found it helpful to review past NIEs to test their accuracy. We discovered that many of these earlier NIEs, including the current NIE 11-3/8 series, were prone to state conclusions without referring to the evidence on which they were based. They rarely indicated the degree of confidence one should place in the judgment expressed or the spread and likelihood of the possibilities. Sometimes sentences were included which in logic had no bearing on the subject under discussion, but which the authors used to convey tendentious impressions.

Although the Team B report is still highly classified, its contents are generally well known. To the extent feasible, we relied on material that was already in the public domain. We found not only that the danger posed by Soviet capabilities was greater than was being reported in the NIEs, but also that there was little evidence to indicate that the Soviets subscribed to our concept of mutual assured destruction (MAD). On the contrary, they appeared to be striving for a nuclear war-fighting, war-winning strategic posture and were molding their doctrine and nuclear capabilities accordingly. This in turn led us to speculate on how our assessments could be improved to provide a more realistic and accurate picture. As a minimum, we recommended that there should be more emphasis on producing net evaluations, and that within the U.S. decision-making structure, there should be a unit whose specific task was to evaluate current and prospective changes in the correlation of forces as they might be viewed by Soviet decision makers, and to estimate the range, probability, and timing of various Soviet strategies and tactical actions consistent with such an evaluation.

On December 2, 1976, Team B submitted its findings to the President's Foreign Intelligence Advisory Board. It did not take long for the existence of the report and the gist of its contents to leak to the press. The reactions, by and large, were hostile. Members of the incoming Carter administration, including the president-elect, generally denounced the report, and at least three congressional committees undertook investigations. Détente was still the conjuring watchword, and in the minds of many people it tended to foreclose serious thought and discussion of our national security problems and how best to deal with them. Still, within a few years, most of the substantive recommendations and many of the organizational and procedural changes we had urged were implemented. Since then our intelligence analyses have improved considerably. That the initial responses to the report by the intelligence community were adverse was to be expected.

Around this same time I also became involved in organizing the Committee on the Present Danger, which I hoped would help restore informed and objective discussion of national security issues. After I left government I found that there were others who shared my view that the United States was entering a dangerous period of strategic disadvantage vis-à-vis the Soviet Union, and that the American public was either unaware of or too complacent about this trend. None of the existing think tanks or other similar institutions was doing the objective analyses and presentations needed to stimulate public awareness. In the country's colleges and universities there was hostility to the discussion of such issues, a carryover no doubt from alienation produced by Vietnam and Watergate. What was missing, I decided, was an effective vehicle that could bring these questions to the public's attention, as Henry Kissinger had said should be done when he called for a national debate on the question of strategic arms and arms control following the 1974 Moscow summit. I was now more than ever ready to take Henry up on his plea.

At first I began meeting informally with Joe Fowler over lunch at the Metropolitan Club, or with Charls Walker, former under secretary of the treasury, over sandwiches at his office. Together with David Packard and Gene Rostow, we agreed that a more formal organization capable of effectively conveying its message should be established. The upshot was the Committee on the Present Danger, established on November 11, 1976, to facilitate a national discussion of the foreign and national security policies of the United States directed toward a secure peace.[2] The com-

---

[2]This was not the first time that concerned citizens had organized for this purpose. Roughly a quarter of a century earlier, in 1950, James Bryant Conant, Tracy Voorhees, Robert Patterson, and others had formed their own Committee on the Present Danger, which had helped to mobilize public support for the Truman administration's Korean War

mittee, which eventually included some 150 men and women, was a non-profit, nonpartisan organization. It was broadly based geographically and by profession. Its membership was distinguished by its expertise in foreign affairs and military matters. Sixty percent of its members were Democrats, forty percent Republicans. Its members believed that the country required a fresh, bipartisan consensus, similar to the bipartisan consensus which had sustained our foreign policy between 1940 and the mid-1960s, to expand the opportunities of and diminish the dangers to the United States of a world in flux.

Shortly after the committee was established, President Carter nominated Paul Warnke to be director of the Arms Control and Disarmament Agency and chief SALT II negotiator. I had known Paul Warnke for a number of years, worked with him in fact as a close colleague, and had considerable respect for his intelligence. During the 1960s he had been one of those who had succeeded me in the ISA job. Since then, his views on defense matters, including arms control, have seemed to me quite wrong. I seriously doubted his appropriateness for the job, either as chief negotiator or as a key adviser to the President on arms control. The more I studied his statements of position on the issues, the more convinced I became that he was not the right man for either role or both.

I learned from a newspaper account of the nomination that the President had asked the Senate Foreign Relations Committee to waive its usual procedure requiring that a nomination not be voted on in less than a week after being submitted. I immediately telephoned Senator Henry Jackson, who was back in his home state of Washington at the time, to inquire whether he or others who shared his views intended to object to the Warnke nomination. Jackson told me that he had not planned to do anything. Over the weekend at my farm I brooded over the problem and wrote a letter to Senator John Sparkman, chairman of the Foreign Relations Committee, expressing my reservations about the nomination. I sent it over to the committee early Monday morning, February 7, 1977. The next day I was scheduled to give an afternoon lecture at the National War College. During the discussion period following my presentation I received a message that there was a telephone call waiting for me from Senator Charles Percy of Illinois. He wanted my opinion on the Warnke nomination. I told him about the letter that I had recently sent Sparkman and summarized its contents. He told me that the chairman had not made

rearmament program. At the time I was a public official, serving as director of the State Department's Policy Planning Staff; I encouraged but took no part in the committee's activities. The second Committee on the Present Danger that I was involved in establishing owed a spiritual kinship to the first, but otherwise they were unrelated.

the letter available to the other members and that he would return to the hearings immediately and ask that that be done.

The result was to extend the hearings on the Warnke nomination, both in the Senate Foreign Relations Committee and in the Senate Armed Services Committee. I was called to testify before both committees in what became a serious debate not only on the nomination of Paul Warnke but on our posture toward the Soviet Union and the entire question of arms control.

Once the hearings were under way, it became apparent that Warnke was desperately eager to soft-pedal his earlier statements on defense and arms control. At one time or another, he had opposed almost every effort to modernize or improve U.S. strategic systems, including construction of the B-1 bomber, the MIRVing of the Minuteman III force, conversion of the Polaris submarines to Poseidons, and construction of the Trident force. Had Warnke's advice in these matters been followed, our strategic forces would have rapidly grown obsolete. As I told the Senate Armed Services Committee, "I think it would be one of such clear inferiority that we would be in serious trouble."

At one point Senator Thomas J. McIntyre, a New Hampshire Democrat who favored the nomination, put me in an awkward position. He asked me whether I thought I was a better American than Warnke. I hesitated to answer but finally said, "I really do." What I meant to say was, "I really do take exception to what I believe to be inconsistent and misleading testimony by Mr. Warnke." After the hearing I asked Senator McIntyre for permission to clarify my reply in the record. He agreed, but the damage had already been done. The hearing had been open to the press and my original reply, without the clarification, to McIntyre's question had been duly reported across the country. The press pounced on that remark and ignored most of the discussion of substantive issues.

On March 9, 1977, the Senate did finally confirm Warnke's nomination as arms control negotiator, but the vote—fifty-eight in favor, forty against—should have been a warning to the Carter administration to adopt a more realistic view of the Soviet Union and of our defense needs.

Aspen and Twentieth Century-Fox

With the controversy over the Warnke nomination barely settled, I found myself becoming engrossed in personal matters having to do with my role in the Aspen Skiing Corporation. My involvement with Aspen went

back a long way. In the early 1930s, William "Billy" Fisk, who had recently graduated from Trinity College, Cambridge, had come to New
York to work for Dillon, Read and Company under my immediate supervision. He had won a world championship as a bobsledder, was an excellent automobile racer, and a first-class skier. One winter Billy asked me
for permission to take a month off to see whether he could find a place
in the Rockies that could be developed for skiing on a par with Saint-
Moritz, Switzerland. I enthusiastically supported the idea. He came back
after a month saying he had found it—Aspen, Colorado. We formed a
syndicate to build ski lifts there but were unable to raise the necessary
capital.

The winter after the Japanese surrender, I received a telephone call
from my brother-in-law, Walter Paepcke. After a recent weekend in
Aspen, Walter had fallen in love with the area. In the nineteenth century
Aspen had been a prosperous silver mining center, but when the price
of silver dropped in the 1890s, the town had fallen on hard times and had
yet to recover. The population, which had once been fifteen thousand,
had dropped to less than three hundred. A run-down abandoned house,
together with its lot, could be bought for fifteen to twenty dollars. Walter
suggested that the three of us devote ourselves to remaking the town into
a center for excellence in body, mind, and beauty. It was agreed over the
phone that Walter would deal with everything having to do with the
mind, including culture, business, and real estate; that my sister, Pussy,
would address herself to music, design, and taste; and that I would address myself to the body, including skiing.

As a result, I organized the Aspen Skiing Corporation and was for
many years its largest stockholder and chairman of the board. During the
first five years it was a financial disaster, periodically on the verge of
failing, because the initial ski trails we cut on Aspen Mountain were too
difficult for all but the most practiced skiers. I eventually put in enough
additional money to bulldoze two of the V-shaped gulches coming down
the side of the mountain into fairly steep, but readily skiable, bowls. After
that it was impossible to keep the skiers away. The problem became one
of building more lifts and developing additional mountains. Whatever
money we made was plowed back into further development, as was every
penny we could borrow.

In order to help finance the enterprise, we eventually sold some skiing
corporation shares to the public; several of the other original stockholders
sold some of their shares concurrently. Among those who acquired an
interest in Aspen Skiing was the Morgan Guarantee Trust Company,

which bought a large block of shares for their clients' pension funds. By the spring of 1976 stock in Aspen Skiing Corporation, which was nationally known by this time, was selling for about twelve dollars a share. One day an officer of the Brunswick Corporation, a maker of athletic equipment, called me and offered to buy us out at thirty-two dollars a share. Aspen Skiing was doing very well, and I thought it would eventually be worth more than Brunswick was ready to pay. So I declined their offer. However, Morgan Guarantee wanted to realize the immediate profits that the Brunswick offer would give them. When they learned that I had turned down the Brunswick offer, they threatened to sue me for maladministration of the company. I decided to hold my ground.

While on a trip to China in the fall of 1977 with other members of the Committee on the Present Danger, I received a message from my son Peter that the Twentieth Century-Fox Corporation was interested in buying Aspen Skiing and was talking of a price in the range of fifty dollars a share. Fox had recently released the highly successful movie *Star Wars* and was looking for secure places to invest its profits. Hence its directors' interest in Aspen. Phyllis and I returned posthaste to Washington via Tokyo, rather than through Europe as we had planned. The next day I flew up to New York to meet with the directors of Twentieth Century-Fox. In a day's time I worked out a complex merger agreement under which those Aspen Skiing Corporation shareholders who wished to do so could exchange their Aspen stock for convertible preferred Twentieth Century-Fox stock. The others could take cash. As part of the transaction, it was agreed that I would continue as chairman of Aspen Skiing Corporation and would also sit on the board of directors of Twentieth Century-Fox.

It took some nine months for all the legal details to be worked out and for the consent of the stockholders of both Aspen and Fox to be obtained. When all was done, the Nitze and Paepcke families owned between them the largest single block of shares in Fox. Thereafter for the next several years the motion picture industry was at the center of my business interests.

I found the entertainment industry a fascinating place, filled with a most varied and interesting assortment of creative people. Princess Grace of Monaco, the former Grace Kelly, and I were the two most junior members of the Fox board of directors in terms of length of service. I found her not only beautiful and charming, but wise and courageous as well. Because of the success of *Star Wars*, the company was doing exceptionally well. But the chairman and chief executive officer, Dennis Stanfill, and I soon came to a basic difference of views. Dennis was a graduate of the U.S. Naval Academy and a former Rhodes scholar; he had left the Navy in 1959 after ten years of service to enter the world of finance and business. His most recent accomplishment had been to rescue Fox during a period when it was doing badly. Almost all of the other directors other than myself owed their appointment to Dennis. He regarded the board as puppets who were supposed to follow his lead without question. The more I saw of Dennis in operation, the more questions I began to have about his direction of the company.

Over a period of time I found that others on the board shared my concern. Warren Hellman, Johnny Vogelstein, and I finally concluded that it made sense for the three of us to buy out all the other shareholders and take the company private. The First National Bank of Boston was prepared to lend us most of the money we would need to finance the offer we contemplated making. The board of directors of Fox recommended acceptance of our offer and everything seemed to be moving forward properly, when our bankers changed their mind. They decided they did not have confidence in Dennis and asked us to relieve him of his job as chief executive officer before consummating the transaction. This resulted in a serious rift among the members of the board. Dennis tried to have Hellman and Vogelstein fired from the board, and it was only with considerable difficulty that we were finally able to muster a majority to reject that idea.

While all this was going on, I received a telephone call at eight o'clock one Saturday morning from Edward Bennett Williams, a distinguished Washington attorney and a friend of long standing. He told me that a client of his, Marvin Davis, an oil tycoon then operating out of Denver, was going to announce at eleven o'clock that morning that he was buying us all out and would then merge Twentieth Century-Fox with a new company he was forming. And that he did. He offered a price some twenty percent higher than Hellman, Vogelstein, and I thought the company was worth. From that point on, until the board of directors finally approved a definitive merger agreement in the spring of 1981, I devoted myself to making sure that the sale to Marvin Davis went through. I particularly regretted being separated from what I thought of as my Aspen Skiing Corporation. But there was no longer any way I could resist the juggernaut.

Confrontation over the SALT II Treaty

Upon returning from China and after working out the merger with Fox, I found my Washington life again immersed in the question of SALT II. Signs were beginning to appear of an impending agreement, and it fell to me, as chairman of policy studies for the Committee on the Present Danger (CPD), to take the lead in trying to interpret for the public and the Congress on behalf of the committee what would be the results and likely effects of such an agreement.

That the committee was destined to play a substantial role in the fate of any SALT II agreement was by now fully established. Slowly but surely, the CPD was making a name for itself. Initially, when the committee was formed in November 1976, no major daily newspaper would even cover the story. But within six months we were beginning to attract national and even international attention. In the spring of 1977 we issued a policy statement, "What Is the Soviet Union Up To?" the response to which far exceeded our expectations in extent and tone. AP and UPI placed excellent and substantial stories, which were widely reprinted. Along with these basic news reports, many of the major newspapers published favorable companion editorials. Additionally, we were gaining coverage on national television. ABC-TV and CBS-TV carried special interviews with Gene Rostow and with me.

An even more encouraging sign was the way in which the committee was being portrayed by the press. Initially, some of the comments were highly negative; we were referred to as "cold warriors," "hawkish," "representatives of the military-industrial complex," and so forth. But by the summer of 1977 the mood of the press had changed. We were now being described as "a public interest group," "an organization comprised of many leading Americans from all segments of the political spectrum," and a "nonpartisan committee," the last being the designation used by the *Washington Post*.

The current state of U.S.–Soviet relations and the strategic balance ranked as the committee's first concern. My principal interest was the SALT II negotiations. Having failed earlier to elicit Soviet agreement to substantial reductions, Carter had retreated to the negotiation of an accord, worked out in September 1977, that extended the SALT I Interim Agreement pending the conclusion of a SALT II treaty modeled on the earlier agreed Vladivostok formula. Although numerous details had yet to be resolved, the basic outline of what Carter envisioned as a SALT II treaty was becoming clear.

I thought that the principal criterion by which one should judge the emerging SALT II agreement was whether it would provide reliable deterrence and enhance crisis stability. In other words, would the resulting balance of forces be such as to assure that the Soviet Union would have no grounds for temptation to execute a preemptive strike in a crisis and such as to deny the Soviet Union any prospect of winning the resulting war were one nevertheless to occur? I firmly believed—and continue to believe—that a sound treaty limiting and reducing strategic offensive arms in a manner to enhance stability would be greatly in our national interest. But I had found from experience and much observation and thought that the SALT negotiations of the 1970s reflected a basic antithesis. Both sides in SALT II wanted a pact, but for discrepant aims—our side to correct the growing imbalance and instability in the strategic arena with its negative impact on international politics, the Soviet side to nail down strategic primacy so as to be in a position to dominate the course of international politics.

To be sure, SALT was not the sole source of our troubles at this time. Carter's summary cancellation of the B-1 bomber, his indecision over the neutron bomb, and slippage on the Trident and MX programs, just to name three instances, were not attributable to the SALT connection. Yet a tendency exemplified in them was all too common to our SALT approach—a tendency to subordinate security policies to hopes of achieving arms control rather than to shaping arms control policies to our security needs.

Taking these various considerations into account, I attempted, sometimes with the help of a former SALT associate, T. K. Jones, and others, to develop for the committee an ongoing analysis of the evolving strategic balance, including my best assessment of the probable impact of the projected SALT II agreement. Accordingly, for nearly three years, I periodically updated and distributed a set of papers and charts setting forth, in full detail, nuclear weapons systems weapon by weapon, the past evolution of the forces of both sides, and the probable further evolution of those forces in both number and quality over the following five years. The tables gave the estimated throw-weight, number of reentry vehicles, their yield, and their accuracy. I then calculated from these estimates the aggregate ability each year of the forces the two sides would possess to destroy hard targets like missile silos, and soft area targets like factories, airfields, and so forth. Among those whose thinking I hoped to influence were the undecided members of the Senate who were likely someday to be voting on the treaty. As the negotiations moved closer to a final agreement, I believed it imperative to give these senators as clear as possible an idea of what the agreement would contain and what its impact would be before the situation became "frozen," leaving them with only a "yes" or "no" decision on ratification.

As I worked through my estimates and computations, the question arose of whether the Soviet civil defense program was of sufficient potential effectiveness to be taken seriously. I was not surprised to find that the Soviets had over the years put an enormous effort into training cadres and providing some prior civil defense training for everyone in the Soviet Union. I concluded that the evidence was quite persuasive that if those segments of the work force (about twenty percent) that the Soviets planned not to evacuate from the cities and industrial plants were provided with 50 to 150 psi blast shelters, and if the rest of the urban population was evacuated, optimally scattered, and occupied fallout shelters for up to two weeks where necessary providing two-hundredfold reduction in exposure to radiation, then even an all-out U.S. attack, optimized under "assured destruction" criteria to kill people and destroy industry, would cause fatalities of less than four percent of the Soviet population, either through blast, fire, or radiation. It was argued by some who disputed these figures that the Soviets could not evacuate their population without our receiving some warning (in which case, presumably, we would launch a preemptive strike) or that in implementing their civil defense plans, foul-ups would occur that would increase the number of casualties. To these criticisms I responded that my calculations fully allowed for the possibility of foul-ups and duly incorporated strategic warning time, though I doubted whether any U.S. president would ever order a preemptive attack on the basis of such evidence. The Soviet program in practice would be imperfect in detail but, overall, could prove highly effective and ought be taken seriously as a factor affecting the strategic balance. The situation of the American population, with no serious civil defense program and having to face the much heavier weight of a Soviet attack, would be quite different.

Finally, Carter's efforts to secure an arms control agreement bore fruit. On June 18, 1979, meeting in Vienna, he and General Secretary Brezhnev joined in signing the SALT II treaty. Generally speaking, the treaty followed the lines I had expected. A limited duration agreement, it was to expire on December 31, 1985. Like the Interim Agreement it superseded, the SALT II treaty concentrated in my opinion on the wrong indices of strategic power—offensive launchers. By so doing it gave both sides the incentive to continue increasing the number of weapons on their missiles, with negative implications for strategic crisis stability. Although the treaty imposed a ceiling of 2,400 (to be reduced to 2,250 by the end of 1981) on the aggregate number of strategic nuclear launch vehicles,[3] and a subceiling of 1,200 on the number of ICBMs and SLBMs that could be MIRVed, the constraints on the deployment of warheads were such as to favor the Soviets, whose missiles were substantially larger than ours and therefore capable of carrying bigger payloads with greater megatonnage. Instead of forcing a reduction in strategic arsenals, there would be a continuous and large increase, especially in megatonnage on the Soviet side, during the term of the treaty. There would be some increase in U.S. capabilities as well, but in net terms the strategic balance would move from a position not far from parity to one of clear Soviet strategic nuclear superiority.

Other provisions of the treaty further undercut the claims of its supporters that it would provide for essential equivalence. What I found especially distressing were its provisions allowing the Soviet Union to have certain unilateral rights, such as the right to have modern large ballistic missiles; our side, in contrast, was allowed none, even if we decided at some future time that we should add them to our arsenal. The Soviets could exercise this option (and already had, with the development of the SS-18), whereas we could not. As a rule, U.S. B-52s and B-1s (if the program were revived) and the USSR's Bears and Bisons were to be counted as "heavy bombers" and as such fell under the ceiling on strategic launch vehicles. However, the Soviet Backfire bomber was to be excluded as were certain Bears and Bisons that had been reconfigured for reconnaissance, tanker, and antisubmarine roles, even though they still retained their bomb bays. At the same time, all U.S. "heavy bombers," including some 230 mothballed B-52s, were to be included under the ceiling.

Over the course of the summer, as the ratification process went forward, I had occasion to testify on the treaty before both the Senate Foreign Relations Committee and the Senate Armed Services Committee. I resisted recommending to the senators that they vote against the treaty, and concentrated on urging them to give careful consideration to possible amendments or changes to make it more equitable and therefore more compatible with our national security needs. I am sure, however, that my disapproval of the treaty as submitted was evident. In my view, if the SALT II treaty as proposed by the administration had been ratified

---

[3]The SALT II documents used the phrase "strategic nuclear delivery vehicles" (SNDVs), which less precisely described this aggregate.

in the form presented to the Senate, the USSR would have been assured a strategic nuclear capability superior to our own.

As the hearings progressed it became increasingly apparent that the administration was losing ground. The questions that I and others persisted in raising about the treaty were creating serious doubts in the minds of a number of key undecided senators as to the wisdom of seeing it ratified. An added complication, because of the recent revolution in Iran and the shah's overthrow, was the loss of our intelligence-gathering stations near the Caspian Sea, without which some aspects of Soviet compliance with the treaty would be hard to verify. However, I did not think that verification was as central a problem as some made it out to be. The treaty was so heavily weighted in the Soviets' favor that I could see no real reason why they should want to cheat. Proponents of SALT II, who now found themselves unexpectedly on the defensive, eventually fell back on the argument that the treaty was "better than no agreement." I dismissed this argument for what it was—a defeatist notion that suggested a loss of confidence in our ability to maintain an adequate deterrent posture without arms control.

With sentiment against the SALT II treaty on the rise, the administration grew desperate. In November 1979 the Senate Foreign Relations Committee voted in favor of recommending ratification, but by a vote of nine to six and with the attachment of twenty specific conditions, some of which would have required renegotiation with the Soviets. The Armed Services Committee was even more critical. It voted ten to seven against the treaty and termed the agreement wholly unacceptable without "major changes."

Had the treaty been put to a vote, it would have been loaded with stringent amendments and reservations or, more likely, it would have gone down to defeat. In either case, the administration would have been seriously embarrassed, something Carter, his popularity now waning, could ill afford as he looked ahead to the 1980 election. The Soviet invasion of Afghanistan in December 1979 gave him the opportunity to ask the Senate to suspend further action on the treaty as part of a package of retaliatory measures. Somewhat earlier, he also had indicated that he would step up certain defense programs. Despite an unprecedented inflation rate, he pledged his support for three percent real growth in military spending, a dramatic reversal of his previous position on defense matters. Even so, in keeping with international practice, he indicated that the United States would abide by the treaty's terms anyway, since it fully intended to honor the treaty should it ever come into force. The Soviets offered similar assurances, but they also announced that they were deferring indefinitely the reduction of their arsenal to the required 2,250 launchers by the end of 1981, as the treaty stipulated. So not only did Carter fail to secure Senate approval; he failed to secure full Soviet compliance as well.

Under the pressure of the election campaign the next year, the Carter administration chose to revive the ratification issue. Having decided to shelve the treaty after Afghanistan, Carter now indicated that he had changed his mind and would press the Senate for action. He wanted to convey the impression that he was the "peace" candidate and that his opponent, Ronald Reagan, was a "war" candidate. The fact that the President, in order to swing the election campaign, was prepared to walk away from the most important sanction in the package of sanctions he had announced after the Soviet invasion of Afghanistan (and had urged our allies to support) could hardly impress either the Soviet Politburo or our allies as to the seriousness of our purpose. To pass over the weaknesses and limitations of SALT II and to overstress its possible benefits could scarcely help us negotiate more equitable and useful arms control agreements in the future.

My own role in the 1980 election campaign was less partisan and more limited than it had been four years earlier. Rather than take sides with one candidate or another, I decided to make myself available to any and all who wished my advice. Officially, the Committee on the Present Danger took no position either, though the fact that one of its members, Ronald Reagan, became the Republican candidate for the presidency was an obvious boost for the committee's cause. Samplings of public opinion indicated that an increasing percentage of the American people shared the basic views of the Committee on the Present Danger and were prepared to support a greater and more expensive defense effort.

As I understood Mr. Reagan's position, it accorded more closely with mine than did Carter's. The expiration date of SALT II was by this time so close to the earliest date by which it could conceivably enter into force—less than five years—that there was little that could be done in that time frame beyond that which Congress had already authorized. After the cutbacks and delays of recent years, there was little, if anything, that the United States was able and wished to do during that time period that ratification of SALT II would prevent from happening. It was probably also true that there was little the Soviet side wished to do during the next five years that it did not already have under way and that it considered not to be permitted by SALT II. A main point on which Reagan and I concurred was that if SALT II were ratified, the Soviets would insist that it be the basis on which the trading on the provisions of SALT III begin.

It seemed to me far better to reject SALT II and to move directly to negotiating a useful SALT III treaty from a clean slate. SALT II would not have much, if any, effect prior to its expiration date, but it could prejudice the possibility of obtaining a useful SALT III treaty.

During the election campaign in 1980, Mr. Reagan asked me to his suite in the Mayflower Hotel in Washington to consult further on the question of arms control. Jeane J. Kirkpatrick, then a professor of political science at Georgetown University, and Lieutenant General Edward Rowny also attended the meeting. Later, I received a telephone call from Mr. Reagan's office that he would like to see me personally and in private. I suggested that he come to my house on Woodley Road for dinner. In the end it was agreed that in addition to Mr. Reagan and myself, the group would include Edwin Meese and Michael Deaver, Mr. Reagan's two closest aides, and Gene Rostow. We had what was, in my opinion, a most useful discussion.

My personal recommendations to Reagan, then and immediately after the election, were that he promptly inform the Soviet Union that he was desirous of serious negotiations on SALT; that he give urgent attention to the issues as soon as his new team was in place; and that he propose that, until a new SALT agreement with the Soviet Union came into force, we take no irreversible action inconsistent with SALT I or SALT II provided that the Soviets behaved likewise. It was essentially this policy that Mr. Reagan adopted following his victory in the 1980 election. Having wandered in an arms control wilderness for so many years, I saw reason to hope that we stood on the threshold of a new era.

19

The INF Negotiations

By the time the Reagan administration took office in 1981 the number one arms control issue had shifted from the SALT II treaty to the growing imbalance in theater weapons, especially in Europe. The problem originated in the Soviet Union's decision in the mid-1970s to deploy substantial numbers of its newly developed SS-20 intermediate-range mobile missile. With a range of over three thousand miles, much improved accuracy, and the capability of carrying three MIRVed warheads, the SS-20 posed a threat to virtually every target of importance in NATO Europe and in Asia as well. The decision to deploy these more precise and more usable weapons soon resulted in a growing disparity of military power in Europe. This was noted by President Ford and Henry Kissinger at the Vladivostok summit.

While Ford and Kissinger were in charge of policy, efforts had been directed in the main toward working out a settlement of the SS-20 problem within the framework of the SALT II negotiations, as part of the resolution of the forward-based systems (FBS) question. Indeed, there were some among Henry's entourage and in the intelligence community who sincerely believed that the Soviets had decided to deploy the SS-20 system exactly for this purpose—as a bargaining chip to get the United States to negotiate on FBS. When Ford's bid to retain the presidency failed, his successor, Jimmy Carter, decided to try to negotiate a somewhat different SALT II agreement from the one Ford and Kissinger had sought. And as Carter did not think that the SS-20s posed a serious threat to Western Europe or to the strategic balance, he saw no reason to include them within the SALT II framework. His interest was in resolving the larger and, from his perspective, more serious problems resulting from the growing imbalance in the U.S. and Soviet intercontinental systems.

It was at this point, in the fall of 1977, that West German Chancellor Helmut Schmidt appeared before the International Institute for Strategic Studies (IISS) in London, urging the United States to take steps to offset the SS-20 deployment. Schmidt was afraid that Carter, in his zeal to reach a SALT II agreement, would make concessions that would weaken or even remove the extended deterrence provided by U.S. strategic weapons. He therefore wanted reassurance, in the form of U.S. deployment of intermediate-range weapons in Europe. This would both counterbalance the Soviet SS-20 threat and add to the coupling of the U.S. nuclear intercontinental capability to the defense of Europe. Carter was not enthusiastic about accepting Schmidt's challenge, but decided that as leader of the Western alliance, he should take some kind of action. Finally, in January 1979, Carter met on the Caribbean island of Guadeloupe with British Prime Minister James Callaghan, French President Valéry Giscard d'Estaing, and Schmidt. There they worked out an arrangement to proceed with the deployment in Western Europe of two new U.S. intermediate-range systems—a force of 108 mobile ballistic missiles, the Pershing II, all of which would be based in West Germany; and a force of 464 ground-launched cruise missiles (GLCMs), most of which would be deployed in other European NATO countries that agreed to accept them. After a further exchange of views, the NATO foreign ministers in December 1979 adopted what they termed the "two track decision" which, in addition to providing for the deployment of the Pershing IIs and GLCMs, called upon the United States and the Soviet Union to enter into negotiations aimed at securing limitations on their respective systems, as the NATO communiqué put it, "consistent with the principle of equality between the sides."

When I first heard about this decision (I was not in the government at the time), I was dubious whether it was a wise move, especially with respect to the deployment of the Pershing IIs. These were improved, longer-range versions of the Pershing Ia, a missile that had been in Europe since the 1960s. The Pershing II was to have a range of 1,800 kilometers (more than twice the range of the Pershing Ia) which would give it the capability to strike Soviet territory, though not enough to threaten Moscow, which the Germans considered too politically sensitive a target. In fact, there were not many strategically significant targets in Russia that the Pershing II could reach. For NATO Europe the most important behind-the-lines targets were the time-sensitive ones, such as the staging bases for second- and third-echelon Warsaw Pact ground forces, virtually all of which were in non-Soviet Eastern Europe. For these targets, the added range of the Pershing II was unnecessary. That job could have been done just as well with a mix of GLCMs and a weapon called the Pershing Ib, which was identical to the Pershing II except for the absence of the second rocket stage, a design that limited its range to around 750 kilometers. In other words, it seemed to me that the case for deploying the Pershing IIs was more political than military.

What also bothered me about the missile decision was its divisive effect on European public opinion, especially West German opinion. Not only did it give the so-called peace movement a ready-made issue; it also threatened to undermine the fragile consensus on defense issues that the West German political parties had struggled so painstakingly to develop and maintain for two decades or more. Among those responsible for that consensus was Herbert Wehner, one of the most influential figures in Schmidt's Social Democratic party, the SPD. A former Communist, Wehner had turned staunchly anti-Soviet. It was partly through Wehner's influence that the SPD had moved away from being a radically left-wing party to being a middle-of-the-road anti-Soviet socialist party that tended to advocate essentially the same defense policies as the other major party, the Christian Democrats. At the time Schmidt made his speech to the IISS in 1977, he still had full SPD support behind him; but by the time of the Guadeloupe meeting fourteen months later, the implications of what he had proposed caused dissension within his party. Wehner and others who made up the left wing of the SPD refused to go along with what they viewed as a militarily superfluous deployment that might wreck chances for easing East-West tensions. Even Schmidt had second thoughts; to maintain his leadership of the party he felt compelled, in effect, to repudiate some of what he had advocated in his IISS speech.

A further complication was the emergence in the late 1970s of a German political movement known as the "Greens," made up of a combination of radical environmentalists, anarchists, leftists, pacifists, and a few hardened Communists of the Trotskyite persuasion. Their strongest appeal was to the young, more liberal-minded who had traditionally gravitated to the left wing of the SPD. At the grass-roots level, SPD organizers found they were losing new voters to the Greens and reacted by endorsing more radical positions themselves, including toughened demands for the elimination of nuclear weapons. The Soviets, for their part, helped to stimulate the peace movement by filtering funds to it and by providing healthy doses of propaganda. They were careful, however, to stay in the background lest their activities become too well known. It was, in sum, a complicated and delicate situation that did not make pursuing a consistent American policy any easier.

Nonetheless, by the time the Reagan administration came into office, I saw no other choice than to proceed with the two-track policy. To hold the Western alliance together, we could not afford to repeat the mistake that President Carter had made with respect to the neutron bomb, which he had first endorsed and then repudiated. If we were to maintain the solidarity of the alliance, we should not make commitments and then abruptly back away from them. I thought that in the case of the Pershing IIs and GLCMs, we had an opportunity to achieve what we wanted through negotiations. It would be advantageous for the West to see these weapons eliminated on both sides, if this could be negotiated with the Soviets. I was therefore in favor of promptly proceeding with INF negotiations. The task of doing so became mine when in July 1981 Eugene Rostow, the new director of the Arms Control and Disarmament Agency, asked me to join him as his candidate for the head of the delegation being assembled to meet in Geneva to negotiate what was then called the "theater nuclear weapons issue."

Behind the eventual name of the talks—the Intermediate-range Nuclear Forces, or INF, negotiations—there is an interesting story. Shortly before being designated as chief INF negotiator, I flew to Europe for preliminary consultations with our allies. At that time nearly everyone in the press and in the United States government was referring to the upcoming talks as either the "Euromissile talks" or the "theater nuclear forces negotiations." During my trip it became clear that our allies disliked this terminology. They thought that the phrase "theater nuclear weapons" gave the wrong impression in that it suggested a disassociation of a nuclear war in Europe from one involving an exchange between the United States and the Soviet Union. What the allies wanted was a coupling of the relatively weak deterrent in Europe to the stronger U.S. intercontinental deterrent. I thought they had a valid point with respect to the name to be given the negotiations and raised the issue at one of our subsequent delegation meetings in Washington. After we had examined the problem from a variety of perspectives, I finally proposed that we call the talks the "intermediate-range nuclear force" negotiations instead of "theater nuclear force" negotiations to establish the concept that the weapons we were to deal with were determined by their range, not by their geographic place of deployment. That was consistent with the line we had taken in SALT, and it seemed to me equally proper in connection with these negotiations.

After some further discussion the entire delegation concurred in the name I suggested we use. Then we all had to persuade our bosses. Generally speaking, people in the State Department, including Secretary of State Alexander Haig, agreed with us, so we had no problem there. The

Joint Chiefs were a little uncertain, but they too were eventually won over, so that by the eve of the talks, everyone in Washington was referring to them as the INF, rather than TNF, negotiations.

The next step was for Haig to persuade the Soviets when he and Gromyko met at the UN in September 1981. Haig's formulation for the title of the talks was "Negotiations for the Reduction and Limitation of Intermediate-range Nuclear Forces in the Context of START"— START being the acronym for Strategic Arms Reduction Talks (the title that President Reagan preferred over SALT), which were to be conducted parallel to the intermediate-range negotiations. Gromyko wanted the title to be "Limitation of Medium Range Nuclear Systems in Europe." His aim was to confine the talks to those weapons deployed in Europe in order to avoid any connection with SALT or START and to leave the Soviets a free hand to deploy whatever they wanted against China and Japan. We continued to insist that the talks deal with all intermediate-range weapons whatsoever. Gradually our view caught on in the press and was the one that prevailed.

What was meant by "intermediate-range" forces became something of a floating concept. My idea was that it should include all ground-based nuclear systems between battlefield-range weapons and intercontinental missiles with a range greater than 5,500 kilometers. The Soviets did not want any of their shorter-range systems (i.e., their SS-21s, with a range of 150 kilometers, and their SS-23s, which had a range of 300 to 500 kilometers) included in the negotiations. Eventually, it came down to discussion of the Pershing IIs and GLCMs on our side, and the SS-4s, SS-5s, and SS-20s on their side.

Shortly after Thanksgiving I arrived in Geneva for the opening round of talks and my first meeting with my Soviet opposite number, Yuli Kvitsinskiy. Before the INF negotiations began on November 30, 1981, I had never met Kvitsinskiy, although I had heard a great deal about him. The day before the first formal meeting between our two delegations was to take place, we met informally for an hour and a half. He spoke English, so we had no need for interpreters. He was forty-four, more than thirty years my junior. I found him, at least superficially, easy to get along with. Unlike many other Soviet negotiators I have known, he had a sense of humor.

From the start we tried to expand the informal contacts between the two delegations as much as we could. Kvitsinskiy and I frequently met one on one, and my wife, Phyllis, and I would invite Kvitsinskiy and his wife, Inga, to dinner, and to all manner of other social gatherings, such as outings on the lake, picnics, and formal receptions. Mrs. Kvitsinskiy was a handsome Ukrainian woman, with blue eyes, pale skin, and black hair; she spoke good French. Phyllis's French was excellent and mine passable. After a period of time we came to know the Kvitsinskiys about as well as it is possible to know a senior Soviet official.

From our casual conversations I learned that Kvitsinskiy came from a family of Polish origin that prided itself on its liberal intellectual background. His grandfather had moved to Russia. His father was a trained chemist and in World War I was inducted into the army as a chemical warfare officer. He ended the war as a colonel, but during the ensuing years of peace was progressively reduced in rank to lieutenant. Kvitsinskiy's aunt was secretary to Marshal Mikhail Tukhachevsky, chief of staff of the Red Army in the 1930s. Just before World War II, Stalin charged Tukhachevsky with treason for having conspired with the Germans. During the "Great Purge" trials, he was "liquidated," as the Soviets put it, as was an uncle of Kvitsinskiy's. His aunt survived but she and the rest of the family were sent to Krasnoyarsk in Siberia. Despite all that had happened to his family, Kvitsinskiy insisted to me that Stalin had been correct in distrusting Tukhachevsky and his associates because of their lingering loyalty to Trotsky. During World War II Kvitsinskiy's father was called back into the Soviet army, retiring after the war, again with the rank of colonel.

In Siberia the Kvitsinskiys continued to pride themselves on being intellectuals. Yuli was taught German before he learned Russian. He told me he had spent five years playing the cello. He did well at school and, through his father's influence, obtained an appointment to Moscow University. There he studied physics but later transferred to languages because he knew German and the examinations were therefore easy for him. He was active in Komsomol, the Communist party's youth organization. After graduation he was sent to the Institute of International Affairs, where he received a degree in jurisprudence and served as head of the Komsomol Bureau. He then went on to serve in Norway under Madame Aleksandra Kollontai, a colleague and contemporary of Lenin's, and in East Germany, where, according to one account I heard, he had been of crucial help in achieving the breakthrough that had led to the 1972 Berlin agreement by being willing to explore a compromise going beyond his instructions. From everything I could learn about Kvitsinskiy, he was not the usual Soviet Foreign Office bureaucrat. He told me with pride that he was one of only six Soviet ambassadors who had been appointed by the Central Committee of the Party rather than by the Ministry of Foreign Affairs.

Kvitsinskiy's sense of humor was sardonic; he did not seem to be a happy man. In repose his mouth turned down at the corners. His long training as a member of the Party was evident. He could elaborate in the finest detail any point of Communist doctrine and its application to any given situation. He was highly sensitive to possible political overtones of anything I said. If I asked a question it seemed barely to cross his mind to concern himself with the facts bearing on the answer to the question; he went directly to speculating on the possible motives that might have caused me to ask that question at that time.

In his formal statements at our plenary meetings he had no hesitation in putting forward a continuous stream of one-sided propaganda arguments which he knew in advance were lacking in factual basis and logic and would therefore be wholly unpersuasive to me and the U.S. delegation or to Washington. He appeared to be under instruction from Moscow to enter these statements into the record so that on the appropriate occasion they could be used by *Pravda* or other Soviet propaganda organs. When in the more informal postplenary discussions, I would demonstrate the errors and lack of logic in Kvitsinskiy's formal statement, he was wholly impervious to embarrassment. Sometimes he would as much as say that what he had stated in the plenary meeting had been on instruction from Moscow; he had had no responsibility for it and was therefore not to blame. On other occasions he would ascribe my remarks to my deputy, Maynard W. "Mike" Glitman, and rebut them with a torrent of misstatements of fact, quotations out of context, ad hominem arguments, or similar polemics which added nothing to the discussion.

In private discussion, away from the ears of his associates, and presumably of the KGB as well, he was generally quite a different man. He could be charming, a good conversationalist, interested in an amazing array of subjects. He appeared to be surprisingly frank in his discussion of Moscow politics, of the character and ability of his superiors, and of speculative possibilities.

Before the first formal negotiating session in the fall of 1981, Kvitsinskiy and I met and quickly agreed on several basic points, agreement on all of which I thought necessary if we were to have a serious negotiation rather than a mere competition for propaganda advantage. There would be no agenda; either side could at any time raise and discuss any subject it wished. We would meet in Geneva for a period of approximately two months and then return to our capitals for two months. (Setting such a schedule in advance would avoid endless useless argument as to which side was prepared to work harder and sit longer before a break.) Kvitsinskiy and I agreed that work with our respective bosses at home would probably be as important as, or more important than, the work the two delegations would have with each other; therefore it was right to give the home front equal time.

We agreed that he and I would attempt to preserve the confidentiality of the negotiations. I made it clear that I had to be free fully to brief the committees of the Congress and our NATO allies, but I believed they also would wish to foster success in the negotiations by maintaining confidentiality. I said I could make no commitment with respect to higher authority in the U.S. executive branch but could assure him with respect to myself and the members of my team. He said the Soviet side was much better disciplined than that of the United States, but admitted that he could give me no assurance as to what *Pravda, Izvestia,* or higher authority in Moscow might say. It was far from an airtight understanding, but for a long time it worked reasonably well; there were no leaks from either delegation.

During the first round, the U.S. delegation took the initiative. We introduced President Reagan's proposal of November 18, 1981, to forgo deployment of our Pershing II and ground-launched cruise missiles if the Soviets would eliminate their SS-20, SS-4, and SS-5 missile systems. This proposal became known as the "zero-zero option," or "zero-zero outcome." We explained the underlying considerations, outlined our view of the essential elements of an agreement designed to meet the interests of the two sides, and in February 1982 tabled the text of a draft treaty which presented in detail the way we proposed the issues involved should be dealt with.

The Soviet delegation used the early sessions in late 1981 and early 1982 to sketch out major elements of their position but left much to be explained later. In contrast to our proposal to eliminate all longer-range INF missiles globally, the Soviets proposed a limit that would pertain to Europe only, permitting NATO and the Soviet Union each three hundred "medium-range" missiles and aircraft, with the proviso that the United States would be allowed to deploy no missiles. (By NATO the Soviets meant the United States, Britain, and France and by "medium-range" they meant systems with a range or combat radius in excess of a thousand kilometers.) In the second round the Soviet side revealed more of their position and finally presented a draft treaty text of their own.

Our delegation had been keeping what we called an "issues book" to which, as one issue after another between the two sides arose, a new section was added. Every word said by anyone of our delegation and every word said by anyone of their delegation on one of those issues were entered into the book under the appropriate section. By the summer of 1982, the issues book contained some thirty-five sections. By that time, each side had reason to believe that it thoroughly understood the other's position, as well as all the ins and outs of the issues that divided us.

The two delegations normally met twice a week in plenary session. In these meetings each side would present a formal statement which represented the official view of its government on whatever question or facet of the INF issue it wanted to address. After these statements were exchanged, the sides would break up into smaller groups for postplenary meetings, where questions were asked and answered about the respective statements or about a side's statement from an earlier session. Though less formal than the plenary meeting, the postplenary sessions were still "on the record." Interpreters were present and both sides took scrupulous notes.

It is my practice to believe what I am told by those with whom I am negotiating until I have evidence that it is false. In the end it turned out that on some important matters, Kvitsinskiy had misled me, and on some it became clear that he had misreported to Moscow what I had said. Still, I continue to believe that much, if not most, of what he said to me was true.

In the spring of 1982, Kvitsinskiy told me that a basic review of Soviet policy toward the INF negotiations was scheduled for that summer in Moscow. He stressed the importance of progress in the negotiations prior to that review. A review of that kind would result in freezing the Soviet position; thereafter it was likely to be much more inflexible. I took his warning seriously.

I also had come to the conclusion that it was important to make progress rapidly, if at all possible. From the beginning of the negotiations it had been my view that the U.S. team in Geneva was negotiating as much, or more, on behalf of the interests of the European members of NATO as it was on behalf of the direct interests of the United States. After all, the SS-20s directly threatened every military installation, airfield, port, rail junction, command center, and city in Western Europe. They did not directly threaten targets in the United States. The U.S. interest was thus indirect; our NATO allies considered their territory to be under direct threat and a threat to them was a threat to us. The European members of NATO were anxious for a prompt agreement.

By the end of June 1982 the members of the U.S. negotiating team were near a consensus that the time had come to cut through the morass of issues and to try to find a basis for a deal. We did not see how we were going to achieve agreement involving substantial movement on the Soviet side unless we were prepared for substantial movement on our side.

My instructions directed me to explore with my opposite number any possibility of significant movement on issues of interest to us. I was not authorized to commit the government to any change in the U.S. position as set forth in my instructions. I saw no way of exploring the possibility of significant Soviet movement without at least indicating the U.S. movement I personally thought commensurate with the movement I was soliciting from them.

I did not think a "step-by-step" exchange of concessions was likely to be the best path to a sound agreement. When two negotiating partners have laid down their formal positions, there are strong reasons against making unilateral concessions. If one side perceives that the other is about to make a move, the first side has an incentive to stand pat and pocket the other side's anticipated concession. This naturally slows down the negotiating process, which is usually slow in any event, particularly when it is the Soviets who are on the other side of the table.

I came to the conclusion that the best hope of solving our problems was to explore informally with Kvitsinskiy a joint package entailing concessions by both sides leading to a mutually acceptable final outcome. Such a package could be developed without commitment by either side and no element would be agreed unless and until all elements were agreed, thereby protecting each side's formal negotiating position.

Indeed, I had had some experience with such explorations during SALT I, when my Soviet counterpart Aleksandr Shchukin and I engaged in informal discussions on limiting ABM radars. Those discussions led to our working out a package proposal for consideration by our respective bosses, Ambassadors Gerard Smith and Vladimir Semenov. Though they rejected one of the features that Shchukin and I valued highly, the package nonetheless remained basically intact and embodied the essential elements of what became the ABM treaty.

I recognized that, while I was authorized to probe for real movement on the issues, the explorations that I had in mind would be seen by some in Washington as going beyond my instructions. However, the potential payoffs seemed immense and I was prepared to run the risk. In any event, the informal nature of the exploration would allow the U.S. government, were it to find the results unsatisfactory, to disavow my efforts.

The Walk in the Woods

At exactly 3 P.M. on July 16, 1982, I was driven to the entrance of the Soviet mission, which occupies a large, partially wooded tract across the Avenue de la Paix from the entrance to the United Nations Palace. The entrance to the compound is through an electronically controlled, militarily guarded gate. As the gate opened, I saw Kvitsinskiy waiting for me on the front steps of the main building. We both were dressed in rough walking clothes. We got into his Mercedes and drove off, my car and driver following behind, in the direction of Lausanne. After about twenty kilometers, we turned off and climbed to the crest of the Jura mountain range, which at that point divides Switzerland from France.

The Mercedes stopped at an open pasture above the little town of St. Cergue on the Swiss side of the border near the crest of the pass. We got out of the car and began to walk up a country road through mountain pastures with a fine view of the higher Jura Mountains behind us. Kvitsinskiy led me to a logging road which appeared to lead down through the woods to the right. He said that in the wintertime he and some of the members of his delegation had gone there from time to time to cross-country ski.

Kvitsinskiy and I walked together along the logging road above St. Cergue. We had planned our informal conversation for weeks. After a few minutes we got down to business. He said that he had decided to consult Gromyko and seek his advice. I said that, as he knew, I had talked with Eugene Rostow, the head of the U.S. Arms Control and Disarmament Agency, who had been in Geneva a few days previously, about our projected walk, but that Rostow and I proposed to talk to no one else about it unless my talk with him led to a positive result.

Kvitsinskiy said Gromyko had told him to insist on compensation for British and French nuclear systems. As it happened, I had presented, in the formal meeting of our two delegations the day before, a major paper setting forth in detail the reasons why compensation for British and French systems was procedurally incorrect, substantively unjustified, and politically impossible for the United States and NATO. I told Kvitsinskiy that my formal statement of the day before on this subject had been completely serious. If his side chose to be adamant on compensation for British and French systems, there was no possibility of a deal.

Over the preceding weeks Kvitsinskiy and I had had a series of private discussions in which we had laid the groundwork for this walk. Now he repeated a point he had made earlier: that his side was adamant in rejecting the U.S. proposal calling for the elimination of all U.S. and Soviet longer-range INF missiles worldwide. He said his people considered that proposal to be a demand for unilateral disarmament by their side; they would never agree to it. I then repeated a point that I had made earlier: President Reagan's zero-zero offer was, in our view, the optimum outcome, both substantively and politically, and we had no intention of backing off from it. If we were to do so, the logical and political basis of our negotiating position would be weakened and from that point on, we would be negotiating from a less strong position. I suggested to Kvitsinskiy that the Soviets' refusal to budge on any part of their position relating to the central issues might be based on similar considerations. He said that that could be true.

I then continued by saying that if this were so, the only way to get to a "well-prepared" summit that fall through the INF route was through an integrated package of the necessary and sufficient elements for a definitive and comprehensive deal. If we could conceive of such a package, no weakening of either side's bargaining position need take place because any agreement between us would be ad referendum to our governments. Unless and not until both governments came to the conclusion that the advantages of the integrated package exceeded in value the costs of the concessions from its current bargaining position would there be any agreement between them.

I asked him whether the interest in Moscow in a "well-prepared" summit that fall was sufficient to justify the attempt to define such a package. He said he was not sure; it was a decision that would have to be taken by higher authority. I said I was equally unsure as to the position on my side.

I said I personally did not want to pass up an opportunity to progress in our negotiations if there was a significant chance that such an opportunity might be made to exist. Kvitsinskiy said he agreed to that.

I said I had given much thought to how such an integrated package might be constructed. I had four memoranda I had prepared earlier in the pocket of my jacket.

At this point in our talk I pulled out of my pocket and showed him the following paper, Paper A, saying that our discussions up to that point had covered most of the ground, but I wanted to be sure he understood what I had in mind. He read the paper and said he understood it.

PAPER A

The only way to proceed is by way of a package solution containing all the necessary and sufficient elements of an agreement. Step by step won't work.

U.S. not *demandeurs*—prepared to take our time, but I personally do not want an opportunity for progress to slip, if it exists.

Gather from our dinner conversation you're backing away from taking any personal initiative or risk in developing a package for the development of which we could take equal responsibility, even though each attributing more of the initiative to the other. You have reported in full to Gromyko. I only in part to Rostow and he and I to no one else.

I am prepared to take more personal risk than you appear to be willing to take in the interest of progress. But only if there is some point in it. If Moscow is adamant in wishing a one-sided deal, or will incorrectly assert that the package I am prepared to discuss is a proposal by my government or that I consider individual parts of the compromise package worth considering apart from the package as a whole, there is no point.

If you think the package as a whole is not acceptable, I will report back to my government that I tried to find some path to a "well prepared" summit this fall based on INF and was unsuccessful.

If you think the matter is worth exploring further, you will know how to reach me in Washington.

By now we were sitting side by side on the top of a pile of felled trees on the edge of the logging road. I showed him Paper B, which outlined the basic premises for a compromise package. He read it with care and commented only on subparagraph e, having to do with China. I said that would become clear when I showed him the next two papers.

PAPER B

What is needed is a package approach. No prospect U.S. will fall off zero/zero unless the alternative is an equitable deal that it knows will stick.

No signs of movement on the Soviet side on matters related to central issue, probably for similar reasons.

What is needed is a package containing a balance of compromises on the significant issues resulting in agreement on all the necessary and sufficient elements of a deal.

Let us accept:

a. that Soviet side will not accept zero/zero,

b. that U.S. will not give on UK/French inclusion or compensation,

c. that Soviet side requires some ceiling on medium-range dual-capable aircraft but that U.S. will agree to no significant reduction in them,

d. that SLCMs [sea-launched cruise missiles] are not an appropriate matter for discussion in INF but can be discussed in START,

e. that Soviet side requires consideration of its China problem, but there can be no export of European problem to Far East,

f. that limits must be equal in appearance and justifiable as to equality of effect.

If one accepted these points, what might a package of the necessary and sufficient elements for an agreement look like?

On thinking about it at your suggestion, it seemed to me that the following 15 elements might balance out in an equitable way.

I said the package I had worked out would not include British and French systems; it would not include sea-based systems; it called for no significant reductions in U.S. dual-capable aircraft; it called for more INF missile warheads in Europe for the U.S. side than for the Soviet side; but it made ten important concessions to the Soviet side. I then showed him Paper C, which listed those concessions. He read it with care but made no comment.

PAPER C

Within those parameters it makes the following concessions to your side:

1. It is not zero/zero.

2. The subceilings are equal in appearance but unequal in effect—ballistic missiles for you, cruise missiles with their longer flight time for us.

3. The limits are based on location, not on characteristics regardless of location.

4. The limits include aircraft.

5. The limits include only aircraft with a combat radius greater than 1000 kms.

6. The limits include FB-III aircraft which are not located in Europe.

7. The limits do not completely ban any present or future systems, including their deployment, production, test and evaluation, etc.

8. The collateral measures are broadened to include U.S. and German Pershing SRINF [short-range INF].[1]

9. The package accepts Soviet terminology, i.e., "medium range" rather than "intermediate range."

10. It provides for some reductions on the U.S. side.

I then showed him Paper D, which outlined the elements of a possible compromise outcome.

PAPER D

An integrated compromise package for consideration by both sides; nothing is agreed, or even proposed, until everything has been agreed.

1. Each side agrees to reduce its "medium-range nuclear delivery systems in Europe" in approximately equal annual increments to no more than 225 such systems by 31 December 1987.

2. Each side agrees to limit its "medium-range nuclear missile delivery systems in Europe" to a subceiling of no more than 75 on each side by the same date.

3. The U.S. agrees, in exercising its rights under the missile subceiling, to deploy only cruise missile systems. The Soviet side agrees, in exercising its right, to deploy only ballistic missile systems.

4. The Soviet side agrees not to deploy "medium-range nuclear missile systems" east of the Urals and west of 80 degrees east, not to deploy more than 75 such systems east of 80 degrees east and not to deploy those within range of targets in NATO Europe.

5. "Europe" includes Spain and the land, islands and inland waters eastward thereof to the Urals, etc.

6. "Delivery systems" are, with respect to missiles, transporter erector launchers and their associated missiles and base facilities; with respect to airplane delivery systems, the airplanes and their immediately associated equipment.

[1]In contrast to British and French nuclear forces, which are under the sole control of the British and French governments, West German Pershing Ia missile systems had nuclear warheads that were under U.S. control.

7. "Medium-range nuclear missile delivery systems" include all missile systems with a range greater than 1000 kilometers and less than 5500 kilometers. "Medium-range airplanes" on the Soviet side presently include Backfire, Badger and Blinder (not Fencer); "medium-range airplanes" on the U.S. side include FB-III and F-III (not F-4 or F-16).

8. The inclusion of Backfire and FB-III in this agreement is without prejudice to their possible treatment in a global context in a SALT/START agreement.

9. New types of airplanes with a combat radius in excess of 1000 kilometers and less than intercontinental will be included as "medium-range delivery systems" subject to agreement between the sides on each such type.

10. New types of "medium-range nuclear missiles" will not exceed existing types in numbers of warheads, i.e., three for Soviet ballistic missile systems and four for U.S. cruise missile systems.

11. The number of "medium-range" nuclear missiles in storage, etc., will not be in excess of normal maintenance and training requirements.

12. All medium-range nuclear delivery systems in Europe that become excess to the relevant limit or sublimit shall be destroyed pursuant to procedures developed in the SCC [Standing Consultative Commission].

13. There will be no increase in the present aggregate number of SS-12/22 and SS-23 missile systems or of Pershing missile systems (whether U.S. or German) deployed in Europe, and such missile systems will not be MIRVed or extended in range beyond that of the present SS-12/22 system.

14. Verification procedures will be worked out and mutually agreed.

15. The sides agree to resume negotiations for further reductions after conclusion of a SALT/START treaty.

When Kvitsinskiy had finished reading the first and second paragraphs, he said his side had hoped to get 150 missile systems. I said that that, in our view, was excessive, that even the 75 was too high from the U.S. perspective. I said he could recall an earlier conversation in which I had asked him whether he was suggesting a division of their proposed 300 ceiling on their side into two subceilings—one of 150 on missiles and the other of 150 on medium-range airplanes. I had taken his 150 on airplanes and added one-half of his 150 on missiles to come out with an overall ceiling of 225 with a subceiling of 75 on missiles.

When he came to the third paragraph, he pointed out that the language would permit the United States to go above 75 systems prior to 1987. I said that was not the intent; if he wanted to make it a paper of joint authorship, we could add the words, "and agrees at no time to exceed 75." He concurred.

When we got to the fourth paragraph, he said he could never sell a reduction to 75 SS-20s in the eastern USSR to his people. He suggested that we change the language to "not to increase the number of such systems presently deployed east of 80 degrees east." I said I understood there were 90 such missiles and suggested we add the number "90" in brackets. He agreed.

When we got to the fifth paragraph, I said I understood his side preferred to define the boundary of Europe by the crest of the Urals rather than 60 degrees east longitude but that I did not know how they described the boundary of Europe south of the Urals; that was what I meant by "etc." He said the Soviet line runs down to the Caspian Sea. He suggested I add the words, "being the geographical border of Europe."

Kvitsinskiy asked what I meant by "the land, islands and inland waters." I replied the landmass of Europe. He said, "What about the islands?" I said that included, for instance, Great Britain and Ireland. He asked about Iceland. I replied, "Maybe, but certainly not the Azores." Kvitsinskiy asked, "Why not the Azores?" I said they were not in Europe; they were a stepping-stone between Europe and America.

He noted the words "and base facilities" in the sixth paragraph and inquired why I had included them. I replied that, if they went down from their present total of approximately 225 operational launchers to 75, the base facilities for some 150 systems would need to be destroyed; otherwise the argument that the Soviets had made that they could not promptly redeploy from the Far East because of lack of base facilities would be untrue.

When we got to the seventh paragraph, he asked me why I had included the FB-111s, which were not in Europe. I said I had included them because to do so was necessary to make it possible to say that the agreement required reductions on both sides; 63 FB-111s plus 165 F-111s currently deployed in Europe equaled 228, which was just over 225. (As the FB-111s were already based in the United States, the package would have forced the removal of 15 F-111s if the U.S. deployed 75 missile launchers in Europe.)

He asked why the eighth paragraph was necessary. I said this package dealt only with aircraft in Europe. START dealt with systems on a worldwide basis. It should be made explicit that the issue of the Backfire bombers on a worldwide basis could be raised in START.

When we got to the ninth paragraph, I commented that this was the formula used with respect to heavy bombers in SALT.

Kvitsinskiy read the tenth paragraph and said that this would give the United States more INF missile warheads in Europe than the Soviet Union. I said that the Pershing missiles were much more threatening than the ground-launched cruise missiles (GLCMs). It was not correct that any warhead could be equated with any other warhead. I asked him whether he would wish us to substitute 75 Pershing IIs for the GLCMs. He replied, "No." I said I understood that the Soviets were testing a longer-range GLCM that could be launched either in an air, ground, or sea mode. He said yes, and added that it took forty-five minutes to switch from one mode to the other.

He made no comment on the eleventh paragraph.

When we got to the twelfth paragraph, I said the words "in Europe" should be struck out; to leave it in would imply that Soviet missiles in the East in excess of 90 would not have to be destroyed.

Kvitsinskiy said that he found the language in the thirteenth paragraph hopeless for him; his people would say that there was no such missile as the SS-23. I said that we had to put in some bottom limit to the shorter-range INF range band. Would he prefer 300, 400, or 500 kilometers? He said 500. He asked what the range of the Pershing Ia was. I said that while I had forgotten the precise range, I thought it was 760 kilometers. In any case, it was less than that of the SS-12/22. He wanted to be sure the provision would cover the range of the Pershing Ib (a missile, as I mentioned earlier, incorporating the Pershing II's accuracy but having the same range as the Pershing Ia) and ensure that its range would not be increased beyond that of the SS-12/22, which the Soviets claimed was 800 kilometers. I said our people estimated SS-12/22 range to be 925 kilometers. We finally agreed on language amended from mine, as follows:

There will be no increase in the aggregate number of missile systems with a range greater than 500 kilometers and up to and including that of the SS-12/22, and such systems will not be MIRVed or their range increased beyond that of the SS-12/22. This provision will cover, on the U.S. side, the Pershing missile (whether U.S. or German).

When we got to the fourteenth paragraph, I said that because the deal outlined in our package provided finite limits, not zero, the verification problem would be serious, and we would need a package of agreed additional measures. It had not been possible to work those out in the absence of knowing the outline of the deal we might finally arrive at on the central and related issues. It was for this reason that I had not gone beyond the language in that bullet.

He said that the fifteenth paragraph would be helpful to him.

He then said it would also be helpful to him if something could be added about a moratorium until our "Statement of Intent" could be transformed into a definitive agreement. I said we would have to limit the time period, otherwise one side could stall forever. I said I would try my hand at drafting a sixteenth paragraph.

It began to rain. His car had driven up to find us. We got into it; his driver got out and disappeared into the woods.

I said I had brought a pad of paper and a pen with me; I assumed he would wish to take full notes on the papers I had gone over. Kvitsinskiy said he had brought his own pad of paper; he took long and complete notes. While he was doing so, I finished drafting the sixteenth paragraph; it read as follows:

> 16. After signature by both sides of this Statement of Intent, and pending a definitive agreement, a moratorium will go into effect on construction activities related to the deployment in Europe of medium-range nuclear ballistic missile delivery systems. A definitive agreement will be concluded in no more than three months from this date.

I asked him whether he had taken down the heading on Paper D. He had not. He took it down word for word.

He said he was troubled that sea-based systems were not included. I said sea-launched cruise missiles could be discussed in START. I had talked to U.S. START negotiator Edward Rowny about it, and he had agreed. I said it was an immensely complicated subject; we certainly should not let ourselves be bogged down in it. As for carrier-based air, we had only two carriers normally in European waters. Each had thirty-eight A-6s and A-7s. The Soviet side should forget about them. We would get endlessly bogged down otherwise. The U.S. Navy was not about to let their conventional capabilities be limited in our negotiations, particularly as the Soviets had put so enormous an effort into arms designed to attack our carriers. The carriers could not be limited without limiting the arms deployed against them. He said he regretted this; they had hoped to get our agreement not to station more than two, or at a maximum three, carriers in European waters. I said it would not go; they should forget it.

Kvitsinskiy raised a final point concerning the freeze on Soviet SS-20s in the eastern portion of the USSR. He noted that the United States would not be limited as to the number of INF missiles it was permitted to deploy in the Far East. I replied that it was better to leave the package as it was. The United States had no intention of deploying such missiles in the Far East; to put in such a limit would get us back into global limitations which would raise other problems. He did not insist further on this point.

Kvitsinskiy said he did not know what the reaction in Moscow would be to our package; the Soviets might reject it out of hand, they might wish to offer substantial amendments. I said I also could not predict Washington's reaction. He asked me where I would be after I returned to the United States. I said for a week in Washington, and then I planned to go to Maine, as I usually do in August. He asked how they could get in touch with me. I said the White House operator could always find me. I said I would go wherever he wanted me to, at whatever time, if it would help get a deal through.

He asked through whom in their embassy they should send a message to me. I replied the only one I knew was Ambassador Dobrynin; I had heard of Aleksandr Bessmertnykh, the number two man at the Soviet embassy, but had never met him. Kvitsinskiy asked me about Oleg M. Sokolov, the number three man. He knew him, he was an experienced man. He would communicate with me through him.

He said he hoped I would say nothing about the substance of our conversations until I heard from him. I did not reply.

At 5:30 P.M. he called loudly for his chauffeur, who then came running from the deep woods. I was driven down to where my car was waiting and we said "good-bye."

Immediately after our meeting I jotted down on a pad a close-to-verbatim reconstruction of my conversation with Kvitsinskiy. Over years of negotiating with the Russians I had trained myself to recollect and immediately get down on paper word by word what had been said. The Soviets are masters at rewriting history to their advantage, so a precise record is essential. Having gotten it down on paper, I had that internal glow that comes from having done something truly constructive. But that glow soon cooled as I thought of all the probable roadblocks ahead.

The Walk's Aftermath

The next morning—Saturday—I talked with Gene Rostow and told him that the "walk" had taken place. However, I held back the details, believing it wisest to give them first to the President or to his national security assistant, Judge William Clark.

On Monday, July 19, I gave the members of the U.S. delegation a general description of the "walk," omitting mention that a specific package had been worked out. I said it was too early to assess whether I had been successful in eliciting a useful reaction from the Soviet side. The delegation sent back a reporting telegram in the same vein. I left for Washington via London the next day.

When I arrived back in Washington, Rostow and I had a preliminary meeting with Judge Clark on the afternoon of July 27. Clark had with him General Richard Boverie, one of his most able NSC assistants. I brought along three copies each of two lengthy memoranda. One was a reporting memorandum describing the "walk in the woods" in full detail, including the four papers I had taken with me on the walk. The other memorandum was an analysis of a number of questions arising from the "walk" with respect to the Soviets, our allies, and public opinion.

Clark and Boverie read my memoranda with care. After an hour or so of discussion, Clark was called out to see the President. Boverie, Rostow, and I continued to talk. Boverie seemed much impressed. He said that it looked to him as though this could be the breakthrough the President had been looking for. As Rostow and I left, Boverie reminded us that Judge Clark had asked that we talk to no one about the walk in the woods until he had been able to brief the President.

A meeting chaired by the President was held several days later at the White House to discuss the walk in the woods. I flew back from my vacation in Maine to be there. Others who attended included Secretary of State George P. Shultz (who had recently replaced Haig after the latter had had a falling-out with Reagan); Secretary of Defense Caspar W. Weinberger; the chairman of the Joint Chiefs, General John W. Vessey, Jr.; CIA Director William J. Casey, Clark, Rostow, and the President's White House triumvirate—Edwin Meese, Michael Deaver, and James Baker. The attitude of all the senior officials seemed to be generally favorable. However, they all thought further study should be given to the package and its various provisions before they could give the President a specific recommendation. As a result, the President issued a memorandum allowing each of the principals to bring one additional person into the circle of those fully informed in order to conduct an urgent analysis of the package.

The basic question was whether Kvitsinskiy had received as favorable a reception in Moscow as I had in Washington. But as the weeks passed, no word came from the Soviet embassy. It seemed to me more and more probable that our package had met with a much colder reception in Moscow. And the more the package received closer attention in Washington, the more concerns began to develop on our side. In order to do the analysis in the depth that the NSC principals thought necessary, more people were brought into the circle of those informed about the walk-in-the-woods package. But unfortunately, none was given full access to my memoranda. As a result, there were some serious misunderstandings about the finer points in the package.

One concern—perhaps the most important—was that the Soviets might not treat the package as a final outcome but instead as a new U.S. proposal, and then try to split the difference between it and the formal Soviet position. My belief is that this was the primary concern of those who had problems with the "walk." Indeed, several officials who opposed the "walk" in the summer of 1982 subsequently told me that they could have accepted it as a final outcome had the Soviets agreed to it; their opposition was based mainly on their fear that the Soviets would abuse our acceptance of the package and turn it against us. Such concerns grew as August passed and there continued to be no word from the Soviet embassy.

I returned to Washington for a further meeting of the NSC principals on September 7. By that time the lines were fairly clearly drawn. State and ACDA, while recognizing that Moscow likely had problems with the package, favored taking a positive approach to it, but did not believe we should commit ourselves to a position. The Pentagon, however, was increasingly concerned about the absence of any contact from Kvitsinskiy. (By that time, seven weeks had elapsed without any word.) They interpreted this to mean that Moscow had rejected the package (as did I) and would seek to pocket our acceptance of it as a concession. They therefore wished to disavow it.

I regretfully concluded that the package had not found favor in Moscow. The package had been designed to be an outcome acceptable to both sides, not as a unilateral change in the U.S. position. If the Soviets were going to reject all or part of the package, it was advisable that we also make it clear that without the Soviet concessions called for by the package, the United States was not prepared to make the concessions the package called upon it to make. I still strongly believed, however, that the direct, informal Nitze-Kvitsinskiy channel should be kept open.

As a result of the September 7 discussion, the President issued a decision paper addressed to Secretary of State Shultz and me. Secretary Shultz was scheduled to see Gromyko in connection with a UN meeting in New York on September 28. I was scheduled to meet with Kvitsinskiy for the beginning of the next round of the INF talks in Geneva on September 29. Neither of us was to initiate a discussion of the walk-in-the-woods package. If Gromyko initiated such a discussion, Shultz would make the point that the United States had examined the package and considered it to be unequal because the United States was not permitted to have in Europe any missiles comparable to the SS-20, and was allowed only slow-flying cruise missiles. In addition, the Soviet Union was permitted to maintain ninety SS-20 missile launchers in the eastern USSR which, given their mobility, could reinforce the SS-20s in European Russia targeted against the West. The United States, however, was fully prepared to continue the exchanges begun in the Nitze-Kvitsinskiy channel. If Gromyko did not raise the subject of the walk-in-the-woods package, but left it to Kvitsinskiy to do so the next day, I was to execute the same instructions.

On September 28 Gromyko did not raise the subject. Secretary Shultz sent me a cable saying he and Gromyko had agreed that both the INF and START negotiations were being handled in a serious and professional manner. Gromyko added, however, that the U.S. position in both negotiations could not be a basis for agreement. Specifically, Gromyko said the zero-zero option was impossible since the Soviets would have to disarm unilaterally. Shultz told Gromyko that it remained to be seen what might come of the walk-in-the-woods procedure, but that he believed this pattern of communications was worthwhile.

On my arrival in Geneva, I was informed that Kvitsinskiy would like to have another walk in the region of St. Cergue on September 29.

This time we walked along a road headed toward a restaurant called the Cave of the Huntsman. Kvitsinskiy lost no time in getting to the point. He said the reaction in Moscow to our package had been wholly negative. He said, "You may as well read what I am instructed to say to you." He then handed me a single typed page. It made the following points:

The Soviet Union will enter into no INF agreement which:
(1) does not provide full compensation for British and French nuclear systems;

(2) limits Soviet systems outside the range of targets in NATO Europe;

(3) does not provide for serious and equal reductions in nuclear-capable medium-range aircraft within range of Europe, whether based on land or on sea; and

(4) is not fully consistent with the principle of "equality and equal security."

Moscow having thus turned down the walk-in-the-woods package, I then executed my instructions precisely as I had been ordered to do. I emphasized, however, that the United States was ready and had authorized me to continue to pursue informal negotiations in our private channel.

Thus, at the beginning of the third round of the INF negotiations in the fall of 1982, the Soviets laid to rest the walk in the woods, as well as any future explorations on a similar informal basis. Kvitsinskiy later confirmed what he had told me earlier, that there had been a basic INF arms control policy review in Moscow that summer. The conclusion reached was that the Soviet Union should not accept any agreement that permitted deployment of even a single Pershing II or ground-launched cruise missile. To do so would put Soviet approval on such U.S. deployments and would undercut the peace, antinuclear, environmentalist, and anti-American movements in Western Europe. The Moscow group had decided that INF could best be used as a political device to sow dissension within NATO and to drive wedges between the United States and its European partners. Soviet acceptance of the walk in the woods or other successful explorations in the Nitze-Kvitsinskiy channel would have undercut that strategy.

The Equal Reductions Episode

From this point on the INF talks in Geneva became much more formal and generally unproductive. However, very near the end the Soviets came up with a most bizarre initiative. The "walk in the park," as the episode came to be known, was mysterious, Byzantine, and ended with my feeling some bitterness toward Kvitsinskiy. It took place during the final month of the final round of the INF negotiations, culminating in the Soviet walkout of November 23, 1983.

The episode had its roots in a late October dinner conversation at our apartment on the Quay Gustav Ador overlooking Lake Geneva. We had invited my executive assistant, Norman Clyne, his wife Alice, several Swiss friends, and Ambassador Kvitsinskiy and his wife. The Kvitsinskiys were somewhat late in arriving. Kvitsinskiy took me aside on entering the apartment and told me that he had been watching a Tass news briefing on Moscow television which he was able to receive via a dish antenna on the roof of the Soviet mission. The Tass broadcast reported on an interview with General Secretary Yuri V. Andropov, who had succeeded Brezhnev in November 1982 upon the latter's death, which would appear in the next day's issue of *Pravda*. In it Andropov, among other things, announced a change in the Soviet INF position. The Soviets were now prepared to reduce the number of their SS-20 launchers within range of NATO Europe to 140 (their preceding position had been that they must have 162 such SS-20 launchers in order to be compensated for the 162 British and French SLBM tubes and IRBM launchers). They were also amending their position with respect to aircraft and with respect to missiles in the Far East.

Later in the evening Kvitsinskiy said, "Why don't you propose equal reductions?" I replied that this sounded to me like a proposal Paul Warnke had made a year earlier, which at the time Kvitsinskiy had told me was no less objectionable to Moscow than the U.S. interim proposal of March 1983 for equal levels of U.S. and Soviet longer-range INF missile warheads. Kvitsinskiy said that what he had in mind was somewhat different. It would bring the total of Soviet SS-20 launchers in Europe down to about 120. Furthermore, it would avoid the issue of compensation for British and French systems, which could be dealt with in "future negotiations."

On November 2, Kvitsinskiy and I met for lunch at La Réserve. After an extended discussion of Andropov's newest proposals, we returned to the subject of Kvitsinskiy's equal reductions suggestion. Kvitsinskiy confirmed that my recollection of what he had suggested was correct. He added that for political reasons his side could not put such a proposal forward; the proposal must appear to come from the U.S. side. I observed that I took it from what Kvitsinskiy had said that if the United States put such a proposal forward, it would be favorably received in Moscow. Kvitsinskiy replied that he had so hinted. I then asked if this also applied to the walk-in-the-woods package, since I had heard that some on the Soviet side had said that that package might also be acceptable to Moscow if the United States put it forward. Kvitsinskiy replied firmly in the negative; should the United States propose such a package formally, he said, the Soviet Union would reject it in its entirety. He added that I seemed to think that statements by the various spokesmen on his side were fully coordinated when, in fact, some on his side spoke out of turn, which much annoyed him.

The next day there was a reception for the two delegations at the residence reserved for the Soviet ambassador to the United Nations Committee on Disarmament. Kvitsinskiy took me out in the garden for a private talk. During our conversation he noted that the point of his suggestion was not only a Soviet reduction to 120 missile systems but a way of deferring the problem of future increases in British and French warheads to future negotiations. He also said that when he had made the suggestion that the United States look at equal reductions ending up with 120 SS-20s in Europe, I had asked him a number of questions and that subsequently I had raised the matter again, asking further questions. Did that indicate any interest on my part? I said that I did not mean to give Kvitsinskiy any false hopes. I asked questions only in order to be sure that I fully understood his suggestion. I also warned him that, personally, I did not think the Soviet offer would be well received in Washington.

On Saturday evening, November 12, Phyllis and I had already gone to bed and were quietly reading when the telephone rang. It was Kvitsinskiy. He said that he had received instructions from Moscow and needed to meet with me the next morning. I suggested we meet in the Botanical Gardens, which was across the Avenue de la Paix from the U.S. delegation's offices, to which he agreed.

When we met on Sunday morning Kvitsinskiy went directly to the business at hand. He said he had been directed to say that Moscow had studied with great care his report of the discussion that he and I had had on the subject of equal reductions. His telegram of instruction officially directed him to tell me that, if the U.S. government were to propose equal reductions of 572 warheads on each side, the Soviet government would accept that proposal and that it was Moscow's view that the remaining issues could be equitably worked out. The Soviet government would reserve the right to raise the issue of British and French forces in an appropriate future negotiating forum. I asked whether, in reporting our previous discussions, he had made it clear to Moscow that the idea of equal reductions had been his and that I had said I did not believe that it would be acceptable to Washington. Kvitsinskiy did not give me a clear answer.

When I reported this conversation back to Washington I included a concluding comment recommending that the State Department promptly inform our NATO allies of the Soviet equal reductions move; I thought that if we failed to do so the Soviets would likely go to them behind our backs.

Kvitsinskiy and I met the following morning, Monday, again in the Botanical Gardens, this time at my request. I told him that President Reagan, after consulting with the U.S. allies, had decided to fill out his September initiatives by proposing a specific global limit of 420 on the number of longer-range missile warheads on each side. I had received instructions the preceding evening to present the number at our next plenary session scheduled for Tuesday morning. To avoid any misunderstanding, I had a paper with me describing this move. I gave it to Kvitsinskiy to read. He said that the answer to this proposal in Moscow would be negative. I pointed out that the proposal left open the question of the level of deployments in Europe as well as the percentage of that level which would consist of Pershing IIs; it thus opened up a wide range of possibilities and seemed to be a useful basis for moving forward toward a mutually acceptable solution. Kvitsinskiy retorted that it did not look hopeful to him.

Shifting to his equal reductions proposal made in our November 13 meeting, Kvitsinskiy asked me when I expected to receive a response from Washington. I said I was not sure. I said that I had a few more questions about Moscow's proposal. In reporting it back to Washington, I had described the Soviet position on compensation for British and French systems to be that such compensation could be addressed "in an appropriate future forum." Was that correct? Kvitsinskiy said it was; however, he amplified that statement with the comment that his instructions had said that the Soviet side would reserve the right to raise the issue of compensation for British and French systems "in this or another forum." I asked what that terminology meant. Kvitsinskiy said "this forum" meant the INF negotiations. As to "another forum," Kvitsinskiy had proposed to Moscow that the forum be START. He said he presumed that was what Moscow had had in mind by "another forum."

At the end of our discussion, I referred to an article that had appeared the day before in London in *The Sunday Times* saying that the first U.S. cruise missiles might arrive in England any day. Kvitsinskiy said that he understood that Britain's defense minister, Michael Haseltine, had promised, upon arrival of the missiles, to make an appropriate announcement in Parliament. I said this was also my understanding. Kvitsinskiy said that if Haseltine were to make that announcement that day or the next he did not believe that the Soviet delegation would be able to meet with the U.S. side on Tuesday as scheduled; he would have to consult Moscow.

I said that would be wholly regrettable; progress had been made during the last few weeks and this was not the time to walk out. Kvitsinskiy replied, "We'll see."

The Soviet delegation did appear for the next day's plenary session, despite the British announcement that the first GLCMs had arrived in the United Kingdom the day before. As instructed, I formally presented the President's proposal for a 420 global warhead limit. That evening my deputy, Mike Glitman, and his wife, Chris, held a reception for both delegations at their residence in Coppet, outside Geneva. I opened my discussion with Kvitsinskiy by noting that Washington was working hard on Moscow's Sunday equal reductions proposal. The heart of the matter was whether Washington, taking the equal reductions proposal as a Moscow initiative, could regard it as opening a possible path to agreement. I proposed thus to advise Washington unless he told me not to do so. Kvitsinskiy agreed that "the heart of the matter" was whether Washington thought the proposal could open a path to agreement; should an agreement eventuate, it would be a joint package.

Kvitsinskiy then again asked me how long I expected it would take for Washington to respond to the Soviet equal reductions initiative. I said I had no way of knowing, but Washington had posed a number of questions. I thought there were the usual divergent viewpoints in Washington and would be surprised if I received an answer in less than five days from then. Kvitsinskiy said he would report to Moscow that I believed there would be at least a five-day delay before I received instructions on how to respond.

I had no doubt in my mind that Kvitsinskiy's equal reductions idea was unacceptable to our side. It seemed to me, however, that rather than reject flatly the Soviet initiative, it would be wiser to come back with a counterproposal using the concept of equal reductions to arrive at a more equitable outcome. After two days of imaginative hard work by the U.S. delegation in Geneva, we came up with a formula which did exactly that.

We sent a telegram back to Washington noting that the Soviet side was positioning itself so that, when it carried out its long-standing threat to break off the talks, they could cite as reasons both the U.S. rejection of Kvitsinskiy's equal reductions proposal and the Bundestag vote as well. (The German Bundestag was scheduled to debate and vote November 21–22 on whether to accept Pershing II deployments and the Soviets appeared to be attempting to isolate the Federal Republic by "ignoring" the earlier arrival of GLCMs in England.) We suggested that the best way to rebut this ploy and reduce pressure on West Germany was for the United States not to reject Kvitsinskiy's proposal but to make a counteroffer, which could pick up the equal reductions idea but modify its method of application in such a way as to produce an outcome consistent with U.S. criteria for an acceptable agreement. We then outlined in the telegram the basic elements of such a U.S. counterproposal.

On Thursday, November 17, while Washington was considering our counterproposal suggestion, the Soviet mission in Geneva and the Soviet embassy in Washington concurrently began to circulate rumors that I had made a proposal to the Soviet side, that Moscow had accepted it, and that Washington had rejected it. At eight o'clock that evening the Soviet embassy in Bonn delivered to the West German Foreign Office a note signed by Soviet Ambassador Semenov asserting that I had made a proposal of equal reductions by 572 warheads on each side, that Moscow had reacted favorably, that Washington had rejected the idea, that the whole thing was a nefarious scheme, and that Moscow was sure the West German government would wish to be informed of the dirty tricks the United States was playing behind its back. The next day similar notes were delivered to other NATO governments. Fortunately, we had already briefed our NATO allies, so they were aware that the facts were the reverse of what the Soviet notes were asserting.

On Saturday, November 19, I received instructions from Washington directing me without delay to convey the following points to Kvitsinskiy with regard to his informal equal reductions proposal of November 13: First, that proposal would leave the Soviet Union with a large force of SS-20 missile systems in Europe while barring the United States from any countering deployments. The United States and its NATO partners had made clear that they could not accept a Soviet monopoly in longer-range INF missiles. Second, while Washington had noted with interest Kvitsinskiy's indication that the Soviet side was willing to drop its explicit demand for compensation for third-country forces, the negotiated outcome of an agreement must provide for equality of rights and limits on a global basis between the United States and the Soviet Union. And finally, while the United States was prepared to study carefully any proposal that the Soviet side might wish to put forward in these negotiations, Washington—and, I added, I personally—found unacceptable Soviet attempts in direct approaches to our allies to misrepresent the informal Soviet suggestion of November 13 as an American proposal.

At my request, Kvitsinskiy came to my office at the Botanic Building at 12:30 that afternoon. Without introduction I handed him a paper containing the above points. After Kvitsinskiy had read the paper I asked if he had any comments. He said the assertion that equal reductions was a Soviet suggestion was incorrect; it was an American proposal. I could not prevent Kvitsinskiy's shameless mendacity from angering me, though I knew it would do no good for me to lose my temper.

I said I could not understand the notes conveyed to NATO governments by Soviet ambassadors. What they contained was simply contrary to fact. Kvitsinskiy objected that all this had been turned into "a filthy thing," asserting that there had been leaks on November 17 by someone on the U.S. side saying the USSR had abandoned the British-French issue. This had been used by Chancellor Helmut Kohl to influence the Bundestag debate. I interjected that the suggestion that the Soviets were willing to drop the British-French issue would not be helpful to Kohl in that debate. Kvitsinskiy asserted that this whole episode was a plot on the U.S. side.

Kvitsinskiy said that on November 13 I had indicated I would do my best on equal reductions. I responded that I had said I would do my best to get an answer to Moscow's proposal. Kvitsinskiy insisted that I had indicated I was hopeful of a positive outcome. I replied that I had made it clear early on in our conversations that I personally saw little hope of the United States reducing from 572 warheads to zero while the Soviet Union maintained a large number of longer-range INF missiles. Insofar as I had not completely rejected the Soviet approach, it was because I had had in mind that the new Soviet position on British and French forces and a formula incorporating equal reductions but producing an equitable, not an unequal, outcome might offer the possibility of opening a way to an acceptable agreement. However, I had made clear to Kvitsinskiy that, overall, I was pessimistic about the concept.

At this point, Kvitsinskiy abruptly left my office. He wandered down the wrong corridor toward the elevator, where a member of our team encountered him. Kvitsinskiy seemed dazed and asked how to get to the "lift." In the elevator on the way out his only remark was: "Everything's finished."

That evening I worried about our heated exchange. On reflection I concluded that while my anger with Kvitsinskiy and with his government for blatantly falsifying the facts was wholly justified, it would be unwise to press the matter. It was important to preserve the channel of communication through Kvitsinskiy.

On Monday morning I invited Kvitsinskiy to lunch at La Réserve. During the luncheon I asked him what the United States should expect to happen on Wednesday, which was the date of our next scheduled plenary. He replied that he expected to receive instructions the next day. I asked if the instructions would be sent out after the Bundestag vote, which was to take place Tuesday. He replied that they would. He added, however, that everything was settled. He would only be able to repeat two pertinent phrases from Andropov's recent *Pravda* interview—that the USSR could not continue the negotiations if the missiles were delivered, and that it could continue if the deliveries were postponed.

I commented that the upcoming period was bound to be rough; Kvitsinskiy agreed. I said I was confident that Semenov's note to the West German government would become public. Kvitsinskiy disagreed, saying there was no reason for it to become public. I told him that Egon Bahr, the spokesman of the Social Democratic party (SPD) on arms control matters, had called me on Friday morning to inquire about a rumored initiative in our negotiations. I had told him that Kvitsinskiy, under instructions, had said that if the United States made the equal reductions proposal, the Soviet government would accept it; I had explained that, although the immediate deal would not be linked to British and French systems, compensation for future increases would be claimed in this or another forum, and the 120 SS-20s would be considered to be partial compensation. Kvitsinskiy said Bahr had called him as well, but he had not wanted to talk on an open line so he had referred Bahr to Semenov.

I asked Kvitsinskiy if he had seen Semenov's note to the Germans. Kvitsinskiy said he had. I said I did not see how the Soviets could have thought the Germans would give the note any credence. Kvitsinskiy said that the initiative was now dead. He said the Semenov note was not directed against me; there was a certain prestige in being known as the author of a proposal. I responded that the Semenov note was aimed at using me against President Reagan.

Wishing to shift the subject, I suggested to Kvitsinskiy that he and I not get into recriminations; the facts were bound to come out. The point was to see whether there was anything the two of us could do to help the negotiating process between the United States and the USSR so that, to the extent possible, we could continue, or rather return to, businesslike discussions. Despite the current serious check, negotiations should continue.

Kvitsinskiy said he did not see where his side could go. His current instructions stopped at the 140 proposal. I said I saw no immediate prospect of a change in my instructions either, but still I thought the sides should keep on trying.

Kvitsinskiy stated that on Wednesday, the twenty-third, he intended to make a short statement. If I made an extended one, he would be prepared to answer. The Soviet side had said that they would call the talks off. He said that he was not authorized to offer any prospect of a resumption. I noted that the Soviet side could always change its mind.

On Wednesday, November 23, the Soviet delegation arrived at our offices in the Botanic Building. The German Bundestag had voted late the previous evening to proceed with deployments. A crowd of peace marchers was in the street with banners and placards; word had spread that the Soviets would probably walk out that day.

In his opening statement, Kvitsinskiy announced that the Soviet delegation "declares this round of negotiations discontinued, without setting any date for resumption." He cited the West German Bundestag vote of November 22 as well as earlier votes by the United Kingdom and Italian parliaments as giving the green light to deployments in those countries. He ended by asserting: "Thus the U.S. and its above mentioned allies knowingly created the situation of which the USSR has warned."

I expressed profound regret at the Soviet decision, calling it as unjustified as it was unfortunate. I noted the progress we had made and expressed the continued commitment of the United States to negotiate until an acceptable accord had been reached.

Thus ended the "walk in the park" episode. Shortly after the negotiations collapsed, Kvitsinskiy submitted an article for publication in *The New York Times* on January 12, 1984. In it he continued to insist that the equal reductions proposal had originated with the United States and that it had been "a tactical move aimed at creating an illusion of progress just when the United States started delivering missiles to Europe." The upshot, Kvitsinskiy insisted, was to thwart what he described as the Soviet Union's efforts to effect "large-scale, meaningful arms cuts." In a typically Kvitsinskiy manner, he completely turned matters around, partly to save face, no doubt, but also to preserve the fiction that his masters in Moscow had gone to such pains to invent.

The question remains as to what actually had gone on on the Soviet side. Had Kvitsinskiy been authorized in advance to make his October 26 suggestion, or did this start as purely a Kvitsinskiy operation? If he had been authorized to do so, was it only the man in Moscow whom Kvitsinskiy wished to protect who had authorized him to do so? How much of our discussions had he accurately reported to Moscow? Who in Moscow authorized his November 13 instructions? Who prepared and authorized the Semenov note to the West German Foreign Office on the seventeenth? Did the Soviets really hope, with the purpose of affecting the Bundestag debate, to catch the United States in a position of not having informed its allies of an important move? Or was the entire scheme a serious effort to explore an endgame ploy leading to U.S. acceptance of a proposal which would have left the USSR with a dominant deployment of SS-20s in Europe with no U.S. offsetting counterdeployments, while doing so in a way in which the Soviets could avoid the United States pocketing their willingness to give up compensation for British and French systems if, in the end, the United States did not agree to the rest of the Soviet proposal? In the event of failure they could deny that they had made any offer whatever by asserting it was my proposal. The answer is probably to be found in a combination of these elements.

20

The Nuclear-Space Talks

Immediately after the Soviets withdrew from the INF negotiations, the United States began the scheduled deployment of Pershing IIs in Germany and ground-launched cruise missiles (GLCMs) in England. I was concerned with the political repercussions, particularly in Germany, of the combination of the start of U.S. INF deployments and the abrupt Soviet withdrawal from the negotiating table. For a week or so, the consequent political debate was on the front pages of all the German newspapers. It was debated in the Bundestag and discussed on television programs. After about two weeks, the INF stories began to appear on the second and third pages of the newspapers rather than on the first page, and after a month or two, an INF story appeared in the newspapers only occasionally. The subject had lost much of its news value.

Protest movements require intense public coverage to maintain their vitality and to attract new adherents. With the diminution of news coverage, the steam seemed to go out of the German and British movements protesting the U.S. deployments. The speed with which this happened surprised me. I believe it was an even greater surprise to Soviet planners in Moscow, who had firmly believed that they could readily exploit these related issues. The organizers of the protest movement in Germany concentrated their efforts upon a large Easter Day protest turnout. But even in this, the results were disappointing to them. About half as many people participated as had done so a year earlier.

As a result of this change in the political climate in Europe, both the Soviet side and the Western powers engaged in an intense review of their respective arms control positions. It was my view that, in the European NATO countries, there remained a serious underlying political problem even though its manifestation in public protest had greatly diminished. There was a consensus among NATO governments that the United States—on behalf of NATO—should seek a resumption of INF and START negotiations with the Soviets. If there were an extended hiatus and the NATO governments were perceived as being opposed to negotiations, public opposition would flare up again.

In the meantime, a great deal of thought and effort was being given in Washington to the negative evolution of the strategic nuclear balance between the United States and the Soviet Union. It had become evident that the intelligence agencies had long underestimated the percentage of the Soviet gross national product going into defense. From about 1970 on, the consensus in the intelligence community had been that some seven to eight percent of Soviet GNP had been allocated to defense. One of the intelligence experts in this field, Bill Lee (on whose expertise I had called before), had long thought it was closer to twelve to thirteen percent.

In the mid-seventies, a man active in the Soviet Gosplan (the Soviet economic planning agency) managed to get out of the Soviet Union. He gave our experts new insights into how the Soviets kept their national accounts. It turned out that most of the cost for Soviet procurement of munitions was accounted for in Soviet statistics under the production of industrial goods. The accuracy of Bill Lee's previous estimates thus appeared to be confirmed.

It was also determined that the Soviet investment in hardened underground shelters for their political, military, and industrial leader cadres was much greater than we had previously thought. The number of hardened targets that we would have to attack in the event of war was also greater than earlier thought. Furthermore, evidence indicated that eventually we would be faced with widespread deployment of Soviet mobile ICBM forces, which would be difficult to target.

A number of proposals had been put forward in interdepartmental meetings to increase the power and, more importantly, the survivability of U.S. ground-based nuclear retaliatory forces. Each of the proposals, however, ran into strong opposition. With respect to mobile systems the difficulty revolved around the interface between such systems and the public—people just don't like to have missiles with nuclear warheads moving about the countryside near their homes and workplaces. Some of our analysts began to revisit the idea of deploying ABM defenses for the protection of missile silos. But the Soviet Union was thought to be in a position to deploy such defenses earlier and more rapidly than the United States; the United States had virtually shut down its ABM program. The Soviets, who had been way behind us in ABM technology in 1972, had continued their development work and had kept their ABM facilities around Moscow in operation. They also were thought to be working even then on technologies more advanced than anything the United States was actively pursuing.

Since the late seventies, a group working under the leadership of retired Lieutenant General Daniel O. Graham, at one time director of the Defense Intelligence Agency, had been examining ideas for advanced space-based ABM defenses along lines the Soviets appeared to be actively exploring. This group called its program the "High Frontier." General Graham had come to the conclusion that such defenses were technologically feasible and should be urgently pursued. He had talked to me about it in the summer of 1980 but I doubted that the work had gone far enough by that time to demonstrate the practicability of such defenses.

The Strategic Defense Initiative

I was taken completely by surprise when President Reagan, on March 23, 1983, made a speech in which he put his full support behind the strategic defense initiative (SDI), or "Star Wars," as the media soon dubbed it. I later learned that the SDI portion of the speech had been put together by a very small group in the strictest secrecy. Those principally involved were Robert "Bud" McFarlane, who was then deputy to Judge William Clark, the President's national security adviser, George A. Keyworth 2d, the President's science adviser, and the President himself. Edward Teller was a strong supporter of the idea. Caspar Weinberger and the Joint Chiefs of Staff were excluded from any knowledge of it, as was the secretary of state.

Two panels were promptly constituted: one under Dr. James C. Fletcher, former director of NASA, to examine what the scientific community could do in the way of outlining promising paths for investigation of the various technologies that together might make such defenses work; and the second one, to examine the military and strategic considerations involved. By the early spring of 1984 these two panels had done a great deal of work, and an SDI office had been created in the Pentagon under Lieutenant General James A. Abrahamson to get on with the project. The Congress had requested a report on the program by the end of March 1984.

A group of us representing the various interested agencies was asked to meet at the Pentagon to go over the draft of that report. It laid out the test program contemplated by the SDI office, which had been carefully tailored to be compatible with the so-called narrow interpretation of the ABM treaty. This had been recommended both by the Pentagon lawyers and by the legal counsel of the Arms Control and Disarmament Agency

(ACDA), where, at that time, I made my offices. I saw no reason then to differ with their judgment and actively supported the report.

The Soviets had reacted immediately to the President's SDI speech, but initially without much force. When Chairman Yuri Andropov died in February 1984, Konstantin U. Chernenko, who succeeded him, lost no time in announcing that the SDI program would result in the militarization of space and that the Soviet Union was strongly opposed to any such result. This argument was without merit. The Soviets had placed many more military satellites in space than had we and they were the only nation in the world with an operational antisatellite system. In the early seventies, the Soviets had successfully tested their co-orbital ASAT interceptor.

On June 29, 1984, the Soviets issued a statement proposing talks on preventing the "militarization" of outer space in Vienna in September. Bud McFarlane, who had replaced Judge Clark as the President's national security adviser in October 1983, believed we should make an immediate response by accepting their offer but proposing that the talks also address the radical reduction of nuclear offensive missiles on a balanced and verifiable basis. I fully agreed with Bud's proposal. That same day the State Department issued a statement accepting the Soviet invitation.

There followed a period of intense staff work within the government to determine the objectives we should seek and the way our arguments should be presented in the event such a meeting actually took place. In a memorandum to McFarlane on July 17, I assessed the Soviet initiative as being designed to block SDI. I suggested that we should translate this initiative into Soviet movement on the issues of greatest interest to us— the stabilizing reduction of strategic (i.e., intercontinental-range) and intermediate-range offensive nuclear forces. I also proposed that the United States should examine the relationship between offensive and defensive systems and the linkage we might draw between them once the Vienna talks were under way.

The Soviets insisted on a stated subject matter of the talks that would favor their approach. We were unwilling to accept their prejudicial formulation. Because of these differences, it proved impossible to settle on an agreed agenda for the Vienna meeting. Consequently, no meeting took place. But after further give-and-take, it was agreed that Secretary of State George Shultz and Soviet Foreign Minister Andrei Gromyko would meet in Geneva on January 7 and 8, 1985, to reach a common understanding on new negotiations covering the whole range of questions concerning nuclear and outer space arms.

It was about this time that Bud McFarlane decided that the work in

Washington on arms control matters needed greater centralization and coordination. He asked me whether I would take on the job, reporting both to the President and to Secretary Shultz. He suggested that I have an office with the NSC staff in the Old Executive Office Building, as well as an office in the State Department.

I was tempted by the offer, although I had had bad experiences before when I had tried to work simultaneously for two bosses. Secretary Shultz vigorously opposed my shuttling between offices in State and the White House. He wanted me to move my office from ACDA on the fifth floor of the State Department building to the seventh floor in an office adjacent to his. I agreed to his proposal. I soon ceased to be on ACDA's payroll as ambassador on arms control matters. I assumed a new title, along with my new offices, and became ambassador-at-large and special adviser to the President and the secretary of state on arms control matters.

The Strategic Concept

The immediate substantive task in November and December 1984 was to prepare the rationale for our position in the upcoming talks with Gromyko. Many of my colleagues wanted to focus the negotiations on INF and START and avoid discussion of defense and space, the subject the Soviets wanted to talk about. I had a different opinion from my colleagues.

At the time we concluded the ABM treaty in 1972, the United States had made a unilateral statement to the Soviet side stressing the interrelation between defensive and offensive capabilities. It stated that if it proved impossible to negotiate a treaty of indefinite duration restraining and reducing offensive weapons, one paralleling the ABM treaty's limitations on defensive weapons, we would regard our supreme national interests to have been jeopardized and would consider ourselves justified in withdrawing from the ABM treaty. The basis for that statement was the fundamental nature of the interrelationship between offense and defense. The excessive Soviet deployments of destabilizing offensive systems forced the United States to consider new defensive systems.

I drafted a set of talking points for Secretary Shultz's use in the January meeting with Gromyko which took the offensive on the essential interrelationship between defense and space issues. Shultz was pleased with the idea of taking what had appeared to be a weak and vulnerable point in our position and turning it into a springboard for attack. He used the talking points to good effect when the meeting with Gromyko took place.

I think a principal factor influencing the Soviets' decision to resume negotiations (in addition to their disappointment with the political consequences of their walking out of the INF negotiations) was President Reagan's decision to initiate the "SDI program." Within the United States government, however, there was little understanding of what the SDI program was to entail. Was it to be a research program only, was it to provide an impenetrable shield, was it to be accomplished within the terms of the ABM treaty and therefore come about as a result of a cooperative transition with the Soviet Union, and, finally, in what time periods were all these things planned to take place? Additionally, since his March 1983 speech, the President had made the long-term objective of banning nuclear weapons a matter of national policy.

During this period, I participated regularly in an interdepartmental body called the Senior Arms Control Policy Group with the unfortunate acronym of SAC-PG, pronounced "Sack-Pig." One of our tasks was to formulate a succinct and understandable statement of objectives for the SDI program.

Many members of the group had doubts as to the adequacy of known technologies to achieve the elimination of nuclear weapons, as the President had envisioned. Of these, some thought the program should concentrate on lesser and more immediately achievable goals, such as contributing to the defense of our nuclear retaliatory facilities. Cap Weinberger wanted the program to concentrate on the more difficult technologies which were bound to take the longest time in order to assure that the entire program could be made to come together in roughly the same time frame.

It seemed to me essential to draft a long-term strategic concept with respect to SDI and its relationship to offensive forces, keeping in mind the President's objective of eventually eliminating nuclear weapons. I thought that if such a concept were to be useful, both internally and for public presentation, it should be short. I remembered the directive given to General Eisenhower on which the Normandy landings and liberation of Europe were based was one paragraph long. At a December 1984 meeting of the SAC-PG, in preparation for the Shultz/Gromyko meeting, I presented a one-paragraph draft statement of the SDI strategic concept that consisted of four sentences:

> For the next five to ten years our objectives should be a radical reduction in the power of existing and planned offensive nuclear

arms as well as the effective limitation of defensive nuclear arms whether land, sea, air, or spaced-based. We should even now be looking forward to a period of transition beginning five or ten years from now, to effective non-nuclear defensive forces, including defenses against offensive nuclear arms. This period of transition should lead to the eventual elimination of all nuclear arms, both offensive and defensive. A nuclear-free world is an ultimate objective to which we, the Soviet Union, and all other nations can agree.

I was surprised at the reaction of the SAC-PG. The representatives of the Defense Department, the JCS, the Arms Control Agency, State, and the CIA all expressed their general agreement. Somewhat revised (e.g., the "five to ten" was made "ten"), the paragraph was approved by the President and thus became part of the policy background Mr. Shultz carried into the January meeting with Foreign Minister Gromyko.

The Shultz/Gromyko Meeting

Geneva was gripped by a numbing cold wave. We were greeted by snow and icy blasts when we arrived in that normally placid lakeside city. The delegations of both sides were large, but the press corps far outnumbered us. The atmosphere in the room where Gromyko and Shultz were closeted with their aides was scarcely warmer. Gromyko—more dour than usual—glumly listened while the secretary gave his opening presentation. He only perked up when Shultz read the four sentences associated with the "strategic concept."

The sides rather quickly agreed to resume negotiations on INF and START, the two areas that had been suspended since November 1983. A third area was more difficult to define. We wanted the talks to be designated "defense and space" and the Soviets insisted on the phrase "space-strike arms." To use the word "defense," said Gromyko, was a euphemism. SDI, he claimed, was a sword of Damocles, designed to deny the Soviet Union the ability to retaliate after an initial attack.

Mr. Gromyko stated the Soviet position unambiguously. He insisted on the nonmilitarization of space. By that he meant a total ban on all arms in space that are "designed to attack" objects in space or on earth and all systems on earth that are "designed to attack" objects in space. He further proposed that all research designed to develop such arms be banned as inconsistent with the basic proposal. To us, the words "designed to" were misleading, since the phrase refers to the intention of a system rather than its capability. The Soviets already had operational interceptor missiles that were capable of destroying satellites, but they had denied this was their intention, thus appearing to escape from their own definition of "space-strike arms."

Gromyko further insisted that all three areas subject to negotiation be discussed in their interrelationship and that no agreement on one was possible without concurrent movement on the other two.

Our talks in Geneva almost came to an abortive end on these issues, with Mr. Gromyko demanding another meeting in Moscow some months later to discuss further the agenda for the negotiations before agreeing to a time and place. Secretary Shultz was unflappable. He threw diversionary talk into the air while working away to move Gromyko toward his basic position. He finally maneuvered Mr. Gromyko into agreeing to resume the bilateral arms control negotiations in March by giving a little here and taking a little there.

After intensive discussions, the sides agreed on a joint communiqué announcing that the two powers would resume arms control negotiations. Each side was to have a single negotiating team, divided into three subgroups: one on INF, another on START, and a third on defense and space. From time to time, the heads of the subgroups were to meet as a team to assure concurrent progress, but most of the negotiations were to be in the subgroups.

The SDI Criteria

Mr. Shultz decided that after the Geneva meeting he would return immediately to Washington to brief the President and the Congress. Bud McFarlane went to Rome, Paris, and then to London, while I debriefed the German, Dutch, and Belgian governments and then met Bud in Paris and returned with him to Washington in his military plane via London. General Edward Rowny, who was also a presidential adviser on arms control, was sent on a similar task to Asia.

On the plane flying back, Bud and I discussed the questions we had run into in our briefings and how we had handled them. I explained that in answering questions on SDI, I had stressed the three-phase strategic concept and had also said that prior to making the transition from the research phase to the deployment phase, we would assure ourselves that the system to be deployed would be survivable; that is, an opponent could not defeat the system by concentrating his attack on it or any one essential part of it. I had also said that we would not deploy it unless we were convinced that it would cost an opponent more to add offsetting offensive military capabilities than it would cost us to add defenses that would negate his response. If this were not so, I said, it would be impossible to be sure that SDI wouldn't lead to an arms race with the economic considerations stacked against us.

These ideas did not originate with me; they were relatively standard ideas that apply generally to the acquisition of new military systems. Frank Miller, a strategic analyst working in Fred Ikle's office in the Pentagon[1] and for whom I have high regard, applied them to SDI, as had Admiral James Watkins, the chief of naval operations.[2]

Bud and I decided it would be useful to draft several paragraphs that could serve as guidance to all those in the executive branch who would be out talking, lecturing, and testifying on the developments at the Shultz-Gromyko meeting. I wrote some paragraphs on the plane as we flew across the Atlantic which Bud then edited. They were then approved by the President and became the official guidance to all interested agencies.

In a speech before the World Affairs Council in Philadelphia on February 20, 1985, I had an opportunity to present these ideas in an authoritative statement of the government's position. The press gave the speech unexpectedly wide and favorable coverage. The three criteria of effectiveness, survivability, and cost-effectiveness at the margin became known as "the Nitze criteria." They were referred to subsequently in official speeches, press conferences, and congressional testimony, and eventually mandated by presidential directive.[3]

Many people, including my former colleagues Robert McNamara and James Schlesinger, considered a cost-effective defense impossible. Bob told me that he doubted that the administration intended to adhere to the criterion of cost-effectiveness in spite of adopting the standard as national policy. Jim Schlesinger applauded the apparent demise of SDI. At an Aspen Institute seminar we both attended at Wye Plantation on the Maryland Eastern Shore, Jim commented that, by definition, a cost-effective defense was not possible. I disagreed. Just because most research

[1] Fred Ikle was then under secretary of defense for policy.
[2] James Watkins, "To Seize the Moment," *U.S. Naval Institute Proceedings* (February 1985), 13–16.
[3] National Security Decision Directive No. 172, May 30, 1985.

and development programs in the past had run into difficulties did not mean this one would. Some programs had turned out better than anticipated.

Others objected strenuously to the criteria, suspecting that it was my way of using SDI strictly as a bargaining chip for START reductions and the end of the program as envisioned by its enthusiastic proponents. This was incorrect. It was my view that deployment of SDI could not and should not be defended unless the United States was reasonably certain that the so-called Nitze criteria could be met. I did not believe technology then in hand had provided that reasonable certainty. But American technology often achieves unanticipated breakthroughs. I did not exclude the possibility that an SDI breakthrough could provide the negotiating leverage to make a favorable overall settlement with the Soviets possible. That consideration argued for full support of the SDI research and development program within the limits of the ABM treaty.

Geneva Redux

With negotiations in Geneva about to resume, the question arose as to who would conduct them. Phyllis's emphysema—from which she had been suffering for several years—had reached the point where her doctor said she could no longer travel with me to Geneva. I recommended to Secretary Shultz that Mike Glitman, my deputy on the INF negotiating team, head the INF delegation; that Max Kampelman deal with defense and space matters and be in overall charge; and that former Senator John Tower be in charge of the START delegation. At my suggestion, the secretary called Senator Tower to ask him to come in for a talk. I was with Mr. Shultz when he came in. He listened carefully to what the secretary had to say—he was visibly moved. The offer was a complete surprise, but John agreed immediately with no reservations. Max Kampelman and Mike Glitman also accepted the secretary's invitations.

Two days before the negotiations began in Geneva, Soviet Chairman Chernenko died after a long illness. He was succeeded by Mikhail Gorbachev, to us a relatively unknown quantity in the Kremlin.

The negotiations opened on March 12, 1985, with the usual flurry of media hype and solemn pronouncements. Viktor Karpov was selected to head the Soviet delegation, while my old nemesis in INF, Yuli Kvitsinskiy, returned to head the subgroup on space-defense. Alexei Obukhov, formerly Karpov's deputy at START, was to lead the negotiations on medium-range weapons. Obukhov, since the breakup of the talks in 1983, had been serving on the U.S. desk in the Soviet Foreign Ministry. As a youth, he had attended the University of Chicago as an exchange student. I was to deal with him more directly several years later.

Our chances of success in Geneva appeared better than in the past but I was not optimistic that there would be a prompt resolution to the complex negotiations facing the delegations. I could only respond to a reporter, when asked in April how the negotiations were going, "about as anticipated," which was, at that point, no progress at all. After an unproductive session, the talks adjourned on April 23, to be resumed the end of May.

The Vienna Meeting

Mr. Shultz had agreed to meet again with Foreign Minister Gromyko in May. The occasion was the celebration in Vienna of the thirtieth anniversary of the signing of the Austrian State Treaty. The U.S. delegation was scheduled to meet with the Soviet delegation for a three-hour session (which extended itself into a six-hour session) the afternoon before the main ceremonies began on May 15.

At the Soviet embassy we met in the same room where, years earlier, we had negotiated the SALT I agreements. We were greeted by Mr. Gromyko, who turned to me and murmured, "A steady man," which I took as a compliment.

The Shultz-Gromyko meeting was a vigorous battle of wits. Mr. Gromyko was determined to set the agenda and pace of the discussions. He urged that we concentrate on the important issue, which he identified as arms control, and leave the minor issues to the end of our discussions in the interest of time.

The secretary agreed, although he insisted on making three points prior to the discussion on arms control. The first was to register our protest over the murder of an American officer, Major Arthur D. Nicholson, Jr., in East Germany on March 24 while he was going about official business under the terms of our agreement; the second was to raise once again the Soviet Union's abysmal record on human rights; and the third—still a continuing problem—was our access rights in Berlin.

Mr. Gromyko abruptly interrupted and said that since the secretary did not wish to address the important subject of arms control, he would do so. And he did—for more than two hours—not only on the subject of arms control but other subjects that took him far afield from arms control as well. I was seated next to Mr. Shultz. As Gromyko went on and on, Shultz began putting together a stack of point papers, one for each of the subjects Gromyko raised. The stack grew steadily from one to two to three inches high by the time Mr. Gromyko finally concluded his monologue at five-thirty. The meeting had been scheduled to adjourn at five.

At that point, Mr. Shultz began to go through his presentation, issue by issue, very leisurely, accurately, and precisely. He ended with a statement deploring the Soviet lack of compliance with the ABM treaty and the unratified SALT II treaty and suggested that the Soviet foreign minister might be interested in reading the speech that I had given on May 1 at the National Press Club which addressed that issue. He handed a copy of the speech to Mr. Gromyko with the comment, "Mr. Minister, if you're nice to Mr. Nitze, I'm sure he will autograph it for you." Mr. Gromyko scowled and said, "I read it within twenty-four hours after Mr. Nitze delivered it."

By the time Mr. Shultz completed his dissertation it was seven-thirty and we had been at the table two and a half hours longer than had been scheduled. Gromyko then proceeded with his response and we finally rose, our backsides aching, at eight-fifteen.

Gromyko asked for a few minutes alone with the secretary. Mr. Shultz agreed and they went off to confer. At first, according to Mr. Shultz, there was an awkward silence, after which Mr. Gromyko said, "Don't you have something to say to me?" "No," replied Shultz, "I thought you had something to say to me." It was evident that Gromyko wanted Shultz to initiate a conversation about a possible summit meeting, but Shultz was not about to be the suppliant in raising the subject. It was alluded to eventually, but to no real point.

In retrospect, Gromyko may have seen the writing on the wall as to his tenure of office. In July he was kicked upstairs as president of the Presidium, nominally a ceremonial position.

The Monday Package

It had become evident shortly after the negotiations began in Geneva in March 1985 that the Russians were primarily concerned with the space-based aspects of SDI. In their view, American battle stations overhead would fulfill Gromyko's prediction of a "sword of Damocles" threatening their homeland. It was then that Kvitsinskiy mentioned to Kampelman the need for a nonwithdrawal clause for the ABM treaty that would offer a form of breakout insurance against an SDI deployment for ten years. The treaty, as negotiated, provides that either side may withdraw after six months' notice if it decides its supreme interests have been jeopardized. The demand for a nonwithdrawal clause became a familiar Russian refrain. The real issue was—and continued to be—which should come first: offensive reductions, or restraints on SDI? The President, of course, had vowed that he would never allow increased restraints on SDI. On the other hand, he had also made the reduction and eventual elimination of nuclear weapons the focal point of his arms control policy.

Working with a few colleagues, I developed a draft schedule of reductions in strategic offensive weapons phased over a period of ten years. These reductions would bring each side down to fifty percent of a 1986 baseline by 1995. The numbers were designed to reduce warheads more than launchers in order to encourage deMIRVing and the development of single reentry vehicle (RV) missiles like Midgetman, and thus enhance crisis stability. We added to this a proposal that the obligation to continue to execute these reductions year by year would be contingent upon both sides continuing to adhere strictly to the ABM treaty. We worked out the provisions of this proposal on a Monday, and needing a completely innocuous title, it became known as the "Monday Package."

Mr. Shultz and Bud McFarlane thought this would be a good time to approach the President for authority for some accommodation on SDI by offering to adhere to the terms of the ABM treaty for a given period of time in return for the deep and stabilizing reductions we all wanted. (This was before the debate began in earnest on the correct interpretation of the treaty. At this point, U.S. policy was to adhere to the so-called narrow interpretation.) Besides, I had little hope that we would be in a position to test an SDI system that met the so-called Nitze criteria before 1995.

Secretary Shultz and Bud McFarlane presented the President with the idea of negotiations with the Soviets to bring about a compromise along the lines of the Monday Package. A START agreement by the end of the year was the tantalizing carrot at the end of the stick. They proposed to Mr. Reagan that I should be the chief advocate of the American position in a secret, exploratory negotiation with someone designated by the Soviet side. The President thought that it was worth a try.

Pentagon civilian officials—particularly Richard Perle[4] and Caspar

---

[4]Richard was assistant secretary of defense for international security policy as well as Weinberger's principal adviser on arms control.

Weinberger—were deliberately excluded from the discussion in the hope that we could achieve decisive progress as a fait accompli. Otherwise, the howls and leaks from Weinberger and Perle and their supporters would have made the project impossible.

Bud and I hoped to enlist the support of the Joint Chiefs of Staff. I discussed the ideas in the Monday Package with the chairman, General John W. Vessey, Jr., and then with the Chiefs as a group. I presented an outline of the proposal as my own idea. The Chiefs raised no objection, but they were careful not to commit themselves to it. Bud McFarlane had said that he would fill them in with the details and obtain their full agreement, but to my disappointment he failed to follow through. Bud and I were both in a delicate and vulnerable position, but on this both of us had agreed that it was so important that the Chiefs fully agree that he should carry the ball.

Using the Monday Package, we prepared talking points for a meeting between Shultz and Soviet Ambassador Anatoly Dobrynin on Monday, June 17, 1985. I was present in the secretary's office, along with Bud McFarlane and Richard Burt,[5] when the meeting was held. Mr. Shultz approached the subject of secret negotiations indirectly, hoping Dobrynin would pick up on the more subtle nuances of the proposal. Mr. Shultz suggested that by engaging in quiet, confidential talks, our two nations might arrive at a compromise that would bring us to an agreement. He suggested that I would be available to meet with whomever the Kremlin might designate to discuss these most important, sensitive issues.

Dobrynin brushed aside the subtle reference to a possible offense-defense trade-off and chose to comment only on the channel suggested. My personal opinion was that Dobrynin—never the grand interpreter of official Washington to Moscow that he was purported by many to be— was negative to the whole idea because of some intrigue being played out in Kremlin politics. In any case, nothing much came of this overture to the Soviets.

The ABM Treaty Interpretation

Earlier in the spring of 1985, the Soviet delegation in Geneva had proposed banning testing and development of space-based missile defenses.

---

[5]Burt was not in on the preparation of the Monday Package, but as assistant secretary of state for European and Canadian affairs, he was the line officer on American-Soviet relations. His presence, unfortunately, added to the constraints already imposed on the discussion.

At the time, the U.S. government considered this already banned by the ABM treaty, but the U.S. Geneva team was unable to find any supporting evidence in their records. As a consequence, they sent back a request that the Pentagon examine the treaty and search its records of the 1972 negotiations.

The Pentagon had recently hired an attorney, Philip Kunsberg, a former New York assistant district attorney who was new to the arms-control business. He was asked to conduct the legal examination. Kunsberg came to the conclusion that there was no evidence that the treaty banned the development and testing (and perhaps not even the deployment) of ABM systems and their components based on "other physical principles," and further that there was no evidence that the Soviets considered themselves bound by such an obligation. As a result, the Pentagon began lobbying for what became known as the "broad" interpretation of the ABM treaty.

On Friday, October 4, 1985, at a meeting of the Senior Arms Control Policy Group chaired by Bud McFarlane, Fred Ikle and Richard Perle pushed for approval of an SDI program that, in my opinion, would go beyond even the broad interpretation of the provisions of the ABM treaty. In particular, they argued that deployment—not just development and testing—of systems and components based on other physical principles was permitted. This became known as the "broader than broad" interpretation.

An extended discussion ensued, in which I argued that the broad, rather than the narrow, interpretation of the ABM treaty was fully justified, but that that did not mean complete freedom from all constraints in the testing, development, and deployment of systems and components based on other physical principles. Bud indicated that he supported my position and, in particular, decided that deployment was not permitted, but he also said that we would return to the subject at a meeting the following Tuesday.

During the night I worried about my part in the discussion earlier that day. Even though I had won on the nondeployment issue, I worried that I had not made clear another concern. I was confident that the Soviets had never committed themselves to the narrow interpretation in a manner which they would consider binding on themselves. Even so, as a result of our recent report to Congress and discussions with Mrs. Margaret Thatcher and other allies, the administration was in a position where it should not implement a decision adopting the broad interpretation without full prior discussion with its allies and with the Congress.

On Saturday morning I drafted a memorandum to Bud clarifying my position in anticipation of the Tuesday meeting he had referred to the previous day. I would not be present at the meeting since I already had been directed to be in Europe for allied consultations on that day.

The next day, Sunday, October 6, Bud appeared on "Meet the Press." He announced, in response to a question, that only deployment of SDI was foreclosed. The ABM treaty, he said, "does indeed sanction research, testing, and development of these new systems."

I immediately informed Secretary Shultz of what had happened. I also revised my Saturday memorandum to take account of Bud's TV appearance. In the revised memorandum, I recommended that we assure the Congress and our allies that we would not implement an expansion of the scope of the SDI program beyond the narrow interpretation.

At a meeting of the National Security Planning Group several days later, the secretary persuaded the President to adopt an amended position; that is, that the permissive interpretation of the treaty was fully justified, but that the United States would continue to observe the more traditional interpretation. National Security Decision Directive 192 was issued accordingly.

The words "broad" and "narrow," as applied to the interpretation of the ABM treaty signed in Moscow and ratified with the advice and consent of the Senate in 1972, became a central issue with the Soviets and also between the Congress and the executive branch.

In a nutshell, the narrow or restrictive interpretation of the treaty would ban the development and testing, as well as deployment, of other than fixed land-based ABM systems or components and those launched into space from fixed land-based launchers. The ban would include those systems based on physical principles other than those whose immediate application in ABM components was understood when the ABM treaty was signed in 1972.

The broad interpretation would allow the "creation" (including research and development) of ABM systems and their components based on "other physical principles," and would prohibit only their deployment without prior consultation and agreement between the parties, as called for in a part of the treaty known as "Agreed Statement D."[6]

In the spring of 1985, I had supported the narrow or traditional interpretation of the treaty along with other members of the Reagan adminis-

---

[6]For a fuller discussion of this complex and troublesome distinction, see the Annex on page 467.

tration in a report on SDI requested by the Congress. My conversion to the so-called broad interpretation began that summer when I read a classified report prepared for the Pentagon by Sid Graybeal, who was retired from government service, and retired Colonel Charles Fitzgerald based on the SALT negotiating records.[7] To my surprise, since I have the highest regard and respect for both of these former SALT colleagues, I found I disagreed with their conclusions relating to limitations on future ABM systems and components. The record as summarized by them seemed to me to demonstrate that the Soviets had never agreed, in a manner they would consider binding on themselves, that research, development, and testing of systems and components based on other physical principles were prohibited under the terms of the treaty. There were, however, certain ambiguities that needed to be addressed, so I urged the secretary to ask his legal counsel, Judge Sofaer, for an informed opinion.

The Soviets, in the meantime, anxious to constrain our strategic defense initiative, leaped in to take advantage of the dissension that developed in Washington over the correct interpretation of the ABM treaty. They claimed that the entire SDI research program was intended to eviscerate the basic provision of the treaty—which was, to ban the deployment of systems or their components capable of intercepting strategic ballistic missiles in flight trajectory or capable of providing territorial defense of either country. Therefore, they argued, the purpose and spirit of the treaty, if not its specific provisions, would be undermined. (This, after the U.S. delegation had tried and failed, over a six-month period in 1971 and 1972, to get the Soviets to accept a definitive prohibition on futuristic systems and their components.)

Furthermore, in 1972, then Soviet Defense Minister Andrei Grechko, in a major statement before the Soviet Presidium shortly after the treaty was signed, said that the ABM treaty "places no limitations on the performance of research and experimental work aimed at resolving the problem of defending the country from nuclear missile strike." Grechko's statement is not conclusive, however, since it is conceivable he had in mind tests into space from permitted fixed ground-based launchers only. But this possibility has been put forward only by American supporters of the narrow interpretation, not by the Soviets.

[7]Colonel Charles L. Fitzgerald and Sidney Graybeal, *SALT I Negotiating History Relating to Limitations on Future ABM Systems and Components Based on "Other Physical Principles"* (Arlington, Va.: System Planning Corporation, March 1985).

Preparation for
the November Summit

Despite the inability of Shultz and Gromyko at their meeting in May to agree on a summit, continuing exchanges finally produced an announcement in July 1985 that the U.S. and Soviet heads of state would confer in November in Geneva. To prepare, we met with Gromyko's successor, Eduard Shevardnadze, in Helsinki at the end of July.

Shevardnadze impressed me as a competent, shrewd, and forceful negotiator. He alone spoke for his delegation throughout the three-hour meeting. The Soviets did agree for the first time to use simultaneous translations, which effectively doubled the time available for discussion. This did not, however, help us resolve our differences at Helsinki.

Yuli Kvitsinskiy accompanied Minister Shevardnadze to Helsinki; it appeared that the new foreign minister thought well of my former counterpart in the INF negotiations. Yuli and I met for dinner at a restaurant in the suburbs of Helsinki. I tried out a version of the Monday Package on him, with more detail than we had given Dobrynin.

Kvitsinskiy looked at me with obvious skepticism: "You've made proposals on both SDI and START. What about INF?"

I told him I thought the walk-in-the-woods formula still made sense.

"Are you ready to give up your Pershing Twos?" he asked.

"Personally," I said, "I can't think of a better outcome to the INF problem than the walk-in-the-woods formula."

"Now," snapped Kvitsinskiy aggressively, "you've covered all three subjects in your proposals," as if to say, and to what end?

"Not at all," I hastened to reply, "they're not proposals *or* solutions; they are my personal thoughts."

The dinner ended without further useful discussion.

The next morning Kvitsinskiy approached Norm Clyne, my chief executive and adviser, and asked him whether I was serious about giving up Pershing II. Norm told him I was always serious, but he reminded Kvitsinskiy that I had been speaking personally the previous evening.

Kvitsinskiy did not seem to want to pursue the matter further. Nevertheless I approached him again in Moscow some two months later on the subject of the Monday Package. Perhaps he felt he did not want to be twice bitten by the "silver fox," as the Soviets had dubbed me. I don't think the walk in the woods had made life in the Kremlin any easier for Yuli.

At the end of the third round of negotiations, Max Kampelman on

November 1 was instructed to introduce a new START proposal in Geneva. We in Washington had based it on elements of the Soviet position tabled on October 25 and on the Monday Package formula. The new proposal called for reductions to 6,000 ballistic missile warheads and air-launched cruise missiles (ALCMs), of which 4,500 of that number were to be ballistic missile warheads and no more than 1,500 of that number were to be heavy ICBM warheads, resulting in a fifty percent reduction in Soviet SS-18s. That implied a limit of 1,500 on air-launched cruise missiles. The Soviets believed that the United States intended to deploy 4,000 ALCMs; I thought a cut to 1,500 would meet one of the Soviet principal concerns. The proposal also included a ban on mobile ICBMs, which did *not* meet Kremlin concerns. That would eliminate the two new systems in the Soviet strategic arsenal under development—the SS-24 and SS-25. Deployment of the latter had already begun.

A ban on mobile MIRVed ICBMs, in my view, would have been stabilizing because it would have reduced the ratio of warheads to targets, but a ban on mobile unMIRVed ICBMs would not have helped and would have eliminated my hope for Midgetman and a truly stabilizing ICBM force.

Bud McFarlane had allowed the ban on mobiles provision to be inserted in the proposal at the insistence of the Pentagon (i.e., Richard Perle) in an effort to halt further deployment of the SS-25. Perle's position was that the provision offered an excellent fallback: one single RV mobile ICBM system for each side—Midgetman for us and the SS-25 for the Soviet Union.

Bud and I had been in disagreement for some time as to whether domestic opposition would allow a mobile deployment of Midgetman. He believed that it would not and that the loss of Midgetman to our strategic posture was unimportant.

Support of Midgetman on the Hill was led by Senators Sam Nunn and Albert Gore, Jr., and Congressman Les Aspin. They were furious when I told them, just before it was formally presented to the Soviets, that the new U.S. proposal would include a ban on Midgetman.

The planning for the 1985 summit necessarily covered many facets. Secretary Shultz, Roz Ridgway,[8] and I were particularly concerned

---

[8]Rozanne L. Ridgway was sworn in as assistant secretary of state for European and Canadian affairs in July 1985, replacing Richard Burt, who had been appointed our ambassador in Bonn.

with the substantive policy issues, the sequence in which they were to be discussed, and the emphasis to be given to each. Shultz was determined that the scope should be comprehensive, that priority should be given to human rights, and then regional issues, such as Afghanistan, Angola, Ethiopia, and Cambodia. The full range of arms control issues would, of course, be included but would not be permitted to dominate the agenda. The Soviet side pressed for an agenda that would be dominated by the nuclear and space issues, and, in particular, by their opposition to SDI.

During the summit, the President and Secretary Shultz succeeded in maintaining the scope and priorities they desired. It turned out to be a media triumph for the President. On the hardest substantive issues—arms control and regional issues—the immediate score was little better than zero-zero. Nevertheless it seemed to me that an important opening had been made in the breadth and depth of Soviet-American relations. With careful nurturing, I thought this could lead to larger steps in the future.

The Fireside Summit

On the morning of the first day of meetings in Geneva, Tuesday, November 19, I met with the President and his other senior advisers at the Pometta Residence on the grounds of the Maison de Sassure, where he and Mrs. Reagan were staying. The group included Secretary Shultz, Donald Regan, the President's chief of staff and his deputy David Thomas, Bud McFarlane, our ambassador to Moscow Arthur A. Hartman, Roz Ridgway, Jack Matlock and Robert Linhard of the White House NSC staff, Bernard Kalb, State Department spokesman, and myself. We went through a final rehearsal of the approach the President would take with Gorbachev during the morning meetings.

President Reagan hosted the first day's talks at Fleur d'Eau, a château made available by the Swiss government. A huge, oval conference table, sixteen feet long, had been shipped to Geneva from New York to accommodate the two heads of state and their advisers.

The President and the Soviet leader agreed, in that first meeting, that there was no point in trying to change the other's government, political system, culture, or ideology. Gorbachev said they must first resolve the issue of war or peace, then they could work on economics, structural change, ecology, sociology, and the needs of the Third World.

The President remarked that one of the factors generating mistrust in the United States was the Marxist-Leninist doctrine that socialist revolutions will prevail around the world, and that the Soviet Union must give them active support. We believe, the President said, that competing factions within nations should settle their differences without outside interference. Gorbachev responded that there were those who regretted that the American, French, and Soviet revolutions had not been suppressed, but revolutions have deep roots and they cannot be imposed from the outside. Moscow and Washington, he said, are not omnipotent.[9]

That afternoon, bundled against the cold wind whipping off Lake Geneva, the two leaders walked over to the pool house with only their interpreters. When they arrived they settled into two overstuffed chairs on either side of the fireplace, where a blazing fire had been prepared. Mr. Reagan had brought with him a manila envelope which contained a set of guidelines I had prepared on the nuclear and space talks.

He handed Gorbachev a Russian translation of the guidelines and the two men studied the two documents for a few minutes. Based on the concept of the Monday Package and our November 1 proposal, the START guidelines proposed a fifty percent reduction in strategic offensive systems, while the defense and space guidelines provided that each side could continue its research and development program for a strategic defense in full accord with the provisions of the ABM treaty. The President stressed, however, that the general secretary could not have one without the other.

"But this allows SDI to continue?" said Gorbachev.

"Yes," said the President, "it must continue."

"Then we just disagree," Gorbachev replied. After that there was little room for agreement.

On the American side, Roz Ridgway headed up the effort to draft a joint communiqué, while I turned my attention to that portion dealing with the nuclear-space talks. We had arrived at tentative agreement with the Soviets prior to the summit on many of the bilateral arms control issues other than START and SDI. In addition the Soviets had proposed extending the time for observing the provisions of the SALT I Interim Agreement and the unratified SALT II treaty to December 31, 1986. We

---

[9]Although Gorbachev's language was not as harsh as Premier Khrushchev's in his 1961 meeting with President Kennedy, his message was unmistakably the same.

had announced our intentions in June of not undercutting the agreements for an indefinite duration, providing the Soviets did not undercut them and providing they were negotiating seriously for meaningful reductions. We further had reserved the right to voice an appropriate response to Soviet violations of these agreements. We were unwilling to change that position.

The President spent some five hours of one-on-one dialogue with Mr. Gorbachev and more than eight hours in plenary discussion over the course of the three-day summit meeting. Gorbachev's opposition to SDI was unwavering. There was no sign of movement from the Soviet position calling for a ban on all SDI research. More encouraging were indications that the Soviets might be willing seriously to discuss all three aspects of the negotiations—START, INF, and space defense—without demanding a prior agreement to ban SDI research when the regular negotiations resumed in Geneva on January 16, 1986. In the joint statement issued at the end of the summit, the sides committed themselves to early progress in the negotiations, including an interim INF agreement, and to the principle of fifty percent reductions in the offensive strategic nuclear arsenals possessed by both countries. On that note, we returned to Washington.

Bud McFarlane was driven out of the administration in early December by unfounded charges by Donald Regan to members of the press, who, in turn, told me. The country, I believe, lost a devoted public servant and I was left with one less friend and ally in the White House. He was replaced by his deputy, Vice Admiral John M. Poindexter.

21

The Search for a
Non-Zero-Sum Outcome

In most games, because of their structure, a gain by one side must
be balanced by an equal loss by the other side, and the sum of the
losses by one side and the gains by the other side is always zero.
There are, however, games in which the aggregate of the gains and
of the losses by the two sides can be unequal and either positive or
negative. In an arms control negotiation, the objective should be to
arrive at a non-zero-sum outcome, where both sides gain and neither side loses.

On the morning of January 15, 1986, at 10:45 A.M., I arrived back at my
office after giving a background briefing with Richard Perle to the White
House press corps. The secretary wanted to see me right away about a
letter the President had just received from Gorbachev. The Soviet leader
had proposed a broad timetable for the elimination of all nuclear weapons
by the end of the century. He added that the process could start only if
the United States joined the Soviet Union in renouncing the development, testing, and deployment of what he called "space strike weapons."
I thought that his proposal for the total elimination of nuclear weapons
was largely a propaganda ploy. But, in any event, it had to be dealt with
substantively and seriously.

The part I found most intriguing was that the first stage of the timetable included the complete elimination of intermediate-range missiles
from Europe, both ballistic and cruise missiles, as a first step toward
ridding the European continent of nuclear weapons. Gorbachev called
for a pledge from Britain and France that they would not enlarge their
nuclear arsenals. This was a significant departure from the Soviets' previous stance, which required compensation for the nuclear weapons of
Britain and France in any agreed count. It was also similar to the zero
option first offered by the Reagan administration in 1981 that had called
for the elimination of intermediate-range nuclear weapons from Asia as

well as Europe. Gorbachev's language was sufficiently broad, however, to require clarification of the details of his proposal. For example, could we work toward a separate INF agreement without linking it to START and space defense?[1]

The Soviet ambassador had already called Mr. Shultz earlier that morning to let him know that an important public announcement would be made in Moscow in a matter of hours. When the secretary asked Dobrynin if the subject matter was going to be the letter the President had just received from the general secretary, Dobrynin said he had no further instructions. It was clear the U.S. government had to be prepared to respond immediately.

After some discussion the secretary left for Fort McNair to deliver a speech on terrorism. He had an appointment with the President at the White House at 2:00 P.M. He asked me to get together three documents for him by 1:30. The first document was to be a one-and-a-half-page summary of Gorbachev's letter; the second a series of talking points that he might use in explaining the letter to the President; and the third a draft statement that the President might issue to the press right away. I was to meet Shultz at Fort McNair, ride with him to the White House for his meeting with the President, and go over the documents with him.

At the White House, we found that Admiral Poindexter had come to the same general conclusion we had. He agreed that the most important item at this point was to issue immediately a positive presidential response to the press.

Adjourning to the Oval Office, Mr. Shultz handed Mr. Reagan the letter along with a summary which he could more easily and quickly read. Shultz went through the talking points with a clear and logical exposition and completed his presentation by handing Mr. Reagan the press statement we had prepared. After some discussion, the President said that he was in favor of the general thrust of our preparations. Originally he had had some reservations because Secretary Weinberger had called with his usual angst after Richard Perle had reported to him what we were proposing. On the whole, however, the President was enthusiastic. His comment to us was, "Why wait until the year two thousand to eliminate all nuclear weapons?"

The new Soviet proposal was introduced at the Geneva negotiations on January 16—the beginning of Round Four. The proposal dropped any

---

[1]This question was clarified by Gorbachev himself in a meeting with Senator Edward Kennedy in Moscow on February 6. The Soviet leader said there was no linkage between an interim INF agreement and other issues.

reference to a ban on SDI research and substituted the Russian word *sozdanize* or "creation"—sometimes translated as "development." The Russians explained that "fundamental" research would be permitted under their new proposal, but "purposeful" research would be banned. This, of course, was their usual doublethink; because the President had announced his intent in his March 1983 speech, our research was "purposeful," while Soviet research was "fundamental" because the Soviets had never announced their intentions.

Problems soon arose with our allies. Bonn insisted that not only SS-20s should be eliminated, but also short-range nuclear missiles that could substitute for them. This was not new, but the Germans made the point again, and at a slightly higher register. Our Asian allies also objected to any agreement that would leave Soviet missiles east of the Urals aimed at them. After heavy infighting in Washington, our Geneva delegation in late February was directed to swing back to the zero option, to reject the freeze on French and British nuclear weapons, and to demand that Soviet SS-20s be eliminated from Asia as well as Europe.

During the seven-month period following Gorbachev's latest proposal, the development of arms control policy within the U.S. government and in the negotiations with the Soviets in Geneva became complex and controversial. One reason for this was the growing concern of the President and his chief of staff Donald Regan about damaging leaks, even from NSC meetings. As a result, a hierarchy of classification levels was created with a decreasing number of people being given access to each higher level of classification, resulting in even greater compartmentalization of the bureaucracy. The highest, but undesignated, level was restricted to the President, Shultz, Weinberger, Regan, and Poindexter. Discussions in this group concerning the drafting of a letter from the President responding to Gorbachev's letter of January 15 were kept secret even from those having access to the highest designated levels of classification, including myself.

The President and his principal advisers were in disagreement, particularly Shultz and Weinberger, over the response to Gorbachev's January 15 letter. The rest of the bureaucracy, unaware of these high-level discussions, continued the debate on a battleground already in disarray, which soon degenerated into a free-for-all between the Pentagon and State Department.

To set the scene here in Washington, on May 27, 1986, the President announced his decision to break with SALT II by the end of the year. This was the culmination of several months of acrimonious debate within the national security bureaucracy. At a SAC-PG meeting Ken Adelman had insisted that, to teach the Russians a lesson, it was necessary to drop our previous policy of "interim restraint" with respect to going beyond the limits of SALT II. I was opposed to this line of thought. Such action would be condemned, not only by our allies, but by most of Congress. The Soviets—not ones to miss a good opportunity to drive a wedge in further—would exploit the opportunity with full vigor. Ken said to me after the meeting that he had come around to thinking I was probably right.

At a White House meeting a few days later, Adelman returned to his previous position and, with the support of Weinberger, convinced the President to drop his commitment to support the numerical limitations of the unratified SALT II treaty. Secretary Shultz tried to swing the decision the other way, but he did not succeed.

The outcry on the Hill following the President's announcement was loud and immediate. Opponents threatened to cut off funding for SDI research and our allies besieged the President with irate letters.[2] Donald Regan tried to shift the blame from the President to the hapless Poindexter. Admiral Poindexter, who was not particularly interested or knowledgeable in arms control and had turned the subject over to his deputy, was somewhat befuddled by the uproar.

As a result, the President backed off his earlier announcement temporarily, indicating that he might reconsider his decision if the nuclear-space talks progressed satisfactorily.

While this was going on, serious discussions continued at the lower levels of the hierarchy concerning a more definitive answer to Gorbachev's January 15 letter proposing the elimination of all nuclear weapons by the end of the century. I prepared a draft based on the ideas of the Monday Package and the approved strategic concept and which received united support in the State Department. I also proposed that the United States offer to adhere strictly to the ABM treaty for five to eight years, which seemed logical since it would be at least that long before we would be able to determine if the SDI program was technically feasible and cost-effective.

This proposal was soon rebutted. Not surprisingly, Weinberger and Perle disapproved of my draft and prepared one of their own. It was circulated by the NSC for comment. Richard Perle asserted that any

---

[2]The President received a setback in August, when Congress handed the executive branch two defeats. First, the House cut the budget for SDI research from $5.3 billion to 3.1 billion; then it voted 225 to 186 to bar funds for the deployment of any strategic systems that would cause the United States to exceed the limits of SALT II.

constraints on deployment of SDI would be a slippery slope to oblivion for the whole program.

I argued that I was not proposing that the United States do away with the SDI program; I was recommending that the United States not decide to deploy SDI until we had something that it made sense to deploy. And that did not appear possible for at least five to eight years.

Weinberger wanted us to propose that the sides *novate* the treaty, a legal term defined by Webster's dictionary as the substitution of a new obligation or contract for an old one by the mutual agreement of all parties concerned. This, Weinberger asserted, would obviate the need for the advice and consent of the Senate. He wanted the Soviets, of course, to accept his version of the substitute treaty. Shultz convinced the President to reject Weinberger's proposal before we opened that particular can of worms.

Nevertheless, I was instructed by Shultz to withdraw my draft and to concentrate my efforts on the NSC draft. At that time, I was not informed about what was transpiring in discussions at the highest level of government on this and related issues.

It turned out that at one of those high-level meetings, Weinberger had suggested that the President, in his response to Gorbachev, propose the total elimination of offensive ballistic missiles. I understand that Shultz responded that he could "go along with that." The President, of course, had been pushing for the elimination of all nuclear weapons since 1983. Poindexter set about expanding that small area of agreement between Shultz and Weinberger into an approved letter from the President to Gorbachev.

I remained unaware of the draft letter being prepared by Poindexter until the end of May, when I received a cable from Mr. Shultz, who was attending a meeting of NATO foreign ministers in Nova Scotia. It contained the text of a draft response to Gorbachev. Mr. Shultz asked that I study the draft and, if I had any problems with it, take them up directly with Poindexter.

The draft proposed that the two sides continue to abide by the ABM treaty for five years. After that period the sides would have two years to negotiate a treaty requiring them to share the benefits of their strategic defense research (or, failing that, each side would have the right to proceed on its own) *and* to share an obligation to dismantle all of their existing ballistic missiles.

I had long considered the elimination of all ballistic missiles non-negotiable; the Soviets have most of their eggs in that one basket. I thought it highly unlikely that they would be willing to give up their land-based ballistic missiles, considering their geographical position. I thought the United States was ahead of the Soviet Union in nonballistic nuclear weapons technology and that the Soviets shared that view.

Not only were we likely to find the proposal nonnegotiable with the Soviets, but it also ignored the interests of our allies. The letter proposed that the United States and the Soviet Union give up all their ballistic missiles, and also that Britain, France, and China do the same. There was no provision for prior consultation with them. The alliance, as I saw it, was once more on the line.

I attempted to see Poindexter, who refused even to return my call. I then called Colonel Robert Linhard, Poindexter's deputy on arms control, and the only person in the White House with a depth of knowledge in the field. Linhard had not seen the draft letter, so I showed him the copy I had received from Shultz. He shared my concerns. We finally managed to get the letter redrafted to call for direct participation in the negotiation of those countries (Britain, France, and China) whose ballistic missiles also would be involved.

Linhard and I were then dispatched to Europe to confer with British and French officials. They were no less appalled than we, but insisted that their countries not be mentioned at all in any such communication with Gorbachev. They wanted no part of it.

Coinciding with these events, the Soviets, in late May, presented their "partial measures" proposal in Geneva, the first part of their version of an offense-defense trade-off. The proposal called for limits on testing and a ban on deployment of antimissile systems, antisatellite (ASAT) weapons, and space-to-earth weapons (i.e., lasers, particle beams, or kinetic-kill vehicles mounted on orbiting space stations). They called this a "strengthening of the ABM treaty." They suggested that a protocol be added to the treaty prohibiting either side from withdrawing from it for fifteen to twenty years and that the sides agree to certain definitions of "development" and of ABM "components." Research, they said, should be frozen at levels reached at the time of an agreement, and prototypes and mock-ups to be used in testing should be banned.

In effect, their proposal would tighten the ABM treaty even more than the so-called narrow interpretation by adding requirements not mentioned or even considered by the treaty's negotiators.

On June 11, 1986, the Soviets put forth a new proposal on the second part of their offense-defense trade-off. As a concession, they abandoned their "reach criterion" for strategic weapons; that is, those systems capable of reaching the territory of the other side. This meant our forward-based systems in Europe would no longer be included under their proposed START limitations. On the negative side, their new proposal would allow the Soviets to retain more nuclear warheads and bombs than their previous position (up from six thousand to eight thousand) and they waffled on reductions in throw-weight. At one time, they had indicated they might agree to reduce their throw-weight by as much as fifty percent, but in June they referred only to "significant reductions" in throw-weight.

In late June, Yuri Dubinin, Moscow's new ambassador in Washington, delivered another letter from Gorbachev to the White House. The Soviet leader promised a significant new proposal on INF at the next round of talks in Geneva in addition to the "concessions" already offered in START and SDI. He stressed that a summit meeting in 1986 would not make sense without "concrete achievements" on nuclear arms control.

The President's letter to Gorbachev, in its final version, was dispatched on July 25 without further reference to our allies. It retained the proposal to eliminate all ballistic missiles but with no time limit. That portion of the letter pertaining to the continued observance of the ABM treaty was promptly leaked. But it was not until August 25 that an article appeared in the *Wall Street Journal* revealing the proposed ban on ballistic missiles. (Surprisingly it caused little comment in the public domain at that time.) Moreover, over the protests of the State Department, the final version of the letter stated that during the interim period in which the sides were to continue to observe the provisions of the ABM treaty, the United States reserved the right to proceed with a program of SDI development and testing, as well as research, "which is permitted" by the ABM treaty.[3]

The proposal of July 25 was interpreted by many as a broad concession to the Soviets on strategic defense in return for deep reductions in offensive weapons. But Weinberger's intent was eventually to deploy SDI, with or without Soviet cooperation, by observing a broader-than-broad interpretation of the ABM treaty in opposition to the Soviet's narrower-than-narrow interpretation.

The Reykjavik Summit

After his letter of July 25 was dispatched to Gorbachev and word leaked to the press, several conservative organizations condemned what they

---

[3]The comma, I might add, preceded the clause "which is permitted," in the final version of the letter.

called the "SDI sellout." As a result the President assured his conservative constituents that SDI was no bargaining chip and that he had no intention of trading it away in exchange for offensive reductions.

This, combined with the disenchantment experienced by our allies over the President's decision to break with SALT II, on the one hand, and to back his conservative SDI advocates, on the other, impelled Mr. Reagan toward the view that a successful summit was necessary to put SDI back on track.

The principal tug-of-war was with the Soviets. In Geneva, the talks were progressing at a snail's pace with each side giving a little here and taking as much as it could get there. Essentially, those talks were stalled.

On July 28, Soviet Deputy Foreign Minister Aleksandr Bessmertnykh, came to Washington to see Roz Ridgway and me. He floated the idea of a so-called expert-level meeting, consisting of four members on each side, to be held in August in Moscow. He assured us the Soviet group would be unrelated to the Geneva negotiating teams and it would be led by someone who could speak with authority for the Kremlin. The United States agreed. I was asked to serve as chairman of our small delegation. The Soviets then placed Karpov in charge and included two members of their Geneva delegation on their team. Despite our irritation at this revision of their proposal, we met in August in Moscow with somewhat larger delegations, including our Geneva arms control ambassadors. We had thirteen hours of intense and, I thought, useful discussion, but we left with empty pockets. A few weeks later the two teams of experts met again in Washington, where both sides presented proposals that moved toward the other. The Soviet experts appeared to favor acceptance of our proposal of a hundred INF warheads on each side in Europe and a hundred in Central Asia and the United States respectively.

On September 19, Eduard Shevardnadze, in Washington for talks with Secretary Shultz, delivered another letter to the President from Mr. Gorbachev. The general secretary suggested that the two leaders should involve themselves personally in order to give momentum to the negotiations. He proposed that they meet halfway between their capitals in Reykjavik, the capital of Iceland, in mid-October, and if things went well, they could plan a full summit in Washington at the end of the year. As an additional incentive, he offered to reduce the period both sides would be required to adhere to the ABM treaty from the "fifteen to twenty years," proposed by the Soviets in May, to "up to fifteen years."[4] He also

---

[4]In a press conference in Moscow, on September 24, First Deputy Foreign Minister Yuli M. Vorontsov said that President Reagan's offer in his letter of July 25 to delay SDI

agreed to global limitations on INF missiles—that is, in both Europe and Asia—but made no suggestion as to what those limitations should be.

The day after Shevardnadze delivered the letter to President Reagan, Dobrynin's deputy in the Central Committee, Georgi Kornienko, said that INF appeared to be the only area of opportunity for progress. Washington devoted the few weeks remaining before the Reykjavik meeting to preparations for closing a deal on INF.

A few days before the meeting, the State Department received reports that Dobrynin, while on a trip to South Asia, had said that Gorbachev was planning to come to Reykjavik with significant new proposals and then trap us into refusing to meet him halfway. My view was, so much the better. I thought we were fairly clear as to the needs of the West, and the further Gorbachev moved to meet those needs, the better off we would be. Despite public opinion pressure created by initial successes in the negotiation, we could then stand firm against going further than we wanted to go; we could pocket what we wished to pocket.

When we arrived at Reykjavik we found that the Soviet delegation differed in its composition from previous delegations. Usually half the members of the Soviet delegation could be associated with the KGB, but this time there were only a handful. Instead, the delegation was flooded with people ordinarily associated with the media, propaganda, psychological warfare, and political dirty tricks. Aleksandr N. Yakovlev, soon to become a full member of the Politburo and propaganda chief, and Valentin M. Falin, president of the Novosti Press Agency, were conspicuous throughout the talks. Falin was well known as a propaganda expert and for his leadership of and guidance to left-wing dissidents in Western Europe, particularly in West Germany.

We were encouraged by the new proposals presented to the President by Gorbachev at the first session on Saturday morning, October 11, but we remained on our guard. In addition to the fifty percent reduction in strategic offensive systems and the zero option in Europe on intermediate-range missiles that had been bouncing on and off the negotiating table for several years, his proposals opened up new ground. The United States, in return, was asked to agree to nonwithdrawal from the ABM treaty for ten to fifteen years and to limit SDI research and testing to the laboratory. To agree with our positions on INF turned out to be of less difficulty for the Soviets than we had anticipated.

The working groups began their work at eight o'clock that evening.

deployment for seven years was unacceptable. The Soviet Union, he said, wanted a guarantee that the ABM treaty would not be broken for "at least fifteen years."

I chaired the American team on arms control and Marshal Sergei Akhromeyev, the chief of staff of the Soviet armed forces, chaired the Soviet team. Richard Perle was on my team along with Max Kampelman, Mike Glitman, Ronald Lehman, Henry "Hank" Cooper (both on our Geneva delegation), Bob Linhard, Admiral Jonathan Howe (deputy chairman of the Military Committee, NATO), General Edward Rowny, and Ken Adelman. The Soviet team, in addition to Marshal Akhromeyev, included Karpov, Falin, Yevgeniy Velikov, and Georgiy Arbatov, an unusual combination for a top-level politico-military negotiation.[5]

We spent a large part of the first six hours of the meeting trying to pin down what "fifty percent reduction" would entail. Akhromeyev explained that the Soviets proposed halving the strategic arsenals of each side "category by category." I was quick to object to that formula. That would mean unequal end points in those categories where one side or the other had the current advantage. For example, the Soviet Union's large relative advantage in ICBM warheads with a hard-target kill capability would remain. I thought the sides must strive for equal end results; this would require unequal reductions where the current levels favored one side.

I suggested that we begin by agreeing on a final numerical ceiling of 6,000 on ballistic missile warheads, including both ICBM and SLBM warheads, plus long-range air-launched cruise missiles, and a 1,600 ceiling on ICBM and SLBM launchers and heavy bombers and then deal with sublimits within those equal end-point aggregates. After much discussion and no agreement, we moved on to INF, then defense and space, and then nuclear testing. We eventually came back to START, but we were still hung up on the issue of equal reductions versus unequal reductions to equal end-points.

At two in the morning, Marshal Akhromeyev rose and said he was leaving the meeting—he then added that he would be back at three. Bob Linhard and I hopped into a car and drove through the frigid Icelandic night to our hotel and woke up Secretary Shultz. He received us in his suite in robe and pajamas, surprisingly alert for that hour. Bob and I reported to him in detail where we were and some of the difficulties we were encountering, including those caused by some of the more obstinate conservative members of our team at the table. Shultz directed me to do what I thought right.

[5]Arbatov, who was already well known to American Kremlinologists, is director of the Institute of U.S. and Canadian Studies; Velikov is a physicist and was then director of the Institute of Atomic Energy in the USSR and former vice president of the USSR Academy of Sciences.

When we reassembled at Hofdi House at three, it became evident that Akhromeyev had awakened his boss too and had received authorization to agree to equal numerical end-levels on warheads and delivery vehicles. It then seemed to me that this opened up a significant prospect for real progress toward a comprehensive agreement.

After we had agreed on 6,000 weapons and a 1,600 delivery-vehicle aggregate, we moved on to the question of how heavy bombers were to be counted within those limits. I had been insisting that armaments on bombers, other than long-range air-launched nuclear armed cruise missiles (ALCMs), should not be counted. Without long-range standoff missiles, it was unlikely our bombers could get to their targets against heavy Soviet air defenses, which were not to be limited.

Akhromeyev objected that defenses could be destroyed and some bombers with gravity bombs and short-range air-to-surface missiles (SRAMs) would get through. We settled on a formula under which bombers equipped only with gravity bombs and SRAMs would count as one, both in the weapons count and in the delivery-vehicle count. Bombers equipped with long-range ALCMs would count in the weapons count for as many ALCMs as they carried and one in the delivery-vehicle count.

I was anxious to nail down sublimits on reentry vehicles (RVs) for ICBMs, heavy ICBMs, and MIRVed and mobile ICBMs. Akhromeyev said that they were amenable to significant reductions in heavy missile warheads (of which we had none), but objected to specific sublimits. With only 6,000 warheads allowed on each side, he said, the Soviet Union would be foolish to keep large numbers of heavy missiles. I suggested a ceiling of 4,500 on ICBM and SLBM warheads with a sublimit of 1,500 on bomber weapons. Akhromeyev objected on the grounds that they didn't want as many as 1,500 countable bomber weapons. At a minimum, I argued, we should insert in the memorandum that our working group would submit to our seniors that either side would have the right to raise the issue of sublimits in future negotiations. Akhromeyev agreed that the issue was of major importance and that either side could later raise the issue, but he did not want that spelled out in the memorandum. I asked for and received Akhromeyev's personal assurance that the issue remained open.

We then moved on to INF. There we ran into further disagreement on levels of intermediate-range nuclear forces in Europe and Asia. I insisted on equal ceilings on both sides of the Urals, whether those ceilings were zero, 100, 200, or 300. It became clear that Akhromeyev was not authorized to negotiate on the Asian level. We did, however, make progress on the issues of duration, verification, and shorter-range systems.

The two sides found themselves far apart on space and defense issues. The Soviet team continued to insist that research and testing on SDI be confined to the laboratory. I suggested language for our memorandum to our superiors that would state the three issues on which we were disagreed: one, the length of the nonwithdrawal period, two, what happened after that period, and three, what happened during that period. Akhromeyev was reluctant to agree with that. I couldn't even get an agreement on how we disagreed.

We worked steadily until 6:30 A.M. drafting our memorandum for inclusion in a final joint communiqué. This is more often than not the time when differences in understanding and perception become obvious. Sea-launched cruise missiles became a glaring problem; on the American side, we didn't know how we could limit those weapons in a verifiable and operationally acceptable manner. While we dealt with that issue in a manner acceptable for inclusion in our joint statement, it has remained a knotty problem. Sublimits on ICBMs, including specific sublimits on heavy ICBMs, also remained unresolved. Most importantly, we were no closer to agreement on space and defense.

As the meeting ended after more than ten hours of intense negotiations, I realized that large doses of mentally induced adrenaline had kept me alert all night. I found Marshal Akhromeyev a challenging negotiator with a clear, well-informed mind. I believe the dark, early morning hours found a mutual respect and admiration in our relationship that are rare in the annals of American-Soviet negotiations. He was tough, determined, but he was trying to get an agreement. He too seemed to thrive on the long hours and short rations during the all-night session. He said it was not unlike the protracted chiefs-of-staff meetings he attended in Moscow. It is always a pleasure to work with someone with a clear, concise mind; I was reminded of my Russian friend Aleksandr Shchukin in earlier negotiations.

I immediately reported to Secretary Shultz the results of our all-night session. Those issues agreed and those that remained unresolved were to be addressed at the ten o'clock meeting between President Reagan and General Secretary Gorbachev. At that meeting, to the surprise of the President and Mr. Shultz, Gorbachev not only proposed a zero INF ceiling in Europe, but offered to come down to one hundred SS-20s in Central Asia, a reduction of almost ninety-three percent in INF RVs in that part of the world. The United States would be allowed one hundred within our national boundaries. The President and Mr. Shultz thought that was acceptable; however, short-range missiles (less than a thousand kilometers) remained an unresolved issue.

The two leaders appeared to accept those ceilings on strategic offensive systems that had been discussed and agreed ad referendum during the course of my all-night session with Akhromeyev, but the space-defense issue continued to loom as a major obstacle.

The morning meeting was supposed to have been the last meeting of the two-day minisummit, but with success almost within reach, the President agreed to another meeting with Gorbachev that afternoon. Shultz and Shevardnadze were to meet with their aides at 2:00 P.M. (it was then 1:30) to try and resolve some of the remaining issues. The rest of us were hurriedly debriefed by the President and Secretary Shultz. Those of us chosen to participate assembled at the negotiating table with Shultz and Shevardnadze and his people. Akhromeyev was missing from the Soviet side of the table, but Karpov and Bessmertnykh were much in evidence. I sat to the secretary's left, with Max Kampelman on my left. Admiral Poindexter was on the secretary's right with Richard Perle and Bob Linhard to his right.

The secretary began by saying that he thought we could clear up some of the minor issues left outstanding from the morning's meeting. Shevardnadze interrupted him and said curtly, "There's only one issue before us, and that is the period of time during which the United States is willing not to withdraw from the ABM treaty and to adhere to it. We are willing to come down to ten years for the nonwithdrawal period (down from fifteen years), but no lower. Without the resolution of this issue, nothing is agreed."

The secretary, as usual, rose to the occasion and remained unflappable. Obviously some bold thinking was required. While he debated with Shevardnadze, I noticed that Bob Linhard was busy scribbling away on his yellow pad. He showed his paper to Perle and Poindexter. Perle gave his initialed approval and Poindexter then handed the paper to Shultz.

The secretary glanced over the paper and then addressed himself to the Soviet foreign minister. He said, "I would like to explore with you an idea that I have not discussed with the President, but please hear me out. We have agreed to fifty percent reductions in strategic offensive systems by the year 1991. What do you think of the elimination of all ballistic missiles by the end of a second five-year period, during which time we will agree not to withdraw from the ABM treaty?"[6]

---

[6]Bob Linhard told me later that this idea had been discussed earlier by Poindexter and Shultz. It somewhat followed President Reagan's July proposal in his letter to Gorbachev, and had been born of an earlier request from Shultz for some "bold ideas." I had suggested time-phased reductions, say, 500 ICBM and SLBM warheads plus long-range cruise missiles per year for nine years that would bring the sides down to 4,500, during which time we

There wasn't much discussion after that because Shevardnadze was not authorized to discuss such a proposal, but he appeared interested. We adjourned at three and joined the President and Donald Regan, who were waiting for us. Shultz outlined our discussions and the proposal for the elimination of all ballistic missiles by 1996. The President, the secretary, Donald Regan, and everyone there, including myself, were in favor of the idea. Richard Perle and Bob Linhard sat down and drafted language for presentation to Gorbachev. We corrected it and the President took it in to the afternoon meeting with Gorbachev.

The proposal met the Soviets' requirement for a ten-year nonwithdrawal assurance, while at the same time upholding our right to continue research, development and testing, "which is permitted by the ABM treaty . . ." and the right for either side to deploy defenses after the completion of the ten-year period and the elimination of all ballistic missiles.

I thought we were ahead of the Soviets in bomber and cruise missile technology and could remain so. As I saw it, ballistic missiles would be the weapon of choice for the Soviets if they were ever to contemplate a first strike. I thought we and our allies would be in a more secure position—as would the Soviets—if all ballistic missiles were eliminated and bombers and cruise missiles, in which we had technical superiority, remained. This would be a better offset to Soviet conventional weapon superiority on land than for the United States to rely on ballistic missiles where the Soviet side also had superiority as measured by most indices of capability.

After about an hour the President came back and said that Gorbachev was unwilling to accept the total elimination of ballistic missiles. Gorbachev had said there was a contradiction in our proposal between the reductions to be made within the first five years and those in the second five years. In the first period strategic offensive weapons were to be reduced by fifty percent, while in the second period all remaining offensive ballistic missiles were to be eliminated. He proposed that the reductions in the second five-year period be consistent with the first period, which would thus result in the elimination of all remaining strategic offensive weapons (not just ballistic missiles).

This would leave short-range ballistic missiles and short-range cruise

would agree not to deploy SDI. I added that there was no magic to the 500 number; it could vary widely, as could the number of years during which the reductions would take place. Carrying that to its extreme end-point would mean reduction to zero on both sides. This, however, was not a recommendation; it was a response to the secretary's request for a bold new idea.

missiles intact. Our European allies, particularly West Germany, would still be under the short-range Soviet nuclear gun. These short-range missiles would be capable of hitting almost every target in Europe when forward deployed.[7] If they were not covered in the agreement, then we would not have accomplished anything constructive for Western security.

We sat down again and revised the language of the first proposal in an effort to meet some of Gorbachev's objections. Mr. Reagan and Mr. Shultz met with Mr. Gorbachev once again. I am uncertain as to the exact exchange that then took place between the President and the general secretary. One thing that is certain is that Gorbachev demanded that all research, development, and testing of SDI be confined to the four walls of a laboratory. Reagan suggested that the issue be set aside to be resolved in Geneva or at a later summit. Gorbachev refused. He said he would never agree to strategic offensive reductions without a corresponding agreement that would assure there would be no sudden breakout or deployment of SDI.

For President Reagan, confining research, development, and testing of SDI to the laboratory was synonymous with consigning it to the trash heap. And that was what Gorbachev wanted to get out of the President at Reykjavik. There were, of course, many other problems still undecided, but the meeting broke up on that issue. As Gorbachev and his delegation walked out of Hofdi House, I was standing at the foot of the stairs going down from the second floor. As he passed me, Akhromeyev turned toward me and said, "It was not my fault."

Shortly afterward, Secretary Shultz gave his press conference and immediately thereafter Roz Ridgway, Max Kampelman, and I gave a background briefing. We then drove to the plane waiting to take us to Brussels, where Shultz was scheduled to debrief the North Atlantic Council the next morning. It had been an intense two-day period.

There was much speculation and criticism in the press, the Congress, and from other segments of society in the United States. Many thought the President and the American delegation had been poorly prepared to deal with a strong, purposeful Soviet leader and his delegation. I disagreed. During those two days the Soviets conceded on many of the INF, START, and nuclear testing issues that had been roadblocks to progress for years. In particular, we won agreement from the Soviets to unequal

[7]The Soviet Union has short-range ballistic missiles with conventional and chemical warheads, in addition to nuclear warheads, targeted on NATO airfields, ports, and bases, for which we have no deployed equivalent.

reductions in order to achieve equal numbers of strategic offensive systems—a crucial concession. We made only small progress on defense and space, but lost no ground. There was some confusion on the total elimination of strategic systems as opposed to the total elimination of ballistic missiles, but Shultz did not permit it to go the wrong way.

Three weeks later, Secretary Shultz and his aides met with Foreign Minister Shevardnadze and his delegation in Vienna. After trading charges and countercharges on human rights issues at the thirty-five-nation Conference on Security and Cooperation in Europe, the secretary and Mr. Shevardnadze met with interpreters at the American embassy to determine what could be preserved from the tentative agreements at Reykjavik. After their meeting, we and our Soviet counterparts at the "expert level" were called in to receive instructions for another working group meeting to last late into the night. The American side consisted of seven members, each of whom, as usual, represented a different faction of the arms control community in the administration.

I found Karpov and Bessmertnykh across the table from me but no sign of Marshal Akhromeyev. One of the first problems I ran into was Karpov's insistence that we had agreed to only two limits for START at Reykjavik, those being the 6,000 ceiling for warheads and 1,600 for delivery vehicles. Furthermore, he insisted that within those limits each side would have complete freedom to mix. There would be no sublimits and the subject was not open for further discussion.

Karpov, of course, had been there at the all-night session, and was well aware—as was almost everyone else at the Vienna negotiating table—that Akhromeyev had agreed with me that sublimits could be raised at another time by either side. After Karpov continued to insist that it had been agreed that the subject of sublimits could not be discussed, I found myself so angry at his arrogant disregard for the truth that I pointed my finger at him and said: "You're a damn liar." (There are times when diplomatic language is simply not adequate. This was one of them.) He shut up. He knew I had seven witnesses at the table who could testify to Akhromeyev's agreement that the subject was still open for discussion.

Both sides presented proposals on how to proceed from there, but no agreement was reached. The U.S. side wanted a joint communiqué that would nail down the progress at Reykjavik and identify where problems remained. The Soviets, on the other hand, wanted a narrower document reflecting their view of our agreements and the direction the talks should take. We could not reach agreement; consequently, no joint communiqué was issued.

Vienna was a partial withdrawal by the Soviets from the progress that had been made at Reykjavik. In addition to the sublimit issue, they withdrew their agreement on the duration and verification of INF limits,[8] they withdrew their agreement on an agenda for talks on nuclear testing, and continued their insistence that all strategic offensive forces be eliminated by 1996, and that all SDI research and testing be restricted to the laboratory.

Both sides tabled proposals at Geneva consistent with their current positions. More time would be needed before there could be further progress. The year ended without a major summit meeting between the two leaders.

[8]They added a provision to their proposal that negotiations should begin on short-range missiles in Europe with a range below 1,000 kilometers, whose current levels were to be frozen. This would give them a clear advantage in the interim as they had many such missiles and the United States had none within the range of 500 to 1,000 kilometers.

22

The View from Moscow

By the end of 1986, much of the forward movement at Reykjavik had vanished and that summit's political liabilities, particularly in NATO Europe, were becoming more apparent. Many here and abroad were concerned by what appeared to have been a close approach to agreement on the total elimination of nuclear weapons. Because of the continuing imbalance in conventional weapons in favor of the Soviet Union, the U.S. side had not proposed this at Reykjavik. We agreed that this could be dangerous.

As 1987 progressed, things got back on track. We made further progress on the START agreement and by December, we had signed the INF treaty. In June 1988 we were able to exchange instruments of ratification of the INF treaty, thus bringing to fruition the negotiations that had started in 1981.

There were radical personnel shifts among those dealing with arms control in the executive branch during 1987. In the White House, Donald Regan, who had been a thorn in all our sides, was replaced as chief of the White House Staff by Howard H. Baker, Jr., in late February.

I went over to Baker's office several times during the initial weeks of his incumbency. Rarely had I seen a happier man; he appeared to have everyone's support. He was anxious to improve the working relationships within the executive branch and, in particular, with the Congress. For a short time it looked as though something approaching bipartisan support for defense and arms control policy, including at least temporary support for SDI funding, was emerging. But after a few weeks it became evident that that was not happening. I suspected that Baker had found the President was a much more determined and forceful man than he had anticipated. In particular, I suspected the President was unwilling to have Baker work out a compromise with Senator Nunn and others in the Congress with respect to SDI.

After Bob McFarlane was succeeded by Admiral Poindexter and Poindexter foundered on the Irangate issue, Frank Carlucci was selected in January 1987 to advise the President on national security matters. When Carlucci became secretary of defense in November 1987, he was replaced by his deputy, Lieutenant General Colin Powell. General Powell proved to be an able staff officer and approached the NSC job in a manner of which I thoroughly approved. Rather than push for policies of his own, he carefully organized the interdepartmental staff work on issues requiring NSC decision, tried to reconcile the diverse and differing approaches of the various agencies, and then faithfully reported them to the President for decision.

The most significant change among the players in the national security field was the resignation of Secretary of Defense Caspar Weinberger on November 17, 1987. Cap had been the focal point of opposition in the administration to Secretary Shultz. They had worked together for years. Shultz had been secretary of the treasury when Cap was director of the Office of Management and Budget under President Nixon. In that capacity Cap had supported—and Shultz had opposed—the politically dangerous, if not unconstitutional, policy of sequestering and refusing to expend funds authorized and appropriated by the Congress. The Congress eventually made such sequestration illegal. When the impeachment of President Nixon was proposed, one of the charges against him was that he had permitted the unconstitutional sequestration of funds.

When Reagan was governor of California, Cap served as his finance director. Since Shultz did not serve with Reagan during that period, Cap could claim greater continuity of support for the President.

Prior to the election of Ronald Reagan to the presidency, both Shultz and Weinberger worked for the Bechtel Corporation, a large worldwide construction firm. Shultz was president and Cap was general counsel and an enthusiastic litigator. Shultz was convinced that so much time and effort going into litigation was diverting attention from their principal business. Steve Bechtel, board chairman, finally directed Cap to stem his instinct for litigation.

These differences in character traits were often evident in the interdepartmental struggles between the State and Defense departments. Shultz emphasized team play; Cap was the more aggressive bureaucratic infighter. Cap's instinct to head into policy fights served the administration badly in its relations with a Congress that was controlled by the Democrats in both Houses after 1986.

He attributed his decision to resign to his wife's persistent health problems. She did indeed have a serious back problem, but there was doubt that this was the whole story. By the fall of 1987 it seemed evident that Cap's influence on the Hill as well as the Pentagon had pretty well run out. He was often no longer able to bring the Joint Chiefs along with him on important issues, and many in the services had become dubious of his leadership.

Richard Perle, Cap's right-hand man on arms control matters, had resigned the previous spring. I admired Richard's intelligence and wit, despite the fact that he and I had tangled repeatedly over important policy issues. Frank Gaffney, one of his deputies and Perle's designated successor, had so irritated a majority of the members of the Senate Armed Services Committee that his confirmation became impossible. When Carlucci returned to the Pentagon from the White House, Gaffney was forced to resign. Kenneth Adelman, who rarely supported Shultz and only somewhat more often me, also resigned in 1987. Much to my pleasure, my former associate on the INF team, General William Burns, was appointed to succeed him.

These personnel changes resulted in a shift in the White House on the problems of arms control. Weinberger and his staff were no longer the main block to a consensus. Carlucci, as secretary of defense, was no longer opposed in principle to what Shultz and I wanted to accomplish. Nevertheless, a number of factors had been at work to slow the pace of developing negotiating positions within the Reagan administration in the early months of 1988.

As I saw it, one of the factors delaying the process on the American side was the harsh questioning of the verifiability of the INF treaty by the Congress. Shultz was the principal administration witness and as usual presented and defended the administration's case with clarity and persuasiveness. I was scheduled to handle the more detailed questions before the Senate Foreign Relations Committee. Senator Jesse Helms began his questioning with a slashing attack on many of the basic concepts and provisions of the treaty, in particular the verification provisions. He so irritated most of the other members of the committee that they devoted most of their time to rebutting him rather than rigorously questioning me.

The principal hearings for executive branch witnesses then shifted to the Intelligence Committee. There Mike Glitman and Admiral William J. Crowe, Jr., chairman of the Joint Chiefs of Staff, were subjected to hard and sometimes antagonistic interrogation. Admiral Crowe and the other Chiefs subsequently expressed shock at the opposition shown to any early consideration of a START treaty, which admittedly would present far more serious verification problems than the INF treaty. The result was to persuade Admiral Crowe that the United States should slow down the process of negotiations and not close on a START or defense and space agreement until we had had sufficient experience with INF to be sure the Soviets were proceeding in accordance with our understanding of its provisions. Only then should we take the risks involved in a broader agreement.

The White House staff did not believe that the administration could carry out measures that were opposed by the Joint Chiefs of Staff. Without JCS support with the Congress, our hands were tied. As a result, not only we in the State Department, but also those on the NSC staff, thought it essential to secure the Chiefs' concurrence in advance on all significant modifications of position.

The periodic meetings Shultz and I had with the Chiefs in their conference room, known as "the Tank," increased in frequency and in breadth of attendance. They now included a number of people from State, Defense, and the NSC staff. The meetings became as important in policy formulation on arms control matters as the SAC-PG meetings at the White House. The result was that the departure of Weinberger, Perle, Gaffney, and Adelman had less effect on the pace of U.S. movement on arms control and security issues than I had hoped.

These, then, were some of the underlying organizational factors helping and hindering our search for acceptable arms control in the last two years of the Reagan administration. Let me turn now to the narrative of those years.

Closing In on an INF Agreement

Efforts to achieve an agreement on intermediate-range nuclear forces (INF) picked up momentum in March 1987, when the Soviets proposed eliminating all such forces from Europe, after having backed off this position after Reykjavik. They also agreed to on-site inspection for the first time. This was followed by a Soviet proposal for follow-on negotiations to eliminate shorter-range nuclear weapons, which the United States identified as those weapons with a range of 500 to 1,000 kilometers.[1]

We agreed with our NATO allies that it was important to maintain our short-range nuclear forces (SNF—under 500 kilometers) and avoid

---

[1] Nuclear weapons with a range of zero to 500 kilometers were identified as short-range nuclear forces (SNF); short-range intermediate nuclear forces (SRINF)—500 to 1,000 kilometers; long-range intermediate nuclear forces (LRINF)—1,000 to 5,500. This last category included our Pershing II.

the denuclearization of Europe. The Bonn government had been concerned in years past that we might overburden the INF negotiations if we were to attempt to limit the short-range weapons (SNF). Three years earlier there had been sounds of discontent emanating from Egon Bahr of the West German Social Democrats (the opposition party) about the Soviet short-range weapons poised within range of West Germany, particularly the SCUD-B missile. I had spoken with officials of Chancellor Helmut Kohl's coalition government on at least two occasions—in 1984 and 1985—to see whether they wished the United States to change its position on these weapons. On both occasions, I was told, no. Now that the United States was approaching a deal with the Soviet Union, Chancellor Kohl—behind closed doors—insisted that we agree to follow-on negotiations with the Soviets on limitations on these short-range weapons. Bonn suddenly had become anxious about the politics of refusing to negotiate about SNF, and perhaps with good reason.

If we arrived at an agreement with the Soviet Union where the short-range weapons (SNF) were the only nuclear forces permitted in Europe, other than strategic forces, they probably would be deployed in East and West Germany. In the event of war, the two Germanies would be the only possible battlefield for such weapons. This, many German officials complained, would put Germans in a "singular" position.[2] Some in Germany even claimed the plan was a conspiracy to kill Germans rather than to contribute to a defense of NATO. This became a serious political issue.

After the Soviet Union insisted that West Germany's Pershing Ia launchers (with a range of over 700 kilometers) be dismantled and that the United States remove the nuclear warheads, Chancellor Kohl's center-right coalition government split in parliamentary debate over the dilemma.

The talks in Geneva became stalled over this issue and verification procedures. Now that the Soviet Union had agreed for the first time to on-site inspection, our military and intelligence officials suddenly became concerned about permitting Russians into our sensitive installations. The Soviet Union apparently had decided it had more to learn from on-site inspection than we did.

While the talks dragged on that summer, Gorbachev, in an interview with an Indonesian newspaper, unexpectedly announced that he was dropping his insistence on retaining a hundred medium-range missiles in

[2]In fact, it is the very singularity of Germany and other NATO countries in Europe that led to the North Atlantic Treaty. The treaty spread the risk facing those closest to the Soviet Union and its satellites to other NATO allies, including the United States and Canada.

Asia and called for a global ban on long-range and short-range intermediate missiles (LRINF and SRINF).

On July 29 the White House announced that the United States had formally accepted the Soviet proposal. But in Geneva the Soviets repeated their demand that the Pershing Ia launchers (all owned by West Germany) be dismantled and that U.S. nuclear warheads be removed from West Germany. Bonn's objections to dismantling the Pershing Ia launchers seemed to be the only remaining obstacle to an INF agreement.

A ban on all medium- and shorter-range missiles significantly simplified the INF verification problems. The United States offered in Geneva a new monitoring plan that called for fewer intrusive on-site inspections and dropped the provision requiring inspectors to be based outside missile production sites. It also modified the provision on surprise inspections. Subsequently, Chancellor Kohl announced that if the United States and the Soviet Union came to an agreement to eliminate all shorter-range and medium-range missiles, West Germany would dismantle its Pershing Ia launchers. He hastened to add, however, that the launchers belonged to his government and were not subject to negotiation in Geneva since any such bilateral agreement could cover only U.S. and Soviet weapons.

The Soviet Union indicated that it "welcomed" Chancellor Kohl's offer and the new U.S. proposal on verification procedures. September brought fresh impetus for the conclusion of an agreement. Work in Geneva went on around the clock drafting the final text of the treaty and its annexes. At one point, Karpov and I estimated the number of remaining issues at about thirty. Two weeks later, Mike Glitman told me the list had grown to more than a hundred. Eventually the two delegations got them all resolved.

The treaty was signed by the President and General Secretary Gorbachev in December at the Washington summit meeting. The contest between the executive branch and the Senate on verification procedures that I mentioned earlier took place the following spring, when the treaty appeared before the Senate for its advice and consent to ratification.

Space Defense and the ABM Treaty

During this period, the SDI issue continued to be an unyielding problem. It almost broke up the January 1985 meeting with Gromyko; it was a pivotal point at the Geneva summit at the end of that year; and it caused the rupture in the minisummit at Reykjavik in October 1986. Not only was it a U.S.–Soviet issue, it was also a serious domestic issue—both within the executive branch and between the executive branch and the Congress.

In the summer of 1986, several senators—Carl D. Levin among them—had demanded to see the documents on which the President had based his October 1985 determination that the broad interpretation of the ABM treaty was fully justified. In December, after Senator Levin and his staff had reviewed the documents, he declared that the study by State Department legal counsel, Abraham Sofaer, on which the President's judgment had been based, was "fatally flawed."

While this was going on, the administration was gearing up for its own intramural disputes. By February 1987 the President had two proposals before him: one was to proceed with testing beyond that which was permitted by the broad interpretation of the ABM treaty, the other was to consider the early phased deployment of a space-based antiballistic missile system. President Reagan had received a December briefing from Caspar Weinberger and Lieutenant General James A. Abrahamson, SDI director, from which Secretary Shultz and I had been excluded. Weinberger and Abrahamson defended the thesis that initiating the first phase of an effective SDI deployment was feasible by 1994. They wished to restructure the SDI program in order to begin testing the components of such a system in space in the relatively near future.

There were two meetings of the National Security Planning Group in February 1987, chaired by the President, to consider these proposals. No consensus developed among the attendees at the meetings—of whom I was one. After the first, we all went back to our respective cells to refine our positions. Others in the State Department helped me prepare talking points for Shultz to take up with the President. On the issue of early phased deployment, I found no persuasive evidence that deployment of a worthwhile system could begin by 1994. The Joint Chiefs of Staff, I pointed out, agreed with that assessment. Moreover, a "phased" deployment was almost a tautology; if and when the United States were to deploy, it would have to be done, incrementally, in phases.

In my mind, there was no pressing need to reverse the decision of 1985. While the new interpretation might indeed be fully justified based on the negotiating record, there were other practical considerations. During the ratification process in the Senate in 1972, testimony by Secretary of Defense Melvin R. Laird and John B. Foster, director of defense research and engineering, in response to questions put to them by Senator Henry M. Jackson, had supported the narrow interpretation of the treaty. New

York Senator James Buckley even voted against the ratification of the treaty because he thought it banned the development and testing of systems based on "other physical principles."

The Soviet Union is obligated by the terms of the treaty and the agreed understandings and interpretations associated with the treaty; it is not bound by the understandings of the Senate during the ratification process if they vary from the text and the negotiating record. But under the United States Constitution, upon the ratification by the President with the advice and consent of the Senate, a treaty becomes the law of the land and is binding under domestic law in the manner understood by the Senate when it gave its consent to ratification, even if that understanding is not binding under international law.

Under those circumstances, it seemed to Judge Sofaer and to me unwise for the President, without full consultation with the Congress, to change his interpretation from that on which ratification had been based. The President has the right under the Constitution to interpret treaties, but the Congress holds the purse strings. Conflict between the two could bring about an unmanageable stalemate.

To avoid a stalemate, I recommended that the President authorize additional legal studies on the ratification record and on subsequent practice of the treaty parties, both of which have a bearing, in international law, on the interpretation of a treaty where the text is ambiguous. I also recommended that the administration consult with the Congress and our allies prior to making any decision to implement the broad interpretation.

Mr. Shultz agreed with these recommendations and showed the talking points to Weinberger. Cap was opposed to some of the points, but agreed that consultation was necessary. Shultz then discussed them with the President and his recently appointed national security adviser, Frank Carlucci. They gave their blessing to Shultz's appearance on the David Brinkley show on Sunday, February 8, 1987, using these talking points.

The President ordered that an extensive study of the negotiating record, the ratification proceedings, and the subsequent practices of the two parties to the ABM treaty be completed by May 1 and then presented to the Congress. In the meantime, Richard Perle (to keep an eye on me, I guess) and I began a swing of European capitals for consultations with our allies. The interpretation of the ABM treaty had become a central issue not only in U.S.–Soviet relations, but in alliance relations as well. The President authorized our negotiators in Geneva to present the broad interpretation to the Soviets.

In mid-March Senator Sam Nunn, chairman of the powerful Armed

Services Committee, released his review of the negotiating record, his summary of the testimony before the Senate before it gave its advice and consent to ratification, and his study of subsequent practices of the parties. These reviews, he said, refuted the administration's position that the broad interpretation was fully justified.

I thought his review of the ratification process to be generally correct, his study of the practices of the parties subsequent to ratification to be irrelevant (neither we nor the Soviets had ever been in a position where we knew how to make or test ABM systems based upon other physical principles), and his review of the negotiating process to be unpersuasive. The latter contained nothing to support the narrow interpretation other than unilateral memoranda of what one or another of our SALT negotiators remembered a Russian negotiator having said to him. Moreover, these oral statements were inconsistent with positions subsequently taken by other Soviet negotiators. The Soviet Union would never consider such evidence legally binding upon itself.

But a majority of the Senate, including a number of the more influential Republicans, joined in support of Nunn in what seemed to them a battle over the powers of the executive branch relative to those of the legislative branch, and of the Senate in particular. The administration was obviously in deep trouble with the Senate.

The only way I could see to make our way through the morass was to work out with the Soviets a way to deal with the hole that had been left in the ABM treaty when we negotiated it in 1972. In 1972 we had no clear idea what ABM capable systems based upon other physical principles might be, or how their components might be defined. Thus we could not design precise limitations on them nor assure effective verification of compliance with them.

Some months earlier, Donald Rice, president of the Rand Corporation, and some of his associates reported to me their discussions with Yevgeniy Velikov, a leading Soviet physicist and director of the USSR atomic energy program, and Roald Sagdeyev, who then ran its space program. The Russian scientists also were concerned that there was no definition for the components of a system based upon "other physical principles" in the ABM treaty. They suggested that the sides should come to agreement on a list of such possible components and then determine thresholds of capability above which these components might be effective in an ABM role. The sides could then agree on what would constitute testing them in an ABM mode. As an example, they suggested that the testing of sensors should be limited only when tested in conjunction with a kinetic-kill vehicle.

I concluded that, while Velikov's ideas would present difficulties because of the administration's existing positions and the mood of many on Capitol Hill, they indicated a path worth considering. I came up with what became known as "Option C" when it was introduced into the interdepartmental and NSC working groups. Option C proposed that the United States negotiate with the Russians as to what technologies we could agree are based on "other physical principles" as they pertain to the ABM treaty. Second, we should agree on their potential components—the parts of those new systems which are comparable to the radars, interceptors, and launchers of the ABM systems based on technologies extant in 1972. Having done that, we might then be able to agree on thresholds of capability (similar to the 3×10^6 provision for phased-array radars in the ABM treaty) above which they would be subject to limitations on how they were tested. Then we could work out the principles of what would constitute "testing in an ABM mode" of such components.

Shortly after these events occurred, Strobe Talbott of the Washington Bureau of *Time* magazine called and asked if I would be willing to see Velikov, who was in Washington and wished to see me. I agreed.

Velikov arrived at my office with two representatives from his embassy in Washington. He elaborated at length on the thoughts he had presented to the Rand people.[3]

I was skeptical that Velikov's proposals represented an official Soviet position, although I believed that both he and Sagdeyev thought their ideas were constructive. The Kremlin sometimes sends out feelers in this form for exploration, and then it'll make up its mind how best to play the hand. Nevertheless I thought that to explore this path further was a proper way to go.

The problem with this formula was, however, that if we agreed to definitions and thresholds of capability, then we might be heading toward constraints that did not appear in the treaty, an outcome that the President already had firmly opposed. The Soviets agreed that there was no way to derive from the language of the ABM treaty a definition of components of a system based on "other physical principles." That was why, incidentally, they had refused to ban the development and testing of futuristic systems and devices in 1972, considering it premature.

I asked a distinguished, young Harvard physicist, Ashton Carter, to

[3]I later got a message from Vorontsov via Max Kampelman in Geneva that Velikov had complained that I wouldn't discuss these matters with him—I only asked questions. He was right; that was all I was authorized to do. If I had gone further, I would have gotten myself into deep trouble.

look into the technical options for early deployment of SDI and how these options might be affected by various interpretations of the ABM treaty. Many SDI proponents considered Ashton a foe of SDI, but he also enjoyed the reputation of being a conscientious and highly respected scientist. He had prepared a report on ballistic missile defense for the United States Office of Technology Assessment in 1984 that was solidly researched and rigorously reasoned. Nevertheless it had put a few noses out of joint. I realized I would be the target of some criticism for pursuing this approach, but I thought it important to find out whether the thresholds under discussion could be negotiated at levels which would allow the testing required for a vigorous SDI research program. The Pentagon, at Weinberger's direction, had refused to conduct the studies necessary to find this out.

Time passed without further word from the Soviets on the matter. We had almost decided that the Kremlin was not interested in further exploration when Shevardnadze, at the foreign ministers' meeting in Moscow in April 1987, proposed that the sides convene a meeting of the Standing Consultative Committee with defense ministers as heads of delegations. He suggested that it might be possible to clear up many important issues, including the matter of permissible and prohibited testing in space.

Weinberger vehemently opposed accepting this proposal. This time he won the ear of the President. Weinberger found an ally in Frank Carlucci, who also objected to talking with the Soviets on this subject. The secretary of defense recommended four new space defense tests that, I believed, would be inconsistent with all but the broadest of broad interpretations of the ABM treaty. To move ahead without coming to an agreement with the Soviets on what testing in space was permitted would, in my estimation, further sour the administration's relations with the Congress on SDI and hurt the prospects not only for the SDI program, but for a successful outcome of the arms control negotiations.

The underlying problem, as previously noted, was that in 1972 the United States and the Soviet Union had left ground not covered in the ABM treaty. I believed the provision dealing with systems based on "other physical principles" needed to be clarified and agreed between the sides. Whether the administration should accept the so-called broad or narrow interpretation was not the central issue. Rather, it was whether the sides could agree on how to fill the gap left in the treaty when we negotiated it in 1972.

The Washington Summit

In September 1987, the Soviets agreed to a summit meeting in Washington before the end of the year. The general secretary and his entourage received a warm welcome in the nation's capital. The meetings began with a ceremony in the White House on Tuesday afternoon, December 8, for the signing of the INF treaty by the President and Mr. Gorbachev.

Shortly after the ceremony, several of us met with Secretary Shultz, Foreign Minister Shevardnadze and Marshal Sergei Akhromeyev, my counterpart at Reykjavik. We agreed that there would be, as usual, two main negotiating levels at this summit. One would be at the level of the general secretary and the President, which would be augmented much of the time by Secretary Shultz and General Colin Powell,[4] and on the Soviet side by Foreign Minister Shevardnadze and Deputy Foreign Minister Bessmertnykh. The other level would be a series of working groups, including one on arms control that I would head on the U.S. side and Marshal Akhromeyev would head on the Soviet side.

The arms control working group met during much of the next day, Wednesday, adjourning shortly after midnight, with serious disagreements on START and defense still outstanding. In the eyes of many in the Reagan administration, Soviet willingness to sever the linkage between INF and START indicated that the Soviets might be willing also to sever the link between reductions in offensive strategic systems and space and defense. I seriously doubted this and our summit negotiations bore this out.

Early the next morning, Thursday, December 10, I reported our disagreements to Secretary Shultz. The sides had achieved some progress with respect to START, but were at a stalemate on the space-defense issue. For example, a fundamental problem remained as to what would be allowed during and after an "agreed period" of nonwithdrawal from the ABM treaty. The Soviet negotiators insisted that if the sides had not come to agreement by the end of the period, the terms of the 1972 ABM treaty would still apply.

Mr. Shultz showed me a "memorandum of conversation" resulting from the President's discussion with the general secretary the day before. At one point, Mr. Gorbachev had said very precisely that after the expira-

---

[4]General Powell had replaced Frank Carlucci as the President's national security adviser in November.

tion of the "agreed period," the United States would be free to decide its own course with respect to deployment of space defenses. The Soviet Union, he had said, had its own program of research, and while it would not itself deploy a space-defense system, he was confident that the Soviet Union could overwhelm any deployment that we might attempt.

If Gorbachev's statement were to be confirmed in the joint communiqué to be issued at the conclusion of the summit, one of the space-defense issues would be on the road to solution.

Mr. Shultz hurriedly dictated a few words based on the general secretary's remarks. He then cleared the sentence on the telephone with Colin Powell and Secretary of Defense Carlucci. The secretary called the Soviet foreign minister and arranged for the two of us to meet with Shevardnadze at the Soviet embassy.

We arrived at the embassy at 8:15 in the morning. Shevardnadze was waiting for us with Karpov and Ambassador Dubinin. After some procedural matters were discussed, the secretary said he had a proposal that might enable the sides to remove almost all of the remaining differences in the joint communiqué on space-defense that had been in controversy the night before. If the Soviet side could agree to the sentence he had drafted and to one other relatively minor change, the sides could then eliminate all the other brackets in the draft communiqué language except for a bracket at the end. Even without removing that last bracket, we would have made enormous progress.

Shevardnadze said that he thought Shultz's proposal was constructive, but that he needed to consult with the general secretary, whom he would not see until 10:30, at which time Mr. Gorbachev had a meeting with the President. Mr. Shultz asked me to go to the White House and have the ten-thirty meeting with the President postponed until 10:45. This I did.

I had barely arrived at the White House when I was told that Marshal Akhromeyev wanted to resume our working group meeting. A small group from both sides assembled in the Cabinet Room after a short delay.

After some strenuous give-and-take, we managed to eliminate all of the remaining brackets in the joint communiqué concerning START. We were not, however, able to remove all of the brackets in the space-defense language. The hours passed. We had been expected to join the President and the general secretary for lunch at 12:30. At two o'clock, members of both delegations, staff, guests, and the press were assembling in the Rose Garden for the closing statements by the two leaders.

About this time Secretary Shultz, accompanied by Colin Powell and Frank Carlucci, joined us in the Cabinet Room. Shevardnadze joined Akhromeyev and Karpov. Intense discussions followed. Akhromeyev had proposed language which involved the words "abide by the ABM treaty as signed and ratified in 1972." We had insisted that the words "and ratified" be eliminated. Secretary Shultz argued that the interpretation of the treaty based on the ratification process was an internal dispute between the administration and the Congress, and the Soviets should keep out of it. Carlucci began to make a proposal on our behalf in which he began with the words, "as signed and . . ." Before he could complete his sentence, however, Marshal Akhromeyev began reading a sentence from a piece of paper in front of him. That sentence did not contain the words "and ratified" and seemed otherwise satisfactory. Shultz immediately interjected, "We buy it."

Akhromeyev had spoken in Russian and his words had been translated to us in English. I was the only one taking precise notes. I dictated from my notes what I believed Marshal Akhromeyev had said and presented it to the Soviet side to see whether it was correct. It was and the deal was made.

The paragraph that had kept the leaders of the two nations cooling their heels in the White House Red Room was adequate to secure agreement on a joint statement for release to the press at the conclusion of the summit, but it would lead to endless wrangling as to its precise meaning. It read as follows:

> Taking into account the preparation of the Treaty on strategic offensive arms, the leaders of the two countries also instructed their delegations in Geneva to work out an agreement that would commit the sides to observe the ABM Treaty, as signed in 1972, while conducting their research, development, and testing as required, which are permitted by the ABM Treaty, and not to withdraw from the ABM Treaty, for a specified period of time. Intensive discussions of strategic stability shall begin not later than three years before the end of the specified period, after which, in the event the sides have not agreed otherwise, each side will be free to decide its course of action.

The meeting broke up and everyone went out to the South Lawn of the White House for the farewell ceremony in a cold December rain. I was left alone in the Cabinet Room gathering my papers and my wits when I realized that I had been sitting in the President's chair throughout the entire session from ten-thirty to two-thirty. Someone came in to tell me that Colin Powell—instead of me—would handle the background press briefing. I made my way to my car and returned to the State Department.

The two leaders hailed the summit as a success of historic proportions with the signing of the INF treaty, the progress toward an agreement for massive reductions in offensive strategic weaponry, and the improvement of relations between the two governments. There had been no progress in delinking START from the space-defense issue, as I mentioned earlier, but we were encouraged. The two leaders had agreed to meet in Moscow sometime in the first half of 1988 with the hope that a START agreement would then be ready for signature.

The wrangling began immediately after the close of the Washington summit. It centered on the phrase "research, development and testing as required, which are permitted by the ABM Treaty." Colin Powell in his background briefing—followed by the President at a press conference the next morning—said that the sides had reached complete agreement with respect to SDI and that we could go forward with whatever testing was required. The Soviets immediately put forward a different interpretation of the phrase. They said it sanctioned required testing only "as permitted by the ABM Treaty," and what was permitted had not been agreed.

Shultz and I thought there was merit to the Soviet point and that we should get on with narrowing the differences between the sides on what testing was permitted by the ABM treaty.

The Moscow Summit

As the last full year of the Reagan administration began, the most immediate and important task I saw lying ahead was to obtain the advice and consent of the Senate to the ratification of the INF treaty. All of our other efforts depended on our success in achieving this step.

It fell to me to explain and defend the INF verification provisions before the Senate Foreign Relations Committee. As I have explained earlier, my first session with the committee was made virtually meaningless by a broadside attack by Senator Helms. Eventually the executive branch had to prepare "authoritative replies" to over 1,300 written questions from various senators. Each reply had to be checked and approved by each agency and department concerned with arms control, including the staff in my small office.

Early on, I transferred my attention to the continuing negotiations with the Soviets on START and defense and space. I considered INF to be essentially completed.

After the Washington summit in December 1987, all of the agencies involved organized their work to come up with positions for the Moscow summit, scheduled for the end of May. Secretary Shultz and his aides met with Soviet Foreign Minister Shevardnadze and his entourage in Moscow in February. There was another meeting in Washington in March between the two foreign ministers, when Shevardnadze had the opportunity to meet with the President. In April, we once again made the long trek to Moscow via Brussels to confer with the North Atlantic Council and a stopover in Helsinki to catch our breath. At each of the Moscow meetings, we had the opportunity to meet with General Secretary Mikhail Gorbachev.

At the meeting in April, Mr. Gorbachev was sharp, eloquent, and at times harshly critical of the United States and its leaders. Mr. Shultz, sitting across the table from him, exhibited his usual aplomb and good judgment. At one point Gorbachev said to Shultz:

"You seem to think that you are always right on matters of foreign policy."

Shultz responded with a wry smile, "Of course I am always right."

The general secretary could not resist joining Shultz in laughter.

There followed a frank discussion between Gorbachev and Shultz that the rest of us followed with intense interest. It covered the gamut of issues that then stood between our two countries, with a give-and-take that was unheard of in our past relationship. The discussion ranged from human rights and arms control, to Afghanistan, the Persian Gulf, and the spread of Muslim fundamentalism.

There were many undercurrents going on in Moscow during the April meeting. In spite of Gorbachev's insistence that all was well in the Politburo, rumors were rampant about what was happening in the Kremlin. I formed an impression at that meeting that the Soviets had decided— probably in February—that the chances of getting agreements on START and space-defense by the May summit date were slight. They had shifted their efforts to put the Soviet Union in the best position to deal with continuing differences at the Moscow summit and thereafter.

After this less than satisfactory meeting, Secretary Shultz was determined nevertheless to keep the momentum going if possible.

The last pre-Moscow summit meeting was held in Geneva in early May. There we achieved final agreement with the Soviets on technical verification issues in the INF treaty. This paved the way for eventual Senate consent to ratification.

The U.S. delegation arrived in Moscow for the summit meeting on Sunday, May 29, 1988. I was pleased to find that Marshal Akhromeyev was once again my opposite number in the working meetings on START and space-defense. I had been sitting across the table from Alexei Obukhov since the Washington summit and found his stance more inflexible and adversarial than Akhromeyev's. When one side refuses to budge one inch toward the other, the negotiations are likely to become stalemated.

Our working groups settled down to address the issues before us at about eight that evening. I spent the next two and a quarter hours laying out the U.S. position on long-range ALCMs and mobile ICBMs, using talking points we had labored over intensively in Washington in order to achieve interdepartmental agreement. Marshal Akhromeyev listened intently and then said, "We will study your proposals overnight and comment tomorrow morning. We will then have points of our own to raise."

The next day I was surprised at the number of my points with which Akhromeyev found it possible to agree. He didn't quibble over small points; he concentrated on major differences—and those differences were indeed serious. He was somewhat more forthcoming on mobile ICBMs than on ALCMs. The Soviet Union wanted to work out limitations on land-based mobile ICBMs. They already had two classes of mobiles deployed while we had none. This problem would have to be resolved if we were going to have an agreement satisfactory to both sides.

The Soviets believed that the United States had an advantage in long-range ALCMs and that we were trying to exploit that advantage. They were fighting hard to block our proposals on these weapons. Nevertheless the sides got quite a lot of work done on this issue during that session.

Akhromeyev emphasized the issue of major concern to him—limitations on nuclear armed sea-launched cruise missiles (SLCMs) and their verification. The U.S. position was that we could not allow Soviet inspectors aboard our submarines or our surface fleet. Our submarines are the baseline of our strategic nuclear defense and contain highly sensitive and classified equipment. As an alternative, I suggested that each side declare the maximum number of SLCMs it proposes to deploy. There would be little incentive to cheat since each side could change its declarations at any time. While declarations would not be rigorously verifiable, there are natural limits to the number of SLCMs either side might wish to deploy on submarines since these weapons compete for space with valuable torpedoes. To give up a number of torpedoes for SLCMs is not a costless switch between armaments.

Akhromeyev insisted that our proposal was slanted in favor of our area of strength—our sea-based systems. He said the Soviet Union relied heavily on land-based systems and that the United States was trying to impose restraints on those systems. The Soviets feel vulnerable at sea.

Although they have spent vast sums building up their navy, they have not achieved the results they had hoped for. In an interview earlier in May with *Washington Post* Chairman Katharine Graham, Mr. Gorbachev said that it was unthinkable to have a START agreement without limits on nuclear-armed SLCMs. I had some thoughts on how we might go about verifying limits on nuclear-armed SLCMs, but our interdepartmental group did not wish to seriously discuss alternatives to a declaratory approach. It is in fact a very difficult and sensitive issue.

Akhromeyev and I had a lively debate on defense and space systems, although we made less progress toward agreement on this issue than I had hoped. In the long run, however, I believe the problem of working out an agreement with the Soviet Union on space and defense is soluble, if for no other reason than that the Soviets are no longer as concerned about our space defense initiative as they were at one time. What they do not want is for us to begin deploying a system before 1997.

The Soviets have taken a different tack than we in their space defense program. As far as we know, they have confined their space weapons research to their laboratories, while at the same time they have moved ahead at a rapid pace with their space-lift and space-based reactor programs. Our space-lift efforts had been mired in technical and fiscal problems for over two years and may well be somewhat limited for the next ten. The Soviets are way ahead of us and have already tested a heavy-lift vehicle. They probably calculate that they can catch up with whatever technology we develop if they can put a lot more weight of weapons and sensors into space than we and do it faster.

On Wednesday afternoon, June 1, the President, who was departing Moscow the next day, and Secretary Shultz each had his own press conference summarizing the progress achieved. Roz Ridgway and I were scheduled to fill in the details with the press later. There were over a thousand international journalists at the press center that evening, representing almost every country on the globe, eager for more information. The Soviet government, for some inexplicable reason, had reserved that hour at the press center for Occidental Petroleum Chairman Armand Hammer to announce that the first championship golf course in the Soviet Union was to be constructed eighteen miles from Moscow. The eighteen-hole golf course, Dr. Hammer said, represented "another step forward in the continuing good relations" between the United States and the Soviet Union. He then proceeded to distribute complimentary golf balls to the surprised journalists. Roz and I, in the meantime, waited in the wings.

We were finally given our turn to appear before the journalists, each equipped with earphones for simultaneous translations. They were starved for details and we answered their questions to the best of our ability. Helen Thomas, senior White House correspondent and UPI reporter, who is given front row center at press conferences—and this one was no exception—asked me whether I was prepared to declare the Cold War over. I answered: "You really wouldn't want the Cold War to turn hot, would you?" Helen was somewhat nettled at this response.

After the Moscow summit, work continued in Geneva to perfect and eliminate brackets from the joint draft texts of the documents being negotiated there. Some progress was made. The review of the ABM treaty, which is required by the terms of the treaty to take place at least every five years, occurred in August with no notable movement by either side. The next opportunity for Shultz and Shevardnadze to have another bilateral meeting was in connection with the latter's visit to New York for the September meeting of the United Nations General Assembly.

A full-scale meeting organized on the lines of preceding bilateral foreign ministers meeting took place in Washington on September 22 and 23, 1988. Again I headed the U.S. working group on arms control, and this time my opposite number was Alexei Obukhov, with whom I had dealt before.

The U.S. side had worked hard interdepartmentally since the Moscow summit to develop positions on the limitation and verification of ALCMs and of mobile ICBMs, were they to be permitted. These positions were designed to meet the concerns expressed by the Soviets at the Moscow summit. We were unable to nail down progress on either of these issues or on others, including the one of primary concern to the Soviets—the limitation and verification of SLCMs.

In space and defense, we tried a different angle. Since American negotiators had not been permitted by the President to pursue the list and threshold approach, my staff and I had devoted much energy over the past year to exploring alternate approaches. For a time I thought the most hopeful alternative was to persuade the Soviets to accept the concept of a test range in space comparable to the limited test ranges on earth provided by Article IV of the ABM treaty. This ran into what appeared to be insuperable problems. We then proposed a twofold approach:

(a) to persuade the Soviets that the sides agree not to object to the other side's sensors in space (their principal function is to provide each side with early warning of the other side's ballistic missile launches—a stabilizing function); and

(b) to agree that each side could have no more than a certain number of test platforms in space—a number so small that they could not possibly constitute a base for a territorial ABM defense.

These proposals had been only tentatively explored with the Soviet side by the time the Shultz-Shevardnadze talks took place in Washington in September 1988 and were not well received by our Soviet counterparts.

In summary, it appeared that no significant progress in the START and defense and space negotiations would be possible during the remainder of the Reagan administration.

What did all this mean for U.S. policy? As I saw it—as we approached the final months of the Reagan administration—in the national security field, the United States should continue on the basic courses of action we had pursued for the past few years.

1. We should renew our search for the optimum way to keep our guard up in the strategic nuclear field, particularly in assuring a survivable and credible deterrent.

2. We should continue to work hard on an arms control approach that we could live with and that should alleviate the most serious and understandable Soviet concerns. Specifically, we should proceed with a START agreement that would exploit the considerable progress we have made toward stabilizing fifty percent reductions in the strategic nuclear forces of both sides. To secure Soviet agreement to a START treaty, we would need to work out a mutually acceptable solution to the defense and space issues.

3. We should concurrently work diligently toward satisfactory arrangements for the reduction of conventional weapons to more nearly equal end-points and to the step-by-step elimination of chemical and biological weapons on a global basis.

Glasnost and Perestroika

I saw no easy panacea. I thought that, while we were on the right road, it was going to take time and patience. The most serious uncertainty was what might evolve from Gorbachev's program of glasnost and perestroika.

It is always hard to judge accurately what is going on at senior levels in Moscow, but glasnost and the frequent high-level meetings between

Washington and Moscow had made the curtain of Soviet secrecy less opaque. During 1987 and the first half of 1988, Secretary Shultz had eleven meetings with Shevardnadze, of which five were in Moscow. At the Moscow meetings, General Secretary Gorbachev received Secretary Shultz and a few of his advisers for three or more hours at each session. These meetings enabled us to get a much richer view of both the man and the policies he was pursuing.

At one of these sessions, Gorbachev told us that the drive for internal reform symbolized by glasnost and perestroika had originated well before he had become general secretary. Three years earlier, during Andropov's leadership, he and Nikolai Ryzhkov (Soviet prime minister) had had serious discussions about necessary changes in the Soviet political structure and in the concepts of its operation. They assigned a number of the younger and brighter men in the Party to conduct studies on necessary fundamental reforms. Some hundred studies resulted. Gorbachev and his supporters thus had a running start when he became general secretary.

Included in these reforms was a drive for glasnost: greater openness in Soviet society, increased freedom to criticize past eras, more realistic discussion of Soviet Party history, and even criticism of current policy and leadership. Perestroika was a drive for fundamental restructuring of the Soviet Party and governmental system designed to reverse many of the defects in the Soviet system identified by Gorbachev, Ryzhkov, and those who had been helping them.

The drive for glasnost was ably directed by Gorbachev and Yakovlev, who shortly was appointed to full membership in the Politburo. It was supported by most of the brighter and more able of the intellectuals. Results were dramatic and widely visible in the fields controlled by them—the arts, the revelation of historical truths, and more apparent freedom for the media.

Perestroika was inherently more difficult. To achieve positive action required the consent (or the outmaneuvering) of a majority of the Politburo. Mr. Gorbachev had some initial success in moving from a solid base of public support against his more ardent opponents in the Politburo. But he subsequently ran into resistance to his proposed changes from a majority of that powerful political body.

Gorbachev called for a Party Conference in the early summer of 1988. He hoped to enlist sufficient support to overwhelm those in the Politburo who opposed his programs. The conference turned out to be less than satisfactory from Gorbachev's point of view. There was much criticism of current policies and of current economic performance. There was, in addition, widespread unwillingness, even on the part of the best and the brightest, to assume additional responsibilities. The majority seemed to be concerned that the pace was too rapid and Gorbachev's reforms too radical.

In order to maintain his position as leader of the Politburo, Gorbachev, on a number of significant issues during the Party Conference, sided with the Politburo majority, which included his principal opponents: Yegor Ligachev, number two man in the Politburo; Andrei Gromyko, then president of the Presidium; KGB chief Viktor Chebrikov; and Mikhail Solomentsev, chairman of the Party Control Commission.[5] At the close of the conference, Gorbachev turned on some who had most ardently supported radical reform such as Boris Yeltsin, whom he brutally humiliated. Gorbachev seemed to be assuming the position of a centrist, attacking those on his left as well as those on his right.

At the Plenum of the Central Committee, which followed shortly thereafter, he appeared to be unable to gain approval of any of the high-level personnel changes he reportedly had been seeking. Even though the general objectives of Gorbachev's reforms were approved, implementation was delayed indefinitely. As a result, it appeared doubtful to me that Gorbachev—in any acceptable period of time and without using extraordinary measures—could carry out his basic domestic reform program. But at the end of September 1988, Gorbachev threatened to take extraordinary measures (what the Soviets call "administrative measures") to circumvent those in the Politburo opposed to perestroika. He thus achieved greater power—in fact, very nearly sole power—but also greater responsibility for achieving success.

With respect to his foreign policy initiatives, Gorbachev ran into less opposition. It had been a long tradition in Soviet foreign policy to outpromise all others in utopian objectives while engaging in the most realistic and cynical policies and tactics. Gorbachev's eloquence, initiative, and tactical brilliance in foreign affairs seem to have impressed even Soviet critics of his domestic reforms. Furthermore, Shevardnadze—a faithful supporter—had control over the Ministry of Foreign Affairs and Yakovlev exercised firm leadership over the propaganda organs.

It is notable that in Ligachev's full-scale attack on Gorbachev and his supporters in July 1988, he mentioned foreign affairs only briefly, while the rest of his speech was devoted to ideological concepts and opposition

---

[5] At a meeting of the Party Central Committee on September 30, 1988, these gentlemen, with the exception of Ligachev, were all retired. Ligachev retained his position as number two man in the Politburo but lost his position as chief ideologist. He became chairman of the CPSU Commission on Agriculture.

to the pace and direction of domestic reform. The basis of his attack was that Gorbachev and his followers maintained that the global struggle against the class enemy—the bourgeoisie led by the United States—was only one factor among a number of others. These other factors included the necessity to avoid global war, preserve the world environment, and return the Soviet Union to world respectability. Ligachev insisted that watering down Communist ideology by denying the primacy of the class struggle would confuse and weaken the Party and could lead it to disaster.

The impact of this internal struggle within the Party was to distract attention from the arms control negotiations. By March 1988 it was already evident to those in official Washington that the Soviet leadership no longer thought it possible to reach agreement on the provisions of a START treaty by the May summit. Furthermore, it appeared probable that they had decided not to move vigorously toward achieving one during the remainder of the Reagan administration.

It seemed to me that success in working out arms control issues might well depend on factors external to arms control. The most likely candidate was the growing economic pressures on the two sides. The economic burden of arms on the average Russian citizen was at least four times that of the analagous burden on the American citizen. The Soviet Union's social structure permits much heavier burdens to be carried, but as the pressure becomes greater, the fragility of that structure increases. The United States was also facing intense budgetary and international balance of payments problems. The decisive race might be between each side's ability to bring its economic structure into balance without prematurely cutting its relative military strength.

End of the Shultz Era

After the 1988 Moscow summit, work on arms control continued, but with a different focus. NATO developed an agreed initial position for anticipated talks with the USSR and the Warsaw Pact on stabilizing reductions in conventional weapons. The negotiations in Vienna produced an agreed mandate within the framework of the Helsinki Accords for those talks. Concurrently, there were important negotiations in Paris directed toward working out the preconditions for a ban on chemical and biological weapons. But in the area of my particular concern—the nuclear and space talks—no serious progress was possible. It became evident that we would have to wait until after the transition from President Reagan to President George Bush for further progress. The Reagan regime had done much, but much also remained to be done.

Some forty of us who had worked most closely with George Shultz during his six and a half years as secretary of state decided to organize under Michael "Mike" Armacost's (under secretary of state for political affairs) leadership a surprise final meeting with the secretary on the afternoon of his departure from the State Department. That day happened to be the two hundredth anniversary of Thomas Jefferson's confirmation as secretary of state in 1789. To commemorate the occasion, Mike had arranged to have a handsome gold medal struck, called the Thomas Jefferson Medal of Merit, along with a citation that all of us signed.

When the secretary and Mrs. Shultz returned from a farewell luncheon at which the President awarded him the Medal of Freedom, we were awaiting him in his office. Mike presented him with the Jefferson medal, read the citation, and then read a number of witty, moving letters from the secretary's friends, including Prime Minister Thatcher, Chairman Gorbachev, Chancellor Kohl, and others. Thereafter several of us in the State Department had an opportunity to speak. Having been in the government longer than others, I was accorded the privilege of speaking first. My remarks were as follows:

"Mr. Secretary, for us old-timers in the government, these years serving in your State Department have been unique. Within a week after you took over, it was evident that the Shultz regime would be different. The aim would be team play, not bureaucratic infighting. What would count was initiative, energy, and courage. We were confident that you would back us up if we ran into personal opposition for pursuing forward-reaching ideas.

"Over the years your thoughts, ideas, and integrity prevailed, thus steadily enhancing the opportunity for constructive work by you and all members of your team.

"The results are there for everyone to see. They cover every aspect of world affairs. The centerpiece has been Western relationships with the Soviet Union and its associates. Six years ago the relationships were wholly adversarial and restricted to trying to make the military aspects of that relationship less immediately dangerous. Gradually you managed to expand the scope and depth of the dialogue. By persistence you raised human rights from a taboo subject to the forefront of the dialogue. You brought regional issues into the realm of productive discussion. Some of the bilateral issues were solved; others have become more manageable.

On the arms control front, from concrete achievement on INF you have opened wide the scope of achievable success across the board from START, defense and space, to balance in conventional forces in Europe and the outlawing of chemical and biological weapons.

"What are the elements of character and leadership that have made that possible? I would list them as follows: Being wholly comfortable within your own skin, a commonsense approach to problems, forthrightness in your relations with others, confidence in the United States and the fundamental ideas informing its spirit.

"The result has been that those of us who have been fortunate to be part of your team have been part of a great experience. We deeply thank you for it."

I believe all of my associates concurred. We were deeply moved as the band struck up and the secretary and Mrs. Shultz got into their car and drove away. The Shultz era had come to an end.

To the Remembrance of Times Past

Karl Marx's *Communist Manifesto* impressed me by its nostalgia for the cultural warmth and beauty of the preindustrial-revolution era. I have a different but analogous nostalgia—a nostalgia for the warmth and beauty of European and American culture prior to the tragedy of the First World War as I remember it from my boyhood. Marx wished to lay the foundations for a totally new society to be made possible by the prior elimination of all existing social structures. I have wished to participate with others in building a new and wider world order in which scope for the further development of the main existing cultural elements would be possible. I have never felt that I was alone in that pursuit.

Over the years I came to believe that this was the wish not only of most Americans, but also of Europeans, including many Russians, and many Asians and Africans as well. We have all seen too much destruction—not only physical destruction but also cultural destruction—to wish more of it.

How has the world done during these years? Not very well. But it could have done worse. And due to the particular circumstances of World War II and its aftermath, we in the United States have had the opportunity to play a particularly important role during the last forty years. It is with those years that most of this book has dealt. During those years, as I saw it, the task was not only to help create a tolerable structure of political and economic order, but also to help defend it while under construction from those who still believed that a better world for them could only be obtained through further widespread tearing down.

We here in the United States described our campaign as the fight for the twin goals of peace and freedom. Have those goals been achieved? No. But I am somewhat more confident of progress during the next decade than I was ten years ago, or even thirty and forty years ago, about the succeeding decades.

With respect to our worldwide economic goals, we were immensely

463

successful in meeting and exceeding goals of expansion in production, development, and trade. Perhaps we were too generous in extending grants, loans, and general economic help while paying inadequate attention to U.S. requirements for our own economic health. We can be faulted, not for lack of generosity, but for inadequate prudence.

We were ill-prepared militarily to help South Korea when she was hit with complete surprise on a Sunday morning, but we nevertheless came immediately to her defense. We outfaced the Soviets in Berlin despite a desperately inferior local military position. We boggled the Bay of Pigs but handled the subsequent Cuban crisis with reasonable competence and tempered success. We permitted ourselves improvidently to become bogged down in Vietnam.

But we then managed to engage the Soviets in serious bilateral strategic arms control negotiations. It is too early to judge how those seemingly endless negotiations have affected our progress toward our twin goals of preserving freedom while moving toward a more solid peace. But that we, together with Gorbachev, have changed the nature of the game is indubitable.

For over forty years I have wrestled with the problem of peace and freedom in a variety of jobs. My overriding concern in all of these has been to serve in such a way as to make a contribution to that goal. Holding high-level office simply for the sake of doing so has never been part of my ambition. When asked to serve as secretary of the navy, I accepted reluctantly, knowing that it would distance me from matters of policy. I was surprised to find that I was not without ability to manage a large organization and therefore I was happy to discover that the job had unexpected rewards. I also found that, in effect, managing the Pentagon as deputy secretary of defense was personally satisfying. But those positions did not divert me from what I had earlier wished to do—that is, to participate with others in dealing with central issues of U.S. foreign and national security policy.

A misconception I wish to avoid is that these forty years of concentration on one set of issues—those connected with my long service in government—represent the most important or enjoyable part of my life. I have consistently put my family ahead of my business or government work. And I have been richly rewarded. I have said little about Phyllis, our four children, my daughters-in-law, their eleven children, and my four great-grandchildren. We have all been intensely involved with one another. Most of us would rather be with other members of our family than with anyone else in the world.

I have dealt only in passing with my years in business. They were not only exciting and productive, but left tangible evidence that we managed to get certain things done. When I drive over the Triboro Bridge in New York, the Golden Gate Bridge or the Oakland Bay Bridge in California, watch certain films, such as *The Turning Point* or *Star Wars,* ride a Greyhound bus, turn on a light in Nebraska, in Milwaukee, or in Kansas City, or wash my hands with Palmolive soap, I am reminded of my role with the enterprises that created them.

And it has not been all work and no play. I have derived enormous pleasure from sports—football, baseball, and soccer at school; football and rowing at college; tennis, skiing, and riding up into my eighties. I have played the piano—badly—but much to my enjoyment (all my children play better than I). I indulged myself in collecting works of art, and not without success. I have traveled, climbed mountains, caught fish, shot quail, played bridge, danced, loved, been loved in return, laughed, and cried.

I have been an uncommonly fortunate man in a troubled world. That, I hope, has enabled me to look at questions of policy with open eyes.

The ABM Treaty Interpretation

Introduction

Over the last two years of the Reagan administration, I urged the State Department's legal counsel, Judge Abraham Sofaer, to complete and circulate his interpretation of the ABM treaty and its impact on testing of ABM systems and components in space. This was discussed at the Tuesday morning breakfasts attended by Secretaries Shultz and Weinberger, and NSC adviser Frank Carlucci (and later Colin Powell). When Carlucci became secretary of defense, he suggested that Sofaer be told to drop the matter so that the Defense Department would have time to deal with it internally. Secretary Shultz agreed.

The various offices in the Pentagon reporting to or through Carlucci found it impossible to resolve their differences. But neither was the order to Sofaer to suspend his work on the subject reversed. As the days of the Reagan administration dwindled, I prepared a paper based on my understanding of the treaty as the result of years of discussion of this and related issues within the executive branch, with the Congress, and with the Soviets. The paper represented my views, not necessarily those of others. I am not a lawyer, but I believe most of the lawyers in the executive branch who dealt with these matters were in general agreement with the views it advanced.[1]

The "Narrow" versus "Broad" Interpretation

Since 1985 the Reagan administration has been racked with dissension over the correct interpretation of the ABM treaty as it applies to ABM

[1] For the reader's convenience, relevant portions of the ABM treaty as signed and ratified in 1972 begin on p. 475.

systems or their components based on "other physical principles" (here-inafter referred to as OPP). The controversy centers on the applicability of Article V of the treaty, which states in paragraph 1:

> Each Party undertakes not to develop, test, or deploy ABM systems or components which are sea-based, air-based, space-based, or mobile land-based.

A. The supporters of the "narrow" interpretation insist that Article V applies to all such systems or components, regardless of the technology employed. They argue that Agreed Statement D, which calls for discussion and agreement prior to deployment in the event "ABM systems based on other physical principles and including components capable of substituting for ABM interceptor missiles, ABM launchers, or ABM radars are created in the future," applies only to fixed, ground-based systems (i.e., those OPP systems whose basing mode is not otherwise banned by Article V) and is intended only to reinforce the ban on deployment of ABM systems and components except as permitted in Article III of the treaty.

B. The supporters of the "broad" interpretation argue that Agreed Statement D is the only place in the treaty that deals specifically with systems based on other physical principles and their components. They contend that Articles III, IV, and V of the treaty apply only to ABM systems and components based on the physical principles that were understood in 1972 to apply to the components defined in Article II (i.e., ABM interceptor missiles, ABM launchers, and ABM radars) and as these technologies might evolve in the future.

A similar dichotomy divides the two camps with respect to the impact of Articles III and IV on the testing of OPP systems and components:

A. The supporters of the "narrow" interpretation insist that the only exception to Article III, which bans the deployment of ABM systems or their components except at two specified deployment areas (later reduced to one) is Article IV, which states that the limitations of Article III shall not apply to ABM systems or their components used for development or testing and located within current or additionally agreed land-based test ranges, and that each party may have no more than a total of 15 ABM launchers at such test ranges. The 1978 supplemental agreement provides that either party may establish additional land-based test ranges without prior agreement, but that the party adding such a range must notify the other party of its location.

B. Supporters of the "broad" interpretation emphasize that Agreed Statement D; and not Articles III, IV, or V, governs systems based on OPP.

1. All supporters of the "broad" interpretation agree that testing OPP systems and their components capable of substituting for ABM interceptor missiles, ABM launchers, or ABM radars is permitted, unless specifically prohibited elsewhere in the treaty, to the extent that such testing is included within the concept of "creation" as used in Agreed Statement D.

2. All supporters of the "broad" interpretation also agree that Agreed Statement D requires that, if OPP systems and their components capable of substituting for ABM components are created, limitations on deployment of such systems and their components will be subject to discussion, in accordance with Article XIII, and shall not be deployed prior to agreement in accordance with Article XIV.

I continue to believe that the "broad" interpretation is fully justified as decided by President Reagan in 1985. There are, however, several additional issues of treaty interpretation among adherents of the broad interpretation:

—What limits does Agreed Statement D place upon OPP systems and their components?

—Are there additional conditions created by the treaty that apply to OPP systems and their components?

—What is the operational meaning of the phrase "other physical principles"?

—Are kinetic-kill vehicles components based on OPP?

—Is an ABM system based on OPP if it includes non-OPP components?

—If so, are its non-OPP components subject to the limitations of Articles V or VI?

Agreed Statement D Limits

Agreed Statement D obligates the parties, in the event ABM systems based on OPP and including components capable of substituting for ABM interceptor missiles, ABM launchers, or ABM radars are created in the future, to discuss specific limitations on such systems and their components. Two issues have arisen with regard to this obligation:

A. The first issue has to do with the point at which the discussions must begin. Some believe that the discussion should be initiated promptly after such systems and their components have been "created." Others argue that they need not begin until a side desires to proceed with deployment. I support the first view.

B. The second issue concerns testing "beyond" the point of "creation." Some believe that, although testing of OPP systems and their components capable of substituting for ABM components is permitted up to the point of "creation," testing beyond this point may not be consistent with Agreed Statement D and, at a minimum, must be discussed. Others argue that Agreed Statement D imposes no obligation with regard to any testing of OPP systems and their components. Again, I support the first view.

My rationale in both cases is based on the intent of Agreed Statement D. The parties are obligated by Agreed Statement D to discuss specific limitations on OPP systems and their components "in order to insure fulfillment of the obligation not to deploy ABM systems and their components except as provided in Article III." The distinction between testing and deployment can become increasingly fuzzy as testing advances further beyond the point of creation, making it necessary to begin discussions at this point to make clear that ABM systems or components are not being deployed. Thus, it is the first view of each of these issues which is the most consistent with the intent of Agreed Statement D.

Application of Other Treaty Provisions to OPP Systems

Paragraph 2 of the basic article of the treaty, Article I, calls for each party not to provide a defense for the territory of its country, not to provide a base for such a defense, and not to deploy ABM systems for a defense of an individual region except as provided for in Article III. Some believe that Article I applies as well to OPP systems and their components; that is, testing of any ABM system or component, even if based on OPP, must comply with this fundamental rule. Others argue that the parties can test

OPP systems as provided in Agreed Statement D, with no reference to Article I, because Article I does not pertain to OPP systems.

I believe that Article I does apply to OPP systems and their components. It seems clear that the treaty was not intended to permit the testing of OPP systems in such a way as to violate the basic premise of the treaty. Moreover, in order for the parties to agree to deployments of OPP systems as provided in Agreed Statement D, they must first amend the ABM treaty as provided in Article XIV. An agreement to amend Article III to allow limited deployment of OPP systems would still leave those systems subject to Article I, unless Article I were amended as well.

In addition, Article VI provides that neither side shall give missiles, launchers, or radars, other than ABM interceptor missiles, ABM launchers, or ABM radars, the capability to counter strategic missiles or their elements in flight trajectory and shall not test them in an ABM mode. Some believe that this creates an additional condition that applies to certain possible components of OPP systems. They argue that, if a device meets the ordinary dictionary definition of being a missile, launcher, or radar, then it is covered by either Article V or VI. If it is an ABM component as defined in Article II, it is then covered by Article V; if it is not a component as defined in Article II, it is covered by Article VI. By constructing and deploying a missile, launcher, or radar for an ABM role or testing it in an ABM mode, it becomes an ABM component under Article II and thus subject to the restraints of Article V. Thus it can be argued that Article VI assures that Article V cannot be evaded by upgrading non-ABM missiles, launchers, or radars, including those based on "other physical principles," into ABM-capable components.

Others claim that ABM systems and their components based on "other physical principles" and capable of substituting for ABM missiles, launchers, and radars are mentioned nowhere else in the treaty other than in Agreed Statement D and that, as a consequence, no aspect of the treaty other than Agreed Statement D has any relevance to OPP systems and their components.

I believe that Article VI does apply to certain possible components of OPP systems, but that Article VI constraints can be made to be no greater than those provided by Article V.[2]

---

[2]If the component in question were declared to be intended for an ABM role pursuant to Article II, subparagraphs 1(a) and 2(c), it would become an "ABM component" and be subject to Article V.

The Meaning of "Other Physical Principles"

Three possible meanings have been suggested for the phrase "other physical principles." These are:

—physical principles other than those whose immediate application in ABM components was understood in 1972;
—physical principles other than those involved in components under development in 1972; and
—physical principles other than those upon which the ABM systems and components specified in Article II of the 1972 treaty were then based.

The first definition is the one that I recollect having had in mind when I originated the term "other physical principles" during the ABM treaty negotiations, and continue to believe to be correct.

Kinetic-Kill Vehicles (KKV)

Two final issues relate to whether kinetic-kill vehicles should be treated as components based on OPP. Some argue that today's KKVs involve characteristics (e.g., optical homing guidance, no nuclear explosive) that were not found in ABM systems in 1972 and are therefore based on OPP. Others point out that BAMBI[3] was a KKV system proposed well before 1972, that other KKV systems were in development in 1972, and that KKVs are, therefore, not necessarily based on "other physical principles."

I believe that the primary KKV being examined by the Strategic Defense Initiative Organization (SDIO)—the space-based interceptor (SBI)—is similar to other KKVs; the application of its physical principles was understood in 1972 and thus is not based on OPP. Moreover, the negotiating record does not support the notion that the absence of a nuclear warhead or the use of a guidance system not based on ABM radars exempts a missile from the constraints of the treaty. Thus, to the extent that a KKV is a "missile" as understood in 1972, it is not based on OPP. On the other hand, other KKVs, such as electromagnetic railguns, may be based on other physical principles.

[3]BAMBI was a concept studied in the early 1960s. It was a boost-phase system using nonnuclear homing interceptors based on satellites.

The second issue is whether an ABM system is based on OPP if it includes non-OPP components and, if so, whether such components are subject to the limitations of Articles V or VI. Some believe that a system can be considered to be based on OPP even if it includes non-OPP components, and that such components are not subject to other treaty limitations because only Agreed Statement D covers OPP systems. Others question whether systems can be considered to be based on OPP if they include non-OPP components. They believe that even if such systems are OPP, their non-OPP components are subject to the limitations of Articles V or VI.

I believe that, while a system may be considered to be based on OPP even if it includes non-OPP components, those components remain subject to the limitations of Articles V or VI. If they were not, circumvention of these articles would be easily accomplished, and the main purpose of the treaty would be undermined. Such circumvention was not the purpose, and should not be the effect, of Agreed Statement D.

Conclusions

To summarize my views, I believe that:

—the broad interpretation is fully justified;

—Agreed Statement D obligates the parties to initiate discussions promptly after OPP systems and their components have been created;

—testing of OPP systems and their components beyond the point of creation may not be consistent with Agreed Statement D and, at a minimum, must be discussed with the Soviet Union;

—Article I of the treaty applies to OPP systems and their components and that Article VI applies to certain possible components of OPP systems;

—the ABM treaty was concluded with the understanding that "other physical principles" meant principles other than those whose application in ABM components was understood in 1972;

—the primary KKV being examined by SDIO—the SBI interceptor—is not based on OPP. Other KKVs, such as electromagnetic railguns, may be based on OPP;

—while a system *may* be considered to be based on OPP even if it includes non-OPP components, those components are subject to the limits of Articles V or VI.

These issues have important implications for the SDI program and for the U.S. position in the defense and space talks. For example, a conclusion that certain kinetic-kill vehicles, including space-based interceptors, are not components of OPP systems would mean that these weapons are subject to Article V of the ABM treaty, even under the broad interpretation, and therefore cannot be developed or tested at the component level in a space-based mode.

Relevant Excerpts
from the ABM Treaty
as Signed and Ratified in 1972

. . . .

ARTICLE I

1. Each Party undertakes to limit anti-ballistic missile (ABM) systems and to adopt other measures in accordance with the provisions of this Treaty.

2. Each Party undertakes not to deploy ABM systems for a defense of the territory of its country and not to provide a base for such a defense, and not to deploy ABM systems for defense of an individual region except as provided for in Article III of this Treaty.

ARTICLE II

1. For the purpose of this Treaty an ABM system is a system to counter strategic ballistic missiles or their elements in flight trajectory, currently consisting of:

(a) ABM interceptor missiles, which are interceptor missiles constructed and deployed for an ABM role, or of a type tested in an ABM mode;

(b) ABM launchers, which are launchers constructed and deployed for launching ABM interceptor missiles; and

(c) ABM radars, which are radars constructed and deployed for an ABM role, or of a type tested in an ABM mode.

2. The ABM system components listed in paragraph 1 of this Article include those which are:

(a) operational;

(b) under construction;

(c) undergoing testing;

Extracted from the 1982 edition of *Arms Control and Disarmament Agreements: Texts and Histories of Negotiations* (Washington, D.C.: United States Arms Control and Disarmament Agency), 139–47.

(d) undergoing overhaul, repair or conversion; or

(e) mothballed.

ARTICLE III

Each Party undertakes not to deploy ABM systems or their components except that:

(a) within one ABM system deployment area having a radius of one hundred and fifty kilometers and centered on the Party's national capital, a Party may deploy: (1) no more than one hundred ABM launchers and no more than one hundred ABM interceptor missiles at launch sites, and (2) ABM radars within no more than six ABM radar complexes, the area of each complex being circular and having a diameter of no more than three kilometers; and

(b) within one ABM system deployment area having a radius of one hundred and fifty kilometers and containing ICBM silo launchers, a Party may deploy: (1) no more than one hundred ABM launchers and no more than one hundred ABM interceptor missiles at launch sites, (2) two large phased-array ABM radars comparable in potential to corresponding ABM radars operational or under construction on the date of signature of the Treaty in an ABM system deployment area containing ICBM silo launchers, and (3) no more than eighteen ABM radars each having a potential less than the potential of the smaller of the above-mentioned two large phased-array ABM radars.

ARTICLE IV

The limitations provided for in Article III shall not apply to ABM systems or their components used for development or testing, and located within current or additionally agreed test ranges. Each Party may have no more than a total of fifteen ABM launchers at test ranges.

ARTICLE V

1. Each Party undertakes not to develop, test, or deploy ABM systems or components which are sea-based, air-based, space-based, or mobile land-based.

. . . .

ARTICLE VI

To enhance assurance of the effectiveness of the limitations on ABM systems and their components provided by the Treaty, each Party undertakes:

(a) not to give missiles, launchers, or radars, other than ABM interceptor missiles, ABM launchers, or ABM radars, capabilities to counter strategic ballistic missiles or their elements in flight trajectory, and not to test them in an ABM mode; and

(b) not to deploy in the future radars for early warning of strategic ballistic missiles attack except at locations along the periphery of its national territory and oriented outward.

Article VII

Subject to the provisions of this Treaty, modernization and replacement of ABM systems or their components may be carried out.

. . . .

Article XIII

1. To promote the objectives and implementation of the provisions of this Treaty, the Parties shall establish promptly a Standing Consultative Commission, within the framework of which they will:

. . . .

(f) consider, as appropriate, possible proposals for further increasing the viability of this Treaty; including proposals for amendments in accordance with the provisions of this Treaty;

. . . .

Article XIV

1. Each Party may propose amendments to this Treaty. Agreed amendments shall enter into force in accordance with the procedures governing the entry into force of this Treaty.

. . . .

Article XV

1. This Treaty shall be of unlimited duration.

2. Each Party shall, in exercising its national sovereignty, have the right to withdraw from this Treaty if it decides that extraordinary events related to the subject matter of this Treaty have jeopardized its supreme interests. It shall give notice of its decision to the other Party six months prior to withdrawal from the Treaty. Such notice shall include a state-

ment of the extraordinary events the notifying Party regards as having jeopardized its supreme interests.

. . . .

1. AGREED STATEMENTS

The document set forth below was agreed upon and initialed by the Heads of the Delegations on May 26, 1972 (letter designations added);

. . . .

[D]

In order to insure fulfillment of the obligation not to deploy ABM systems and their components except as provided in Article III of the Treaty, the Parties agree that in the event ABM systems based on other physical principles and including components capable of substituting for ABM interceptor missiles, ABM launchers, or ABM radars are created in the future, specific limitations on such systems and their components would be subject to discussion in accordance with Article XIII and agreement in accordance with Article XIV of the Treaty.

. . . .

[F]

The Parties agree not to deploy phased-array radars having a potential (the product of mean emitted power in watts and antenna area in square meters) exceeding three million, except as provided for in Articles III, IV and VI of the Treaty, or except for the purposes of tracking objects in outer space or for use as national technical means of verification.

. . . .

Acknowledgments

During the course of writing this book I received help and assistance from many quarters. For taking the time and patience to read and comment on early drafts of the manuscript, I would like to thank my dear friend and former colleague, Louis J. Halle; Evan Thomas of *Newsweek;* Don Oberdorfer of *The Washington Post;* C. L. Sulzberger, and Anthony R. Dolan. Many of my friends and associates gave me the benefit of their advice and own recollections. For this I would like to thank Charles Burton Marshall, always a source of wise ideas and sound advice; Admiral Elmo R. Zumwalt, Jr.; Rear Admiral Horace B. Robertson, Jr.; Rear Admiral John R. Lee; James C. Cooley; Glenn T. Seaborg; and Judge Abraham Sofaer.

The original editor of this book was Harold Evans, whom I found to be invariably understanding and insightful. It later proved impossible for him to continue with the project. Subsequently, John Herman, editorial director of Grove Weidenfeld, took over in a thoroughly competent manner. I would also like to express my appreciation to Ronald L. Easley and System Planning Corporation for providing much welcomed logistical support. For all manner of help and encouragement, I also need to thank Jo McClenny, Bonnie Bailey, Barbara Jacobi, Nancy Jenkins, and Norman Clyne. I likewise owe a debt to Donald O. Cooke, who arranged access to my Defense Department files, and to John Lehman, who did the same for my Navy papers. George P. Shultz, one of this country's most able and dedicated public servants, was a source of continual moral support.

I owe a special appreciation for her help and encouragement to Carol Laise.

Finally, I need to thank my collaborators, Ann M. Smith and Steven L. Rearden, for helping me collect and organize much of the material that went into this book.

P.H.N.
Washington, D.C.

Index

About the Authors

Paul H. Nitze has been a key figure in Washington since the Roosevelt administration. Among the many positions he has held are Director of the State Department Policy Planning Staff, Secretary of the Navy, Deputy Secretary of Defense, arms control negotiator, and Ambassador at Large and Special Adviser to the President and Secretary of State on Arms Control Matters.

Ann M. Smith was staff assistant to Paul Nitze from 1969 to 1979, and has collaborated with him since 1982 on the preparation of these memoirs.

Steven L. Rearden is a Harvard-trained historian specializing in national security affairs.